P9-BYA-288

THE FACTS ON FILE DICTIONARY OF

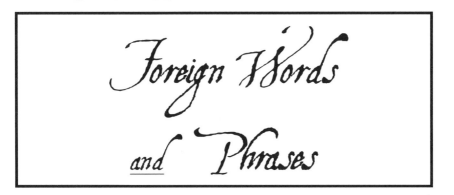

Foreign Words

and Phrases

THE FACTS ON FILE DICTIONARY OF

Foreign Words and Phrases

MARTIN H. MANSER

Associate Editor: David H. Pickering

Checkmark Books®

An imprint of Facts On File, Inc.

The Facts On File Dictionary of Foreign Words and Phrases

Copyright © 2002 by Martin H. Manser

All rights reserved. No part of this book may be reproduced or utilized in any form or by any means, electronic or mechanical, including photocopying, recording, or by any information storage or retrieval systems, without permission in writing from the publisher. For information contact:

Checkmark Books
An imprint of Facts On File, Inc.
132 West 31st Street
New York NY 10001

Library of Congress Cataloging-in-Publication Data
Manser, Martin H.
 The Facts On File dictionary of foreign words and phrases / Martin H. Manser; associate editor, David H. Pickering.
  p. cm.
 Includes index.
 ISBN 0-8160-4458-9 (hc: acid-free paper) ISBN 0-8160-4459-7 (pbk: acid-free paper)
 1. English language—Foreign words and phrases—Dictionaries. I. Title: Dictionary of foreign words and phrases. II. Pickering, David, 1958–. III. Title.
PE1670.M26 2002
422′.4′03—dc21   2001042302

Checkmark Books are available at special discounts when purchased in bulk quantities for businesses, associations, institutions or sales promotions. Please call our Special Sales Department in New York at (212) 967-8800 or (800) 322-8755.

You can find Facts On File on the World Wide Web at http://www.factsonfile.com

Text design by Sandy Watanabe
Cover design by Cathy Rincon

Printed in the United States of America

MP Hermitage 10 9 8 7 6 5 4 3 2

This book is printed on acid-free paper.

Contents

Introduction

The American poet and essayist Ralph Waldo Emerson described the English language as "the sea which receives tributaries from every region under heaven." This dictionary has been compiled as an accessible guide to expressions that are derived from foreign languages. Some such words and phrases have been fully assimilated into the language *(igloo, bonanza);* others are still thought of as foreign *(de rigueur, magnum opus).*

Words and phrases that have become part of the English language cover a wide range of fields: entertainment *(flamenco, soirée),* food and drink *(filo, goulash, lager, rijsttafel),* language and literature *(portmanteau, Sturm und Drang),* law *(force majeure, virgo intacta),* music *(allegro, largo, nocturne),* politics and economics *(glasnost, laissez-faire, ombudsman),* and religion *(Corpus Christi, Rosh Hashanah).*

Headwords

Entries are arranged in strict alphabetical order. Letter-by-letter alphabetical order is followed:

fusilli

futon

fu yung

Hyphens are ignored:

faux amis

faux-naïf

faux pas

Accents are included in the headword if that is how the word is usually rendered in English:

> **café**
>
> **coup d'état**
>
> **più**

Words with the same spelling but with different etymologies are shown as separate entries:

> **forte (1)** (f<u>or</u>tay, for<u>tay</u>) FRENCH [*fort* strong] *noun* a person's speciality or strong point
>
> **forte (2)** (f<u>or</u>tay, for<u>tay</u>) ITALIAN [derived from Latin *fortis* strong] *adjective* in music. . .

Variant spellings of the headword are shown:

> **coup d'état** (koo day<u>ta</u>, koo d<u>ă</u><u>ta</u>), **coup d'etat** FRENCH. . .
>
> **coupé** (<u>koo</u>pay), **coupe** FRENCH. . .

Pronunciation

A pronunciation of the word or phrase in American English is shown for each entry, except for cross-references.

A respelling system is used to show pronunciations:

a (c<u>a</u>b)	er (thi<u>r</u>st)
ă (<u>a</u>bout, robb<u>er</u>)	f (<u>f</u>ine)
ah (c<u>ar</u>)	g (<u>g</u>et)
air (b<u>ear</u>)	h (<u>h</u>and)
ay (d<u>a</u>y, st<u>a</u>te)	i (<u>i</u>ll)
b (<u>b</u>ut)	ī (tr<u>y</u>)
ch (<u>ch</u>ip)	j (<u>j</u>olly)
d (<u>d</u>anger)	k (<u>c</u>an)
e (s<u>e</u>ll)	kh (lo<u>ch</u>)
ee (f<u>ee</u>t)	ks (mi<u>x</u>)
eer (cl<u>ear</u>)	kw (<u>qu</u>ell)

l (<u>l</u>ie)	s (<u>s</u>ilent)
m (<u>m</u>ole)	sh (<u>sh</u>ut)
n (<u>n</u>ine)	t (<u>t</u>ip)
ng (lo<u>ng</u>er)	th (<u>th</u>eater)
n(g) (restaur<u>an</u>t, b<u>on</u> t<u>on</u>)	TH (<u>th</u>is)
o (f<u>o</u>g)	u (l<u>u</u>ck)
ō (teleph<u>o</u>ne)	uu (b<u>u</u>lletin)
oi (pl<u>oy</u>)	v (<u>v</u>ery)
oo (gl<u>ue</u>)	w (<u>w</u>et)
oor (p<u>oor</u>)	y (<u>y</u>oung)
or (s<u>ore</u>)	yoo (<u>u</u>nisex)
ow (c<u>ow</u>)	yoor (<u>Eur</u>opean)
p (<u>p</u>ink)	z (fi<u>zz</u>)
r (<u>r</u>ed)	zh (fu<u>s</u>ion)

Stress is shown by an underscore in the pronunciation:

> **flügelhorn** (<u>floo</u>gălhorn) GERMAN. . .

> **fons et origo** (fonz et o<u>rī</u>gō) LATIN. . .

Where a word or phrase has more than one pronunciation, these are given, separated by a comma:

> **fondant** (<u>fon</u>don(g), <u>fon</u>dănt) FRENCH. . .

Etymology

The language of origin is shown in SMALL CAPITALS after the pronunciation:

> **jodhpurs** (<u>jod</u>părs) HINDI [after Jodhpur, India] *plural noun* a style of riding breeches. . .

> **Kaaba** (<u>kā</u>bă) ARABIC [cubic building] *noun* the square stone shrine. . .

The meaning of the word or phrase in the original language is given after the language of origin:

> **ménage à trois** (maynahzh a <u>twa</u>, menahzh a <u>twa</u>) FRENCH [household of three] *noun phrase* a domestic arrangement in which three people live together in the same household (usually understood to imply a sexual relationship. . .

> **kiosk** (<u>kee</u>osk) FRENCH [*kiosque,* derived from Turkish *kiushk* pavilion, ultimately from Persian *kushk* portico] *noun* a small stall, booth, pavilion. . .

Significant changes in spelling between the original language and English are shown in the etymology:

> **feme covert** (feem <u>ko</u>vărt) FRENCH [covered woman, from *femme* woman and *couverte* covered] *noun phrase.* . .

> **feme sole** (feem <u>sō</u>l) FRENCH [single woman, from *femme* woman and *seule* alone] *noun phrase.* . .

Eponymous words include the name (with birth and death dates) that they are derived from:

> **jacquard** (zha<u>kard</u>) FRENCH [after Joseph-Marie Jacquard (1752–1834), inventor of the Jacquard loom] *noun* a piece of fabric woven on a Jacquard loom, or the loom on which such material is made. . .

Toponymous words include the place-name that they are derived from:

> **faience** (fay<u>ons</u>) FRENCH [after Faenza, Italy] *noun* colorful tin-glazed earthenware. . .

> **marathon** (<u>ma</u>răthăn, <u>ma</u>răthon) GREEK [after Marathon, Greece, where the Greeks defeated the Persians in 490 B.C., the news of the victory being rushed to Athens by a long-distance runner] *noun* a long-distance race run over a course of 26 miles 385 yards. . .

Additional background information may be included in the etymology:

> **veni, vidi, vici** (waynee, weedee, <u>wee</u>kee; vaynee, veedee, <u>vee</u>chee) LATIN [I came, I saw, I conquered, as quoted by Julius Caesar (100–44 B.C.) on his victory over Pharnaces, king of Pontus, at Zela in 47 B.C.] *interjection.* . .

Grammatical information

The part of speech is shown for all entries, indicating the grammatical behavior of the English word or phrase:

> **obi** (ōbee) JAPANESE [belt] *noun* a sash worn round the waist as part of traditional Japanese dress. . .

> **siesta** (seeestă) SPANISH [from Latin *sexta hora* sixth hour, noon] *noun* a midday or afternoon nap or short rest. . .

Words that function as plural nouns in English are shown thus:

> **facetiae** (făseeshīī) LATIN [plural of *facetia* a jest, witticism] *plural noun* witticisms or short, typically pornographic, stories. . .

Where the word or phrase is used in English with more than one part of speech these are shown after a swung dash (~):

> **fête** (fayt), **fete** FRENCH [festival] *noun* a festival, fair, or party: *"'Will you be at Madame Rolandaky's fete?' asked Anna, to change the conversation"* (Leo Tolstoy, *Anna Karenina,* 1873–77). ~*verb* to celebrate or pay honor to.

Headwords that consist of more than one word in English are given the part of speech "*. . .phrase*":

> **jolie laide** (zholee layd) FRENCH [pretty ugly] *noun phrase* a woman who is deemed sexually attractive despite the fact that she is not conventionally beautiful. . .

> **laborare est orare** (laborahree est orahree) LATIN [to work is to pray] *verb phrase* hard work is a form of prayer.

Grammatical information—especially plurals of nouns—is given whenever it is not clear what the form might be:

> **falsetto** (folsetō) ITALIAN [diminutive of *falso* false] *noun* (*plural* **falsetti,** folsetee) a singer with a high-pitched voice, above tenor. . .

> **feu de joie** (fō dă zhwa) FRENCH [fire of joy] *noun phrase* (*plural* **feux de joie**) a fusillade of guns fired in salute. . .

The pronunciation of plurals is shown, except where they are pronounced in the same way as the singular form or where the pronunciation follows normal English rules:

> **faux pas** (fō pa) FRENCH [false step] *noun phrase* (*plural* **faux pas,** fō pahz) a mistake or social blunder. . .

fungus (fungăs) LATIN [probably derived from Greek *sphoggos* or *spoggos*, sponge] *noun* (*plural* **fungi,** fungee, funjee, fungī) a class of. . .

sphinx (sfinks) GREEK [after the Sphinx winged monster of Greek mythology, probably from *sphiggein* to draw tight] *noun* (*plural* **sphinxes** or **sphinges,** sfinjeez) a winged female monster with a woman's head and a lion's body. . .

stadium (staydeeăm) LATIN [from Greek *stadion*] *noun* (*plural* **stadiums** or **stadia,** staydeeă) a large sports ground or other arena. . .

Definitions

The English meaning of the word or phrase of foreign origin is given:

kaffeeklatsch (kafeeklach, kafiklach) GERMAN [coffee gossip] *noun* informal conversation over cups of coffee, or a meeting at which such conversation takes place. . .

In some cases, developments of the meaning of the word or phrase are explained:

smorgasbord (smorgăsbord) SWEDISH [*smörgås* sandwich and *bord* table] *noun* a buffet including a wide variety of hot and cold dishes, such as meat and fish dishes, pickles, cheeses, and salads, and, by extension, any mixture of diverse elements: *"The committee came up with a compromise, a smorgasbord of initiatives and resolutions."*

moiré (moray, mwahray), **moire** (moray, mwahray, mwahr) FRENCH [*moirer* to give a watered appearance to] *noun* a watered fabric or a fabric or other material with a rippled or wavy texture, or appearance; can also refer to the shimmering patterns produced when geometric patterns are superimposed on each other slightly out of alignment.

passe-partout (paspertoo, paspahrtoo), **passepartout** FRENCH [pass everywhere] *noun* a master key or pass that allows the holder to cross borders etc. at will; can also refer to a frame or border in which a picture may be displayed.

Background or usage information is also sometimes included in the definition:

j'accuse (zhakooz) FRENCH [I accuse] *noun phrase* an allegation or charge, typically against official injustice (in imitation of Émile Zola's famous article beginning with the words "J'accuse" published in the newspaper *L'Aurore* on January 13, 1898, and relating to the Dreyfus affair, alleging that a Jewish army officer convicted of treason had been wrongly condemned by the French military.)

jacquerie (zhakree, zhakăree) FRENCH [derived from the archetypal peasant name Jacques] *noun* a peasant uprising, specifically the 1358 Jacquerie revolt in northern France, or the peasantry in general. . .

per procurationem (per prokyooratee<u>o</u>năm) LATIN [by agency] *adverb phrase* by proxy, on the authority of a deputy or agent. ~*abbreviated forms* **per pro, p.p.** Strictly speaking, when used in a letter the abbreviation *p.p.* should precede the name of the person signing the letter. "In modern usage the abbreviation is frequently interpreted as 'for and on behalf of' and placed before the name of the person on whose behalf the letter is signed. This 'incorrect' sequence is so well-established that the correct usage could lead to misunderstanding" (*Bloomsbury GoodWord Guide,* edited by Martin H. Manser.)

Occasionally words and phrases are described as slang or informal as appropriate:

cojones (kǎh<u>o</u>niz) SPANISH [from *cojón* testicle] *plural noun* (slang) balls, guts, courage.

cushy (<u>kuu</u>shee) HINDI [from *khush* pleasant] *adjective* (informal) easy, pleasant, untaxing. . .

Examples

Many entries have examples to show the use of the word or phrase. Some examples are constructed as typical uses of the word or phrase; others are citations from works of English literature and the *Oxford English Dictionary*:

façon de parler (fason(g) dǎ pahr<u>lay</u>) FRENCH [way of speaking] *noun phrase* (*plural* **façons de parler**) a manner of speech or a formulaic phrase or figure of speech: *"Interlopers from the rich end of town were immediately identifiable by their façon de parler."*

kursaal (<u>ker</u>sarl) GERMAN [*Kur* cure and *Saal* hall, room] *noun* a public building at a health resort: *"Down the road a piece was a Kursaal—whatever that may be—and we joined the human tide to see what sort of enjoyment it might afford. It was the usual open-air concert, in an ornamental garden, with wines, beer, milk, whey, grapes, etc. . ."* (Mark Twain, *A Tramp Abroad,* 1880).

Abbreviated and derived forms

Abbreviated (shortened), derived and related forms are shown as appropriate:

per annum (per <u>an</u>ăm) LATIN [through the year] *adverb phrase* annually, yearly, every year, for each year, by the year: *"The enterprise brings in over two million dollars per annum."* ~*abbreviated forms* **p.a., per an.**

nemine contradicente (neminay kontrǎdi<u>ken</u>tay) LATIN [no one contradicting] *adverb phrase* unanimously, with no one dissenting. ~*abbreviated form* **nem. con.**: *The resolution was passed nem. con.*

fiancé (fee<u>on</u>say, feeons<u>ay</u>) FRENCH [past participle of *fiancer* to betroth, promise] *noun* a man who is engaged to be married: *"Even if you are engaged, I am sure your fiancé would wish you to go into society rather than be bored to death"* (Leo Tolstoy, *War and Peace*, 1863–69). ~*noun, feminine* **fiancée** (fee<u>on</u>say, feeons<u>ay</u>) a woman who is engaged to be married.

siffleur (si<u>flǎr</u>) FRENCH [whistler, *siffler* to whistle] *noun* a person who whistles (especially one who entertains publicly by whistling). ~*noun, feminine* **siffleuse** (si<u>flerz</u>).

Cross-references

Cross-references are supplied at alternative points where users might expect an entry, except where the cross-reference would be immediately next to the main entry.

shivaree *See* CHARIVARI.

shmooze *See* SCHMOOZE.

Index

The index at the back of the book lists the main headwords of words and phrases in alphabetical order of the source language.

Conclusion

We hope that users of this book will find it to be not only an informative work of reference but also a fascinating guide for anyone who enjoys delving into the treasure trove of English words.

Martin H. Manser

David H. Pickering

Entries A to Z

a

abacus (a̠băkăs) LATIN [from Greek *abax* slab] *noun* (*plural* **abacuses,** a̠băkăsiz, or **abaci,** a̠băsee, a̠băkee) a simple instrument on which mathematical calculations can be done by moving beads or balls along rods, wires, or grooves.

à bas (a ba̠) FRENCH [toward below] *interjection* down with (someone or something)!

abattoir (a̠bătwahr) FRENCH [slaughterhouse, from *abattre* to beat down, to fell] *noun* a slaughterhouse for the killing and preparation of fresh meat.

abbé (aba̠y) FRENCH [from Latin *abbas* abbot] *noun* title used by a member of the French secular clergy (specifically a priest who does not have any official duties): *"It was here that the brave Abbé wrote a book with his own blood, with a pen made of a piece of iron hoop, and by the light of a lamp made out of shreds of cloth soaked in grease obtained from his food. . ."* (Mark Twain, *Innocents Abroad,* 1869).

à bientôt (a beea̠nto̅) FRENCH [until soon, before long] *interjection* so long! until next time! good-bye!

ab initio (ab ănishee̅o̅) LATIN [from the beginning] *adverb phrase* from the start, from the outset.

à bon chat, bon rat (a bon sha bon ra̠) FRENCH [to a good cat, a good rat] *adverb phrase* used to express the idea that it takes cunning to get the better of cunning.

ab origine (ab ărijănee) LATIN [from the beginning] *adverb phrase* from the beginning of creation, from the beginning of the world. *"If one is ab origine a fool, one becomes so more than ever, seeing that, however much one may try not to forget what one has learnt, there will dawn upon one, sooner or later, the revelation that one's knowledge is all rubbish'"* (Ivan Turgenev, *Fathers and Sons,* 1862).

aborigine (abărijănee) LATIN [*ab origine* from the beginning] *noun* a member of the indigenous people of a particular region (especially of Aus-

1

tralia). ~*adjective* of or relating to aborigine peoples or aborigine culture: *"These cave paintings are among the finest examples of aborigine art ever discovered."*

ab ovo (ab ōvō) LATIN [from the egg] *adverb phrase* from the beginning. *"Is it possible that we are so absolutely, so innocently, so ridiculous? ab ovo"* (D. H. Lawrence, *Mornings in Mexico*, 1927).

abseil (ab sayl) GERMAN [*abseilen, from ab* down and *Seil* rope] *verb* to lower oneself quickly down a cliff, wall, etc. by sliding down a rope; to rappel.

ab urbe condita (ab erbay kondeetă) LATIN [since the city was founded] *adverb phrase* from the founding of the city of Rome (used in Roman dating systems).

A.C. *see* ANTE CHRISTUM.

academia (akădeemeeă) LATIN [from Greek *akademia* academy, from Akademos, the grove where Plato taught his pupils] *noun* the academic world, academic life in general: *"He spent his whole adult life in the rarefied world of academia."*

a cappella (a kăpelă), **a capela** ITALIAN [at chapel, in chapel style] *adverb phrase* (music) unaccompanied, without instrumental backing: *"The group was obliged to sing a cappella after the accompanist failed to turn up."* ~*adjective phrase* (music) unaccompanied, without instrumental backing.

accelerando (achelărandō) ITALIAN [accelerating, from Latin *accelerandum*] *adverb* (music) getting faster. ~*adjective* (music) getting faster: *"'Arabia's time at last has come!' He is interrupted by a chorus of triumphant Arabs (twelve-eight time, accelerando)"* (Honoré de Balzac, *Gambara*, 1837). ~*noun* (music) a gradual increase in speed. ~*abbreviated form* **accel.**

accolade (akălayd) FRENCH [embrace, *accoler* to embrace, from Italian *accollare* to embrace about the neck] *noun* an award, a salute, a public acknowledgment of achievement: *"The Child Mordred was properly rebuked and denied the accolade, though, like the others, he seemed to have assumed the title already"* (Booth Tarkington, *Penrod*, 1914).

accouchement (ăkooshmon(g)) FRENCH [delivery, labor, from *accoucher* to give birth] *noun* confinement in childbirth, labor, lying-in.

accoutrement (ăkootrămănt, ăkootărmănt), **accounterment** FRENCH [equipment] *noun* accessories, trappings, equipment: *"She sat on the floor, surrounded by all the accoutrements of college life."*

à cheval (a shăval) FRENCH [on horseback] *adverb phrase* astride, with a leg on each side; can also refer to a ploy in gambling in which stakes are placed simultaneously on two chances.

achkan (<u>atch</u>kan) HINDI [*ackan*] *noun* a knee-length coat in the style worn by men in India and neighboring countries: *"Several movie stars have been photographed in recent months wearing an achkan, the latest fad to hit the fashion pages."*

achtung (<u>ak</u>tăng) GERMAN [attention] *interjection* look out! watch out!: *"Achtung, guys, the foreman's coming over."*

acme (<u>ak</u>mee) GREEK [from *akme* highest point, culmination] *noun* the highest point of something, the zenith, the peak of perfection: *"There was not a sound of life save that acme and sublimation of all dismal sounds, the bark of a fox, its three hollow notes being rendered at intervals of a minute with the precision of a funeral bell"* (Thomas Hardy, *Far from the Madding Crowd*, 1874).

acropolis (<u>ak</u>ro<u>pă</u>lăs) GREEK [*akropolis* upper city, *akros* peak and *polis* city] *noun* a citadel or raised, usually fortified part of a city (after the Acropolis in Athens): *"Further on, some remains of a gigantic aqueduct; here the high base of an Acropolis, with the floating outline of a Parthenon; there traces of a quay, as if an ancient port had formerly abutted on the borders of the ocean, and disappeared with its merchant vessels and its war-galleys"* (Jules Verne, *20,000 Leagues Under the Sea*, 1870).

acte gratuit (akt gra<u>twee</u>) FRENCH [gratuitous act] *noun phrase* (*plural* **actes gratuits**) a gratuitous, impulsive, or random action.

actualité (aktyoo<u>ali</u>tay) FRENCH [current events] *noun* the objective facts of the matter, the truth: *"The assertions of the minister appeared to be at conflict with the evident actualité of the political situation."*

actus Dei (aktăs <u>day</u>ee) LATIN [act of God] *noun phrase* an act of God, an act of nature (typically a storm, earthquake, or other unpredictable natural catastrophe or phenomenon over which man has no control): *"If the court rules that the flood was an actus Dei, the insurance company won't have to pay out."*

actus reus (aktăs <u>ray</u>ăs) LATIN [a guilty act] *noun phrase* (in law) a wrongful act giving rise to legal proceedings: *"The prosecution argued that without a valid actus reus no crime had actually been committed."*

acumen (<u>a</u>kyămăn) LATIN [a point, sharpness, from *acuere* to sharpen, from *acus* needle] *noun* (*plural* **acumina,** akyoo<u>mee</u>nă) shrewdness, discernment, insight, acuteness of perception: *"He sung a good song, told a good story, and could crack a severe jest with all the acumen of Shakespeare's jesters, though without using, like them, the cloak of insanity"* (Walter Scott, *The Antiquary*, 1816).

A.D. *See* ANNO DOMINI; ANTE DIEM.

ad absurdum (ad ab<u>ser</u>dăm) LATIN [to an absurd thing] *adverb phrase* to the point of absurdity: *"The professor seemed determined to pursue his theory ad absurdum."*

adagio (ă<u>dah</u>jeeō, ă<u>dah</u>zheeō) ITALIAN [at ease, from *ad* to and *agio* ease] *adverb* (music) at a relaxed, slow tempo. *~noun* a piece of music written in a relaxed, slow tempo. *~adjective* of or relating to such a piece of music: *"The boots beat time with his head, as he looked gently round at Mr. Trott with a smile of pity, and whistled an adagio movement"* (Charles Dickens, *Sketches by Boz*, 1836–37).

ad astra per ardua (ad astră per <u>ahr</u>dyooă) LATIN [to the stars through difficulty] *noun phrase* through difficulty to the stars (advising that those who seek to attain an ambitious target must expect difficulties along the way): *"Grandfather looked with resigned dismay upon the wreckage of his prototype glider: 'Ad astra per ardua,' he said to himself."* See also PER ARDUA AD ASTRA.

A.D.C. See AIDE-DE-CAMP.

addendum (ă<u>den</u>dăm) LATIN [that which must be added, neuter of *addendus,* gerundive of *addere* to add] *noun* (*plural* **addenda,** ă<u>den</u>dă) an addition, an appendix, something added to a book, document, etc.: *"'But they tasted just as good,' added Bob, by way of note or addendum, after a moment's pause"* (George Eliot, *The Mill on the Floss,* 1860). *~abbreviated form* **add.**

ad eundem (ad eeăndăm) LATIN [abbreviation of *ad eundem gradum* to the same grade] *adverb phrase* to the same degree, rank, or class (usually in reference to honorary degrees awarded by a university or other institution to those who have studied elsewhere). *~abbreviated form* **ad eund.**

à deux (a <u>dă</u>) FRENCH [by two] *adjective phrase* for two people, involving two people (usually in private together). *~adverb phrase* privately between just two people: *"They dined à deux each evening in a cosy restaurant up a narrow back street."*

ad finem (ad <u>feen</u>ăm) LATIN [to the end] *adverb phrase* to the end (a bibliographical instruction in a text advising the reader to read from a certain point to the end of the passage). *~abbreviated form* **ad fin.**

ad hoc (ad <u>hok</u>) LATIN [to this, for this] *adverb phrase* for this special purpose, in this particular case. *~adjective phrase* improvised or dedicated to a specific end or purpose: *"The governor has decided to set up an ad hoc committee to look into the problem."*

ad hominem (ad <u>hom</u>ănăm) LATIN [to the person] *adverb phrase* appealing to a person's emotions rather than to his or her intellect; can also refer to a personal attack on someone rather than a considered criticism of his or her views or deeds. *~adjective phrase* personal, aimed at or directed against an individual.

ad idem (ad i̱dem) LATIN [to the same thing] *adjective phrase* agreed, in agreement, on the same point.

adieu (adyoo, adya̱) FRENCH [with God] *interjection* (*plural* **adieus** or **adieux,** adyoo, adya̱, adyooz, adya̱z) go with God! good-bye!: "*And, farewell, friends; / Thus Thisbe ends: Adieu, adieu, adieu*" (William Shakespeare, *A Midsummer Night's Dream,* c. 1595). ~*noun* a farewell, a leave-taking.

ad infinitum (ad infa̱nı̄ta̱m) LATIN [to the infinite] *adverb phrase* without end, indefinitely: "*I think I rave in a kind of exquisite delirium. I should wish now to protract this moment ad infinitum; but I dare not*" (Charlotte Brontë, *Jane Eyre,* 1847). ~*adjective phrase* without end, indefinitely.

ad initium (ad ini̱sheea̱m) LATIN [at the beginning] *adverb phrase* at the beginning, from the start. ~*abbreviated form* **ad init.**

ad interim (ad i̱nta̱rim) LATIN [to meanwhile] *adverb phrase* for the time being, meanwhile, temporarily: "*The assistant principal will run the school ad interim until a new principal is appointed.*" ~*adjective phrase* temporary. ~*abbreviated form* **ad int.**

adios (adeeo̱s) SPANISH [with God] *interjection* good-bye! farewell!: "'A

pretty scholar,' laughed the Lakeman. 'Adios, Senor!' and leaping into the sea, he swam back to his comrades*" (Herman Melville, *Moby-Dick,* 1851).

ad lib (ad li̱b), **ad-lib** LATIN [abbreviation of *ad libitum* at pleasure] *adverb phrase* without restraint, spontaneously. ~*adjective phrase* unrestrained, spontaneous. ~*verb* to deliver a spontaneous, extemporized speech or performance: "*The actors were forced to ad lib until the stagehands could free the jammed curtain.*" ~*noun* something said, written, or done spontaneously.

ad litem (ad lı̄ta̱m) LATIN [for the suit] *adjective phrase* (law) as legal guardian for another. ~*adverb phrase* (law) as legal guardian for another.

ad litteram (ad li̱ta̱ram) LATIN [to the letter] *adverb phrase* to the letter, exactly.

ad locum (ad lo̱ka̱m) LATIN [to the place] *adverb phrase* (in bibliographical references) at the place. ~*abbreviated form* **ad loc.**

ad majorem Dei gloriam (ad ma̱yora̱m dayee gloreea̱m) LATIN [for the greater glory of God] *adverb phrase* for the greater glory of God (motto of the Jesuit order). ~*abbreviated form* **A.M.D.G.**

ad nauseam (ad no̱zeea̱m) LATIN [to sickness] *adverb phrase* interminably,

5

to an excessive or sickening degree: "*She rattled on about her discovery ad nauseam.*"

adobe (ădōbee) SPANISH [*adobar* to plaster, from Arabic *at-tub* brick] *noun* a simple brick made from sun-dried earth or straw, or a building made of such bricks: "*The house and several outbuildings were constructed of adobe, which, according to Belding, retained the summer heat on into winter, and the winter cold on into summer*" (Zane Grey, *Desert Gold*, 1913).

Adonis (ădōnis) GREEK [after the beautiful youth of Greek and Roman mythology with whom the goddess of love Aphrodite fell in love] *noun* an exceptionally handsome young man: "'*Humph! my beau must be an Adonis indeed, Matilda, the admired of all beholders, if I am to be contented with him alone*" (Anne Brontë, *Agnes Grey*, 1845).

ad personam (ad persōnăm) LATIN [to the person] *adverb phrase* (of an argument) designed to appeal to a person's emotions rather than to their intellect. ~*adjective phrase* of or relating to such an appeal.

ad referendum (ad refărendăm) LATIN [for referring] *adverb phrase* for further consideration (usually by a higher authority).

ad rem (ad rem) LATIN [to the thing] *adverb phrase* to the purpose, rele-vantly, to the point: "*The evidence offered in the company's defense was hardly ad rem.*" ~*adjective phrase* relevant.

adroit (ădroit) FRENCH [*à* toward and *droit* right, from Latin *directus* straight] *adjective* clever, dexterous, skillful, resourceful: "*He told her about the election, and Anna knew how by adroit questions to bring him to what gave him most pleasure—his own success*" (Leo Tolstoy, *Anna Karenina*, 1874–76).

ad valorem (ad vălorăm) LATIN [according to strength] *adjective phrase* in proportion to the value of the goods or property: "*The new tax will be raised ad valorem.*" ~*abbreviated form* **ad val.**

ad verbum (ad verbăm) LATIN [to a word] *adverb phrase* verbatim, word for word, to the word: "*The reporter took down the statement ad verbum.*" ~*adjective phrase* verbatim, word for word, to the word.

ad vivum (ad veevăm) LATIN [according to life] *adverb phrase* (of portraits etc.) from life, lifelike. ~*adjective phrase* lifelike.

advocatus diaboli (advăkahtăs deeabălee) LATIN [advocate of the devil] *noun phrase* (*plural* **advocati diaboli,** advăkahtee deeabălee) a devil's advocate, a person appointed to find faults (originally, an official of the Roman Catholic Church appointed to question a nominee's suitability for beatification or canonization).

aegis (ee̯jăs), **egis** GREEK [*aigis* goatskin, a reference to the goatskin shield of the god Zeus] *noun* auspices, sponsorship, patronage, authority, protection, direction, guidance: *"It's a new series of books produced under the aegis of the Department of Education."*

aegrotat (ī̯grōtat) LATIN [he is sick, from *aegrotare* to be ill] *noun* a certificate confirming that a student is too ill to attend an examination, lecture, etc.; can also refer to a degree awarded to a student despite the fact that he or she has missed examinations through illness: *"The teacher was reluctant to give the boys an aegrotat in case it served as a precedent."*

aeolian (ayō̯leeăn, eeō̯leeăn) GREEK [after Aeolus, the Greek god of the wind] *noun* powered by the wind (usually referring to musical instruments that are sounded by the wind): *"A low moan issued from the aeolian harp as the wind stirred the strings."*

aeon (ee̯on), **eon** GREEK [*aion* age] *noun* an age, an immensely long period of time: *"Certainly, too, we shall awake, and live again and again shall sleep, and so on and on, through periods, spaces, and times, from aeon unto aeon, till the world is dead, and the worlds beyond the world are dead, and naught liveth save the Spirit that is Life"* (H. Rider Haggard, *She*, 1887).

affaire (ă̯fair) FRENCH [affair, abbreviated from *affaire d'amour* love affair or *affaire de coeur* affair of the heart, *à faire* to do] *noun* a love affair or scandal, sensation, event: *"The next day's paper had these additional particulars. 'The Tragedy in the Rue Morgue. Many individuals have been examined in relation to this most extraordinary and frightful affair,' (The word 'affaire' has not yet, in France, that levity of import which it conveys with us). . ."* (Edgar Allan Poe, "The Murders in the Rue Morgue," 1841).

affaire d'amour *See* AFFAIRE.

affaire de coeur *See* AFFAIRE.

affaire d'honneur (ă̯fair do̯ne̯r) FRENCH [affair of honor] *noun phrase* (*plural* **affaires d'honneur**) an argument or conflict involving a challenge to a person's honor, a duel: *"The young duke considered the insult an affaire d'honneur and immediately challenged his critic to a duel."*

afficionado *See* AFICIONADO.

affidavit (afă̯day̯vit) LATIN [he/she has made an oath, from *affidare* to declare on oath] *noun* a written statement made under an oath before a magistrate of other court official: *"Will you do me the favor to mention (as it may interest her) that I have something to tell her on her return in reference to the person who copied the affidavit in the Chancery suit, which so powerfully stimulated her curiosity"* (Charles Dickens, *Bleak House*, 1852–53).

afflatus (ăf̲l̲a̲y̲tăs) LATIN [act of blowing or breathing on, from *afflare* to blow on] *noun* (*plural* **afflatus** or **afflatuses**, ăf̲l̲a̲y̲tăsiz) inspiration or knowledge (especially when apparently imparted from divine or supernatural sources): *"Through me the afflatus surging and surging, through me the current / and index"* (Walt Whitman, *Leaves of Grass,* 1855).

aficionado (ăfishă̲n̲a̲h̲dō, ăfiseeă̲n̲a̲h̲dō), **afficionado** SPANISH [amateur, from the past participle of *aficionar* to inspire affection, ultimately from Latin *affectio* favorable disposition] *noun* a person who has a particular interest in or enthusiasm for something: *"He likes to think of himself as an aficionado of the arts."* ~*noun, feminine* **aficionada** (ăfishă̲n̲a̲h̲dă, ăfiseeă̲n̲a̲h̲dă), **afficionada** a female who has a particular interest in or enthusiasm for something.

a fortiori (ay forshee̲o̲r̲e̲e̲, ay forteē̲o̲r̲e̲e̲) LATIN [from the stronger] *adverb phrase* with greater reason or force, much more, even more so, all the more. ~*adjective phrase* more certain, more conclusive.

aga (a̲h̲gă) **agha** TURKISH [master, lord, from Mongolian *aqa*] *noun* (formerly) the rank of a military commander in the Ottoman Empire; also used more generally as a courtesy title in rural Turkish communities: *"Then the Princess bade an aga of the eumuchry go down and barter the old lamp for a new*

lamp" (Richard Burton, "Aladdin; or, The Wonderful Lamp," *Arabian Nights,* 1885–88). Aga khan is the title of the spiritual leader of the Nizari sect of Ismaili Muslims.

agape (aga̲h̲pay, a̲g̲ăpay) GREEK [brotherly love] *noun* (*plural* **agapes** or **agapae**, a̲g̲ăpee) a love feast or feast of fellowship among early Christians; can also refer to God's love for the human race.

agenda (ă̲j̲e̲n̲dă) LATIN [things to be done, neuter plural of *agendum,* from *agere* to do] *noun* a list of matters to be dealt with, or an underlying plan, policy, or program. ~*adjective* of or relating to an agenda: *"'Meanwhile,' he glanced at his agenda paper, 'I have one or two more points to bring before the meeting'"* (Arthur Conan Doyle, "The Valley of Fear," 1914–15).

agent provocateur (azhon(g) prōvok̲ă̲t̲e̲r̲, ayjănt prōvokă̲t̲e̲r̲) FRENCH [provoking agent] *noun phrase* (*plural* **agents provocateurs**) a spy, a secret agent who incites others to commit incriminating acts while pretending to be in sympathy with them: *"The proper business of an 'agent provocateur' is to provoke. As far as I can judge from your record kept here, you have done nothing to earn your money for the last three years"* (Joseph Conrad, *The Secret Agent,* 1907).

aggiornamento (ăjornă̲m̲e̲n̲tō) ITALIAN [updating, from *aggiornare* to update] *noun* the modernization or updating of an institution or organization.

agitprop (ăjătprop) RUSSIAN [*agitatsiya* agitation and *propagandy* propaganda] *noun* propaganda, especially that of a political (orginally, communist) kind: *"Severe penalties were imposed on anyone suspected of actively spreading agitprop against the government."*

agnostic (ăgnostik) GREEK [*agnostos* unknown, coined by the biologist T. H. Huxley (1825–95)] *noun* a person who professes uncertainty about the existence or nonexistence of God. ~*adjective* of or relating to agnosticism: *"'Oah yes. I have met him several times at Benares, and also at Buddh Gaya, to interrogate him on religious points and devil-worship. He is pure agnostic—same as me'"* (Rudyard Kipling, *Kim,* 1901).

Agnus Dei (agnăs dayee) LATIN [Lamb of God] *noun phrase* the Lamb of God, Jesus Christ; can also refer to the Christian symbol of the lamb and flag, representing Christ, or to a musical setting of a Christian prayer for peace beginning with these words that forms a part of the Mass.

agog (ăgog) FRENCH [*en gogues* in mirth] *adjective* eager, enthusiastic, excited: *"They found the stone house agog with excitement"* (Lucy Maud Montgomery, *Anne of Avonlea,* 1909). ~*adverb* eagerly, enthusiastically, excitedly.

agora (agără) GREEK [assembly, *ageirein* to gather] *noun* (*plural* **agoras** or **agorae,** agaree) a marketplace or gathering place.

agoraphobia (agrăfōbeeă, agărăfōbeeă) GREEK [fear of the marketplace, from *agora* marketplace and *phobos* fear, coined by German psychologist Carl Westphal in 1871] *noun* an irrational fear of open spaces: *"Agoraphobia kept the old woman inside her house for most of the last thirty years of her life."*

ahimsa (ăhimsă) SANSKRIT [non-violence, from *a* non and *himsa* violence] *noun* the doctrine of refraining from causing harm to any living thing, as propounded by the Buddhist, Hindu, and Jain religions.

à huis clos (a wee klō) FRENCH [in a closed door] *adverb phrase* in secret, behind closed doors: *"The meeting was held à huis clos."*

aide-de-camp (ayd dă kom(g)), **aid-de-camp** FRENCH [assistant of the camp] *noun* (*plural* **aides-de-camp**) an assistant, especially a military aide: *"The general's aide-de-camp was ordered to communicate with the enemy's headquarters."* ~*abbreviated form* **A.D.C.**

aide-mémoire (ayd memwahr) FRENCH [memory aid, from *aider* to aid and *mémoire* memory] *noun* (*plural* **aide-mémoires**) something that serves as a reminder, a means of jogging the memory, a memorandum: *"At the end of the talk the great man checked his aide-mémoire, a tiny piece of paper, to see if there was anything he had omitted."*

aigrette (ay<u>gret</u>, <u>ay</u>gret) FRENCH [egret's plume] *noun* a tuft of feathers or spray of gems worn in the hair or on a hat: *"The admirable roundness of the wrist was well set off by a bracelet which encircled it, and which also was ornamented and clasped by a magnificent aigrette of jewels—telling, in words that could not be mistaken, at once of the wealth and fastidious taste of the wearer."* (Edgar Allan Poe, "The Spectacles," 1844).

aiguille (ay<u>gweel</u>, ay<u>gwee</u>) FRENCH [needle] *noun* a needle-like pinnacle of rock.

aikido (ī<u>kee</u>dō) JAPANESE [mutual spirit art, from *ai* together, *ki* spirit, and *do* way] *noun* Japanese art of self-defense in which an opponent's momentum is turned against him.

aileron (<u>ay</u>lăron) FRENCH [*aile* wing] *noun* a hinged flap along the trailing edge of an aircraft wing that is adjusted as the aircraft banks in order to maintain balance: *"Inspection of the wreckage after the crash revealed that one of the ailerons was missing."*

à la (ă lă), **a la** FRENCH [to the, *à la mode de* in the manner of] *preposition* after the manner of, in the manner of, in the style of, as done by.

à la carte (ă lă <u>kahrt</u>), **a la carte** FRENCH [by the menu, by the bill of fare] *adverb phrase* from a menu on which each item is separately priced. *~adjective phrase* from a menu on which each item is separately priced: *"Because it was his birthday, he decided to treat them both to dishes from the à la carte menu."* *~abbreviated form* **a.l.c.**

à la française (ă lă fron<u>sayz</u>, a lă fron-<u>sez</u>) FRENCH [from *à la mode française* in the French manner] *adjective phrase* in the French style, after the French fashion. *~adverb phrase* in the French style, after the French fashion: *"Every detail of the décor was done à la française."*

à la grecque (ă lă <u>grek</u>) FRENCH [in the Greek manner] *adjective phrase* food served in a sauce of olive oil, lemon juice, and seasoning.

à la mode (ă lă <u>mōd</u>), **a la mode** FRENCH [according to the fashion] *adjective phrase* fashionable, stylish, chic, up-to-date: *"The luxuriously rich are not simply kept comfortably warm, but unnaturally hot; as I implied before, they are cooked, of course à la mode."* (Henry David Thoreau, *Walden; or, Life in the Woods*, 1854). Also, served with ice cream.

à la russe (ă lă <u>roos</u>) FRENCH [in the Russian manner] *adverb phrase* in the Russian manner. *~adjective phrase* in the Russian manner.

albino (al<u>bī</u>nō) PORTUGUESE [from Spanish *albo* white, itself from Latin *albus* white] *noun* a human being or other living creature that is congenitally deficient in pigment (usually resulting in a pale skin, colorless hair, and pink eyes): *"'Griffin,' answered the Voice—'a younger student, almost an albino, six feet high, and broad, with a pink and white face and red eyes—who won the medal for chemistry'"* (H. G. Wells, *The Invisible Man,* 1897). ~*adjective* of or relating to albinism.

album (<u>al</u>băm) LATIN [white tablet, *albus* white] *noun* a book with blank pages suitable for pasting in newspaper clippings, photographs, and other memorabilia; can also refer to a long-playing record or to any collection of writings or pictures in book form: *"For Rosamond never showed any unbecoming knowledge, and was always that combination of correct sentiments, music, dancing, drawing, elegant note-writing, private album for extracted verse, and perfect blond loveliness, which made the irresistible woman for the doomed man of that date"* (George Eliot, *Middlemarch,* 1871–72).

a.l.c. See À LA CARTE.

alcazar (al<u>kaz</u>ăr) SPANISH [from Arabic *al-kasr* the captain] *noun* a Spanish palace or fortress: *"The great tower of the alcazar still bears the scars of ancient bombardments."*

alcove (<u>al</u>kōv) FRENCH [from Spanish *alcoba,* ultimately from Arabic *al-qubbah* arch] *noun* a recess, nook, niche: *"He sat at his desk in the dark alcove."*

al dente (al <u>den</u>tay, al <u>den</u>tee) ITALIAN [to the tooth] *adjective phrase* lightly cooked (so as to remain slightly firm). ~*adverb phrase* lightly cooked (so as to remain slightly firm): *"The vegetables should be cooked al dente, so that they are still crisp to eat."*

alea jacta est (<u>a</u>leeă yaktă <u>est</u>) LATIN [the die has been cast, attributed to Julius Caesar (100–44 B.C.) when he crossed the Rubicon] *noun phrase* the die is cast, it is too late to go back.

alert (ă<u>lert</u>) FRENCH [*alerte,* itself from Italian *all'erta* on the lookout] *adjective* watchful, ready to act. ~*noun* a state of watchfulness or readiness. ~*verb* to warn others of something, to advise others to be ready.

al fine (al <u>fee</u>nee) ITALIAN [to the end] *adverb phrase* (music) to the end of the piece.

alfresco (al<u>fres</u>kō), **al fresco** ITALIAN [in the open] *adjective* open-air. ~*adverb* in the open air, out-of-doors: *"If the weather stays fine we shall eat alfresco."*

algebra (<u>al</u>jăbră) ARABIC [*al-jabr* the reduction] *noun* a form of arithmetic in which letters are substituted for numbers but continue to be treated in a mathematical way, or a book containing such calculations: *"His studies in binary code and Boolean algebra contributed to the devising of* *computer circuitry that is crucial to modern digital telecommunications."*

alias (a̱yleeăs, a̱ylyăs) LATIN [abbreviation of *alias dictus* at other times called, otherwise] *noun* (*plural* **aliases,** a̱yleeăsiz, a̱ylyăsiz) an assumed name. *~adverb* also called, otherwise known as: *"This dreadful threat had the desired effect, and through the two remaining fields the three pair of small legs trotted on without any serious interruption, notwithstanding a small pond full of tadpoles, alias 'bullheads,' which the lads looked at wistfully"* (George Eliot, *Adam Bede,* 1859).

alibi (a̱lăbī) LATIN [elsewhere, *alius* other] *noun* (in law) a defensive plea that a person was elsewhere at the time that an offense was committed; also used more generally to refer to any excuse designed to escape punishment or blame: *"'Writing? Rot! What's he writing? He's breaking you in, my dear; that's what he's doing: establishing an alibi'"* (Edith Wharton, *Glimpses of the Moon,* 1922).

aliyah (aẖleeyah), **aliya** HEBREW [*aliya* ascent] *noun* the immigration of Jews to Israel.

alla breve (ală bre̱v, ală bra̱yvee) ITALIAN [according to the breve] *noun phrase* (in music) a symbol indicating that a passage should be played in duple or quadruple time, with two minim beats in a bar. *~adverb phrase* (in music) to be played in duple or quadruple time, with two minim beats in a bar. *~adjective phrase* (in music) of or relating to a passage to be played in duple or quadruple time, with two minim beats in a bar.

Allahu akbar (alahoo a̱kbahr) ARABIC [Allah is great, from *al ilah* the God] *noun phrase* God is great (Islamic chant).

allée (ala̱y) FRENCH [Old French *aler* to go] *noun* a tree-lined walk through a garden or park.

allegretto (alăgre̱tō) ITALIAN [diminutive of *allegro* merry] *adverb* (in music) to be played at a medium-fast pace. *~adjective* (in music) medium-fast. *~noun* (*plural* **allegrettos** or **allegretti,** alăgre̱tee) a medium-fast pace, or a piece of music to be played at a medium-fast pace: *"I have heard an Italian conductor (no longer living) take the adagio of that symphony at a lively allegretto, slowing down for the warmer major sections into the speed and manner of the heroine's death song in a Verdi opera. . ."* (George Bernard Shaw, *Treatise on Parents and Children*).

allegro (ăle̱grō, ăla̱ygrō) ITALIAN [merry] *noun* (*plural* **allegri,** ăle̱gree, ăla̱ygree) a piece of music written to be played at a brisk pace. *~adverb* (in music) to be played at a brisk pace. *~adjective* (in music) brisk, lively.

alleluia *See* HALLELUJAH.

alligator (a̲l̲ăgaytăr) SPANISH [*el lagarto* the lizard, ultimately from Latin *lacertus* lizard] *noun*   a broad-snouted reptile of the crocodilian group, native to the Southeastern United States and other parts of the world: *"Under the shore his boat was tied, / And all her listless crew / Watched the gray alligator slide / Into the still bayou"* (Henry W. Longfellow, "The Quadroon Girl," 1842).

alma mater (almă m̲a̲htăr, almă m̲a̲ytăr) LATIN [fostering mother] *noun phrase* (*plural* **alma maters,** almă m̲a̲htrăz or **almae matres,** almă m̲a̲ytreez)   a school, college, or university where an individual has been educated: *"The U. is my own Alma Mater, and I am proud to be known as an alumni, but there are certain instructors there who seem to think we ought to turn the conduct of the nation over to hoboes and roustabouts"* (Sinclair Lewis, *Babbitt,* 1922).

aloe vera (alō v̲e̲eră) LATIN [true aloe, *aloe* and *vera* true] *noun phrase*   an aloe, the source of an extract used in the preparation of skin-care and other health products.

aloha (ăl̲ō̲hah) HAWAIIAN [*aloha* love] *interjection*   a customary word of greeting or farewell among Hawaiians.

alpaca (alp̲a̲kă) SPANISH [Aymara *allpaqa*] *noun*   a sheeplike domesticated mammal *(Lama pacos)* of South America, and the fine wool for which it is prized: *"The peasants piled the mules high with bales of alpaca."*

alpenstock (a̲l̲penstok) GERMAN [Alpstick, from *Alpen* Alps and *stock* staff] *noun*   a long iron-tipped staff traditionally used by mountain walkers: *"The last we saw of him he was striding into the mist, stabbing the path ahead with his ancient alpenstock."*

alpha (a̲l̲fă) GREEK [first letter of the Greek alphabet] *noun*   the first letter of the Greek alphabet, used to indicate the first in a sequence or ranking.

al segno (al s̲a̲ynyō) ITALIAN [from the sign] *adverb phrase*   (in music)   repeat from the sign indicating the beginning of a particular passage.

alter ego (oltăr e̲e̲gō, oltăr e̲g̲ō) LATIN [another I] *noun phrase* (*plural* **alter egos**)   a person's second or other self, or an intimate friend: *"Over the months they became very close, behaving almost as each other's alter ego."*

alto (a̲l̲tō) ITALIAN [high, from Latin *altus* high] *noun*   a contralto singer or a musical instrument with a lower range than treble or soprano. ~*adjective*   of or relating to a voice or musical instrument with an alto range: *"They are offering lessons on the alto saxophone."*

alumnus (ăl̲ă̲mnăs) LATIN [pupil, foster son, from *alere* to nourish] *noun* (*plural* **alumni,** ăl̲ă̲mnee, or **alumnae,**

ălămnnee, ălămnī) a former student of a particular school, college, university, or other organization: *"He was rewarded by seeing Maggie let her work fall and gradually get so absorbed in his wonderful geological story that she sat looking at him, leaning forward with crossed arms and with an entire absence of self-consciousness, as if he had been the snuffiest of old professors and she a downy-lipped alumnus"* (George Eliot, *The Mill on the Floss*, 1860). ~*noun, feminine* **alumna** (ălămnă) a female who has attended a particular school, college, university, or other organization.

A.M. *See* ANTE MERIDIEM.

amanuensis (ămanyooensis) LATIN [secretary, from *servus a manu* slave with secretarial duties] *noun* (*plural* **amanuenses,** ămanyooenseez) a person who is employed to take dictation or make copies of manuscript: *"Nicholas briefly replied, that he wanted to know whether there was any such post to be had, as secretary or amanuensis to a gentleman"* (Charles Dickens, *Nicholas Nickleby*, 1838–39).

amaretto (ămaretō) ITALIAN [diminutive of *amaro* bitter] *noun* (*plural* **amaretti,** ămaretee) a type of macaroon made with bitter almonds, or a liqueur made with almonds: *"The cardinal usually enjoys a small glass of amaretto after dinner."*

amateur (ămăter, ămăchăr) FRENCH [lover, from Italian *amatore* lover, ultimately from Latin *amare* to love] *noun* a person who pursues a particular interest, line of study, sport, or other activity on an unpaid, nonprofessional basis, usually out of pure enthusiasm for it; can also refer to someone who lacks experience or competence in something, especially in comparison to a professional: *"Oh no, Lady Caroline. I have only had one husband as yet. I suppose you look upon me as quite an amateur"* (Oscar Wilde, *A Woman of No Importance*, 1893). ~*adjective* of or relating to an amateur pursuit, or to someone who lacks professional expertise or competence in something.

amazon (amăzăn), **Amazon** GREEK [*Amazon*] *noun* a member of a mythological race of female warriors (fabled to cut off a breast in order to pull their bows) and by extension any physically powerful or imposing female: *"'I may not be a Amazon, Miss Floy, and wouldn't so demean myself by such disfigurement, but anyways I'm not a giver up, I hope'"* (Charles Dickens, *Dombey and Son*, 1846–48).

ambiance (ombeeons, ambeeons), **ambience** FRENCH [atmosphere, *ambiant* ambient, ultimately from Latin *ambire* to go round] *noun* the atmosphere or character of a particular place, person, or thing; or, more generally, the immediate environment or surroundings: *"She stood quite motionless for a minute or two, taking in the ambiance of the place."*

ambrosia (am<u>brō</u>zhǎ, am<u>brō</u>zeeǎ) LATIN [immortality, from Greek *ambrotos* immortal] *noun* the elixir of the gods (variously identified as either food, drink, or perfume) in Roman and Greek mythology, and thus anything with a delightful taste or scent: *"And as I sat I fell into conversation with a god-like stranger who sipped some golden ambrosia"* (Robert Service, *Ballads of a Bohemian*, 1920).

A.M.D.G. *See* AD MAJOREM DEI GLORIAM.

ameba *See* AMOEBA.

âme damnée (am dam<u>nee</u>) FRENCH [damned soul] *noun phrase* (*plural* **âmes damnées**) a willing servant or devotee, a stooge.

amen (ay<u>men</u>, ah<u>men</u>) LATIN [from Hebrew *amen* truly, verily] *interjection* so be it (spoken at the end of a prayer or to express approval): *"For thine is the kingdom, the power, and the glory, for ever and ever. Amen."* (Lord's Prayer). ~*noun* an expression of approval or assent.

amende honorable (ǎmend onǎ<u>rah</u>blǎ) FRENCH [honorable amends] *noun phrase* (*plural* **amendes honorables**) a public apology or open acknowledgment of error.

amicus curiae (ameekǎs <u>kyoo</u>riee, ameekǎs <u>kyoo</u>reeī) LATIN [a friend of the court] *noun phrase* (*plural* **amici curiae**, ameekee <u>kyoo</u>riee, ameesee <u>kyoo</u>reeī) an individual or organization invited by a court to advise on a case in which the individual or organization is not otherwise involved. ~*abbreviated form* **am. cur.**

amigo (a<u>mee</u>gō, ǎ<u>mee</u>gō) SPANISH [friend, from Latin *amicus*] *noun* friend, comrade: *"It is a fan I am looking for. I cannot understand how Antonia could—Well! Have you found it, amigo?"* (Joseph Conrad, *Nostromo*, 1904).

amnesia (am<u>nee</u>zhǎ, am<u>nee</u>zeeǎ) GREEK [forgetfulness] *noun* forgetfulness or loss of memory due to brain injury, illness, or other condition: *"Research is being undertaken to determine whether people who suffer from amnesia can still remember their general knowledge of objects."*

amoeba (ǎ<u>mee</u>bǎ), **ameba** LATIN [from Greek *amoibe* change] *noun* (*plural* **ameobas** or **amoebae,** ǎ<u>mee</u>bee) a single-celled water-dwelling microorganism with a constantly changing shape belonging to a large genus of protozoans: *"The Life Force either will not or cannot achieve immortality except in very low organisms: indeed it is by no means ascertained that even the amoeba is immortal"* (George Bernard Shaw, *Treatise on Parents and Children*).

amok (ǎ<u>mǎk</u>, ǎ<u>mok</u>), **amuck** MALAY [*amoq* frenzied] *adverb* in a wild, frenzied, uncontrollable manner: *"It is true, I might have resisted forcibly with more or less effect, might have run 'amok' against society; but I preferred that society should run 'amok' against me, it being the desperate party"* (Henry David Thoreau, *Walden; or, Life in the Woods,* 1854). ~*adjective* wild, frenzied, uncontrollable.

amontillado (ămontilah̄dō) SPANISH [in the manner of Montilla, Andalusia] *noun* a pale-colored medium dry Spanish sherry: *"Luchresi cannot tell Amontillado from Sherry"* (Edgar Allan Poe, "The Cask of Amontillado," 1846).

amoretto (amăretō) ITALIAN [diminutive of *amore* love, ultimately from Latin *amor* love] *noun* (*plural* **amorettos** or **amoretti,** amăretee) a cupid or cherub: *"Carved amoretti adorn the tomb at each corner."*

amoroso (amărōsō) ITALIAN [from Latin *amorosus* amorous, from *amor* love] *noun* (*plural* **amorosos** or **amorosi,** amărōsee) a lover, a gallant; also the name of a sweetened oloroso sherry: *"Singular though it may seem, Winterbourne was vexed that the young girl, in joining her amoroso, should not appear more impatient"* (Henry James, *Daisy Miller,* 1879). ~*adverb* (in music) to be played tenderly. ~*adjective* (in music) tender.

amor omnia vincit *See* AMOR VINCIT OMNIA.

amor patriae (amor patriee) LATIN [love of country] *noun phrase* patriotism, love of one's country.

amor vincit omnia (amor vinchit omneeă), **amor omnia vincit** LATIN [love conquers all] *noun phrase* love conquers all, love overcomes all difficulties: *"We spent our wedding night in a huge four-poster bed on which was inscribed the legend 'amor vincit omnia'."*

amour (amoor) FRENCH [love, ultimately from Latin *amare* to love] *noun* a love affair or a lover: *"The papers will quickly tire of reporting her amours."*

amourette (amăret) FRENCH [little love affair] *noun* a brief, relatively insignificant, love affair: *"'My dear Menteith,' said Montrose, very kindly, 'were you one of the gay cavaliers of Whitehall, who are, in their way, as great self-seekers as our friend Dalgetty, should I need to plague you with inquiring into such an amourette as this?'"* (Walter Scott, *A Legend of Montrose,* 1819).

amour propre (amoor propră) FRENCH [love of oneself] *noun phrase* self-esteem, self-love, vanity: *"I smiled inwardly; and strange to say, though my amour propre was excited not disagreeably by the conquest, my better feelings remained untouched"* (Charlotte Brontë, *The Professor,* 1857).

amphora (amfără) LATIN [from Greek *amphoreus,* from *amphi* around and *phoreus* bearer] *noun* (*plural* **amphoras** or **amphorae**, am̲fáree, am̲fā́rī) a two-handled jar or vase with a narrow neck and oval body, of a type associated with ancient Greek culture: *"This potsherd had, in my judgment, once been a part of an ordinary amphora of medium size"* (H. Rider Haggard, *She*, 1887).

amuck *See* AMOK.

anabasis (an̲ahbásăs) GREEK [a going up, inland march, recalling a retreat by Greek warriors from the Persian Empire, as recorded in the *Anabasis* of Xenophon (c. 430–c. 355 B.C.)] *noun* (*plural* **anabeses**, an̲ahbásees) a military advance or expedition, especially one going inland or up-country in difficult circumstances.

anaemia *See* ANEMIA.

anaesthesia *See* ANESTHESIA.

analgesia (anăljée̱zheeă, anăljée̱ezeeă) GREEK [painlessness, from *an* not and *algos* pain] *noun* insensibility to pain through the use of drugs or other remedies.

analysis (ănalăsăs) GREEK [a breaking up, from *analyein* to break up] *noun* (*plural* **analyses**, ănaláseez) a detailed examination or study of something, or the breaking down of a thing into its constituent elements: *"Marilla was not given to subjective analysis of her thoughts and feelings"* (Lucy

Maud Montgomery, *Anne of Green Gables*, 1908).

anaphrodisiac (anafrădize̱eăk) GREEK [not belonging to Aphrodite] *adjective* discouraging sexual desire: *"The seeds of the poppy are traditionally believed to have an anaphrodisiac effect upon those who consume them."* See also APHRODISIAC.

anathema (ănathămă) GREEK [something devoted to evil, from *anatithenai* to set up] *noun* (*plural* **anathemas** or **anathemata**, ănathămahtă) a curse, or a person or thing that inspires loathing in others: *"Lydia was sure that Lucy was a great deal too good for him. Cecilia had wondered where he would go to—a form of anathema which had brought down a rebuke from her mother"* (Anthony Trollope, *The Eustace Diamonds*, 1873).

ancien régime (onsyon(g) rayzhee̱m) FRENCH [old regime] *noun phrase* (*plural* **anciens régimes**) the system of government of France prior to the 1789 revolution and, by extension, any former social or political system or other mode of things that has become outdated: *"The ancien régime was utterly swept away when the army took over."*

andante (an̲dantay, an̲dantee) ITALIAN [walking, present participle of *andare* to go] *adverb* (in music) to be played moderately slowly. ~*adjective* (in music) moderately slow. ~*noun* (*plural*

andantes) a piece of music to be played at a moderately slow pace: *"The grand piano was a splendid instrument, the symphony was well performed. At least, so it seemed to Nekhludoff, who knew and liked that symphony. Listening to the beautiful andante, he felt a tickling in his nose, he was so touched by his many virtues"* (Leo Tolstoy, *Resurrection,* 1899–1900).

andantino (andanteenō) ITALIAN [diminutive of *andante* walking] *adverb* (in music) to be played at a pace slightly faster than andante. ~*adjective* (in music) slightly faster than andante. ~*noun* a musical piece to be played at an andantino pace.

androgynous (androjănăs) GREEK [*androgynos* hermaphrodite] *adjective* of neither one sex nor the other, or having the characteristics of both sexes: *"No one will suppose that the marsupials still remained androgynous, after they had approximately acquired their present structure"* (Charles Darwin, *The Descent of Man,* 1871).

android (android) GREEK [*androeides* manlike] *noun* a robot with a human form: *"The space station of the future will be operated largely by robots, possibly in the form of androids."*

anemia (ăneemeeă), **anaemia** LATIN [from Greek *anaimia* bloodlessness] *noun* a lack of blood or a shortage of red blood cells in the blood, resulting in a pasty complexion; also used more generally to refer to anything deemed bloodless or lacking in vitality: *"The doctors diagnosed anemia and the patient was confined to bed."*

anesthesia (anăstheezhă), **anaesthesia** LATIN [from Greek *anaisthesia* insensibility, from *aisthanesthai* to perceive] *noun* a loss of sensation (through the use of drugs or other techniques): *"The patients began to emerge from their anesthesia after some 12 hours."*

angelus (angălăs) LATIN [angel, abbreviation of *Angelus Domini* angel of the lord, from Greek *aggelos* messenger] *noun* a devotional prayer on the subject of the Incarnation that is recited in Catholic churches in the morning, at noon, and at sunset each day (named after the opening word); can also refer to the bell rung when the prayer is recited: *"The sound of the angelus bell tolling in the village church drifted to them on the noonday breeze."*

angina pectoris (anjīnă pektoris) LATIN [strangling of the chest, from Greek *anchone* strangling and *pectoris* of the breast] *noun phrase* a heart disease causing painful spasms in the chest.

angst (ankst) GERMAN [*Angst* fear, anguish, dread] *noun* a feeling of apprehension, anxiety, or insecurity: *"His music shows a barely disguised angst."*

anima (anămă) LATIN [soul] *noun* (*plural* **animas** or **animae,** anămī) the self, a person's inner self, or the feminine aspect of an individual's personality (such as in psychoanalysis).

anima mundi (anămă <u>mă</u>ndee) LATIN [mind of the world] *noun phrase* world soul, the underlying power that controls the universe.

animato (ană<u>mah</u>tō) ITALIAN [animated, from Latin *animatus*] *adverb* (in music) to be played with animation. ~*adjective* (in music) animated.

animus (<u>a</u>nămăs) LATIN [mind] *noun* (*plural* **animuses** or **animi,** <u>a</u>nămee, <u>a</u>nămī) the mind, the spirit; can also refer to ill will or hostility toward someone or something. Also used in psychoanalysis to refer to the masculine aspect of an individual's personality: *"Dorothea had observed the animus with which Will's part in the painful story had been recalled more than once; but she had uttered no word, being checked now, as she had not been formerly in speaking of Will, by the consciousness of a deeper relation between them which must always remain in consecrated secrecy"* (George Eliot, *Middlemarch,* 1871–72).

ankh (ank) EGYPTIAN [life, *nh* live] *noun* a cross topped by a loop (a symbol of life in ancient Egypt).

annex (<u>ă</u>neks), **annexe** FRENCH [Old French *annexe* joined, ultimately from Latin *annectere* to bind to] *noun* something added on as an expansion or appendix of the main part (typi-

cally an extension to a house): *"The workshop was housed in an annex at the back of the building."* ~*verb* to attach; to incorporate (territory) into one's own.

anno Domini (anō <u>do</u>mănee) LATIN [in the year of the Lord] *adverb phrase* in the year of the Lord (used in Christian chronology, indicating the number of years that have passed since the birth of Christ). ~*abbreviated form* **A.D.**

anno hegirae (anō hij<u>ī</u>ree, anō <u>hi</u>jăree) LATIN [in the year of the Hegira] *adverb phrase* in the year of the migration (used in Islamic chronology, indicating the number of years that have passed since the Hegira migration to Medina led by the prophet Muhammad in A.D. 622). ~*abbreviated form* **A.H.**

anno regni (anō <u>reg</u>nee) LATIN [in the year of the reign] *adverb phrase* in the year of the reign (of a particular monarch). ~*abbreviated form* **A.R.**

annus horribilis (anăs ho<u>ri</u>bilis) LATIN [horrible year, based on *annus mirabilis*] *noun* a year of misfortune and disaster: *"After matrimonial troubles in the royal family and a fire at Windsor Castle, Queen Elizabeth II said that 1992 had been an annus horribilis."*

annus mirabilis (anăs mi<u>rah</u>bălăs) LATIN [wonderful year, after John Dryden's poem *Annus Mirabilis: The Year of Wonders* (1667)] *noun* (*plural* **anni**

mirabiles, anee mi<u>rah</u>băleez) a remarkable year, a year of wonders: *"With regard to astronomy, this year has been something of an annus mirabilis."*

anonymous (ă<u>non</u>ămăs) LATIN [from Greek *anonymos* anonymous, from *a* non and *onyma* name] *adjective* not named, unidentified, of unknown authorship; can also refer to anything that lacks distinctiveness, character, or originality: *"The performers looked out from the stage onto a sea of anonymous spectators."*

anorak (<u>an</u>ărak) DANISH [from Inuit *annoraaq*] *noun* a weatherproof hooded pullover jacket.

anorexia (ană<u>rek</u>seeă) LATIN [no appetite, from Greek *a* non and *orexis* appetite] *noun* loss of appetite.

anorexia nervosa (ană<u>rek</u>seeă ner<u>vō</u>să) LATIN [nervous loss of appetite] *noun phrase* an eating disorder in which sufferers develop an obsessive desire to lose weight, even at the risk of their own health. *"Self-induced vomiting has been associated with the psychiatric diagnosis of anorexia nervosa and a newly proposed disorder named bulimia" (Journal of the American Medical Association,* 1978).

Anschluss (<u>an</u>shlăs) GERMAN [connection, political union, from *anschliessen* to join] *noun* (*plural*

Anschlusses or **Anschlüsse** a political or economic union of two countries (often applied specifically to the annexation of Austria by Germany in 1938): *"Memories of the 1938 Anschluss still cloud diplomatic relations between the two countries."*

ante (<u>an</u>tee) LATIN [before] *noun* a stake put up by a player in gambling, or more generally any payment made in advance: *"The one-eyed man upped the ante by $1,000."*

antebellum (antee<u>bel</u>ăm), **antebellum, ante bellum** LATIN [from *ante bellum* before the war] *adjective* of or relating to the period before the outbreak of a war (often referring specifically to the Civil War): *"'On My Journey Home,' hymn by Isaac Watts, found in many of the southern country songbooks of the ante bellum period" (Harriet Beecher Stowe, Uncle Tom's Cabin,* 1852).

antechamber (<u>an</u>teechaymbăr) FRENCH [from Italian *anti* before and French *chambre* room] *noun* an anteroom, an outer room leading to another principal room, a waiting room: *"He was beckoned into the vast, drafty antechamber and had to wait until the prince appeared an hour later."*

ante Christum (antee <u>kris</u>tăm) LATIN [before Christ] *adverb phrase* before Chirst (sometimes used as an alternative to B.C. in Christian chronology to refer to the period before Christ's birth). ~*abbreviated form* **A.C.**

ante diem (antee deeem) LATIN [before the day] *adverb phrase* before the day appointed; early. ~*adjective phrase* of or relating to something done before the time appointed. ~*abbreviated form* **A.D.**

ante meridiem (antee mărideeăm) LATIN [before noon] *adjective phrase* before noon, in the morning, between midnight and midday. ~*abbreviated form* **A.M.**

ante mortem (antee mortăm), **ante-mortem** LATIN [before death] *adjective phrase* before death, preceding death.

antenna (antenă) LATIN [sail yard, from Greek *keraioi* horns] *noun* (*plural* **antennae**, antenee, anteni) one of a pair of appendages (or feelers) on the heads of crustanceans, insects, and other creatures; can also refer to a radio or television aerial or, more generally, to any special sensitivity or receptiveness: *"With a frightful qualm, I turned, and I saw that I had grasped the antenna of another monster crab that stood just behind me."* (H. G. Wells, *The Time Machine*, 1895).

ante partum (antee pahrtăm) **ante-partum** LATIN [before birth] *adjective phrase* before childbirth.

ante rem (antee rem) LATIN [before the thing] *adverb phrase* (in philosophy)

existing previously to something else. ~*adjective phrase* already existing.

anti (antee) GREEK [against] *prefix* against, opposing. ~*adjective* opposed to, against: *"Many parents are antismoking considering the grave risks to their children's health."* ~*noun* a person who is opposed to someone or something.

antipasto (anteepastō) ITALIAN [before food] *noun* (*plural* **antipasti**, anteepastee) an appetizer or dish of hors d'oeuvres in the Italian style, often served as the first course of a meal.

antipodes (antipădeez), **Antipodes** GREEK [*antipous* having the feet opposite] *noun* the opposite side of the earth and the peoples who live there (often taken to refer to Australasia and its inhabitants): *". . .he, coming up from the antipodes rather unsteadily, after an apparently violent journey, proved to be Mr Wopsle in a high-crowned hat, with a necromantic work in one volume under his arm"* (Charles Dickens, *Great Expectations*, 1860–61).

antithesis (antithăsăs) GREEK [opposition, *antitithenai* to oppose] *noun* (*plural* **antitheses**, antithăseez) a counter-thesis, a contrast of ideas, the opposite of something: *"So far from being a Bishop Blougram (as the rumour went) he was, in fact, the very antithesis of that subtle and worldly-wise ecclesiastic"*

(Lytton Strachey, *Eminent Victorians,* 1918).

A.O.C. See APPELLATION CONTRÔLÉE.

à outrance (a oo<u>trons</u>), **à l'outrance** FRENCH [to excess] *adverb phrase* to the limit, to the utmost, to death, unsparingly: *"She persecuted her former husband à outrance."*

apartheid (ă<u>pahr</u>tīt, ă<u>pahr</u>tayt) AFRI-KAANS [apartness, from Dutch *apart* apart and *heid* hood] *noun* a policy of racial segregation (usually referring specifically to the policy of the former government of South Africa): *"The discredited policy of apartheid has left a bitter legacy among its victims."* ~*adjective* of or relating to a policy of racial segregation.

aperçu (apă<u>rsoo,</u> apă<u>rsee</u>) FRENCH [a glimpse, past participle of *apercevoir* to perceive] *noun* a brief summary, sketch, or outline, or an immediate impression or understanding of something.

aperitif (ăperă<u>teef</u>), **apéritif** FRENCH [aperient, ultimately from Latin *apertus* open] *noun* an alcoholic drink consumed as an appetizer: *"The guests were offered an aperitif on the terrace before coming inside for the main meal."*

apex (<u>ay</u>peks) LATIN [extremity, summit] *noun* (*plural* **apexes** or **apices,** <u>ay</u>păseez) the peak, summit, or cul-mination of something: *"At sound of this, the cry of Life plunging down from Life's apex in the grip of Death, the full pack at Buck's heels raised a hell's chorus of delight"* (Jack London, *Call of the Wild,* 1903).

apfelstrudel (apfăl<u>strood</u>ăl) GERMAN [apple whirlpool] *noun* a dessert comprising flaky pastry with an apple filling: *"She paled a little at the suggestion that a plateful of apfelstrudel would not interfere with her diet."*

aphasia (ă<u>fay</u>zhă) GREEK [*aphatos* speechless] *noun* loss or impairment of the power to understand written or spoken language (through psychological trauma or damage to the brain).

aphrodisiac (afră<u>deez</u>eeak) GREEK [*aphrodisia* sexual pleasures, neuter plural of *aphrodisios* of Aphrodite] *noun* a food, drug, perfume, lotion, or anything else that is reputed to arouse sexual desire: *"This question of the Censorship reminds me that I have to apologize to those who went to the recent performance of Mrs Warren's Profession expecting to find it what I have just called an aphrodisiac"* (George Bernard Shaw, *Mrs Warren's Profession,* "The Author's Apology," 1898). ~*adjective* of or relating to something that is reputed to arouse sexual desire.

à pied (a pee<u>ay</u>) FRENCH [by foot] *adverb phrase* walking, on foot: *"Because the horses are exhausted we shall have to proceed à pied."*

aplomb (ăplom) FRENCH [perpendicularity, from *à plomb* according to the plummet] *noun* poise, self-assurance, self-confidence: *"Jude Fawley, with the self-conceit, effrontery, and aplomb of a strong-brained fellow in liquor, threw in his remarks somewhat peremptorily. . ."* (Thomas Hardy, *Jude the Obscure*, 1895).

apocrypha (ăpokrăfă), **Apocrypha** GREEK [things hidden away, from *apokryphos* obscure, from *apokryptein* to hide] *noun* writings or statements of uncertain authorship or doubtful authenticity (often referring specifically to the collection of Jewish writings from the period between about 300 B.C. and A.D. 100). Certain books that were included in early Latin and Greek versions of the Scriptures were excluded from the Hebrew Scriptures. The Roman Catholic Church confirmed the acceptance of most of the books as part of the Scriptures. The Protestant view is that the books of the Apocrypha should be read "for example of life and instruction of manners" rather than to establish doctrine.

apogee (apăjee), **apogée** FRENCH [from the earth, from Greek *apogaion*, neuter of *apogaois* far from the earth] *noun* the highest point, peak, or culmination of something; can also refer to the most distant point in the orbit of an object around the earth: *"Seek ye Bombast Paracelsus, / Read what Flood the Seeker tells us / Of the Dominant that runs / Through the cycles of the Suns— / Read my story last and see / Luna at her apogee."* (Rudyard Kipling, "Consequences," 1886).

à point (a pwan(g)) FRENCH [to the point] *adverb phrase* to the point, just enough.

apologia (apălōjeeă) GREEK [a speech in defense] *noun* (*plural* **apologias** or **apologiae,** apălōjeeī) a written apology or defense of a position, opinion, or action: *"The bishop published an apologia in defense of his decision."*

a posteriori (ah postăreeoree, ay postăreeoree) LATIN [from the latter] *adjective phrase* inductive, empirical, based on observed facts. ~*adverb phrase* empirically, inductively.

apotheosis (ăpotheeōsăs) GREEK [deification, from *apotheoun* to deify] *noun* (*plural* **apotheoses,** ăpotheeōseez) the quintessence of something, the perfect model or ideal; in its original sense can refer to the deification of a human being: *"She disappeared in a kind of sulphurous apotheosis, and when a few years later Medora again came back to New York, subdued, impoverished, mourning a third husband, and in quest of a still smaller house, people wondered that her rich niece had not been able to do something for her"* (Edith Wharton, *The Age of Innocence,* 1920).

app. *See* APPENDIX.

apparatchik (apăratchik) RUSSIAN [agent of the bureaucracy, from *apparat* political machine] *noun* (*plural* **apparatchiks** or **apparatchiki,** apăratchikee) a person who blindly obeys the demands of his or her superiors, usually within a party political context (often referring to the Communist establishment of the former Soviet Union): "*The president appeared briefly, surrounded by apparatchiks.*"

apparatus criticus (apărătăs krităkăs) LATIN [critical equipment] *noun phrase* (*plural* **apparatus critici,** apărătăs krităsī) additional material in a document offering variant readings and versions of a text or critical comment upon it.

appassionato (ăpasiănahtō) ITALIAN [impassioned] *adjective* (in music) with passion or feeling.

appellation contrôlée (apălayshăn kontrolay) FRENCH [controlled designation] *noun phrase* controlled name, a guarantee on French wine bottles (or food) confirming that the wine originates from a particular region and has been made in accordance with that region's standards of production. ~*abbreviated form* **A.O.C.**

appendix (ăpendiks) LATIN [addition, supplement, from *appendere* to weigh] *noun* (*plural* **appendixes** or **appendices,** ăpendăseez) an appendage or supplement, usually referring to additional material attached to the end of a book or other piece of writing: "*This testimony, so long as I live, and so long as my descendants have any legal right in my books, I shall cause to be republished, as an appendix to every copy of those two books of mine in which I have referred to America*" (Charles Dickens, *American Notes,* 1842). In anatomy, the **vermiform appendix** is a wormlike tube, closed at the end, that extends from the cecum of the large intestine. ~*abbreviated form* **app., appx., apx.**

appliqué (ăpleekay) FRENCH [applied, past participle of *appliquer* to put on, ultimately from Latin *applicare* to apply] *noun* an artistic or decorative technique in which cut-out patches of cloth or paper are attached to a larger piece of material. ~*verb* to decorate material in such a way.

appx *See* APPENDIX.

après (apray) FRENCH [after] *preposition* after, following.

après moi le déluge (apray mwah lă deloozh, apray mwah lă delooj) FRENCH [after me the deluge] *adverb phrase* when we have gone, disaster will follow; used to indicate that the existing order of things is unlikely to last after one's own period of influence: "'*Après moi le déluge,*' murmured the president as he surveyed the massed ranks of his opponents.*" The less common variant **après nous le deluge** (apray noo lă delooj) is attributed to Madame de Pompadour (1721–64), predicting the fall of France against the Prussians in 1757.

après-ski (apray <u>skee</u>) FRENCH [after skiing] *noun* a time of relaxation and social activity after a day's skiing. ~*adjective* of or relating to social activity after a day's skiing: *"Many people seem to go up into the mountains just for the après-ski fun and games."*

a priori (ay pree<u>or</u>ee, ah prī<u>or</u>ee) LATIN [from the former] *adjective phrase* deductive, presumptive, derived by reasoning, rather than being based on actual observed facts: *"The most plausible instances of a priori concepts are the formal concepts of logic"* (*The Fontana Dictionary of Modern Thought*). ~*adverb phrase* intuitively, presumptively, deductively.

apropos (aprăp<u>ō</u>) FRENCH [*à propos* to the purpose] *adverb* opportunely, pertinently, seasonably, incidentally, by the way. ~*adjective* relevant, pertinent, opportune, appropriate. ~*preposition* **à propos** concerning, regarding, with respect to: *"You shall go there one day, and find them blundering through half the nautical terms in Young's Dictionary, apropos of the 'Nancy' having run down the 'Sarah Jane,' or Mr Peggotty and the Yarmouth boatmen having put off in a gale of wind with an anchor and cable to the 'Nelson' Indiaman in distress. . ."* (Charles Dickens, *David Copperfield*, 1849–50).

apx. *See* APPENDIX.

aqua (ăk̲wă) LATIN [water] *noun* (*plural* **aquae,** ak̲wī, ak̲wee) water, or the color of water.

aqua fortis akwă <u>for</u>tis), **aquafortis** LATIN [strong water] *noun phrase* nitric acid: *"The dissolving of silver in aqua fortis, and gold in aqua regia, and not vice versa, would be then perhaps no more difficult to know than it is to a smith to understand why the turning of one key will open a lock, and not the turning of another."* (John Locke, *Essay Concerning Human Understanding*, 1690).

aqua regia (akwă <u>rej</u>ă) LATIN [royal water] *noun phrase* (*plural* **aquae regiae,** akwī <u>rej</u>eeī) a concentrated mixture of nitric and hydrochloric acid used to dissolve gold, platinum, and other metals.

aquarium (ăk̲waireeăm) LATIN [*aquarius* pertaining to water] *noun* (*plural* **aquariums** or **aquaria,** ăk̲waireeă) a water-filled tank, pond, or other container for keeping live fish, plants, and other aquatic life; can also refer to a place where a collection of such aquatic plants and animals are kept: *"The aquarium has been restocked with a dozen or so exotic fish of various sizes."*

aquatint (ăk̲wătint) ITALIAN [*acqua tinta* dyed water] *noun* an etching process permitting the reproduction of tones resembling watercolor washes; an artwork made by such a process: *"He came home with a fine aquatint of the house and garden."*

aqua vitae (akwă <u>vee</u>tī) LATIN [water of life] *noun phrase* brandy, whisky, or another type of strong alcoholic liquor: *"Ah, where's my man? give me some aqua vitae: / These griefs, these woes, these sorrows make me old"* (William Shakespeare, *Romeo and Juliet*, c. 1595).

arabesque (ară<u>besk</u>) FRENCH [from Italian *arabesco* Arabic] *noun* an artistic or decorative style characterized by elaborate, intertwined, flowing lines and scrollwork; also refers to a ballet posture in which the dancer stands with one leg extended horizontally backward and, in music, to a passage that is heavily ornamented: *"Not Art but Nature traced these lovely lines, / And carved this graceful arabesque of vines; / No organ but the wind here sighs and moans, / No sepulchre conceals a martyr's bones."* (Henry W. Longfellow, "My Cathedral," 1880). ~*adjective* decorated with arabesques.

arbiter (<u>ah</u>bităr) LATIN [judge, mediator] *noun* a judge, a mediator with power to decide a dispute; can also refer to a person who enjoys great influence over something: *"To whom these most adhere / He rules a moment: Chaos umpire sits, / And by decision more embroils the fray / By which he reigns: next him, high arbiter, / Chance governs all."* (John Milton, *Paradise Lost*, 1667).

arbiter elegantiae (ahrbiter eli<u>ga</u>nteeī) LATIN [from *arbiter elegantiarum* judge of elegance] *noun phrase* (*plural* **arbitri elegantiae**, ahbitree eli<u>ga</u>nteeī) an authority on taste or social etiquette.

arboretum (ahrbă<u>ree</u>tăm) LATIN [plantation of trees, from *arbor* tree] *noun* (*plural* **arboretums** or **arboreta**, ahbă<u>ree</u>tă) a plot of land where rare trees and shrubs are cultivated for scientific or educational purposes: *"The arboretum has been open to the public since the spring and has proved a popular tourist attraction."*

arcade (ahr<u>kayd</u>) FRENCH [from Italian *arcata* arch, from *arco* bow] *noun* an arched gallery, covered passageway, or avenue, often with shops on either side; can also refer to an amusement center with coin-operated game machines: *"Several shops in the arcade are empty, but plenty of interest has been shown in the site by local companies."*

arcadia (ahr<u>kay</u>deeă) GREEK [after Arcadia, a mountainous region of ancient Greece] *noun* a place where a peaceful life of rustic pleasure can be enjoyed: *"If you were not born in Arcadia, you linger in fancy on its margin; your thoughts are busied with the flutes of antiquity, with daffodils, and the classic poplar, and the footsteps of the nymphs, and the elegant and moving aridity of ancient art"* (Robert Louis Stevenson, *The Wrecker*, 1892).

arcana (ahr<u>kah</u>nă) LATIN [plural of *arcanum* mystery, from *arcanus* secret, from *arca* chest] *plural noun* mysterious facts or secrets (typically to be revealed only to a select few); sometimes referring specifically to the elixirs formerly sought by alchemists: *"He endeavored to initiate me into the bewildering arcana of their religious experiences."*

arc de triomphe ark dă <u>tree</u>omf) FRENCH [arch of triumph] *noun* (*plural* **arcs de triomphe**) a triumphal arch.

archipelago (arkăpelă<u>g</u>ō) ITALIAN [*arcipelago* chief sea] *noun* a large body of water containing numerous islands, or an island chain: *"The whole archipelago was swamped by a tidal wave."*

arena (ă<u>ree</u>nă) LATIN [sandy place] *noun* the central area in a Roman amphitheater, where gladiatorial contests took place, and, by extension, any space suitable for public entertainment or sporting contests. Also used more generally for any sphere of activity or competition or for a place where any debate or exchange of views can be held: *"They are considered one of the top bands in the arena of modern dance music."*

argot (<u>ahr</u>găt, <u>ahr</u>gō) FRENCH [slang, jargon] *noun* the language, vocabulary, and idiom of a particular group or class of people, often devised as a means of private communication: *"...the argot of the French underworld."*

argumentum ad hominem (ahrgyoo-mentăm ad <u>hom</u>ănăm) LATIN [reason-ing to the person] *noun phrase* (*plural* **argumenta ad hominem,** ahgyoo-mentă ad <u>hom</u>ănăm) a personal attack, or an argument that aims to appeal to a person's emotions rather than to their intellect: *"Thirdly, a third way is to press a man with consequences drawn from his own principles or concessions. This is already known under the name of argumentum ad hominem"* (John Locke, *Essay Concerning Human Understanding,* 1690).

argumentum ex silentio (ahrgyoo-mentăm eks sī<u>len</u>teeō, ahgyoomentăm eks sī<u>lent</u>sheeō) LATIN [argument from silence] *noun phrase* (*plural* **argumenta ex silentio**) an argument based on a lack of evidence to the contrary.

Argus (<u>ahr</u>găs) GREEK [after the giant Argos, who had 100 eyes, from *argos* shiny, bright] *noun* (*plural* **Arguses**) a person who is constantly watchful, a vigilant guardian.

aria (<u>ah</u>reeă) ITALIAN [air, melody, ultimately from Greek *aer* air] *noun* a tune or melody, specifically one featuring a solo voice with instrumental accompaniment: *"At a piano, singing an aria from Bellini, sat a young and very beautiful woman, who, at my entrance, paused in her song, and received me with graceful courtesy"* (Edgar Allan Poe, "The System of Dr. Tarr and Prof. Fether," 1845).

armada (ahr<u>mah</u>dă) SPANISH [from Latin *armata* army, fleet, from *armatus,* past participle of *armare* to arm] *noun* a fleet of warships or, more generally, a large group of boats, vehicles, or aircraft: *"To secure the possession of this land required the co-operation of a land force, which I agreed to furnish. Immediately commenced the assemblage in Hampton Roads, under Admiral D. D. Porter, of the most formidable armada ever collected for concentration upon one given point"* (Ulysses S. Grant, *Personal Memoirs*, 1885).

Armageddon (ahrmăgĕdăn) GREEK [from Hebrew *har megiddon* hill of Megiddo, the site of the final battle between good and evil predicted in the Book of Revelation 16:16, possibly derived from Megiddo, N Israel] *noun* a decisive final battle or confrontation, expected to lead to the utter annihilation of one or both sides: *"Privately the manager feared that the forthcoming game would prove the team's Armageddon."*

armoire (ahrmwahr) FRENCH [from Latin *armarium*] *noun* a tall cupboard or wardrobe: *"The best item in the auction catalog was, in his opinion, a French armoire with elaborate carvings."*

arpeggio (ahrpejeeō, ahrpejō) ITALIAN [like a harp, *arpegiare* to play on the harp, *arpa* harp] *noun* (*plural* **arpeggios**) a rapid series of notes of a chord played on a musical instrument: *"Lise, my daughter, was sitting before a book, and the old nurse, with my youngest child, was beside the table,*

turning the cover of something or other. In the parlor I heard a slow arpeggio, and his voice, deadened, and a denial from her" (Leo Tolstoy, *The Kreutzer Sonata*, 1889).

arrière-pensée (areeair-ponsay) FRENCH [behind-thought, *arrière* behind and *pensée* thought] *noun* (*plural* **arrière-pensées**) an afterthought, a mental reservation, a concealed thought, an ulterior motive.

arrivé (areevay) FRENCH [having arrived, past participle of *arriver* to arrive] *noun* a person who has risen rapidly to fame or success. ~*adjective* successful.

arrivederci (areevăderchee, areevădairchee) ITALIAN [until we meet again] *interjection* goodbye for now, farewell for the present, until next time: *"The youth left with a final 'arrivederci' and a wave of his hand."*

arriviste (ariveest), **arrivist** FRENCH [go-getter, from *arriver* to arrive] *noun* an upstart, an ambitious newcomer seeking success, wealth, social status, or critical praise: *"The old hands were inclined to dismiss him as an empty-headed arriviste interested only in the money to be made."*

arrondissement (ărondismon(g)) FRENCH [roundness, district, *arrondir* to make round] *noun* a chief division of a French department, or an administrative ward of a French city:

"Within three months of settling in the Rue Vanneau, Madame Marneffe had entertained Monsieur Crevel, who by that time was Mayor of his arrondissement and Officer of the Legion of Honor" (Honoré de Balzac, *Cousin Bette*, 1846–47). ~abbreviated form **arron.**

arroyo (ăroiō) SPANISH [stream, gutter] *noun* a watercourse, gully, or creek.

arsenal (ahrsnăl, ahrsănăl) ITALIAN [*arsenale* dock, ultimately from Arabic *dar sina'ah* workshop] *noun* a store of weapons and munitions or, more generally, any store or reserve: "*She still had a few weapons left in the arsenal with which to impress her superiors.*"

ars gratia artis (ahrz grahteeă ahrtis) LATIN [art for the sake of art] *noun phrase* art for art's sake (rather than for financial reward).

ars longa, vita brevis (ahrz longă veetă brevis) LATIN [art long, life short] *noun phrase* art is long, life is short (emphasizing that a work of art outlives its creator): "'*Ars longa,*' said Captain Wragge, pathetically drifting into Latin—'vita brevis! Let us drop a tear on the lost opportunities of the past, and try what the present can do to console us*'*" (Wilkie Collins, *No Name*, 1862).

artiste (ahrteest) FRENCH [performer] *noun* a performing artist, an entertainer: "*The show featured several promising new artistes.*"

art nouveau (ahrt noovō) FRENCH [new art, originally named after a shop in Paris] *noun phrase* the ornamental and artistic style characterized by flowing lines and foliate designs that became popular in the late 19th century: "*Art nouveau relished the sinuous line.*"

ashram (ashram) SANSKRIT [*asrama* hermitage] *noun* a hermitage or religious retreat in India, or any group of people sharing similar spiritual aims: "*Her parents met in a hippie ashram run by an emaciated Indian guru with a taste for cheap bourbon.*"

asphyxia (asfikseeă, ăsfikseeă) GREEK [stopping of the pulse, *a* non and *sphyxis* pulsation] *noun* suffocation resulting from a lack of oxygen or an excess of carbon dioxide in the body.

assassin (ăsasin) ARABIC [*hashshashin, hashshash* one who takes hashish] *noun* a person who commits murder, typically for political motives or for payment (originally a reference to members of a secret Muslim order that murdered Christians during the Crusades while under the influence of hashish): "*Police across the nation have been warned to keep a sharp lookout for the assassins.*"

assegai (asăgī), **assagai** ARABIC [*az-zaghaya*] *noun* an iron-tipped spear of the type used by the Zulu warriors of southern Africa.

asylum (ăsīlăm) LATIN [from Greek *asylos* inviolable and *sylon* right of seizure] *noun* a place of retreat or sanctuary, or the granting of official protection to a refugee by a nation, embassy etc.; can also refer to an institution where the mentally or physically ill may be treated or confined: *"A merchant in Hopeton last winter donated three hundred yards of wincey to the asylum. Some people said it was because he couldn't sell it, but I'd rather believe that it was out of the kindness of his heart, wouldn't you?"* (Lucy Maud Montgomery, *Anne of Green Gables,* 1908).

atelier (ateleeay) FRENCH [workshop, studio, Middle French *astelier* woodpile, a diminutive of *astele* splinter] *noun* an artist's or craftsman's studio or workshop: *"Above this floor was a large atelier, which had been increased in size by pulling down the partitions—a pandemonium, in which the artist and the dandy strove for preeminence"* (Alexandre Dumas, *The Count of Monte Cristo,* 1844).

a tempo (ah tempō) ITALIAN [in time] *adverb phrase* (in music) returning to the original tempo.

atman (atmăn) SANSKRIT [breath, soul] *noun* in Hinduism, the spirit or innermost essence of an individual, or the world soul.

atoll (atol) MALDIVIAN [*atolu*] *noun* a coral island comprising a central lagoon surrounded by a reef: *"The atoll was devastated by its use for nuclear tests over two decades."*

à tort et à travers (a tor ay a travair) FRENCH [with wrong and with fault] *adverb phrase* at random, haphazardly, indiscriminately, recklessly, heedlessly.

atrium (aytreeăm) LATIN [central court] *noun* (*plural* **atriums** or **atria,** aytreeă) the central room in a Roman house and, subsequently, the main hall or portico of a modern house (often with a glass roof): *"Standing in the shade of the dull passage, and looking through the doorway, he beheld the atrium of a Roman house, roomy and rich to a fabulous degree of magnificence"* (Lew Wallace, *Ben Hur,* 1880).

à trois (a twa) FRENCH [for three] *adjective phrase* for three persons: *"They decided to spend the evening à trois."*

attaché (atăshay, ătashay) FRENCH [attached, past participle of *attacher* to attach] *noun* a person with expertise in a particular field (sometimes pertaining to trade or the military) who works with the diplomatic staff of an embassy or legation: *"He had now finished his breakfast; but he was drinking a small cup of coffee, which had been served to him on a little table in the garden by one of the waiters who looked like an attaché"* (Henry James, *Daisy Miller,* 1879).

aubade (ōbahd) FRENCH [Old Provençal *aubada, auba* dawn] *noun* a piece of music or a poem celebrating the dawn or written to be performed at daybreak: *"His series of aubades are now considered among his finest poems."*

auberge (ōbairzh) FRENCH [shelter, Provençal *alberga* lodging] *noun* a French inn or tavern: *"I have no goal. When I am weary I stop at some / auberge; / when I am rested I go on again"* (Robert Service, *Ballads of a Bohemian*, 1920).

au beurre (ō ber) FRENCH [with butter] *noun phrase* (in French cuisine) cooked in butter.

au contraire (ō kontrair) FRENCH [to the contrary] *adverb phrase* on the contrary: *"The suave young man shook his head and murmured, 'Au contraire, my dear fellow, au contraire.'"*

au courant (ō kooron(g)) FRENCH [in the current] *adjective phrase* up-to-date, well-informed, conversant, abreast, cognizant: *"The senator has been kept au courant with events ever since the crisis started."*

auditor (ōdităr) LATIN [hearer, *auditus* act of hearing, *audire* to hear] *noun* a person who has the authority to examine and verify financial accounts, or more generally any person who hears or listens: *"I was an involuntary spectator and auditor of whatever was done and said in the kitchen of the adjacent vil-* lage inn—*a wholly new and rare experience to me"* (Henry David Thoreau, *Civil Disobedience*, 1849).

auditorium (odătoreeăm) LATIN [lecture room, place for listeners] *noun* (*plural* **auditoriums** or **auditoria,** ordătoreeă) the part of a theater or other public building where the audience sits: *"But the populace, seeing in that title an allusion damaging to Barbicane's project, broke into the auditorium, smashed the benches, and compelled the unlucky director to alter his playbill"* (Jules Verne, *From the Earth to the Moon*, 1865).

au fait (ō fay) FRENCH [to the point] *adjective phrase* well-informed, conversant, familiar, competent, expert: *"She claimed to be au fait with the layout of the palace."*

Aufklärung (owfklahrăng) GERMAN [clearing up] *noun* enlightenment (usually referring specifically to the philosophical movement called the Enlightenment that swept European culture during the 18th century): *"Indeed there would have been something peculiarly fitting in the idea that the boy-actor, whose beauty had been so vital an element in the realism and romance of Shakespeare's art, should have been the first to have brought to Germany the seed of the new culture, and was in his way the precursor of that Aufklärung or Illumination of the eighteenth century. . ."* (Oscar Wilde, *Lord Arthur Savile's Crime*, 1891).

au fond (ō <u>fon(g)</u>) FRENCH [to the bottom] *adverb phrase* at heart, fundamentally, basically, deep down, on the whole.

auf Wiedersehen (owf <u>vee</u>dărzayn) GERMAN [till seeing again] *interjection* farewell! good-bye!: *"'Auf Wiedersehen, darling,' she called out as she ascended the stairs."*

au gratin (ō <u>grah</u>tăn, ō <u>gra</u>tăn) FRENCH [with the burnt scrapings from the pan] *adjective phrase* (in French cuisine) covered with grated cheese or breadcrumbs and browned.

au lait (ō <u>lay</u>) FRENCH [with milk] *adjective phrase* (in French cuisine) prepared or served with milk: *"They finished the evening with a café au lait and a chocolate."*

au naturel (ō nată<u>rel</u>, ō nachă<u>rel</u>) FRENCH [in the natural] *adverb phrase* in a natural condition, naked, bare, plain: *"The guests were shocked to see their host appear au natural on the top balcony."*

au pair (ō <u>pair</u>) FRENCH [on even terms] *noun phrase* (*plural* **au pairs,** ō <u>pairz</u>) a young man or woman (usually of foreign nationality) who lives with a family free of charge in exchange for performing various domestic duties, often so as to learn the family's native language: *"We are hoping that the au pair will do the ironing for us."* ~*adjective phrase* of or relating to such an arrangement or to a person involved in such an exchange.

au pied de la lettre (ō peeay dă la <u>let</u>ră) FRENCH [to the foot of the letter] *adverb phrase* to the letter, literally.

au poivre (ō <u>pwah</u>vră) FRENCH [with pepper] *adjective phrase* (in French cuisine) cooked with pepper: *"Steak au poivre was the only item on the menu that he fancied."*

aura (<u>or</u>ă) GREEK [breeze] *noun* (*plural* **auras** or **aurae,** or<u>ī</u>) an atmosphere, an emanation, a distinctive impression, character, or quality: *"Enough, then, that I not only recognized my natural body for the mere aura and effulgence of certain of the powers that made up my spirit, but managed to compound a drug by which these powers should be dethroned from their supremacy, and a second form and countenance substituted. . ."* (Robert Louis Stevenson, *The Strange Case of Dr. Jekyll and Mr. Hyde,* 1886).

au revoir (ō ră<u>vwah</u>, or ră<u>vwah</u>) FRENCH [till seeing again] *interjection* good-bye! until we meet again! ~*noun* an expression of farewell: *"They parted with a volley of au revoirs and shakes of the hand."*

aurora (ă<u>ror</u>ă) LATIN [after Aurora, Roman goddess of the dawn] *noun* (*plural* **auroras** or **aurorae,** ă<u>ror</u>ee) dawn, or the light of dawn: *"We sat in* *the aurora of a sunrise which was to put out all the stars"* (Ralph Waldo Emerson, "The Poet", 1844).

aurora australis (ărorӑ ostra̱ylis) LATIN [southern dawn] *noun phrase* the southern lights, the aurora visible in the Southern Hemisphere.

aurora borealis (ărorӑ bōreea̱lis) LATIN [northern dawn, coined by French physicist and philosopher Pierre Gassendi (1592–1655)] *noun phrase* the northern lights, the aurora visible in the Northern Hemisphere.

au sérieux (ō sereeǎ̱) FRENCH [with seriousness] *adverb phrase* seriously.

auspices (o̱spӑsăz, o̱spӑseez) LATIN [plural of *auspex* diviner by birds, from *avis* bird and *specere* to look at] *plural noun* patronage, guidance: *"The idea of her being indebted to Mrs Elton for what was called an introduction—of her going into public under the auspices of a friend of Mrs Elton's—probably some vulgar, dashing widow, who, with the help of a boarder, just made a shift to live!"* (Jane Austen, *Emma*, 1815).

auteur (ōter) FRENCH [author] *noun* a film director whose influence over the filmmaking process is such that he is effectively also the author of the piece: *"Like other auteurs of his generation, he rewrote screenplays to the extent that they were barely recognizable as anything but his own work."*

autobahn (o̱tōbahn) GERMAN [expressway, *Auto* car and *Bahn* road] *noun* (*plural* **autobahns** or **autobahnen**, o̱tōbahnăn) an expressway in a German-speaking country: *"German autobahns are generally easier on the driver than expressways elsewhere in Europe."*

auto-da-fé (otō-dӑ-fa̱y, owtō-dӑ-fa̱y) PORTUGUESE [act of faith] *noun* (*plural* **autos-da-fé,** owtōz dӑ fa̱y) the pronouncement of judgment upon heretics by the Inquisition, followed by their public execution.

automaton (orto̱mӑtăn) GREEK [*automatos* self-acting] *noun* (*plural* **automatons** or **automata,** orto̱mӑtӑ) a robot, a self-operating mechanical device, a person who acts in an involuntary, machinelike way: *"'Mason!— the West Indies!' he said, in the tone one might fancy a speaking automaton to enounce its single words; 'Mason!—the West Indies!' he reiterated. . ."* (Charlotte Brontë, *Jane Eyre,* 1847).

automobile (o̱rtӑmӑbeel) FRENCH [from Greek *auto* self and Latin *mobile* movable] *noun* a motor vehicle: *"This is the age of the automobile."*

autoroute (o̱rtōroot) FRENCH [car route, *automobile* car and *route* route] *noun* an expressway in a French-speaking country.

autostrada (orto̱strahdӑ) ITALIAN [car street, *automobile* car and *strada* street] *noun* (*plural* **autostradas** or **auto-**

strade (ortōstrahday) an express-way in an Italian-speaking country.

autres temps, autres moeurs (ōtră ton(g) ōtră mer) FRENCH [other times, other customs] *interjection* one should change one's behavior to suit one's environment or circumstances.

avalanche (avălanch) FRENCH [alpine French dialect *lavanche* a mountainside snowfall, from *avaler* to go down] *noun* a sudden rush, flood, or fall of some-thing (originally a fall of snow, rock, or earth down a mountainside): *"Polly was startled on entering the Shaws' door, by Maud, who came tumbling down stairs, sending an avalanche of words before her. . ."* (Louisa May Alcott, *An Old-Fashioned Girl*, 1870).

avant-garde (avon(g)-gard, avont-gard) FRENCH [vanguard] *noun* (*plural* **avant-gardes**) those pio-neers who are in the forefront of a particular field or movement, typi-cally courting controversy with their unorthodox methods and progres-sive views. ~*adjective* of or relating to those who are at the forefront of a particular field or movement: *"Such avant-garde thinking has caused uproar in the halls of academe."*

avanti (ăvantee) ITALIAN [before] *interjection* forward! first: *'Avanti! Yes! That is all cares for. To be first some-where—somehow—to be first with these English"* (Joseph Conrad, *Nostromo*, 1904).

avatar (avătahr) SANSKRIT [*avatara* descent, *avatari* he descends] *noun* the incarnation of a Hindu god in earthly form and by extension the embodiment of any idea or philosoph-ical concept; can also refer to a new phase in a person's or other entity's existence: *". . .and honest Alan, who was a grim old fire-eater in his day has in this new avatar no more desperate purpose than to steal some young gentleman's attention from his Ovid, carry him awhile into the Highlands and the last century, and pack him to bed with some engaging images to mingle with his dreams"* (Robert Louis Stevenson, *Kidnapped*, 1886).

ave (ahvay) LATIN [hail] *interjection* hail! farewell! welcome!

ave atque vale (ahvay atkwee vahlay) LATIN [hail and farewell] *interjection* hello and good-bye!

avec plaisir (avek playzeer) FRENCH [with pleasure] *adverb phrase* with pleasure: *"The man smiled when he received the order to kill his rival. 'Avec plaisir,' he replied, with a smirk."*

ave Maria (ahvay măreeă) LATIN [hail Mary] *noun phrase* hail Mary (the opening words of a prayer to the Vir-gin Mary).

avoirdupois (avărdăpoyz) FRENCH [to have weight, Old French *avoir de pois* goods sold by weight] *noun* a series of units of weight based on a pound of 16 ounces: *"Janet is a dear soul and very nice looking; tall, but not over-tall;*

stoutish, yet with a certain restraint of out-line suggestive of a thrifty soul who is not going to be overlavish even in the matter of avoirdupois" (Lucy Maud Montgomery, *Anne of the Island,* 1915).

à votre santé (a votră son<u>tay</u>) FRENCH [to your health] *interjection*   to your health! (a drinking toast).

ayatollah (īă<u>tol</u>ă) PERSIAN [*ayatullah* sign of God, from Arabic *aya* sign and *allah* God] *noun*   a leader of the Muslim Shiite religion in Iran; also used more generally of any person of influence or power: *"The ayatollahs have ruled that all international contact must be subject to their scrutiny."*

baas (bahs) DUTCH [master] *noun* master, boss (especially in former use by black employees of white Europeans in South Africa): *"'Baas,' he gasped, 'Baas, how did you know?' 'I knew,' I replied grandly, 'in the same way that I know everything. Show me the diamond'"* (H. Rider Haggard, *Finished,* 1917).

babu (<u>bah</u>boo), **baboo** HINDI [father] *noun* a courtesy title addressed to Hindu gentlemen, or to Hindu clerks who speak English (or derogatively of Hindus who have only superficial knowledge of English): *"He had the noise of the Bay of Bengal and a Bengali Babu for company; nothing more."* (Rudyard Kipling, "His Chance in Life," 1887).

babushka (bă<u>boosh</u>kă) RUSSIAN [grandmother, *baba* old woman] *noun* an old Russian woman, or a triangular folded headscarf of the sort typically worn by such women: *"Ivan's daughter-in-law replied: 'You see, babushka, my hen flew into your yard this morning. Did she not lay an egg there?'"* (Leo Tolstoy, *The Kreutzer Sonata,* 1889).

baccalaureate (bakă<u>lor</u>eeat) FRENCH [*baccalauréat* diploma, from Latin *baccalaureus* bachelor, itself ultimately from *bacca lauri* laurel berry] *noun* a bachelor's degree, as awarded by universities and colleges. ~*abbreviated form* **Bac.**

baccarat (bakă<u>ră</u>) FRENCH [from *baccara* (of unknown meaning)] *noun* a card game in which players gamble against the dealer: *"Here, amid the blaze of crowded baccarat tables, he caught sight of Lord Hubert Dacey, seated with his habitual worn smile behind a rapidly dwindling heap of gold"* (Edith Wharton, *The House of Mirth,* 1905).

bacchanalia (bakă<u>nay</u>leeă) LATIN [things connected with Bacchus, the Greek and Roman god of wine] *noun* (*plural* **bacchanalia** or **bacchanalias**) a wild, festive gathering of music, dance, and drinking originally celebrated in honor of Bacchus but now in more general usage: *"The morning after the bacchanalia in the saloon of the palace, the divan was covered with young patricians"* (Lew Wallace, *Ben Hur,* 1880).

bacillus (bă<u>sil</u>ăs) LATIN [small staff, *baculus* staff] *noun* (*plural* **bacilli,** bă<u>sil</u>ī, bă<u>sil</u>ee) a rod-shaped bacterium of a class including numerous saprophytes and parasites, many of which cause diseases: *"Scientists have worked around the clock trying to isolate the bacillus."*

backsheesh *See* BAKSHEESH.

bacterium (bak<u>teer</u>eeăm) LATIN [from Greek *bakteria* staff] *noun* (*plural* **bacteria,** bak<u>teer</u>eeă) an example of a very large, widely-distributed group of parasitic or saprophytic single-celled microorganisms important for their roles in biochemical and pathenogenic processes.

badinage (badănahzh) FRENCH [joking, from *badiner* to joke, itself from *badar* to gape] *noun* humorous banter, playful repartee: *"They enjoyed listening to the badinage of the old men, who had obviously known one another for years and years."*

bagatelle (bagă<u>tel</u>) FRENCH [trifle, from Italian *bagatella*] *noun* one of several games in which players attempt to roll balls into scoring areas and by extension any trifling or frivolous matter. Also used to refer to a short, lighthearted musical composition or poem.

bagel (<u>bayg</u>ăl) YIDDISH [from *beygel,* itself possibly from German *bõugel* ring] *noun* a hard ring-shaped roll.

bagnio (<u>ban</u>yō) ITALIAN [from *bagno* bath, itself from Latin *balneum* bath] *noun* a public bath or Asian prison (recalling the Turks' use of the Roman baths at Constantinople as a prison). Also an alternative term for a brothel or bordello: *"How the prodigal drinks and sports at the bagnio"* (W. M. Thackeray, *English Humourists,* 1858).

baguette (ba<u>get</u>) FRENCH [rod, from Italian *bacchetto,* itself from Latin *baculum* staff] *noun* a long, thin roll or loaf of white bread and, by extension, a gem cut into a rectangular shape.

bain-marie (ban(g) mă<u>ree</u>) FRENCH [bath of Maria, from Latin *balneum Mariae,* from Greek *kaminos Marias* furnace of Maria (legendary Jewish alchemist identified as Miriam, sister of Moses)] *noun* (*plural* **bains-marie**) a type of double saucepan in which food can be heated slowly over hot water, or a dish prepared in such a vessel: *"While Sylvie and the man were upstairs, Mlle. Michonneau, who came down first, poured the contents of the phial into the silver cup belonging to Vautrin— it was standing with the others in the bain-marie that kept the cream hot for the morning coffee"* (Honoré de Balzac, *Le Père Goriot,* 1834).

baklava (bahklă<u>vah</u>) TURKISH *noun* a dessert comprising thin pastry, nuts, and honey or syrup.

baksheesh (<u>bak</u>sheesh, bak<u>sheesh</u>), **backsheesh** PERSIAN [*bakhshish* present, *bakhshidan* to give] *noun* a bribe, gratuity, or tip paid to secure or reward another's service (originally in the Middle East alone, but now used more widely): *"Add a hundred for the cost of the last trip—Gad, won't Torp stare to see me!—a hundred and thirty-two leaves seventy-eight for baksheesh—I shall need it—and to play with"* (Rudyard Kipling, *The Light that Failed*, 1890).

balaclava (balăklahvă) RUSSIAN [after Balaclava, Crimea, site of a battle in the Crimean War, 1881] *noun* a knit covering for the head and neck after the type originally worn by soldiers fighting in the Crimea: *"Most of the climbers wore sweaters and thick balaclavas to protect themselves from the cold."*

balalaika (balălīkă) RUSSIAN [stringed instrument] *noun* a triangular, three-stringed musical instrument of Russian origin: *"All of a sudden there was a great uproar of shouting, singing and the balalaika, and from the tavern a number of big and very drunken peasants came out, wearing red and blue shirts and coats thrown over their shoulders"* (Fyodor Dostoyevsky, *Crime and Punishment*, 1866).

ballerina (balăreenă) ITALIAN [female ballet dancer, *ballare* to dance] *noun* a female ballet dancer.

ballet (balay) FRENCH [from Italian *ballo* dance] *noun* a form of theatrical classical dance in which dancers mime to music, or the music accom-

panying this. Also used to refer to a dance company or group performing classical ballet.

ballista (bălĭstă) LATIN [from Greek *ballein* to throw] *noun* (*plural* **ballistae,** bălĭstee) in historical warfare, a large military engine resembling a huge crossbow formerly used to hurl stones, bolts, or other missiles at an enemy: *"If his mother were there in living burial, what could he do for her? By the strong hand, nothing. An army might beat the stony face with ballista and ram, and be laughed at."* (Lew Wallace, *Ben Hur*, 1880).

ballot (balăt) ITALIAN [from *ballotta* bullet, itself from *balla* ball] *noun* a vote or system of secret voting (originally through the selection of small differently colored balls): *"On the fifth day came the elections of the district marshals. It was rather a stormy day in several districts. In the Selezniovsky district Sviiazhsky was elected unanimously without a ballot, and he gave a dinner that evening"* (Leo Tolstoy, *Anna Karenina*, 1874–76).

balti (boltee) URDU [bucket] *noun* a style of Indian cookery of northern Pakistani origins in which highly spiced food is prepared in metal pans.

bambino (bambeenō) ITALIAN [*bambo* child, simple] *noun* (*plural* **bambinos** or **bambini,** bambeenee) a child, a baby (occasionally referring specifically to the infant Christ).

bandanna (bandanǎ) HINDI [*badhnu* tie-dyeing] *noun* a large, colorful handkerchief usually worn around the head or neck: *"He took Judge Thornton aside and whispered the important question to him,—in his distress of mind, mistaking pockets and taking out his bandanna instead of his white handkerchief to wipe his forehead"* (Oliver Wendell Holmes, *Elsie Venner*, 1861).

bandit (bandit) ITALIAN [*bandito,* past participle of *bandire* to banish] *noun* (*plural* **bandits** or **banditti,** banditee) an outlaw who lives by plunder and robbery, usually with violence: *"The countryside outside the capital is dangerous for foreigners, being peopled chiefly by army deserters and bandits."*

bandolier (bandǎleer), **bandoleer** FRENCH [from Old Spanish *bando* band, sash] *noun* a leather belt worn over the shoulder and across the breast, usually in order to carry cartridges for a gun: *"One, having taken off his shako, carefully loosened the gathers of its lining and drew them tight again; another, rubbing some dry clay between his palms, polished his bayonet; another fingered the strap and pulled the buckle of his bandolier, while another smoothed and refolded his leg bands and put his boots on again"* (Leo Tolstoy, *War and Peace*, 1863–69).

bangle (bangǎl) HINDI [*bangri* bracelet of glass] *noun* an ornamental bracelet or anklet: *"The girl toyed anxiously with the bangle on her wrist."*

banquette (banket) FRENCH [from Italian *banchetta,* itself from *banca* bench] *noun* a long upholstered bench; can also refer to a raised step running along the inside of a parapet or trench or to a sidewalk: *"The four sides of the stockade had been manned by that time. Lingard, ascending the banquette, looked out and saw the lagoon shrouded in white, without as much as a shadow on it, and so still that not even the sound of water lapping the shore reached his ears"* (Joseph Conrad, *The Rescue,* 1920).

banshee (banshee), **banshie** IRISH [*bean sidhe* fairy woman] *noun* in Irish and Scottish folklore, a supernatural spirit that utters unearthly wails as a warning of approaching death in the family: *"They were a species of tutelary sprite, or Banshee; although winged and feathered differently from most other guardian angels"* (Nathaniel Hawthorne, *The House of the Seven Gables,* 1851).

banzai (banzī) JAPANESE [from Chinese, ten thousand years] *interjection* may you live ten thousand years (used as a battle cry or as a cheer): *"All the people cheered and shouted 'Banzai' to the Emperor."* ~*adjective* reckless, suicidal.

barbecue (bahrbǎkyoo), **barbeque** SPANISH [*barbacoa* framework for cooking meat over a fire, probably from Haitian Taino *barboka*] *noun* a grill on which food can be cooked over a fire in the open air, and by extension a social gathering at which barbecued food is cooked and consumed, or the food itself: *"We like to throw a barbecue for all our friends every summer."* ~verb to cook on a barbecue.

barcarole (<u>bah</u>kărōl, bahkă<u>rōl</u>), **barcarolle** FRENCH [from Italian *barcaruolca* boatman's song, from *barca* barge] *noun* the traditional song of Venetian gondoliers with a rhythm suggestive of rowing. By extension any piece of music with a similar beat.

bar mitzvah (bah <u>mitz</u>vă) HEBREW [*bar miswah* son of the law] *noun phrase* a religious ceremony at which a Jewish boy is recognized as having come of age with responsibility for his own religious and ethical duties, celebrated on his 13th birthday: *"A boy's bar mitzvah is one of the most important days in his life."* See also BAT MITZVAH.

baroque (bă<u>rok</u>, ba<u>rok</u>) FRENCH [*barroque* irregularly shaped, from Portuguese *barroco* irregularly shaped pearl] *noun* an ornamental style in the arts that flourished in Europe in the 17th and 18th centuries. ~adjective of or relating to such a style or, more generally, grotesque, complex, or exaggerated: *"Other pictures were two watercolors in baroque frames; one being the Amalfi monk on a pergola wall, while the second was a yard-wide display of iris blossoms"* (Booth Tarkington, *Alice Adams*, 1921).

barouche (bă<u>roosh</u>) GERMAN [*Barutshce*, from Italian *baroccio*, ultimately from Latin *birotus* two-wheeled] *noun* a four-wheeled horse-drawn carriage with two double seats facing each other under a folding hood for the passengers and a single seat in front for the driver: *"He gave me his arm, and the two officers courteously bowed me out, and we found at the door a phaeton or barouche with a postilion and post horses"* (Charles Dickens, *Bleak House*, 1852–53).

barracks (<u>bar</u>ăks) FRENCH [*baraque* hut] *plural noun* a building or series of buildings, usually on a military base, used to house soldiers: *"An agreement was reached and the soldiers returned to their barracks."*

barrage (<u>ba</u>razh) FRENCH [*barrer* to bar] *noun* a barrier placed in a watercourse to alter the flow, or alternatively a shower or discharge of words, explosives, protests, etc.: *"Strike me dead / If the Huns ain't strafing the road ahead / So the convoy can't get through! / A barrage of shrap, and us alone; / four rush-cases—you hear 'em moan?"* (Robert Service, *Ballads of a Bohemian*, 1920). ~verb to shower with words, explosives, protests, etc.

barre (bahr) FRENCH [from Latin *barra*] *noun* a horizontal bar used by dancers for their exercises.

barrio (<u>ba</u>reeō) SPANISH [from Arabic *barri* of the open country] *noun* a district within a larger urban conglomeration in a Spanish-speaking country (or a Spanish-speaking district within a U.S. town or city): "*A crime wave has swept through the barrios of the city in recent months.*"

bas bleu (ba blă) FRENCH [blue stocking] *noun phrase* (*plural* **bas bleus**) a bluestocking, a woman with strong intellectual or academic interests.

basilica (băsilăkă, băzilăkă) LATIN [royal palace, from Greek *basilike* royal, from *basileus* king] *noun* a Christian church, typically one with a nave higher than its aisles: "*While, contrasting strangely with the wondrous radiance around them, the huge bronze pine-tree in the middle of the Place, and the wide front of the Basilica, rose up in gloomy shadow, indefinite and exaggerated, lowering like evil spirits over the joyous beauty of the rest of the scene. . .*" (Wilkie Collins, *Antonina*, 1850).

basmati (bazmahtee, bazmatee) HINDI [fragrant] *noun* a variety of aromatic long-grain rice.

basque (bask) FRENCH [after the Basque region of the western Pyrenees, from Latin *Vasco*] *noun* a tight-fitting bodice for women: "*The actress wore a bright red basque and fishnet stockings.*"

bas-relief (bah răleef, bah răleef, bas răleef), **bas relief** FRENCH [low relief, *bas* low and *relief* raised work, from Italian *basso-rilievo* low relief] *noun* (*plural* **bas reliefs**) a form of sculpture in which the carved image projects slightly above the surface of the surrounding wood or stone, or an example of such work: "*The whole story of the pharoah's reign is carved in bas-relief on a stone column.*"

bassinet (basănet), **bassinette** FRENCH [*bassin* basin] *noun* a wickerwork bed or carrying basket for a baby with a curved hood, or a baby carriage with a similar shape: "*The baby was carried into the room in an old-fashioned bassinet.*"

basso profondo (baso profundo) ITALIAN [deep bass] *noun phrase* (*plural* **bassos profundos** or **bassi produndi**, basee profundee) in music, a rich heavy bass voice, or a singer with such a voice.

bastille (basteel) FRENCH [after the Bastille fortress prison in Paris, from Old Provençal *bastida* fortified town, itself from *bastir* to build] *noun* a strong prison or jail, especially one with a stern appearance or reputation.

bathos (baythos) GREEK [depth] *noun* the lowest point, the nadir of something, an anticlimax, humiliation; also similar to pathos, indicating sentimentalism or a descent into triteness: "*I was quite willing to answer your uncle any questions he could ask about money. Indeed, I had no secret from him on any subject. But when he subjected me to cross-examination, forcing me into a bathos of poverty, as he thought, I broke down*"

(Anthony Trollope, *Ayala's Angel,* 1881).

batik (ba<u>teek</u>) JAVANESE [painted] *noun* hand-printed dyed fabric of a type first produced in Java, Indonesia. ~*adjective* of or relating to fabric of this type.

bat mitzvah (baht <u>mitz</u>vă), HEBREW [*bat miswah* daughter of the law] *noun phrase* a religious ceremony at which a Jewish girl is recognized as having come of age with responsibility for her own religious and ethical duties, for a girl aged 12 or 13: *"A girl's bat mitzvah is one of the most important days in her life."* See also BAR MITZVAH.

baton (<u>bat</u>on(g), bă<u>ton</u>(g)) FRENCH [stick, from Latin *bastum* stick] *noun* a staff, rod, or stick (especially one wielded by the conductor of an orchestra or choir): *"His mood was lively: he twirled the stick through his fingers like a drum-major's baton, and whistled loudly"* (Booth Tarkington, *Alice Adams,* 1921).

Bauhaus (<u>bow</u>hows) GERMAN [architecture house, after the school for architecture founded by Walter Gropius (1883–1969) in 1919] *adjective* of or relating to the principles of the German Bauhaus school of architecture, aiming for a synthesis of art and technology.

bayonet (bay<u>ă</u><u>net</u>) FRENCH [after Bayonne, France, where such weapons were first made] *noun* a steel blade that may be attached to the muzzle of a rifle for use in close combat: *"The regiment advanced with fixed bayonets."* ~*verb* to stab an enemy with a bayonet.

bayou (<u>bī</u>yoo, <u>bī</u>ō) FRENCH [creek, Louisiana French from Choctaw *bayuk* small stream] *noun* a marshy creek or small river: *"On Saturday, early in the morning, the beauty of the place graced our cabin, and proud of her fair freight the gallant little boat glided up the bayou"* (Mark Twain, *Life on the Mississippi,* 1883).

bazaar (bă<u>zah</u>) PERSIAN [*bazar* market] *noun* an oriental market and, by extension, a department store or arcade of shops; can also refer to a fair for the sale of miscellaneous or secondhand goods (often to raise money for charity): *"We visited the charming book bazaar in Istanbul."*

béarnaise (bayă<u>nayz</u>, bair<u>nayz</u>) FRENCH [after Béarn, France] *noun* a rich sauce made with egg yolks, butter, wine, vinegar, and seasonings. ~*adjective* a dish prepared with such a sauce.

beau (bō) FRENCH [beautiful, from Latin *bellus* pretty] *noun* (*plural* **beaus** or **beaux,** bōz) a woman's male escort or boyfriend; occasionally also used to refer to a fashionable man who prides himself on his appearance or clothing: *"The other girls did not think very much of their friend's latest beau."*

beau geste (bō <u>zhest</u>) FRENCH [fine gesture] *noun phrase* (*plural* **beau gestes** or **beaux gestes**) a noble deed or generous gesture.

beau ideal (bō īdeeăl) FRENCH [*beau idéal* ideal beauty] *noun phrase* (*plural* **beau ideals**) a model or conception of perfect beauty.

beau monde (bō <u>mond</u>) FRENCH [fine world] *noun phrase* (*plural* **beau mondes,** bō <u>mondz</u>, or **beaux mondes,** bō <u>mond</u>) the world of fashion and high society: "*The Countess Lidia Ivanovna was a friend of her husband's, and the center of that one of the coteries of the Peterburg beau monde with which Anna was, through her husband, in the closest rapport*" (Leo Tolstoy, *Anna Karenina,* 1874–76).

beaux arts (bō <u>zah</u>), **beaux-arts** FRENCH [beautiful arts] *plural noun* the fine arts: "*Over the decades he has carefully nurtured a reputation as a connoisseur of les beaux arts.*"

béchamel (bayshă<u>mel</u>) FRENCH [after its creator, the 18th-century French courtier Louis de Béchamel, steward of Louis XIV] *noun* a rich white sauce, often flavored with carrots, onions, and seasoning: "*The meat was served in a simple béchamel sauce.*"

bedouin (<u>bed</u>ooin), **beduin** FRENCH [from Arabic *badawi* desert-dweller] *noun* a nomadic Arab of the desert regions of North Africa, Syria, or the Arabian Peninsula: "*The story was that she had been kidnapped by bedouin tribesmen, but her parents refused to believe any such thing.*"

begum (<u>bay</u>găm) HINDI [*begam*] *noun* a Muslim noblewoman; also used as a courtesy title for a married Muslim woman: "*He went to India with his capital, and there, according to a wild legend in our family, he was once seen riding on an elephant, in company with a Baboon; but I think it must have been a Baboo—or a Begum*" (Charles Dickens, *David Copperfield,* 1849–50).

behemoth (bă<u>hee</u>măth, bee<u>ă</u>măth) HEBREW [beasts] *noun* a creature or something else of monstrous dimensions or strength: "*And the hippopotami heard my call, and came, with the behemoth, unto the foot of the rock, and roared loudly and fearfully beneath the moon.*" (Edgar Allan Poe, "Silence—A Fable," 1845).

beige (bayzh) FRENCH *noun* a yellowish brown color (similar to that of undyed wool). ~*adjective* of or relating to such a color: "*She selected a beige dress for her mother's inspection.*"

bel canto (bel <u>kan</u>tō) ITALIAN [beautiful singing] *noun phrase* a style of operatic singing in which emphasis is given to purity and smoothness of tone as well as excellence of technique.

belle (bel) FRENCH [beautiful, the feminine of *beau* beautiful, fine, from Latin *bellus* beautiful] *noun* a beautiful girl or woman: *"That evening she was definitely the belle of the ball."*

Belle Époque (bel epok) FRENCH [beautiful epoch] *noun phrase* the golden age, the fine age (usually referring to life in France or England, loosely spanning the last decade of the 19th century and the first decade of the 20th century): *"His memories of the Belle Époque were dominated by his recollections of hours spent in an intimate Paris bistro."*

belles-lettres (bel letră), **belles lettres** FRENCH [fine letters] *plural noun phrase* the world of literature, especially writing of a serious or sophisticated nature: *"And notwithstanding, moreover, a certain habitual contempt for his understanding, especially on affairs of genius and taste, on which Blattergowl was apt to be diffuse, from his hope of one day fighting his way to a chair of rhetoric or belles lettres. . ."* (Walter Scott, *The Antiquary*, 1816).

Benedictus (benidiktăs) LATIN [praise be, blessed, past participle of *benedicere* to commend, bless] the song or hymn of thanksgiving (Luke 1:68–79) uttered by Zacharias at the birth of his son John the Baptist.

bene esse (benee essee) LATIN [to be well] *noun phrase* well-being, welfare, or prosperity.

ben trovato (ben trōvahtō) ITALIAN [well found] *adjective phrase* appropriate, characteristic, even if not actually true (of stories, etc.): *"It was a good anecdote, although I suspect it was ben trovato rather than factually accurate."*

beret (beray) FRENCH [from Gascon *berret* cap] *noun* a round peakless flat soft woollen cap of a type traditionally worn by French peasants and workers, but since widely adopted as an item of military uniform and appropriated by high fashion: *"The outfit was completed with various accessories in pink and a red beret worn at a jaunty angle."*

berg (berg) AFRIKAANS [from Dutch *berg*] *noun* a mountain: *"The leader of the expedition eyed the distant bergs with misgivings."*

berserk (bărzerk) OLD NORSE [from *berserkr*, itself from *bjorn* bear and *serkr* shirt, a reference to ancient Viking warriors who worked themselves into a frenzy before going into battle convinced of their invulnerability] *adjective* frenzied, wild, mad: *"The young man's berserk behavior at the airport surprised his friends."*

beta (baytă, beetă) GREEK [second letter of the Greek alphabet] *noun* the second letter of the Greek alphabet, used to indicate the second in a sequence or ranking.

bête noire (bet nwahr, bayt nwahr) FRENCH [black beast] *noun phrase* (*plural* **bêtes noires,** bet <u>nwahrz</u>, bayt <u>nwahrz</u>) a person or thing that is greatly detested or feared by a particular individual or body: "*The question of Europe has been the British government's bête noire for several years now.*"

bey (bay) TURKISH [chief, gentleman, *beg* governor] *noun* the rank of provincial governor in the Ottoman Empire or alternatively that of ruler of Tunisia, also formerly used as a courtesy title in Egypt and Turkey: "*They tell me of California and Texas, of England and the Indies, of the Hon. Mr. ——— of Georgia or of Massachusetts, all transient and fleeting phenomena, till I am ready to leap from their court-yard like the Mameluke bey*" (Henry David Thoreau, *Walden; or, Life in the Woods,* 1854).

bhaji (<u>bah</u>jee) HINDI [fried vegetables, *bhrajj* to fry] *noun* in Indian cuisine, a fritter made with onions or other vegetables: "*She was disappointed that the dinner for two did not include onion bhajis.*"

bhangra (<u>ban</u>gră) PANJABI *noun* a traditional Punjabi folkdance or alternatively a genre of popular dance music combining traditional Punjabi musical styles with modern funk or rock music.

bibelot (bee<u>bă</u>lō) FRENCH [trinket, *bel* beautiful] *noun* (*plural* **bibelots,** bee<u>bă</u>lōz) a trinket, curio, or small decorative object: "*. . .the thrill of snapping up a jewel or a bibelot or a new*

'*model' that one's best friend wanted.*" (Edith Wharton, *Glimpses of the Moon,* 1922).

bibliomania (biblee<u>ō</u><u>may</u>neeă) GREEK [book passion, *biblio* book and *mania* enthusiasm] *noun* an obsessive interest in collecting books: "*One look inside the old man's library confirmed her suspicion that she was dealing with an advanced case of bibliomania.*"

bidet (bee<u>day</u>) FRENCH [small horse, *bider* to trot] *noun* a bathroom fixture used for washing the genital and anal regions: "*His grandmother never figured out what the bidet was really for and used it to wash her underwear in.*"

bien entendu (beean(g) onton<u>doo</u>) FRENCH [well heard] *adverb phrase* naturally, of course, it goes without saying.

bijou (bee<u>zhoo</u>) FRENCH [from Breton *bizou* ring] *adjective* delicate, small but elegant: "*I soon found Briony Lodge. It is a bijou villa, with a garden at the back, but built out in front right up to the road, two stories.*" (Arthur Conan Doyle, "A Scandal in Bohemia" from *The Adventures of Sherlock Holmes,* 1891).

bildungsroman (<u>bil</u>dungsrō<u>man</u>) GERMAN [*Bildung* education and *Roman* book] *noun* a novel in which the psychological and spiritual development of a youthful central character is the main subject.

billabong (bilăbong) AUSTRALIAN ABORIGINAL [after the Billibang (Bell) River, *billa* water and *bang* channel] *noun* a side channel of a river, a stagnant backwater, or a dry streambed that fills with water only at certain times: *"The search party following the footprints in the mud through a maze of marshy billabongs."*

billet-doux (bilee doo, bilay doo) FRENCH [sweet note] *noun* (*plural* **billets-doux,** bilay dooz, bilee dooz) a love letter.

biltong (biltong) AFRIKAANS [from Dutch *bil* rump and *tong* tongue] *noun* strips of dried meat.

bimbo (bimbō) ITALIAN [baby] *noun* (*plural* **bimbos** or **bimboes**) a slang term for a physically attractive but apparently unintelligent young woman (or, more rarely, young man): *"Any woman who succeeds as a top model has to work hard to convince the press not to label her a bimbo."*

biretta (băretă), **beretta,** **birretta** ITALIAN [from *beretta,* ultimately from Latin *birrus* cloak with a hood] *noun* a stiff square cap of a type worn by Roman Catholic and other clergy: *"'Beautiful!' remarked Bickley, 'but why don't you put on your surplice and biretta?' (Being very High-Church Bastin did wear a biretta on festival Sundays at home)."* (H. Rider Haggard, *When the World Shook,* 1919).

biriyani (bireeanee), **biryani, biriani** URDU [from Persian *biriyan* fried, grilled] *noun* in Indian cuisine, a dish of spiced meat or vegetables, served with rice.

bistro (beestrō, bistrō) FRENCH [café] *noun* a café, small restaurant, or wine bar.

bivouac (bivooak, bivăwak, bivwack) FRENCH [extra watch, from Swiss German *biwacht,* from *bi* by and *wacht* guard, referring originally to the patrols voluntarily undertaken by citizens of Aargau and Zürich in Switzerland during the 18th century] *noun* a rudimentary encampment in the open air (usually without a tent or more substantial shelter): *"We reckoned the improvements of the art of war among the triumphs of science, and yet Napoleon conquered Europe by the bivouac, which consisted of falling back on naked valor, and disencumbering it of all aids."* (Ralph Waldo Emerson, *Essays,* 1841). ~*verb* to make a bivouac shelter or to spend time in such an encampment.

bizarre (băzahr, bizahr) FRENCH [from Italian *bizzarro* angry] *adjective* extraordinary, odd, weird, eccentric, outlandish, peculiar, grotesque: *"His posture combines a surreal exaggerated style with a bizarre sense of humor."* ~*noun* something of a bizarre nature.

blancmange (blămonj, blămonzh) FRENCH [*blanc manger* white food] *noun* a gelatinous milk-based dessert dish.

blanquette (blon<u>ket</u>) FRENCH [*blanc* white] *noun* a meat or fish stew prepared in a white sauce: *"They serve a very good blanquette of veal at that restaurant."*

blasé (blah<u>zay</u>), **blase** FRENCH [satiated, exhausted, past participle of *blaser* to exhaust, to satiate] *adjective* unconcerned, indifferent, apathetic: *"One gets pale, and old, and sadly fagged out, with all this dissipation, pleasant as it is. I feel quite blasé, already"* (Louisa May Alcott, *An Old-Fashioned Girl*, 1870).

blitz (blits) GERMAN [*Blitzkrieg* lightning war] *noun* an intensive aerial attack or other military campaign relying on surprise and overwhelming force; any energetic, concentrated effort to get something done: *"His bedroom was transformed following a blitz by his mother and the cleaning lady."* ~*verb* to launch a sudden violent attack on an enemy, or to conduct any intense campaign.

bloc (blok) FRENCH [block, from Dutch *blok* or German *block*] *noun* a combination of individuals, groups, political parties, or nations in pursuit of shared interests or to provide mutual support: *"The parties of the left have joined in a bloc to overwhelm the government."*

blond (blond) FRENCH [from Latin *blundus* yellow] *adjective, masculine* fair-haired, flaxen-haired (referring to a man or boy): *"The older man ran an affectionate hand through the lad's matted blond hair."* ~*noun, masculine* a fair-haired man or boy. ~*adjective, feminine* **blonde** (blond) fair-haired, flaxen-haired (referring to a woman or girl) ~*noun, feminine* **blonde** a fair-haired woman or girl.

bodega (bo<u>day</u>gă) SPANISH [from Greek *apotheke* storehouse] *noun* a wine merchant's shop or a bar in a Spanish-speaking country: *"I saw John Henry Menton casually in the Bodega just now and it will cost me a fall if I don't . . . wait awhile. . . .We're on the right lay, Bob, believe you me"* (James Joyce, *Ulysses,* 1922). Also, a Hispanic grocery store.

Boer (bor, bō̆ă) DUTCH [farmer, countryman] *noun* an Afrikaner, a South African of Dutch or Huguenot lineage. ~*adjective* of or relating to the Boer community in South Africa.

boeuf bourguignon (bŭf <u>borgee</u>-nyon(g)) FRENCH [beef of Burgundy] *noun phrase* a beef casserole cooked in red wine.

boîte (bwat) FRENCH [box] *noun* a nightclub or small restaurant.

bolas (<u>bō</u>lăs), **bola** (<u>bō</u>lă) SPANISH [*bola* ball] *noun* (*plural* **bolas** or **bolases,** <u>bō</u>lăsăz) a weighted cord thrown to bring down livestock, etc.: *"Although the ostrich in its habits is so shy, wary, and solitary, and although so fleet in its pace, it is caught without much difficulty by the Indian or Gaucho armed with* the bolas" (Charles Darwin, *The Voyage of the Beagle,* 1839).

bolero (bălairō) SPANISH *noun* a variety of traditional Spanish dance or the music played to accompany it: *"The waltz, some delicious measure, lapsing, bathing me in bliss, / The bolero to tinkling guitars and clattering castanets"* (Walt Whitman, *Leaves of Grass,* 1855). Can also refer to a short jacket with an open front worn by both men and women.

Bolshevik (bolshevik), **bolshevik** RUSSIAN [member of the majority, *bolshoi* big] *noun* a member or supporter of the Russian Social Democratic Party that staged the 1917 November Revolution in Russia and, by extension, any individual suspected of holding radical left-wing or revolutionary views: *"Her uncle would have nothing to do with her new boyfriend, having decided from the outset that he was a bolshevik with undersirable views about the monarchy."* ~*adjective* of or relating to the Bolshevik political movement or Bolshevik principles. ~*abbreviated form* **bolshie, bolshy.**

bombe (bom, bomb) FRENCH [bomb] *noun* a frozen ice-cream dessert, usually made in a rounded bomblike mold.

bona fide (bōnă fīdee) LATIN [in good faith] *adverb phrase* done in good faith, sincerely. ~*adjective phrase* genuine, valid, legitimate, sincere, honest: *"But on the other hand, if a man through any cause falls into bona fide misfortune the State supports him in the position of life to which he belongs"* (H. Rider Haggard, *Allan Quatermain,* 1887).

bona fides (bōnă fīdeez, bōnă fidz) LATIN [good faith] *noun phrase* good faith, sincerity, honesty; can also refer to a person's credentials: *"The customs officials had checked his bona fides at length at the border post."*

bonanza (bănanză) SPANISH [fair weather, ultimately from Greek *malakos* soft] *noun* a lucky success or fount of great prosperity or profit (originally applied chiefly to productive gold and silver mines): *"The campaign will likely turn into yet another multimillion-dollar bonanza for the advertisers."* ~*adjective* of or relating to such a source of great wealth or prosperity.

bon appétit (bon apătee) FRENCH [good appetite] *interjection* enjoy your meal: *"The waiter wished them bon appétit and left them to their own company."* See also BUON APPETITO.

bonbon (bonbon), **bon-bon** FRENCH [*bon* good] *noun* a candy with a fondant center: *"Oh! thank you, Arthur; and may I have the bonbon too? I had no notion that Lady Clementina liked sweets. I thought she was far too intellectual"* (Oscar Wilde, *Lord Arthur Savile's Crime,* 1891).

bongo (bongō) SPANISH [of American Spanish origin] *noun* (*plural* **bongos** or **bongoes**)   a drum, usually one of a pair, that is played with the hands.

bonhomie (bonămee) FRENCH [*bon-homme* good-natured man]   *noun* friendliness, affability, geniality, good nature, a friendly manner: *"There is some defect in one of his feet. His address is frank, and his whole manner noticeable for bonhomie"* (Edgar Allan Poe, "Von Kempelen and His Discovery," 1850).

bonjour (bonzhoor) FRENCH [good day] *interjection*   hello, good day.

bon marché (bon(g) mahshay) FRENCH [good market]   *adjective* cheap.

bon mot (bon(g) mō) FRENCH [good word] *noun phrase* (*plural* **bons mots** or **bon mots,** bon(g) mōz)   a quip, clever remark, witticism: *"Many of the famous man's celebrated bon mots were inspired by his dislike of strong-willed women."*

bonne (bon) FRENCH [feminine of *bon* good] *noun*   a French maidservant or nursemaid.

bonne bouche (bon boosh), **bonne-bouche** FRENCH [good mouth] *noun phrase* (*plural* **bonnes bouches**)   a delicacy, a titbit, a morsel of food.

bonne femme (bon fam) FRENCH [good wife, in the manner of a good housewife] *adjective phrase*   in cookery, words to describe a dish prepared simply and garnished with fresh vegetables and herbs.

bonsai (bonsī, bonzī) JAPANESE [tray planting, from *bon* tray and *sai* to plant] *noun*   the art of growing dwarfed plants and trees, or an example of this art: *"She first became interested in bonsai as a very young girl."*

bonsoir (bonswahr) FRENCH [good night] *interjection*   good evening, good night: *"'No, you can tell them to take away the samovar,' answered Nikolai Petrovich, and he got up to meet her. Pavel Petrovich said 'bonsoir' to him abruptly, and went to his own study"* (Ivan Turgenev, *Fathers and Sons,* 1862).

bon ton (bon(g) ton(g)) FRENCH [good tone] *noun phrase* (*plural* **bons tons**)   a fashionable style, in the style of high society, good taste.

bon vivant (bon(g) veevon(g)) FRENCH [a good living person] *noun phrase* (*plural* **bons vivants** or **bon vivants**)   a person who enjoys good living, or a person with refined, sophisticated tastes, an epicure: *"He is something of a bon vivant—I doubt that he has ever eaten a hamburger in his life."*

bon viveur (bon(g) viver) FRENCH [good liver] *noun phrase* (*plural* **bons viveurs** or **bon viveurs**)   a person who indulges freely in the good things in life: *"His father is a bon viveur* *of the old school, rarely home before the early hours."*

bon voyage (bon(g) voi<u>ahzh</u>, bon(g) vwoi<u>yahzh</u>) FRENCH [good voyage] *interjection* farewell, have a pleasant trip: *"The old lady wished them bon voyage with tears in her eyes."*

boomerang (<u>boo</u>mărang) AUSTRALIAN ABORIGINAL [from Kamilaroi *bumarin*] *noun* a bent hardwood throwing club used as a self-returning weapon by native Australians and since widely adopted as a plaything. Also applied to any remark, act, or scheme that seems likely to rebound on its originator: *"What she had undertaken in vain conquest of Glenn's pride and Flo Hutter'sWestern tolerance she had found to be a boomerang."* (Zane Grey, *Call of the Canyon,* 1921). ~*verb* to act like a boomerang, rebounding on the originator.

boondocks (<u>boon</u>doks) TAGALOG [mountain] *plural noun* rough, relatively inaccessible, remote country, a rural region or region that is considered remote or distant from a main center of activity; sometimes abbreviated colloquially to *boonies: "The firm is to relocate somewhere out in the boondocks."*

bordello (bor<u>del</u>ō) ITALIAN [brothel, from Latin *bordellum*] *noun* a brothel: *"The two young men suddenly realized that what they had assumed was a boarding house was really a bordello."*

borscht (borsht), **borsch, bortsch** RUSSIAN [*borshch*] *noun* a hot or cold soup made from beets and often served with sour cream.

bossa nova (bosă <u>nō</u>vă) PORTUGUESE [new trend] *noun phrase* a genre of rhythmic Brazilian dance music similar to the samba but with a stronger jazz element, or a dance performed to such music.

bouclé (boo<u>klay</u>), **boucle** FRENCH [curly, past participle of *boucler* to curl] *noun* an uneven woven or knitted yarn with a looped or curled ply.

boudoir (<u>boo</u>dwah) FRENCH [place to sulk in, from *bouder* to sulk, to pout] *noun* a woman's bedroom or private dressing room: *"A light was shining through the door of the little hall-room which served Janey as a dressing-room and boudoir, and her brother rapped impatiently on the panel"* (Edith Wharton, *The Age of Innocence,* 1920).

bouffant (<u>boo</u>fon(g)) FRENCH [from present participle of *bouffer* to puff, to swell] *noun* a piled-up or puffed-out hairstyle or dress style. ~*adjective* of or relating to such a style: *"Everyone wore towering bouffant hairstyles in those days."*

bouillabaisse (booyă<u>bes</u>, booyă<u>bayz</u>) FRENCH [from Modern Provençal *bouiabaisso,* itself from *boui* boil and *abaisso* down] *noun* in French cuisine, a highly seasoned fish stew cooked in water or white wine.

bouillon (booyon(g)) FRENCH [from Old French *boillir* to boil] *noun* in French cuisine, a thin soup made from lean beef.

boulevard (boolǎvahrd) FRENCH [rampart, from Middle Dutch *bolwerc* bulwark] *noun* a street or avenue, especially one that is broad and elegant in appearance: "*They spent the afternoon strolling along the fashionable Paris boulevard.*"

boulevardier (boolǎvahrdeeay, boolǎvahrdeeǎ) FRENCH [person of the boulevard] *noun* a person who frequents the fashionable boulevards of a city, a person of taste and urbanity: "*For an instant he stood, resplendent, with the leisurely air of a boulevardier concocting in his mind the route for his evening pleasures*" (O. Henry, *Strictly Business*, 1910).

bouquet (bookay) FRENCH [thicket, from *bois* wood] *noun* a bunch or nosegay of flowers: "*She rustled forward in radiant loveliness, smiling and chattering, carrying a large bouquet, and attended by Mr Giovanelli*" (Henry James, *Daisy Miller*, 1879). It can also refer to the aroma of wine or perfume, and more generally to any complimentary remark or praise.

bouquet garni (bookay gahrnee) FRENCH [garnished bouquet] *noun phrase* (*plural* **bouquets garnis**, bookayz gahrnee) a selection of herbs bound together and used to flavor soups, meat dishes, and other foods.

bourgeois (boorzhwah, buzhwah) FRENCH [middle-class, from Old French *borjois*] *adjective* middle-class, materialistic, capitalistic, reactionary, mediocre: "*It's ridiculous to say of a man got up in correct tailor clothes, but there was a funereal grace in his attitude so that he might have been reproduced in marble on a monument to some woman in one of those atrocious Campo Santos: the bourgeois conception of an aristocratic mourning lover*" (Joseph Conrad, *The Arrow of Gold*, 1919). ~*noun* a man who belongs to the middle classes or who espouses conventional middle-class values. ~*noun, feminine* **bourgeoise** (boorzhwahz, buzhwahz) a woman of the middle classes.

bourgeoisie (borzhwahzee, boorzhwahzee) FRENCH [the bourgeois class] *noun* the middle classes: "*It is when it calls itself aristocracy or aestheticism or a superiority to the bourgeoisie that its inherent weakness has in justice to be pointed out*" (G. K. Chesterton, *Heretics*, 1908).

bourguignon *See* BOEUF BOURGUIGNON.

bourse (boors) FRENCH [purse] *noun* a European money market or stock exchange (especially the Paris stock exchange): *"So instead of going to the Folies Bergère I spent all evening in the Omnium Bar near the Bourse. . ."* (Robert Service, *Ballads of a Bohemian,* 1920).

boutique (boo<u>teek</u> FRENCH [shop, from Old Provençal *botica,* ultimately from Greek *apotheke* storehouse] *noun* a shop selling fashionable specialties and luxury items: *"This jacket came from a wonderful little boutique we found last week."*

boutonnière (bootă<u>neer</u>) FRENCH [buttonhole, from *bouton* button] *noun* a flower or posy worn in a lapel buttonhole.

bouzouki (bă<u>zoo</u>kee) GREEK [from *mpouzouki,* from Turkish *bozuk* spoiled, roughly made] *noun* a Greek musical stringed instrument with a long neck.

boyar (boi<u>yahr</u>), **boyard** RUSSIAN [from *boyarin* grandee, lord] *noun* a member of the senior Russian aristocracy (prior to the reign of Peter the Great): *". . .doubtless more than one aged lady sighs as she drives by the deserted palace of the boyar and recalls the old days and her vanished youth"* (Ivan Turgenev, *A Hunter's Notes,* 1847–51).

bra *See* BRASSIÈRE.

Brahman, Brahmin (<u>brah</u>măn, brāmăn) SANSKRIT [from *brahman*

sacred utterance] *noun* a Hindu of the highest priestly caste: *"Take notice, further, that the law, so born with them, forbade a man of one caste becoming a member of another; the Brahman could not enter a lower order; if he violated the laws of his own grade, he became an outcast, lost to all but outcasts like himself"* (Lew Wallace, *Ben Hur,* 1880). Hence, a person of considerable intellect and learning: *"He is one of the Brahmins whose influence over the president has come in for criticism in recent months."*

brasserie (bras<u>ree</u>, brasă<u>ree</u>) FRENCH [brewery, from Middle French *brasser* to brew] *noun* a small informal restaurant serving wine, beer, and relatively simple dishes: *"The city has plenty of bars and brasseries where it is possible to spend a lively evening in excellent company."*

brassière (bră<u>zir</u>, brăse<u>er</u>), **brassiere** FRENCH [little camisole, from *brassière* bodice, from Old French *braciere* arm protector] *noun* an undergarment for women designed to cover and support the breasts. ~*abbreviated form* **bra.**

bratwurst (<u>brat</u>werst, <u>brat</u>verst, <u>brat</u>versht) GERMAN [from *brat* spit and *wurst* sausage] *noun* a German pork sausage.

bravado (bră<u>vah</u>dō) SPANISH [from *bravada,* itself from Old Italian *bravare* to show off, to challenge] *noun* a pretense of bravery, bluster, boasting, swaggering: *"They may add, too, that at Trafalgar it was in effect nothing less than a challenge to death; and death came; and that but for his bravado the victorious Admiral might possibly have survived the battle. . ."* (Herman Melville, *Billy Budd*, 1924).

bravo (brahvō) ITALIAN [brave, courageous] *interjection* (*plural* **bravos**) well done! good! ~*noun* a shout of approval or approbation, a cheer. ~feminine **brava** (brahvă) a shout praising a female performer.

bravura (brăvooră) ITALIAN [bravery, from *bravo* brave] *noun* a brilliant, stylish, or spirited display of virtuosity, technical skill, daring, or agility: *"The conductor launched with great bravura into a brilliant interpretation of Beethoven's Ninth Symphony."* ~*adjective* showy, ostentatious, ornate.

bric-a-brac (brik-ă-brak), **bric-à-brac** FRENCH [from *à bric et à brac* at random] *noun* a miscellaneous collection of items (typically inexpensive ornaments or curios), bits and pieces, odds and ends, knickknacks: *"The shop was full of bric-a-brac, ranging from ornamental brasses and memorabilia to bits of military uniform and old books."*

bricolage (breekōlazh, brikōlazh) FRENCH [from *bricoler* to putter about] *noun* a construction made with whatever is conveniently at hand.

brio (breeō) ITALIAN *noun* verve, vivacity, liveliness.

brioche (breeōsh) FRENCH [from *brier* to knead] *noun* in French cuisine, a light, sweet bread, roll, or bun: *"The only things he could find to eat were a stale brioche and an apple."*

briquette (briket), **briquet** FRENCH [from *brique* brick] *noun* a brick-shaped block or slab of coal dust, charcoal, or other material suitable as fuel: *"He piled a few charcoal briquettes up under the barbecue."*

brochette (brōshet) FRENCH [from *broche* spit, pointed tool] *noun* a skewer, or food cooked on a skewer.

brochure (brōshoor) FRENCH [stitching, from *brocher* to sew, referring to the stitching holding a pamphlet together] *noun* a pamphlet or booklet: *"This brochure, the work of an American named Locke, had a great sale."* (Jules Verne, *From the Earth to the Moon,* 1865).

brogue (brōg) IRISH [from *barrog* accent] *noun* a regional dialect or local accent: *"'The question lies in a nutshell,' said Laurence, with that sweet Connaught brogue which always came to him when he desired to be effective—'here it is'"* (Anthony Trollope, *Phineas Finn,* 1869).

bronco (bronkō), **broncho** SPANISH [rough, wild] *noun* a mustang, a wild or only partly broken horse.

brouhaha (broohahhah) FRENCH [uproar] *noun* uproar, hubbub, fuss, commotion: *"'Yes,' he answered, modestly, 'I enjoy the brouhaha, if you choose to consider it such, of all this quarrelsome menagerie of noise-making machines, brought into order and harmony by the presiding genius, the leader...'"* (Oliver Wendell Holmes, *Over the Teacups*, 1891).

brunet, brunette (broonet) FRENCH [from *brun* brown] *noun* a person with brown hair: *"That night he dreamed again about the mysterious brunette."* ~*adjective* brown, dark.

brusque (brăsk, broosk) FRENCH [from Italian *brusco* sour, tart, itself from Latin *bruscus* butcher's broom (a spiny plant)] *adjective* abrupt, blunt, short, offhand: *"Marilla, brusque and tearless, pecked Anne's cheek and said she supposed they'd hear from her when she got settled."* (Lucy Maud Montgomery, *Anne of the Island*, 1915).

brut (broot) FRENCH [rough, raw] *adjective* (of wine, champagne, etc.) very dry: *"Under an assumed name he drank, I've just been informed by my butler, an entire pint bottle of my Perrier-Jouet, Brut, '89; wine I was specially reserving for myself"* (Oscar Wilde, *The Importance of Being Earnest*, 1895).

brutum fulmen (brootăm fălmăn) LATIN [random thunderbolt] *noun* (*plural* **bruta fulmina**, brootă fălmeenă) an empty threat, a mere noise. *"The sermons of priests these days are often seen simply as bruta fulmina."*

buckaroo (băkăroo, băkăroo), **buckeroo** SPANISH [from *vaquero* cowboy, itself from Latin *vaca* cow] *noun* a cowboy, a cowherd.

buenas noches (bwenăs notchăs) SPANISH [good night] *noun phrase* good night.

buffet (băfay) FRENCH [sideboard, from Old French *bufet*] *noun* an informal meal laid out on a sideboard or table with the intention that diners help themselves to food; can also refer to the sideboard or sidetable itself or to a place where snacks and light meals are served: *"Bartley took his arm and they went together into the station buffet"* (Willa Cather, *Alexander's Bridge*, 1912).

bulgur (bălgăr), **bulghur** TURKISH [from Persian *bulgur* bruised grain] *noun* dried cracked wheat.

bulimia (băleemeeă) GREEK [*boulimia* great hunger] *noun* a pathological craving for food, or an eating disorder in which bouts of compulsive overeating are followed by self-induced vomiting, resulting in weight loss or depression.

bulletin (buulătin) FRENCH [from *bullette* notice, from Latin *bulla* edict] noun   a brief news item or announcement, or a periodical publication: *"Other announcements may be found in the weekly church bulletin."*

bungalow (băngălō) HINDI [from *bangla* in the Bengal style] *noun*   a single-story house: *"The bungalow was sold eventually to an elderly couple with a dog."*

buon appetito (bon apăteetō) ITALIAN [good appetite] *interjection*   enjoy your meal. See also BON APPÉTIT.

bureau (byoorō) FRENCH   [desk, ultimately from Latin *burra* shaggy cloth]   *noun*   (*plural* **bureaus,** byoorōz, or **bureaux** byoorō)   a writing desk with drawers, or a low chest of drawers. Can also refer to an official administrative unit, office, or government department, or to a branch of a news service or other commercial agency.

bureaucracy (byoorōkrăsee) FRENCH [from *bureaucratie,* from *bureau,* desk, office] *noun*   officialdom, especially with regard to unwieldy government organizations that appear to be excessively bound by their own rules and regulations: *"The politicians plan to reduce bureaucracy in our schools."*

bureau de change (byoorō dă shonzh) FRENCH [office of change] *noun* (*plural* **bureaux de change**)   foreign exchange office, currency exchange office: *"They got a good rate of exchange at the local bureau de change."*

burger (bergă) GERMAN [abbreviation of hamburger, after *Hamburger* of Hamburg, Germany] *noun*   a flat, round patty of fried or grilled ground beef, typically served in a soft bun: *"She had eaten only a burger and fries since the weekend."*

burlesque (berlesk) FRENCH [comic, droll, from Italian *burlesco,* from *burla* joke] *noun*   a caricature, parody, travesty, mockery, exaggeration, distortion (originally a theatrical genre or piece of writing aiming to ridicule through humor): *"Most of the magazine consisted of political burlesques and skits."* ~*adjective* mocking, parodying, jocular. ~*verb* to mock, parody, caricature.

burro (bărō, boorō) SPANISH [from *borrico,* itself from Latin *burricus* small horse] *noun*   a donkey, especially one used as a pack animal: *"The sailors, the Indian, and the stolen burro were never seen again"* (Joseph Conrad, *Nostromo,* 1904).

bustier (băsteeay, boosteeăy) FRENCH [from *buste* bust, ultimately from Latin *bustum* tomb] *noun*   a tight-fitting strapless bodice or top for women.

butte (byoot) FRENCH [knoll] *noun* an isolated hill or mountain with steep sides and a flat, narrow top: *"Above him he saw the black fringe of pinon and pine, and above that the bold peak, bare, yellow, like a desert butte"* (Zane Grey, *Lone Star Ranger,* 1915).

bwana (bwahnă) KISWAHILI [from Arabic *abuna* our father] *noun* master, boss, sir.

c

c., ca. *See* CIRCA.

cabal (kăbal) FRENCH [from *cabale* intrigue, ultimately from Hebrew *qabbalah* received lore, revived in England in 1672 in reference to the political grouping comprising the ministers Clifford, Arlington, Buckingham, Ashley, and Lauderdale, whose initials formed the word *cabal*] *noun* a group of persons who engage together in public intrigue: *"'And now,' he continued, turning to Lady Mary and speaking in English, 'let me be asking of our gallants yonder what make them to be in cabal with highwaymen'"* (Booth Tarkington, *Monsieur Beaucaire,* 1900).

caballa (kăbahlă, kabălă), **cabbala, cabbalah, kabala, kabbala** HEBREW [from *qabbalah* received lore] *noun* a body of secret or occult knowledge (originally referring specifically to medieval rabbinical teachings): *"The old man had been schooled in the secrets of the caballa as a young man."*

caballero (kabălairō, kabăyairō) SPANISH [horseman, from Latin *caballarius* hostler] *noun* a skilled horseman, cavalier, or gentleman in a Spanish-speaking country: *"The General, bewildered and dismayed by the resounding streets, welcomed his deliverer as a caballero with a most disinterested heart"* (O. Henry, *Strictly Business,* 1910).

cabana (kăbană, kăbanyă) SPANISH [from *cabaña* hut] *noun* a simple beach house, often with an open side facing the seashore or a swimming pool, or any simple cabin offering basic shelter.

cabaret (kabăray, kabăray) FRENCH [restaurant, nightclub, ultimately from Old Picard *camberet* little room] *noun* a nightclub or restaurant where customers seated at tables can enjoy music, dancing, and other entertainment; can also refer to the floor show presented at such a venue: *"That blond-haired chap across the way / With sunny smile and voice so mellow, / He sings in some cheap cabaret, / Yet what a gay and charming fellow!"* (Robert Service, *Ballads of a Bohemian,* 1920).

cabbala *See* CABALLA.

cabriole (<u>k</u>abreeōl) FRENCH [caper] *noun* (in ballet) a leap in which one leg is extended and the other drawn up next to it; can also refer to the curved, tapering leg of a piece of furniture.

cabriolet (kabreeōl<u>ay</u>) FRENCH [diminutive of *cabriole* caper] *noun* a one-horse carriage with two wheels and a folding hood and, by extension, a car (or convertible) with a folding top: *"It was within a week of the close of the month of July, that a hackney cabriolet, number unrecorded, was seen to proceed at a rapid pace up Goswell Street. . ."* (Charles Dickens, *Pickwick Papers*, 1837).

cacciatore (kachă<u>tore</u>e) ITALIAN [hunter] *adjective* (in Italian cuisine) cooked with tomatoes and herbs (and sometimes also with wine): *"The latest addition to their range of frozen foods is a chicken cacciatore."*

cache (kash) FRENCH [hiding-place, from *cacher* to hide] *noun* a secret store or hiding place, or the things hidden in such a place: *"The cache had been found and rifled; the seven hundred thousand pounds were gone!"* (Robert Louis Stevenson, *Treasure Island*, 1883). ~*verb* to hide items in a secret place.

cachepot (<u>k</u>ashpō, kashăpō), **cachepot** FRENCH [pot hiding place, from *cacher* to hide and *pot* pot] *noun* an ornamental container for a flowerpot.

cachet (ka<u>shay</u>) FRENCH [seal, stamp, from *cacher* to hide, to press] *noun* prestige, recognition, honor (originally a seal or other mark of official approval): *"Though he is too modest to admit it, Lord Doak gives a cachet to our smart quartier such as it has not received since the ever-memorable visit of the Earl of Sittingbourne"* (Sinclair Lewis, *Babbitt*, 1922).

cachou (kă<u>shoo</u>, <u>k</u>ashoo) FRENCH [from Portuguese *cachu*, from Malay *kacu*] *noun* a pastille or lozenge taken to sweeten the breath: *"He was eating cachous to disguise the smell of cigarettes."*

cadastre (kă<u>das</u>tăr), **cadaster** FRENCH [land survey, from Italian *catastro* list, ultimately from Greek *katastichon* notebook] *noun* an official register of land ownership compiled for tax purposes.

cadaver (kă<u>da</u>văr) LATIN [from *cadere* to fall] *noun* a corpse, a human body: *"The stale cadaver blocks up the passage— the burial waits no longer. / Allons! yet take warning!"* (Walt Whitman, *Leaves of Grass*, 1855).

caddy (<u>k</u>ad<u>ee</u>) MALAY [from *kati*] *noun* (*plural* **caddies**) a small box, chest, or tin in which tea is stored: *"Her grandmother kept the key in an old caddy that still smelled of stale tea leaves."*

cadeau (kadō) FRENCH [gift] *noun* (*plural* **cadeaux**) a present: *"Sir, you have now given me my 'cadeau'; I am obliged to you: it is the meed teachers most covet—praise of their pupils' progress"* (Charlotte Brontë, *Jane Eyre*, 1847).

cadenza (kădenză) ITALIAN [cadence] *noun* (in music) an elaborate or improvised passage towards the end of a composition allowing a performer to demonstrate his or her technical skill: *"A few brass instruments awake in the orchestra, announcing the Prophet's first triumph (in a broken cadenza)"* (Honoré de Balzac, *Gambara*, 1837).

cadet (kădet) FRENCH [from Gascon *capdet* chief, ultimately from Latin *caput* head] *noun* a person who is studying at a military academy or in training to join one of the armed services or the police, or more generally a younger brother or son or the younger branch of a family: *"It was the night of a little party at the Doctor's, which was given on the occasion of Mr Jack Maldon's departure for India, whither he was going as a cadet, or something of that kind: Mr Wickfield having at length arranged the business"* (Charles Dickens, *David Copperfield*, 1849–50).

cadre (kadray, kahdray, kahdree, kahdă) FRENCH [framework, executive, from Italian *quadro*, from Latin *quadrus* square] *noun* a core group of trained personnel working together as a unit within a larger organization; also, a group of activists in a communist or other revolutionary, organization.

caduceus (kădooseeăs, kădjooshăs) LATIN [from Greek *karykeion* herald's staff, from *karyx* herald] *noun* (*plural* **caducei,** kădooseeī, kădyoosheeī) a staff decorated with a representation of two entwined snakes and two wings, as carried by heralds and used as an insignia of the medical profession: *"O thou great thunder-darter of Olympus, / Forget that thou art Jove, the king of gods and, / Mercury, lose all the serpentine craft of thy / Caduceus, if ye take not that little, little less / Than little wit from them that they have!"* (William Shakespeare, *Troilus and Cressida*, c. 1601).

caesura (sizoоră), **cesura** LATIN [act of cutting, from *caedere* to cut] *noun* (*plural* **caesuras** or **caesurae,** sizooree, sizhooree) a pause, specifically a break in the middle of a line of verse marking an interruption in the rhythm: *"In Old English verse the caesura was used rather monotonously to indicate the half line."* (J. A. Cuddon, *A Dictionary of Literary Terms*, 1976).

café (kăfay), **cafe** FRENCH [coffee, from Turkish *kahve*] *noun* a coffee shop, a small restaurant where snacks, drinks, and light meals are available: *"We stopped at the first café we came to and entered. An old woman seated us at a table and waited for orders."* (Mark Twain, *Innocents Abroad*, 1869).

café au lait (kafay ō lay) FRENCH [coffee with milk] *noun phrase* (*plural* **cafés au lait**) coffee served with milk (often hot milk). ~*adjective phrase* of the color of café au lait, pale brown.

café noir (kafay nwahr) FRENCH [black coffee] *noun phrase* (*plural* **cafés noirs**) coffee served without milk or cream.

cafeteria (kafăteereeă) SPANISH [from American Spanish *cafetería* coffeehouse, ultimately from French *café* coffee] *noun* a restaurant or lunchroom where customers usually select food at a counter or serve themselves and then eat at tables.

cafetière (kafeteeair) FRENCH [coffeepot, from *café* coffee] *noun* a coffeemaking machine, a coffee percolator.

caftan (caftan), **kaftan** TURKISH [from Persian *qaftan*] *noun* a full-length cotton or silk garment with long sleeves, as worn by men throughout the Middle East: "'*And here is your servant,*' *he added, indicating a boy with close-cropped hair, who had come in with him, wearing a long blue caftan with holes in the elbows and a pair of boots which did not belong to him*" (Ivan Turgenev, *Fathers and Sons*, 1862).

cagoule (kăgool), **kagoule** FRENCH [cowl] *noun* a lightweight waterproof coat that is put on over the head: "*The boys pulled their cagoules off over their heads once the rain had stopped.*"

calamari (kalămahree) ITALIAN [plural of *calamaro,* from Latin *calamarium* ink pot] *plural noun* (in Italian cuisine) a dish of squid.

caldera (kaldairă, koldairă) SPANISH [from Latin *caldaria* cauldron] *noun* a wide volcanic crater caused by the collapse of the cone of a volcano: "*The helicopter flew low over the lava-filled caldera.*"

caliber (kalăbăr) FRENCH [from Old Italian *calibro,* itself from Arabic *qalib* shoemaker's last] *noun* the diameter of a bullet or artillery shell, or the bore of a gun used to fire such bullets or shells; may also refer to the diameter of any cylindrical object "'*Shore it's funny how a bullet can floor a man an' then not do any damage,*' *said Ladd.* '*I felt a zip of wind an' somethin' like a pat on my chest an' down I went. Well, so much for the small caliber with their steel bullets. Supposin' I'd connected with a .405!*'" (Zane Grey, *Desert Gold,* 1913). Can also be used more generally to express a degree of excellence, importance, merit, or moral quality.

calico (kalăkō) HINDU [after Calicut, India] *noun* a white cotton cloth originally of Indian manufacture; can also refer to a blotched or piebald animal (the patterns supposedly resembling printed calico cloth). ~*adjective* of or relating to calico cloth or patterns: "*Arrayed in a new calico dress, with clean, white apron, and high, well-starched turban, her black polished face glowing with satisfaction, she lingered, with needless punctiliousness, around the arrangements of the table, merely as an excuse for talking a little to her mistress*" (Harriet Beecher Stowe, *Uncle Tom's Cabin*, 1852).

caliph (ka̱ylif), **calif**, **khalifa**   ARABIC [from *khalifah* successor] *noun*   title borne by a successor of Muhammad as the head of Islam.

calliope (kăli̱ăpee, ka̱leeo̱p) GREEK [after Calliope, the Greek muse of heroic poetry, from *kalliope* beautiful voice] *noun*   a steam-operated pipe organ: "*Claude and his mules rattled into Frankfort just as the calliope went screaming down Main Street at the head of the circus parade*" (Willa Cather, *One of Ours*, 1922).

calvados (kalvădo̱s) FRENCH [after Calvados, France] *noun*   apple brandy, traditionally made in the Calvados region of Normandy.

calyx (ka̱yliks) LATIN [from Greek *kalyx* husk, shell, from *kaluptein* to hide] *noun* (*plural* **calyxes** or **calyces**, ka̱ylăseez)   the outer whorl of sepals of a flower.

camaraderie (kamăra̱hdăree, kamra̱hdree) FRENCH [comradeship, from *camarade* comrade] *noun*   friendship, comradeship, good fellowship, mutual trust: "*There was a great sense of camaraderie in the theater that evening.*"

camarilla (kamări̱lă, kamăreeă) SPANISH [small room, diminutive of *camara* chamber] *noun*   a clique, a cabal, a group of scheming advisers.

cameo (ka̱meeo̱) FRENCH [from Old French *camau*] *noun*   a small gem or medallion carved in relief, or alternatively a short sequence or small role in a play, film, or book: "*Her face, encompassed by the blackness of the receding heath, showed whitely, and without halflights, like a cameo*" (Thomas Hardy, *The Return of the Native*, 1878).

camera lucida (kamără loosădă) LATIN [light chamber] *noun phrase*   an optical device that projects a virtual image of an object onto a plane surface by means of a prism so that it can be traced.

camera obscura (kamără obskooră) LATIN [dark room] *noun phrase* (*plural* **camera obscuras**)   an optical device that projects an image of an object onto a surface in a darkened enclosure by means of a lens: "*Academics debate the extent of the use of the camera obscura in renaissance art.*"

ça m'est égal (sa met ayga̱hl) FRENCH [that is equal to me] *interjection*   it's all the same to me, I don't mind.

camisole (kamăsōl) FRENCH [from Provençal *camisolla,* from *camisa* shirt] *noun* a sleeveless underbodice for women, or a short négligé jacket: *"Mrs O'Dowd, the good housewife, arrayed in curl papers and a camisole, felt that her duty was to act, and not to sleep, at this juncture"* (William Makepeace Thackeray, *Vanity Fair,* 1847–48).

camorra (kămoră), **Camorra** ITALIAN [a shirt, or possibly from Spanish *camorra* dispute, quarrel] *noun* a secret criminal organization, often referring specifically to a clandestine society that was founded in Naples, Italy, around 1820: *"The local hoods had gathered together to form a sort of camorra to protect their interests."*

camouflage (kameflahzh, kameflahj) FRENCH [disguise, from *camoufler* to disguise, to cover up] *noun* the use of paint, netting, or other means to disguise military equipment by making it merge into the immediate surroundings; also used more generally of any attempt to conceal something or deceive others. ~*adjective* of or relating to a design, pattern, or combination of colors intended to disguise or conceal something. ~*verb* to disguise something in such a manner: *"You can camouflage all you want to, but you know darn well that these radicals, as you call 'em, are opposed to the war. . ."* (Sinclair Lewis, *Main Street,* 1920). ~*abbreviated form* **cam.**

campanile (kampăneelee) ITALIAN [bell tower, from *campana* bell] *noun* (*plural* **campaniles** or **campanili,** kampăneelee) a freestanding bell tower: *"The campanile next to the cathedral was badly damaged in the earthquake."*

campesino (kampăseenō) SPANISH [field-worker, from *campo* field, country, ultimately from Latin *campus* field] *noun* (*plural* **campesinos,** kampăseenōz) a Latin American farmer or peasant.

campus (kampăs) LATIN [field, plain] *noun* (*plural* **campuses** or **campi,** kampee) the site of a university, college, or school, including associated buildings and grounds, or the university or college itself: "The group had the right to hold meetings on the campus without prior official approval."

canaille (kănī, kănayl) FRENCH [from Italian *canaglia* pack of dogs, from *cane* dog] *noun* the general populace, the masses, the rabble, the mob: *"Canaille / of the gutter, up! Away! / You've battened on me for a bitter-long day; / But I'm driving you forth, and forever and aye, / Hunger and Thirst and Cold"* (Robert Service, *Ballads of a Bohemian,* 1920).

canapé (kanăpay, kanăpee) FRENCH [sofa, from Latin *canopeum* mosquito net] *noun* an appetizer, usually in the form of a piece of bread, toast, or a cracker topped with cheese, caviar, anchovies, meat spread, or other morsels: *"He helped himself from a plate of canapés as he waited for the lady of the house to come down."*

canard (kănahrd) FRENCH [duck, from *vendre des canards à moitié* to half-sell ducks] *noun*   a hoax, an unfounded report; can also refer in aeronautics to a small airfoil located in front of the wing of some aircraft to increase stability: *"The idea that staring at the moon induces madness is a canard of considerable longevity."*

cancan (kankan) FRENCH [from *canard* duck] *noun*   a lively dance, originally from France, in which female dancers perform series of high kicks while wearing full ruffled skirts: *"Crowds flocked to the theater to see the scandalous new dance called the cancan."*

candelabrum (kandălahbrăm) LATIN [from *candela* candle] *noun* (*plural* **candelabra,** kandălahbră) a branched ornamental candlestick or lightholder: *"An eight-branched candelabrum stood on a little table near the head of a sofa."*

ça ne fait rien (sa nă fay reean(g)) FRENCH [that means nothing] *noun phrase*   it does not matter.

cannelloni (kanălōnee) ITALIAN [from *cannello* cane stalk] *plural noun*   (in Italian cuisine) a variety of tube-shaped or rolled pasta with a meat, fish, cheese, or other filling, served in sauce.

canoe (kănoo) SPANISH [*canoa,* from Carib *kanawa*] *noun*   a small lightweight boat with pointed bow and stern, propelled by paddles: *"It was a man, a living man, an Indian, a fisherman, a poor devil who, I suppose, had come to glean before the harvest. I could see the bottom of his canoe anchored some feet above his head"* (Jules Verne, *20,000 Leagues Under the Sea,* 1870). ~*verb* to paddle such a boat.

cantabile (kantahbilay, kantahbilee) ITALIAN [from Latin *cantabilis* that may be sung] *adverb*   (in music) in a flowing manner. ~*adjective* (in music) smooth, flowing. ~*noun* a passage of music in a smooth, flowing style.

cantaloupe (kantălōp) FRENCH [after Cantalupo, the former papal villa near Rome where the first European cantaloupe melons were grown] *noun*   a variety of melon with orange flesh.

cantata (kăntahtă) LATIN [feminine of *cantatus,* past participle of *cantare* to sing] *noun*   (in music) a composition for one or more voices, usually combining solos, choruses, and recitatives, with instrumental accompaniment: *"He conducted me into a chamber, where I found a great quantity of music: he gave me some to copy, particularly the cantata he had heard me singing, and which he was* *shortly to sing himself"* (Jean-Jacques Rousseau, *Confessions,* 1782–89).

cantatrice (kăntătrees) FRENCH/ITALIAN [female singer, from Latin *cantatrix,* feminine of *cantator* singer] *noun (plural* **cantatrices,** kăntătreeseez, *or* **cantatrici,** kăntăttreechee) a female opera singer, or other professional singer.

cantina (kanteenă) SPANISH [canteen, from Italian *cantina* wine cellar] *noun* a barroom or saloon; can also refer in Italy to a wine shop.

canto (kantō) ITALIAN [song, from Latin *cantus* song] *noun* a division of a long poem: *"This last work comprised an epic poem of several dozen cantos."*

canton (kantăn) FRENCH [from Italian *canto* corner, from Latin *canthus* corner] *noun* a small district or an administrative division of a country (specifically of France or Switzerland): *"Voters in several cantons have recently shown a new enthusiasm for candidates representing the far right."*

cantor (kantor) LATIN [singer, from *canere* to sing] *noun* a choir leader; in Jewish religious services, an official who chants or sings and also leads the prayers in a synagogue.

canyon (kanyăn) SPANISH [from *cañón* tube, ultimately from Latin *canna* reed] *noun* a narrow, steep-sided valley: *"They crossed the gap between the*

multi-storey buildings, which gave great canyon-like elevations."

capo (kapō) ITALIAN [chief, from Latin *caput* head] *noun* the head of a branch of the Mafia, or of a similar criminal organization: *"The capos meet regularly to decide what to do about rivals on the waterfront."*

cappuccino (kapăcheenō) ITALIAN [Capuchin, referring to the color of the habit worn by Capuchin monks] *noun* an espresso coffee topped with frothy milk or cream.

capriccio (kăpreecheeō) ITALIAN [caprice, ultimately from *capro* goat] *noun* (in music) a piece of instrumental music written in a lively, flowing style; can also refer to any whim, trick, or prank: *"Will this capriccio hold in thee? art sure?"* (William Shakespeare, *All's Well That Ends Well,* c. 1602).

caprice (kăprees) FRENCH [from Italian *capriccio* shudder, head with the hair standing on end, from *capo* head and *riccio* hedgehog] *noun* a whim, fancy, an unpredictable change of mind, impulsiveness: *"Adam dared not plead again, for Dinah's was not the voice of caprice or insincerity"* (George Eliot, *Adam Bede,* 1859).

carabiner (kară beenăr) GERMAN [abbreviation of *Karabinerhaken* carabiner's hook] *noun* a spring-hinged oblong metal ring used by climbers to connect ropes: *"The leading climber ran the rope through a carabiner and waited for the next man to join him on the ledge."*

carabiniere (karăbinee<u>air</u>) ITALIAN [soldier armed with a carbine, from French *carabine* carbine] *noun* (*plural* **carabinieri,** karăbinee<u>air</u>ee) a member of the Italian national police force.

carafe (kă<u>raf</u>, kă<u>rahf</u>) FRENCH [from Italian *caraffa,* itself from Arabic *gharrafah* drinking vessel] *noun* a flask, usually made of glass, from which water, wine, or other beverages may be served: *"His eye fell upon a carafe of water on a chair at his bedside; he seized upon it with a shaking hand and drank half its contents before he set it down"* (Booth Tarkington, *His Own People,* 1907).

caravanserai (kară<u>van</u>să<u>rī</u>), **caravansary** PERSIAN [from *karwan* caravan and *sarai* inn, palace] *noun* a type of hostelry in the Middle East constructed round a central court where caravans of travelers can rest at night: *"The necromancer acknowledged his kindness in many words and, thanking him for his good offices, returned to his cell in the caravanserai"* (Richard Burton, "Aladdin; or, The Wonderful Lamp," *Arabian Nights,* 1885–88).

carbonara (kahrbon<u>ah</u>ră) ITALIAN [in the manner of a charcoal maker] *noun* (in Italian cuisine) a dish of hot pasta served in a sauce with such ingredients as cheese, bacon, or ham.

carcinoma (kahrsă<u>nō</u>mă) GREEK [*karkinoma* cancer, itself from *karkinos* crab] *noun* (*plural* **carcinomas** or **carcinomata,** kahrsă<u>nō</u>mătă) a cancerous tumor of epithelial origin, specifically one that is malignant in nature.

cargo (<u>kah</u>rgō) SPANISH [load, charge, from *cargar* to load] *noun* (*plural* **cargos** or **cargoes**) goods or merchandise for transport, freight: *"Lighten ship! Lively, now, lively, men! Heave the whole cargo overboard!"* (Mark Twain, *Captain Stormfield's Visit to Heaven,* 1909).

caries (<u>kai</u>reez) LATIN [decay] *plural noun* tooth or bone decay: *"Treatments for dental caries have made huge technological strides in the last decade."*

carillon (<u>ka</u>rilăn, <u>ka</u>reeahn, kă<u>ril</u>yăn) FRENCH [bells, from Old French *quarregnon* peal of four bells, from Latin *quaternio* set of four] *noun* a musical instrument comprising a set of chromatically tuned bells that are struck by hammers connected to a keyboard, or a piece of music written for such an instrument.

caritas (<u>ka</u>ritas) LATIN [love, care] *noun* charity, Christian love.

carousel (kară<u>sel</u>, kară<u>zel</u>), **carrousel** FRENCH [a knight's tournament, from *carrousel,* from Italian *carosello*] *noun* a merry-go-round; can also refer to a circular conveyor belt, as at an airport: *"The children clamored for a ride on the carousel."*

carpe diem (kahrpay de̲e̲em) LATIN [seize the day, quoting the Roman poet Horace (65–8 B.C.)] *noun phrase* seize the opportunity when it presents itself, no time like the present, do not waste time: *"'Carpe diem,' he said laughing. Do you know what 'carpe diem' means? . . .This is what it means. As an hour for joy has come, do not let any trouble interfere with it'"* (Anthony Trollope, *Ayala's Angel*, 1881).

carte blanche (kahrt blonsh̲, kahrt blonch̲) FRENCH [white card] *noun phrase* (*plural* **cartes blanches**) free license to do what one wishes, full discretionary power, freedom of action; can also refer to a document left blank for another party to fill in as he or she wishes: *"I only ask you to give me carte blanche. I'm not going to offer you my protection . . .Though, indeed, why shouldn't I protect you?"* (Leo Tolstoy, *Anna Karenina*, 1873–77).

carte des vins (kahrt day va̲n(g̲)) FRENCH [list of wines] *noun phrase* a wine list.

carte de visite (kahrt dă vize̲et), **carte-de-visite** FRENCH [visiting card] *noun phrase* (*plural* **cartes de visite**) a visiting card, a calling card: *"The stranger declined to leave behind his carte de visite, indicating instead that he would call again later."*

carte d'identité (kahrt dido̲ntătay) FRENCH [identity card] *noun phrase* (*plural* **cartes d'identité**) an identity card, ID card: *"The soldier demanded to see their cartes d'identité."*

carte du jour (kahrt doo zho̲or) FRENCH [card of the day] *noun phrase* (*plural* **cartes du jour**) a menu: *"The waiter produced the carte du jour for their inspection."*

cartel (kahrte̲l) FRENCH [coalition, from Italian *cartello* placard] *noun* a coalition of political or commercial groups in pursuit of their own interests; *"The government is looking into accusations that the companies are operating as a cartel."* Can also refer to a written agreement between warring nations.

cartouche (kahrto̲osh), **cartouch** FRENCH [from Italian *cartoccio,* from *carta* paper] *noun* in Egyptian hieroglyphics, an oblong outline enclosing the name of a pharoah of ancient Egypt and by extension an ornamental frame, usually in the shape of a scroll; *"Whether this was the cartouche of the original Kallikrates, or of some prince or Pharaoh from whom his wife Amenartas was descended, I am not sure. . ."* (H. Rider Haggard, *She,* 1887). Can also refer to a gun cartridge with a paper case.

casa (kah̲să, ka̲să) SPANISH / ITALIAN [cottage] *noun* a house, a dwelling: *"'My casa is your casa,' the man said with a grin."*

Casanova (kasănōvă) ITALIAN [after the Italian adventurer and lover Giacomo Girolamo Casanova (1725–98)] *noun* a man who has a reputation as a seducer of women: *"As a young man, the count had been considered something of a Casanova."*

casbah (kazbah), **kasbah** ARABIC [qasbah] *noun* the native quarter of a North African town.

cascara (kaskahră) SPANISH [abbreviated from *cascara sagrada* sacred bark, from *cascar* to crack] *noun* the dried bark of a buckthorn *(Rhamnus purshiana)* used as a purgative.

casino (kăseenō) ITALIAN [little house, from Latin *casa* house] *noun* a room or building used for gambling and other amusements: *"All these tricks and turns of the show were upon him with a spring as he descended the Casino steps and paused on the pavement at its doors"* (Edith Wharton, *The House of Mirth,* 1905).

Cassandra (kăsandră, kăsahndră) GREEK [Kassandra, the prophetess daughter of King Priam of Troy] *noun* a person who habitually predicts misfortune, a prophet or prophetess of doom: *"I do not know why, but his wandering words struck me cold; the proverbial funeral bell at the marriage feast was nothing to them. I suppose it was because in a flash of intuition I knew that they would come true and that he was an appointed Cassandra"* (H. Rider Haggard, *When the World Shook,* 1919).

casserole (kasărōl) FRENCH [saucepan, ultimately from Greek *kyathos* ladle] *noun* a cooking pot with a lid, or a dish baked or served in such a pot: *"'Just be so good as to let me get to the fire, Mr Hunsden; I have something to cook.' (An interval occupied in settling a casserole on the fire; then, while she stirred its contents:). . ."* (Charlotte Brontë, *The Professor,* 1857). ~*verb* to cook food in a casserole.

cassette (kăset, kaset) FRENCH [diminutive of *casse* case] *noun* a flat container or case loaded with photographic film, magnetic tape, or similar material to facilitate ease of use: *"There were 40 or 50 audio cassettes on the display table."*

cassis (kăsees) FRENCH [blackcurrant] *noun* blackcurrant liqueur: *"She poured some cassis into the wine in the vain hope that this would make it more palatable."*

cassoulet (kasălay) FRENCH [diminutive of *cassolo* stew pan, ultimately from *casso* ladle] *noun* a casserole of meat baked with white beans and herbs.

castrato (kastrahtō, kăstrahtō) ITALIAN [castrated, past participle of *castrare* to castrate] *noun* (*plural* **castratos** or **castrati,** kastrahtee, kăstrahtee) a singer who has been castrated at an early age in order to retain his high-pitched singing voice in adulthood: *"Whereat the castrato cried out and said: 'Allah! Allah! O my lord, these are sandals for the treading of thy feet, so thou mayst wend to the wardrobe.'"* (Richard Burton, "Story of the Larrikin and the Cook," *Arabian Nights,* 1885–88).

casus belli (kahsăs belee, kaysăs beli̅) LATIN [occasion of war] *noun phrase* an event or situation that is seen as justifying or causing hostilities or that is used as an excuse for declaring war: *"The invasion of the island could constitute a casus belli in the eyes of the international community."*

catachresis (katăkreesăs) GREEK [misuse, from *katachresthai* to misuse] *noun* (*plural* **catachreses,** katăkreeseez) the use of a word in the wrong context, misuse of language.

catafalque (katăfolk, katăfalk) ITALIAN [from *catafalco,* probably from *catafalicum* scaffold] *noun* an elaborate structure erected over or around the coffin at a funeral or lying in state, or a structure on which the coffin is placed or carried in procession: *"The dead president lay upon the catafalque, surrounded by his grieving people."*

catalysis (katalăsis) GREEK [*kataluein* to dissolve] *noun* (*plural* **catalyses,** katalăseez) the chemical process of increasing the rate of a reaction without consuming or chemically changing the material concerned; also used more widely to refer to the provocation or encouragement of an exchange between parties or the precipitation of change in general.

catamaran (katămăran, katămăran) TAMIL [from *kattumaram* tied wood, from *kattu* to tie and *maram* wood, tree] *noun* a boat with twin hulls: *"The technology of the catamaran has advanced so far that it is now possible to sail around the world in such vessels."*

catastrophe (katastrăfee) GREEK [overturning, from *katastrephein* to overturn] *noun* a calamity, disaster, or total failure; can also refer to the dénouement of a novel, play, or other story: *"The region faces economic catastrophe with the loss of thousands of jobs."*

catechesis (katăkeesis) GREEK [*katekhesis* instruction by mouth] *noun* (*plural* **catacheses,** katăkeeseez) oral instruction, often referring specifically to the teaching of Christianity.

catechumen (katăkyoománkyooman) FRENCH [from Latin *catechumenus,* itself from Greek *katechoumenos* being instructed] *noun* a convert to Christianity prior to baptism, or one being taught in Christian doctrine before joining the church.

catharsis (katharsis), **katharsis** GREEK [purification, from *katharsis,* from *kathairein* to cleanse] *noun* (*plural* **catharses,** kătharseez) purification of the emotions: "*The whole episode served as something of a catharsis in the young man's life.*"

catheter (kathătăr, kathtăr) GREEK [*kathienai* to send down] *noun* a hollow tube through which fluids may be injected into or withdrawn from a body or by means of which a passageway or canal may be kept open: "*He was shocked to see his aunt in hospital, dependent upon catheters and drugs.*"

caudillo (kotheeyō, kotheelyo) SPANISH [small head, from Latin *capitellum*, diminutive of *caput* head] *noun* (*plural* **caudillos,** kordeeyōz, kordilyōz) a military or political leader in a Spanish-speaking country.

causa sine qua non (cowză sīnay kwah nōn) LATIN [cause without which not] *noun phrase* (*plural* **causae sine quibus non,** cowzī sinee kweebăs nōn) the immediate and indispensable cause of something happening: "*Poverty is the causa sine qua non of most acts of vandalism and other petty crimes.*" See also SINE QUA NON.

cause célèbre (koz săleb, koz sălebră), **cause celebre** FRENCH [celebrated case] *noun* (*plural* **causes célèbres, causes celebres**) a notorious affair, scandal, case, person, or thing: "'*It's difficult to say what it is, but it may yet be a cause célèbre,*' said the Assistant Commis-

sioner" (Joseph Conrad, *The Secret Agent,* 1907).

ça va sans dire (sa va son deer) FRENCH [that goes without saying] *interjection* it goes without saying, it stands to reason.

caveat (kaveeat) LATIN [let him beware, from *cavere* to be on guard] *noun* (*plural* **caveats**) a warning to others to beware or to be careful, a proviso: "*He recommended a vacation in Europe, but then qualified the recommendation with a lengthy list of caveats.*"

caveat emptor (kaveeat emptor) LATIN [let the buyer beware] *interjection* buyer beware, at the buyer's own risk (a warning to a purchaser that he or she can have no recourse to the law if due care is not exercised in making a purchase): "*But I say that if my story be right the doctrine of Caveat emptor does not encourage trade*" (Anthony Trollope, *Phineas Redux,* 1876). ~*abbreviated form* **c.e.**

cave canem (kayvee kaynăm) LATIN [beware of the dog] *interjection* beware of the dog.

Cdt. *See* COMMANDANT.

c.e. *See* CAVEAT EMPTOR.

cedilla (sădilă) SPANISH [diminutive of *zeda,* letter Z] the diacritical mark as on ç in French, Portuguese, and other languages to show that it has the sound of *s*.

ceilidh (<u>ka</u>ylee) GAELIC [from Old Irish *céilide* visit] *noun*   a Scottish or Irish barn dance, usually featuring live folk music: *"There is a ceilidh in the village hall every Friday during the summer."*

ceinture (sant(y)oor, <u>san</u>chăr) FRENCH [from Latin *cinctura* girdle, from *cingere* to gird] *noun*   a belt or sash worn round the waist.

census (<u>sen</u>săs) LATIN [register of citizens and property, from *censere* to assess] *noun* (*plural* **censuses,** <u>sen</u>săsiz) an official count of the population of a city, region, or nation: *"The 1991 census found that 47 percent of Brazilians considered themselves black or brown; 51 percent said they were white."*

cerebellum (seră<u>bel</u>ăm) LATIN [little brain, diminutive of *cerebrum* brain] *noun* (*plural* **cerebellums** or **cerebella,** seră<u>bel</u>ă)   the lower rear part of the brain that controls the muscles, posture, balance, and various mental processes.

cerebrum (se<u>ree</u>brăm) LATIN [brain] *noun* (*plural* **cerebrums** or **cerebra,** se<u>ree</u>bră)   the front, main part of the brain that is considered the seat of conscious mental processes, including movement, memory, and speech.

cerise (să<u>rees</u>, să<u>reez</u>) FRENCH [cherry] *noun*   a cherry red color. ~*adjective*

of or relating to such a color: *"She hunted along the stale-smelling corridors with their wallpaper of cerise daisies and poison-green rosettes, streaked in white spots from spilled water, their frayed red and yellow matting, and rows of pine doors painted a sickly blue"* (Sinclair Lewis, *Main Street,* 1922).

certiorari (sersheeără<u>rah</u>ree) LATIN [to be informed] *noun* (*plural* **certioraris**) a writ issued by a superior court ordering the production of the records of a lower court or other judicial body to enable inspection for irregularities.

c'est la guerre (say la <u>gair</u>) FRENCH [that is the war] *interjection*   that is what happens in wartime, we must resign ourselves to the situation.

c'est la vie (say la <u>vee</u>) FRENCH [that is life] *interjection*   that is what happens in life, life is like that, we must resign ourselves to the situation, such is life; used to express resignation when confronted with an unpleasant or difficult situation: *"We spent years campaigning for a new expressway. Now that it's been built, the volume of traffic is even greater and noisier—oh well, c'est la vie, I suppose."*

cesura   See CAESURA.

cetera desunt (ketără <u>dee</u>sănt, setără <u>dee</u>sănt) LATIN [the other things are missing] *noun phrase*   the rest is missing (usually referring to missing portions of manuscript).

ceteris paribus (ketăris păribăs, setăris păribăs) LATIN [other things being equal] *adverb phrase* other things being equal, assuming nothing else changes. ~*abbreviated form* **cet. par.**

cf. *See* CONFER.

cha-cha (chah-chah), **cha-cha-cha** SPANISH [imitative of the rhythm of the dance] *noun* a lively ballroom dance of Latin American origin, or the music that accompanies it.

chacun à son goût (shakăn a son(g) goo) FRENCH [each to his own taste] *interjection* everyone to his or her own taste, there is no accounting for taste: "*'I can't believe he likes that music,'* she sighed, *'but chacun à son goût, as the French say.'*"

chador (chadah, chadă), **chaddar, chadar, chuddar** URDU [from Persian *cadar* sheet, veil] *noun* a large cloth worn as a headscarf, veil, and shawl by Muslim women: "*Many of the younger women protested publicly against the wearing of the chador.*"

chagrin (shăgran(g)) FRENCH [rough skin] *noun* a sense of anxiety or ruefulness provoked by embarrassment, humiliation, or disappointment. ~*verb* to provoke such a feeling in a person: "*'But,' he added, with an air of chagrin, which he endeavored, though unsuccessfully, to conceal, 'had I been aware that what I then believed a soldier's conduct could be so construed, shame would have been added to the list of reasons'*" (James Fenimore Cooper, *The Last of the Mohicans*, 1826).

chaise (shayz) FRENCH [chair] *noun* a light horse-drawn carriage, typically with two wheels and a folding hood: "*For now the chaise creaked upon its springs, and Mrs. Varden was inside; and now it creaked again, and more than ever, and the locksmith was inside; and now it bounded once, as if its heart beat lightly, and Dolly was inside. . .*" (Charles Dickens, *Barnaby Rudge*, 1841).

chaise longue (shayz long) FRENCH [long chair] *noun* (*plural* **chaise longues** or **chaises longues**) a type of sofa or couch with a single backrest at one end: "*At length, upon a peremptory call for 'Madame Lalande,' she arose at once, without affectation or demur, from the chaise longue upon which she had sat by my side, and, accompanied by one or two gentlemen and her female friend of the opera, repaired to the piano in the main drawing-room*" (Edgar Allan Poe, "The Spectacles," 1844).

chalet (shalay, shalay) FRENCH [from Old French *chasel* farmstead] *noun* a Swiss-style wooden house reminiscent of the huts originally built by Alpine herdsmen; sometimes also used for any wooden cottage or house (especially vacation houses): "*'Much worse,' said Agatha. 'I think we had better get under the veranda of the old chalet. It* *is not half a minute's walk from here'"* (George Bernard Shaw, *An Unsocial Socialist*, 1887).

chambré (shom<u>bray</u>, <u>shom</u>bray) FRENCH [past participle of *chambrer* to bring to room temperature] *adjective* at room temperature (specifically referring to wine).

chamois (<u>sha</u>mee, <u>sham</u>wah), **chammy, shammy** FRENCH [after the chamois antelope] *noun* a piece of soft leather made from the skin of the chamois antelope, or from sheepskin: *"The children helped clean the car with a chamois leather."*

chandelier (shand<u>ă</u>leer) FRENCH [candlestick] *noun* a branched candlestick or light fitting suspended from a ceiling: *"Over the well of the staircase hangs a great chandelier with wax lights, which illumine a large eighteenth-century French tapestry. . ."* (Oscar Wilde, *An Ideal Husband*, 1895).

chanson (shon<u>son</u>(g)) FRENCH [song, from Latin *cantio* song] *noun* a song (especially one suitable for music hall or cabaret): *"In France, for instance, he would write a chanson; / In England a six canto quarto tale; / In Spain, he'd make a ballad or romance on / The last war— much the same in Portugal. . ."* (Lord Byron, *Don Juan*, 1819–24).

chanson de geste (shonson(g) dă <u>zhest</u>) FRENCH [song of heroic deeds] *noun phrase* (*plural* **chansons de geste**) an epic poem about heroic deeds of the type written by medieval French poets.

chanteuse (shon<u>te(r)z</u>, shon<u>tooz</u>) FRENCH [a female singer] *noun* a female singer of ballads or other popular songs: *"However, the management is appreciative if they accept the invitation of some dignitary of the army, of administration, or of finance, who seeks the honor of hearing from the chanteuse, in a private room and with a company of friends not disposed to melancholy, the Bohemian songs of the Vieux Derevnia"* (Gaston Leroux, *The Secret of the Night*, 1914).

Chanukah *See* HANUKKAH.

chaos (<u>kay</u>os) GREEK [from *khaos* chasm, gulf] *noun* a state of utter confusion or disorganization (originally referring to the disordered condition of the universe when it was first formed): *"As Rose stood by him watching the ease with which he quickly brought order out of chaos, she privately resolved to hunt up her old arithmetic and perfect herself in the four first rules, with a good tug at fractions, before she read any more fairy tales"* (Louisa May Alcott, *Eight Cousins*, 1875).

chaparajos (shap<u>ăray</u>hōs, chap<u>ăray</u>-hōs), **chaparejos** SPANISH [from *chaparreras*, from *chaparro* dwarf evergreen oak] *noun* strong leather leggings worn over the trousers by western ranch hands to protect themselves from thorny vegetation. ~*abbreviated form* **chaps.**

chaparral (shapӑ<u>ral</u>) SPANISH [from *chaparro* dwarf evergreen oak] *noun* an impenetrable thicket of dwarf evergreen oaks or other shrubs and trees: *"One winter he was out in the Pink Cliffs with a Mormon named Shoonover, an' they run into a lammin' big grizzly track, fresh an' wet. They trailed him to a clump of chaparral, an' on goin' clear round it, found no tracks leadin' out"* (Zane Grey, *Last of the Plainsmen,* 1908).

chapati (chӑ<u>pah</u>tee), **chappati** HINDI [from *capati,* from *capana* to roll out] *noun* (in Indian cuisine) a round flat cake of unleavened bread.

chapeau (shap<u>ō</u>, shӑp<u>ō</u>) FRENCH [hat] *noun* (*plural* **chapeaus** or **chapeaux**) a hat.

chaperon (<u>sha</u>pӑr<u>ō</u>n), **chaperone** FRENCH [hood, cape] *noun* an older person who acts as an escort in public for young unmarried women to ensure that they do not get into trouble or misbehave: *"'It is a sort of thing,' cried Mrs. Elton emphatically, 'which I should not have thought myself privileged to inquire into. Though, perhaps, as the Chaperon of the party—I never was in any circle. . .'"* (Jane Austen, *Emma,* 1815). ~*verb* to act as a chaperon for someone.

chaps *See* CHAPARAJOS.

charabanc (<u>sha</u>rӑbang) FRENCH [from *char à bancs* carriage with benches] *noun* a motor coach: *"He smiled ironically, looking at the raven horse, and was already deciding in his own mind that this smart trotter in the charabanc was only good for promenade. . ."* (Leo Tolstoy, *Anna Karenina,* 1874–76).

charade (shӑ<u>rayd</u>, shӑ<u>rahd</u>) FRENCH [riddle, from Provençal *charrado* chat, entertainment] *noun* an absurd pretense, a farce, a pointless or empty act: *"What charade Colonel Dent and his party played, what word they chose, how they acquitted themselves, I no longer remember. . ."* (Charlotte Brontë, *Jane Eyre,* 1847). Can also refer to a parlor game in which the players try to guess a solution from clues acted out in mime.

chargé d'affaires (shahrzhay dӑ<u>fair</u>) FRENCH [one charged with affairs] *noun* (*plural* **chargés d'affaires**) a diplomatic rank below that of ambassador (especially one who assumes the duties of an ambassador or minister when the latter is absent): *"Matters were left in the hands of a chargé d'affaires until a new ambassador was appointed."* ~*abbreviated form* **chargé.**

charisma (kӑ<u>riz</u>mӑ) GREEK [from *kharisma* favor, from *kharis* grace] *noun* (*plural* **charismas** or **charismata,** kӑ<u>riz</u>mӑtӑ) personal charm, magnetism, star appeal, personal aura: *"He* *is the only presidential candidate with any personal charisma at all."*

charivari (shiva<u>ree</u>, <u>shiv</u>aree), **shivaree** FRENCH [possibly from Latin *caribaria* headache] *noun* a raucous mock serenade or cacophony (originally raised by the local populace, using pots, pans, and other noise makers to express disapproval of a marriage): *"Wants to know if they can't be run in for this awful crime. It seems they made a dreadful charivari at the village boundary, threw a quantity of spell-bearing objects over the border, a buffalo's skull and other things . . ."* (Rudyard Kipling, "The Enlightenments of Pagett, M.P.").

charlotte (<u>shahr</u>lăt) FRENCH [possibly after the girls' name Charlotte] *noun* a dessert dish comprising layers of stewed fruit and custard or other filling layered with breadcrumbs, sponge cake, or biscuits.

chassé (sha<u>say</u>), **sashay** FRENCH [chased, from *chasser* to chase] *noun* a dance step in which one foot slides into the place of the other. ~*verb* to perform such a step.

chasseur (sha<u>ser</u>) FRENCH [hunter, from *chasser* to chase] *noun* a hunter; can also refer to a light cavalryman (especially in the French army): *"After passing a chasseur regiment and in the lines of the Kiev grenadiers—fine fellows busy with similar peaceful affairs—near the shelter of the regimental commander, higher than and different from the others,*

Prince Andrew came out in front of a platoon of grenadiers before whom lay a naked man" (Leo Tolstoy, *War and Peace*, 1863–69).

chassis (<u>cha</u>see, <u>sha</u>see) FRENCH [from *châssis*, ultimately from Latin *capsa* case] *noun* (*plural* **chassis**) the basic frame of a motor vehicle, aircraft, or other machine, around which the body is constructed: *"The factory makes the basic chassis for the new car, but the body is built elsewhere."*

château (sha<u>tō</u>), **chateau** FRENCH [mansion, from Latin *castellum* castle] *noun* (*plural* **châteaus** or **châteaux**) a French castle, mansion, or country house; can also refer to a wine-growing estate.

chatelaine (<u>sha</u>tălayn) FRENCH [from *châtelaine*, feminine of *chatelain* castellan, ultimately from Latin *castellanus* occupant of a castle] *noun* the lady of the manor, the mistress of a château or of some other large household or establishment; Can also refer to a clasp worn at the waist to which may be attached keys, a purse, a watch, and other items: *"Daisy found it impossible to keep her eyes off her 'pitty aunty,' but attached herself like a lap dog to the wonderful chatelaine full of delightful charms"* (Louisa May Alcott, *Little Women*, 1868–9).

chaud-froid (shō<u>frwah</u>) FRENCH [hot-cold: the hot cooked meat is allowed to become cold before it is served] *noun* a dish of cold meat in an aspic sauce.

chauffeur (sho̱făr, sho̱fer) FRENCH [stoker, from *chauffer* to heat] *noun* a person who is employed to drive a private motor vehicle: *"Rumors began to circulate about her friendship with the chauffeur."* ~*verb* to work as the driver of a motor vehicle.

chef (shef) FRENCH [head, abbreviated from *chef de cuisine* head of the kitchen] *noun* a cook in a restaurant or hotel: *"The hotel has advertised for a new chef."*

chef d'oeuvre (shay dervră, shay derv), **chef-d'oeuvre** FRENCH [leading work] *noun phrase* (*plural* **chefs d'oeuvre**) a masterpiece (especially in the arts): *"Critics consider this work to be his chef d'oeuvre."*

chemin de fer (shăman(g) dă fair) FRENCH [railroad] *noun phrase* (*plural* **chemis de fer** a variety of baccarat (card game).

chemise (shămeez) FRENCH [shirt, from Latin *camisia* shirt] *noun* a loose-fitting one-piece undergarment or dress for women: *"A chemise buttoned upon the right shoulder, and passing loosely over the breast and back and under the left arm, but half concealed her person above the waist, while it left the arms entirely nude"* (Lew Wallace, *Ben Hur*, 1880).

chenille (shăneel) FRENCH [hairy caterpillar, ultimately from Latin *canis* dog] *noun* a fabric or yarn with a velvety pile used in embroidery, etc.: *"She had the mark of a scald on her bosom, which a scanty piece of blue chenille did not entirely cover, this scar sometimes drew my attention, though not absolutely on its own account"* (Jean-Jacques Rousseau, *Confessions*, 1782–89).

cheongsam (chongsam) CHINESE [from Mandarin *changshan* long gown] *noun* an oriental-style dress with a slit skirt and high neck.

cherchez la femme (shairshay la fam) FRENCH [find the woman] *interjection* look for the woman (in the belief that where there is trouble a woman is generally found to be at the bottom of it), find the underlying cause: *"The journalist winked at him knowingly. 'Cherchez la femme,' he whispered, wagging his forefinger."*

chérie (shăree) FRENCH [dear] *noun* darling: *"I love every minute I spend with you, ma chérie."*

cherub (cherăb) HEBREW [from *kerubh* supernatural being] *noun* (*plural* **cherubs, cherubim,** cherăbim) an angel of a type usually depicted as a small, rather plump, winged child; by extension, any child with an angelic disposition or appearance: *"Winged figures representing cherubim were located above the ark of the covenant in the Most Holy Place"* (M. Selman, M. Manser,

Macmillan Dictionary of the Bible, 1998).

che sarà, sarà (kay săr<u>ah</u> sărah) ITALIAN [what will be will be] *interjection* what will happen will happen regardless of what anyone does: *"The old man threw up his hands in a gesture of resignation: 'che sarà, sarà.'"*

chevalier (shăvă<u>lir</u>) FRENCH [horseman, ultimately from Latin *caballus* horse] *noun* a cavalier or knight and, by extension, any honorable or chivalrous man: *"Among certain grizzled sea-gossips of the gun decks and forecastle went a rumor perdue that the Master-at-arms was a chevalier who had volunteered into the King's Navy by way of compounding for some mysterious swindle whereof he had been arraigned at the King's Bench"* (Herman Melville, *Billy Budd,* 1924).

chevron (<u>she</u>vron) FRENCH [rafter, probably from Latin *caprio* rafter] *noun* a V-shaped figure or pattern (as used in heraldry, badges of military rank, or signposts): *"Bad bends on the road are clearly marked by large chevron signs."*

chez (shay) FRENCH [from Latin *casa* cottage] *preposition* at the house of, at the home of: *"Come and dine chez moi tonight."*

chiaroscuro (keeahră<u>skooro</u>) ITALIAN [bright dark, from *chiaro* clear and *oscuro* obscure] *noun* the interplay of light and shade (as in paintings).

~*adjective* of or relating to the interplay of light and shade: *"Not that Mr. Wakem had not other sons besides Philip, but towards them he held only a chiaroscuro parentage, and provided for them in a grade of life duly beneath his own"* (George Eliot, *The Mill on the Floss,* 1860).

chiasmus (kī<u>az</u>măs, kee<u>az</u>măs) GREEK [*chiasmos,* from *chiazein* to place crosswise, to mark with a chi] *noun* (*plural* **chiasmi,** kī<u>az</u>mī, kee<u>az</u>mī) a figure of speech in which two grammatical elements in a pair of parallel phrases or clauses are reversed, as in *"He went to London, to Los Angeles went she."*

chic (sheek) FRENCH [style, probably from German *Schick* skill] *noun* stylishness, elegance, vogue. ~*adjective* stylish, fashionable, in vogue, elegant, smart: *"The new mall features chic boutiques and restaurants."*

chicane (shi<u>kayn</u>) FRENCH [subterfuge, deception, from *chicaner* to quibble] *noun* a sharp double-bend on a motor-racing track: *"Several cars came off the track at the frist chicane."*

Chicano (chi<u>kah</u>nō, shi<u>kah</u>nō) SPANISH [from *mexicano* Mexican] *noun* an American of Mexican origin, especially a male. ~*adjective* of or relating to Chicanos, Mexican American. ~*noun, feminine* **chicana** (chi<u>kah</u>nă, shi<u>kann</u>ă) an American girl or woman of Mexican origin.

chichi (<u>shee</u>shee, <u>chee</u>chee) FRENCH [pretentiousness] *noun* affected manners, preciosity, fussiness. ~*adjective* precious, pretentious, fussy, afftected: *"She moved into a chichi little apartment on the edge of town."*

chiffon (shi<u>fon</u>, <u>shi</u>fon) FRENCH [rag, from *chiffe* old rag] *noun* a soft sheer fabric of silk, nylon, rayon, or similar material. ~*adjective* of or relating to such fabric: *"He was confronted by three small girls in yellow chiffon dresses."*

chignon (<u>sheen</u>yon) FRENCH [from Middle French *chaignon* chain, nape, from Latin *catena* chain] *noun* a knot or coil of hair worn by women at the nape of the neck: *"The form of her head was so good that she could dare to carry it without a chignon, or any adventitious adjuncts from an artistes shop"* (Anthony Trollope, *The Eustace Diamonds,* 1873).

chile *See* CHILI.

chile con carne *See* CHILI CON CARNE.

chili (<u>chi</u>lee), **chile, chilli** SPANISH [from *chile,* from Nahuatl *chilli*] *noun* hot pepper made from the pod of the pepper *Capsicum annuum* (var. *longum*), or a meat or vegetable dish prepared with hot peppers or hot pepper sauce.

chili con carne (chilee kon <u>kah</u>nee), **chilli con carne, chile con carne** SPANISH [chili with meat] *noun phrase* a Mexican stew of ground beef and usually beans, prepared with chopped chili peppers.

chilli *See* CHILI.

chilli con carne *See* CHILI CON CARNE.

chimera (kī<u>mee</u>ră, kă<u>mee</u>ră), **chimaera** GREEK [*chimaira* she-goat, monster] *noun* an illusion, a phantasm, a wild fancy, an imaginary creature or monster or a creature made up of several different species: *"In the middle of these cogitations, apprehensions, and reflections, it came into my thoughts one day that all this might be a mere chimera of my own, and that this foot might be the print of my own foot, when I came on shore from my boat. . ."* (Daniel Defoe, *Robinson Crusoe,* 1719–20).

chinoiserie (sheen<u>wahz</u>ree, sheen<u>wahz</u>ăree, sheenwahz<u>ă</u><u>ree</u>) FRENCH [from *chinois* Chinese] *noun* a style in the decorative arts and furniture imitative of Chinese designs: *"A fad for chinoiserie pervaded all branches of decorative art in England in the wake of expanded trade contacts with the Far East."*

chinos (<u>chee</u>nōz) SPANISH [from *chino* toasted] *plural noun* trousers of cotton twill cloth: *"He selected a white shirt and a pair of chinos from the pile of clothes on the bed."*

chintz (chints) HINDI [from *chit*] *noun* (*plural* **chintzes**) a printed calico (originally of Indian origin) or glazed cotton fabric: *"The gentle breeze stirred the yellow chintz curtains."*

chipolata (chipălahtă) FRENCH [from Italian *cipollata* dish of onions] *noun* a small sausage.

Chi-Rho (kī-rō, kee-rō) GREEK [from the Greek letters *chi* and *ro*] *noun* (*plural* **Chi-Rhos**) monogram representing the name of Christ (after the first two letters of the name).

chop suey (chop sooee) CHINESE [from Cantonese *tsaap sui* mixed bits] *noun phrase* (*plural* **chop sueys**) (in Chinese cuisine) a dish of rice mixed with meat, fish, bean sprouts, bamboo shoots, water chestnuts, onions, mushrooms, and soy sauce.

chorizo (chăreezō, chăreesō) SPANISH *noun* a highly seasoned pork sausage.

chow mein (chow mayn) CHINESE [from *chao mian* fried noodles] *noun phrase* (in Chinese cuisine) a dish of fried noodles mixed with meat, mushrooms, and vegetables.

chuddar *See* CHADOR.

chutney (chătnee) HINDI [from *chatni*] *noun* a savory sauce or relish containing fruits, vinegar, sugar, and spices.

chutzpah (hătspă, kătspă), **chutzpa** YIDDISH [from Hebrew *huspah*] *noun* self-confidence, audacity, effrontery, gall: *"The child even had the chutzpah to volunteer to go to the police station himself."*

ciao (chow) ITALIAN [I am your slave, from Latin *sclavus* slave] *interjection* good-bye, farewell, greetings, hello: *"'Ciao, my friends, I will be back in the morning,' he called over his shoulder."*

cicatrice (sikătrees) LATIN [feminine of *cicatrix*] *noun* a scar, or a mark resembling a scar: *"Captain Mitchell exhibited willingly the long cicatrice of a cut over his left ear and temple, made by a razor-blade fastened to a stick. . ."* (Joseph Conrad, *Nostromo*, 1904).

cicerone (sisărōnee) ITALIAN [after the Roman orator Cicero (106–43 B.C.)] *noun* (*plural* **cicerones** or **ciceroni**) a guide who conducts tourists on a sightseeing tour: *"Here renewed greetings passed: the young ladies shook hands; and Oldbuck, completely in his element, placed himself as guide and cicerone at the head of the party, who were now to advance on foot towards the object of their curiosity"* (Walter Scott, *The Antiquary*, 1816).

cicisbeo (cheechăzbayō) ITALIAN *noun* (*plural* **cicisbeos** or **cicisbei**, cheechăzbayee) the male lover of a married woman: *"He was moreover the cicisbeo, or rather the complaisant chevalier of the Countess of Boufflers, a great friend also to D'Alembert, and the Chevalier de Lorenzi was the most passive instrument in* her hands" (Jean-Jacques Rousseau, *Confessions,* 1782–89).

ci-devant (see-dă<u>von</u>) FRENCH [formerly, heretofore] *adjective* former, late. ~*adverb* formerly.

cineast (<u>sin</u>eeast, <u>sin</u>eeăst), **cineaste, cinéaste** FRENCH [from *ciné* cinema and *-aste* (after *enthusiaste* enthusiast)] *noun* a person with an enthusiasm for the cinema; can also refer to a moviemaker.

cinéma vérité (sinămă veri<u>tay</u>) FRENCH [cinema truthfulness] *noun phrase* a style of moviemaking emphasizing realism: *"That movie is now regarded as a masterpiece of cinéma vérité."*

cinquecento (chinkwee<u>chen</u>tō) ITALIAN [five hundred] *noun* the 16th century (especially in relation to Italian art, literature, and history). See also QUATTROCENTO.

circa (<u>ser</u>kă) LATIN [around] *preposition* around, about, approximately (especially in relation to dates): *"The writer William Browne was born circa 1590."* ~*abbreviated form* **c., ca., cir.**

cire perdue (seer pair<u>doo</u>) FRENCH [lost wax] *noun phrase* a technique of bronze casting in which a mold is contructed around a wax model, which is then melted and replaced by metal.

clairvoyance (klair<u>voi</u>yăns) FRENCH [clear-sightedness, from *clair* clear and *voyant* seeing] *noun* the power to perceive objects that cannot be detected through the natural senses, or intuitive knowledge of things: *"He was wondering all the time over the extraordinary clairvoyance of the publisher, who had looked through so many thick folds, broadcloth, lining, brown paper, and seen his poems lying hidden in his breast-pocket"* (Oliver Wendell Holmes, *The Guardian Angel,* 1867).

claque (klak) FRENCH [applauders, from *claquer* to clap] *noun* a group of people who are hired to applaud a performance and, by extension, any group of sycophantic or self-seeking admirers: *"'Wever, Monsieur Braulard, the leader of the claque, got him out of that. He wears gold earrings, and he lives by doing nothing, hanging on to women, who are fools about these good-looking scamps'"* (Honoré de Balzac, *Cousin Bette,* 1846–47).

claqueur (kla<u>ker</u>) FRENCH [applauder, from *claquer* to clap] *noun* a person who is hired as a member of a claque: *"Such were his tastes and passions: his antipathies were not less lively. He detested three things: a Jesuit, a gendarme, and a claqueur at a theater"* (William Makepeace Thackeray, *The Paris Sketch Book of Mr. M. A. Titmarsh,* 1840).

claret (<u>kla</u>răt) FRENCH [clear] *noun* a full-bodied red wine of a type produced in the Bordeaux region of

France. ~*adjective* deep red (after the color of claret wine): *"The curtains were of a deep claret color."*

cliché (klee<u>shay</u>, <u>klee</u>shay), **cliche** FRENCH [stereotype, from *clicher* to stereotype] *noun* an overused or trite expression, idea, theme, or character: *"His speech was full of clichés and bad jokes."* ~*adjective* hackneyed, stereotyped, trite.

clientele (klĭăn<u>tel</u>, kleeăn<u>tel</u>), **clientèle** FRENCH [from *clientèle*, ultimately from Latin *cliens* client] *noun* the patrons or customers of a commercial establishment: *"The clientele of the hotel were largely traveling salesmen and drifters."*

clique (kleek, klik) FRENCH [set, gang, from *cliquer* to make a noise, from Middle Dutch *klikken* to click] *noun* an exclusive group of people who work together in pursuit of their common interest: *"A man once came a considerable distance to ask me to lecture on Slavery; but on conversing with him, I found that he and his clique expected seven eighths of the lecture to be theirs, and only one eighth mine; so I declined"* (Henry David Thoreau, *Life Without Principle,* 1863).

clochard (klō<u>shar</u>) FRENCH [from *clocher* to limp] *noun* a vagrant or tramp.

cloche (klosh) FRENCH [bell] *noun* a glass or plastic cover used to protect young plants in cold weather; can also refer to a type of woman's hat vaguely in the shape of a bell: *"She wore bobbed hair under a cloche hat."*

cloisonné (kloiză<u>nay</u>, klahză<u>nay</u>), **cloisonne** FRENCH [past participle of *cloisonner* to partition] *noun* a type of enamelwork, usually applied to metal. ~*adjective* of or relating to such enamelwork: *"He picked up the cloisonné vase"* (Sinclair Lewis, Main *Street,* 1920).

cocotte (ko<u>kot</u>) FRENCH [hen, darling, from *coq* rooster] *noun* a prostitute, a woman of easy virtue: *"'Get along to your sovereign mistress,' she said to him (there was at that time in Wiesbaden a certain princess di Monaco, who looked surprisingly like a cocotte of the poorer sort); 'what do you want to stay with a plebeian like me for?'"* (Ivan Turgenev, *Torrents of Spring,* 1870).

coda (<u>kō</u>dă) ITALIAN [tail, from Latin *cauda* tail] *noun* the concluding part of a piece of music, literature, or ballet: *"At this moment a harlequin and columbine, dancing to the music of the band in the garden, which has just reached the coda of a waltz, whirl one another into the room"* (George Bernard Shaw, *You Never Can Tell,* 1899).

codex (<u>kō</u>deks) LATIN [tablet, block of wood, from *caudex* tree trunk] *noun* (*plural* **codices,** <u>kō</u>diseez, <u>koh</u>diseez) a manuscript book containing ancient or medieval texts; can also refer to any collection of rules.

coffee (<u>ko</u>fee) TURKISH [from *kahve,* itself from Arabic *qahwa*] *noun* a hot drink made from the roasted and ground seeds of the coffee plant.

cogito, ergo sum (kogitō airgō <u>sum</u>) LATIN [I think, therefore I am, coined by French philosopher René Descartes (1596–1650)] *interjection* I think, therefore I am (used to express the notion that the fact that an individual is capable of thought constitutes a proof of his or her existence).

cognac (<u>ko</u>nyak, <u>kō</u>nyak) FRENCH [after Cognac, France] *noun* a superior brandy made in the departments of Charente and Charente-Maritime, France: *"The general never went on campaign without at least a couple of cases of good cognac."*

cognomen (kog<u>nō</u>măn, <u>kog</u>nămăn) LATIN [from *nomen* name] *noun* (*plural* **cognomens** or **cognomina,** kog<u>nō</u>mănă) a name or title (often referring specifically to a surname or family name): *"He had been long identified with the Bailie, and he was vain of the cognomen which he had now worn for eight years; and he questioned if any of his brethren in the Council had given such universal satisfaction"* (Walter Scott, *Chronicles of the Canongate,* 1827).

cognoscente (konyă<u>shen</u>tee, kognă<u>shen</u>tee, konyă<u>sen</u>tee, kognă<u>sen</u>tee) ITALIAN [a person who knows, from Latin *cognoscere* to know] *noun* (*plural*

cognoscenti, konyă<u>shen</u>tee, kognă<u>shen</u>tee, konyă<u>sen</u>tee, kognă<u>sen</u>tee) a person with expert knowledge of something (especially of the fine arts), a connoisseur: *"The gallery became very popular with the cognoscenti of the art world."*

coiffeur (kwa<u>fer</u>) FRENCH [hairdresser, from *coiffer* to dress the hair] *noun* a male hairstylist: *"Hearing why he had come, the Princess was half-humorously, half-seriously angry with him, and sent him home to dress and not to hinder Kitty's hairdressing, as Charles the coiffeur was just coming"* (Leo Tolstoy, *Anna Karenina,* 1874–76). ~*noun, feminine* **coiffeuse** (kwa<u>ferz</u>) a female hairstylist.

coiffure (kwa<u>fyur</u>) FRENCH [hairstyle, from *coiffer* to dress the hair] *noun* a hairstyle: *"No wonder that with her admirably dressed, abundant hair, thickly sprinkled with white threads and adding to her elegant aspect the piquant distinction of a powdered coiffure. . ."* (Joseph Conrad, *Chance,* 1914).

coitus (<u>kō</u>ătăs, <u>kō</u>eetăs, <u>koi</u>tăs) LATIN [union, from *coire* to go together] *noun* sexual intercourse.

coitus interruptus (<u>kō</u>ătăs intă<u>ră</u>ptăs, <u>kō</u>eetăs intă<u>ră</u>ptăs, koităs intă<u>ră</u>ptăs) LATIN [interrupted sexual intercourse] *noun phrase* sexual intercourse in which the penis is withdrawn before ejaculation to avoid conception.

cojones (kăhōniz) SPANISH [from *cojón* testicle] *plural noun* (slang) balls, guts, courage.

collage (kolazh) FRENCH [gluing, from *coller* to glue] *noun* an artistic technique in which pieces of paper, fabric, or other materials are glued onto a surface to create an image or pattern: *"The class worked together on the collage over several weeks."* Can also refer more generally to any muddled or confusing miscellany of ideas or impressions.

collecteana (kolektayneeă) LATIN [collected things, neuter plural of *collectaneus* collected] *plural noun* collected writings, an anthology of written passages.

collegium (kălegeeăm, kălaygeeăm) LATIN [college, guild] *noun* (*plural* **collegiums** or **collegia,** kălegeeă, kălaygeeă) a group in which power and authority is divided equally among the members.

col legno (kol legnō) ITALIAN [with the wood] *adverb phrase* (of violins and other stringed instruments) played with the wooden back of the bow.

colloquium (kălōkweeăm) LATIN [conversation] *noun* (*plural* **colloquiums** or **colloquia,** kălōkweeă) an academic conference or seminar during which specialists each deliver their views on a particular subject: *"The society will host a colloquium on the topic of historical linguistics next spring."*

cologne *See* EAU DE COLOGNE.

coloratura (kălărătooră, kălărăchooră) ITALIAN [colored, from the past participle of Latin *colorare* to color] *noun* (in vocal music) an elaborate ornamentation, or a singer who specializes in such music. ~*adjective* of or relating to such ornamentation: *"She developed into a very fine coloratura soprano, appearing at leading opera houses throughout Europe."*

colossus (kălosăs) LATIN [from Greek *kolossos* a huge statue] *noun* (*plural* **colossuses** or **colossi,** kălosee) a giant, or a thing of gigantic proportions: *"'Dombey,' said the Major, defiantly, 'I know better; a man of your mark—the Colossus of commerce—is not to be interrupted'"* (Charles Dickens, *Dombey and Son,* 1846–48).

coma (kōmă) GREEK [*koma* deep sleep] *noun* a state of deep unconsciousness produced by injury, illness, or drugs; can also refer more generally to a state of lethargy or inactivity: *"The household convulsion had made her herself again. The temporary coma had ceased, and activity had come with the necessity for it"* (Thomas Hardy, *Far From the Madding Crowd,* 1874).

comedienne (kămeedien) FRENCH [from *comédienne* actress in comedy] *noun* a woman comedian: *"They hung mainly on the problematical good-will of an ancient comedienne, with whom Mrs.*

Farlow had a slight acquaintance. . ." (Edith Wharton, *The Reef,* 1912).

commandant (kom<u>ă</u>ndănt) FRENCH [commander, from *commander* to command] *noun*   a commanding officer: *"It was not the Colonel that brought Bobby out of Simla, but a much more to be respected Commandant"* (Rudyard Kipling, "Only A Subaltern," 1888). ~*abbreviated form* **Cdt., Comdt.**

commandeer (kom<u>ă</u>n<u>deer</u>) AFRIKAANS [from French *commander* to command] *verb*   to take possession of property or goods by force; to force a person into military service: *"Among them was the pimply clerk, who had been inspired to commandeer a pitchfork from a hardware store"* (Booth Tarkington, *The Conquest of Canaan,* 1905).

commando (kă<u>mand</u>ō) AFRIKAANS [from *kommando* military unit, from Dutch *commando* command, from Portuguese *comandar* to command, ultimately from Latin *commandare* to command] *noun*   a specialized military unit trained to carry out raids on an enemy, or a member of such a unit: *"The commandos were sent in first to disrupt enemy communications."*

comme ci, comme ça (kom <u>see</u> kom sa) FRENCH [like this, like that] *adverb phrase*   so-so, middlingly.

commedia dell'arte (kă<u>may</u>deeă del <u>ahr</u>tay, kă<u>mee</u>deeă delahrtay) ITAL-IAN [comedy of art] *noun phrase*   a genre of largely improvised theatrical comedy featuring stock characters and slapstick action that first became popular in 16th-century Italy: *"Many of the characteristics of the Italian commedia dell'arte were absorbed into the English pantomime via the harlequinade."*

comme il faut (kom eel <u>fō</u>) FRENCH [as it should be] *adverb phrase*   properly, as necessary, as dictated by accepted standards. ~*adjective phrase* proper, as it should be: *"I implore you, my dear Miss Vavasor, to remember what you owe to God and man, and to carry out an engagement made by yourself, that is in all respects comme il faut, and which will give entire satisfaction to your friends and relatives"* (Anthony Trollope, *Can You Forgive Her?,* 1864).

commissar (<u>kom</u>ăsah) FRENCH [from Russian *komissar,* from German *Kommissar,* ultimately from Latin *commissarius* agent] *noun*   a person who heads a government department or occupies a senior political position (especially in communist countries).

commissariat (komă<u>sa</u>reeat) LATIN [from *commissarius* agent] *noun*   a board of commissioners, or a government department (especially in a Communist country); can also refer to an organization responsible for providing supplies for an army: *"Crops in the region were confiscated on the order of the army commissariat."*

commissionaire (kămishǎ<u>nair</u>), **com-missionnaire** FRENCH [from Latin *committere* to commit] *noun* a uniformed door-attendant at a hotel, theater, etc.: "*. . .I am sure she and her daughter enjoyed themselves hugely in the shops, from one of which I shall never forget Irene emerging proudly with a commissionaire, who conducted her under an umbrella to the cab where I was lying in wait*" (J. M. Barrie, *The Little White Bird,* 1902).

commode (kă<u>mōd</u>) FRENCH [suitable, convenient, from Latin *commodus* fit, useful] *noun* a small chest of drawers; can also refer to a piece of furniture housing a chamber pot or washbasin: "*The drawers of her commode stood open, giving glimpses of dainty trifles, which she was tying up with bright ribbons*" (Louisa May Alcott, *Rose in Bloom,* 1876).

communard (<u>kom</u>yoonahrd) FRENCH [ultimately from Latin *communis*] *noun* a person who lives in a commune (originally a supporter of the 1871 Paris Commune).

communiqué (kom<u>yoo</u>nǎkay) FRENCH [communicated, past participle of *communiquer* to communicate] *noun* an official bulletin or press release: "*The press department has issued several communiqués since yesterday.*"

compadre (kompahdray) SPANISH [godfather] *noun* a benefactor, accomplice, companion, friend.

compagnon de voyage (kompanyon(g) dǎ voi<u>yazh</u>) FRENCH [companion of the voyage] *noun phrase* a traveling companion.

compendium (kom<u>pen</u>deeǎm) LATIN [profit, shortcut, from *compendere* to weigh together] *noun* (*plural* **compendiums** or **compendia,** kom<u>pen</u>deeǎ) a collection or compilation of writings, table games, etc.; can also refer to a summary or abstract of a larger work: "*An easy substitute for this labor was found in a digest or compendium of the work noticed, with copious extracts—or a still easier, in random comments upon such passages as accidentally met the eye of the critic, with the passages themselves copied at full length*" (Edgar Allan Poe, "Exordium," 1842).

compere (<u>kom</u>pair), **compère** FRENCH [godfather] *noun* a master of ceremonies, a host of a television or radio program. ~*verb* to announce the acts during a theatrical entertainment or a television or radio program: "*The next decision to be made was who to choose to compere the show.*"

compos mentis (kompǎs <u>men</u>tǎs) LATIN [master of one's mind] *adjective phrase* sane, lucid, of sound mind: "*Personally, I doubt that the old lady is totally compos mentis.*"

compote (<u>kom</u>pōt) FRENCH [from Latin *compostus,* from *componere* to put together] *noun* a dessert consisting of fruit preserved or stewed in syrup: *"She served up a delicious fresh fruit compote."*

compte rendu (kompt ron<u>doo</u>) FRENCH [account rendered] *noun phrase* (*plural* **comptes rendus**) a financial statement or, more generally, a report or summary: *"In this manner I went through the whole extent of the science; and the written outline of it which resulted from my daily compte rendu, served him afterwards as notes from which to write his Elements of Political Ecomomy"* (John Stuart Mill, *Autobiography,* 1873).

con *See* CONTRA.

con amore (kon ă<u>mor</u>ay) ITALIAN [with love] *adverb phrase* (in music) tenderly; can also mean in a wider context with love, with enthusiasm, with delight.

con brio (kon <u>bree</u>ō) ITALIAN [with vigor] *adverb phrase* (in music) to be played briskly, energetically.

concerto (kon<u>chair</u>tō) ITALIAN [from *concertare* to bring into harmony] *noun* (*plural* **concertos** or **concerti,** kon<u>chair</u>tee) a musical composition, usually in three movements, written for one or more soloist instruments and orchestra: *"The new concerto was greeted with wild enthusiasm."*

concerto grosso (kon<u>chair</u>tō <u>gros</u>ō, kon<u>chair</u>tō <u>grōs</u>ō) ITALIAN [big concerto] *noun phrase* (*plural* **concerti grossi,** kon<u>chair</u>tee <u>gros</u>ee, kon<u>chair</u>-

tee <u>grō</u>see) an orchestral composition in which solo instruments are backed by a full orchestra.

concessionaire (konseshă<u>nair</u>), **concessionnaire** FRENCH [concessionary, from *concession,* ultimately from Latin *concedere* to concede] *noun* the owner or operator of a concession permitting the running of a refreshment stand, souvenir both, or other small business outlet: *"All the concessionaires running stands in the foyer have been invited to a meeting to discuss the problem."*

concierge (kons<u>yairzh</u>) FRENCH [janitor, ultimately from Latin *conservus* fellow slave] *noun* a person who serves as doorkeepr or porter for an apartment building or hotel.

concordat (kă<u>kor</u>dat) FRENCH [from the past participle of Latin *concordare* to agree] *noun* an agreement, a compact (especially one between a government and a religious body referring to ecclesiastical matters): *"The Concordat afterwards, in the sixteenth century, gave to the kings of France the absolute right of presenting to all the great, or what are called the consistorial, benefices of the Gallican Church"* (Adam Smith, *The Wealth of Nations,* 1776).

concours d'élégance (konkor dele<u>gons</u>) FRENCH [contest of elegance] *noun phrase* a parade of automobiles in which the vehicles are judged on the grounds of appearance.

condominium (kondămineeăm) LATIN [joint ownership, from *dominium* domain] *noun plural* **condominiums** or **condominia,** kondămineeă) a type of apartment building or complex in which residents own individual units of the property and pay common maintenance charges; can also refer to a territory that is jointly controlled by two or more other states: *"They moved into a new condominium overlooking the river."* ~*abbreviated form* **condo** (kondō).

condottiere (kondoteeairee) ITALIAN [from *condotta* a contract, ultimately from *condurre* to hire, to conduct] *noun* (*plural* **condottieri,** kondoteeairee) a mercenary soldier (referring originally to the mercenaries employed by many postmedieval European armies).

conduit (kondwit, kondooăt, kondwăt, kondit) FRENCH [pipe, culvert] *noun* a pipe, channel, or ditch for conveying water or other liquids; can also be used more generally of any means of distribution of money, goods or information: *". . .therefore I give thee leave and licence to go when thou wilt to my fountain, my conduit, and there to drink freely of the blood of my grape, for my conduit doth always run wine"* (John Bunyan, *The Holy War,* 1682).

con espressione (kon espreseeōnee, kon espreseeōnay) ITALIAN [with expression] *adverb phrase* (in music) to be played expressively, with feeling.

confer (kănfer) LATIN [compare, from *conferre* to bring together] *verb* compare with (instruction to a reader to consult a relevant passage elsewhere). ~*abbreviated form* **cf.**

confetti (kănfetee) ITALIAN [plural of *confetto* candy, from Latin *confectus,* past participle of *conficere* to prepare] *plural noun* tiny scraps of colored paper in a variety of shapes that are traditionally tossed in celebration, such as over a newly married couple by guests at the wedding: *"The happy couple were still picking pieces of confetti out of their hair the following morning."*

confidant (konfădont, konfădont) FRENCH [from Italian *confidenate* confident] *noun* a person in whom another confides: *"Fix made up his mind that, if worst came to worst, he would make a confidant of Passepartout, and tell him what kind of a fellow his master really was"* (Jules Verne, *Around the World in 80 Days,* 1873). ~*noun, feminine* **confidante** a female in whom another confides.

confrere (konfrair), **confrère** FRENCH [colleague, from Latin *confrater* brother] *noun* a comrade, a colleague, a fellow: *"Ha, ha! You see? You are my confrere"* (Booth Tarkington, *Monsieur Beaucaire,* 1900).

confrérie (konfreree) FRENCH [confraternity, brotherhood] *noun* an association of individuals who share the same interests or who work in the same trade.

con moto (kon mōtō) ITALIAN [with movement] *adverb phrase* (in music) to be played in a spirited manner.

connoisseur (konă̆ser, konă̆soor) FRENCH [Old French for *connaisseur* good judge, ultimately from Latin *cognoscere* to know] *noun* an expert, a person who has a thorough knowledge of a particular subject: *"'Don't say no,' returned the little woman, looking at me with the aspect of a connoisseur; 'a little bit more eyebrow?'"* (Charles Dickens, *David Copperfield*, 1849–50).

conquistador (konkeestădor, kănkeestădor, konkistădor, kănkweestădor) SPANISH [conqueror, ultimately from Latin *conquirere*] *noun* (*plural* **conquistadors** or **conquistadores**, konkeestădoreez, kănkweestădorez, konkistădorez, kănkwistădorez) a person who conquers (originally referring specifically to the Spanish conquerors of Latin America): *"The whole building, which, for all I know, may have been contrived by a Conquistador farmer of the pearl fishery three hundred years ago, is perfectly silent"* (Joseph Conrad, *Nostromo*, 1904).

consensus (kănsensăs) LATIN [agreement, from *consentire* to assent] *noun* (*plural* **consensuses**, kănsensăseez) unanimity, general agreement, accord: *"All parties eventually reached a*

consensus on their future approach to tobacco products."

conservatoire (konservătwahr) FRENCH [from Italian *conservatorio* conservatory, ultimately from Latin *conservare* to keep] *noun* an academy of music or another of the performing arts (especially in France): *"The son was a fellow student of mine at the Conservatoire. He was killed the second winter of the war"* (Willa Cather, *One of Ours*, 1922).

console (konsōl) FRENCH [possibly from *consolider* to consolidate] *noun* a control panel for an electric or electronic system; can also refer to the keyboard of an organ or to a cabinet housing a television or other apparatus: *"The technicians took the top off the console and started to inspect the tangle of wires inside the machine."*

consommé (konsămay) FRENCH [past participle of *consommer* to complete, from Latin *consummare* to finish up] *noun* a clear soup made with meat stock: *"The thin consommé had done little to satisfy their hunger."*

consortium (konsorsh(ē)ĕm, konsorteeăm) LATIN [fellowship] *noun* (*plural* **consortiums** or **consortia**, konsorsh(e)ĕm, konsorteeă) an association, society, or group of organizations formed to pursue shared interests: *"The consortium have held a meeting and have agreed to delay further progress on the project."*

con spirito (kon spirătō, kōn spirătō) ITALIAN [with spirit] *adverb phrase* (in music) to be played in a lively manner.

consul (konsăl) LATIN [possibly from *consulere* to consult] *noun* a diplomat who represents his or her country's commercial interests abroad and who provides assistance as required to his or her state's citizens in that country: *"The consul managed to sort out visas for all the tourists but could not help with transportation."*

contagion (kontayjăn) LATIN [*com* together and *tangere* to touch] *noun* a contagious disease or infection; can also refer more widely to the working any kind of influence: *"He had caught the contagion of the excitement, and he felt that in some way he must do a great thing for John Thornton"* (Jack London, *The Call of the Wild,* 1903).

conte (kont) FRENCH [story] *noun* a short adventure story or tale.

continuum (kontinyooăm) LATIN [neuter of *continuus* continuous, from *continere* to hold together] *noun* (*plural* **continuums** or **continua,** kontinyooă) a continuous whole, or an unbroken series, sequence, or progression.

contra (kontră) LATIN [against] *preposition* against, in opposition to. ~*adverb* on the contrary, contrariwise. ~*abbreviated form* **con.**

contralto (kontraltō) ITALIAN [from *contra* against and *alto* high] *noun* (*plural* **contraltos**) a singer with a range below mezzo-soprano but above tenor: *"The choir is very short of contraltos."* ~*adjective* of or relating to a contralto voice or part.

contra mundum (kontră măndăm) LATIN [against the world] *adverb phrase* contrary to general opinion, opposing everyone: *"'It's a game,' he said, 'an odd game—but the chances are all for me, Mr. Griffin, in spite of your invisibility. Griffin contra mundum—with a vengeance!'"* (H. G. Wells, *The Invisible Man,* 1897).

contrapposto (kontrăpostō) ITALIAN [set opposite, ultimately from Latin *contraponere* to contrapose] *noun* (*plural* **contrapposti,** kontrăposttee) (in art and sculpture) a pose in which the upper body is turned in a different direction from the lower body.

contretemps (kontrăton(g)) FRENCH [against time, from *contre* counter and *temps* time] *noun* an unfortunate event, a moment of embarrassment or humiliation; can also refer to a difference of opinion, an argument: *"There had been one contretemps; for a man and his wife had driven up while they were still emptying their revolvers into the silent body"* (Arthur Conan Doyle, "The Valley of Fear," 1914–15).

conversazione (konvărsatseeōnee) ITALIAN [conversation] *noun* (*plural* **conversaziones** or **conversazioni,**

konvărsateeōnee) a social gathering for conversation, particularly about the arts or culture: *"On entering upon the twenty-fifth year of his incumbency in Marylebone, and the twenty-eighth of his ministry in the diocese of London, it was thought a good idea to have an 'Evening Conversazione and Fete'"* (Oliver Wendell Holmes, *Over the Teacups,* 1891).

coolie (ko͟olee), **cooley** HINDI [from *kuli*] *noun* an unskilled laborer (especially one from the Far East): *"The rickshaw was pulled by an elderly coolie with a long white beard."*

coq au vin (cok ō va͟n(g)) FRENCH [cock in wine] *noun phrase* (in French cuisine) chicken cooked in wine.

coquette (co͟ket) FRENCH [feminine of *coquet,* diminutive of *coq* cock] *noun* a flirtatious woman, a woman who trifles with men's affections: *"She thought she had a good deal of the coquette in her, and I've no doubt that with time and training she would have become a very dangerous little person, but now she was far too transparent and straightforward by nature even to tell a white lie cleverly"* (Louisa May Alcott, *An Old Fashioned Girl,* 1870).

coram (ko͟răm) LATIN [before] *preposition* in the presence of, before.

cor anglais (kor o͟n(g)lay) FRENCH [English horn] *noun phrase* (plural **cors anglais,** korz o͟n(g)lay) the English horn, a woodwind instrument in the oboe family, slightly lower in pitch than the oboe.

cordillera (kordăly͟eră, kordăl͟eră) SPANISH [mountain chain, from *cordilla,* diminutive of Latin *chorda* cord] *noun* a series of parallel mountain ridges (often referring specifically to ranges in the Andes).

cordon (ko͟rdăn) FRENCH [cord, band] *noun* a line of persons or military posts to prevent passage: *"A mockery to the yeomen over ale, / And laughter to their lords: but those at home, / As hunters round a hunted creature draw / The cordon close and closer toward the death, / Narrow'd her goings out and comings in. . ."* (Alfred Lord Tennyson, *Enoch Arden,* 1864). ~*verb* to set up a cordon to prevent passage.

cordon bleu (kordon bl͟ă) FRENCH [blue ribbon] *noun phrase* (*plural* **cordons bleus**) a person of superior skill, rank, or distinction. ~*adjective* of or relating to a person or event of the first order or rank: *"Her son is now working as a cordon bleu chef."*

cordon sanitaire (kordon san͟etair) FRENCH [sanitary cordon] *noun phrase* (*plural* **cordon sanitaires** or **cordons sanitaires**) a protective barrier set up against a threat of some kind (typically against infection or against invasion by a hostile nation): *"The police have set up a cordon sanitaire around the hospital."*

corniche (kor<u>neesh</u>) FRENCH [from *cornice* cornice] *noun*   a coastal road built along the edge of a cliff and often commanding panoramic views: *"'I can't very well ride out alone. A solitary amazon swallowing the dust and the salt spray of the Corniche promenade would attract too much attention'"* (Joseph Conrad, *The Arrow of Gold,* 1919).

cornucopia (kornă<u>kō</u>peeă, kornyă<u>kō</u>peeă) LATIN [from *cornu copiae* horn of plenty] *noun*   (in decorative art) a goat's horn filled with fruit, flowers, and corn, representing abundance; also used more generally to refer to any abundant supply or inexhaustible store of something: *"But now if he have lost his cornucopia of ready-money, what else had he to lose?"* (Thomas Carlyle, *The French Revolution,* 1837).

corona (kă<u>rō</u>nă) LATIN [garland, crown] *noun* (*plural* **coronas** or **coronae,** kă<u>rō</u>nee)   a luminous glow or halo around the sun, moon, or other luminous object: *"The sun's corona was clearly visible during the eclipse."*

corps (kor) FRENCH [body, staff, from Latin *corpus* body] *noun* (*plural* **corps,** korz)   a military unit comprising two or more divisions; can also refer to any substantial body of individuals working in cooperation or engaged in the same activity: *"In the spring of 1917 I again served with my Corps; but on the entry of the United States into the War I*

joined the army of my country" (Robert Service, *Ballads of a Bohemian,* 1920).

corps de ballet (kor dă ba<u>lay</u>) FRENCH [company of the ballet] *noun phrase* **corps de ballet,** kor dă ba<u>lay</u>, korz dă ba<u>lay</u>)   a ballet ensemble (excluding the principal dancers and soloists): *"The announcement provoked protests from the corps de ballet."*

corps d'élite (kor day<u>leet</u>) FRENCH [élite body] *noun* (*plural* **corps d'élite,** kor day<u>leet</u>, korz day<u>leet</u>)   a body of picked troops (or other select personnel): *"The marines have long been considered a corps d'élite among the armed forces."*

corps diplomatique (kor diplō mă<u>teek</u>) FRENCH [diplomatic body] *noun*   the diplomatic staff of a particular government: *"He quickly realized he had offended the etiquette of the international corps diplomatique."*

Corpus Christi (korpăs <u>kris</u>tee) LATIN [body of Christ] *noun phrase*   a Roman Catholic festival celebrated on the Thursday after Trinity Sunday in honor of the Eucharist.

corpus delicti (korpăs dă<u>lik</u>tī, korpăs dă<u>lik</u>tee) LATIN [body of the crime] *noun phrase* (*plural* **corpora delicti,** korpŏră dă<u>lik</u>tī, korpŏră dă<u>lik</u>tee)   the physical object on which a crime has been committed, or the sum of the evidence indicating that an offense has taken place: *"The prosecution needs* *to establish a corpus delicti if they are to win this case."*

corral (kărahl) SPANISH [enclosure, from *corro* ring, probably ultimately from Latin *currale* enclosure for vehicles] *noun* a fenced area for keeping livestock; can also refer to a ring of wagons positioned for defense: *"I keep remembering locoed horses I used to see on the range when I was a boy. They changed like that. We used to catch them and put them up in the corral, and they developed great cunning"* (Willa Cather, *Alexander's Bridge,* 1912). *~verb* to enclose livestock in a pen or to marshal support, votes, and the like; can also refer to the drawing up of wagons in a circle for defense.

corrida (kăreedă) SPANISH [act of running] *noun* a bullfight, or the sport of bullfighting in general.

corrigendum (korăjendăm) LATIN [that which must be corrected, from *corrigere* to correct] *noun* (plural **corrigenda,** korăjendă) a correction to a printed text, usually detailed on a separate sheet.

corroboree (kărobăree) AUSTRALIAN ABORIGINAL [from Dharuk *garaabara*] *noun* a lively festivity held by native Australians to mark important events; by extension, any noisy gathering or disturbance.

cortege (kortezh), **cortège** FRENCH [from Italian *corteggio,* from *corteggiare*

to court] *noun* a retinue of attendants (often referring specifically to a funeral procession): *"The torch-bearers shook their torches, scattering a shower of sparks into the river, and the cortege moved off, leaving Almayer agitated but greatly relieved by their departure"* (Joseph Conrad, *Almayer's Folly,* 1894).

corvette (korvet) FRENCH [from Middle Dutch *korf* basket, kind of ship] *noun* a fast, lightly armed escort ship smaller than a frigate or destroyer but larger than a gunboat: *"I chose this place, because, having served last in a little corvette, I knew I should feel more at home where I had a constant opportunity of knocking my head against the ceiling"* (Charles Dickens, *The Mystery of Edwin Drood,* 1870).

cosmonaut (kozmănot) RUSSIAN [universe sailor, from *kosmonavt,* from Greek *kosmos* cosmos and *navt* sailor] *noun* an astronaut in the Russian (formerly Soviet) space program: *"Three cosmonauts were killed in the explosion."*

cosmos (kozmăs, kozmōs) GREEK [universe, world, order] *noun* the universe (especially when regarded as a harmonious whole): *"Astronomers are probing the hidden secrets of the cosmos."*

cossack (kosak) RUSSIAN [from Turkic *kozak* adventurer] *noun* a person from southern Russia, especially a man serving with one of the Cossack light cavalry units in prerevolutionary Russia; also (lowercased) used colloquially to mean a wild person, someone who lashes out suddenly and violently in a heavy-handed manner: *"At the foot of the hill lay wasteland over which a few groups of our Cossack scouts were moving"* (Leo Tolstoy, *War and Peace,* 1863–69).

costumier (kostyoomeeă) FRENCH [from *costumer* to costume] *noun* a person who sells or makes clothing, especially theatrical costumes.

cot (kot) HINDI [from *khat* bedstead] *noun* a small collapsible bed; in Great Britain, also a baby's crib.

coterie (kōtăree) FRENCH [tenants holding land together] *noun* an exclusive circle of friends or colleagues: *"I do not give this as the gossip of a coterie; I am persuaded that it is the belief of a very considerable portion of the country"* (Mark Twain, *Life on the Mississippi,* 1883).

cotillion (kōtilyăn, kătilyăn), **cotillon** FRENCH [from *cotillon* petticoat] *noun* a ballroom dance similar to the quadrille, or a formal ball.

couchant (koochon(g)) FRENCH [lying down, present participle of *coucher* to lie down] *adjective* lying down, in a prone position (as used in reference to animals in heraldic designs): *"The main column is surrounded by four huge lions couchant."*

couchette (kooshet) FRENCH [little bed] *noun* a sleeping compartment in a train, ferry, or other vehicle, or a bed in such a compartment.

coulis (koolee) FRENCH [flowing] *noun* (in French cuisine) a sauce made from puréed vegetables of fruit: *"The ice cream was served with a delicious banana coulis."*

coup (koo) FRENCH [stroke, ultimately from Greek *kolphos* blow with the fist] *noun* (*plural* **coups,** kooz) a masterstroke, a successful act, feat, or move: *"Getting such a big star to join the squad is a considerable coup for the team."* See also COUP D'ÉTAT.

coup de grâce (koo dă gra, koo dă gras), **coup de grace** FRENCH [stroke of mercy] *noun phrase* (*plural* **coups de grăce,** koo dă gras) a final, fatal blow, a death blow, a decisive, finishing act or event: *". . .the young Count of Tierra-Nueva brought the bull to his knees, and having obtained permission from the Infanta to give the coup de grace, he plunged his wooden sword into the neck of the animal with such violence that the head came right off, and disclosed the laughing face of little Monsieur de Lorraine, the son of the French Ambassador at Madrid"* (Oscar Wilde, *A House of Pomegranates,* 1891).

coup de main (koo dă man(g)) FRENCH [stroke of the hand] *noun phrase* (plural **coups de main,** koo dă man(g)) a surprise attack, a raid.

coup d'état (koo day<u>ta</u>, koo dă<u>ta</u>), **coup d'etat** FRENCH [stroke of state] *noun* (*plural* **coups d'état,** koo day<u>ta</u>, or **coups d'états,** koo day<u>taz</u>) the overthrowing of a government by the use of force, a revolution; can also refer to a sudden change in government policy: *"The rebels staged a coup d'état but failed to win international recognition for the new regime."* ~*abbreviated form* **coup.**

coup de théâtre (koo dă tay<u>a</u>tră), **coup de theatre** FRENCH [stroke of theater] *noun phrase* (*plural* **coups de théâtre,** koo dă tay<u>a</u>tră) a sudden, dramatic turn of events during a theatrical performance and by extension any unexpected, sensational action or event; can also refer to a brilliant theatrical success.

coup d'oeil (koo <u>doi</u>) FRENCH [stroke of the eye] *noun* (*plural* **coups d' oeil,** koo <u>doi</u>) a glance, a quick look.

coupé (koo<u>pay</u>), **coupe** (koop) FRENCH [past participle of *couper* to cut] *noun* an enclosed automobile with two doors and two or four seats (originally referring to a horse-drawn carriage with seats for just two passengers).

courier (<u>kă</u>reeăr) FRENCH [ultimately from Latin *currere* to run] *noun* a messenger (especially a diplomat who carries official messages to and fro); can also refer to a tourist's guide or representative of a travel agency: *"The post of the morning had brought a letter to*

the secretary from a courier then at Venice. It contained startling news of Ferrari" (Wilkie Collins, *The Haunted Hotel,* 1879). ~*verb* to send by courier.

couscous (<u>koos</u>koos) FRENCH [from Arabic *kuskus,* from *kaskasa* to beat] *noun* (in Tunisian cuisine) a dish of semolina served with meat or vegetables.

couture (koo<u>toor</u>) FRENCH [from Old French *cousture* sewing, ultimately from Latin *consuere* to sew together] *noun* the making and selling of fashionable clothing for women, dressmaking.

couturier (koo<u>toor</u>eăr, koo<u>toor</u>eeā) FRENCH [dressmaker] *noun* a person, or business, manufacturing and selling fashionable clothing: *"In his youth he ranked among the most respected couturiers in Paris."* ~*noun, feminine* **couturiere** (koo<u>toor</u>eeăr) a female couturier.

coyote (kī<u>yō</u>tee) SPANISH [from Nahuatl *coyotl*] *noun* a wolflike North American animal *(Canis latrans),* a prairie wolf: *"Jack strained his hearing, yet caught no sound, except the distant yelp of a coyote"* (Zane Grey, *Heritage of the Desert,* 1910).

cranium (<u>kray</u>neeăm) LATIN [from Greek *kranion* skull, from *kara* head] *noun* (*plural* **craniums** or **crania,** <u>kray</u>neeă) the skull: *"In the gorilla and certain other monkeys, the cranium of the adult male presents a strongly-marked sagittal crest, which is absent in the* *female...*" (Charles Darwin, *The Descent of Man,* 1871).

crape *See* CREPE.

cravat (krăvat) FRENCH [from *cravate,* itself from *Cravate* Croatian, where the fashion for such neckties originated] *noun* a necktie or band worn around the neck: "*He was dressed in knickerbockers, with red stockings, which displayed his poor little spindle-shanks; he also wore a brilliant red cravat*" (Henry James, *Daisy Miller,* 1879).

crèche (kresh, kraysh) FRENCH [manger, crib] *noun* a day nursery for young children: "*The crèche is licensed to take up to 40 children at any one time.*"

credo (kreedō, kraydō) LATIN [I believe] *noun* a creed, a set of doctrines or principles (often in reference to Christian belief, especially to the Apostles' or Nicene Creed): "*Self-sufficiency became the credo by which they planned their lives.*"

crème (krem), **creme** FRENCH [cream] *noun* (in French cuisine) cream.

crème brûlée (krem broolay) FRENCH [scorched cream] *noun phrase* (in French cuisine) a dessert dish of custard cream topped with caramelized sugar.

crème caramel (krem karămel) FRENCH [caramel cream] *noun phrase* (in French cuisine) a custard served with caramel sauce.

crème de la crème (krem dă la krem, krem dă lă krem) FRENCH [cream of the cream] *noun phrase* the very best, the best of the best: "*No one would buy. Caviare. Do the grand. Hock in green glasses. Swell blowout. Lady this. Powdered bosom pearls. The elite. Creme de la creme*" (James Joyce, *Ulysses,* 1922).

crème de menthe (krem dă menth, krēm-, -mint) FRENCH [cream of mint] *noun phrase* a sweet mint-flavored liqueur.

crème fraîche (krem fresh), **crème fraiche** FRENCH [fresh cream] *noun* (in French cuisine) a thickened, slightly soured cream.

Creole (kreeōl) FRENCH [from *créole,* from Spanish *criollo,* itself from Portuguese *crioulo* white person born in the colonies] *noun* a person born in the West Indies or Latin America of European descent, or more generally a person of mixed French or Spanish and black descent; can also refer to the language spoken by the black population of southern Louisiana. *~adjective* of or relating to the creoles or to creole culture: "*Society loves creole natures, and sleepy, languishing manners, so that they cover sense, grace, and good-will; the air of drowsy strength, which disarms criticism. . .*" (Ralph Waldo Emerson, "Manners," 1844).

crepe (krayp), **crêpe, crape** FRENCH [from Old French *crespe* curled, frizzed, ultimately from Latin *crispus* curled] *noun* a light fabric or paper with a crinkled surface; can also refer to a type of thin pancake; also a type of rubber especially used for shoe soles. ~*adjective* of or relating to crepe fabric.

crêpe suzette (krayp soo<u>zet</u>) FRENCH [probably after Suzette, the nickname of early-20th century French actress Suzanne Reichenberg] *noun phrase* (*plural* **crêpes suzette** or **crêpe suzettes**) (in French cuisine) a dessert dish comprising a folded or rolled pancake with a hot orange-butter filling, traditionally served in flaming liqueur.

crescendo (krǎ<u>shen</u>dō) ITALIAN [increasing, from Latin *crescere* to grow] *noun* (*plural* **crescendos** or **crescendi,** krǎ<u>shen</u>dee) (in music) a gradual increase in volume; also used more widely to describe any increase in intensity, force, or loudness: *"For Anne the real excitement began with the dismissal of school and increased therefrom in crescendo until it reached to a crash of positive ecstasy in the concert itself"* (Lucy Maud Montgomery, *Anne of Green Gables,* 1908). ~*adverb* (in music) to be played with increasing volume. ~*abbreviated form* **cres., cresc.**

cretin (<u>krē</u>tin) FRENCH [from *crétin* wretch, ultimately from Latin *christianus* Christian] *noun* an idiot, a lout, a fool, also, a person suffering from cretinism, a congenital thyroid deficiency.

crevasse (krǎ<u>vas</u>) FRENCH [from Old French *crevace*] *noun* a fissure (often referring to a crevice or chasm in a glacier); can also refer to a breach in a riverbank or levee.

cri de coeur (kree dǎ <u>ker</u>), **cri du coeur** FRENCH [cry of the heart] *noun phrase* (*plural* **cris de coeur**) a cry from the heart, a passionate appeal, an expression of genuine desire or emotion: *"Her protest at her treatment was a real cri de coeur."*

crime passionnel (kreem pasyǎ<u>nel</u>) FRENCH [passion-related crime] *noun* (*plural* **crimes passionnels**) a crime of passion, a murder or other crime prompted by love, sexual jealousy, or other emotions: *"The papers interpreted the affair as a crime passionel and accordingly gave it plenty of coverage."*

crise de coeur (kreez dǎ <u>ker</u>) FRENCH [crisis of heart] *noun phrase* (*plural* **crises de coeur**) an emotional crisis.

crise de conscience (kreez dǎ <u>kon</u>syons) FRENCH [crisis of conscience] *noun phrase* a crisis of conscience: *"The bishop suffered something of a crise de conscience in the wake of the executions."*

crise de foi (kreez dǎ <u>fhwah</u>) FRENCH [crisis of faith] *noun phrase* a crisis of faith, a severe attack of doubt.

criterion (krīteereeăn) GREEK [from *kriterion* standard, test, from *krinein* to judge] *noun* (*plural* **criterions** or **criteria,** krīteereeă) a standard by which something may be judged; can also refer to a characteristic feature or trait: *"By what objective criteria can you measure a child's education?"*

critique (krăteek, kriteek) FRENCH [from Greek *kritike* criticism] *noun* a critical analysis or discussion: *"Marianne's indignation burst forth as soon as he quitted the room; and as her vehemence made reserve impossible in Elinor, and unnecessary in Mrs. Jennings, they all joined in a very spirited critique upon the party"* (Jane Austen, *Sense and Sensibility*, 1811).

crochet (krōshay) FRENCH [from Old French *croche* hook] *noun* a type of needlework in which a hooked needle is used to interlock looped stitches. ~*verb* to produce crochet work.

croissant (krwason(g)) FRENCH [crescent] *noun* a flaky pastry roll, often baked in a crescent shape: *"Breakfast consisted of a large cup of coffee and some croissants."*

croix de guerre (krwa dă gair) FRENCH [cross of war] *noun phrase* a French military decoration first awarded in 1915.

cromlech (kromlek) WELSH [bent stone] *noun* a dolmen or circle of dolmens; can also refer to any megalithic tomb.

croque-monsieur (krokmăsyer) FRENCH [munch-sir] *noun* a toasted ham and cheese sandwich.

croquette (krōket) FRENCH [from *croquer* to crunch] *noun* a small ball of ground meat, fish, or potato coated in breadcrumbs and fried.

croupier (kroopeeăr, kroopeeă) FRENCH [rider on the croup of a horse] *noun* a member of the staff at a gambling casino who collects bets and pays out money at a gaming table: *"At that moment the croupier raked it all up, and carried it all away; but Alice did not see that this had been done"* (Anthony Trollope, *Can You Forgive Her?*, 1864).

crouton (krootăn) FRENCH [from *croûton*, diminutive of *croûte* crust] *noun* a small piece of fried or toasted bread served with soup or as a garnish.

crudités (kroodeetay, kroodătay) FRENCH [plural of *crudité* rawness, ultimately from Latin *cruditas* indigestion] *plural noun* pieces of raw vegetable served as an hors d'oeuvre.

crux (krăks) LATIN [cross, torture] *noun* (*plural* **cruxes,** krăksiz or **cruces,** krooseez) the main point (of an argument or theory) or a problem, a difficulty; can also refer to a climactic moment of some kind: *"This bit* *of the path was always the crux of the night's ramble, though, before starting, her apprehensions of danger were not vivid enough to lead her to take a companion"* (Thomas Hardy, *Far From the Madding Crowd*, 1874).

cuesta (<u>kwest</u>ă) SPANISH [slope, from Latin *costa* side, rib] *noun*   a hill or ridge with a sharp drop on one side.

cui bono (kwee <u>bō</u>nō) LATIN [to whose advantage?, as quoted by the Roman orator Cicero (106–43 B.C.)] *interjection*   who stands to gain? (expressing the theory that responsibility for an act usually rests with the person who stands to profit most from it).

cuisine (kwi<u>zeen</u>) FRENCH [kitchen, cooking, from Latin *coquere* to cook] *noun*   cookery, the preparation of food (especially when considered as an art).

cul-de-sac (kăl-dă-sak) FRENCH [bottom of the sack] *noun* (*plural* **cul-de-sacs** or **culs-de-sac**)   a street that comes to a dead end, a blind alley: *"And so, as I came trotting out of that cul de sac, full of satisfaction with my own cleverness, he turned the corner and I walked right into his handcuffs"* (Mark Twain, *A Connecticut Yankee*, 1889).

culottes (<u>koo</u>lots, <u>kyu</u>lots, -<u>lots</u>) FRENCH [knee-breeches] *plural noun* a divided skirt. *See also* SANSCULOTTE.

culpa (<u>kăl</u>pă) LATIN [fault, blame] *noun* (*plural* **culpae**)   neglect or negligence that is punishable by law.

cum (kăm) LATIN [with] *preposition* along with, together with, and.

cum laude (kăm <u>low</u>dă, kăm lowdē) LATIN [with praise] *adverb phrase*   with honors, with distinction: *"He graduated cum laude from college at the ripe old age of 21."* ~*adjective phrase* with honors, with distinction. *See also* MAGNA CUM LAUDE, SUMMA CUM LAUDE.

cummerbund (<u>kă</u>mărbănd) HINDI [from *kamarband* loin band, from Persian *kamar* waist and *band* band] *noun* a broad waistband worn as part of a man's formal dress; also used in women's fashion: *"He appeared on the terrace wearing a white jacket and red cummerbund."*

cupola (<u>kyoo</u>pălă) ITALIAN [from Latin *cupula* little cask, from *cupa* cask] *noun* a rounded vault or dome constructed on a circular base or, more generally, any small tower or similar structure on a roof: *"The cupola of the cathedral, which is seen at its best from the bridge about twenty paces from the chapel, glittered in the sunlight, and in the pure air every ornament on it could be clearly distinguished"* (Fyodor Dostoyevsky, *Crime and Punishment*, 1866).

curia (<u>kyoo</u>reeă) LATIN [court, senate house] *noun* (*plural* **curias** or **curiae**, <u>kyoo</u>reeī)   a court of justice, or the senior administration of the Roman Catholic church.

curragh (kără, kărăk), **currach** IRISH GAELIC [coracle] *noun*   a large coracle of a type used in western Ireland.

curriculum (kărikyălăm) LATIN [running, course, from *currere* to run] *noun* (*plural* **curriculums** or **curricula,** kărikyălă)   a program of study, the range of courses offered by an educational establishment: *"From two sides this system of education was beginning to be assailed by the awakening public opinion of the upper middle classes. On the one hand, there was a desire for a more liberal curriculum; on the other, there was a demand for a higher moral tone"* (Lytton Strachey, *Eminent Victorians,* 1918).

curriculum vitae (kărikyălăm veetī) LATIN [course of life] *noun phrase* (*plural* **curricula vitae,** kărikyălă veetī)   a formal summary of a person's career, experience, or qualifications to date, ~*abbreviated form* **c.v.**

curry (kăree) TAMIL [from *kari* sauce] *noun* (*plural* **curries**)   a highly spiced dish prepared in the Indian manner; also, the sauce or powder used to prepare this dish. ~*verb* to prepare a dish of curry.

cursor (kersă) LATIN [runner, from *currere* to run] *noun*   a slide or other movable implement used to mark a position in surveying, mathematics, and other fields; also, a flashing element or cue on a computer monitor to indicate position.

cushy (kuushee) HINDI [from *khush* pleasant] *adjective*   (informal) easy, pleasant, untaxing: *"His cousin had landed a very cushy job with an insurance company."* **c.v.** See CURRICULUM VITAE.

czar (zahr), **tsar** RUSSIAN [from *tsar,* ultimately from Latin *Caesar* emperor] *noun*   the emperor of Russia; also used more widely of any high-ranking official who wields considerable authority: *"Metrov repeated a saying that had reached him through a most trustworthy source, reported as having been uttered on this subject by the Czar and one of the ministers"* (Leo Tolstoy, *Anna Karenina,* 1874–76).

da capo (dah k̲a̲pō, dǎ k̲ā̲pō) ITALIAN [from the head] *adverb phrase* in music, repeat from the beginning: *"It was one of his favorite caravansaries, and so silent and swift would be the service and so delicately choice the food, that he regretted the hunger that must be appeased by the 'dead perfection' of the place's cuisine. Even the music there seemed to be always playing da capo"* (O. Henry, *Strictly Business*, 1910). ~*adjective phrase* of or relating to a passage of music to be repeated from the beginning. ~*abbreviated form* **D.C., d.c.**

d'accord (dak̲o̲r) FRENCH [of accord] *interjection* all right, OK.

dacha (d̲a̲chǎ), **datcha** RUSSIAN [grant of land] *noun* (*plural* **dachas, datchas**) in Russia, a country cottage or villa used for summer retreats and other occasions: *"The count and his family planned to spend the summer at their dacha in the hills."*

dachshund (d̲ǎ̲kshund, d̲ǎk̲sǎnt) GER-MAN [badger dog] *noun* a breed of long-bodied, short-legged dogs of German origin: *"The black cat was doz-ing in the sunlight at her feet, and Joe's dachshund was scratching a hole under the scarlet geraniums and dreaming of bad-gers"* (Willa Cather, *Troll Garden and Other Stories*, 1905).

dacoit (dǎk̲oit̲), **dakoit** HINDI [from *dakait,* itself from *daka* gang-rob-bery] *noun* a bandit of India or Myanmar (Burma), usually a mem-ber of a gang of such robbers; also used more widely of any armed rob-ber or thug.

dado (d̲a̲ydō) ITALIAN [die, cube] *noun* (*plural* **dados, dadoes**) in architec-ture, the pedestal of a column between the cornice and the base, or alternatively the lower part of an inte-rior wall when decorated differently from the upper part: *"A visitor . . . would, if his taste lay that way, admire the wall decoration of Lincrusta Walton in plum color and bronze lacquer, with dado and cornice; the ormolu consoles in the cor-ners; the vases on pillar pedestals of veined marble with bases of polished black wood, one on each side of the window. . ."* (George Bernard Shaw, *You Never Can Tell,* 1898).

dal (dahl), **dahl** HINDI [split pulses] *noun* in Indian cooking, spiced and often pureed legumes.

dahl *See* DAL.

Dalai Lama (dalī lahmă, dalā lahmă) MONGOLIAN [from *dalai* ocean and *lama* priest] *noun* the spiritual head of Tibetan Buddhism: *"The Dalai Lama appeared briefly before the cameras after meeting the queen."*

dal segno (dal saynyō) ITALIAN [from the sign] *adverb phrase* in music, repeat from the sign indicating the beginning of a particular passage. ~*abbreviated form* **D.S.**

dame d'honneur (dam donēr) FRENCH [lady of honor] *noun phrase* a lady-in-waiting or maid of honor.

damnosa hereditas (damnōsă hereditas) LATIN [ruinous inheritance] *noun phrase* an unrewarding or otherwise burdensome inheritance: *"To be left the guardian of Mameena! Talk of a 'damnosa hereditas,' a terrible and mischievous inheritance—why, this was the worst that ever I heard of"* (H. Rider Haggard, *Child of Storm,* 1913).

damnum (damnăm) LATIN [damage, loss] *noun* (*plural* **damna,** damnă) legal term for a loss, wrong, or damage sustained by a person or property.

dan (dan) JAPANESE *noun* one of several advanced grades of proficiency in judo, karate, and other martial arts; also applied to a person who has attained one of these grades.

danse macabre (dahns măkahbră) FRENCH [macabre dance] *noun phrase* (*plural* **danses macabres**) the dance of death: *"The danse macabre, with its prancing skeletons and lamenting mortals, was a favorite subject of medieval artists."*

danseur (donser) FRENCH [from *danser* to dance] *noun* a male ballet dancer. ~*noun, feminine* **danseuse** (donsŭz) a ballerina.

dashiki (dasheekee) WEST AFRICAN [probably from Yoruban *dansiki*] *noun* a loose, brightly colored pullover shirt of a type widely worn in West Africa and the United States.

data (daytă, dată, dahtă) LATIN [plural of *datum,* neuter past participle of *dare* to give] *noun* facts, details, information: *"We are left to interpret the vast amounts of data produced by computers."*

daube (dōb) FRENCH *noun* a stew of braised meat cooked with vegetables, wine, herbs, and spices: *"The king opened his eyes with delight, and, while cutting some of the faisan en daube, which was being handed to him, he said: 'That is a dish I should very much like to taste, Monsieur du Vallon. Is it possible! a whole lamb!'"* (Alexandre Dumas, *Louise de la Vallière,* 1850).

dauphin (d<u>ō</u>fan(g), dō<u>fan</u>(g)) FRENCH [from Old French *daulphin,* originally a family name adopted as a title of the lords of Viennois or Dauphiné] *noun* title borne by the eldest son of a king of France: *"Yes, my friend, it is too true— your eyes is look-in' at this very moment on the pore disappeared Dauphin, Looy the Seventeen, son of Looy the Six-teen and Marry Antonette."* (Mark Twain, *Huckleberry Finn,* 1884). ~*noun, feminine* **dauphine** (dō<u>feen</u>) title borne by a dauphin's wife.

D.C., d.c. *See* DA CAPO.

debacle (dee<u>bah</u>kăl, dee<u>bak</u>ăl), **débâcle** (day<u>bah</u>kăl) FRENCH [collapse, from *débâcler* to clear] *noun* a comprehensive disaster, fiasco, or defeat: *"But it may yet be asked, how has the solid basalt been moved? Geologists formerly would have brought into play the violent action of some overwhelming debacle; but in this case such a supposition would have been quite inadmissible. . ."* (Charles Darwin, *Voyage of the Beagle,* 1839).

de bene esse (dee benay <u>es</u>ay) LATIN [of well-being] *adverb phrase* valid for the time being (a legal term used specifically of evidence taken in advance from a person who is expected to be too ill to come to court personally, to be referred to if he or she is in fact unable to attend court when the case eventually gets under way).

debonair (debă<u>nair</u>) FRENCH [from *débonnaire* good-natured, itself from *de bon aire* of good nature, of good family] *adjective* suave, urbane, nonchalant, carefree: *"Ah! what avails that she was fair, / Luminous, blithe, and debonair? / The storm has stripped her of her leaves; / The Lily floats no longer!— She hath perished"* (William Wordsworth, "The Egyptian Maid," 1835).

debris (dă<u>bree</u>, day<u>bree</u>, <u>day</u>bree), **débris** FRENCH [from Middle French *débriser* to break to pieces] *noun (plural* **debris** or **débris,** dă<u>breez</u>, day<u>breez</u>, <u>day</u>breez) fragments, remnants, wreckage, ruins, rubbish: *"We examined the debris of the old shanty scattered about by the storm."*

debut (<u>day</u>byoo, day<u>boo</u>), **début** FRENCH [beginning, from *débuter* to make the first stroke] *noun* a first appearance (in the theater or in society, for example): *"Thenceforth, certain of herself, certain of her friends in the house, certain of her voice and her success, fearing nothing, Carlotta flung herself into her part without restraint of modesty . . . She was no longer Margarita, she was Carmen. She was applauded all the more; and her debut with Faust seemed about to bring her a new success, when suddenly . . . a terrible thing happened"* (Gaston Leroux, *Phantom of the Opera,* 1911). ~*verb* to make a first appearance or to introduce something or someone in public for the first time.

debutante (<u>deb</u>yootont) FRENCH [present participle of *débuter* to make the first stroke] *noun, feminine* a young woman making her first appearance (in society or on the stage, for example): *"Some weeks elapse; and, during this interval, the public, at a loss where to procure an opinion of the debutante, have necessarily no opinion of him at all for the nonce"* (H. W. Longfellow, "The Spanish Student," 1842–43). ~*noun, masculine* **debutant** (<u>deb</u>yootant) a person making a debut.

déclassé (daycla<u>say</u>) FRENCH [degraded, past participle of *déclasser* to degrade] *adjective* lower, inferior, degraded. ~*noun* a person who has been degraded or reduced in status or social standing. ~*noun, feminine* **déclassée.**

décolletage (daykolă<u>tahzh</u>, dekolă<u>tahzh</u>, daykol<u>tahzh</u>, dekol<u>tahzh</u>) FRENCH [low-cut neck, from *décolleter* to expose the neck] *noun* a low-cut neckline of a woman's dress, that leaves the shoulders and neck exposed: *"He could not help but admire her décolletage as she made her grand entrance into the ballroom."*

décolleté (daykolă<u>tay</u>, dekolă<u>tay</u>) FRENCH [low-necked, past participle of *décolleter* to expose the neck] *adjective* having a low-cut neckline or wearing a low-cut neckline that leaves the neck and shoulders exposed.

decor (day<u>kor</u>, de<u>kor</u>), **décor** FRENCH [decoration, from *décorer* to decorate] *noun* decoration, furnishings or (in the theater) the setting or scenery: *"The decor needs some attention but otherwise the apartment is ready for immediate occupation."*

decorum (di<u>kor</u>ăm) LATIN [neuter singular of *decorus* seemly, from *decor* beauty, grace] *noun* propriety, good conduct, polite behavior, or seemliness: *"Miss Churchill, however, being of age, and with the full command of her fortune—though her fortune bore no proportion to the family-estate—was not to be dissuaded from the marriage, and it took place, to the infinite mortification of Mr. and Mrs. Churchill, who threw her off with due decorum"* (Jane Austen, *Emma,* 1816).

decoupage (daykoo<u>pazh</u>), **découpage** FRENCH [act of cutting out, from *decouper* to cut up] *noun* an artistic technique in which pictures or patterns are constructed out of pieces of cut-out paper, fabric, or other material.

decoy (<u>dee</u>koi, di<u>koi</u>) DUTCH [from *de kooi* the cage] *noun* someone or something that is used as a lure: *"Now harkee, mate; you will not beg, you will not rob; so be it. But I will tell you what you WILL do. You will play decoy whilst I beg"* (Mark Twain, *The Prince and the Pauper,* 1882). ~*verb* to lure or entice through the use of a decoy.

decrescendo (deekră<u>shend</u>ō) ITALIAN [decreasing, present participle of decrescere to decrease] noun (plural **decrescendos** in music, an instruction for a particular passage to be played with a gradual reduction in volume: *"After the gradual cessation of all sound and movement on the faithful river, only the ringing of ships' bells is heard, mysterious and muffled in the white vapour from London Bridge right down to the Nore, for miles and miles in a decrescendo tinkling, to where the estuary broadens out into the North Sea. . ."* (Joseph Conrad, *The Mirror of the Sea*, 1906). ~*adverb* to be played with decreasing volume.

de facto (di fak̄tō, day fak̄tō) LATIN [from the act] *adverb phrase* actually, in reality. ~*adjective phrase* actual, in effect: *"Although neither side had declared war, a de facto state of war between the two countries existed."*

Defensor Fidei See FIDEI DEFENSOR.

de fide (day feeday) LATIN [from faith] *noun phrase* as a matter of faith, of the faith.

dégagé (daygahzhay) FRENCH [past participle of *dégager* to set free] *adjective* nonchalant, carefree, relaxed, unconstrained, disinterested.

de gustibus non est disputandum (day goostibăs non est dispyootandăm) LATIN [concerning tastes, it is not to be disputed] *noun* there is no point arguing about other people's tastes: *"One of the most deplorably false of them is*

the antique adage, De gustibus non est disputandum—there should be no disputing about taste"* (Edgar Allan Poe, *Ballads and Other Poems*, 1842). ~*abbreviated form* **de gustibus.**

de haut en bas (dă ō ton ba) FRENCH [from top to bottom] *adverb phrase* arrogantly, contemptuously, in a condescending manner: *"The landlady looked at him de haut en bas, rather pitying, and at the same time, resenting his clear, fierce morality"* (D. H. Lawrence, *Sons and Lovers*, 1913).

Dei gratia (dayee grahteeă) LATIN [by the grace of God] *adverb phrase* by the grace of God, by divine favor (usually referring to rule by divine right): *"The monarch or the sovereign assembly only hath immediate authority from God to teach and instruct the people; and no man but the sovereign receiveth his power Dei gratia simply; that is to say, from the favor of none but God. . ."* (Thomas Hobbes, *Leviathan*, 1651). ~*abbreviated form* **D.G.**

déjà vu (dayzhah voo, dayzhah vyoo) FRENCH [already seen] *noun phrase* the psychological phenomenon in which a person has the sense of having experienced something before, even though to the best of his or her knowledge they have never actually done so. Also used of anything that is overly familiar, hackneyed, or unoriginal: *"The whole show had a distinct air of déjà vu, with hardly an original idea in it."*

de jure (dee jŭree, day <u>yooree</u>) LATIN [from right] *adverb phrase* by right: *"In all things which regard the external relations of the individual, he is de jure amenable to those whose interests are concerned, and if need be, to society as their protector"* (John Stuart Mill, *On Liberty*, 1859). ~*adjective phrase* legitimate, lawful.

del. *See* DELINEAVIT.

delicatessen (delikă<u>tes</u>ăn) GERMAN [plural of *Delikatesse* delicacy] *noun* a store or counter in a store selling ready-to-eat food products: *"The new supermarket boasts an excellent delicatessen, with a wide range of meat and cheeses."* ~*abbreviated form* **deli.**

delineavit (delinee<u>ay</u>vit) LATIN [he/she drew it] *noun* he/she drew it (identifying the artist of a particular drawing or painting). ~*abbreviated form* **del.**

delirium (dă<u>li</u>reeăm) LATIN [from *delirare* to deviate, to leave the furrow] *noun* (*plural* **deliriums** or **deliria,** dă<u>li</u>riă) a state of mental disturbance or frenzied excitement.

delirium tremens (dă<u>li</u>reeăm <u>tre</u>mens) LATIN [trembling madness] *noun* violent delirium characterized by uncontrollable trembling, a consequence of prolonged alcohol abuse: *"They—that is, Vronsky—had a trainer, an Englishman, first-rate in his own line, but a drunkard. He's completely given up to drink—delirium tremens—and the family*

were cast on the world" (Leo Tolstoy, *Anna Karenina*, 1873–77). ~*abbreviated form* **d.t.'s.**

delphic (<u>del</u>fik) GREEK [after the Oracle dedicated to Apollo in the ancient Greek city of Delphi] *adjective* ambiguous, obscure: *"The old man's reply was positively delphic, leaving us none the wiser."*

delta (<u>del</u>tă) GREEK [fourth letter of the Greek alphabet] *noun* something triangular in shape (thus resembling the triangular symbol for the Greek letter delta), especially the roughly triangular area of land enclosed or traversed by the mouths of a river: *"Always Florida's green peninsula— always the priceless delta of Louisiana— always the cotton-fields of Alabama and Texas, Always California's golden hills and hollows, and the silver mountains of New Mexico—always soft-breath'd Cuba. . ."* (Walt Whitman, *Leaves of Grass*, 1891–92).

deluxe (di<u>luks</u>, dee<u>luks</u>), de luxe FRENCH [of luxury] *adjective* luxurious, elegant, choice, superior or top quality. ~*adverb* luxuriously, sumptuously.

dementia (di<u>men</u>chă) LATIN [madness, from *demens* mad] *noun* (*plural* **dementias** or **dementiae,** di<u>men</u>sheeī) mental disorder, or a state of fanaticism, folly, or wildness bordering on insanity: *"It seemed to him that every conviction, as soon as it became effective,* turned into that form of dementia the gods send upon those they wish to destroy" (Joseph Conrad, *Nostromo*, 1904).

demimondaine (dămeemon<u>dayn</u>, de-mee<u>mon</u>dayn), **demi-mondaine** FRENCH [from *demi-monde* half-world] *noun* (*plural* **demimondaines** or **demi-mondaines**) a woman of the demi-monde, living on the fringes of respectable society and thus not very respectable herself.

demimonde (<u>dem</u>eemond), **demi-monde** FRENCH [from *demi-monde* half-world] *noun* a class of women living on the fringes of respectable society, usually of doubtful reputation and often maintained by wealthy lovers; also used more loosely of prostitutes in general: *"The doctor was a good-looking man and still young. He had a superb practice among the gay world, and being very merry by nature and ready to laugh and joke in the friendliest way with the demimonde ladies with whom, however, he never went farther, he charged very high fees and got them paid with the greatest punctuality"* (Émile Zola, *Nana*, 1880).

demi-pension (dămi pons<u>yon</u>(g), demi pons<u>yon</u>(g)) FRENCH [half-board] *noun* in French-speaking countries, a hotel offering bed, breakfast, and one other meal each day.

demi-sec (dămi <u>sek</u>, demi <u>sek</u>) FRENCH [half dry] *adjective* medium dry (of wine).

demitasse (<u>dem</u>eetas) FRENCH [half-cup] *noun* a small coffee-cup

démodé (daymō<u>day</u>) FRENCH [out-moded, past participle of *démoder* to go out of fashion] *adjective* out of date, outmoded, obsolete, unfashionable.

demoiselle (demwă<u>zel</u>) FRENCH [unmarried woman] *noun* (*plural* **demoiselles** or **desmoiselles** a young lady or girl: *"The darkness came on fast. We must camp, of course. I found a good shelter for the demoiselle under a rock, and went off and found another for myself"* (Mark Twain, *A Connecticut Yankee in King Arthur's Court*, 1889).

de mortuis nil nisi bonum (day <u>morty</u>-oois nil neesi bō<u>nă</u>m) LATIN [about the dead, nothing except good] *noun phrase* do not speak ill of the dead: *"De mortuis nil nisi bonum is an excellent injunction—even if the dead in question be nothing but dead small beer"* (Edgar Allan Poe, "Never Bet The Devil Your Head," 1845). ~*abbreviated form* **de mortuis.**

denim (<u>den</u>im, <u>den</u>ăm) FRENCH [short for *serge de Nîmes*, serge of Nîmes, a hardwearing material first made in Nimes, France] *noun* durable cotton fabric originally used chiefly for working clothes, but now in wide use for work and casual clothing. ~*adjective* relating to a garment made of such fabric: *"The park and streets were buzzing with strikers, young men in blue denim* *shirts, old men with caps"* (Sinclair Lewis, *Babbitt,* 1922).

de nos jours (day nō zhoor) FRENCH [of our days] *adjective phrase* of our time, contemporary: *"He is not the first poet to have been labelled the Lord Byron de nos jours."*

denouement (daynoomon(g), daynoo-mon(g)), **dénouement** FRENCH [untying, unravelling, from *desnouer* to untie] *noun* the final outcome or issue of a plot or situation: *"He was not sorry for the denouement of his visit: he only wished it had come sooner, and spared him a certain waste of emotion"* (Edith Wharton, *The Age of Innocence,* 1920).

de novo (di nōvō, day nōvō, dee nōvō) LATIN [from new] *adverb phrase* over again, afresh, anew: *"None of my writings have been either so carefully composed, or so sedulously corrected as this. After it had been written as usual twice over, we kept it by us, bringing it out from time to time, and going through it de novo, reading, weighing, and criticizing every sentence"* (John Stuart Mill, *Autobiography,* 1873).

deoch an doris *See* DOCH-AN-DORRIS.

Deo gratias (dayō grahtiäs, dayō grah-siäs) LATIN [thanks to God] *interjection* thanks be to God. *~abbreviated form* **D.G.**

Deo volente (dayō volentay, deeo volentee) LATIN [God be willing] *adverb*

phrase God willing, if God wills. *~abbreviated form* **D.V.**

dépassé (daypasay) FRENCH [passed] *adjective* surpassed, outmoded, outdated, out-of-date. See also PASSÉ.

depot (deepō, depō) FRENCH [from *dépôt* deposit, depository, itself from Latin *depositum,* neuter past participle of *deponere* to place, put away] *noun* a store, cache, or place where supplies or vehicles are kept. Also used to refer to a train or bus station or other commercial center or base.

de profundis (day prōfundis) LATIN [from the depths, the opening words of Psalm 130] *noun phrase* out of the depths (usually, of sorrow or despair). *~adverb phrase* out of the depths (usually, of sorrow or despair).

déraciné (dayrasinay) FRENCH [uprooted, past participle of *déraciner* to uproot] *adjective* displaced, dislodged, uprooted.

de rigueur (dă reeger) FRENCH [in strictness] *adjective phrase* required, compulsory, obligatory, expected: *"Every one has subjects of conversation, ladies for instance . . . people in high society always have their subjects of conversation, c'est de rigueur, but people of the middle sort like us, thinking people that is, are always tongue-tied and awkward"* (Fyodor Dostoyevsky, *Crime and Punishment,* 1866).

dernier cri (dernyay <u>cree</u>) FRENCH [last cry] *noun phrase* the latest fashion, the last word in fashion, style or design: *"They wore dresses and skirts that they were told were the dernier cri."*

derriere (deree<u>air</u>), **derrière** FRENCH [back part, behind] *noun* (slang) the buttocks, behind, rear, posterior (slang): *"He aimed a kick at his tormentor's derriere but thought better of it at the last moment."*

dervish (<u>der</u>vish) TURKISH [beggar, from Persian *darvish* religious mendicant] *noun* a member of one of several ascetic Muslim religious orders bound by vows of poverty and austerity; usually associated with religious fanatics who dance feverishly and whirl about as part of their religious devotions: *"It befell one day of the days that as he was sitting about the quarter at play with the vagabond boys, behold, a dervish from the Maghrib, the Land of the Setting Sun, came up and stood gazing for solace upon the lads"* (Richard Burton, "Aladdin; or, The Wonderful Lamp," *Arabian Nights,* 1885–88).

desaparecido (desapără<u>seedō</u>) SPANISH [disappeared one] *noun* (*plural* **desaparecidos**) the disappeared (usually referring to the thousands of Argentine citizens who vanished, allegedly on the orders of the country's authoritarian military rulers, during the 1970s and early 1980s).

deshabille (dayză<u>beel</u>, dayză<u>bil</u>), **dishabille** (disă<u>beel</u>, disă<u>bil</u>), **déshabillé** (dayză<u>beey</u>ay) FRENCH [undressed, past participle of *déshabiller* to undress] *noun* casual dress, or a state of partial undress. *"Madame Hohlakov had been slightly ailing for the last three weeks: her foot had for some reason swollen up, and though she was not in bed, she lay all day half-reclining on the couch in her boudoir, in a fascinating but decorous deshabille"* (Fyodor Dostoyevsky, *The Brothers Karamazov,* 1880).

desideratum (disidă<u>rah</u>tăm, dizidă<u>rah</u>tăm) LATIN [neuter of *desideratus,* past participle of *desiderare* to desire] *noun* (*plural* **desiderata,** disidă<u>rah</u>tă, dizidă<u>rah</u>tă) a requirement, or something needed or desired as essential: *"The thing that will logically extinguish him is perhaps still a desideratum in Constitutional civilization"* (Thomas Carlyle, *The French Revolution,* 1837).

dessert (di<u>zert</u>) FRENCH [from *desservir* to clear the table] *noun* a sweet course, the final course of a meal: *"There was none of the strong ale here, of course, but wine and dessert—sparkling gooseberry for the young ones, and some good sherry for the mothers"* (George Eliot, *Adam Bede,* 1859).

détente (day<u>tont</u>, de<u>tont</u>, day<u>tahnt</u>), **detente** FRENCH [relaxation, easing] *noun* (*plural* **détentes**) a period of relaxation in tension, usually referring to political relations between opposed nations (and the policies connected with this): *"An uneasy détente existed between the management and the rebellious workforce as the two sides considered their future strategies."*

detour (<u>dee</u>toor, di<u>toor</u>) FRENCH [*détour* turning away, from *détorner* to divert, turn away] *noun* a deviation from the direct or normal course or route. ~*verb* to make such a deviation from the direct or normal course or route: *"'Yes, that's to be taken for granted,' retorted the celebrated doctor, again glancing at his watch. 'Beg pardon—but is the Iauzsky bridge finished yet, or must one still make a detour?' he asked"* (Leo Tolstoy, *Anna Karenina,* 1874–76).

detritus (di<u>trī</u>tăs) LATIN [rubbing away, from the past participle of Latin *deterere* to wear away] *noun* (*plural* **detritus**) debris, remnants, particles, rubbish as in *"the emotional detritus of a failed marriage."* Also used in geology to describe sand, gravel, and rocks produced by erosion: *"The geologists examined vast mounds of detritus across the valley."*

de trop (dă <u>trō</u>) FRENCH [of too much] *adjective phrase* superfluous, too much, excessive, unwelcome: *"Julia felt uncomfortable—she felt herself to be de trop; and making an incoherent excuse, she had scarcely taken a seat on a sofa, before she arose, left the room, and ran up stairs again"* (James Fenimore Cooper,

Autobiography of a Pocket-Handkerchief, 1843).

deus ex machina (dayăs eks <u>ma</u>kină, dayăs eks <u>ma</u>sheenă) LATIN [a god out of a machine] *noun phrase* (*plural* **dei ex machina,** dayee eks <u>ma</u>kină, dayee eks <u>ma</u>sheenă) an artificial ending or convenient but contrived solution to a difficulty (referring to the traditional appearance in classical drama of a god, lowered on an artificial cloud, toward the end of a play to resolve the action on the stage): *"It is the deus ex machina who, by suspending that resistance, makes the fall of the curtain an immediate necessity, since drama ends exactly where resistance ends"* (George Bernard Shaw, *Mrs. Warren's Profession,* 1898).

Deus vobiscum (dayăs vō<u>bis</u>kăm) LATIN [God with you] *noun phrase* may God be with you: *"'Nay, then, if wilful will to water, wilful must drench.—Deus vobiscum, most doughty Athelstane!'—he concluded, loosening the hold which he had hitherto kept upon the Saxon's tunic"* (Walter Scott, *Ivanhoe,* 1819).

deva (<u>day</u>vă) SANSKRIT [a god, a shining one] *noun* in Hindu, Buddhist and Vedic mythology, a god or divine spirit.

D.G. *See* DEI GRATIA; DEO GRATIAS.

dharma (<u>dahr</u>mă, <u>der</u>mă) SANSKRIT [law, statute, decree] *noun* in Hindu and Buddhist philosophy, the fundamental law of the universe and an individual's duty to live according to the basic principles of nature and universal truth.

dhoti (dōtee) HINDI *noun* (*plural* **dhotis**) a man's loincloth, as worn by Indian men: *"A strange old man in a dhoti glared balefully at the tourists as they leveled their cameras at him."*

dhow (dow), **dow** ARABIC [*dawa,* probably from Marathi *daw*] *noun* a lateen-rigged Arabian sailing boat with one or two masts and a low waist: *"A gentle breeze fills the huge sails of our dhow, and draws us through the water that ripples musically against our sides"* (H. Rider Haggard, *She,* 1887).

diaeresis (dīăreesis), **dieresis** GREEK [*diairesis* division, from *diairein* to divide] *noun* (*plural* **diaereses,** dīăreeseez, **diereses**) a sign placed over a vowel denoting that it should be pronounced as an independent syllable; also used in poetry to mark a place where the end of a foot coincides with the end of a word.

diagnosis (dīăgnōsis) GREEK [*diagignoskein* to distinguish] *noun* (*plural* **diagnoses,** dīăgnōseez) an analysis, investigation or examination, or the decision resulting from such analysis: *"A more exact diagnosis can only be made if we obtain a blood sample."*

diamanté (deeămahntay) FRENCH [like a diamond, from *diamant* diamond]

adjective of or relating to fabric decorated with sequins or artificial jewels to achieve a sparkling effect: *"She accepted the award with a white-toothed smile, a thousand lights reflecting on her fabulous diamanté gown."*

diaspora (dīaspără, deeaspără) GREEK [a scattering, dispersion, from *diaspeirein* to scatter] *noun* the Jewish community resident in parts of the world other than Israel; by extension any group of people linked by nationality or religion who have dispersed and settled far from their original homeland.

dibbuk *See* DYBBUK

dictum (diktăm) LATIN [neuter of *dictus* word] *noun* (*plural* **dictums** or **dicta,** diktă) a statement, formal pronouncement, saying, or maxim: *"Apart from her studies Anne expanded socially, for Marilla, mindful of the Spencervale doctor's dictum, no longer vetoed occasional outings"* (Lucy Maud Montgomery, *Anne of Green Gables,* 1908).

didgeridoo (dijăreedoo), **didjeridoo, didgeridu** AUSTRALIAN ABORIGINAL [Yolngu language, of imitative origin] *noun* an aboriginal wind instrument comprising a long wooden or bamboo tube.

dieresis *See* DIAERESIS.

dies irae (deeayz eeray, deeayz eeră) LATIN [day of wrath] *noun phrase* the

111

Day of Judgment, or the name of a medieval hymn on the theme of the Last Judgment, frequently sung or recited at requiem masses; also used more generally in relation to any day of reckoning.

dies non (d̄eez non) LATIN [non day] *noun phrase* in the commercial or legal world, a day on which no business is done.

Dieu et mon droit (dyă ay mon(g) d̲w̲a̲) FRENCH [God and my right] *noun phrase* God is my right (motto on the royal arms of England dating from the reign of Richard I).

diktat (d̲ik̲tat) GERMAN [something dictated, from Latin *dictare* to dictate] *noun* an official order or command, often severe and inflexible in nature: *"The director issued an immediate diktat prohibiting any further experiments without his express permission."*

dilemma (dă̲lem̲ă, dī̲lem̲ă) LATIN [probably from Greek *dilemmatos* involving two assumptions, an ambiguous proposition] *noun* a difficult choice between two equally imperfect alternatives, or a problematic, even perilous predicament in which such a choice must be made: *"The Canadian then said, 'Sir, we must do all we can to get out of this dilemma. Let us signal them. They will then, perhaps, understand that we are honest folks'"* (Jules Verne, *20,000 Leagues Under the Sea,* 1870).

dilettante (dĭl̲ă̲tont, dĭl̲ă̲tant, dĭlă̲tant̲, dĭlă̲tont̲) ITALIAN [a lover, present participle of *dilettare* to delight] *noun* (*plural* **dilettantes** or **dilettanti,** dĭlă̲tant̲ee, dĭlă̲tont̲ee) a lover or connoisseur of the arts, usually an amateur who has enthusiasm but little serious knowledge or professional experience of the artistic world: *"He had dawdled over his cigar because he was at heart a dilettante, and thinking over a pleasure to come often gave him a subtler satisfaction than its realization"* (Edith Wharton, *The Age of Innocence,* 1920). ~*adjective* having a superficial knowledge of the arts.

diminuendo (diminyoo̲wen̲dō) ITALIAN [diminishing, from Latin *diminuendum,* gerund of *diminuere* to lessen] *adverb* in music, decreasing in volume. ~*adjective* decreasing in volume. ~*noun* a gradual decrease in volume: *"He moved his left hand out into the air as if he were suggesting a diminuendo to an orchestra"* (Willa Cather, *The Song of the Lark,* 1915).

dim sum (dim s̲ăm̲) CHINESE [from *dim* speck and *sum* heart] *noun* a traditional steamed Chinese food comprising small portions of such items as cooked chicken, dumplings, and rice balls and usually served as a snack meal.

dinero (di̲nair̲ō) SPANISH [money, from Latin *denarius* silver coin] *noun* money (slang): *"It was a pretty fishy arrangement, but he was seduced by the* *promise that he would receive plenty of dinero for his contribution to the enterprise."*

Ding an sich (ding an <u>zik</u>, ding an <u>zish</u>) GERMAN [a thing in itself] *noun phrase* (*plural* **Dinge an sich**) in philosophy, the underlying reality beneath superficial appearances.

dinghy (<u>din</u>gee) HINDI [from *dingi* small boat] *noun* (*plural* **dinghies**) a small rowing or sailing boat, sometimes inflatable and often used as a tender or lifeboat for a larger vessel.

dingo (<u>din</u>gō) AUSTRALIAN ABORIGINAL [Dahruk language, wild dog] *noun* a species of wild dog (*Canis dingo*) of Australia.

diorama (dīă<u>rah</u>mă) GREEK [*dia* through and *orama* view, imitative of *panorama*] *noun* a scenic painting, stage or film setting, tableau or display with three-dimensional figures: *"The memory has as many moods as the temper, and shifts its scenery like a diorama"* (George Eliot, *Middlemarch,* 1871–72).

diploma (dă<u>plō</u>mă) LATIN [passport, from Greek *diploma* folded paper, from *diploun* to double] *noun* (*plural* **diplomas** or **diplomata,** dip<u>lō</u>mahtă) an official document, usually awarded by a school, college, university, or other educational institution, certifying that the recipient has graduated from that institution, and giving details

of an academic qualification, honor, or privilege conferred upon the holder: *"I'm expecting to receive my college diploma next year."*

dipsomania (dipsă<u>may</u>neeă, dipsă<u>may</u>nyă) LATIN [madness of thirst, from Greek *dipsa* thirst and Latin *mania* madness] *noun* a craving for alcohol, alcoholism: *"Her husband is a pleasant man, but his the pallor of his cheeks and the redness of his nose suggests dipsomania."*

Directoire (deerek<u>twahr</u>, dee<u>rek</u>twah) FRENCH [after the Directoire group of five officials who ruled France in the years 1795–99] *adjective* of or relating to the style of decoration reminiscent of classical Greek and Roman design that was popular in France during the last decade of the 18th century: *"I am glad to see that many of the most charming women in Paris are returning to the idea of the Directoire style of dress"* (Oscar Wilde, *Shorter Prose Pieces*).

dirigisme (diri<u>zhi</u>zăm), **dirigism** FRENCH [planning, from *diriger* to direct] *noun* (*plural* **dirigismes**) economic and social planning, especially control of the economy and society by the state.

discotheque (<u>dis</u>kătek, diskă<u>tek</u>), **discothèque** FRENCH [record library, from *disque* record, influenced by *bibliothèque library*] *noun* a venue or event for dancing to pop music: *"The* whole team was photographed by the press going into a discotheque the night before the big game." ~abbreviated form **disco** (dĭskō).

diseuse (deezerz) FRENCH [one who tells, feminine of *diseur,* from *dire* to say] *noun* a professional woman speaker or reciter: "*She is making quite a reputation as a diseuse at intimate comedy venues around the country.*"

dishabille *See* DESHABILLE.

disjecta membra (disjektă membră) LATIN [scattered limbs] *noun phrase* scattered, remains, usually referring to fragments of a literary work or other written material: "*She led the way westward past a long line of areas which, through the distortion of their paintless rails, revealed with increasing candour the disjecta membra of bygone dinners. . .*" (Edith Wharton, *The House of Mirth,* 1905).

distingué (deestangay, distangay, distangay) FRENCH [past participle of *distinguer* to distinguish] *adjective* distinguished in manner or appearance, illustrious, elegant: "*He has taken to wearing a frock coat and floral waistcoat in the mistaken belief that this makes him look distingué.*" ~*adjective, feminine* **distinguée.**

distrait (distray, distray) FRENCH [distracted, past participle of *destraire,* from Latin *distrahere* to distract, pull asunder] *adjective* dis-

tracted, absentminded: "*Stapleton was talking with animation, but the baronet looked pale and distrait. Perhaps the thought of that lonely walk across the ill-omened moor was weighing heavily upon his mind*" (Arthur Conan Doyle, *The Hound of the Baskervilles,* 1902). ~*adjective, feminine* **distraite** (distrayt, distrayt).

ditto (dĭtō) ITALIAN [having been said, from Tuscan dialect *detto* said, from Latin *dicere* to say] *adverb* as before, as aforesaid, likewise. ~*noun* (*plural* **dittos**) the aforesaid, something already mentioned (to avoid repetition at length): "'*I shouldn't!' Alice exclaimed indignantly. 'Besides, if I'M only a sort of thing in his dream, what areYOU, I should like to know?' 'Ditto' saidTweedledum. 'Ditto, ditto' cried Tweedledee*" (Lewis Carroll, *Through the Looking-Glass,* 1871). ~*verb* to repeat something already mentioned or done, to make a duplicate copy of something. ~*adjective* similar. ~*abbreviated form* **do.**

diva (deevă) ITALIAN [goddess, from Latin *divus* god] *noun* (*plural* **divas,** deevăz, or **dive,** deevee) a prima donna, a distinguished female singer in opera, concerts, or other performances: "*And it had needed Carlotta's incomprehensible and inexcusable absence from this gala night for the little Daae, at a moment's warning, to show all that she could do in a part of the program reserved for the Spanish diva!*" (Gaston Leroux, *Phantom of the Opera,* 1910).

divan (di<u>van</u>) TURKISH [from Persian *diwan* bench, account book] *noun* a couch suitable for use as a bed, usually lacking either headboard or footboard: *"The woman stretched out on the divan and sighed deeply."*

divertimento (divertimen<u>to</u>) ITALIAN [diversion, from *divertire* to divert] *noun* (*plural* **divertimenti,** diverti<u>men</u>tee, or **divertimentos**) a light instrumental chamber work in several movements, or an entertainment or amusement of any kind.

divertissement (di<u>ver</u>tismănt, di<u>ver</u>tizmănt, dī<u>ver</u>tismon(g)) FRENCH [diversion, amusement] *noun* an entertainment or diversion of any kind, or, in music, an operatic interlude (often in the form of a brief ballet) or a series of operatic extracts played on the same program: *"In the carnival following the conclusion of the year 1753, the Devin was performed at Paris, and in this interval I had sufficient time to compose the overture and divertissement"* (Jean-Jacques Rousseau, *Confessions,* 1782–89).

divorcé (divor<u>say</u>, divor<u>see</u>, di<u>vor</u>say) FRENCH [divorced, past participle of *divorcer* to divorce] *noun* a divorced man: *"She married a divorcé with two children."* ~*noun, feminine* **divorcée** (di<u>vor</u>see, di<u>vor</u>say, di<u>vor</u>say) a divorced woman.

dixit (<u>dik</u>sit) LATIN [he has spoken] *verb* referring to a statement already made.

djellaba *See* JELLABA.

djinn *See* JINNI.

do. *See* DITTO.

doch-an-dorris (dok ăn <u>do</u>ris), **deoch an doris** SCOTTISH GAELIC [drink of the door] *noun* a parting drink.

doctrinaire (doktră<u>nair</u>) FRENCH [pedantic, illiberal, from *doctrine* doctrine] *adjective* dogmatic, dictatorial. ~*noun* a person who holds strict views or adheres to a particular theory or doctrine, regardless of practical considerations: *"Who wants to be consistent? The dullard and the doctrinaire, the tedious people who carry out their principles to the bitter end of action, to the reductio ad absurdum of practice"* (Oscar Wilde, *Intentions,* 1891).

dogma (<u>dog</u>mă) GREEK [*dokein* to seem] *noun* (*plural* **dogmas,** <u>dog</u>măz, or **dogmata,** dog<u>mah</u>tă) an established opinion, prescribed doctrine, or code of belief: *"Stooping over, he kissed on the fair cheek his fellow-man, a felon in martial law, one who though on the confines of death he felt he could never convert to a dogma; nor for all that did he fear for his future"* (Herman Melville, *Billy Budd,* 1924).

dolce (<u>dol</u>chay) ITALIAN [sweet] *adjective* soft, smooth. ~*adverb* in music, to be played in a soft or smooth manner.

115

dolce vita (dolchi v<u>ee</u>tă) ITALIAN [sweet life] *noun phrase*   the soft life, a life of self-indulgence and luxury: *"In his mind's eye he saw himself in a villa overlooking the sea, cocktail in hand, living the dolce vita."*

dollar (d<u>o</u>lăr) DUTCH [from German *Taler,* abbreviation of *Joachimstaler,* after Sankt Joachimsthal of Bohemia, where taler coins were first manufactured] *noun*   the basic monetary unit of many countries, or a coin or bill with the value of one dollar: *"As I was walking on the beach here in my last visit, looking for shells and pebbles, just after that storm which I have mentioned as moving the sand to a great depth, not knowing but I might find some cob-money, I did actually pick up a French crown piece, worth about a dollar and six cents, near high-water mark, on the still moist sand, just under the abrupt, caving base of the bank"* (Henry David Thoreau, *Cape Cod,* 1865).

dolmen (d<u>o</u>lmăn) FRENCH [from Breton *tol* table and *men* stone] *noun*   a megalithic monument consisting of a huge stone slab supported by two or more stone pillars, often built originally as a burial chamber: *"Again, M. Dupont found thirty per cent of perforated bones in the caves of the Valley of the Lesse, belonging to the Reindeer period; whilst M. Leguay, in a sort of dolmen at Argenteuil, observed twenty-five per cent to be perforated; and M. Pruner-Bey found twenty-six per cent in the same condition in bones from Vaureal"* (Charles Darwin,

The Descent of Man, 1871). See also CROMLECH.

doloroso (dolăr<u>o</u>s<u>o</u>) ITALIAN [painful] *adjective*   in music, plaintive, soft, and pathetic.

dominatrix (domi<u>na</u>triks) LATIN [she who dominates, feminine of *dominator* he who dominates] *noun* (*plural* **dominatrices,** domi<u>na</u>triseez)   a woman who dominates her partner in sadomasochistic sex, or more generally a woman who is domineering in character.

domino (d<u>o</u>min<u>o</u>) SPANISH [from Latin *dominus* master] *noun* (*plural* **dominos** or **dominoes**)   a long hooded cloak, often with half mask, as worn at costume parties and masquerades: *"What does your blockhead father when he and Mrs. Rudge have laid their heads together, but goes there when he ought to be abed, makes interest with his friend the doorkeeper, slips him on a mask and domino, and mixes with the masquers"* (Charles Dickens, *Barnaby Rudge,* 1841).

Dominus vobiscum (dominăs v<u>o</u>biskăm) LATIN [the Lord with you] *noun phrase*   May the Lord be with you.

don (don) SPANISH [from Latin *dominus* master] *noun*   a Spanish nobleman or gentleman. Also used as a title for university professors in Britain and more widely applied to any person of consequence, including high-ranking members of the Mafia: *"The dons who rule the waterfront would never allow such interference from the unions in their murky affairs."*

doner kebab (dŏnăr kăbab, dōnăr kăbab) TURKISH [rotating kebab] *noun phrase* a Turkish dish comprising slices of meat cut from a large piece of lamb roasted on a rotating spit.

Don Juan (don wahn, don jooăn) SPANISH [after the legendary Spanish nobleman and rake Don Juan] *noun* a good-looking male who has a reputation as a libertine and seducer of women: *"Tales of his many sexual conquests appeared to confirm his reputaton as the Don Juan of the district."*

donnée (donay) FRENCH [given, feminine past participial adjective of *donner* to give] *noun* a given fact or basic assumption.

doppelgänger (dopălgangăr), **doppelganger** GERMAN [double-goer, from *doppel* double and *gänger* goer] *noun* a person's spectral double, also sometimes applied to a person who is strikingly similar in appearance to another individual: *"The stranger was so similar in appearance to the king that he might have been his doppelgänger."*

do-si-do (dō see dō), **do-se-do** FRENCH [from *dos-à-dos* back-to-back] *noun* a square dance sequence in which partners circle one another back-to-back.

dossier (dosyay, doseeay) FRENCH [bundle of documents, from *dos* back] *noun* a file of papers relating to a particular subject: *"The police officer looked through a whole dossier of evidence about the crimes."*

double entendre (dooblă ontondră) FRENCH [double meaning] *noun phrase* (*plural* **double entendres**) a word or phrase that can be interpreted as having more than one meaning, one of which is usually risqué in nature: *"This was greeted with an irreverent laugh, and the youth blushed deeply, and tried to look as if he had meant to insinuate what knowing people called a 'double entendre'"* (Edith Wharton, *The Age of Innocence*, 1920).

douche (doosh) FRENCH [from Italian *doccia*, from *doccia* water pipe] *noun* a jet of water or a device for producing a jet of water: *"He fixed a pail of water up in a tree, with a bit of ribbon fastened to the handle, and when Daisy, attracted by the gay streamer, tried to pull it down, she got a douche bath that spoiled her clean frock and hurt her little feelings very much"* (Louisa May Alcott, *Little Men*, 1871). ~*verb* to direct a jet of water at something.

dow See DHOW.

doyen (doiăn, dwayen) FRENCH [from Latin *decanus* dean, oldest member] *noun* a person with expert knowledge or unrivalled experience in a particular field and thus considered

117

senior to others in the same group or category of people. ~noun, feminine **doyenne** (doi<u>en</u>, dwa<u>yen</u>) a woman with particular knowledge or experience of a subject.

draconian (drăk<u>ō</u>neeăn), **Draconian** GREEK [after the authoritarian Athenian lawgiver Drakon, or Draco] *adjective* severe, harsh, cruel: *"Will the courts ever stop issuing draconian punishments for such petty crimes?"*

dragée (dra<u>zhay</u>) FRENCH [from Old French *dragie*, possibly from Latin *tragemata* sweetmeats] *noun* a sugarcoated nut or sweet with a hard sugar coating; also applied to sugarcoated pills containing drugs or medicine.

drama (<u>drah</u>mă) GREEK [deed, act, play, from *dan* to do] *noun* a stage play, or the theater as a whole; also applied more generally to any situation or event in which conflicting forces come into play: *"The drama unfolded in the full glare of national publicity."*

dramatis personae (dramătis pers<u>ō</u>nee, dramătis pers<u>ōn</u>ī) LATIN [characters of a drama] *noun phrase* the cast of a play or other public performance, or the characters in a novel, poem, or drama; also used more widely of the participants involved in any particular event: *"I am afraid we should get a good deal confused even in reading our Shakespeare if we did not look back now and then at the dramatis personae"* (Oliver Wendell Holmes, *Over the Teacups,* 1891).

dramaturge (<u>dram</u>ăterj), **dramaturg** (<u>dram</u>ăterg) GREEK [*dramatourgos* drama worker] *noun* a dramatist, a person with skills and experience of theatrical writing and techniques.

dressage (dră<u>sahzh</u>, dre<u>sahj</u>) FRENCH [dressing, preparing, from *dresser* to train] *noun* the practice of training horses to perform drill movements with minimal guidance by the rider, or a competition in which such skills are displayed and tested: *"The team came away with gold medals in the showjumping and dressage events."*

droit (droit, drwah) FRENCH [right, from neuter of Latin *directus* just, straight] *noun* a legal right or claim, or the law in general.

droit du seigneur (drwah due say<u>ny</u>-<u>oor</u>), **droit de seigneur** FRENCH [right of the lord] *noun phrase* the supposed right of a feudal lord to claim the virginity of his vassal's bride on her wedding night: *"She was a commoner, and had been sent here on her bridal night by Sir Breuse Sance Pite, a neighboring lord whose vassal her father was, and to which said lord she had refused what has since been called le droit du seigneur, and, moreover, had opposed violence to violence and spilt half a gill of his almost sacred blood"* (Mark Twain, *A Connecticut Yankee,* 1889).

D.S. *See* DAL SEGNO.

duce (<u>doo</u>chay), **Duce** ITALIAN [leader, title borne by Fascist dictator Benito Mussolini (1883–1945), from Latin *dux* leader] *noun* leader (generally used derogatively). See also FÜHRER.

duenna (doo<u>en</u>ă, dyoo<u>en</u>ă) SPANISH [governess, from Latin *domina* mistress] *noun* a Spanish or Portuguese governess, usually a woman of mature years who traditionally acted as chaperon to younger unmarried women: *"Well; what do you think my senior duenna did—the female one, I mean? She took my own carriage, and posted off after Mr. Palliser as hard as ever she could, leaving the male duenna on the watch"* (Anthony Trollope, *Can You Forgive Her?*, 1864).

duffle (<u>dŭ</u>făl), **duffel** DUTCH [after the town of Duffel, Belgium] *noun* a coarse woollen material used for making bags, coats, and other items ~*adjective* of or relating to garments made of such material: *"The captain arrived on the bridge in a blue duffle coat and steel helmet."*

dulce et decorum est (dŭlchay et de<u>kor</u>ăm est) LATIN [abbreviated form of *dulce et decorum est pro patria mori* it is sweet and fitting to die for one's country, from the *Odes* of the Greek poet Horace (65–8 B.C.)] *noun phrase* it is right and proper to die for one's own country: *"Sacred to the memory of George Osborne, Junior, Esq., late a Captain in his Majesty's—the regiment of foot, who fell on the 18th of June, 1815, aged 28 years, while fighting for his king and country in the glorious victory of Waterloo. Dulce et decorum est pro patria mori"* (William Makepeace Thackeray, *Vanity Fair*, 1847–48).

duma (<u>doo</u>mă), **douma** RUSSIAN [council] *noun* the lower house of the postcommunist Russian legislature (formerly the national legislature in prerevolutionary Russia).

dumdum (<u>dăm</u>dăm), **dum dum** HINDI [after the arsenal in the town of Dum Dum, near Calcutta, India] *noun* a type of hollow-nosed bullet that expands explosively on hitting its target, with devastating effect: *"The dumdum bullets used by the rebels inflicted serious wounds upon government troops."*

dummkopf (<u>dăm</u>kopf) GERMAN [dumb head, from *dumm* stupid and *Kopf* head] *noun* a blockhead, stupid person, idiot.

dungarees (dăngă<u>reez</u>) HINDI [from *dugri*] *plural noun* a set of working overalls made from coarse hard-wearing denim fabric: *"Most of the workers wear dungarees and broad-brimmed hats when toiling in the fields."*

duomo (<u>dwō</u>mō) ITALIAN [dome, from Latin *domus* house] *noun* (*plural* **duomos** or **duomi**, <u>dwō</u>mee) an Italian cathedral: *"Even in our own day a Milanese merchant could leave five hundred thousand francs to the Duomo, to regild the colossal statue of the Virgin that* *crowns the edifice"* (Honoré de Balzac, *Cousin Bette,* 1846).

duplex (<u>doo</u>pleks) LATIN [twofold] *noun* an apartment with rooms on two floors, or otherwise divided into two separate parts: *"His brother lives in a luxurious duplex with commanding views of the city." ~adjective* twofold, double, having two parts.

durbar (<u>der</u>bahr) HINDI [from *darbar* court, from Persian *dar* door and *bar* audience] *noun* a formal reception or court held in the presence of royalty: *"The ambassador presented his new attaché to the prince at a durbar the following week."*

duvet (d(y)oo<u>vay</u>, <u>d(y)oo</u>vay) FRENCH [down] *noun* a thick quilt used as a bed covering instead of blankets and sheets: *"She pulled the duvet up over her head and told him she intended to stay in bed all day."*

D.V. *See* DEO VOLENTE.

dybbuk (<u>di</u>băk), **dibbuk** YIDDISH [from Hebrew *dibbuq* ghost, from *dabaq* to cling] *noun* (*plural* **dybbuks, dibbuks, dybbukim** or **dibukkim,** dibă<u>keem</u>) in Jewish mythology, a malevolent wandering spirit that seeks to possess living mortals and can only be driven out by exorcism.

e

easel (<u>ee</u>zăl) DUTCH [from *ezel* ass, from Latin *asinus* ass] *noun*   a three-legged frame for supporting an artist's canvas or blackboard: "*More than a dozen artists worked at easels in the studio.*"

eau de Cologne (ō dă kă<u>lōn</u>), **eau-de-Cologne** FRENCH [water of Cologne, after Cologne, Germany] *noun phrase* (*plural* **eaux de Cologne,** ō dă kă<u>lōn</u>, ōz dă kă<u>lōn</u>)   a scented perfume first manufactured at Cologne, Germany: "*He doused himself liberally in eau de Cologne and admired himself in the mirror.*" ~*shortened form* **cologne.**

eau de Nil (ō dă <u>neel</u>), **eau-de-Nil** FRENCH [water of the Nile] *noun phrase*   a pale green color: "*Her face had turned the same hue of eau-de-Nil as her dress.*"

eau de toilette (ō dă twah<u>let</u>) FRENCH [toilet water] *noun phrase*   a lightly scented perfume.

eau de vie (ō dă <u>vee</u>), **eau-de-vie** FRENCH [water of life, after Latin *aqua vitae*] *noun phrase* (*plural* **eaux de vie,** ō dă <u>vee</u>, ōz dă <u>vee</u>)   a clear brandy distilled from fermented fruit juice: "*He kindles this heap in a twinkling, and produces a jorum of hot brandy and water; for that bottle of his keeps company with the seasons, and now holds nothing but the purest eau de vie*" (Charles Dickens, *Pictures from Italy,* 1846).

ecce homo (echee, eksee <u>hō</u>mō) LATIN [see the person] *interjection*   behold the man. ~*noun phrase* a depiction of Jesus wearing a crown of thorns (recalling the words spoken to the crowd by Pontius Pilate when Jesus was brought before him): "*The party took note of the sacred spot, and moved on. We passed under the 'Ecce Homo Arch,' and saw the very window from which Pilate's wife warned her husband to have nothing to do with the persecution of the Just Man*" (Mark Twain, *The Innocents Abroad,* 1869).

ecce signum (ekee <u>sig</u>năm) LATIN [see the sign] *interjection*   behold the sign (or proof).

echelon (<u>esh</u>ălon(g), <u>ech</u>ălon(g)), **échelon** FRENCH [rung of a ladder, from *échelle* ladder] *noun* a military formation in which units are staggered in a series of steps, or, more generally, any step, level, or grade, or the individuals who have attained that grade: *"After years in the junior post, she eventually made her way into the upper echelons of the organization."*

echt (ekt) GERMAN [genuine] *adjective* genuine, authentic, pure.

éclair (ay<u>klair</u>, e<u>klair</u>, i<u>klair</u>) FRENCH [lightning] *noun* a pastry filled with whipped cream or custard and topped with icing: *"He resolutely refused to consider adopting any diet that precluded consumption of chocolate éclairs."*

éclat (ay<u>kla</u>) FRENCH [splinter, burst, from *éclater* to burst out] *noun* brilliant success, radiance, splendor, a dazzling effect, acclaim, or an ostentatious or pompous display: *"The distressing explanation she had to make to Harriet, and all that poor Harriet would be suffering, with the awkwardness of future meetings, the difficulties of continuing or discontinuing the acquaintance, of subduing feelings, concealing resentment, and avoiding éclat, were enough to occupy her in most unmirthful reflections some time longer. . ."* (Jane Austen, *Emma*, 1816).

ecru (<u>ay</u>kroo, <u>e</u>kroo), **écru** FRENCH [raw, unbleached] *noun* a light brown, unbleached color. ~*adjective* unbleached, beige in color.

editio princeps (ayditeeō <u>prin</u>keps, idisheeō <u>prin</u>seps) LATIN [first edition] *noun phrase* (*plural* **editiones principes,** ayditeeōnăs <u>prin</u>kăpăs, idisheeōneez <u>prin</u>săpăs) the first printed edition of a literary work previously known only in manuscript form: *"He had the scent of a slowhound, sir, and the snap of a bull-dog. He would detect you an old black-letter ballad among the leaves of a law-paper, and find an editio princeps under the mask of a school Corderius"* (Walter Scott, *The Antiquary,* 1816). ~*abbreviated form* **E.P., e.p.**

effendi (e<u>fen</u>dee) TURKISH [master, from Greek *authentes* lord, master] *noun* a title of respect reserved for men of authority, education, or property in Arab or eastern Mediterranean cultures: *"The shopkeeper eyed the stranger suspiciously. 'Can I be of service, effendi?' he inquired in a hostile tone."*

effluvium (e<u>floo</u>veeăm) LATIN [a flowing out] *noun* (*plural* **effluviums** or **effluvia,** e<u>floo</u>veeă) an outflowing of some kind, especially of evil-smelling waste material.

e.g. *See* EXEMPLI GRATIA.

ego (<u>ee</u>gō, <u>e</u>gō) LATIN [I] *noun* (*plural* **egos**) the self or self-respect, self-esteem, egotism, arrogance: *"His father's ego had been bruised by the encounter, and no words passed between them all the way home."*

eidolon (īdōlǎn) GREEK [phantom, idea] *noun* (*plural* **eidolons** or **eidola,** īdōlǎ) an insubstantial image, or ideal.

eisteddfod (īstedfod) WELSH [session, from *eistedd* to sit and *bod* being] *noun* (*plural* **eisteddfods** or **eisteddfodau,** īstedfodī) a competitive Welsh festival of the arts: *"This year's eisteddfod includes appearances by many performers from beyond Welsh borders."*

élan (aylahn, elan) FRENCH [outburst, impetus, from *élancer* to hurl, rush forth] *noun* enthusiasm, spirit, vivacity, zest.

élan vital (aylahn veetahl) FRENCH [vital spirit] *noun phrase* the life force, the creative principle, motivating power.

El Dorado (el dǎrahdō), **Eldorado** SPANISH [the gilded one, after the fabled city of gold sought by 16th-century Spanish conquistadores in South America] *noun* a place where fabulous wealth or opportunity is reputed to be found: *"The town has become a real El Dorado for those seeking peace and quiet in an exotic setting."*

elite (ayleet, eleet), **élite** FRENCH [choice, pick, past participle of *élire* to choose] *noun* the choice, the cream, or the best part of something, often referring to the most select persons in society: *"Many people still think that England is run by a small, privileged elite."*

elixir (eliksǎr) ARABIC [*al-iksir,* probably from Greek *xerion* drying powder] *noun* a medicinal preparation, formerly one alleged to have the power to cure all ills, to bestow the gift of everlasting life, or to have the power of turning base metal into gold: *"As, put the case, / That some great Man, in state, he have the Gout, / Why you but send three droppes of your Elixir, / You help him straight: There you have made a Friend"* (Ben Jonson, *The Alchemist,* 1610).

ellipsis (ilipsis) GREEK [omission, from *elleipsis* ellipse, from *elleipein* to leave out] *noun* (*plural* **ellipses,** ilipseez) a series of dots, asterisks, or other marks indicating the omission of one or more words in a piece of writing, a pause, or a sudden change in topic; such an omission.

El Niño (el neenyō), **el Niño** SPANISH [the Christ child, referring to the coincidence of the phenomenon with the Christmas period] *noun phrase* (*plural* **El Niños,** el neenyōz) a southward flow of warm surface water that occurs periodically in the east Pacific, exerting a profound influence upon world weather patterns and ecology. Also, **La Niña,** a climactic fluctuation in the equatorial pacific that results in cooler water than usual off of coastal Peru and Ecuador: *"Scientists have tentatively blamed the rise in rainfall upon the climactic changes resulting from El Niño."*

Elysium (ilizeeăm) GREEK [from *Elysion pedion* plain, field] *noun* (*plural* **Elysiums** or **Elysia**, ilizeeă) the paradise where the dead dwell according to Greek and Roman mythology; by extension, any place or state of contentment: *"I suppose this Halifax would have appeared an Elysium, though it had been a curiosity of ugly dullness"* (Charles Dickens, *American Notes*, 1842). ~*adjective* **Elysian** (ilizeeăn) of or relating to Elysium, or anything blissful or delightful.

embargo (embahrgō, imbahrgō) SPANISH [attachment, arrest, from *embargar* to bar, to restrain] *noun* (*plural* **embargoes**, embahrgōz, imbahrgōz) a prohibition or impediment to something, especially an official order preventing commercial contacts with a particular state: *"The company is accused of trying to break the oil embargo."* ~*verb* to impose an embargo, thus preventing commercial activity or transportation.

embarras de choix (ombara dă shwa) FRENCH [embarrassment of choice] *noun phrase* a bewildering variety of options, too much to choose from.

embarras de richesse (ombara dă reeshes) FRENCH [embarrassment of wealth] *noun phrase* (*plural* **embarras de richesses**) an embarrassment of riches, an overabundance of wealth, information, opportunities, or resources.

embonpoint (om(g)bon(g)pwan(g)) FRENCH [from *en bon point* in good condition] *noun* plumpness, stoutness (often referring to a woman). ~*adjective* plump, stout.

embouchure (ombooshoor) FRENCH [from *s'emboucher* to put into the mouth, discharge by mouth] *noun* the position of a musician's mouth and lips and tongue in playing a wind instrument; also refers to the mouthpiece of a wind instrument: *"The child needs to practice her embouchure if she is to progress further on the clarinet."*

embourgeoisement (emboorzhwahz-mănt) FRENCH [from *embourgeoiser* to make bourgeois] *noun* the adoption of bourgeois values, interests, or opinions: *"The old man shook his head sadly, regretting the embourgeoisement of his children's generation."*

embrasure (imbrayzhă, embrayzhă) FRENCH [from *embraser* to widen an opening] *noun* an opening in a wall or parapet for the firing of cannon, or more generally a recess for a door or window: *"She sat with him in the adjoining room, in the embrasure of the window, for the rest of the evening"* (Henry James, *Daisy Miller*, 1879).

embroglio *See* IMBROGLIO.

emeritus (imerităs) LATIN [well-deserved, past participle of *emereri* to deserve] *adjective* of or relating to an honorary title retained after retirement: *"Unlike most of his contemporaries, he refused to use the honorary title of professor emeritus except when undertaking public speaking engagements."* ~noun (plural **emeriti,** i̱meritee, i̱meritī) a person who after retirement retains an honorary title equivalent to that held during his or her working life. ~noun, feminine **emerita** (e̱merită).

émigré (e̱migray), **emigré** FRENCH [past participle of émigrer to emigrate] noun an emigrant, a person obliged to live in exile: *"The émigrés gather in the same bar most evenings to exchange nostalgic memories of the old country."* ~noun, feminine **émigrée, emigrée.** ~adjective of or relating to an émigré or a life in exile.

éminence grise (emănons greez) FRENCH [gray eminence, after the nickname of Cardinal Richelieu's confederate Père Joseph François du Tremblay (1577–1638)] noun (plural **éminences grises**) a confidential agent who exerts enormous influence behind the scenes without holding any official position: *"For years the wily old man had acted as a sort of éminence grise, pulling strings and bending ears on behalf of the president."*

emir (e̱meer, ay̱meer) ARABIC [amir commander] noun a ruler, lord, or commander in an Islamic country.

emporium (impo̱reeăm, empo̱reeăm) GREEK [emporion place of trade, mar-

ket] noun (plural **emporiums** or **emporia,** impo̱reeă, empo̱reeă) a commercial center or store, a retail outlet: *"San Francisco was no longer the legendary city of 1849—a city of banditti, assassins, and incendiaries, who had flocked hither in crowds in pursuit of plunder; a paradise of outlaws, where they gambled with gold-dust, a revolver in one hand and a bowie-knife in the other: it was now a great commercial emporium"* (Jules Verne, *Around the World in 80 Days,* 1873).

en avant (on avo̱n(g)) FRENCH [in advance] interjection phrase forward, onward: *"The officers ordered the company forward with shouts of 'en avant!' and much brandishing of swords."*

en banc (on bo̱n(g)) FRENCH [on the bench] adverb phrase in full court. ~adjective phrase in full court.

en bloc (on blok) FRENCH [in a block] adverb phrase all together, collectively, as a body: *"The estate of Silas Deemer being in the hands of an administrator who had thought it best to dispose of the 'business,' the store had been closed ever since the owner's death, the goods having been removed by another 'merchant' who had purchased them en bloc"* (Ambrose Bierce, *Can Such Things Be?*). ~adjective phrase made or done as one, all together.

en brochette (on bro̱shet) FRENCH [on a skewer] adjective phrase cooked on a skewer.

enceinte (on<u>sant</u>) FRENCH [pregnant, from Latin *inciens* being with young, from Greek *enkyos* pregnant] *adjective* pregnant: *"I mean that M. de Nargonne, your first husband, being neither a philosopher nor a banker, or perhaps being both, and seeing there was nothing to be got out of a king's attorney, died of grief or anger at finding, after an absence of nine months, that you had been enceinte six"* (Alexandre Dumas, *The Count of Monte Cristo, 1844–45*).

enchanté (onshon<u>tay</u>) FRENCH [enchanted, past participle of *enchanter* to charm, to enchant, from Latin *incantare* to chant a magic formula against] *verb* charmed, enchanted, delighted (usually in response when being introduced to someone).

enchilada (ench<u>ă</u><u>lah</u>d<u>ă</u>) SPANISH [feminine of *enchilado,* past participle of *enchilar* to season with chili] *noun* a filled tortilla rolled and baked with chili sauce.

en clair (on <u>klair</u>) FRENCH [in clear] *adverb phrase* in plain language, clearly. ~*adjective phrase* clear, unambiguous.

enclave (<u>on</u>klayv) FRENCH [enclosure, from *enclaver* to enclose] *noun* a region, area, or community that is entirely enclosed within foreign territory or otherwise alien surroundings: *"The hotel provided an enclave for the expatriate community."*

encomium (enk<u>ō</u>meeăm) GREEK [*enkomion* eulogy, panegyric] *noun* (*plural* **encomiums** or **encomia,** enk<u>o</u>meeă) an expression of praise, a eulogy: *"'This part was raised by order of the first of the Seleucidae. Three hundred years have made it part of the rock it rests upon.' The defence justified the encomium. High, solid, and with many bold angles, it curved southwardly out of view"* (Law Wallace, *Ben Hur,* 1880).

encore (<u>on</u>kor) FRENCH [again, once more, possibly from Latin *hanc horam* within this hour] *interjection* again! (in requesting that a performance be repeated). ~*noun* a request by an audience for a performance of some kind to be repeated, or the repeated performance itself; a request for the performers to follow up with a performance of an additional (usually brief) work. *"No doubt he had applauded for an 'encore' when he danced with Ella Dowling, gave Ella the same genial look, and said, 'That's splendid!' When the 'encore' was over, Alice spoke to him for the first time"* (Booth Tarkington, *Alice Adams,* 1921). ~*verb* to repeat a performance, or request that it be repeated.

en croûte (on <u>kroot</u>) FRENCH [in crust] *adverb phrase* cooked in. ~*adjective phrase* cooked in pastry: *"The next item on the menu was boeuf en croûte, beautifully presented surrounded with glazed vegetables."*

en famille (on fa<u>mee</u>) FRENCH [in family] *adverb phrase* at home, with one's family, informally: *"I always call her Henny, en famille, and I look upon you as almost one of us since our travels"* (James Fenimore Cooper, *Autobiography of a Pocket-Handkerchief,* 1843).

enfant terrible (onfon(g) tăreeb, onfon(g) tăreeblă) FRENCH [terrible child] *noun phrase (plural* **enfants terribles**) an unruly child or a person who is known for unorthodox or outrageous behavior, often applied to avant-garde figures in the arts world: *"'Am I worse than other people, or better? I think I'm worse.' 'Enfant terrible, enfant terrible!' repeated Betsy"* (Leo Tolstoy, *Anna Karenina,* 1874–76).

enfant trouvé (onfon(g) troovay) FRENCH [found child] *noun phrase (plural* **enfants trouvés**) an abandoned child with unknown parents, a foundling.

en fête (on fet) FRENCH [in festival] *adjective phrase* in a festive mood or holiday spirit, or wearing gala attire.

enfilade (enfălayd) FRENCH [from *enfiler* to thread on a string] *noun* in military jargon, a position offering command over the entire length of a line, or gunfire directed from such a position: *"As soon as the first line left the trenches it was subjected to an enfilade from the right flank."* ~*verb* to rake the entire length of a line of troops with gunfire.

engagé (ongazhay) FRENCH [engaged, past participle of *engager* to engage]

adjective committed (to a political cause, for example).

en garde (on gard) FRENCH [on guard] beware, watch out! (traditionally used as a challenge in fencing): *"The two rivals raised their blades and with challenges of 'en garde' circled one another warily."*

enigma (enigmă) GREEK [*ainigma,* from *ainos* fable] *noun (plural* **enigmas** or **enigmata,** enigmahtă) a mystery or puzzle, something or someone considered difficult to understand: *"She had drawn lines in the shape of a cross over the sphinx and sent him a message to say that the solution of the enigma was the cross"* (Ivan Turgenev, *Fathers and Sons,* 1862).

en masse (on mas) FRENCH [in a mass] *adverb phrase* in a body, as a whole, as one, collectively: *"Then the March family turned out en masse, and Jo exerted herself to some purpose, for people not only came, but stayed, laughing at her nonsense, admiring Amy's taste, and apparently enjoying themselves very much"* (Louisa May Alcott, *Little Women,* 1868–69).

ennui (onwee) FRENCH [annoyance, from Latin *in odio,* from *mihi in odio est* it is hateful to me] *noun (plural* **ennuis**) boredom, tedium, listlessness: *"She threw down the book and surrendered herself to the ennui that had been threatening her all morning."* ~*adjective* **ennuyant** (onweeon) FRENCH [boring, present participle of *ennuyer* to bore] boring.

Enosis (in̄ōsis) GREEK [from *henosis* union, from *henoun* to unite] *noun* a political movement seeking the union of Greece and Cyprus.

en papillote See PAPILLOTE.

en passant (on pa<u>son</u>(g)) FRENCH [in passing] *adverb phrase* in passing, incidentally, by the way: *"We merely suggest, en passant, that some of our best citizens might deem it a wonderful and beauteous thing if, in addition to paying the fine, Mr. Louden could serve for the loyal Happy his six months in the Bastile!"* (Booth Tarkington, *Conquest of Canaan*, 1905).

en pension (on <u>pon</u>syon(g), on <u>pon</u>shon(g)) FRENCH [in board and lodging] *adverb phrase* living in lodgings or as a boarder. ~*adjective phrase* living in lodgings or as a boarder.

en plein air (on plan <u>air</u>) FRENCH [in full air] *adverb phrase* in the open air.

enragé (on<u>ra</u>zhay) FRENCH [enraged, mad, past participle of *enrager* to enrage] *noun* a fanatic or enthusiast.

en rapport (on ra<u>por</u>) FRENCH [in connection, in contact] *adjective phrase* in harmony, in agreement: *"It would appear that the negotiators are now en rapport about the future course of the project."*

en route (on <u>root</u>) FRENCH [on the way] *adverb phrase* on the way, along the way, in transit: *"The documents are en route and will be with you by tomorrow."* ~*adjective phrase* on the way, along the way, in transit.

ensemble (on<u>som</u>băl) FRENCH [together, from Latin *insimul* at the same time] *noun* a group (of musicians, actors, or performers) working as a whole to produce a single effect; also applied to parts of machinery and sets of clothing: *"The whole ensemble was topped off with a jaunty little cloche hat with a yellow feather stuck in it."*

en suite (on <u>sweet</u>) FRENCH [in succession] *adverb phrase* in a series, in succession, in a row, or connected, leading to another, or part of a matching set. ~*adjective phrase* in a series, in succession, or connected, leading to another, or part of a matching set: *"They want to reserve a bedroom with an en suite bathroom."*

entente (on<u>tont</u>) FRENCH [arrangement, understanding] *noun* an agreement or understanding between nations on a common course of action.

entente cordiale (ontont kordee<u>al</u>) FRENCH [cordial understanding, hearty agreement] *noun phrase* (*plural* **ententes cordiales**) a cordial or friendly agreement or working relationship, especially between governments: *"The entente cordiale between*

Britain and France in 1904 formed the basis of Anglo-French cooperation in World War I."

entourage (ontoo<u>rahzh</u>, <u>on</u>toorahzh) FRENCH [circle of friends, from *entourer* to surround] *noun* a person's retinue, attendants, or associates, or more rarely a person's surroundings or environment: "*The queen arrived with her entourage around midnight.*"

entr'acte (<u>on</u>trakt) FRENCH [between the acts, from *entre* between and *acte* act] *noun* an interval during a play, or a dance or piece of music played during such an interval: "*A trio of fiddlers entertained the audience during the entr'acte.*"

en train (on <u>tran(g)</u>) FRENCH [in train] *adverb phrase* in train, under way, afoot.

en travesti (on <u>tra</u>vestee) FRENCH [in travesty] *adverb phrase* wearing the clothes of the opposite sex: "*As an actor he was always being asked to perform en travesti, usually in light comedy and revue.*"

entrechat (<u>on</u>trăshah) FRENCH [from Italian *capriola intrecciata* complicated caper] *noun* in ballet, a leap during which a dancer strikes the heels together or crosses the legs several times in quick succession.

entrecôte (<u>on</u>trăkot), **entrecote** FRENCH [between rib] *noun* a sirloin steak cut from between the ribs:

"*The minister dined off an entrecote steak, washed down with a bottle of good red wine.*"

entrée (<u>on</u>tray, on<u>tray</u>), **entree** FRENCH [entrance] *noun* an entrance, or permission to enter; alternatively, the first part of a piece of music or public performance: "*The old woman racked her brains trying to decide which connection she should exploit to secure the best entrée into society for her young niece.*" Also refers to the main course of a meal (originally a dish served between the fish course and the main meat course).

entremets (ontră<u>mayz</u>, <u>on</u>trămayz) FRENCH [between-dish, from Latin *intermissus,* past participle of *intermittere* to intermit] *plural noun* a side dish, a dish served between the main courses of a meal (sometimes referring to the dessert).

entre nous (ontră <u>noo</u>) FRENCH [between us] *adverb phrase* between ourselves, in confidence: "*His answer was, 'I have given out that she is to sail on Saturday next; but I may let you know, entre nous, that if you are there by Monday morning, you will be in time, but do not delay longer'*" (Benjamin Franklin, *Autobiography,* 1793).

entrepôt (<u>on</u>trăpō) FRENCH [warehouse, from *entreposer* to put between, to store] *noun* a storehouse or an intermediate port or staging post for trade, where goods for import and export may be stored temporarily: *"The great trade of Rouen and Bordeaux seems to be altogether the effect of their situation. Rouen is necessarily the entrepot of almost all the goods which are brought either from foreign countries, or from the maritime provinces of France, for the consumption of the great city of Paris"* (Adam Smith, *Wealth of Nations,* 1776).

entrepreneur (ontrăprăner) FRENCH [from *entreprendre* to undertake] *noun* a person who pursues an independent course in business, typically setting up and running his or her own projects or companies: *"He was a bold entrepreneur who enjoyed arranging profitable business deals."*

entrez (ontray) FRENCH [you enter] *verb* enter (in response to a knock on the door etc.): *"Next day at ten o'clock Levin, who had already gone his rounds, knocked at the room where Vassenka had been put for the night. 'Entrez!' Veslovsky called to him"* (Leo Tolstoy, *Anna Karenina,* 1874–76).

environs (envīrănz, envīărănz) FRENCH [area, vicinity, plural of *environ* surrounding] *plural noun* the immediate vicinity or neighborhood, often referring to the outlying areas of an urban district: *"The unsalubrious environs did little to encourage patrons to venture out to the restaurant."*

envoi (envoi), **envoy** FRENCH [message, from *envoyer* to send] *noun* the concluding words or section of a piece of poetry or other writing, often a commendation or dedication from the author.

en voyage (on voyahzh) FRENCH [on a journey] *adverb phrase* while traveling: *"The lamps are lighted up all of a sudden. The music plays the old air from John of Paris, Ah quel plaisir d'etre en voyage"* (William Makepeace Thackeray, *Vanity Fair,* 1847).

eo nomine (eeō nominee) LATIN [by that name, ablative of *id nomen* that name] *adverb phrase* by or under that name, in that name.

E.p., e.p. *See* EDITIO PRINCEPS.

épater les bourgeois (aypatay lay borzhwa) FRENCH [to amaze the bourgeois, attributed to Alexandre Private d'Anglemont (d. 1859)] *adverb phrase* in order to shock conventional society: *"You refer to things not generally known by your readers without explanation—a thing which inferior people do to 'épater les bourgeois'"* (Oliver Wendell Holmes, *Letters*).

epaulette (epălet, epălet), **epaulet** FRENCH [from *épaulette,* from *épaule* shoulder, ultimately from Latin *spatula* spoon (after the shape)] *noun* an ornamental shoulder piece commonly attached to military uniforms, ranging from a simple loop or tab to a more elaborate trimming indicating the rank of officer: *"As a major he wore a smart scarlet uniform with gold epaulettes."*

épée (epay, aypay) FRENCH [from Latin *spatha* spoon, sword] *noun* a fencing or duelling sword with a triangular blade having a sharp point but no cutting edge: *"He picked up the fallen épée and found that there was blood on the point."*

ephemera (efemără) GREEK [plural of *ephemeron* on a day] *noun* (*plural* **ephemeras** or **ephemerae,** efemăree) something of transitory nature or significance; also applied to collections of everyday printed or written items (such as tickets or posters) that were never intended to last beyond their immediate use: *"He had a vast collection of railroad travel ephemera."*

epithalamium (epăthălaymeeăm) GREEK [*epithalamion* bridal chamber] *noun* (*plural* **epithalamiums** or **epithalamia,** epăthălaymeeă) a song or poem written in celebration of a wedding.

epitome (epitămee) GREEK [*epitemnein* to cut short] *noun* a summary or abstract of a written document, or the embodiment of something: *"Thus Uncle Venner was a miscellaneous old gentleman, partly himself, but, in good measure, somebody else; patched together, too, of different epochs; an epitome of times and fashions"* (Nathaniel Hawthorne, *The House of the Seven Gables,* 1851).

e pluribus unum (ay ploorăbăs oonăm) LATIN [out of many, one] *noun phrase* one out of many (motto of the United States of America): *"The more you examine the structure of the organs and the laws of life, the more you will find how resolutely each of the cell-republics which make up the E pluribus unum of the body maintains its independence"* (Oliver Wendell Holmes, *Medical Essays,* 1883).

ergo (ergō) LATIN [therefore] *adverb* therefore, hence, consequently: *". . .he that loves my / flesh and blood is my friend: ergo, he that kisses / my wife is my friend"* (William Shakespeare, *All's Well that Ends Well,* c. 1602).

Eros (eeăros) GREEK [after Eros, the Greek god of love, from *eros* sexual love] *noun* sexual desire, the personification of erotic enjoyment; also used to refer to the sexual urge.

erotica (erotikă) GREEK [*erotika*] *noun* works of art, literature, and other media that depict sexual love: *"His collection of erotica was much admired by his friends."*

errare humanum est (erahree hoomahnăm est) LATIN [to err is human] *noun phrase* it is only human to make mistakes: *"In short, doctor, although I know you to be the most conscientious man in the world, and although I place the utmost reliance in you, I want, notwithstanding my conviction, to believe this axiom, errare humanum est"* (Alexandre Dumas, *The Count of Monte Cristo,* 1844).

erratum (e<u>rah</u>tăm) LATIN [from *erratus,* neuter past participle of *errare* to err] *noun* (*plural* **errata,** e<u>rah</u>tă) an error, a mistake (especially in a printed or written work; also, a printed list identifying such errors and giving their corrections): *"I wrote him an ingenuous letter of acknowledgment, crav'd his forbearance a little longer, which he allow'd me, and as soon as I was able, I paid the principal with interest, and many thanks; so that erratum was in some degree corrected"* (Benjamin Franklin, *Autobiography,* 1793).

ersatz (<u>er</u>sats, er<u>zats</u>) GERMAN [from *Ersatz* substitute, replacement] *noun* a substitute or inferior imitation. ~*adjective* substitute, imitation, fake, inferior: *"He grimaced as he swallowed a mouthful of gray ersatz coffee, then put the cup down."*

escargot (es<u>kah</u>gō) FRENCH [snail, from Provençal *escaragol*] *noun* an edible snail.

escritoire (eskră<u>twah</u>) FRENCH [writing desk, from Latin *scriptorium*] *noun* a writing table, writing desk, or bureau: *"The note arriving at maturity, the diddler, with the diddler's dog, calls upon the friend, and the promise to pay is made the topic of discussion. The friend produces it from his escritoire, and is in the act of reaching it to the diddler, when up jumps the diddler's dog and devours it forthwith"* (Edgar Allan Poe, "The Devil in the Belfry," 1839).

esophagus (ī<u>so</u>făgăs), **oesophagus** GREEK [from *oisophagos,* from *oisein* to be going to carry and *phagein* to eat] *noun* (*plural* **esophagi** ī<u>so</u>făgī, ī<u>so</u>făjī) the canal leading from the mouth to the stomach; the gullet.

esoterica (eesō<u>te</u>rikă) GREEK [from *esoterika* inner things] *noun* mysterious or arcane items reserved for inspection by a select few; often referring specifically to pornographic writings: *"The rest of the shelves were filled with volumes of esoterica, ranging from diaries to bestselling blockbusters."*

espadrille (<u>es</u>pădril, es<u>pă</u><u>dril</u>) FRENCH [from Provençal *espardilhos,* ultimately from Greek *sparton* rope] *noun* a type of sandal with a canvas upper and a flexible rope sole: *"The sailors wore espadrilles and barely made a sound as they ran about the decks."*

esplanade (<u>es</u>plănayd, esplă<u>nayd</u>) FRENCH [level space, from Italian *spianare* to level] *noun* a stretch of level ground suitable for walkers, usually running alongside a shore, river, or road: *"Rearward of the structure which graced the entrance-way—a purely Grecian pile—he stood upon a broad esplanade paved with polished stone. . ."* (Lew Wallace, *Ben Hur,* 1880).

espressivo (espre<u>see</u>vō, es<u>pre</u>sivō) ITALIAN [expressive, from Latin *exprimere* to express] *adverb* in music, an instruction for a passage to be played with expression. ~*adjective* in music, expressive.

espresso (espresō) ITALIAN [from *caffè espresso* pressed out coffee, squeezed coffee] *noun* strong coffee brewed by forcing steam or boiling water through ground coffee beans: *"The woman chose a seat near the door and ordered an espresso from one of the waiters."* ~*adjective* of or relating to such coffee, or a place where such coffee is served.

esprit (espree) FRENCH [spirit, from Latin *spiritus* spirit] *noun* liveliness of wit or vivacity, sprightliness, zest: *"The interviewers are usually impervious to such demonstrations of charm and esprit."*

esprit de corps (espree de kor) FRENCH [spirit of body] *noun phrase* team spirit, public spirit, the enthusiasm, devotion, or sense of honor shared by the members of a particular group or organization: *"It's not that I don't approve of the Mingotts' esprit de corps; but why Newland's engagement should be mixed up with that Olenska woman's comings and goings I don't see,"* Mrs. Archer grumbled to Janey, the only witness of her slight lapses from perfect sweetness" (Edith Wharton, *The Age of Innocence,* 1920).

esprit de l'escalier (espree dă leskalyay), **esprit d'escalier** FRENCH [wit of the stair, attributed to the French philosopher Denis Diderot (1713–84)] *noun phrase* a clever or witty rejoinder that a person thinks of only after the opportunity for it has passed.

esse (esee) LATIN [being, from *esse* to be] *noun* in philosophy, the essential being or essence of someone or something.

estaminet (estaminay) FRENCH [from Walloon *staminé* byre] *noun* a small café, bistro, or bar: *"'There's not much to do here, by way of amusement,' said the Major. 'A movie show tonight, and you can get anything you want at the estaminet,— the one on the square, opposite the English tank, is the best'"* (Willa Cather, *One of Ours,* 1922).

estrus (estrăs), **oestrus** (eestrăs) GREEK [*oistros* gadfly, frenzy] *noun* a period during the monthly cycle in female mammals marking the point when they will most readily accept mates and are most likely to conceive; heat; the rut: *"The dog should come into estrus within a few days."*

et al. See ET ALIBI; ET ALII.

et alibi (et alăbī) LATIN [and elsewhere] *adverb phrase* and elsewhere (used in bibliographical references). ~*abbreviated form* **et al.**

et alii (et aleeī), **et alia** (et aleeă) LATIN [and others] *adverb phrase* and others. ~*abbreviated form* **et al.**

et cetera (et setără, et setră) LATIN [and others] *adverb phrase* and the rest, and so on, and so forth: *"To him, Patroclus; tell him I humbly desire the / valiant Ajax to invite the most valorous Hector / to come unarmed to my tent, and to procure / safe-conduct for his person of the magnanimous / and most illustrious six-or-seven-times-honored / captain-general of the Grecian army, Agamemnon, / et cetera"* (William Shakespeare, *Troilus and Cressida,* c. 1601). ~*noun phrase* (*plural* **etceteras**) odds and ends, sundries, extras. ~*abbreviated form* **etc.**

ethos (<u>ee</u>thos) GREEK [custom, character] *noun* the character, nature, values, or beliefs of an individual, group, region, or age: *"Virtue, then, being of two kinds, intellectual and moral, intellectual virtue in the main owes both its birth and its growth to teaching (for which reason it requires experience and time), while moral virtue comes about as a result of habit, whence also its name (ethike) is one that is formed by a slight variation from the word ethos (habit)"* (Aristotle, *Nicomachean Ethics,* fourth century B.C.).

etiquette (<u>e</u>tiket, <u>e</u>tikăt) FRENCH [from *étiquette* ticket, label] *noun* the rules of personal conduct that individuals are expected to observe in polite society or in ceremonial circumstances: *". . .the few gun-room officers there at the time had, in due observance of naval etiquette, withdrawn to leeward the moment Captain Vere had begun his promenade on the deck's weather-side. . ."* (Herman Melville, *Billy Budd,* 1924).

et sequens (et <u>sek</u>wenz) LATIN [abbreviation of *et sequentes* and the following one] *noun phrase* and the following (in bibliographical references, etc.). ~*abbreviated form* **et seq.** (*plural* **et seqq.** or **et sqq.**).

et tu, Brute? (et <u>too</u> brootay) LATIN [and you, Brutus?, from the accusation reputedly leveled by the dying Julius Caesar against his friend Brutus after the latter revealed himself as one of the conspirators involved in Caesar's assassination] *interjection* you also, Brutus? (an accusation of betrayal leveled against a friend suspected of betraying the speaker, usually spoken in jest).

étude (ayt(y)<u>oo</u>d), **etude** FRENCH [study] *noun* a musical composition written or played as a technical exercise or for the sake of displaying virtuosity: *"He consented to play two brief Chopin études for the assembled company, but refused point-blank to play anything from his new opera."*

euphoria (yoo<u>fo</u>reeă) GREEK [*euphoros* healthy] *noun* a state of well-being or a feeling of elation, exhilaration, joy, optimism: *"Euphoria swept over him when he heard the news of his success."*

eureka (yoo<u>ree</u>kă) GREEK [from Greek *heureka* I have found it, as supposedly uttered by Archimedes (287–212 B.C.) while in his bath when he worked out the principle of specific discovery] *interjection* an expression of triumph usually uttered on making a discovery of some kind: *"When he remembered suddenly his steward's wife he must have exclaimed eureka with particular exultation"* (Joseph Conrad, *Chance,* 1914).

euthanasia (yoothănayzeeă) GREEK [a good death, from *eu* good and *thanatos* death] *noun* the practice of procuring the painless death of someone facing terminal illness; mercy killing: *"The review board asked the doctor to explain his views on euthanasia."*

événement (evenămon(g)) FRENCH [event, happening, as applied to the student riots and strikes that took place in Paris and elsewhere in 1968] *noun* an outbreak of public disorder, civil unrest: *"The événements of 1968 exerted a profound and lasting influence upon the French psyche."*

ex (eks) LATIN [former, used as a prefix] *noun* (*plural* **exes, **eksiz) a person who formerly held a particular post or position; a former spouse, partner, lover: *"She has few good things to say about her ex."* ~*adjective* former, outdated.

ex (eks) LATIN [out of, from] *preposition* out of, from, free from, without, excluding.

ex animo (eks animō) LATIN [from the heart] *adverb phrase* in earnest, sincerely, heartily.

ex ante (eks antee) LATIN [from before] *adjective phrase* predicted, based on prior expectations. ~*adverb phrase* in advance, beforehand.

ex cathedra (eks kătheedră) LATIN [from the chair] *adverb phrase* with official authority, authoritatively: *"An aged shepherd whom they had used as a guide, or who had approached them from curiosity, listened with mouth agape to the dissertations on foss and vellum, ports dextra, sinistra, and decumana, which Sir John Clerk delivered ex cathedra, and his learned visitor listened with the deference to the dignity of a connoisseur on his own ground"* (Walter Scott, *The Antiquary,* 1816). ~*adjective phrase* official, authoritative.

excelsior (ekselseeor, ekselseeăr) LATIN [higher, from *excelsus* high] *interjection* upward! higher! (motto of New York State).

excerpta (ekserptă, ekzerptă) LATIN [extracts, things selected] *plural noun* extracts, clippings, selections (of a book, piece of music, etc.): *"The committee was presented with a file of excerpta from the national press."*

excreta (ekskreetă) LATIN [things separated, neuter plural of *excretus* separated, from *excernere* to excrete] *plural noun* waste matter, excretions (especially body waste, feces, urine, excrement).

ex curia (eks kooreeă) LATIN [out of court] *adverb phrase* away from court. ~*adjective phrase* away from court.

excursus (ekskersăs) LATIN [excursion, from *excurrere* to run out] *noun* (*plural* **excursus** or **excurses,** ekskerseez) in written documents, an appendix or digression in which a topic is explored in further detail: *"Nafferton filed that, and asked what sort of people looked after Pig. This started an ethnological excursus on swineherds, and drew from Pinecoffin long tables showing the proportion per thousand of the caste in the Derajat"* (Rudyard Kipling, "Pig," 1887).

ex delicto (eks dăliktō) LATIN [from a crime] *adverb phrase* as a consequence of an offence or fault. ~*adjective phrase* of or relating to the consequence of an offense or fault.

exeat (ekseeat) LATIN [let him or her go out, third person singular present subjunctive of *exire* to go out] *noun* in the theater, a stage direction indicating that a particular character should leave the stage.

exegesis (eksăjeesis) GREEK [explanation, interpretation, from *exegeisthai* to explain, to interpret] *noun* (*plural* **exegeses,** eksăjeeseez) an explanation or critical examination of a text (especially scriptural texts): *"He was a preacher renowned for his careful exegesis of the New Testament letters."*

exemplar (ekzemplahr, ekzemplăr) LATIN [from *exemplum* example, model] *noun* an ideal example or standard specimen: *"Boldwood's deep attachment was a matter of great interest among all around him; but, after having been pointed out for so many years as the perfect exemplar of thriving bachelorship, his lapse was an anticlimax somewhat resembling that of St. John Long's death by consumption in the midst of his proofs that it was not a fatal disease"* (Thomas Hardy, *Far from the Madding Crowd,* 1874).

exempli gratia (ekzemplee gra`yshă) LATIN [for the sake of example] *adverb phrase* for example, for instance. ~*abbreviated form* **e.g.**

exemplum (ekzemplăm) LATIN [example, model] *noun* (*plural* **exempla,** ekzemplă) example, model; also used to refer to a short story with a message or moral.

exeunt (ekzeeănt) LATIN [they go out, from *exire* to go out] *noun* a stage direction indicating that two or more characters leave the stage. ~*verb* two or more characters leave the stage (stage direction).

exeunt omnes (ekzeeănt omnayz) LATIN [they all go out, from *exire* to go out] *verb phrase* all the characters leave the stage (stage direction).

ex facie (eks fayshee) LATIN [from the face] *adverb phrase* apparently, on the face of it.

ex gratia (eks grayshă) LATIN [from grace] *adjective phrase* as a favor, voluntary, gratuitory: *"The company made several ex gratia payments on the understanding that the money would not be used to buy shares in their rivals."* ~*adverb phrase* as a favor, voluntarily, gratuitously.

ex hypothesi (eks hīpothăsee) LATIN [from a hypothesis] *adverb phrase* by hypothesis, hypothetically, supposedly.

exigeant (ekzijănt), **exigent** FRENCH [from Latin *exigere* to exact] *adjective* exacting, demanding, requiring immediate attention.

exit (ekzit, egzit) LATIN [he or she goes out, from *exire* to go out] *noun* a stage direction indicating that a character leaves the stage; also in more general usage for any way out or departure: *"The comedian made a rapid exit from the stage, pausing only to snarl a sharp word at his tormentors."* ~*verb* a character leaves the stage (stage direction, but also in more general usage).

ex libris (eks leebris, eks libris) LATIN [from the books] *noun phrase* from the library of (as printed on bookplates identifying a book's owner). ~*abbreviated form* **ex lib.**

ex nihilo (eks neeălō, eks nīălō) LATIN [out of nothing, from *ex nihilo nihil fit* nothing is made out of nothing] *adverb phrase* from nothing: *"He believes that God created the universe ex nihilo."* ~*adjective phrase* from nothing.

exodus (eksădăs, egzădăs) GREEK [*ex-* out of and *hodos* way] *noun* (*plural* **exoduses,** eksădăsiz, egzădăsiz) an emigration or mass departure: *"They were part of the exodus of Jews from Eastern Europe."* ~*abbreviated form* **exod.**

ex officio (eks ăfisheeō, eks ăfiseeō), **ex officiis** (eks ăfisheeis, eks ăfiseeis) LATIN [from the office] *adverb phrase* by virtue of a person's office or position. ~*adjective phrase* by virtue of a person's office or position: *"Ten chances but you plead your own cause, man, for I may be brought up by a sabre, or a bowstring, before I make my pack up; then your road to Menie will be free and open, and as you will be possessed of the situation of comforter ex officio, you may take her with the tear in her ee', as old saws advise"* (Walter Scott, *Chronicles of the Canongate,* 1827). ~*noun phrase* a person who acts in an ex officio role. ~*abbreviated form* **ex off.**

exordium (egzordeeăm) LATIN [introduction, from *exordiri* to begin] *noun* (*plural* **exordiums** or **exordia,** egzordeeă) the beginning or introduction (usually of a piece of writing or speech): *"'Mr. Varden,' returned the other, perfectly composed under this exordium; 'I beg you'll take a chair. Chocolate, perhaps, you don't relish? Well! it IS an acquired taste, no doubt"* (Charles Dickens, *Barnaby Rudge,* 1841).

exotica (egzotikă) LATIN [from *exotika,* from the neuter plural of Latin *exoticus* exotic] *noun* objects or things of an exotic or mysterious nature: *"Various items of exotica spilled out of the suitcase."*

ex parte (eks pahrtee), **ex-parte** LATIN [from a side] *adverb phrase* from or on one side only (especially in legal proceedings). *~adjective phrase* one-sided, partisan.

ex pede Herculem (eks pedee herky-oolăm) LATIN [from the foot, Hercules] *adverb phrase* to work out the entirety of something from a small piece of information about it (recalling how the Greek mathematician Pythagoras attempted to calculate the height of Hercules form the size of his foot).

exposé (ekspōzay), **expose** FRENCH [exposition, report, past participle of *exposer* to set out, display] *noun* an exposure of sensational or discrediting facts (usually in the media); also applied more generally of any explanation of facts or ideas: *"Full details of their affair appeared in a searing exposé in the newspapers the following day."*

ex post (eks pōst) LATIN [from after] *adjective phrase* based on fact; factual, objective. *~adverb phrase* retrospectively.

ex post facto (eks pōst faktō), **ex postfacto** LATIN [from something done afterward] *adjective phrase* after the fact, retrospective: *"An act done . . . may be made good by matter ex post facto, that was not so at first"* (Tom-

lin's *Law Dictionary,* 1835). *~adverb phrase* retrospectively.

expresso *See* ESPRESSO.

ex professo (eks profesō) LATIN [from the professed thing, *profiteri* to declare] *adverb phrase* professedly, as claimed: *". . . you will have some difficulty in understanding why the leading society of Soulanges (all the town, in fact) thought this quasi-queen a beauty,—unless, indeed, you remember the succinct statement recently made 'ex professo,' by one of the cleverest women of our time, on the art of making her sex beautiful by surrounding accessories"* (Honoré de Balzac, *Sons of the Soil,* 1823–26).

ex proprio motu (eks prōpreeō mōtoo) LATIN [by one's own motion] *adverb phrase* voluntarily, of a person's own accord.

ex silentio (eks silenteeō, eks silensheeō) LATIN [from silence] *adverb phrase* lacking evidence to the contrary.

extempore (ekstempăree), **ex tempore** LATIN [from *ex tempore* out of the time, ablative of *tempus* time] *adverb* in an extemporaneous, unpremeditated, unprepared manner: *"SNUG Have you the lion's part written? pray you, if it / be, give it me, for I am slow of study. / QUINCE You may do it extempore, for it is nothing but roaring"* (William Shakespeare, *A Midsummer Night's Dream,* c. 1595). *~adjective* extemporaneous, unpremeditated, unprepared.

extra muros (ekstră myooros) LATIN [beyond the walls] *adjective phrase* external, outside the walls. ~*adjective* **extramural** concerned with the external policies of an organization or institution.

extraordinaire (ekstrordinair) FRENCH [extraordinary] *adjective* extraordinary, remarkable, unusual.

extravaganza (ekstravăganză) ITALIAN [from *estravaganza* extravagance] *noun* a lavish or spectacular display, event, show, or entertainment: *"In a minute or two afterwards he rose from his chair, paced the room at a very rapid rate, which was his practice in certain moods of mind, then made a dead halt, and bursting into an extravaganza of laughter, 'James,' cried he, 'I'll tell you what Byron should say to me when we are about to accost each other. . .'"*

(J. G. Lockhart, *Life of Sir Walter Scott,* 1837–38).

extra vires (ekstră vīreez) LATIN [beyond power] *adjective phrase* beyond the scope of a body's legal authority. ~*adverb phrase* beyond the scope of a body's legal authority.

ex-voto (eks vōtō), **ex voto** LATIN [from *ex voto* from a vow] *noun* (*plural* **ex-votos**) a votive offering or gift: *"On every picture 'Ex voto' was painted in yellow capitals in the sky. Though votive offerings were not unknown in Pagan Temples, and are evidently among the many compromises made between the false religion and the true, when the true was in its infancy, I could wish that all the other compromises were as harmless"* (Charles Dickens, *Pictures from Italy,* 1845). ~*adjective phrase* votive, according to a vow.

f *See* FORTE (2).

façade (făsahd) FRENCH [front] *noun* the front of a building, or a false or superficial appearance: *"The indistinct summit of the facade was notched and pronged by chimneys here and there, and upon its face were faintly signified the oblong shapes of windows, though only in the upper part"* (Thomas Hardy, *Far From the Madding Crowd*, 1874).

facetiae (făseesheeī) LATIN [plural of *facetia* a jest, witticism] *plural noun* witticisms or short, typically pornographic, stories: *"At the head of the 'Facetiae' in the morning's paper, Lousteau inserted the following note. . ."* (Honoré de Balzac, *A Distinguished Provincial at Paris*, 1839).

facile princeps (făkilă prinkeps, făsilee prinseps) LATIN [easily first] *noun phrase* clearly the first or foremost, the leader in a particular field: *"I saw a good deal of Robert Brown, 'facile Princeps Botanicorum,' as he was called by Humboldt"* (Charles Darwin, *Autobiography*, 1887).

façon de parler (fason(g) dă pahrlay) FRENCH [way of speaking] *noun phrase* (*plural* **façons de parler**) a manner of speech or a formulaic phrase or figure of speech: *"Interlopers from the wealthy end of town were immediately identifiable by their façon de parler."*

facsimile (făksimilee) LATIN [imperative of *facere* to make and *simile* like] *noun* a faithful replica or precise reproduction of something, often a copy of written material transmitted electronically: *"Each utensil—spoon, fork, knife, plate—had a letter engraved on it, with a motto above it, of which this is an exact facsimile: MOBILIS IN MOBILI N"* (Jules Verne, *20,000 Leagues Under the Sea*, 1869). ~*abbreviated form* **fax** (faks).

facta non verba (faktă non verbă) LATIN [deeds not words] *noun phrase* the time has come to take action rather than simply talk about doing something.

factotum (faktōtăm) LATIN [imperative of *facere* to do and *totum* all] *noun* (*plural* **factotums**) a person or employee who has responsibility for a range of general tasks or activities; a person who does all his master's work: *"'Dmitri! Eh, Dmitri! Gallop off to our Moscow estate,' he said to the factotum who appeared at his call"* (Leo Tolstoy, *War and Peace*, 1863–69).

faience (fay<u>ons</u>) FRENCH [after Faenza, Italy] *noun*   colorful tin-glazed earthenware of the type developed at the town of Faenza, Italy, sometimes applied to any type of glazed ceramic: *"The smile, you see, is perfect—wonderful / As mere Faience! a table ornament / To suit the richest mounting"* (George Eliot, *Middlemarch*, 1871–72).

fainéant (<u>fa</u>yneeon(g)) FRENCH [third person singular of *faire* to do and *néant* nothing] *noun*   a lazy person or idler: *"And then, out comes the red truth; and he dares to tell me, to my face, that my patent must be suppressed for the present, for fear of disgusting that rascally coward and fainéant. . ."* (Walter Scott, *Waverly*, 1814). ~*adjective* lazy, indolent.

fait accompli (fayt ăkom<u>plee</u>, fet ăkom<u>plee</u>) FRENCH [accomplished fact] *noun phrase* (*plural* **faits accomplis,** fayt ăkom<u>pleez</u>, fet ăkom<u>pleez</u>)   a deed that is irreversibly done or settled by the time others first know about it: *"Europe adjusts itself to a fait accompli, and so does an individual character—until the placid adjustment is disturbed by a convulsive retribution"* (George Eliot, *Adam Bede*, 1859).

fajita (fa<u>heeta</u>) MEXICAN SPANISH [diminutive of *faja* sash, belt] *noun*   a dish of marinated beef or chicken cut into strips and served in sauce as the filling of a flour tortilla.

fakir (fă<u>keer</u>, fayker) ARABIC [poor man] *noun*   a Muslim or Hindu religious ascetic or mendicant monk: *"Then he occupied himself with the education of this son, and when the boy waxed strong and came to the age of seven, he brought him a fakir, a doctor of law and religion, to teach him in his own house, and charged him to give him a good education and instruct him in politeness and good manners"* (Richard Burton, "The Tale of Three Apples," *Arabian Nights*, 1885–88). Also used as a negative term for a charlatan or fake.

falafel (fă<u>lahfă</u>l) ARABIC *noun*   a ball or patty of spiced ground vegetables or beans, fried and typically served with pita bread.

falsetto (fol<u>set</u>ō) ITALIAN [diminutive of *falso* false] *noun* (*plural* **falsetti,** fol<u>set</u>ee)   a singer with a high-pitched voice, above tenor. ~*adjective* sung in an artificially high-pitched voice, above tenor: *"Someone could be heard within dancing frantically, marking time with his heels to the sounds of the guitar and of a thin falsetto voice singing a jaunty air"* (Fyodor Dostoyevsky, *Crime and Punishment*, 1866).

fandango (fan<u>dang</u>ō) SPANISH *noun* (*plural* **fandangos, fandangoes**)   a lively Spanish or South American dance usually performed by two dancers accompanied by guitar and castanets; also applied to the music itself. Also used satirically of foolish, ridiculous, or improper behavior or speech.

fanfaronade (fanfarănayd) FRENCH [bragging, derived from Spanish *fanfarrón* braggart] *noun* empty boasting or bluster: *"The rivals for governor tried to outwit one another with their fanfaronades."*

fantasia (fantayzhă) ITALIAN [fantasy] *noun* a musical composition distinguished by its fanciful structure or else incorporating selections from other works: *"His new work, a fantasia that rejected the conventional forms of the day, was received with some puzzlement by its first audience."*

farandole (farăndōl) FRENCH [probably derived from Portuguese *fa* make and *roundelo* round dance] *noun* a lively communal chain dance from Provençal, France, or the music associated with it.

farce (fahrs) FRENCH [stuffing] *noun* a stage comedy featuring ridiculous situations and exaggerated characters, and thus "stuffed" for laughs, or more generally a state of affairs that has descended into laughable chaos: *"After the bride broke down in giggles the ceremony was quickly reduced to a farce."*

farceur (fahrser) FRENCH [derived from *farcer* to joke] *noun* a writer or performer of farce, or more broadly a practical joker or trickster: *". . .and Jake Offutt (a gang-politician, a small manufacturer, a tobacco-chewing old farceur who enjoyed dirty politics, business diplomacy, and cheating at poker) had only ten per cent. . ."* (Sinclair Lewis, *Babbitt*, 1922).

farci (fahrsee) FRENCH [past participle of *farcir* to stuff] *adjective* stuffed, usually with forcemeat.

farouche (faroosh) FRENCH [wild, derived from Latin *foras* out of doors] *adjective* wild, or shy, sullen, unsociable: *"But he was by nature farouche; his soul revolted against dinner parties and stiff shirts; and the presence of ladies—especially of fashionable ladies—filled him with uneasiness"* (Lytton Strachey, *Eminent Victorians*, 1918).

farrago (fărahgō) LATIN [mixed fodder] *noun* (*plural* **farragos** or **farragoes**) a jumble, confused mixture, or hodgepodge: *"The less I understood of this farrago, the less I was in a position to judge of its importance; and an appeal so worded could not be set aside without a grave responsibility"* (Robert Louis Stevenson, *The Strange Case of Dr. Jekyll and Mr. Hyde,* 1886).

fascia (fayshă, faysheeă) LATIN [band] *noun* (*plural* **fasciae,** fayshiee, or **fascias,** fayshăz) an instrumental panel, dashboard or, in architecture, a horizontal piece of boarding, band of wood, or nameplate above a shop window: *"He ran an appreciative hand over the walnut fascia so evocative of a forgotten era of motoring."* Also, in anatomy, a sheet of connective tissue surrounding a muscle or organ.

fata morgana (fahtă morg<u>ah</u>nă) ITALIAN [fairy Morgana] *noun phrase* Morgan le Fay, the treacherous fairy sorceress identified as the sister of the legendary King Arthur and sometimes described as living in Calabria, Italy. Also, a mirage, especially one seen in the Straits of Messina between southern Italy and Sicily; by extension anything that is illusory in nature.

fatwa (f<u>ă</u>twă) ARABIC [legal ruling, from *afta* to give a legal decision] *noun* ruling or decree issued by a religious authority on a point of Islamic law: *"The ayatollah's fatwa was widely condemned in the Western press."*

fauna (f<u>ah</u>nă) LATIN [after Fauna, Roman goddess of the groves] *noun* (*plural* **faunas** or **faunae,** <u>fah</u>nee, <u>fah</u>nī) animal life, especially the range of wildlife typical of a given place or environment, as distinct from the flora (plant life) of the area: *"But it appeared that she had come once as a small child, when the geography of the place was entirely different, and the fauna included certainly flamingoes and, possibly, camels"* (Virginia Woolf, *Night and Day,* 1919).

faute de mieux (fōt dă <u>mee</u>ă) FRENCH [want of better] *adverb phrase* for want of better, in the absence of anything better being available. ~*adjective phrase* accepted in the absence of a better alternative: *"He has taken something more than his fair share in the cathedral services, and has played the violoncello daily to such audiences as he could collect, or, faute de mieux, to no audience at all"* (Anthony Trollope, *The Warden,* 1855).

fauteuil (fō<u>toi</u>, f<u>ō</u>toi) FRENCH [armchair] *noun* an upholstered chair with arms, typically such a seat in a theater: *"Already the cold sweat started on my brow, already I glanced back over my shoulder at the closed door, when, to my unspeakable relief, my eye, wandering mildly in the direction of the stove, rested upon a second figure, seated in a large fauteuil beside it"* (Charlotte Brontë, *The Professor,* 1857).

fauve (f<u>ō</u>v) FRENCH [wild animal] *noun* an artist associated with fauvism, an early-20th-century school of art favoring the unrestrained use of color. ~*adjective* of or relating to fauvism or artists associated with the movement.

fauvism (f<u>ō</u>visăm) FRENCH [from *fauve* wild animal] *noun* an early-20th-century French art movement favoring the unrestrained use of color.

faux (fō) FRENCH [false] *adjective* artificial or imitation, used especially in relation to fashion and interior design:

"You have a 'faux air' of Nebuchadnezzar in the fields about you, that is certain: your hair reminds me of eagles' feathers; whether your nails are grown like birds' claws or not, I have not yet noticed" (Charlotte Brontë, *Jane Eyre*, 1847).

faux amis (fōz a<u>mee</u>) FRENCH [false friends] *noun phrase* words from two different languages that have different meanings despite being misleadingly similar or identical in appearance: *"The French word 'assister' and the English word 'assist' are faux amis apt to cause confusion; French 'assister' means 'to attend.'"*

faux-naïf (fō-nī<u>eef</u>) FRENCH [from *faux* false and *naïf* ingenuous] *noun* a person who makes a pretense of innocence. ~*adjective* of or relating to a person or work of art purposely projecting a misleadingly simple or artless appearance.

faux pas (fō <u>pa</u>) FRENCH [false step] *noun phrase* (plural **faux pas,** fō <u>pahz</u>) a mistake or social blunder: *"She blushed crimson, suddenly conscious of the faux pas she had committed in mentioning his name."*

favela (fa<u>ve</u>lă) PORTUGUESE [after Favela, the name of a hill near Rio de Janeiro, Brazil] *noun* a humble shelter or shanty typical of the slums located on the outskirts of many cities.

fax *See* FACSIMILE.

fecit (<u>fay</u>kit) LATIN [he/she made, he/she did] *verb* made by, done by (usually in relation to a work of art): *"Certainly, sir; for the Dutch Antiquaries claim Caligula as the founder of a lighthouse, on the sole authority of the letters C.C.P.F., which they interpret Caius Caligula Pharum Fecit"* (Walter Scott, *The Antiquary*, 1816).

feldsher (<u>feld</u>shăr) GERMAN [*feld* field and *scherer* barber or surgeon] *noun* a medical auxiliary or medical practitioner lacking formal qualifications.

felix culpa (fayliks <u>kul</u>pa) LATIN [happy fault] *noun phrase* a lucky mistake or error that turns out to have beneficial consequences.

felucca (fe<u>luu</u>kă) ITALIAN *noun* a single-sailed boat of the Mediterranean region, still in use today on the Nile: *"She had wanted to annex that apparently quiet and steady young man, affectionate and pliable, an orphan from his tenderest age, as he had told her, with no ties in Italy except an uncle, owner and master of a felucca, from whose ill-usage he had run away before he was fourteen"* (Joseph Conrad, *Nostromo*, 1904).

feme covert (feem <u>ko</u>vărt) FRENCH [covered woman, from *femme* woman and *couverte* covered] *noun phrase* a married woman who enjoys protection in law through her husband.

feme sole (feem <u>sōl</u>) FRENCH [single woman, from *femme* woman and *seule* alone] *noun phrase* a legal term for an unmarried woman, widow, or divorcée, or formerly a woman who trades in business independently of her husband.

femme de chambre (fam dă <u>shom</u>bră, fem dă <u>shom</u>bră) FRENCH [woman of the chamber] *noun phrase* a chambermaid, a lady's maid: *"The femme de chambre arrived to turn down the bed."*

femme du monde (fam dă <u>mond</u>, fem dă <u>mond</u>) FRENCH [woman of the world] *noun phrase* a worldly woman, or a woman of sophistication or society: *"In Paris she quickly acquired a reputation as a femme du monde, playing host to scores of artists and, more importantly, their aristocratic patrons."*

femme fatale (fam fa<u>tal</u>, fem fa<u>tal</u>) FRENCH [fatal woman] *noun phrase* (*plural* **femmes fatales,** fam fa<u>tal</u>, fem fa<u>tal</u>, fam fa<u>tals</u>, fem fa<u>tals</u>) a dangerously seductive woman likely to use her mysterious allure to entice admirers into difficult situations: *"She specialized in playing the kind of unflappable femme fatale who provokes dutiful wives to heights of jealous fury."*

femme savante (fam sav<u>on</u>(<u>g</u>)) FRENCH [learned woman] *noun phrase* an erudite or scholarly woman (often used derogatively): *"In the process of winning recognition as a femme savante, she unfortunately had discarded the last traces of the little charm she had once had."*

feng-shui (fung <u>shway</u>, feng <u>shoo</u>ee) CHINESE [from *feng* wind and *shui* water] *noun* belief system based on the notion that buildings and landscape features are inhabited by spirits who must be appeased so that people can live in harmony with the environment. Introduced to the West in recent years as a lifestyle skill, as expressed through interior decoration in particular: *"Put quite simply, feng shui is a method of arranging our environment to be as beneficial as possible to us"* (Richard Craze, *Feng Shui,* 1999).

ferae naturae (ferī nat<u>yoor</u>ī) LATIN [of wild nature] *adjective phrase* undomesticated (used especially of wild animals): *"The lower classes, in this duel of Authority with Authority, Greek throttling Greek, have ceased to respect the City-Watch: Police-satellites are marked on the back with chalk (the M signifies mouchard, spy); they are hustled, hunted like ferae naturae"* (Thomas Carlyle, *History of the French Revolution,* 1837).

fest (fest) GERMAN [feast] *noun* a celebration or festive gathering: *"One of the liveliest banquets that has recently been pulled off occurred last night in the annual Get-Together Fest of the Zenith Real Estate Board, held in the Venetian Ball Room of the O'Hearn House"* (Sinclair Lewis, *Babbitt,* 1922); Also used to mean "occasion" or "meeting" and combined with other words, e.g., *songfest, gabfest.*

146

festina lente (festeenă lentă) LATIN [make haste slowly] *noun phrase* more haste, less speed: *"Recollect yourself, I pray, And be careful what you say— As the ancient Romans said, festina lente"* (Gilbert and Sullivan, *Iolanthe,* 1882).

Festschrift (festshrift) GERMAN [from *Fest* celebration and *Schrift* writing] *noun* a celebratory volume of writings by various authors compiled as a special commemorative tribute to a scholar, often on his or her retirement: *"This volume, a Festschrift presented to the professor on his 60th birthday, contains 15 papers written by appreciative scholars."*

feta (fetă) GREEK [from *tyri pheta* slice of cheese] *noun* crumbly white cheese made from sheep's or goat's milk.

fête (fayt, fet), **fete** FRENCH [festival] *noun* a festival, fair, or party: *"'Will you be at Madame Rolandaky's fete?' asked Anna, to change the conversation"* (Leo Tolstoy, *Anna Karenina,* 1873–77). ~*verb* to celebrate or pay honor to.

fête champêtre (fet shompetră) FRENCH [rural festival] *noun phrase* a garden party or pastoral entertainment: *"To-morrow morning, sir, we give a public breakfast—a fête champêtre—to a great number of those who have rendered themselves celebrated by their works and talents"* (Charles Dickens, *Pickwick Papers,* 1837).

fête galante (fet galon(g)) FRENCH [courteous festival] *noun phrase* rural or outdoors entertainment.

fettucine (fetoocheenee) ITALIAN [diminutive of *fetta* slice or ribbon] *plural noun* a form of ribbon-shaped pasta, also the name for a dish of this.

fetus (feetăs) LATIN [offspring] *noun* an unborn child, usually from three months after conception, or other unborn or unhatched vertebrate: *"It is now possible to detect a range of physical abnormalities through examination of the unborn fetus."*

feu d'artifice (fō dahrtifis) FRENCH [fire of artifice] *noun phrase* (*plural* **feux d'artifice,** fō dahtifis) a firework or firework display.

feu de joie (fō dă zhwa) FRENCH [fire of joy] *noun phrase* (*plural* **feux de joie)** a fusillade of guns fired in salute, or more generally a celebration.

feuilleton (făyăton(g), foiyăton(g), fooiton(g)) FRENCH [diminutive of *feuillet* sheet of paper] *noun* a section of a newspaper devoted to entertainment, or a novel or other litrary work published in installments: *"'The press has fallen heir to the Woman,' exclaimed Rastignac. 'She no longer has the quality of a spoken feuilleton—delightful calumnies graced by elegant language'"* (Honoré de Balzac, *Another Study of Woman,* 1842).

fez (fez) TURKISH [after the town of Fez, Morocco] noun (plural **fezzes** or **fezes**) a flat-topped brimless felt hat, often red and decorated with a tassel, worn by men in various countries of the eastern Mediterranean: *"He was wearing another elegant English suit with a bright little fez on his head"* (Ivan Turgenev, *Fathers and Sons,* 1862).

FF. *See* FORTISSIMO.

fiancé (feeonsay, feeonsay) FRENCH [past participle of *fiancer* to betroth, promise] noun a man who is engaged to be married: *"Even if you are engaged, I am sure your fiancé would wish you to go into society rather than be bored to death"* (Leo Tolstoy, *War and Peace,* 1863–69). ~noun, feminine **fiancée** (feeonsay, feeonsay) a woman who is engaged to be married.

fiasco (feeaskō) ITALIAN [from *fare fiasco* to make a bottle] noun (plural **fiascoes**) a disastrous or chaotic failure: *"Lucetta was rather addicted to scribbling, as had been shown by the torrent of letters after the fiasco in their marriage arrangements, and hardly had Elizabeth gone away when another note came to the Mayor's house from High-Place Hall"* (Thomas Hardy, *The Mayor of Casterbridge,* 1886).

fiat (feeat, feeăt) LATIN [let it be done] noun an order, decree, or authorization, typically as issued by an official organization, but sometimes used of old saws and sayings: *"But 'he that mar-ries her marries her name.' This fiat somewhat soothed himself and wife"* (Alfred, Lord Tennyson, *Enoch Arden,* 1864).

fiche (feesh) FRENCH [slip of paper] noun a microfiche, a document reduced to compressed form on a small piece of paper, plastic, or other material.

Fidei Defensor (fidī difensor), **Defensor Fidei** LATIN [defender of the faith] noun phrase Title conferred by the papacy upon Henry VIII prior to the Reformation, and subsequently borne by succeeding English monarchs.

fiesta (feeestă) SPANISH [feast] noun a religious festival or public holiday held to mark the feast day of a saint, and thus any festival or holiday: *"They went on strike regularly (every bull-fight day), a form of trouble that even Nostromo at the height of his prestige could never cope with efficiently; but the morning after each fiesta, before the Indian market-women had opened their mat parasols on the plaza, when the snows of Higuerota gleamed pale over the town on a yet black sky, the appearance of a phantom-like horseman mounted on a silver-gray mare solved the problem of labor without fail"* (Joseph Conrad, *Nostromo,* 1904).

filet (feelay, filit) FRENCH [net] noun decorative lace with a square mesh.

filet mignon (feelay meenyon(g)) FRENCH [small fillet] noun phrase a thick slice of tender meat cut from the small end of a beef tenderloin: *"For breakfast I had a grilled filet mignon and some scrambled eggs."*

filioque (filiōkway) LATIN [and to the Son] *noun* extract of the Nicene Creed, which asserts that the Holy Spirit emanates both from God the Father and his Son. The notion is rejected by the Eastern Orthodox Church, and thus the term can also be used to denote a point of issue between two disagreeing parties.

filius populi (filiăs popyooli) LATIN [son of the people] *noun phrase* an illegitimate son.

fille de joie (fee dă zhwa) FRENCH [girl of pleasure] *noun phrase (plural* **filles de joie***)* a prostitute: *"He had seen Venice, Milan, Florence, Bologna, and Naples leisurely, as he wished to see them, as a dreamer of dreams, and a philosopher; careless of the future, for an artist looks to his talent for support as the fille de joie counts upon her beauty"* (Honoré de Balzac, *Cousin Pons,* 1847).

film noir (film nwahr) FRENCH [black film] *noun phrase* a cinema genre characterized by dark themes and somber atmosphere, typically depicting the criminal underworld: *"As a director he proved to be one of the masters of film noir."*

filo (feelō) GREEK [from *phullo* leaf] *noun* a type of pastry dough usually cooked in layers of very thin sheets.

fils (fees) FRENCH [son] *adjective* junior, sometimes appended to surnames where father and son share the same first name in order to distinguish between them.

finale (finahlee) ITALIAN [final] *noun* the end or closing part of something: *"This wretched note was the finale of Emma's breakfast"* (Jane Austen, *Emma,* 1816).

fin de guerre (fan dă gair) FRENCH [end of war] *adjective phrase* of or relating to the period immediately following warfare: *"Traders reopened their shops in an ebullient fin de guerre wave of optimism."*

fin de saison (fan dă sayzon(g)) FRENCH [end of season] *noun phrase* the end of the social season. ~*adjective phrase* of or relating to the end of the social season: *"The gathering had an unmistakable fin de saison atmosphere about it."*

fin de siècle (fan dă seeairkăl) FRENCH [end of the century] *adjective phrase* of or relating to the last years of a century, usually to the end of the 19th century and typically hinting at an overriding atmosphere of decadence and anxiety inspired by a heightened sense of changing times: *"The rooms were decorated in a florid, fin de siècle style."*

fines herbes (feenz erb, feen erb) FRENCH [fine herbs] *plural noun* a mixture of fresh chopped herbs used as seasoning in cookery.

finesse (fi<u>nes</u>, fee<u>nes</u>) FRENCH [delicacy, perception] *noun* refinement, skill, or adroitness in doing something, or a trick or stratagem employed in the course of a game or dispute: *"Having conceived the idea he proceeded to carry it out with considerable finesse"* (Arthur Conan Doyle, *The Hound of the Baskervilles,* 1902).

finis (fi<u>n</u>is, fi<u>n</u>ee, fi<u>nee</u>), **fini** LATIN [limit, end, conclusion] *noun* the end or conclusion of something: *"Next Year . . . must be the finis of this long agnostic tragedy"* (Thomas Carlyle, *The History of Frederick II of Prussia called Frederick the Great,* 1865).

fino (fee<u>n</u>ō) SPANISH [fine] *noun* a pale, very dry sherry.

fjord (fee<u>o</u>rd, fyord), **fiord** NORWEGIAN [derived from *fjördr* firth] *noun* a narrow, deep, steep-sided inlet of the sea (often referring to such inlets along the Norwegian coast): *"From our new Cape Horn in Denmark, a chain of mountains, scarcely half the height of the Alps, would run in a straight line due southward; and on its western flank every deep creek of the sea, or fiord, would end in 'bold and astonishing glaciers'"* (Charles Darwin, *The Voyage of the Beagle,* 1839).

fl. *See* FLORUIT.

flagellum (flaj<u>e</u>lăm) LATIN [diminutive of *flagrum* scourge] *noun* (*plural* **flagellums** or **flagella,** flaj<u>e</u>lă) a whiplike appendage, as encountered in various plants, animals, and microorganisms.

flagrante delicto *See* IN FLAGRANTE DELICTO.

flair (flair) FRENCH [sense of smell] *noun* a natural skill, talent, or aptitude in doing something; can also refer to flamboyance in style: *"Their latest marketing campaign seems to lack flair."*

flak (flak) GERMAN [abbreviated form of *Fliegerabwehrkanonen,* from *Flieger* flyer, *Abwehr* defense, and *Kanonen* cannons] *noun* antiaircraft fire; or, by extension, critical comments or other opposition: *"The fighters dived through a curtain of flak from the antiaircraft battery."*

flambé (fl<u>om</u>bay) FRENCH [past participle of *flamber* to flame, to singe] *adjective* of or relating to a dish served in flaming liquor. ~*verb* to prepare or serve food in burning liquor.

flamenco (flă<u>men</u>kō) SPANISH [Fleming, of the gypsies] *noun* a lively gypsy dance of Andalusian origin, also the guitar music to which it is usually danced.

flèche (flesh) FRENCH [arrow] *noun* a small, slender spire of wood or stone rising from a roof.

fleur-de-lis (fler-dă-<u>lee</u>, fler-dă-<u>lees</u>) FRENCH [flower of the lily] *noun* a heraldic or artistic floral device based on the iris, best known as a symbol of the royal family of France.

flor.   *See* FLORUIT.

flora (flŏrǎ) LATIN [after Flora, the Roman goddess of flowers, from *flos* flower] *noun* (*plural* **floras** or **florae**, flŏrī) plant life, especially the range of plants typical of a given place or environment, as distinct from the fauna (animal life) of the area, or a catalog of plants associated with a particular place or environment: *"The most isolated islands once possessed a far more abundant flora than they now have."*

floreat (flŏriat) LATIN [may he/she/it flourish] *interjection* a wish that someone or something will prosper or thrive, as sometimes encountered in slogans and mottoes: *"Floreat Regina!"*

floruit (flŏrooit) LATIN [he/she/it flourished] *verb* flourished, as sometimes given in biographies of artists whose birth and death dates are unsure: *"St. Hugh of Lincoln (floruit 1170–1200)."* ~*noun* the period of time during which a person or thing flourished. ~*abbreviated form* **fl.; flor.**

flotilla (flǎtĭlǎ) SPANISH [diminutive of *flota* fleet] *noun* a small fleet of boats or ships, or more generally a substantial number of things: *"After the flotilla was chased away from the*

coast, the villagers dispersed and returned to their homes."

flu   *See* INFLUENZA.

flügelhorn (floogǎlhorn) GERMAN [from *Flügel* wing and *Horn* horn] *noun* a valved brass wind instrument with a larger bore than a cornet.

focus (fŏkǎs) LATIN [hearth, fireplace] *noun* (*plural* **focuses** or **foci**, fŏkī, fŏsī) a point on which all attention is concentrated; a point at which an image, idea, or something else becomes clear and sharp: *"The focus of the discussion shifted from children's education to the role of women in modern society."* ~*verb* to devote special attention to something, or to isolate a particular image, idea, or something else until it becomes clear.

foehn (fern), **föhn** GERMAN [warm wind] *noun* a warm, dry wind often encountered in the lee of the Alps.

föhn   *See* FOEHN.

foie gras (fwah grā) FRENCH [fat liver] *noun phrase* paté made from the liver of a specially fattened goose: *"And even then I didn't know whom I had there, opposite me, busy now devouring a slice of pate de foie gras"* (Joseph Conrad, *The Arrow of Gold,* 1919).

folie à deux (folee a dǎ) FRENCH [madness by two] *noun phrase* a foolish, delusional, or mistaken belief that is shared by two closely associated persons: *"The prosecution's version of events suggested the existence of a folie à deux between the two defendants."*

folie de grandeur (folee dă gron<u>der</u>) FRENCH [madness by greatness] *noun phrase* (*plural* **folies de grandeur**) delusions of grandeur: *"He [Clive James] said he 'snivelled at his desk' and he wrote what even some of his friends saw as his suicide note. 'It might have been folie de grandeur [to write it], but I don't think so. On that occasion I was as close as a pathologically solipsistic man can be to self denial. All I could see even in the mirror was her [Princess Diana's] face'* (the *Guardian*, May 29, 2001).

fondant (<u>fon</u>dănt) FRENCH [present participle of *fondre* to melt] *noun* a soft creamy paste of sugar, water, and flavoring commonly used as cake icing or in confectionery: *"The top of the cake was decorated with candles set in thick pink fondant."*

fondue (fon<u>dyoo</u>, <u>fon</u>dyoo) FRENCH [past participle of *fondre* to melt] *noun* a traditional Swiss dish of flavored melted cheese into which pieces of bread, meat, and fruit may be dipped: *"The fondue craze lasted perhaps three years before falling into apparently permanent disfavor among New York's fashionable middle-class hostesses."* Also, a dish in which pieces of food are dipped into hot broth or melted chocolate.

fons et origo (fonz et <u>orī</u>gō) LATIN [fount and origin] *noun phrase* the original source or foundation of something: *"He fixed the old man with a stony glare, clearly considering him the fons et origo of all his present afflictions."*

force de frappe (fors dă <u>frap</u>) FRENCH [strike force] *noun phrase* a military strike force, specifically a force capable of delivering a nuclear attack.

force majeure (fors ma<u>zher</u>) FRENCH [superior force] *noun phrase* an irresistible or uncontrollable power, or an unforeseen event such as the outbreak of war that prevents parties to a contract from completing their obligations as planned: *"Their insurance policy did not apply in cases of force majeure."*

forte (1) (<u>for</u>tay, for<u>tay</u>) FRENCH [from *fort* strong] *noun* a person's speciality or strong point: *"As far as the piano is concerned, sentiment is my forte. I keep science for Life"* (Oscar Wilde, *The Importance of Being Earnest*, 1895).

forte (2) (<u>for</u>tay, for<u>tay</u>) ITALIAN [derived from Latin *fortis* strong] *adjective* (in music) loud. ~*adverb* (in music) played or sung loudly: *"She had to sing forte in order to be heard above the roar of the sea."* ~*abbreviated form* **f.**

fortissimo (for<u>tisi</u>mō) ITALIAN [superlative of *forte,* ultimately from Latin *fortis* strong] *adjective* (in music) very loud. ~*adverb* (in music) played or sung very loudly: *"But now, immediately before the third quatrain or chorus, sung fortissimo, with emphatic raps of the table, which gave the effect of cymbals and drum together, Alick's can was filled, and he was bound to empty it before the chorus ceased"* (George Eliot, *Adam Bede*, 1859). ~*abbreviated form* **ff.**

forum (fŏrăm) LATIN [derived from *fores* door] *noun* ((*plural* **forums** or **fora,** fŏră) a public square or meeting place, or a publication, program, or other medium for public discussion: *"What is called eloquence in the forum is commonly found to be rhetoric in the study"* (Henry David Thoreau; *Walden; or, Life in the Woods*, 1854).

foyer (fŏiyăr, fŏiay) FRENCH [hearth] *noun* an entrance hallway or lobby, particularly of a hotel, theater, cinema, or other large building: *"'Gentlemen, gentlemen,' he stammered, 'do please make haste. They've just rung the bell in the public foyer'"* (Émile Zola, *Nana*, 1880).

fracas (frăkah, frăkăs) FRENCH [din, derived from Italian *fracassare* to shatter] *noun* an outbreak of noise, uproar, clamor, often the result of a quarrel or brawl: *"And at the beginning of the whole fracas I said — I've said right along — that we ought to have entered the war the minute Germany invaded Belgium"* (Sinclair Lewis, *Main Street*, 1920).

Fraktur (fraktoor) GERMAN [breaking, so called because of the curlicues that

broke up the continuous line of a word] *noun* a style of typeface formerly used for typesetting German.

framboise (frombwaz, frombwahz) FRENCH [raspberry] *noun* a liqueur made from raspberries, or something with a color of raspberry. ~*adjective* of or relating to a raspberry color.

franc-tireur (fron(g)-tirer) FRENCH [free shooter] *noun* a sharpshooter or guerrilla fighting independently of the regular armed forces: *"The column was harried by franc-tireurs all the way to the coast."*

franglais (fronglay) FRENCH [from *français* French and *anglais* English] *noun* an informal variety of the French language in which much use is made of British and American words and phrases: *"Nothing arouses the wrath of a certain breed of patriotic Frenchman so much as the idea that practicality will force pure French to submit to such bastardized forms as franglais."*

frankfurter (frankferter) GERMAN [after Frankfurt am Main, Germany] *noun* a cured, usually skinless, cooked beef or pork sausage (also called hot dog).

frappé (frapay) FRENCH [past participle of *frapper* to strike, to chill] *adjective* chilled or partly frozen. ~*noun* a drink served iced or chilled or thickened with crushed ice.

Frau (frow) GERMAN [woman] *noun* a title borne by a German married woman.

fräulein (froilīn) GERMAN [diminutive of *Frau* woman] *noun* an unmarried German woman, or a governess.

fresco (freskō) ITALIAN [fresh, cool] *noun* (plural **frescoes**) an artistic technique in which paint is applied directly to moist plaster, or a painting executed in this manner: *"The articles of furniture, which stood out from the walls, were duplicated on the floor distinctly as if they floated upon unrippled water; even the panelling of the walls, the figures upon them in painting and bas-relief, and the fresco of the ceiling were reflected on the floor"* (Lew Wallace, *Ben Hur*, 1880).

fricassee (frikǎsee) FRENCH [feminine past participle of *fricasser* to cut up and stew in sauce] *noun* a dish in which the meat is sliced and fried or stewed in a white sauce. ~*verb* to prepare meat in such a way.

frisson (freeson(g)) FRENCH [shiver, derived from Latin *frigere* to be cold] *noun* a thrill or shudder of excitement or emotion: *"The news of his death caused a frisson of fear to run down her spine."*

fromage frais (fromarzh fray) FRENCH [fresh cheese] *noun phrase* soft curd cheese: *"The child took a small pot of fromage frais from her lunchbox."*

frottage (frŏtahzh) FRENCH [friction, derived from *frotter* to rub] *noun* the practice of rubbing one's body against other people for the purposes of sexual excitement; alternatively, the artistic technique of making impressions of textured material by rubbing a pencil over a sheet of paper laid on top of it.

fruits de mer (frwee dǎ mair) FRENCH [fruits of the sea] *noun phrase* a dish of seafood usually comprising a variety of shellfish.

fugue (fyoog) FRENCH [flight, derived from Latin *fuga* flight] *noun* a contrapuntal musical composition based on repetitions and elaborations of one or more themes: *"The spot at which their instrumentation rose loudest was a place called Ten Hatches, whence during high springs there proceeded a very fugue of sounds"* (Thomas Hardy, *The Mayor of Casterbridge*, 1886).

führer (fyoorǎr) GERMAN [leader, derived from Old High German *fuoren* to lead] *noun* title assumed in 1934 by Nazi leader Adolf Hitler (1889–1945), and since used of any official or bureaucrat who behaves in a despotic manner.

fulcrum (fulkrǎm) LATIN [bedpost, derived from *fulcire* to prop] *noun* (*plural* **fulcrums** or **fulcra**, fulkrǎ) a prop, or the point of support on which a lever turns or hinges: *"The head and neck were moved frequently, and* *apparently with force; and the extended wings seemed to form the fulcrum on which the movements of the neck, body and tail acted"* (Charles Darwin, *The Voyage of the Beagle,* 1839).

fungus (fŭngăs) LATIN [probably derived from Greek *sphoggos* or *spoggos,* sponge] *noun* (*plural* **fungi,** fŭngee, fŭnjee, fŭngī) a class of spore-producing, chlorophyll-lacking plantlike organisms including mildews, molds, mushrooms, rusts, and yeasts: *"I was startled by a great patch of vivid scarlet on the ground, and going up to it found it to be a peculiar fungus, branched and corrugated like a foliaceous lichen, but deliquescing into slime at the touch. . ."* (H. G. Wells, *The Island of Dr. Moreau,* 1896).

funicular (fyoonĭkyoolăr, fănĭkyoolă) ITALIAN [derived from Latin *funis* rope] *noun* a cable railway in which an ascending car is usually counterbalanced by another descending car. ~*adjective* of or relating to such a railway system: *"It is possible to reach the top of the cliff by means of a short funicular railway."*

furioso (fyooriōsō) ITALIAN [furious, violent] *adverb* with great strength or vigor, especially in music. ~*adjective* vigorous, forceful.

furore (fyooror) ITALIAN [rage, derived from Latin *furere* to rage] *noun* a general commotion, fuss, or uproar, variously motivated by anger, indignation,

excitement, or enthusiasm: *"Joe was not of the nation that keeps us forever in a furore with fugues and fruit"* (O. Henry, *Strictly Business,* 1910).

fuselage (fyoosălazh) FRENCH [derived from *fuselé* spindle-shaped] *noun* the central body section of an aircraft, including the cargo and crew areas: *"The fuselage of the plane was peppered with bulletholes."*

fusillade (fyoozălayd, fyoozălahd) FRENCH [derived from *fusiller* to shoot] *noun* a volley of shots fired simultaneously or in quick succession; by extension, any similar noise, such as applause, or sustained barrage (of criticisms, etc.): *"At all events it drew from him a furious fusillade of artillery and musketry, plainly heard but not felt by us"* (Ulysses S. Grant, *Personal Memoirs,* 1885–86).

fusilli (fyoosĭli) ITALIAN [diminutive of Italian dialect *fuso* spindle] *noun* a type of twisted or spiral-shaped pasta.

futon (footon) JAPANESE *noun* a low-slung wooden bed frame with a cotton-filled mattress, or simply the mattress itself laid out on a mat on the floor for sleeping: *"No fashionable modern home is complete without a futon that can be folded away when not in use."*

fu yung (foo yung) CHINESE [hibiscus] *noun phrase* a Chinese dish of eggs cooked with beansprouts, onions, and various other ingredients.

gaffe (gaf) FRENCH [blunder] *noun* (*plural* **gaffes**) a social or diplomatic blunder or indiscretion; also used more generally of any mistake: *"The ambassador made futile attempts to prevent the press from hearing about his unfortunate gaffe."*

gaga (ga̱hgah) FRENCH [crazy] *adjective* crazy, insane, foolish, senile, or wildly enthusiastic: *"All the kids went completely gaga when they learned of their team's success."*

gala (ga̱ylă, ga̱lă, ga̱hlă) ITALIAN [merrymaking, derived via Spanish from Middle French *gale* festivity, pleasure] *noun* (*plural* **galas**) a celebration or festival: *"It was to be a gala occasion and every man, woman and child in the settlement had assembled on the green"* (Zane Grey, *Betty Zane,* 1904). *~adjective* of or relating to such a celebration or festivity.

galabiya (galăḇīyă), **gallabiya, galabieh, galabia** ARABIC [Egyptian variant of *jallabiyya*] *noun* a long, loose-fitting gown of the type widely worn in Egypt and other Arabian countries: *"His wife chose a black galabiyah with gold spangles to take home as a souvenir of the trip."*

galant (ga̱lănt, ga̱la̱nt, gă̱lon(g)t) FRENCH [gallant] *adjective* courteous, charming, polite, or gentlemanly: *"War is one of the gifts of life; but, alas! no war appears so very necessary when time has laid its soothing hand upon the passionate misunderstandings and the passionate desires of great peoples. 'Le temps,' as a distinguished Frenchman has said, 'est un galant homme'"* (Joseph Conrad, *The Mirror of the Sea,* 1906).

galette (ga̱let) FRENCH [flat cake] *noun* a thin pastry cake, usually with a fruit or chocolate filling.

gallabiya *See* GALABIYA.

galleon (ga̱leeăn) SPANISH [from *galeón*] *noun* a large square-rigged sailing ship that constituted significant parts of the navies of Spain, England, and other countries between the 15th and 18th centuries: *"But, seeing that the treasure must fall into the enemy's hands, he burnt and scuttled every galleon, which* *went to the bottom with their immense riches"* (Jules Verne, *20,000 Leagues Under the Sea,* 1869).

galleria (galăree̱ă) ITALIAN [gallery] *noun* a shopping arcade, or a shop within such an arcade: *"His mother now works in a stylish galleria selling designer clothing to the nouveau riche of the town."*

gallimaufry (galămo̱rfree) FRENCH [from Middle French *galimafrée* stew] *noun* (*plural* **gallimaufries**) a hodgepodge, medley or jumble: *"Mas- ter, there is three carters, three shepherds, / three neat-herds, three swine-herds, that have made themselves / all men of hair, they call themselves Saltiers, and they have a dance which the wenches / say is a gallimaufry of gambols, because they are / not in't. . ."* (William Shakespeare, *The Winter's Tale,* 1611).

gambit (ga̱mbit) ITALIAN [from *gam- betto* act of tripping someone, from *gamba* leg] *noun* a calculated move or stratagem, or an opening remark in a conversation or negotiation: *"So now once again you know exactly how we stand, and it is clear that I must plan some fresh opening move, for this gambit won't work"* (Arthur Conan Doyle, "The Adventure of the Illustrious Client," *The Adventures of Sherlock Holmes,* 1891–93).

gamin (ga̱măn, ga̱min) FRENCH [mean- ing unknown] *noun* a street urchin or waif: *"The gamin—the street Arab— of Paris is the dwarf of the giant. Let us not exaggerate, this cherub of the gutter some- times has a shirt, but, in that case, he owns but one; he sometimes has shoes, but then they have no soles; he sometimes has a lodging, and he loves it, for he finds his mother there; but he prefers the street, because there he finds liberty"* (Victor Hugo, *Les Misérables,* 1862).

gamine (ga̱mee̱n, ga̱meen) FRENCH [feminine of *gamin*] *noun* a small girl who spends much of her time in the streets. ~*adjective* of or relating to a girl or young woman with a mischie- vous, playful manner.

ganja (ga̱njă) HINDI [hemp] *noun* marijuana.

garage (gă̱rahzh, gară̱hi) FRENCH [act of docking, from *garer* to dock] *noun* a shelter or repair shop for motor vehi- cles: *"This morning he was darkly pre- pared to find something wrong, and he felt belittled when the mixture exploded sweet and strong, and the car didn't even brush the door-jamb, gouged and splintery with many bruisings by fenders, as he backed out of the garage"* (Sinclair Lewis, *Babbitt,* 1922). ~*verb* to keep in a garage, or to take a motor vehicle to a garage for repair, etc.

garam masala (gă̱răm mă̱sahlă) URDU [hot spices] *noun phrase* a mixture of ground spices used in Indian cuisine.

garçon (gahrso̱n(g)) FRENCH [boy, ser- vant] *noun* (*plural* **garçons**) a waiter: *"Garcon, fetch a brandy quick . . . / There!*

I'm feeling better now. / Let's collaborate, we two. / You the Mummer, I the Bard; / Oh, what ripping stuff we'll do, / Sitting on the Boulevard!" (Robert Service, *Ballads of a Bohemian*, 1920).

garni (gahrnee, gahrnee) FRENCH [garnished] *adjective* of or relating to a dish served with a garnish or sauce of some kind.

Gastarbeiter (gastahrbītăr) GERMAN [guestworker] *noun* (*plural* **Gastarbeiter, Gastarbeiters**) a foreign or immigrant worker (especially one working in Germany): *"There have been several serious riots in recent weeks over the issue of Gastarbeiters, who are accused of taking jobs that would otherwise go to German workers."*

Gasthaus (gasthows) GERMAN [guesthouse] *noun* (*plural* **Gasthaüser,** gasthoizăr) a guesthouse or inn (especially one in Germany).

gastronome (gastrănōm) FRENCH [from *gastronomie* gastronomy, itself derived from Greek *gastronomia* stomach law] *noun* a person with a love of and serious interest in good food: *"'But first,' he hastily continued, perceiving, with the unerring instinct of an old gastronome, that the inviting refreshments on Vetranio's table had remained untouched, 'permit me to fortify my exhausted energies by a visit to your ever-luxurious board'"* (Wilkie Collins, *Antonina*, 1850).

gateau (gatō), **gâteau** FRENCH [cake] *noun* (*plural* **gateaus,** gatōz, **gateaux** or **gâteaux,** gatō) a rich, often multilayered, cake: *"She felt her determination to stick to the diet start to fail as she stared at the enormous gateau, oozing cream and melting chocolate."*

gauche (gōsh) FRENCH [left, clumsy, awkward] *adjective* lacking in grace, elegance, tact or social experience: *"I wish I had Her constant cheek; I wish that I could sing / All sorts of funny little songs, / Not quite the proper thing. / I'm very gauche and very shy, / Her jokes aren't in my line; / And, worst of all, I'm seventeen / While She is forty-nine"* (Rudyard Kipling, "My Rival," 1886).

gaucherie (gōshăree) FRENCH [left-handedness, clumsiness, derived from *gauche* left, clumsy, awkward] *noun* (*plural* **gaucheries**) a tactless, awkward, or clumsy act or manner: *"He had made his entrance into the 'great world' and he meant to hold his place in it as one 'to the manor born.' Its people should not find him lacking: he would wear their manner and speak their language—no gaucherie should betray him, no homely phrase escape his lips"* (Booth Tarkington, *His Own People*, 1907).

gaucho (gowchō) SPANISH [probably from Araucanian *kaucu*] *noun* (*plural* **gauchos,** gowchōz) a cowboy of the South American pampas, typically of mixed European and American Indian descent: *"The boy was little else than a young Gaucho when he first came to Rock-*

land; for he had learned to ride almost as soon as to walk, and could jump on his pony and trip up a runaway pig with the bolas or noose him with his miniature lasso at an age when some city-children would hardly be trusted out of sight of a nursery-maid" (Oliver Wendell Holmes, *Elsie Venner,* 1859–60).

gavotte (găvot) FRENCH [from Old Provençal *gavot* person from Gap, in the French Alps] *noun* a dance of French peasant origin, or the music to accompany such a dance.

gazette (găzet, gazet) FRENCH [newspaper, from Italian *gazetta,* referring to news sheets that were sold for the price of a *gazeta* (a low-value Venetian coin)] *noun* a newspaper, periodical, or journal: *"If it had concerned either of the political parties, depend upon it, it would have appeared in the Gazette with the earliest intelligence"* (Henry David Thoreau, *Walden,* 1854).

gazpacho (găspachō) SPANISH *noun* (*plural* **gazpachos**) a spicy Spanish soup prepared from tomatoes, peppers, and other chopped raw vegetables, usually served cold: *"A reaping-hook fits my hand better than a governor's scepter; I'd rather have my fill of gazpacho than be subject to the misery of a meddling doctor. . ."* (Miguel de Cervantes Saavedra, *Don Quixote,* 1605).

gefilte (găfĭltă) YIDDISH [stuffed, filled] *adjective* stuffed (usually referring to

gefilte fish, balls of minced fish cooked in fish stock or tomato sauce).

gegenschein (gaygănshīn) GERMAN [counterglow, from *gegen* against and *Schein* shine, light] *noun* a faint glow in the sky that sometimes appears opposite the sun, probably as the result of sunlight reflecting on dust particles.

geisha (gayshă) JAPANESE [art person, from *gei* art and *sha* person] *noun* (*plural* **geisha** or **geishas**) a Japanese girl or woman who is specially trained in the arts of conversation, song and dance to provide entertaining company for men.

gemutlich (gemootlik, gemootlish), **gemütlich** GERMAN [pleasant, comfortable] *adjective* agreeable, friendly, genial, sociable.

gendarme (zhan(g)dahrm) FRENCH [policeman, ultimately from *gens d'armes* men of arms] *noun* (*plural* **gendarmes**) a police officer (especially one in a French-speaking country): *"Burgo, when he first got to the door leading out of the salon, had paused a moment, and, turning round, had encountered the big gendarme close to him"* (Anthony Trollope, *Can You Forgive Her?,* 1864). ~abbreviated form **gend.**

gendarmerie (zhan(g)dahrmăree) FRENCH [constabulary, derived from *gendarme* policeman] *noun* a police station, or the police force as a whole (especially in a French-speaking country): *"Mounted Gendarmerie gallop distracted; are fired on merely as a thing running; galloping over the Pont Royal, or one knows not whither"* (Thomas Carlyle, *History of the French Revolution*, 1837).

generalissimo (jenărălĭsĭmō) ITALIAN [chief general, superlative of *generale* general] *noun (plural* **generalissimos**) the commander in chief of the combined armed forces or of two or more armies: *"Old-Dragoon Drouet is our engineer and generalissimo; valiant as a Ruy Diaz:—Now or never, ye Patriots, for the Soldiery is coming; massacre by Austrians, by Aristocrats, wars more than civil, it all depends on you and the hour!"* (Thomas Carlyle, *History of the French Revolution*, 1837).

genesis (jenăsis) GREEK [*gignesthai* to be born] *noun (plural* **geneses,** jenăseez) the beginning, origin, or creation of something: *"'Could you not prevail to know the genesis of projection, as well as the continuation of it?' Nature, meanwhile, had not waited for the discussion, but, right or wrong, bestowed the impulse, and the balls rolled"* (Ralph Waldo Emerson, "Nature," 1836).

genie (jeenee) FRENCH [*génie*, from Arabic *jinni* demon] *noun (plural* **genies, genii,** jeeneeī) a supernatural being of Arabian and Muslim mythology, credited with the power to cast spells, change shape, and per-

form magic; also used of anyone who demonstrates an unusual talent to grant wishes or get difficult things done: *"I see him yet standing there like a pigmy out of the Arabian Nights before the huge front of some malignant genie. He was daring destiny, and he was unafraid"* (Jack London, *The Sea-Wolf*, 1904).

genius (jeenyăs, jeeneeăs) LATIN [guardian spirit, inclination, from *gignere* to beget] *noun* (plural **geniuses, genii,** geneeī) the attendant spirit of a place or person; by extension, any unusual talent, ability or intellectual capacity or the person who possesses it: *"'Anne says Paul is a genius,' said Mrs. Sloane. 'He may be. You never know what to expect of them Americans,' said Mrs. Andrews. Mrs. Andrews' only acquaintance with the word 'genius' was derived from the colloquial fashion of calling any eccentric individual 'a queer genius'"* (Lucy Maud Montgomery, *Anne of Avonlea*, 1909).

genius loci (lōsee, lōkee) LATIN [the tuterlary deity of a place] *noun phrase* (plural **genii loci,** jeeneeī lōsee, jeeneeī lōkee) the attendant spirit of, or the pervading atmosphere or associations of, a particular place: *"He was a soldier. His sudden appearance was to darkness what the sound of a trumpet is to silence. Gloom, the genius loci at all times hitherto, was now totally overthrown, less by the lantern-light than by what the lantern lighted"* (Thomas Hardy, *Far from the Madding Crowd*, 1874).

genre (<u>zhon</u>ră, <u>zhahn</u>ră, <u>jon</u>ră) FRENCH [kind, sort, gender] *noun* (*plural* **genres**) a category, kind, style, or species of artistic, literary, or other creative work, or more generally any genus, sort, or type. *"His clothes were new and the indescribable smartness of their cut, a genre which had never been obtruded on her notice before, astonished Mrs. Fyne, who came out into the hall with her hat on; for she was about to go out to hear a new pianist (a girl) in a friend's house"* (Joseph Conrad, *Chance*, 1913).

genteel (jen<u>teel</u>, zhon<u>teel</u>) FRENCH [from *gentil* gentle] *adjective* polite, elegant, stylish, or aristocratic: *" 'True, true.' said Joseph Poorgrass. 'The Balls were always a very excitable family. I knowed the boy's grandfather—a truly nervous and modest man, even to genteel refinery"* (Thomas Hardy, *Far from the Madding Crowd*, 1874).

genus (<u>jee</u>năs, jenăs) LATIN [birth, race, kind] *noun* (*plural* **genuses, genera**, <u>jen</u>ără) a kind, class, or group sharing identical or similar characteristics (especially living organisms): *"Cats and lynxes belong to the genus Felis."*

geopolitik (jee<u>ō</u><u>pol</u>itik), **Geopolitik** GERMAN [geopolitics] *noun* the study of the influence of geography, economy, and other forces upon politics and policies that are based upon such considerations.

germ (jerm) FRENCH [from *germe*, from Latin *gignerre* to beget] *noun* a microorganism, or the tiny beginning of a larger development, movement, or idea.

gesellschaft (<u>ge</u>zelshahft) GERMAN [companionship, society] *noun* (*plural* **gesellschafts, gesellschaften**) a class of social integration based upon impersonal relationships, or a society constructed upon such relationships.

gesso (<u>jes</u>ō) ITALIAN [gypsum] *noun* (*plural* **gessoes**) a paste of plaster of paris or gypsum used as a base in painting or gilding or in making bas-reliefs.

gestalt (gă<u>sh</u>talt, gă<u>sh</u>tolt, gă<u>sh</u>talt) GERMAN [shape, form] *noun* (*plural* **gestalts, gestalten**, gă<u>sh</u>taltăn, gă<u>shol</u>tăn, gă<u>sh</u>taltăn) a structure or pattern of biological, psychological, or physical elements combining to create something greater than the sum of its constituent parts.

gestapo (ges<u>tah</u>pō, ges<u>tap</u>ō) GERMAN [from *Geheime Staatspolizei* secret state police] *noun* (*plural* **gestapos**) a secret-police organization or other covert agency suspected of underhand tactics, especially one sharing similarities with the ruthless Gestapo police that operated in Nazi Germany: *"The social service agency was accused of behaving like the Gestapo, splitting up families and causing much needless distress."*

gesundheit (gă<u>zunt</u>hīt) GERMAN [health] *interjection* a response wishing good health to someone who has just sneezed.

geyser (gīzer) ICELANDIC [after the Geyser hot spring in Iceland, from *geysa* to rush forth] a natural hot spring from which hot water and steam gushes periodically and, by extension, a gas-operated hot-water heater: *"Now, unless the sandbank had been submitted to the intermittent eruption of a geyser, the Governor Higginson had to do neither more nor less than with an aquatic mammal, unknown till then, which threw up from its blow-holes columns of water mixed with air and vapour"* (Jules Verne, *20,000 Leagues Under the Sea*, 1869).

gharry (garee) HINDI [from *gari* horse-drawn cart] *noun* (*plural* **gharries**) a horse-drawn cab or carriage of a type traditionally used in India and other countries.

ghat (gat), **ghaut** HINDI [from *ghat*] *noun* in India, a flight of steps leading down to the riverbank, used for bathing, cremations, and other rituals.

ghee (gee), **ghi** HINDI [from Sanskrit *ghrta,* past participle of *ghr* to sprinkle] *noun* clarified liquid butter, as used in Indian cuisine.

ghetto (getō) ITALIAN [Jewish quarter, from Venetian dialect *gheto* foundry, referring to the section of Venice with a foundry where most of Venice's Jews were forced to live] *noun* (*plural* **ghettos, ghettoes**) a quarter of a city in which members of the Jewish or other minority community are obliged to congregate for political, legal, economic, or other reasons: *"He passed over the river, and saw the lanterns hanging to the masts of the ships. He passed over the Ghetto, and saw the old Jews bargaining with each other, and weighing out money in copper scales"* (Oscar Wilde, *The Happy Prince and Other Tales,* 1888). Also used more generally to refer to any slum quarter.

ghi *See* GHEE.

ghoul (gool) ARABIC [from *ghul*] *noun* in Arabian legend, an evil demon that robs graves to feed on the dead; also used more generally of any monster, demon, or someone who has similar characteristics or tastes: *"Do you suppose I eat like an ogre or a ghoul, that you dread being the companion of my repast?"* (Charlotte Brontë, *Jane Eyre,* 1847).

gigolo (jigălō, zhigălō) FRENCH [ladies' man] *noun* (*plural* **gigolos**) a man who dances with women for money, or is paid or otherwise rewarded to act as a companion, escort, or lover of wealthy (typically older) women: *"As a young man he tried to make ends meet by offering himself as a gigolo to the bored wives of rich businessmen."*

gigot (jigăt, zheegō) FRENCH [from *gigue* fiddle, from its shape] *noun* (*plural* **gigots,** jigăts, zheegōz) a leg of meat (usually lamb or mutton).

163

gingham (gin(g)ăm) FRENCH [from Malay *genggang* striped cloth] *noun* dyed cotton fabric with a plain weave: *"The brown gingham and the blue print will do you for school when you begin to go"* (Lucy Maud Montgomery, *Anne of Green Gables*, 1908). ~*adjective* of or relating to such fabric.

ginseng (jinseng, jinseng) CHINESE [from *ren* man and *shen* herb] *noun* the perennial herb *(Panax schinseng or Panax quinquefolius)* having an aromatic root with various purported medicinal properties.

giocoso (zheeăkōsō) ITALIAN [merry] *adverb* in music, an instruction to play a passage merrily or joyously.

girandole (jirăndōl) FRENCH [from Italian *girandola* from late Latin *gyrare* to gyrate] *noun* a revolving or radiating firework or jet of water, or alternatively an ornate candelabrum or cluster design in jewelry: *"'Ingenious,' remarked Hunsden; 'whether true or not is another question. Meantime, don't you feel your little lamp of a spirit wax very pale, beside such a girandole as Lucia's?"* (Charlotte Brontë, *The Professor*, 1857).

giro (jīrō) ITALIAN [from Greek *gyros* circuit] *noun* European banking system that facilitates the direct transfer of funds between account holders without the transfer of actual cash: *"Payments will be made by giro to reduce the risk of claimants getting their money late."*

gite (zheet), **gîte** FRENCH [lodging] *noun* a holiday home of the type widely offered to visitors in rural parts of France and other French-speaking countries: *"Last year we spent the summer in a gite on the French coast."*

glacé (glasay) FRENCH [past participle of *glacer* to freeze, to ice] *adjective* of or relating to something that has a glossy or glazed surface, as though frozen: *"Maria Nikolaevna was dressed that day very much 'to her advantage,' as our grandmothers used to say. She wore a pink glacé silk dress, with sleeves à la Fontange, and a big diamond in each ear"* (Ivan Turgenev, *Torrents of Spring*, 1870).

glasnost (glaznost) RUSSIAN [publicity, public information] *noun* official government policy promoting unrestrained discussion of important issues and freedom of news and information, as adopted by the Soviet regime in the 1980s: *"The press demanded greater access to secret government files, arguing that any refusal would be tantamount to a denial of the spirit of glasnost that the country's leaders professed themselves to be so eager to promote."*

glissade (glisayd) FRENCH [slide, from *glisser* to slip] *noun* in dancing, a sliding or gliding step as though on ice. Also used to refer to an expanse of ice on a mountainside: *"Along their track lay the villages of the hill-folk—mud and earth huts, the timbers now and then rudely carved with an axe—clinging like* *swallows' nests against the steeps, huddled on tiny flats half-way down a three-thousand-foot glissade . . ."* (Rudyard Kipling, *Kim,* 1901).

glissando (glisandō) ITALIAN [sliding, from French *glisser* to slip, to slide] *noun* (*plural* **glissandos, glissandi,** glisandee) in music, a rapid slide up or down a scale. ~*adjective* of or relating to a passage of music to be played in such a manner.

glockenspiel (glokănspeel, glokăn-shpeel) GERMAN [bell-play, from *Glocke* bell and *Spiel* play] *noun* (*plural* **glockenspiels**) a musical instrument in which tuned metal bars are struck with two mallets.

gloire (glwah) FRENCH [glory] *noun* glory, especially the glory of France as a nation: *"Thousands of French soldiers were sacrificed on the Somme in the cause of 'la gloire,' there being little prospect otherwise of any material gain."*

gloria See GLORIA IN EXCELSIS; GLORIA PATRI.

Gloria in Excelsis (gloreeă in ekschelsis, gloreeă in ekselsis) LATIN [glory on high] *noun phrase* a Christian prayer in praise of God on high (the "greater doxology"). ~*abbreviated form* **gloria.** Also, a sacred musical setting of this prayer.

Gloria Patri (gloreeă patree) LATIN [glory to the Father] *noun phrase* a Christian prayer in praise of God the

Father (the "lesser doxology"). ~*abbreviated form* **gloria, G.P.**

glossolalia (glosălayleeă) GREEK [from *glossa* tongue and *lalia* talk] *noun* (*plural* **glossolalias**) speaking in tongues, the gift of tongues (as employed in Pentecostal churches).

gnocchi (nokee, nyokee) ITALIAN [plural of *gnocco,* from *nocchio* knot in wood] *plural noun* a type of potato, flour, or semolina dumplings, usually served in sauce.

gnome (nōm) GREEK [thought, from *gignoskein* to know] *noun* (*plural,* **gnomae,** nōmī, or **gnomes**) a maxim, adage, proverb, or aphorism.

gnomon (nōmăn) GREEK [interpreter, from *gignoskein* to know] *noun* the pointer on a sundial, or any pillar, column, or shaft erected vertically for similar purposes: *"Exactly as the gnomon of the official dial up in the citadel pointed the second hour half gone, the legion, in full panoply, and with all its standards on exhibit, descended from Mount Sulpius. . ."* (Lew Wallace, *Ben Hur,* 1880).

go (gō) JAPANESE *noun* Japanese board game played on a checkered black-and-white board in which players attempt to gain control of the greater area of territory.

golem (gōlăm, gōlăm) YIDDISH [from *goylem,* fool, derived from Hebrew *golem* shapeless mass] *noun* an artificial human being of Jewish legend, usually described as a figure of clay endowed with life through magic: *"The children's grandmother had been forbidden to frighten the children with tales about the golem, but she was soon prevailed upon to forget the injunction."*

gondola (<u>gon</u>dălă) ITALIAN [Venetian dialect, probably from Middle Greek *kontoura* small vessel] *noun* a long, narrow, flat-bottomed boat with a high pointed prow and stern, as seen on the canals of Venice: *"The Venetian gondola is as free and graceful, in its gliding movement, as a serpent. It is twenty or thirty feet long, and is narrow and deep, like a canoe; its sharp bow and stern sweep upward from the water like the horns of a crescent with the abruptness of the curve slightly modified"* (Mark Twain, *Innocents Abroad,* 1869). Also applied to the passenger compartment of an airship or dirigible, which sometimes bears a vague resemblance in shape to the boats of Venice, and to the enclosed cars suspended from cables as on ski lifts.

gong (gong) MALAYSIAN [imitative of the sound a gong makes] *noun* a disk-shaped percussion instrument that is struck with a padded hammer to produce sound: *"Oh, Timballoo! how happy we are, / We live in a sieve and a crockery jar! / And all night long, in the starlight pale, / We sail away, with a pea-green sail, / And whistle and warble a moony song / To the echoing sound of a coppery gong"* (Louisa May Alcott, *Eight Cousins,* 1875).

Götterdämmerung (gertă<u>damă</u>rung), **götterdämmerung** GERMAN [twilight of the gods, the title of the climactic opera in Wagner's *Ring Cycle*] *noun* (*plural* **Götterdammerüngen,** gertă<u>damă</u>rungăn) the end of the world, or the total collapse of a political, social or economic system, with its accompanying chaos.

gouache (gwahsh) FRENCH [from Italian *guazzo,* puddle] *noun* in art, a technique of painting with opaque water-soluble pigment, a picture painted with such pigment or the pigment itself: *"Lydie, who had been taught music by Schmucke, was herself a musician capable of composing; she could wash in a sepia drawing, and paint in gouache and water-color"* (Honoré de Balzac, *Scenes from a Courtesan's Life,* 1839–47).

goujon (<u>goo</u>zhon(g) FRENCH [from Latin *gobius* goby] *noun* a strip of fish or chicken, usually deep-fried.

goulash (<u>goo</u>lash) HUNGARIAN [from *gulyashus* herdsman's meat] *noun* a highly seasoned meat and vegetable stew: *"She prepared them a hearty goulash, conscious that it might be days before they ate their next hot meal."*

gourmand (<u>goor</u>mond, goor<u>mond</u>) FRENCH [greedy, gluttonous, from Middle French *gourmant*] *noun* (*plural*

gourmands) a glutton, a person who loves food and drink to excess: *"Look at your knife-handle, there, my civilized and enlightened gourmand, dining off that roast beef, what is that handle made of?—what but the bones of the brother of the very ox you are eating?"* (Herman Melville, *Moby Dick*, 1851). ~*noun, feminine* **gourmande** (*plural* **gourmandes**).

gourmandise (goormon<u>deez</u>) FRENCH [from *gourmand*] *noun* gluttony, or appreciation of and indulgence in good food and drink: *"'Oh, if I was permitted a vice it would be the gourmandise!' Could I resist that? No. I gave her a gooseberry"* (Mark Twain, *Horse's Tale*, 1907).

gourmet (goor<u>may</u>) FRENCH [from *groumet* wine taster] *noun* (*plural* **gourmets**) an epicure, a connoisseur of food and drink: *"Indeed, when she had her own supper, she joined the Kennicotts, and how ludicrous it was to suppose that Maud was a gourmet of emotions Carol saw in the fact that she talked not to one of the town beaux but to the safe Kennicott himself!"* (Sinclair Lewis, *Main Street*, 1920). ~*adjective* of or relating to fine food and drink or to a person with an interest in and knowledge of good food and drink.

goy (goi) YIDDISH [from Hebrew *goy* people, nation] *noun* (*plural* **goys** or **goyim,** goiăm) derogatory term for a non-Jew or Gentile: *"Relentless persecution of Jews, century after century, in* nation after nation, left a legacy of bitter sayings: 'Dos ken nor a goy' ('That, only a goy is capable of doing')"* (L. Rosten, *The Joys of Yiddish*, 1968).

G.P. *See* GLORIA PATRI; GRAND PRIX.

gracias (<u>gra</u>seeăs, <u>gra</u>thiăs) SPANISH [thanks] *noun* thank you: *"She seemed the incarnation of girlish scorn and wilful passion. 'Gracias, senor,' she replied, mockingly. 'Adios.' Then she flashed out of his sight"* (Zane Grey, *Desert Gold*, 1913).

gracioso (grasee<u>ō</u>s<u>ō</u>) SPANISH [agreeable, amusing] *noun* (*plural* **graciosos**) a buffoon or clown in traditional Spanish comedy.

gradatim (grad<u>ay</u>tim, gray<u>day</u>tim) LATIN [by steps] *adverb* by degrees, gradually.

Graf (grahf) GERMAN [count] *noun* (*plural* **Grafen,** <u>grah</u>făn) a rank of German nobility: *"Graf von Ferdinand Zeppelin was a well-known pioneer of flight."* ~*noun, feminine* **Gräfin** (<u>grah</u>făn).

graffiti (gră<u>fee</u>tee) ITALIAN [plural of *graffito*, from *graffiare* to scratch] *plural noun* words or symbols painted, written or incised on a wall or other surface (usually one in general public view): *"No one knew for certain who was responsible for the graffiti on the lavatory door, but several people had their suspicions."*

grand coup (gron(g) <u>koo</u>) FRENCH [big blow] *noun phrase* (*plural* **grands**

coups) a bold move or decisive stroke: *"The acquisition of the company by its main rivals was a stunning grand coup that took the markets entirely by surprise."* See also COUP.

grand cru (gron(g) <u>kroo</u>) FRENCH [great vintage] *noun phrase* (*plural* **grands crus**) fine wine, wine of superior quality.

grande cuisine (grond kwi<u>zeen</u>) FRENCH [grand cooking] *noun phrase* high quality or fashionable cooking: *"It was a meal in the best traditions of French grand cuisine, with the best ingredients and mouth-watering sauces."*

grande dame (grond <u>dahm</u>) FRENCH [great lady] *noun phrase* (*plural* **grandes dames,** grond <u>dahms</u>) a mature woman of considerable status or influence, typically of distinguished bearing and noble birth: *"Still she did not forget that Anna, her sister-in-law, was the wife of one of the most important personages in Petersburg, and was a Petersburg grande dame"* (Leo Tolstoy, *Anna Karenina,* 1874–76).

grandee (gran<u>dee</u>) SPANISH [from grande great, large] *noun* a high-ranking nobleman, originally of Spanish or Portuguese society but now used more widely of any high-ranking or influential person: *"I was bound to see more of him, so I invited him to come out to Marco's Sunday, and dine with us. Marco was appalled, and held his breath: and when the grandee accepted, he was so*

grateful that he almost forgot to be astonished at the condescension" (Mark Twain, *A Connecticut Yankee in King Arthur's Court,* 1889).

grande passion (grond <u>pas</u>yon(g) FRENCH [grand passion] *noun phrase* (*plural* **grandes passions**) an intense love affair or overwhelming passion for someone or something: *"But a really grande passion is comparatively rare nowadays. It is the privilege of people who have nothing to do"* (Oscar Wilde, *A Woman of No Importance,* 1893).

Grand Guignol (gron(g) gi<u>nyol</u>) FRENCH [great punch, after the Grand Guignol Theater, Paris] *noun phrase* a melodramatic style of theatrical entertainment of particularly bloody or gruesome character.

grandioso (grandee<u>o</u><u>so</u>) ITALIAN [from Latin *grandis* grand] *adverb* in music, to be played in a majestic, broad manner. ~*adjective* of or relating to music of an imposing, noble style.

grand jeté (gron(g) jă<u>tay</u>) FRENCH [big leap] *noun phrase* (*plural* **grands jetés**) in ballet, a big jump or leap (occasionally used more widely of any major advance or move): *"He completed his solo with a grand jeté performed with apparently effortless ease."*

grand luxe (gron(g) <u>looks</u>) FRENCH [great luxury] *noun phrase* the height of luxury.

grand mal (gron(g) <u>mal</u>) FRENCH [great sickness] *noun phrase*   severe epilepsy. See also PETIT MAL.

grand prix (gron(g) <u>pree</u>), **Grand Prix** FRENCH [big prize] *noun phrase* (*plural* **grands prix,** gron(g) <u>preez</u>) a contest at the highest level, often referring to international Formula One motor racing but also applicable to equestrianism, cycling, tennis, and other activities: *"Do you remember, my dear Madame de Camps, that in 1831 you and I went together to the Beaux-Arts to see the exhibition of works which were competing for the Grand Prix in sculpture?"* (Honoré de Balzac, *Deputy of Arcis,* 1847). ~*abbreviated form* **G.P.**

grand seigneur (gron(g) sen<u>yoor</u>) FRENCH [great lord] *noun* (*plural* **grands seigneurs**) a great nobleman or aristocrat, typically of French background: *"Mills hardly deigned to answer that he didn't know anything about his cousin's movements. 'A grand seigneur combined with a great connoisseur,' opined the other heavily"* (Joseph Conrad, *The Arrow of Gold,* 1919).

grand siècle (gron(g) see<u>ye</u>klă) FRENCH [the great century] *noun phrase* (*plural* **grands siècles**) the classical or golden age, often referring specifically to the reign of Louis XIV of France (1638–1715).

gran turismo (gran tyoo<u>riz</u>mō) ITALIAN [great touring] *noun phrase*   high-performance, high-specification (of automobiles). ~*abbreviated form* **G.T.**

grappa (<u>gra</u>pă) ITALIAN [Italian dialect for grape stalk] *noun*   brandy distilled from the remains of the grapes after winemaking.

gratin (<u>gra</u>tăn, <u>grah</u>tăn) FRENCH [from *grater* to grate] *noun*   a method of cooking in which grated cheese or breadcrumbs is sprinkled on food and then cooked to form a thin brown crust: *"The waiters reported that they objected to their breakfasts, and especially to the eggs. Thereupon (to translate the Frenchman's own way of putting it) he exhausted himself in exquisite preparations of eggs. Eggs à la tripe, au gratin . . . and so on"* (Wilkie Collins, *I Say No,* 1884).

gratis (<u>gra</u>tis, <u>grah</u>tis) LATIN [ablative plural of *gratia* favor] *adverb*   freely, gratuitously: *"They spoke to me with great humanity, and said, they were sure the captain would carry me gratis to Lisbon, whence I might return to my own country. . ."* (Jonathan Swift, *Gulliver's Travels,* 1726). ~*adjective* free, without charge.

gravadlax   *See* GRAVLAX.

gravamen (gră<u>vah</u>măn) LATIN [burden, from *gravare* to weigh on, oppress] *noun* (*plural* **gravamens** or **gravamina,** gră<u>vah</u>mănă)   the substance or gist of a complaint, accusation, or grievance.

169

gravida (gravădă) LATIN [feminine of *gravidus*, from *gravis* heavy] *noun* (*plural* **gravidas** or **gravidae,** gravădee) a pregnant woman.

gravitas (gravitas) LATIN [seriousness] *noun* gravity, solemnity, or high seriousness: "*The inspector listened to their story with suitable gravitas.*"

gravlax (gravlaks), **gravlaks, gravadlax** (gravadlaks) SWEDISH [buried salmon] *noun* salmon cured with salt, dill, and other spices.

grazioso (gratseeōsō) ITALIAN [gracious] *adverb* in music, an instruction for a passage of music to be played gracefully. ~*adjective* of or relating to a passage of music to be played gracefully.

grenadine (grenădeen, grenădeen) FRENCH [from *grenade* pomegranate] *noun* a cordial syrup flavored with pomegranate juice.

grimace (grimăs, grimays) FRENCH [from *grimache*] *noun* a facial expression of disapproval or disgust: "'*You're a damned rogue,*' *says the old gentleman, making a hideous grimace at the door as he shuts it.* '*But I'll lime you, you dog, I'll lime you!*'" (Charles Dickens, *Bleak House,* 1852–53). ~*verb* to make such a face.

gringo (gringō) SPANISH [foreigner, gibberish, from *griego* Greek, stranger] *noun* (*plural* **gringos**) a foreigner in Spain or in Spanish-speaking Latin America, usually applied to white-skinned non-Hispanics, especially of Anglo-Saxon background: "*The peasants could not make up their minds whether the stranger was the man they had been waiting for or just another lazy gringo down on his luck.*" ~*adjective* of or relating to a gringo or anything foreign.

grisette (grizet) FRENCH [cheap, unbleached cloth, as worn by French shopgirls, from *gris* grey] *noun* (*plural* **grisettes**) a French working girl or shopgirl, typically coquettish in character. Also applied to such young women who supplemented their income with part-time prostitution: "*Still Adrienne thought herself the obliged party, in times as critical as those which then hung over France, in being permitted to toil for a sum that would barely supply a grisette, accustomed all her life to privations, with the coarsest necessaries*" (James Fenimore Cooper, *Autobiography of a Pocket-Handkerchief,* 1843).

gros point (gro pwan(g)) FRENCH [large point] *noun phrase* a form of embroidery in which stitches are worked over a double-thread canvas.

grotesque (grōtesk) FRENCH [from Italian *grottesco* of a grotto or cave] *adjective* bizarre, fanciful, distorted, or hideous: "*The effect is said to be unspeakably absurd: and if I may judge from a print of this ceremony which I have in my possession; and which I am informed* *by those who have visited the chapel, is perfectly accurate; it must be infinitely grotesque."* (Charles Dickens, *American Notes,* 1842).

grotto (gro̱to̱) ITALIAN [cavern] *noun* a cavern, or an artificial recess or retreat with cave-like qualities: *"They retreated by the same passage which had admitted them to the prior's secret seat of observation, and when they issued from the grotto into the wood, the birds which began to chirp, and even to sing, announced that the dawn was advanced"* (Walter Scott, *The Antiquary,* 1816).

G.T. *See* GRAN TURISMO.

guacamole (gwaka̱mo̱lee) SPANISH [from Nahuatl *ahuacatl* avocado and *molli* sauce] *noun* a Mexican dish of pureed or mashed avocado mixed with seasonings.

guano (gwahno̱) SPANISH [from Quechua *huanu* dung, fertilizer] *noun* (*plural* **guanos**) a natural fertilizer made from the droppings of seabirds or bats: *"Of course they might be made into guano, and Cape Cod is not so fertile that her inhabitants can afford to do without this manure,—to say nothing of the diseases they may produce."* (Henry David Thoreau, *Cape Cod,* 1865).

gueridon (ge̱rida̱n(g)), **guéridon** FRENCH [after Gueridon, a traditional character in French farces and songs] *noun* a small (usually round and often elaborately carved) ornamental table or stand.

guerrilla (geri̱la̱, ga̱ri̱la̱) SPANISH [little war, diminutive of *guerra* war] *noun* (*plural* **guerrillas**) an irregular soldier, typically one belonging to a band of such fighters and usually engaged in raids and acts of sabotage behind enemy lines. ~*adjective* of or relating to such fighters or their campaigns and tactics: *"That aim was attained in the first place of itself, as the French ran away, and so it was only necessary not to stop their flight. Secondly it was attained by the guerrilla warfare which was destroying the French."* (Leo Tolstoy, *War and Peace,* 1863–69).

guillotine (gi̱lăteen, geeăteen) FRENCH [after French physician Joseph Ignace Guillotin (1738–1814), who proposed the use of the guillotine during the French Revolution] *noun* a decapitating machine in which the head of the condemned prisoner is cleanly severed by a heavy falling blade with a diagonal cutting edge: *"According to the received code in such matters, it would have been nothing short of duty, in a politician, to bring every one of those white heads under the axe of the guillotine"* (Nathaniel Hawthorne, *The Scarlet Letter,* 1850). Also used of smaller devices designed to cut paper. ~*verb* to cut off someone's head (or a piece of paper, etc.) using a guillotine.

guitar (gita̱hr, ga̱tahr) SPANISH [guitarra from Greek *kithara]* *noun* a string instrument with six strings, played with the fingers or a pick: *"She was a fearless and familiar little thing, who asked disconcerting questions, made precocious comments, and possessed outlandish arts, such as dancing a Spanish shawl dance and singing Neapolitan love-songs to a guitar"* (Edith Wharton, *The Age of Innocence,* 1920).

gulag (go͞olag) RUSSIAN [from *Glavnoe upravlenie ispravitel no-trudovykh lagerei* chief administration of corrective labor camps] *noun* a Soviet prison camp, one of a system of such camps set up by the Communist regime in the USSR for the confinement of political prisoners and other criminals: *"Thousands of dissidents were carried off from their homes and sent to a miserable death in the gulags, their disappearance barely noticed by the foreign press."*

gung-ho (gung hō) CHINESE [from *gonghé,* from *Zhongguo Gongye Hezuo She* Chinese Industrial Cooperative Society, but interpreted as meaning "work together" and adopted as a slogan by U.S. Marines during World War II] *adjective* eager, enthusiastic, overzealous: *"The colonel was very gung-ho about their chances of victory."*

Gurkha (gerkă) NEPALESE [after the Gurkha people of Nepal] *noun* a member of the warlike Rajput clan of Nepal, often referring to soldiers from Nepal serving in the British or Indian army: *"The Gurkhas established a fearsome reputation in the jungle campaigns against the Japanese."*

guru (go͞oroo, gǎroo) HINDI [from *guru* heavy, venerable] *noun* (*plural* **gurus**) in Hinduism, a spiritual guide or religious teacher, but also used in a much wider context of any influential instructor or popular expert: *"'I am no Khitai, but a Bhotiya (Tibetan), since you must know—a lama—or, say, a guru in your tongue.' 'A guru from Tibet,' said Kim. 'I have not seen such a man. They be Hindus in Tibet, then?'"* (Rudyard Kipling, *Kim,* 1901).

gusto (gustō) ITALIAN [taste, pleasure] *noun* enthusiasm, vigor, vitality, relish, enjoyment, delight: *"Penrod brought the bottle down, surprisingly full after so much gusto, but withheld it from Sam; and the two scuffled for its possession"* (Booth Tarkington, *Penrod,* 1914).

gutta-percha (gǎtă perchă) MALAYSIAN [from *getah* sap, latex and *percha* scrap, rag] *noun* a rubbery plastic substance derived from the latex of various Malaysian trees, variously used in dentistry, electrical insulation, and elsewhere.

gym *See* GYMNASIUM.

gymkhana (jimkahnă) HINDI [from *gedkhana* ball court] *noun* a festival of sporting contests and athletic displays, most often a series of competitive equestrian events: *"Miss Venner did* *not know what magnum opus meant; but she knew that Captain Kerrington had won three races at the last Gymkhana"* (Rudyard Kipling, "Wressley of the Foreign Office," 1887).

gymnasium (jim<u>nay</u>zeeăm) GREEK [*gymnazein* to exercise naked] *noun* (*plural* **gymnasiums** or **gymnasia,** jim<u>nay</u>zeeă) an indoor sports facility suitable for a range of sports and gymnastics: *"The Zenith Athletic Club is not athletic and it isn't exactly a club, but it is Zenith in perfection. It has an active and smoke-misted billiard room, it is represented by baseball and football teams, and in the pool and the gymnasium a tenth of the members sporadically try to reduce"* (Sinclair Lewis, *Babbitt,* 1922). ~*shortened form:* **gym.**

h

h.a.   *See* HOC ANNO.

habeas corpus (haybeeăs <u>kor</u>păs) LATIN [you should have the body] *noun phrase* a common law writ under which a party may be summoned to court, or else protected against illegal imprisonment through investigation of the legitimacy of that person's detention: *"Trip up a policeman in such a scramble, and he will take it in good spirit; but mention the words 'Habeas Corpus,' and he'll lock you up if he can"* (Anthony Trollope, *Phineas Finn,* 1869).

habitat (<u>hab</u>ĭtat) LATIN [he, she, or it inhabits] *noun* a place or environment that a particular person, plant, or animal normally frequents; often referring to a person's domestic surroundings: *"The Arctic is the natural habitat of the polar bear."*

habitué (ha<u>bich</u>yooay, hă<u>bich</u>yooay) FRENCH [past participle of *habituer* to frequent] *noun* a person who regularly frequents a particular place or kind of place, such as nightclubs or theaters: *"'Darm their nasty ways,' said Tony to Mr. Larry Twentyman, who was one of the popular habitués of the hunt; 'they runs one a top of another's brushes, till there ain't a 'ound living knows t'other from which"* (Anthony Trollope, *Ayala's Angel,* 1881).

hacienda (hasee<u>en</u>dă) SPANISH [derived from Latin *faciendus,* things to be done, gerundive of *facere* to do] *noun* (*plural* **haciendas**)   a large Spanish-style country estate or plantation, or the main building within such an estate: *"Our first day's ride was northward along the seacoast. After dark we reached the Hacienda of Quintero, the estate which formerly belonged to Lord Cochrane"* (Charles Darwin, *Voyage of the Beagle,* 1839).

hac lege (hac <u>le</u>gay) LATIN [with this law] *noun phrase*   under this law or regulation.

Hades (<u>hay</u>deez), **hades** GREEK [after Haides, god of the underworld] *noun* the underworld, or hell, or the god who rules the abode of the dead: *"She stood fearfully at the extreme edge of a stupendous cliff, where it sheered dark and forbidding, down and down, into what*

175

seemed red and boundless depths of Hades" (Zane Grey, *Call of the Canyon*, 1924).

hadj *See* HAJJ.

hadji *See* HAJJI.

hafiz (<u>hah</u>fiz) PERSIAN [from Arabic *hafiz*, one who memorizes or guards] *noun* a Muslim who has memorized the Koran.

ha-ha (<u>hah</u> hah) FRENCH [from *haha*, probably inspired by the cry of surprise that might greet the discovery of a concealed barrier] *noun* a ditch with a sunken retaining wall, used in parks and gardens to create a barrier to livestock without defacing the landscape: "*Farm animals were kept out of the park by the discreet use of a ha-ha.*"

haiku (<u>hī</u>koo) JAPANESE [from *hai* amusement, entertainment and *ku* sentence] *noun* (*plural* **haiku** or **haikus**) a Japanese verse form consisting of three unrhymed lines with a total of 17 syllables (5-7-5), typically on the topic of nature or the seasons: "*She spent the morning trying to compose a haiku about a raindrop on a leaf.*"

hajj (haj), **hadj** ARABIC [pilgrimage] *noun* the pilgrimage to the sacred mosque at Mecca that all Muslims are expected to make during their lifetimes as a matter of religious duty: "*Devotees may excuse themselves from making the hajj on the grounds of physical disability or a range of other inconveniences.*"

hajji (<u>ha</u>jee), **hadji** ARABIC [pilgrim] *noun* (*feminine* **hajja**, <u>ha</u>jă, or **hadja**) a person who has successfully completed the pilgrimage to the sacred mosque at Mecca that all Muslims are expected to make during their lifetimes as a matter of religious duty.

haka (ha<u>k</u>ă) MAORI *noun* a ceremonial war dance of the Maori people of New Zealand: "*The New Zealand rugby squad is famous for its performance of the haka before major internationals matches.*"

hakim (1) (<u>hah</u>kim), **hakeem** ARABIC [ruler, from *hakama* to pass judgment] *noun* (*plural* **hakims** or **hakeems**) a judge, ruler, or administrator in a Muslim country: "*The hakim said that at any time we may return to the Plains, for we do no more than skirt the pleasant places. The hakim is full of learning; but he is in no way proud*" (Rudyard Kipling, *Kim*, 1901).

hakim (2) (hă<u>keem</u>) ARABIC [wise man] *noun* (*plural* **hakims**) a physician in a Muslim country.

halakah (hala<u>k</u>ă, hală<u>kah</u>), **halacha** (HEBREW [that which one walks by, way, from *halak,* to walk] *noun* that part of Talmudic writing that deals with Jewish religious law.

halal (hă<u>lal</u>), **hallal** ARABIC [lawful, according to religious law] *adjective* of or relating to meat slaughtered and prepared in a ritual manner according to Islamic holy law: *"The store carries an impressive range of halal meats."* ~*noun* meat that has been slaughtered and prepared in a ritual manner according to Islamic holy law.

halcyon (<u>hal</u>seeăn, <u>hal</u>syăn) GREEK [*alkuon* kingfisher] *adjective* peaceful, calm, prosperous, or idyllic. ~*noun* in Greek myth, a legendary bird that was believed to calm the waves by magic in order to nest at sea during the winter solstice, often identified with the kingfisher: *"Then for the teeming quietest, happiest days of all! / The brooding and blissful halcyon days!"* (Walt Whitman, "Halcyon Days," *Leaves of Grass,* 1891–92 version).

hallal *See* HALAL

hallelujah (halay<u>loo</u>yă, hali<u>loo</u>yă), **halleluiah, alleluia** HEBREW [praise ye the Lord, from *hallelu* praise and *Yah* God] *interjection* an expression of praise, joy, or thanks: *"In heaven, all the redeemed are shouting 'Hallelujah!'"* ~*noun* a shout or song of praise, joy, or thanksgiving.

hände hoch (handee <u>hok</u>) GERMAN [hands up] *noun phrase* an instruction to a prisoner to put his or her hands in the air to indicate surrender, in imitation of Allied troops to captured German soldiers in the two world wars: *"The boy pointed his stick threateningly and growled 'hände hoch!' just as he had seen soldiers in the movies do."*

Hanukkah (<u>ha</u>nukă), **Hanukah, Chanukah** HEBREW [dedication] *noun* an eight-day Jewish holiday commemorating the rededication of the Temple of Jerusalem in 165 B.C.

hara-kiri (hară <u>ki</u>ree), **hari-kari** (haree <u>ka</u>ree) JAPANESE [from *hara* belly and *kiri* cutting] *noun* Japanese tradition of ritual suicide by disembowelment and cut throat, associated with the aristocratic samurai class; also formerly employed as a form of capital punishment imposed by feudal courts in Japan. Commonly applied today to any apparently deliberate self-harming act or policy: *"The opposition reveled in the government's apparent act of hara-kiri, knowing that these latest tax increases would lose millions of votes in the election."*

Hare Krishna (haree <u>krish</u>nă) HINDI [O Krishna] *noun phrase* a religious movement based on Hindu principles, founded by Surami Prabhupada and dedicated to worship of the god Krishna, or one of its adherents: *"As a teenager she had flirted with the idea of taking up Hare Krishna."*

harem (<u>ha</u>răm, <u>he</u>răm) TURKISH [sanctuary, derived from Arabic *haram* something forbidden] *noun* the wives, concubines, and various female servants and relatives of a single Muslim man, or the part of a building in which they live, often secluded from contact with the outside world. Also applied to female animals of certain species who share a single mate.

haricots verts (harikō <u>vair</u>) FRENCH [green beans, possibly after Aztec *ayacotli*] *plural noun* a variety of bean *(Phaseolus vulgaris)* with edible green pods.

hari-kari *See* HARA-KIRI.

hashish (ha<u>sheesh</u>, <u>ha</u>sheesh, <u>ha</u>shish), **hasheesh** ARABIC [from *hasis,* dry herb] *noun* the concentrated resin of the female cannabis plant *(Cannabis sativa)* that has a narcotic effect if smoked, chewed, or drunk: *"Having neither opium nor hashish on hand, and being desirous of filling his brain with twilight, he had had recourse to that fearful mixture of brandy, stout, absinthe, which produces the most terrible of lethargies"* (Victor Hugo, *Les Misérables,* 1862). ~*abbreviated form* **hash.**

hasta la vista (astă la <u>vee</u>stă) SPANISH [until the sight] *interjection* goodbye, until we meet again, or, see you again: *"He rose his arm in salute as he drove away, calling a final 'Hasta la vista, baby' over his shoulder."*

hasta mañana (astă man<u>ya</u>nă) SPANISH [until tomorrow] *interjection* see you tomorrow.

hatha yoga (hată <u>yō</u>gă) SANSKRIT [from *hatha* force and *yoga* yoga] *noun phrase* a system of physical exercise and breathing control that developed as a Hindu discipline.

hausfrau (<u>hows</u>frow) GERMAN [wife, from *Haus* house and *Frau* woman] *noun* (*plural* **hausfraus** or **hausfrauen,** <u>hows</u>frowăn) a housewife: *"Their host was a hausfrau with a brittle smile and bad teeth."*

haute bourgeoisie (ōt boorzhah<u>zee</u>) FRENCH [high bourgeoisie] *noun phrase* the upper middle or professional class.

haute couture (ōt koo<u>toor</u>, ōt koo<u>choor</u>) FRENCH [high sewing] *noun phrase* high fashion, or the top design houses that dictate current fashion and the products they produce: *"Few people can afford to fill their wardrobe with examples of modern haute couture."* ~*abbreviated form* **couture.**

haute cuisine (ōt kwi<u>zeen</u>) FRENCH [high cooking] *noun phrase* elaborate or fashionable, high-quality cuisine, as offered at the best restaurants and hotels: *"The hotel is noted for its haute cuisine, the work of its internationally famous chef."*

haute école (ōt e<u>kol</u>) FRENCH [high school] *noun phrase* in horse riding, an advanced level of dressage; sometimes applied to music and other arts.

haute monde *See* HAUT MONDE.

haute noblesse (ōt nō<u>bles</u>) FRENCH [high nobility] *noun* the upper echelons of the nobility.

haute politique (ōt poli<u>teek</u>) FRENCH [high politics] *noun phrase* politics as conducted at the most senior or rarefied levels: *"The two ambassadors were deep in conversation on matters of haute politique."*

hauteur (ō<u>ter</u>, hō<u>ter</u>) FRENCH [from *haut* high] *noun* (*plural* **hauteurs**) haughtiness, arrogance, or condescension of manner: *"Now they were men and women of the world, very supercilious men and women; the boys condescended to Babbitt, they wore evening-clothes, and with hauteur they accepted cigarettes from silver cases"* (Sinclair Lewis, *Babbitt*, 1922).

haut monde (ō <u>mond</u>), **haute monde** (ōt <u>mond</u>) FRENCH [high world] *noun phrase* fashionable or high society.

haut-relief (ōre<u>leef</u>) FRENCH [high relief] *noun* a sculpture or carving in high relief: *"The pulpit is decorated with figures of angels in haut-relief."*

haut ton (ō ton(g)) FRENCH [high tone] *noun phrase* high fashion: *"An air of extreme haut ton, however, pervaded her whole appearance; she wore in a graceful and degage manner, a large and beautiful winding-sheet of the finest India lawn. . ."* (Edgar Allan Poe, "King Pest"). ~*abbreviated form* **ton.**

H.C. *See* HONORIS CAUSA; HORS CONCOURS.

hegemony (he<u>je</u>mănee he<u>ge</u>mănee, <u>he</u>jemōnee) GREEK [from *hegemon* leader] *noun* domination or influence over others: *"Moscow regards its energy partnership with the EU as an important instrument with which to restore hegemony over the Commonwealth of Independent States"* (*Guardian*, November 21, 2000).

hegira (he<u>jee</u>ră, he<u>jă</u>ră), **hejira, hijra** (hijră) ARABIC [from *hijrah* flight, departure] *noun* a journey made to escape danger or unpleasantness, after the journey made by the prophet Muhammad from Mecca to Medina in A.D. 622 to escape persecution (marking the start of the Muslim era): *"'This is the argument of my opera.' He paused. 'The first act,' he went on, 'shows Mahomet as a porter to Kadijah, a rich widow with whom his uncle placed him. He is in love and ambitious. Driven from Mecca, he escapes to Medina, and dates his era from his flight, the Hegira'"* (Honoré de Balzac, *Gambara*, 1837).

Heimweh (<u>hīm</u>vay) GERMAN [home woe] *noun* homesickness.

helix (<u>hee</u>liks) GREEK [from *eilyein* to roll, wrap] *noun* (*plural* **helixes,** <u>hee</u>liksez, or **helices,** <u>hee</u>liseez) a spiral or coil: *"The whole external shell may be considered a rudiment, together with the various folds and prominences (helix and anti-helix, tragus and anti-tragus, &c.) which in the lower animals strengthen and support the ear when erect, without adding much to its weight"* (Charles Darwin, *The Descent of Man*, 1871).

herculean (herkyoo<u>lee</u>ăn, herky<u>ă</u>leeăn) LATIN [after Hercules, itself meaning glory of Hera, from Greek Hera and *kleos* glory] *adjective* of or relating to something colossal, mammoth, or daunting in scale, power, intensity, or difficulty, in reference to the legendary Greek hero Hercules: *"Cataloging the thousands of new library books is certainly a herculean task."*

herpes (<u>her</u>peez) LATIN [from *herpein* to creep] *noun* a group of inflammatory viral diseases of the skin and nervous system.

Herr (hair) GERMAN [mister, sir, lord, master] *noun* (*plural* **Herren,** <u>he</u>ren) courtesy title among German speakers for a man.

Herrenvolk (<u>her</u>ănfōk, <u>her</u>ănfōlk) GERMAN [master race] *noun* a people who believe they are superior to all other races and destined to rule the world, a concept espoused by the Nazi Party in Germany in the 1930s and 1940s.

Hezbollah *See* HIZBOLLAH.

hiatus (hī<u>ay</u>tăs) LATIN [opening, cleft, gap, from *hiare* to yawn] *noun* (*plural* **hiatuses,** hī<u>ay</u>tăsiz) an interruption or break in continuity or time: *"The long street which connected Moonstone with the depot settlement traversed in its course a considerable stretch of rough open country, staked out in lots but not built up at all, a weedy hiatus between the town*

and the railroad" (Willa Cather, *The Song of the Lark,* 1915).

hibachi (hi<u>bach</u>i) JAPANESE [from *hi* fire and *hachi* bowl] *noun* a Japanese pot or brazier for burning charcoal for heating purposes; also a variety of portable outdoor cooking equipment resembling a barbecue.

hic et ubique (hic et <u>oo</u>bikway) LATIN [here and everywhere] *adverb* here and everywhere.

hic iacet (hic <u>yak</u>et), **hic jacet** LATIN [here lies] *noun phrase* here lies, an epitaph or inscription on a tombstone. ~*abbreviated form* **H.J.**

hic sepultus (hic se<u>pul</u>tăs), **hic sepultus est** (hic se<u>pul</u>tăs est) LATIN [here buried, here is buried] *noun phrase* here is buried, an epitaph or inscription on a tombstone. ~*abbreviated form* **H.S.**

hidalgo (hi<u>dalg</u>ō) SPANISH [from Old Spanish *fijo dalgo,* son of something, son of property] *noun* (*plural* **hidalgos,** hi<u>dalg</u>ōz) a member of the lower Spanish aristocracy, or someone who behaves like an aristocrat or aspires to become one: *"A procession of noble boys, fantastically dressed as TOREADORS, came out to meet her, and the young Count of Tierra-Nueva, a wonderfully handsome lad of about fourteen years of age, uncovering his head with all the grace of a born hidalgo and grandee of Spain, led her solemnly in to a little gilt* and ivory chair that was placed on a raised dais above the arena" (Oscar Wilde, *A House of Pomegranates,* 1891).

hijra   *See* HEGIRA.

hinterland   (<u>hin</u>tărland, <u>hin</u>tărlănd) GERMAN [hinder land, the land behind] *noun*   an interior region or part of the countryside remote from the city: *"Few venture into the hinterland for fear of wolves and roaming bands of brigands."*

hippodrome   (<u>hip</u>ădrōm) GREEK [*hippos* horse and *dromos* racecourse] *noun*   a course for chariot or horse races and, by extension, an arena or theater used for a variety of entertainments: *"And Aladdin also took horse with his Mamelukes, he mounting a stallion whose like was not among the steeds of the Arab al-Arba, and he showed his horsemanship in the hippodrome, and so played with the jarid that none could withstand him. . ."* (Richard Burton, "Aladdin; or, The Wonderful Lamp," *Arabian Nights,* 1885–88).

Hizbollah   (hiz<u>bol</u>ă), **Hizbullah** (hiz<u>bul</u>ă), **Hezbollah** (hez<u>bol</u>ă) ARABIC [party of god] *noun*   a militant Shiite Muslim organization.

H.J.   *See* HIC IACET.

H.M.P.   *See* HOC MONUMENTUM POSUIT.

hoc anno   (hok <u>an</u>ō) LATIN [in this year] *noun phrase*   in this year. ~*abbreviated form* **h.a.**

hoc loco   (hok <u>lō</u>kō) LATIN [in this place] *noun phrase*   in this place.

hoc monumentum posuit   (hok mon-yoo<u>ment</u>ăm pozyooit) LATIN [he/she erected this monument] *noun phrase* he/she erected this monument. ~*abbreviated form* **H.M.P.**

hoc tempore   (hok temp<u>or</u>ay, hok <u>temp</u>ăray) LATIN [at this time] *noun phrase*   at this time.

hoc titulo   (hok <u>tit</u>yoolō) LATIN [with this title] *noun phrase*   under this title (used in bibliographical references).

hoi polloi   (hoi pă<u>loi</u>) GREEK [the many] *noun phrase*   the common herd, the ordinary people, the masses: *"The cost of the tickets for the concert was ridiculously high in an attempt to keep out the hoi polloi."*

hollandaise   (<u>hol</u>ăndayz) FRENCH [from *hollandais,* Dutch] *noun*   a rich sauce made with butter, eggs, lemon juice or vinegar, and white wine, often served with fish. ~*adjective* of a dish served with such a sauce.

hombre   (<u>hom</u>bray, <u>om</u>bray) SPANISH [man] *noun*   informal term for a man, an equivalent of "guy" or "fellow."

homme d'affaires   (hom da<u>fairz</u>, om da<u>fairz</u>) FRENCH [man of affairs] *noun phrase* (*plural* **hommes d'affaires**)   a professional or business man: *"This promotion established his reputation as an* *homme d'affaires with access to people of influence throughout the banking world."*

homme de lettres (hom dă letră, om dă letră) FRENCH [man of letters] *noun* (*plural* **hommes de lettres**) a literary man: *"There are plenty of men of the world who ought to be aware, since the knowledge of such subtle distinctions is their province, that you cannot insult a French writer more cruelly than by calling him un homme de lettres—a literary man"* (Honoré de Balzac, *Le Cousin Pons,* 1847).

homme d'esprit (hom despree, om despree) FRENCH [man of wit] *noun* (*plural* **hommes d'esprit**) a witty man or a man with a strong sense of humor: *"The passing of his legendary homme d'esprit was greatly regretted by many people, who missed his debonair humor."*

homme du monde (hom doo mond, om doo mond) FRENCH [man of the world] *noun* (*plural* **hommes du monde**) a gentleman or man-about-town, a man who moves in high society: *"Her uncle was a suave homme du monde who stayed up till dawn several times a week gambling and drinking with the cream of society."*

homme du peuple (hom doo peplă, om doo peplă) FRENCH [man of the people] *noun* (*plural* **hommes du peuple**) a man of humble origins, or one who acts as though he comes from the ranks of the ordinary peo-ple: *"As a candidate for governor, he worked hard to retain his image as an homme du peuple."*

homme moyen sensuel (hom moiyen sensyooel, om moiyen sensyooel) FRENCH [average sensual man] *noun phrase* an average man of normal appetites and desires, the man in the street.

homo (hōmō) LATIN [human being] *noun* (*plural* **homos**) the genus to which the human race belongs, or an individual member of the human race. Also used as a slang term for a homo-sexual.

Homo sapiens (hōmō sapiănz) LATIN [wise man, from *homo* human being and *sapiens* wise, intelligent] *noun phrase* the primate species to which human beings belong, human beings regarded as a species.

homo sui juris (hōmō sooi jooris, hōmō sooi yooris) LATIN [a human of one's own law] *noun phrase* a person who is deemed in law to be in full control of his or her own affairs.

homunculus (hōmănkyălăs) LATIN [diminutive of *homo* human being] *noun* (*plural* **homunculi,** hōmăn-kyălee) a little man or person of diminutive proportions: *"Then came a yelling, a crashing among the branches, and a little pink homunculus rushed by us shrieking"* (H. G. Wells, *The Island of Dr. Moreau,* 1896).

honcho (honchō) JAPANESE [squad leader, from *han* squad and *cho* head, chief] *noun* (*plural* **honchos**) a person in charge, typically the boss or head of a company or organization: *"Lucas has been the head honcho around here since the death of the chairman."*

honi soit qui mal y pense (onee swa kee mal ee pons) FRENCH [shamed be he who thinks bad of it] *noun phrase* shame on him who thinks evil of it, the motto of the Order of the Garter: *"And nightly, meadow-fairies, look you sing, / Like to the Garter's compass, in a ring: / The expressure that it bears, green let it be, / More fertile-fresh than all the field to see; / And 'Honi soit qui mal y pense' write / In emerald tufts, flowers purple, blue and white. . ."* (William Shakespeare, *The Merry Wives Of Windsor*, 1597).

honorarium (onăraireeăm) LATIN [that which is honorary] *noun* (*plural* **honorariums** or **honoraria**, onăraireeă) a gift or reward made to someone for services rendered on an otherwise unpaid, voluntary basis: *"That his bill, including the honorarium of the barristers, would sooner or later be paid out of the estate, he did not doubt—but a compromise would make the settlement easy and pleasant"* (Anthony Trollope, *Lady Anna*, 1873–4).

honoris causa (onōris cowză) LATIN [for the sake of honor] *adverb phrase* as a token of respect, usually applying to degrees and other qualifications awarded on an honorary basis. ~*abbreviated form* **H.C., h.c.**

hookah (hookă), **hooka** ARABIC [from *huqqah* bottle of a water pipe] *noun* a variety of tobacco pipe with a long flexible tube by means of which the smoke of burning tobacco, marijuana, or other substance is drawn through a container of water and thus cooled: *"She stretched herself up on tiptoe, and peeped over the edge of the mushroom, and her eyes immediately met those of a large caterpillar, that was sitting on the top with its arms folded, quietly smoking a long hookah, and taking not the smallest notice of her or of anything else"* (Lewis Carroll, *Alice's Adventures in Wonderland*, 1865).

hoop-la (hooplah), **houp-la** FRENCH [hey there] *interjection* exclamation to draw attention to some physical movement or trick: *"The ringmaster shouted 'hoop-la' every time the dog jumped over the stool."* ~*noun* a hullabaloo or commotion, or alternatively a game in which participants attempt to win prizes by tossing hoops over pegs or other objects.

hors concours (or konkoor) FRENCH [out of the competition] *adverb phrase* in the manner of a person or thing that cannot compete. ~*adjective* not competing for a prize, excluded from competition; or without equal, beyond comparison. ~*abbreviated form* **H.C.**

hors de combat (or dă kombă) FRENCH [out of combat] *adverb phrase* disabled, out of action, or unable to participate further: *"As there was no time to be lost, the scout immediately set about effecting so necessary a precaution; and when he had gagged the Indian, his enemy might safely have been considered as 'hors de combat'"* (James Fenimore Cooper, *The Last of the Mohicans,* 1826). ~*adjective phrase* of or relating to someone or something in such a condition.

hors de question (or dă kestyon(g)) FRENCH [out of the question] *adverb phrase* out of the question.

hors d'oeuvre (or dervră, or derv) FRENCH [outside of the work] *noun* (*plural* **hors d'oeuvres** or **hors d'oeuvre**) a savory dish served as an appetizer before the main course; by extension, any preliminary event or incident: *"The guests will be offered a choice of hors d'oeuvres made with the freshest ingredients."*

hosanna (hōzană), **hosannah** GREEK [from Hebrew *hoshiahnna* pray save us] *interjection* praise the Lord: *"At Jesus' triumphal entry into Jerusalem, the crowds shouted, 'Hosanna to the Son of David!'"* ~*noun* a shout of praise addressed to God.

hospice (hospis, hospăs) FRENCH [poorhouse, hospital] *noun* (*plural* **hospices**, hospisiz, hospăsiz) a hospital for patients close to death: *"The old woman was cared for in a hospice during the final months of her life."* Alternatively, a lodging for travelers, pilgrims, or the homeless, typically run by a religious order.

hôtel de ville (otel dă vil) FRENCH [town hall] *noun* (*plural* **hôtels de ville**) a town hall in a French-speaking country: *"Saint Antoine's blood was up, and the blood of tyranny and domination by the iron hand was down—down on the steps of the Hotel de Ville where the governor's body lay—down on the sole of the shoe of Madame Defarge where she had trodden on the body to steady it for mutilation"* (Charles Dickens, *A Tale of Two Cities,* 1859).

hotelier (hōtelyer, ōtelyay) hôtelier FRENCH [hotelkeeper] *noun* the owner or manager of a hotel: *"She quickly recognized the new arrival as an internationally famous businessman and hotelier."*

houp-la See HOOP-LA.

houri (hooree, heree), **huri** PERSIAN [*huri,* from Arabic *ahwar,* having black eyes] *noun* one of the lovely young virgins who according to Muslim mythology attend upon devout believers in paradise; by extension, any beautiful young woman: *"Grandfather Smallweed has been gradually sliding down in his chair since his last adjustment and is now a bundle of clothes with a voice in it calling for Judy. That houri, appearing, shakes him up in the usual manner and is charged by the old gentleman to* remain near him." (Charles Dickens, *Bleak House*, 1852–53).

howdah (<u>how</u>dă) URDU [from Arabic *hawdaj*] noun   a covered seat or litter mounted on the back of an elephant or camel: "*When thou art old, Kala Nag, there will come some rich rajah, and he will buy thee from the Government, on account of thy size and thy manners, and then thou wilt have nothing to do but to carry gold earrings in thy ears, and a gold howdah on thy back, and a red cloth covered with gold on thy sides, and walk at the head of the processions of the King*" (Rudyard Kipling, *The Jungle Book*, 1894–95).

howitzer (<u>how</u>itsăr) DUTCH [from Czech *houfnice* ballista, catapult] noun a short-barrelled cannon used to fire shells at a steep angle: "*The barbers snatched steaming towels from a machine like a howitzer of polished nickel and disdainfully flung them away after a second's use*" (Sinclair Lewis, *Babbitt*, 1922).

H.S.   *See* HIC SEPULTUS.

hubris (<u>hyoo</u>bris), **hybris** GREEK [from *hybris* violence provoked by insolence] noun   arrogant pride or excessive self-confidence: "*His critics were apt to accuse him of excessive hubris, but he remained popular among other writers of his generation.*"

hula (<u>hoo</u>lă), **hula-hula** (hoolă-<u>hoo</u>lă) HAWAIIAN noun   a Polynesian dance featuring rhythmic gyrations of the hips and fluid arm movements.

humanum est errare (hoo<u>mah</u>năm est erahree) LATIN [to err is human] noun to make a mistake is a human characteristic: "*'Prince, humanum est errare, but. . .' replied the doctor, swallowing his r's, and pronouncing the Latin words with a French accent*" (Leo Tolstoy, *War and Peace*, 1863–69).

hummus (<u>hă</u>măs, <u>hoo</u>măs) ARABIC [chickpeas] noun   ground mixture of chickpeas, sesame paste, and seasonings of Middle Eastern origin, commonly used as a dip or sandwich spread.

huri   *See* HOURI.

hurricane (<u>hă</u>rikayn, <u>hă</u>răkayn, <u>hă</u>rikăn, <u>hă</u>răkăn) SPANISH [*huracán*, from Taino *hurakan*] noun   a tropical cyclone with winds of 74 miles per hour (118 kilometers per hour) or more; by extension, any wild outburst of activity or noise: "*The Yeehats were dancing about the wreckage of the sprucebough lodge when they heard a fearful roaring and saw rushing upon them an animal the like of which they had never seen before. It was Buck, a live hurricane of fury, hurling himself upon them in a frenzy to destroy*" (Jack London, *Call of the Wild*, 1903).

husky (<u>hă</u>skee) INUIT [abbreviation of *Huskemaw* or *Uskemaw* Eskimo] noun (*plural* **huskies**) a breed of heavy-coated working dog of Arctic regions.

hussar (hă<u>zah</u>) HUNGARIAN [highway robber, from Serbo-Croat *husar* pirate] *noun* a light cavalryman, after the light cavalry units that formed part of the Hungarian armed forces from the 15th century: *"If you'd been a cadet in the army, or a young hussar, you wouldn't have talked like that, but would have drawn your sabre to defend all Russia"* (Fyodor Dostoyevsky, *The Brothers Karamazov*, 1880).

hutzpah *See* CHUTZPAH.

hybris *See* HUBRIS.

Hydra (hī<u>drǎ</u>), **hydra** GREEK [*hudra* water serpent] *noun* (*plural* **hydras**) in Greek and Roman mythology, a nine-headed monster killed by Hercules that had the power to replace each severed head with two new ones unless the wound was cauterized; also used of any situation that gets yet more complicated each time action is taken to resolve a particular aspect of it: *"Before the passage, horrid Hydra stands, / And Briareus with all his hundred hands; / Gorgons, Geryon with his triple frame; / And vain Chimaera vomits empty flame"* (Virgil, *Aeneid*, c. 19 B.C.).

hydrophobia (hī<u>dro</u>fōbiǎ) GREEK [*hudrophobos* water-fearing] *noun* rabies, or the morbid fear of water that accompanies the disease: *"'Water!' cried the captain; 'he never drinks it; it's a sort of fits to him; fresh water throws him into the hydrophobia; but go on—go on with the arm story'"* (Herman Melville, *Moby-Dick*, 1851).

hyperbole (hī<u>per</u>bolee) GREEK [overshooting, excess, from *hyper* over and *ballein* to throw] *noun* (*plural* **hyperboles**) extravagant exaggeration or overstatement: *"I'd marry the W—of Babylon rather than do anything dishonourable! No reflection on you, my dear. It is a mere rhetorical figure – what they call in the books, hyperbole'"* (Thomas Hardy, *Jude the Obscure*, 1895).

hypochondriac (hī<u>po</u>kon<u>d</u>riak) GREEK [*hypochondria* under the cartilage, the abdomen] *noun* a person who suffers from hypochondria, depression caused by imaginary physical ailments (originally believed to be seated in the abdomen): *"He was clearly a confirmed hypochondriac, and I was dreamily conscious that he was pouring forth interminable trains of symptoms, and imploring information as to the composition and action of innumerable quack nostrums, some of which he bore about in a leather case in his pocket"* (Arthur Conan Doyle, *The Sign of Four*, 1890).

hypostasis (hī<u>post</u>ǎsis) GREEK [*hyphistasthai* to stand under, support] *noun* (*plural* **hypostases**, hī<u>post</u>ǎseez) sediment in a fluid; in philosophy, the foundations of reality; in theology, the union of the divine and human natures in the person of Jesus Christ.

hypothesis (hīpŏthăsis) GREEK [*hypotithenai* to suppose, put under] *noun (plural* **hypotheses,** hīpŏthăseez) a theory or proposition advanced for the sake of argument or in order to test its validity: *"Several different hypotheses have been proposed to explain the origins of human language."*

i

i.a.   *See* IN ABSENTIA; INTER ALIA.

ibidem (ib̲idem, ib̲ǎdem) LATIN [in the same place] *adverb*   in the same place, often used in footnotes to indicate references to the same book, chapter or page of a book, or author ~*abbreviated form* **ib.** or **ibid.**

ich dien (ik d̲eeǎn) GERMAN [I serve] *noun*   I serve, the motto of the Prince of Wales: *"He bore as his crest three white ostrich feathers, with the motto ICH DIEN, signifying in English 'I serve.' This crest and motto were taken by the Prince of Wales in remembrance of that famous day, and have been borne by the Prince of Wales ever since"* (Charles Dickens, *A Child's History of England,* 1854).

icon (ī̲kon) GREEK [*eikon* likeness, from *eikenai* to resemble] *noun* (*plural* **icons**)   a pictorial representation, often a religious image and an object of reverence, and more generally any person, event, or thing that achieves symbolic or cult status: *"Since her death, Princess Diana has been revered almost as an icon."*

id (id) LATIN [it] *noun* (*plural* **ids**)   in psychoanalytic theory, the part of the psyche in which an individual's inherited, instinctive impulses reside: *"Freud's writings on the id had a lasting effect upon analysis, and their influence is still profound today."*

id.   *see* IDEM.

idée fixe (iday f̲eeks) FRENCH [fixed idea] *noun phrase* (*plural* **idées fixes**)   an obsession or set idea: *"The duke has some idée fixe about marrying a commoner."*

idée reçue (iday re̲soo, eeday re̲soo) FRENCH [received idea] *noun phrase* (*plural* **idées reçues**)   a view or opinion that is generally accepted and rarely subjected to critical analysis, even though it may be outdated or otherwise invalid.

idem (ī̲dem, i̲dem) LATIN [the same] *pronoun*   something already mentioned (as in a document), usually a reference to an author or book previously cited: *"Freda Johnson,* Revolution in Farming, *1985; idem,*

Agricultural Techniques, *1997."* ~*abbreviated form* **id.**

idem quod (īdem <u>kwod</u>, idem <u>kwod</u>) LATIN [the same through the same] *pronoun* the same as, namely. ~*abbreviated form* **I.Q.** or **i.q.**

idem sonans (īdem <u>sō</u>nans, <u>i</u>dem <u>sō</u>nans) LATIN [sounding the same] *adjective* in legal terminology, the rule that the wrong spelling of an important word in a document does not invalidate the document, if the mistakenly spelled word sounds the same as the intended word.

id est (id <u>est</u>) LATIN [that is] *adverb phrase* that is, that is to say. ~*abbreviated form* **i.e.**

idiot savant (idyō sa<u>von</u>(<u>g</u>)) FRENCH [learned idiot] *noun phrase* (*plural* **idiots savants** or **idiot savants**) a person who displays brilliance in a particular field, despite being otherwise slow, ignorant, or mentally deficient: *"The doctor made one of the first real studies of the mysterious genius of those who have often been dubbed 'idiots savants.'"*

i.e. *See* ID EST.

igloo (<u>i</u>gloo) INUIT [from *iglu* house] *noun* (*plural* **igloos**) a temporary dome-shaped Inuit shelter made from blocks of packed snow; also used of similarly-shaped structures made in other materials: *"It takes just a few hours to complete an igloo using traditional ice saws."*

ignis fatuus (ignis <u>fach</u>ăwăs) LATIN [foolish fire] *noun phrase* (*plural* **ignes fatui,** ignez <u>fach</u>ăwee) a will-of-the-wisp, a ghostly phosphorescent light resulting from burning methane emitted by decomposing organic material occasionally seen over marshy ground; also used more generally to refer to anything deceptive or misleading: *"When they were clear of the priory, and had gained the little meadow in which it stands, Dousterswivel could perceive the torches which had caused him so much alarm issuing in irregular procession from the ruins, and glancing their light, like that of the ignis fatuus, on the banks of the lake"* (Walter Scott, *The Antiquary,* 1816).

ignoramus (ignă<u>ray</u>măs) LATIN [we do not know] *noun* (*plural* **ignoramuses,** ignă<u>ray</u>măsiz, or **ignorami,** ignă<u>ray</u>mee) a stupid or ignorant person: *"I get your idea, Sandy. He couldn't interest me. He would be an ignoramus in such things—he would bore me, and I would bore him"* (Mark Twain, *Captain Stormfield,* 1909).

ignorantia juris neminem excusat (igno<u>ran</u>tia yooris neminem eksyoozat) LATIN [ignorance of the law excuses no one] *noun phrase* ignorance of the law does not constitute a valid defense for a person who breaks the law.

IHS (ī aych <u>es</u>) LATIN [from *Iesus Hominum Salvator* Jesus, Savior of

Men] *abbreviation* Christian symbol for Jesus.

ikebana (ikabáhnă, ikeebáhnă, ikibáhnă)) JAPANESE [flower arranging, from *ikeru* to arrange and *hana* flower] *noun* the Japanese art of flower arranging.

illuminati (iloomináhtee) ITALIAN [plural of *illuminato,* enlightened, from Latin *illuminatus* lighted, *illuminated*] *plural noun* those who have, or claim to have, special knowledge of a subject: *"The prophets are employed in excusing the ways of men. Most reverend seniors, the illu-minati of the age, tell me, with a gracious, reminiscent smile, betwixt an aspiration and a shudder, not to be too tender about these things—to lump all that, that is, make a lump of gold of it"* (Henry David Thoreau, *Life Without Principle,* 1863).

imago (imáhgō, imáygō) LATIN [image, copy] *noun* (*plural* **imagoes,** imáhgōz, imáygōz, or **imagines,** imáhgăneez, imáygăneez, imáyjăneez) an insect in its mature, winged state of development; also an idealized, unconscious self-image.

imam (imáhm, eemáhm) ARABIC [leader, from *amma* to lead the way] *noun* (*plural* **imams**) the officiating priest who leads the prayers in a mosque, or more generally a religious, political, or ideological leader in a Muslim country, in the case of Shiite Islam claiming descent from Muhammad himself.

imbroglio (imbrōliō), **embroglio** ITALIAN [muddle, from *imbrogliare* to entangle, confuse] *noun* (*plural* **imbroglios, embroglios**) a state of confusion resulting in embarrassment, perplexity, misunderstanding, or brawling: *"It was appointed of Fate that, in this wide-weltering, strangely growing, monstrous stupendous imbroglio of Convention Business, the grand First-Parent of all the questions, controversies, measures and enterprises which were to be evolved there to the world's astonishment, should be this Question of King Louis"* (Thomas Carlyle, *History of the French Revolution,* 1837).

imp *See* IMPRIMATUR.

impasse (ímpas, ámpas) FRENCH [deadlock, dilemma, from *im* not and *passer* to pass] *noun* (*plural* **impasses**) deadlock, or a predicament from which there is no apparent escape; also, a road that comes to a dead end: *"Negotiations between the two sides in the trade dispute have reached an impasse."*

impasto (impástō) ITALIAN [from *impastare* to make into a paste] *noun* (*plural* **impastos**) artistic technique in which pigment is thickly applied to the canvas or panel, or the pigment itself thus applied; also used to refer to a style of ceramics in which the decoration is raised in relief.

impedimenta (impediméntă) LATIN [from *impedimentum* impediment, hindrance] *plural noun*   equipment, luggage, or supplies, especially when viewed as encumbrances creating an obstacle to progress: *"When retrieved, our impedimenta would consist of her parasol and dressing-bag, and my dressing-case. My stick and gloves were in the hall, and I decided to let them go"* (Dornford Yates, *The Brother of Daphne,* 1914).

impetus (<u>imp</u>ătăs) LATIN [assault, from *impetere* to attack] *noun* (*plural* **impetus** or **impetuses**)   forward motion or an impulse, stimulus, incentive, or driving force: *"The new principal's fresh thinking has provided the impetus to improve school standards."*

impresario (imprăs<u>ah</u>riō, imprăz<u>ah</u>riō) ITALIAN [from *impresa* undertaking, enterprise] *noun* (*plural* **impresarios**)   a person who produces, promotes, manages, or conducts an opera, concert, or theatrical company or who puts on or sponsors entertainment of some kind: *"Among the directors of the theater was a rich and luxurious general officer, in love with an actress, for whose sake he had made himself an impresario"* (Honoré de Balzac, *Two Brothers,* 1830).

imprimatur (imprăm<u>ah</u>tăr, imprimah-tăr) LATIN [let it be printed] *noun* (*plural* **imprimaturs**)   in the Roman Catholic church, a license permitting the printing or publishing of a religious work; more generally, any expression of official approval for something. Also used of the publisher's name and address, together with the date of publication, that is usually printed on the title page of a book. ~*abbreviated form* **imp.**

imprimis (impr<u>ee</u>mis, imprīmis) LATIN [from *im primis* among the first] *adverb* in the first place (usually introducing a list of items): *"This inventory I afterwards translated into English, and is, word for word, as follows: 'IMPRIMIS, In the right coat-pocket of the great man-mountain' (for so I interpret the words QUINBUS FLESTRIN) 'after the strictest search, we found only one great piece of coarse-cloth, large enough to be a foot-cloth for your majesty's chief room of state"* (Jonathan Swift, *Gulliver's Travels,* 1726).

impromptu (impr<u>om</u>too, impromp-choo) FRENCH [extemporaneously, from Latin *in promptu* in readiness] *noun* (*plural* **impromptus**)   a musical composition or something else that is put together without prior planning or preparation. ~*adjective* of or relating to something that is put together without prior planning or preparation: *"He had hardly returned from the marquee with the prize in his hand, when it began to be understood that Wiry Ben proposed to amuse the company, before the gentry went to dinner, with an impromptu and gratuitous performance—namely, a hornpipe. . ."* (George Eliot, *Adam Bede,* 1859). ~*adverb* done or improvised on the spur of the moment, without prior planning or preparation.

imshi (<u>im</u>shee), **imshee** ARABIC [imperative of *misi* to go] *verb*   go away (originally military slang): *"'Go! Imshi, Vootsak,—get out!' The man departed, staggering and dazed"* (Rudyard Kipling, *The Light That Failed*, 1890).

in absentia (in ab<u>sen</u>chyă) LATIN [in absence] *adverb phrase* in the absence of a person or persons etc. ~*abbreviated form* **I.A.** or **i.a.**

in abstracto (in ab<u>strak</u>tō) LATIN [in the abstract] *adverb phrase* from an abstract point of view.

inamorata (inamă<u>rah</u>tă) ITALIAN [past participle of *innamorare* to enamour, inspire with love] *noun* (*plural* **inamoratas**) a female lover or girlfriend: *"Mme. Coquenard recognized her present, and could not at first comprehend this restitution; but the visit of Porthos soon enlightened her. The anger which fired the eyes of the Musketeer, in spite of his efforts to suppress it, terrified his sensitive inamorata"* (Alexandre Dumas, *The Three Musketeers*, 1844). ~*noun, masculine* **inamorato** (inamă<u>rah</u>tō) (*plural* **inamoratos**) a male lover or boyfriend.

in articulo mortis (in arh<u>tik</u>yoolō mortis) LATIN [in the moment of death] *adverb phrase* at the point of death, in extremis.

in camera (in <u>kam</u>ără) LATIN [in a chamber] *adverb* privately, secretly, behind closed doors: *"The committee met in camera to debate the question at length."* ~*adjective* private, secret.

incipit (in<u>sip</u>it, in<u>kip</u>it, <u>in</u>sipit, <u>in</u>kipit) LATIN [it begins, third-person singular present indicative of *incipere* to begin] *noun* here begins, the first words of a manuscript, as employed in many medieval documents and books.

incognito (inko<u>gnee</u>tō) ITALIAN [from Latin *incognitus* unknown, from *in* un- and *cognoscere* to know] *adverb* with a concealed or false identity: *"When my goods had been all sold, I left Paris to go and live incognito as a parlor-boarder in the Convent of the Ursuline nuns of Pondevaux"* (Wilkie Collins, *The Fair Penitent*, 1857). ~*adjective* of or relating to a concealed or false identity. ~*noun* (*feminine* **incognita**, inko<u>gnee</u>tă, *plural* **incognitos, incognitas**) a person who goes under a concealed or false identity.

incommunicado (inkomyoonikahdō), **incomunicado** SPANISH [from *incomunicado* not in communication, the past participle of *incomunicar* to deprive of communication] *adverb* without access to communication, or in solitary confinement: *"The hostages were held incommunicado for several weeks."* ~*adjective* without means of communication.

inconnu (ankă<u>noo</u>, an<u>kă</u>noo) FRENCH [stranger] *noun* (*plural* **inconnus**) a stranger or unknown person: *"...rushing at the rate of double drink-money: an*

Unknown 'Inconnu on horseback' shrieks earnestly some hoarse whisper, not audible, into the rushing Carriage-window, and vanishes, left in the night." (Thomas Carlyle, History of the French Revolution, 1837).

in concreto (in kon<u>kree</u>tō) LATIN [in concrete] adverb phrase set in concrete, from a concrete point of view.

in corpore (in <u>kor</u>păray) LATIN [in the body] adverb phrase in substance.

incubus (<u>in</u>kyăbăs) LATIN [a person who lies upon, from incubare to lie on] noun (plural **incubi,** <u>in</u>kyăbee, or **incubuses,** <u>in</u>kyăbăsez) a supernatural demon reputed to have sexual intercourse with women while they are asleep or to induce oppressive nightmares, or any person who behaves in a similarly stealthy, demonic manner: ". . .I thought she might assist me with her experience; never dreaming she would prove a usurper, a tyrant, an incubus, a spy, and everything else that's detestable" (Anne Brontë, Agnes Grey, 1847).

incunabulum (inkyoo<u>nah</u>byoolăm) LATIN [swaddling clothes or bands holding a baby in a cradle] noun (plural **incunabula,** inkyoo<u>nah</u>byoolă) a book printed prior to the 16th century, or anything else belonging to an early period or at an early stage of development.

in curia (in <u>kyoo</u>riă) LATIN [in court] noun phrase in open court.

indecorum (indi<u>ko</u>răm) LATIN [that which is unbecoming, from neuter singular of indecorus unseemly] noun lack of decorum, or impropriety: "One would say, that Nature, like untrained persons, could not sit still without nestling about or doing something with her limbs or features, and that high breeding was only to be looked for in trim gardens, where the soul of the trees is ill at ease perhaps, but their manners are unexceptionable, and a rustling branch or leaf falling out of season is an indecorum" (Oliver Wendell Holmes, Elsie Venner, 1861).

index (<u>in</u>deks) LATIN [forefinger, spy, that which discloses, from indicare to indicate] noun (plural **indexes,** <u>in</u>deksiz, **indices,** <u>in</u>dăseez) an alphabetical list of references at the end of a book or document, or anything that lists, points out, or guides: "The infallible index of true progress is found in the tone the man takes" (Ralph Waldo Emerson, "Heroism," 1844). ~verb to compile such an index.

Index Librorum Prohibitorium (indeks librorăm prō<u>hi</u>bi<u>to</u>răm) LATIN [index of prohibited books] noun phrase the Roman Catholic Church's official list of books that members of the church are forbidden to read.

inertia (in<u>er</u>shă, in<u>er</u>sheeă) LATIN [lack of skill, inactivity] noun a state of rest, motionlessness, apathy, or inactivity: "For the first few days he reproached himself for his inertia; then *he began to seek reasons for justifying it"* (Edith Wharton, *Glimpses of the Moon,* 1922).

in esse (in <u>e</u>see) LATIN [in existence] *adjective phrase* existing, in actual fact.

in ex *See* IN EXTENSO.

in excelsis (in eks<u>chel</u>sis, in ek<u>sel</u>sis) LATIN [on high, in the highest] *adverb phrase* superlatively, in the highest or utmost degree.

in extenso (in eks<u>tens</u>ō) LATIN [in length, from *extensus,* the past participle of *extendere* to stretch out] *adverb phrase* in full, in its entirety. *~abbreviated form* **in ex.**

in extremis (in ek<u>stree</u>mis, in ik<u>stree</u>mis) LATIN [in the extreme] *adverb phrase* at the point of death, in extreme difficulty, in extreme circumstances: *"In the interests of secrecy, he was told only to use the radio in extremis."*

inf. *See* INFRA.

in facie curiae (in fasee <u>kooree</u>ī) LATIN [in the face of the court] *adverb phrase* before the court.

in facto (in <u>fak</u>tō) LATIN [in fact] *adverb phrase* in actual fact.

infanta (in<u>fan</u>tă) SPANISH / PORTUGUESE [feminine of *infante* infant] *noun (plural* **infantas**) a younger daughter of a Spanish or Portuguese king (and thereby not the heir to the throne), or the wife of an infante: *"Although she was a real Princess and the Infanta of Spain, she had only one birthday every year, just like the children of quite poor people, so it was naturally a matter of great importance to the whole country that she should have a really fine day for the occasion"* (Oscar Wilde, *A House of Pomegranates,* 1891).

infante (in<u>fan</u>tee, in<u>fan</u>tă) SPANISH / PORTUGUESE [infant] *noun (plural* **infantes**) a younger son of a Spanish or Portuguese king (and thereby not the heir to the throne): *". . .I will make the same to take no rest, and to roam the seven regions of the earth more thoroughly than the Infante Don Pedro of Portugal ever roamed them, until I have disenchanted her"* (Miguel de Cervantes Saavedra, *Don Quixote,* 1605).

inferno (in<u>fern</u>ō) ITALIAN [hell, from Latin *infernus* below] *noun (plural* **infernos** or **inferni,** in<u>fern</u>ee) hell, or a place that suggests comparison with hell or the fires of hell: *"All the stories that can be found in old manuscripts will never prevent the going out of the fires of the legendary Inferno"* (Oliver Wendell Holmes, *Over the Tea-Cups,* 1891).

in flagrante delicto (in flă<u>grantay</u> di<u>likt</u>ō) LATIN [while the crime is blazing] *adverb phrase* to be caught out while doing something forbidden or disapproved of, typically used of a couple surprised while engaging in illicit sexual activity: *"Nana, her arms round Prulliere's neck, was drawing him toward her when Fontan, with comically furious mimicry and an exaggerated imitation of the face of an outraged husband who surprises his wife in FLAGRANTE DELICTO,* appeared at the back of the grotto" (Émile Zola, *Nana,* 1880).

influenza (inflooenză) ITALIAN [influence, from medieval Latin *influentia,* inspired by the belief that epidemics are due to the influence of the stars] *noun* a contagious viral disease, the symptoms of which include fever, weakness, muscular aches and pains, and inflammation of the respiratory mucous membrane, or any disease giving rise to similar ailments: *"How sorry I am! But colds were never so prevalent as they have been this autumn. Mr. Wingfield told me that he has never known them more general or heavy—except when it has been quite an influenza"* (Jane Austen, *Emma,* 1815). ~*abbreviated form* **flu** (floo).

infra (infră, infrar) LATIN [below, under] *adverb* later or below, a bibliographical reference directing the reader to something following in the text. ~*abbreviated form* **inf.**

infra dig (infră dig) LATIN [from *infra dignitatem,* below dignity] *adjective phrase* undignified, beneath one's dignity: *"He considered the suggestion that he do the work himself decidedly infra dig."*

ingénue (anjănoo, hanzhănoo), **ingenue** FRENCH [feminine of *ingénu* ingenuous, innocent] *noun* (*plural* **ingénues**) a naive, unsophisticated young woman or girl, or the role of such a woman in a play, or an actress specializing in such parts: *"The fact is, the old lady believed Rebecca to be the meekest creature in the world, so admirably, on the occasions when her father brought her to Chiswick, used Rebecca to perform the part of the ingenue; and only a year before the arrangement by which Rebecca had been admitted into her house, and when Rebecca was sixteen years old, Miss Pinkerton majestically, and with a little speech, made her a present of a doll. . ."* (William Makepeace Thackeray, *Vanity Fair,* 1847–48). ~*adjective* of or relating to someone of a naive, unsophisticated character.

in infinitum (in infinītăm) LATIN [into the endless] *adverb phrase* to infinity, without end.

in jure (inyoori, in jooray) LATIN [in law] *adverb phrase* according to law, in court: *"The barrister suggested that his client's argument had little strength in jure."*

in lieu, in lieu of *See* LIEU.

in loc. cit. *See* IN LOCO CITATO.

in loco (in lōkō) LATIN [in place] *adverb phrase* instead of, in place of. ~*abbreviated form* **in loc.**

in loco citato (in lōkō si<u>tah</u>tō) LATIN [in the place cited] *adverb phrase* in the place mentioned. ~*abbreviated form* **in loc. cit.**

in loco parentis (in lōkō pă<u>ren</u>tis) LATIN [in the place of a parent] *adverb phrase* assuming the authority or responsibility of a parent: *"Teachers act in loco parentis during school hours."*

in medias res (in meediăs <u>rayz</u>) LATIN [into the middle of things] *adverb phrase* into the heart of the matter, into the midst of everything, without preamble (especially of a narrative or plot): *"'I will even do as Horace says, sir,' I answered, smiling, 'and carry you in medias res.' He nodded as if he was well pleased, and indeed his scrap of Latin had been set to test me"* (Robert Louis Stevenson, *Kidnapped,* 1886).

in memoriam (in mă<u>mor</u>iăm) LATIN [for memory] *noun phrase* in memory of, to the memory of, or a poem or notice in memory of a deceased person: *"A statue was raised in memoriam of the great hero."*

in nomine (in <u>nom</u>inay, in <u>nom</u>inee) LATIN [in the name] *noun phrase* in the name of.

innuendo (inyoo<u>en</u>dō, inyoo<u>wen</u>dō) LATIN [by hinting, from *innuere* to hint, signify, nod to] *noun* (*plural* **innuendos, innuendoes**) an insinuation, hint, or oblique allusion: *"'Anyhow, he—eventually—married her.' There were volumes of innuendo in the way the 'eventually' was spaced, and each syllable given its due stress"* (Edith Wharton, *The Age of Innocence,* 1920).

in ovo (in <u>ō</u>vō) LATIN [in the egg] *adverb phrase* in embryo, or at an embryonic stage of development: *"The project seemed doomed to fail while still in ovo."*

in parvo (in <u>pah</u>rvō) LATIN [in little] *adverb phrase* in microcosm, in miniature, on a small scale.

in perpetuum (in per<u>pet</u>yooăm, in per<u>pet</u>jooăm) LATIN [in perpetuity] *adverb phrase* for ever, for all time, in perpetuity: *"Under the terms of his will, the charity was to receive $1,000 per annum in perpetuum."*

in personam (in per<u>sō</u>nam) LATIN [against the person] *adverb phrase* legal term for an action to enforce a liability or obligation against a particular individual: *"The city council hopes to institute a legal action in personam against the mayor."*

in petto (in <u>pet</u>ō) ITALIAN [in the breast] *adverb phrase* in private, secretly (especially in relation to the appointment of cardinals by the Pope in private rather than before the governing body of the church).

in posse (in <u>po</u>see) LATIN [in being able] *adjective phrase* in possibility, potentially (rather than actually existing).

in principio (in prin<u>chi</u>peeō, in prin<u>si</u>peeō) LATIN [in origin] *adverb phrase* at first, in the beginning. ~*abbreviated form* **in pr.**

in propria persona (in prōpriă persōnă) LATIN [in one's own person] *adverb phrase* personality, in one's own proper person (specifically, in law, instead of being represented by a lawyer): *"It was so seldom that I met Miss Wyllys, that for a time my mind was undecided. But, of course, I should have written you word, if anything had been finally settled; even if you had not come to look after me in propria persona"* (Susan Fenimore Cooper, *ElinorWyllys,* 1846).

in re (in r<u>ay</u>, in r<u>ee</u>) LATIN [in the thing, in the matter] *preposition phrase* concerning, in the matter of.

in rem (in r<u>em</u>) LATIN [against a thing] *adjective phrase* against a thing (especially in relation to legal actions concerning rights to, the status of, and the titles to property): *"The company launched an action in rem against several individuals who were alleged to have committed breaches of copyright."*

in rerum natura (in rayrăm <u>na</u>chyooră) LATIN [in the nature of things] *adverb phrase* in the physical world, existing, genuine: *"Answer—and for once in thy long, useless, and evil life, let it be in the words of truth and sincerity,—hast thou such a coach?—is it in rerum natura?—or is this base annunciation a mere swindle on the incautious to beguile*

them of their time, their patience, and three shillings of sterling money of this realm?" (Walter Scott, *The Antiquary,* 1816).

INRI (<u>in</u>ree) LATIN [abbreviation of *Jesus Nazarenus Rex Judaerum* Jesus the Nazarene King of the Jews, the words inscribed on Christ's cross on the orders of Pontius Pilate] *noun* Jesus of Nazareth, King of the Jews.

in s. *See* IN SITU.

in saecula saeculorum (in sekyoolă sekyoo<u>lor</u>ăm) LATIN [to the ages of ages] *adverb phrase* for ever, for all time, to eternity: *"Humans will strive to push back the limits of knowledge in saecula saeculorum."*

in se (in s<u>ay</u>) LATIN [in itself] *adverb phrase* in itself, of itself, intrinsically (used chiefly in philosophical discussion).

inshallah (in<u>sh</u>alah), **in sha Allah** ARABIC [if Allah wills] *interjection* if Allah wishes, by the grace of God: *"Shams al-Din replied, 'Thy slave shall stand in thy presence tomorrow, Inshallah, if it be God's will'"* (Richard Burton, trans., "The Tale of the Three Apples," *Arabian Nights,* 1885–88).

insignia (in<u>si</u>gneeă) LATIN [plural of *insigne* badge, mark, derived from *insignis* distinguished by a mark] *noun* (*plural* **insignia** or **insignias**) a badge or official emblem of rank, honor, or authority: *"Any landsman observing this gentleman, not conspicuous by his stature and wearing no pronounced insignia, emerging from his cabin to the open deck, and noting the silent deference of the officers retiring to leeward, might have taken him for the King's guest, a civilian aboard the King's-ship, some highly honorable discreet envoy on his way to an important post"* (Herman Melville, *Billy Budd*, 1924).

in situ (in s<u>it</u>yoo) LATIN [in position] *adverb phrase* in its natural or original position: *"Everything has been left in situ in case the forensic experts need to make a record."* ~ *abbreviated form* **in s.**

insomnia (in<u>som</u>neeă) LATIN [from *insomnis* sleepless] *noun* inability to get adequate sleep, sleeplessness: *"Mr. Gould, senior, did not desire the perpetual possession of that desolate locality; in fact, the mere vision of it arising before his mind in the still watches of the night had the power to exasperate him into hours of hot and agiated insomnia"* (Joseph Conrad, *Nostromo*, 1904).

insouciance (in<u>soo</u>seeons, in<u>soo</u>syons) FRENCH [heedlessness, from *in* and *soucier* to trouble, disturb] *noun* (*plural* **insouciances**) nonchalance, unconcern, indifference: *"By the selection of horses, the magnificence of the chariot, the attitude, and display of person—above all, by the expression of the cold, sharp, eagle features, imperialized in his countrymen by sway of the world through so many generations, Ben-Hur knew Messala unchanged,* as haughty, confident, and audacious as ever, the same in ambition, cynicism, and mocking insouciance*"* (Lew Wallace, *Ben Hur*, 1880).

instanter (in<u>stan</u>tă) LATIN [urgently, vehemently] *adverb* instantly, immediately, at once: *"'It's gude to have a friend at court,' he said, continuing his heartless harangues to the passive auditor, who neither heard nor replied to them; 'few folk but myself could hae sorted ye out a seat like this—the Lords will be here incontinent, and proceed instanter to trial'"* (Walter Scott, *The Heart of Midlothian*, 1818).

in statu quo (in statyoo <u>kwō</u>, in stachoo <u>kwō</u>) LATIN [in the state in which, abbreviated from *in statu quo ante* in the original state] *adverb phrase* in the former condition, in the same states as before, as always: *"'And what state is your militia actually in?' 'Awful! It is what my boss, the judge, sometimes calls a "statu quo"'"* (James Fenimore Cooper, *Autobiography of a Pocket-Handkerchief*, 1843).

int. *See* INTERIM.

intacta *See* VIRGO INTACTA.

intaglio (in<u>ta</u>leeō, in<u>tah</u>leeō, in<u>ta</u>gleeō) ITALIAN [engraving, from *intagliare* to engrave, cut] *noun* (*plural* **intaglios** or **intagli**) an engraving or figure sunk in relief in stone or other hard material; also applied to such images printed or stamped in relief on paper.

~*adjective* of or relating to such an image: *"It was an antique intaglio stone in an Etruscan setting,—a wild goose flying over the Campagna"* (Oliver Wendell Holmes, *Mortal Antipathy,* 1885).

int. al. *See* INTER ALIA.

intelligentsia (intelijentseeă, intelăjentseeă) RUSSIAN [*intelligentsiya,* from Latin *intelligentia* intelligence] *noun* (*plural* **intelligentsias**)   the intellectual or cultural elite within a society or nation: *"The worst menace to sound government is not the avowed socialists but a lot of cowards who work under cover— the long-haired gentry who call themselves 'liberals' and 'radicals' and 'non-partisan' and 'intelligentsia' and God only knows how many other trick names!"* (Sinclair Lewis, *Babbitt,* 1922).

inter alia (intăr ayleeă, intăr ahleeă) LATIN [among other things] *adverb phrase*   together with other things, in addition to other things: *"If you are going to be in London for a few days, I believe you can be very useful to me, at a considerable expense and trouble to yourself, in the way of buying accoutrements; inter alia, a sword and a saddle,—not, you will understand, for my own use"* (Thomas Carlyle, *Life of John Sterling,* 1851). ~*abbreviated form* **i.a.** or **int. al.**

inter alios (intăr ayleeos, intăr ahleeos) LATIN [among others] *adverb phrase*   among other people, among other persons.

interim (intărim, intărăm) LATIN [meanwhile] *noun* (*plural* **interims**)   an interlude or interval of time: *"In the interim until the new law is passed we shall continue to sell these products as before."* ~*adjective* temporary, provisional, for the meantime. ~*adverb* meanwhile. ~*abbreviated form* **int.**

intermezzo (intămetsō) ITALIAN [intermediate thing, from Latin *intermedius* intermediate] *noun* (*plural* **intermezzo,** intămetsō, or **intermezzi,** intămetsee)   a brief interlude or diversion, or in music a short movement between major sections of an opera or other lengthy composition: *"As they lifted the casket, Paine began playing on the orchestrelle Schubert's 'Impromptu,' which was Jean's favorite. Then he played the Intermezzo; that was for Susy; then he played the Largo; that was for their mother"* (Mark Twain, *What is Man and Other Essays,* 1906).

inter nos (intăr nōs) LATIN [between us] *adverb phrase*   between ourselves.

internuncio (intărnunseeō) ITALIAN [*internunzio,* from Latin *inter* between and *nuntius* messenger] *noun* (*plural* **internuncios**)   a go-between, mediator, or messenger between two parties; also a rank borne by a papal representative or ambassador: *"He was asked by the president to act as internuncio between the two sides."*

inter partes (intăr pahrteez) LATIN [between parties] *adjective phrase* between the parties (usually parties to a legal case).

interregnum (intărĕgnăm) LATIN [from *inter* between and *regnum* reign] *noun* (*plural* **interregnums** or **interregna**, intărĕgnă) the period between two successive reigns or regimes, or a temporary interruption or pause in the normal run of things: *"Upon a dim, warm, misty day, toward the close of November, and during the strange interregnum of the seasons which in America is termed the Indian Summer, Mr. Bedloe departed as usual for the hills"* (Edgar Allan Poe, "A Tale of the Ragged Mountains," 1844).

inter se (intăr say), **inter sese** LATIN [among themselves] *adverb phrase* between themselves, among themselves.

inter vivos (intă vīvōs, intă veevōs) LATIN [between the living] *adverb phrase* between living persons (especially in relation to gifts made between parties who are both still alive). ~*adjective phrase* of or relating to deals or gifts made between living parties.

intifada (intifahdă) ARABIC [shaking off] *noun* an uprising (specifically, the Palestinian rebellion against the Israeli occupation in 1987): *"The intifada provoked fears that the whole of the region would be ignited in a wave of violence."*

in toto (in tōtō) LATIN [on the whole] *adverb phrase* completely, entirely, totally, wholly: *"The enterprise cost him several million dollars in toto."*

intra muros (intră myooros) LATIN [within the walls] *adjective phrase* internal, relating to the internal politics of an organization or institution.

in transit (in tranzit) LATIN [from *in transitu* in passage] *adverb phrase* on the way: *"The parcel is in transit and should be with you tomorrow."* ~abbreviated form **in trans.**

intra vires (intră vīreez) LATIN [within the powers] *adverb phrase* within the scope, within the powers (usually in relation to the authority of a court, corporation, or government body): *"The Secretary argued that his decision was intra vires, but critics argued that he had acted beyond his powers."*

introit (introit) FRENCH [from Latin *introitus* entrance] *noun* an entrance or the opening of a religious office or passage of sacred music: *"The chorister chants with joy the introit for paschal time."*

in utero (in yootărō) LATIN [in the uterus] *adverb phrase* in the womb, before birth: *"Serious defects can now be detected while the baby is still in utero."* ~*adjective phrase* of or relating to life in the womb or before birth.

inv. *See* INVENIT.

in vacuo (in vakyooō) LATIN [in a vacuum] *adverb phrase* in a vacuum, without context.

invenit (in<u>vay</u>nit) LATIN [he/she invented it] *verb* he/she invented it, discovered it, designed it. ~*abbreviated form* **inv.** or **invt.**

invenit et delineavit (invaynit et deli-nee<u>ah</u>vit) LATIN [he/she designed and drew it] *verb* he/she designed and drew it. ~*abbreviated form* **inv. et del.**

inv. et del. *See* INVENIT ET DELINEAVIT.

in vino veritas (in <u>vee</u>nō veritas) LATIN [in wine, truth] *noun phrase* there is truth in wine (or, a person who drinks alcohol is more likely to reveal the truth of things).

in vitro (in <u>vee</u>trō) LATIN [in glass] *adverb phrase* in a test tube, outside the living body, in an artificial environment. ~*adjective phrase* of or relating to an environment outside the living body: *"Big advances have been made in the field of in vitro fertilization in recent years."*

in vivo (in <u>vee</u>vō) LATIN [in the living] *adverb phrase* within the living body (of a plant or animal). ~*adjective phrase* of or relating to an environment within the living body (of a plant or animal).

invt. *See* INVENIT.

iota (<u>ī</u>ŏtă) GREEK [ninth letter of the Greek alphabet, considered the smallest of the letters] *noun* a very small amount, a scrap or bit: *"I do not believe one iota of what you have said."*

ipse dixit (ipsee <u>dik</u>sit, ipsay <u>dik</u>sit) LATIN [he himself said it] *noun phrase* (*plural* **ipse dixits**) an unproved assertion or saying.

ipso facto (ipsō <u>fak</u>tō) LATIN [by the fact itself] *adverb phrase* by the very fact, by that very fact, thereby: *"The room was empty, so, ipso facto, this could not have been the way they had come."*

irredenta (iree<u>den</u>tă) ITALIAN [unredeemed, from *irredenta Italia* unredeemed Italy] *noun* (*plural* **irredentas**) a territory that has close historical, cultural, or ethnic links with a particular state while not being part of it politically: *"They annexed Tibet, but they had argued themselves into the belief that this was ancient Chinese territory, China irredenta"* (*Punch,* February 1, 1967).

_j_

jabot (zha<u>bō</u>) FRENCH [bird's crop] *noun* an ornamental lace or cloth frill, as attached to the neckband of men's shirts in the 18th century or as attached to the front of women's blouses and dresses in modern times: *"About Vida's new jabot which made her look thirty-two (Vida's estimate) or twenty-two (Raymie's estimate). . ."* (Sinclair Lewis, *Main Street,* 1920).

j'accuse (zha<u>kooz</u>) FRENCH [I accuse] *noun phrase* an allegation or charge, typically against official injustice (in imitation of Émile Zola's famous article beginning with the words "J'accuse" published in the newspaper *L'Aurore* on January 13, 1898, and relating to the Dreyfus affair, alleging that a Jewish army officer convicted of treason had been wrongly condemned by the French military).

jacquard (zha<u>kahrd</u>) FRENCH [after Joseph-Marie Jacquard (1752–1834), inventor of the Jacquard loom] *noun* a piece of fabric woven on a Jacquard loom, or the loom on which such material is made: *". . .from a hand loom to a Jacquard—a Jacquard that weaves fair forms and wondrous flowers beyond Arachne's utmost dream. . ."* (Robert Green Ingersoll, *A Thanksgiving Sermon,* 1897).

jacquerie (zha<u>kree</u>, zhakă<u>ree</u>) FRENCH [derived from the archetypal peasant name Jacques] *noun* a peasant uprising, specifically the 1358 Jacquerie revolt in northern France, or the peasantry in general: *"Look around and consider the Eves of all the world that we know, consider the faces of all the world that we know, consider the rage and discontent to which the Jacquerie addresses itself with more and more of certainty every hour"* (Charles Dickens, *A Tale of Two Cities,* 1859).

j'adoube (zha<u>doob</u>) FRENCH [I repair, I adjust] *interjection* a formulaic expression used by chess players to signify that they wish to adjust the position of a piece on the board without actually moving it to another square.

jäger (<u>yay</u>gă) GERMAN [from *jagen* to hunt, to pursue] *noun* a sharpshooter in the German or Austrian armies, or a hunter or footman in huntsman's costume.

jai alai (hī lī, hī ălī) BASQUE [from *jai* holiday, festival, and *alai* merry] *noun* a game resembling handball, played on a three-walled court by two or four players who use a long, curved wicker basket strapped to the wrist to catch and throw a small, hard ball against the front wall.

jalapeño (halăpeenō, halăpeenyo) SPANISH [of Jalapa, Mexico] *noun* a small, dark green hot chili pepper.

jalousie (jalăsee) FRENCH [jealousy] *noun* a variety of blind or shutter with adjustable horizontal slats allowing light and air into a room but blocking bright sunlight and rain: *"Shafts of pale sunlight seeped between the slats of the jalousies."*

jambalaya (jambălīă) FRENCH [from Provençal French *jambalaia* dish of rice, ham, and seafood] *noun* a muddle or jumble, or the Louisiana dish after which it takes its name.

janissary (janăsăree) TURKISH [from *yeni* new and *ceri* soldier] *noun* a member of an élite corps of soldiers; originally a unit of the Turkish army founded in the 14th century: *". . .in Pumpernickel itself, the last Transparency but three, the great and renowned Victor Aurelius XIV built a magnificent bridge, on which his own statue rises, surrounded by water-nymphs and emblems of victory,* *peace, and plenty; he has his foot on the neck of a prostrate Turk—history says he engaged and ran a Janissary through the body at the relief of Vienna by Sobieski. . ."* (William Makepeace Thackeray, *Vanity Fair*, 1847–48).

janitor (janităr) LATIN [doorkeeper, derived from *janus* arch, door] *noun* a caretaker, porter, or other person entrusted with the cleaning and maintenance of a building: *"Among the many billets which I have filled in America during my wandering life, I was once janitor and sweeper out of the laboratory at York College"* (Arthur Conan Doyle, "A Study in Scarlet," 1887).

japonaiserie (zhapănayzăree) FRENCH [from *japonais* Japanese] *noun* a decorative or artistic style based on Japanese motifs and characteristics; also furniture and decorative objects in this style: *"Salerooms in London and New York were suddenly swamped with items of japonaiserie."*

jardinière (jardiniair, zhardiniair) FRENCH [female gardener, from *jardin* garden] *noun* an ornamental ceramic flowerpot or flowerpot holder: *"Mrs. Newland Archer's drawing-room was generally thought a great success. A gilt bamboo jardiniere, in which the primulas and cinerarias were punctually renewed, blocked the access to the bay window. . ."* (Edith Wharton, *The Age of Innocence*, 1920). Can also refer to a garnish for meat made with glazed, diced, or boiled vegetables.

jaspé (<u>zha</u>spay) FRENCH [marbled] *adjective* mottled, marbled, veined, or variegated.

jawohl (ya<u>vol</u>) GERMAN [yes indeed] *interjection* yes, affirmative (usually spoken in response to a command): *"The foreman looked at the manager with distaste. 'Jawohl, mein führer,' he muttered under his breath."*

jehad *See* JIHAD.

jellaba (<u>je</u>labă), **djellaba** ARABIC [gown] *noun* a loose-fitting long-sleeved, often hooded, gown of the type commonly worn by men in Egypt and other parts of North Africa.

je ne sais quoi (zhă nă say <u>kwa</u>) FRENCH [I do not know what] *noun phrase* an indefinable or inexpressible quality or characteristic, as of style or appearance: *"I still think the recipe lacks that certain je ne sais quoi."*

jet d'eau (<u>zhe</u> dō) FRENCH [jet of water] *noun phrase* an ornamental fountain or the pipe from which it rises.

jeté (zhă<u>tay</u>) FRENCH [past participle of *jeter* to jump] *noun* (in ballet) a hop or jump from one leg to another, with one foot extended forward: *"The dancer executed a jeté with athletic precision, arms raised and head turned sideways."*

jeu de mots (zhă dă <u>mō</u>) FRENCH [play of words] *noun phrase* a play on words, or pun.

jeu d'esprit (zhă des<u>pree</u>) FRENCH [play of wit] *noun phrase* a witticism or an example of clever, humorous writing.

jeune premier (zhăn pre<u>myă</u>) FRENCH [first young man] *noun phrase* an actor who takes the juvenile lead in a play or film, usually performing the part of a young hero or lover: *"Perceiving all the advantages of such a connection, Lucien played his lover's part as well as it could have been acted by Armand, the latest jeune premier at the Comedie Francaise"* (Honoré de Balzac, *Scenes from a Courtesan's Life,* 1839–47). Also used in a wider context for any young man who emerges as a leading talent or personality among his contemporaries.

jeunesse dorée (zhănes do<u>ray</u>) FRENCH [gilded youth] *noun phrase* the wealthy, sophisticated, and fashionable young. Originally applied to the wealthy young counterrevolutionaries who combined to bring Robespierre's Reign of Terror to an end in France in 1794: *"But the young man of today has no bad quarter of an hour. 'You are a mercantile old brick with money and a daughter. I am a jeunesse dorée—gilded by blood and fashion, though so utterly impecunious!'"* (Anthony Trollope, *Ayala's Angel,* 1881).

jihad (<u>ji</u>hăd) ARABIC [struggle, effort, contest] *noun* a crusade or holy war that is launched as a matter of religious duty in defense of Islamic principles or beliefs; can also refer to any personal crusade based on spiritual conviction: *"The ayatollahs announced a jihad against their ideological enemies."*

jinni (<u>jee</u>nee, <u>ji</u>nee), **djinn** ARABIC [demon] *noun* a supernatural being of Arabian and Muslim mythology, credited with the power to cast spells, change shape, and perform magic: *"And behold, it was a Jinni, huge of height and burly of breast and bulk, broad of brow and black of blee, bearing on his head a coffer of crystal"* (Richard Burton, trans., "Story of King Shahryar and his Brother," *Arabian Nights,* 1885–88).

jodhpurs (<u>jod</u>părs) HINDI [after Jodhpur, India] *plural noun* a style of riding breeches cut wide at the hip and close-fitting at the calf: *"She stared with horror at the splash of mud on her previously pristine jodhpurs."*

joie de vivre (zhwa dă <u>veev</u>ră) FRENCH [joy of living] *noun phrase* enjoyment of life or general enthusiasm for living: *"This setback did nothing to dent his customary joie de vivre."*

jojoba (hă<u>hō</u>bă) SPANISH *noun* a shrub or small tree *(Simmondsia chinensis)* native to SW North America, and the liquid wax produced from its edible seeds, which has various commercial uses.

jolie laide (zholee <u>layd</u>) FRENCH [pretty ugly] *noun phrase* a woman who is deemed sexually attractive despite the fact that she is not conventionally beautiful: *"Strangely, the terrible scars on*

the face of his 'jolie laide' only served to heighten his fascination."

jongleur (zhong<u>ler</u>) FRENCH [jester, derived from Old French *jogleour* juggler] *noun* an itinerant medieval entertainer or minstrel, usually skilled in performing songs, poetry, and acrobatics: *"She hastily ran over the contents, which were expressed both in Arabic and French, and when she had done, she laughed in bitter anger. 'Now this passes imagination!' she said; 'no jongleur can show so deft a transmutation!'"* (Walter Scott, *The Talisman,* 1825).

jour de fête (zhoor dă <u>fet</u>) FRENCH [day of festival] *noun phrase* a festival or birthday.

journal intime (zhoornal an<u>teem</u>) FRENCH [intimate journal] *noun phrase* a diary or other confessional writing.

jubilate (joobă<u>lah</u>tay, yoobă<u>lah</u>tay) LATIN [rejoice] *noun* a joyous outburst of song or triumphant shouting: *"The soothing sanity and blitheness of completion, / the pomp and hurried contest-glare and rush are done; / Now triumph! transformation! jubilate!"* (Walt Whitman, *Leaves of Grass,* 1891–92). Can also refer specifically to Psalm 100 and musical settings of this psalm.

judo (<u>joo</u>dō) JAPANESE [from *ju* weak, gentle and *do* art, way] *noun* a Japanese martial art in which participants wrestle using balance and leverage to throw their opponent: *"Children are* being offered the chance to try judo and other martial arts at school."

Jugendstil (<u>yoo</u>gănsteel, <u>yoo</u>gănshteel) GERMAN [from *Jugend* youth and *Stil* style] *noun* a German name for the art nouveau style or movement in the arts.

juggernaut (<u>jă</u>gărnot) HINDI [from *Jagannath,* lord of the world, whose festival is marked by the hauling of a huge many-wheeled wagon] *noun* an unstoppable force or object that crushes everything in its path; by extension, commonly applied to heavy trucks: *". . .if you are patient because you think it a duty to meet insult with submission, you are an essential sap, and in no shape the man for my money; if you are patient because your nature is phlegmatic, flat, inexcitable, and that you cannot get up to the pitch of resistance, why, God made you to be crushed; and lie down by all means, and lie flat, and let Juggernaut ride well over you"* (Charlotte Brontë, *The Professor,* 1857).

ju-jitsu (joo<u>jit</u>soo) JAPANESE [from *ju* weak, gentle and *jutsu* arts] *noun* a Japanese and Chinese system of unarmed combat reliant upon the use of wrestling holds, throws, and blows to the body of an opponent.

juju (<u>joo</u>joo) HAUSA [probably from French *jouer* to play] *noun* a fetish, amulet, or charm, or the supernatural power associated with such objects: *"Fear of the power of juju prevented many of the locals from speaking to the police."*

jujube (<u>joo</u>joob, <u>joo</u>joobee) FRENCH [from Greek *zizuphos* zizyphus tree] *noun* a tree (genus *Ziziphus*) of the buckthorn family and the edible plumlike fruit it produces. Also the name of a fruit-flavored gumdrop or lozenge originally flavored with fruit from the jujube tree.

julienne (jooli<u>en</u>, zhooli<u>en</u>) FRENCH [after the girl's name Julienne] *noun* a dish of vegetables cut into strips, or a consommé made with vegetables prepared in this manner. ~*adjective* of or relating to a dish, garnish, or soup consisting of vegetables cut into strips: *"The main dish was served with a side dish of julienne vegetables."*

Junker (<u>yun</u>kăr, <u>yoon</u>kăr) GERMAN [from Old German *juncherro* young lord] *noun* a young Prussian aristocrat, typically one representing the traditional militaristic values of the German landowning nobility: *"'I wasn't long in the artillery; I'm a junker, in reserve,' he said, and he began to explain how he had failed in his examination"* (Leo Tolstoy, *Anna Karenina,* 1873–77).

junta (<u>huun</u>tă, <u>jun</u>tă) SPANISH/PORTUGUESE [feminine of *junto* joined] *noun* a political faction or clique that assumes political power, typically after a military coup or revolution, or by extension any group of people operating in close association for a common purpose: *"The military junta seized control of the television station last night."*

jura in re (zhoorǎ in ray) LATIN [rights against something] *noun phrase* rights in a matter.

jure divino (zhooree diveenō) LATIN [by divine right] *adverb phrase* by divine right, with the authority of God.

jure humano (zhooree hyoomahnō) LATIN [by human law] *adverb phrase* by human law, rather than divine right or natural justice.

jure mariti (zhooree mareetee) LATIN [by right of a husband] *adverb phrase* by the right of a husband, through the husband.

jure uxoris (zhooree ǎksoris) LATIN [by right of a wife] *adverb phrase* by the right of a wife, through the wife.

jus canonicum (yǎs kǎnonikǎm) LATIN [canon law] *noun phrase* church law, ecclesiastical law: "*The bishops sought to maintain the precedence of jus canonicum.*"

jus civile (yǎs siveelee) LATIN [civil law] *noun phrase* civil law, domestic law.

jus cogens (yǎs kōjens) LATIN [compelling law] *noun phrase* in international law, a law that must be observed whatever the circumstances or wishes of the parties involved.

jus divinum (yǎs diveenǎm) LATIN [divine law] *noun phrase* divine law: "*. . .the more scrupulous Presbyterians, who held that even the pronouncing the name*

of the 'Lords Spiritual' in a Scottish pulpit was . . . an acknowledgment of prelacy, and that the injunction of the legislature was an interference of the civil government with the jus divinum of Presbytery. . ." (Walter Scott, *The Heart of Midlothian,* 1818).

jus gentium (yǎs genteeǎm, yǎs jenteeǎm) LATIN [law of nations] *noun phrase* international law.

jus mariti (yǎs mareetee) LATIN [right of a husband] *noun phrase* the legal rights of a husband over the property of his wife.

jus naturae (yǎs natyoorī, yǎs natyooree) LATIN [law of nature] *noun* natural law, the law common to all mankind, established on basic principles of right and wrong: "*In strict philosophy, a limitation of the rights of war seems to imply nonsense and contradiction. Grotius himself is lost in an idle distinction between the jus naturae and the jus gentium, between poison and infection*" (Edward Gibbon, *The History of the Decline and Fall of the Roman Empire,* 1776–88).

jus primae noctis (yǎs preemī noktis) LATIN [right of the first night] *noun* droit du seigneur, the right of a feudal lord to claim the virginity of his vassal's bride on her wedding night: "*The right of a baron to deflower the brides of his underlings on their wedding night has frequently been questioned as a matter of historical fact.*"

jusqu'au bout (zhăskō boo) FRENCH [up to the end] *adverb phrase* to the very end; until a conclusion is reached: *"In 1916, the generals were unanimous in their belief that the campaign should be pursued jusqu'au bout."*

jus sanguinis (yăs sangwinis) LATIN [right of blood] *noun phrase* in law, the rule that a child's citizenship depends upon that of its parents: *"The argument over the child's nationality was eventually decided on the basis of jus sanguinis."*

jus soli (yăs sōlee) LATIN [right of the soil] *noun phrase* in law, the rule that a child's citizenship depends on its place of birth: *"The court eventually accepted his plea for citizenship on the grounds of jus soli."*

juste milieu (jăst milyă) FRENCH [fair mean] *noun phrase* the happy medium or middle course, used especially of government policy: *"You will put him in a fury; he'll try to be calm, though inwardly fuming; but, all the same, you will enlighten a man of talent as to the peril in which he really stands; and you will also have the satisfaction of laming the horses of the 'juste-milieu' in their stalls. . ."* (Honoré de Balzac, *Daughter of Eve,* 1838–39).

juvenilia (joovănileeă) LATIN [youthful things, neuter plural of *juvenilis* young] *plural noun* the immature works of a composer, artist, or writer, or alternatively works intended primarily for the young: *"In later years the old man found this and other of his juvenilia embarrassing in the extreme."*

Kaaba (<u>kah</u>bă) ARABIC [cubic building] *noun* the square stone shrine in the court of the great mosque at Mecca, Saudi Arabia to which all Muslims turn in their daily prayers: *"For a pilgrimage is what it is. The devotees come from the very ends of the earth to worship their prophet in his own Kaaba in his own Mecca"* (Mark Twain, *What is Man and Other Essays,* 1906).

kabala *See* CABALLA.

kabuki (kă<u>boo</u>kee) JAPANESE [song and dance art] *noun* a genre of traditional Japanese drama combining dance, stylized movement, and music: *"Several European writers were influenced by performances of kabuki in the early years of the century."*

kaddish (<u>kah</u>dish) ARAMAIC [from *qaddis* holy] *noun* a Jewish liturgical prayer spoken in each of the three daily services in synagogues and also in the course of mourning rituals: *"The mourners listened to the recital of the kaddish in complete silence."*

kaffeeklatsch (<u>ka</u>feeklach, <u>ka</u>fiklach) GERMAN [coffee gossip] *noun* informal conversation over cups of coffee, or a meeting at which such conversation takes place: *"Her clothes always smelled of savory cooking, except when she was dressed for church or kaffeeklatsch, and then she smelled of bay rum or of the lemon-verbena sprig which she tucked inside her puffy black kid glove"* (Willa Cather, *The Song of the Lark,* 1915).

kaffiyeh (kă<u>fee</u>yă), **keffiyeh** ARABIC [after Al Kufa, Iraq] *noun* an Arabic headdress comprising a folded square of cloth kept in place by a cord: *"Street hawkers pressed the band of tourists with kaffiyehs to take home as souvenirs."*

kaftan *See* CAFTAN.

kagoule *See* CAGOULE.

kai (kī) MAORI [food] *noun* food: *"The soldiers were offered some kai at the canteen."*

kairos (<u>kī</u>ros) GREEK [right time] *noun* the most propitious time for something, or the critical point.

kaiser (kīzăr) GERMAN [emperor, ruler, derived from Latin *Caesar* emperor] *noun* title borne by the former emperor of Germany and Austria: *"A remarkable man this Von Bork— a man who could hardly be matched among all the devoted agents of the Kaiser"* (Arthur Conan Doyle, "His Last Bow," 1917).

kakemono (kakămōnō) JAPANESE [hanging object] *noun* a vertical Japanese calligraphic scroll or picture, usually unframed and painted on paper or silk: *"The museum has acquired several fine examples of Japanese kakemono."*

kama (kahmă) SANSKRIT [love] *noun* love.

Kama Sutra (kahmă sootră) SANSKRIT [love rule] *noun* the title of an ancient Sanskrit treatise on the subject of sexual technique and thus any reference source detailing sexual practices: *"He was surprised to find a new edition of the Kama Sutra in the library's reference section."*

kamerad (kamărad, kamărahd) GERMAN [comrade] *interjection* I surrender: *"When it got nothing by screaming and stiffening, however, it suddenly grew quiet; regarded him with pale blue eyes, and tried to make itself comfortable against his khaki coat. It put out a grimy little fist and took hold of one of his buttons. 'Kamerad, eh?' he muttered, glaring*

at the infant. 'Cut it out!'" (Willa Cather, *One of Ours,* 1922).

kamikaze (kamikahzee) JAPANESE [divine wind, recalling a typhoon that fortuitously scattered the invading fleet of Kublai Khan in 1281] *noun* a pilot in a Japanese suicide squadron, as employed against Allied shipping in the latter stages of World War II; since applied more widely to anyone who behaves with suicidal recklessness with regard to their own safety. ~*adjective* of or relating to a suicide attack, or to a person who shows little regard for his or her own welfare: *"The kamikaze tactics of the Japanese air force caused considerable consternation among the crews."*

kana (kahnă) JAPANESE [false character] *noun* a Japanese system of syllabic writing that includes characters useful for the transliteration of foreign words.

kanaka (kănakă, kanăkă) HAWAIIAN [person] *noun* a South Pacific islander or native Hawaiian: *"I see only one mistake: the cook is not a Chinaman; he is a Kanaka, and, I think, a Hawaiian"* (Robert Louis Stevenson, *The Wrecker,* 1892).

kangaroo (kangăroo) AUSTRALIAN ABORIGINE [from Guugu Yimidhirr *ganurru*] *noun* an herbivorous leaping marsupial (family *Macropodidae*) of Australia and New Guinea, distinguished by its small head, sturdy hind legs, and long, thick tail.

kanji (kanjee) JAPANESE [from Chinese *han zi* Chinese characters] *noun* a Japanese system of writing based on Chinese characters.

kaolin (kayōlin) CHINESE [after Gaoling hill, Jiangxi province, China, from *gaoling* high hill] *noun* a high quality white clay used in ceramics manufacture and medicine, first imported to Europe from Gaoling hill in China: "*The supply of kaolin was severely disrupted by the outbreak of war.*"

kapellmeister (kăpelmīstăr) GERMAN [choir master] *noun* a choir or orchestra director: "*Rosamond played admirably. Her master at Mrs. Lemon's school (close to a county town with a memorable history that had its relics in church and castle) was one of those excellent musicians here and there to be found in our provinces, worthy to compare with many a noted Kapellmeister in a country which offers more plentiful conditions of musical celebrity*" (George Eliot, *Middlemarch*, 1871–72).

kaput (kăpuut, kăpoot) GERMAN [tired, exhausted, derived from French *être capot* to be without tricks in piquet] *adjective* finished, defeated, destroyed, dead, broken, unable to function, or hopelessly outmoded: "*The radio went kaput after the accident.*"

karakul (karăkăl) RUSSIAN [after the village of Karakul, Uzbekistan] *noun* a breed of hardy, wiry-coated sheep from Uzbekistan, raised primarily for the curly fleeces of newborn lambs of the breed.

karaoke (kareeōkee) JAPANESE [empty orchestra] *noun* the pastime of singing along with a prerecorded backing track; also the electronic device used to play the recorded background music. ~*adjective* of or relating to such music-making: "*A karaoke machine was installed in the bar and proved an instant success.*"

karate (kărahtee) JAPANESE [empty hand] *noun* a system of defensive unarmed combat in which an opponent is disabled with kicks and punches: "*She had been trained in karate since childhood.*"

karma (kahrmă) SANSKRIT [fate, deed] *noun* destiny, fate, or, in Hindu and Buddhist theory, the influence that an individual's actions has upon his or her migration to a new plane of existence: "*They are diametrically opposed to the philosophy of Karma and of reincarnation, which are the tenets of theosophy*" (Mary Baker Eddy, *Pulpit and Press*, 1895).

karoshi (kărōshee) JAPANESE *noun* [from *karo* overwork and *shi* death] death through overwork.

kasbah *See* CASBAH.

kashrut (kash<u>root</u>) HEBREW [fitting] *noun* the body of Jewish dietary laws encompassing both the preparation and consumption of food.

katakana (kată<u>kah</u>nă) JAPANESE [side kana] *noun* a form of the kana writing system, which incorporates symbols for many foreign words and scientific terms.

katharsis *See* CATHARSIS.

katzenjammer (<u>kat</u>zănjamăr) GERMAN [from *Katze* cat and *Jammer* wailing, distress] *noun* a harsh noise or confused and discordant uproar, as of the caterwauling of cats; can also refer to a hangover, headache, or distress in general.

kayak (<u>kī</u>ak) INUIT [from *qayak*] *noun* a one- or two-person Eskimo canoe made of animal skins and propelled by paddles, with one or more circular openings for the occupants. Also used of any other small boat based on a similar design. ~*verb* to paddle such a canoe: *"In the end, they settled on kayaking for two weeks in the Rockies."*

kebab (ki<u>bab</u>, kă<u>bab</u>), **kebob** (ki<u>băb</u>, kă<u>băb</u>) ARABIC [possibly derived via Turkish *kebap* from Persian] *noun* cubes of marinated meat grilled or roasted with vegetables on a skewer: *"That evening, they dined off kebabs covered in chili sauce."*

kedgeree (<u>kej</u>ăree) HINDI [from Sanskrit *khicca*] *noun* a dish of rice, beans, lentils, and white or smoked fish, sometimes served with hard-boiled eggs and cream: *"In former times, hunters in England would have kedgeree for breakfast before their day's sporting activities."*

keffiyeh *See* KAFFIYEH.

kendo (<u>ken</u>dō) JAPANESE [sword art] *noun* Japanese sport of fencing with two-handed bamboo swords: *"Interest in the Japanese art of kendo has increased significantly in recent years."*

kepi (<u>ke</u>pee, <u>kay</u>pee) FRENCH [from German *kappi* cap] *noun* a peaked military cap, with a flat top and cloth visor to shield the neck from sunburn: *"The chin strap of his kepi was gilt, and on his sleeve there was a little strip of gold"* (Vicente Blasco Ibáñez, *The Four Horsemen of the Apocalypse,* 1919).

ketchup (<u>kech</u>ăp) MALAY [from *kechap* fish sauce] *noun* a seasoned condiment made from puréed tomatoes: *"The children poured ketchup on their hamburgers."*

khaki (<u>ka</u>kee, <u>kah</u>kee) URDU [dust-colored] *noun* a dusty brownish yellow color, as widely used for military uniforms. ~*adjective* of or relating to this color, or to uniforms or other garments of a khaki color: *"But little they cared for the Native Press, / The worn white soldiers in Khaki dress, / Who tramped through the jungle and camped in the byre, / Who died in the swamp and were tombed in the mire, who gave up their lives,* at the Queen's Command, / For the Pride of their Race and the Peace of the Land" (Rudyard Kipling, "The Ballad of Boh Da Thone," 1888).

khalifa   See CALIPH.

khan (kahn) TURKISH [from *han* prince] *noun*   a ruler of certain parts and peoples of medieval central Asia, including China and Mongolia: *"But to our subject: a brave Tartar khan— / Or 'sultan,' as the author (to whose nod / In prose I bend my humble verse) doth call / This chieftain— somehow would not yield at all. . ."* (Lord Byron, *Don Juan,* 1819–24).

khat (kat) ARABIC [from *qat*] *noun*   a shrub *(Catha edulis)* grown in Africa and the Middle East for its leaves and buds, which have stimulant properties when chewed or drunk as tea: *"The bearers sat in the shade, chewing khat and brushing away the flies."*

kia-ora (keeă ŏră) MAORI [be well] *interjection*   good luck, or an expression of greeting.

kibbutz (ḵibuuts) HEBREW [from *qibbus* gathering] *noun (plural* **kibbutzim,** ḵibuutism)   a communal settlement or collective farm in Israel run as a cooperative by and on behalf of its own members: *"Several students arranged to spend their vacation working on a kibbutz in the Holy Land."*

kibbutznik (ḵibuutsnik) HEBREW [from *qibbus* gathering] *noun*   a member of a kibbutz: *"A mob of angry kibbutzniks blocked the main entrance into the settlement."*

kibitzer (ḵibitsăr, ḵăbitsăr) YIDDISH [from German *kiebitzen* to be an onlooker, from *Kiebitz* lapwing, peewit, or onlooker] *noun*   a person who offers unwanted advice or opinions, particularly to players of card games.

kiblah (ḵiblă) ARABIC [from *qibla* that which is opposite] *noun*   the direction in which Muslims turn to pray (specifically, toward the Kaaba at Mecca).

kiddush (ḵidoosh, ḵidăsh) HEBREW [from *qiddush* sanctification] *noun*   a formal blessing pronounced on holy days by the head of the household in Jewish homes, usually over wine or bread: *"The priest led them in the recital of the kiddush for one last time."*

kimono (kămōnō) JAPANESE [clothes, from *ki* wearing and *mono* thing] *noun*   a long robe with a broad sash and wide sleeves, the traditional Japanese dress, or more generally any loose-fitting dressing gown or robe in a vaguely Japanese style: *"Mrs. Dyer was superfeminine in the kimono in which she received Carol. Her skin was fine, pale, soft, suggesting a weak voluptuousness"* (Sinclair Lewis, *Main Street,* 1920).

kinder, kirche, küche (kindăr kerkă kookă, kindăr kerchă koochă) GERMAN [children, church, cooking] *noun*

215

phrase the domestic concerns of motherhood, religious duty, and household responsibilities that are the traditional domain of German womanhood, as fostered by the Nazi regime in the 1930s but now considered outdated.

kindergarten (kĭndăgahrtăn) GERMAN [children's garden, from *Kinder* children and *Garten* garden] *noun* a nursery school or class for children of preschool age: *"The foreign words in these two letters, the first of which was written during a visit to the kindergarten for the blind, she had been told months before, and had stowed them away in her memory"* (Helen Keller, *Story of My Life,* 1903). ~*adjective* of or relating to schools or classes for children of preschool age.

kinesis (kăneesis, kīneesis) GREEK [movement] *noun* movement or motion, the undirected movement of an organism as a response to an external stimulus.

kinetic (kinetik, kīnetik) GREEK [from *kinein* to move] *adjective* of or relating to the motion of physical bodies and the forces involved; can also refer to anything that has its own natural, precipitate forward motion: *"He studied the kinetic energy of moving water."*

kiosk (keeosk) TURKISH [from *kiushk* pavilion, ultimately from Persian *kushk* portico] *noun* a small stall, booth, pavilion, or other modest structure, usually with open sides and typically used for selling merchandise to the public or to provide shelter for public telephones: *"Sometimes about the painted kiosk / The mimic soldiers strut and stride, / Sometimes the blue-eyed brigands hide / In the bleak tangles of the bosk"* (Oscar Wilde, *Charmides and Other Poems, 1913*).

kir (keeăr) FRENCH [named after Canon Félix Kir, who devised the recipe] *noun* an alcoholic drink comprising white wine and cassis: *"They offered the doctor a small glass of kir, which he accepted with a smile."*

kirsch (keersh) GERMAN [from *Kirsche* cherry and *Wasser* water] *noun* a dry brandy made in Germany and Switzerland from the fermented juice of the black morello cherry: *"He wanted to joke about it, but she swept off, looking like a queen. Clarisse, who had propped herself against a wall in order to drink a quiet glass of kirsch, was seen to shrug her shoulders"* (Émile Zola, *Nana,* 1880).

kismet (kizmet, kizmăt, kizmit) TURKISH [from Arabic *qismah* portion, lot] *noun* fate, fortune, destiny: *"It's predestined on the face of it. Yes, tell him it's Kismet. Kismet, mallum? (Fate! Do you understand?)"* (Rudyard Kipling, *Kim,* 1901).

kithara (kithără) GREEK *noun* an ancient Greek and Roman stringed instrument resembling a lyre with a box-shaped body.

kitsch (kich) GERMAN [trash] *noun* something that appeals to popular, often sentimental, taste but is generally regarded as lacking any real artistic merit or taste. ~*adjective* of or relating to something that appeals to popular taste while lacking any real artistic merit or taste: *"The woman's room was full of kitsch ornaments and knickknacks from her seaside holidays."*

kiwi (<u>kee</u>wee) MAORI *noun* a flightless bird of New Zealand; also, the national symbol of the country and by extension a nickname for anyone from New Zealand: *"The Kiwis fly in next week for a rugby tour of three countries."*

kleptomania (kleptō<u>may</u>nyă, kleptă<u>may</u>nyă) GREEK [madness of a thief, from *kleptes* thief and *mania* mania] *noun* a compulsion to steal, regardless of economic benefit or of the risk involved: *". . . just as when a youthful nobleman steals jewellery we call the act kleptomania, speak of it with a philosophical smile, and never think of his being sent to the house of correction as if he were a ragged boy who had stolen turnips"* (George Eliot, *Middlemarch*, 1871–72).

klutz (klăts) YIDDISH [from *klots* wooden beam, from Middle High German *kloz* lumpy mass] *noun* an oaf, fool, or clumsy person: *"'The man is a klutz,' Levi observed with a shrug. 'A big disappointment to his mother.'"*

knackwurst (<u>nok</u>werst, <u>nok</u>verst) GER-MAN [from *knacken* to crackle and *Wurst* wurst] a variety of German seasoned sausage: *"He ordered a plate of knackwurst and rye bread to accompany the tankard of golden beer."*

knapsack (<u>nap</u>sak) GERMAN [from German and Danish *knappen* to make a snapping sound, to eat and *sack* sack] *noun* a bag used to carry personal belongings, clothing, or supplies on the back: *"The moment he read it, he packed his knapsack, bade adieu to his fellow pedestrians, and was off to keep his promise, with a heart full of joy and sorrow, hope and suspense"* (Louisa May Alcott, *Little Women*, 1868–69).

Knesset (kă<u>nes</u>it, <u>nes</u>it) HEBREW [gathering] *noun* the parliament of Israel: *"There was uproar in the Knesset when the announcement was made."*

knout (nowt) RUSSIAN [*knut*, from Old Norse *knútr* knot] *noun* a scourge or whip for flogging: *"So the Tatars have taught us, and they left us the knout as a remembrance of it"* (Fyodor Dostoyevsky, *The Brothers Karamazov*, 1880).

koan (<u>kō</u>ahn) JAPANESE [public matter, from *ko* public and *an* matter, proposition] *noun* (in Zen Buddhism) a paradoxical riddle that may be employed for the purposes of mediatation.

kobold (<u>kō</u>bold, <u>kō</u>băld) GERMAN [goblin] *noun* in German folklore, a mischievous breed of goblin that lives underground, typically in silver mines and similar places, or alternatively in the home: *"In remote areas, domestic mishaps are to this day often blamed on the malevolent interference of a kobold, or goblin."*

kofta (<u>kof</u>tă) URDU [from *koftah* pounded meat] *noun* (in Middle Eastern cuisine) a meat or fish rissole.

kohl (kōl) ARABIC [from *kuhl*] *noun* a type of black makeup for the eyes, derived from powdered lead suphide or antimony sulphide, as developed at an early date in Egypt and Arabia: *"Then she turned them over and behold, the kitchen wall clave asunder, and therefrom came a young lady, fair of form, oval of face, perfect in grace, with eyelids which kohl lines enchase"* (Richard Burton, "The Fisherman and the Jinni," *Arabian Nights*, 1885–88).

kohlrabi (kōl<u>rah</u>bee) GERMAN [from Italian *cavolo rapa* cabbage turnip] *noun* a variety of cabbage *(Brassica oleracea gongylodes)* with a turnip-like edible stem.

koine (<u>koi</u>nee) GREEK [feminine singular of *koinos* common, ordinary] *noun* the Greek language as spoken in the eastern Mediterranean area in the Hellenistic and Roman periods, and by extension the standard language or dialect of a particular area.

kolkhoz (<u>kol</u>koz) RUSSIAN [collective farm, from *kollektivnoe* collective and *khozyaistvo* farm] *noun* a collective farm, as organized in the former Soviet Union: *"For decades, agricultural revenue depended largely upon the kolkhoz, an inherently inefficient setup that served only to encourage the lazy and self-serving."*

Kol Nidre (kol <u>nī</u>dray, kol <u>nī</u>dră) ARAMAIC [all the vows] *noun phrase* an Aramaic prayer sung on the eve of Yom Kippur (after the opening words of the prayer): *"The pillar of the cloud appears. A fife and drum band is heard in the distance playing the Kol Nidre"* (James Joyce, *Ulysses*, 1922).

kop (kop) AFRIKAANS [from Dutch *kop* head] *noun* an isolated hill or peak: *"Sentries were posted on the kop overlooking the village in case of a surprise attack."*

kore (<u>ko</u>ray) GREEK [maiden, girl] *noun* in Greek art, a statue of a fully-clothed young woman: *"The best find of the day was a Greek kore, in near-perfect condition."*

korma (<u>kor</u>mă) URDU [from Turkish *kavurma*] *noun* a mild curry dish of meat or fish: *"The korma was excellent, served with naan bread and chutney."*

kosher (<u>ko</u>shă) YIDDISH [from Hebrew *kaser*, fit, proper] *noun* food that has been prepared and cooked in such a way to meet the requirements of Jewish dietary law. ~*adjective* of or relating to food that has been prepared and cooked in a ritual manner according to Jewish dietary law. More generally applied to anything that has been honestly acquired or otherwise passes muster and is not in some way fake or illegitimate: *"Are you sure these designer suits are kosher?"*

kouros (ko͟oros) GREEK [from *koros* boy] *noun* in Greek art, a statue of a naked boy or young man.

kowtow (ko͟wtow, kowto͟w) CHINESE [from *kou* to knock and *tou* head] *verb* to submit slavishly to the wishes of another or generally to act in a fawning, obsequious manner (a reference to the ancient Chinese custom of indicating reverence to another person by kneeling and touching the ground with one's forehead): *"He was reluctant to kowtow to the management in such a humiliating manner."*

kraal (krahl) AFRIKAANS [from Portuguese *curral* pen, enclosure] *noun* a stockade for domestic livestock, or an enclosed village community in central or southern Africa: *"Cattle belonging to the tribe are kept safe from lions in a kraal of thorns."* ~*verb* to enclose animals in such a pen.

kraken (kra͟ykăn, krah͟kăn) NORWEGIAN *noun* in Norwegian legend, a mythical sea monster of vast proportions: *"There seems some ground to imagine that the great Kraken of Bishop Pontoppodan may ultimately resolve itself into Squid"* (Herman Melville, *Moby-Dick,* 1851).

kremlin (kre͟mlin), **Kremlin** RUSSIAN [*kreml* citadel] *noun* the citadel of a Russian city or town, or specifically the center of the government (and, by extension, the top echelon of the Communist Party) in Moscow during the Soviet era: *"The interpreter addressed an old porter and asked if it was far to the Kremlin"* (Leo Tolstoy, *War and Peace,* 1863–69). Occasionally employed in jocular use with reference to any government or management head office.

kriegspiel (kre͟egspeel) GERMAN [wargame] *noun* a wargame in which military forces are represented by small blocks moved about on a map, used for training purposes.

krill (kril) NORWEGIAN (from *kril* fish fry) *noun* a small planktonic crustacean or other larval creature that provides the basic diet for many larger ocean-dwelling animals and fish: *"Each year the fleet harvests thousands of tons of krill."*

kris (krees) MALAY [from *keris*] *noun* a traditional dagger with a jagged serpentine blade: *"Hassim unsheathed his kris and held it in his hand"* (Joseph Conrad, *The Rescue,* 1920).

kudos (k(y)o͟odos, k(y)oodo͟s) GREEK [from *kydos,* glory, praise] *noun* fame, prestige, renown, reputation, as won in recognition of some deed or achievement: *"In the first place, Bellairs had made his last advance with a smile of gratified vanity, and I could see the creature was glo-*

rying in the kudos of an unusual position and secure of ultimate success" (Robert Louis Stevenson, *The Wrecker,* 1892).

kukri (<u>koo</u>kree) NEPALI [from *khukuri*] *noun* the broad, curved knife of the Ghurkas: *"The leader of the brigands drew his kukri menacingly across his throat."*

kulak (<u>koo</u>lak) RUSSIAN [fist, tightfisted person, from Turkic *kul* hand] *noun* a wealthy peasant farmer or merchant in prerevolutionary Russia, a class subsequently made a particular target of the Stalinists: *"The kulaks found few defenders among the peasants who had formerly been their vassals."*

kultur (kuul<u>toor</u>) GERMAN [from Latin *cultura* culture] *noun* culture, particularly state-controlled culture or culture that contributes toward the evolution of society in general. Sometimes taken to refer specifically to German culture during the Nazi era, which adherents considered superior to that of other nations: *"Sudden I heard my Captain say: / 'Voila! Kultur has passed this way, / And left us a monument'"* (Robert Service, *Ballads of a Bohemian,* 1921).

Kulturkampf (<u>kuul</u>terkampf, <u>kuul</u>tă-kampf) GERMAN [from *kultur* culture and *kampf* conflict] *noun* the cultural struggle between civil and religious authorities, especially over education and religious posts (usually referring specifically to the clashes that took place between the Roman Catholic Church and Bismarck's government in Germany during the late 19th century).

Kulturkreis (<u>kuul</u>terkrīs) GERMAN [culture circle] *noun* an area of culture, or culture in general.

kümmel (<u>koo</u>măl) GERMAN [caraway seed, from Old High German *kumin* cumin] *noun* a colorless cordial or sweet liqueur flavored with cumin and caraway seeds.

kung fu (kăng <u>foo</u>) CHINESE [from *gong* merit and *fu* master] *noun* the Chinese art of unarmed self-defense: *"Kung fu incorporates several disciplines, including judo and karate."*

kursaal (<u>ker</u>sahl) GERMAN [from *Kur* cure and *Saal* hall, room] *noun* a public building at a health resort: *"Down the road a piece was a Kursaal— whatever that may be—and we joined the human tide to see what sort of enjoyment it might afford. It was the usual open-air concert, in an ornamental garden, with wines, beer, milk, whey, grapes, etc. . ."* (Mark Twain, *A Tramp Abroad,* 1880).

kvass (kă<u>vas</u>) RUSSIAN [from *kvas*] *noun* a weak beer distilled from fermented rye and other cereals in parts of eastern Europe: *"As they were walking back over the cut grass, the old man called Levin's attention to the little girls and boys who were coming from different directions, hardly visible through the long grass, and along the road toward the mowers, carrying* *sacks of bread that stretched their little arms, and lugging small pitchers of kvass, stopped up with rags"* (Leo Tolstoy, *Anna Karenina,* 1873–77).

kvetch (kăvech) YIDDISH [from *kvetshn* to squeeze, to pinch, from German *quetschen* to crush, to press] *verb* to gripe or complain at length. ~*noun* a person who is always complaining or is in some other way objectionable.

Kyogen (kīōjen) JAPANESE *noun* a brief comic interlude performed in the course of an evening of Noh drama.

Kyrie eleison (kireeay elayzon) GREEK [from *kyrie* lord and *eleeson* to have mercy, to have pity] *noun* in the Christian church, a short prayer beginning with these words, often set to music: *"The notes of the Kyrie eleison soared up into the vaults of the cathedral roof."*

kyu (kyoo) JAPANESE [class] *noun* one of six grades of proficiency in Japanese martial arts such as karate and judo.

la (la) FRENCH [the] *adjective* the (usually preceding the name of a woman and variously suggesting admiration or contempt for the person concerned): *"Her voice equalled that of la Dietrich herself."*

laager (<u>lah</u>găr) AFRIKAANS [from German *Lager,* itself from Old German *legar* couch] *noun* an encampment of wagons or armed vehicles drawn up in a defensive position, or more generally any defensive or entrenched position or policy: *"In front of the house . . . was arranged an arc of wagons, placed as they are in a laager and protected underneath by earth thrown up in a mound and by boughs of the mimosa thorn"* (H. Rider Haggard, *Marie,* 1912).

laborare est orare (laborahree est o<u>rah</u>ree) LATIN [to work is to pray] *verb phrase* hard work is a form of prayer.

labyrinth (<u>lab</u>ărinth) GREEK [from *labyrinthos* maze] *noun* a maze or any intricate or complicated situation (recalling the Cretan maze constructed by Daedulus in which lurked the dreaded Minotaur): *"Not because*

Paris was not Rome, nor because it was Paris; but because hidden away somewhere in that vast unheeding labyrinth was the half-forgotten part of himself that was Susy. . ." (Edith Wharton, *Glimpses of the Moon,* 1922).

lachrymae rerum *See* LACRIMAE RERUM.

laconic (lă<u>kon</u>ik) GREEK [*lakonikos* Laconian, of Laconia, the Greek district of which Sparta was the capital, referring to the terseness of speech with which the inhabitants were traditionally associated] *adjective* using minimal words, terse, concise: *"He explained the situation in a few laconic phrases."*

lacrimae rerum (lakrimī <u>ray</u>răm), **lachrymae rerum** LATIN [tears of things, quoting the *Aeneid* by the Roman poet Virgil (70–19 B.C.)] *noun phrase* the sadness of life, the tragedy that is inherent in ordinary human existence.

lacuna (lă<u>koo</u>nă, lă<u>kyoo</u>nă) LATIN [pool, pit, gap, from *lacus* lake] *noun* (*plural* **lacunas** or **lacunae,** lăkoonī, lăkyoonī) a gap, a blank space, a hiatus, a missing part, a defect.

lager (lăhgăr) GERMAN [from *Lagerbier* beer made for keeping, from *Lager* storehouse and *Bier* beer] *noun* a light beer that matures in storage (as originally made in Germany or Bohemia): "*The bar was well stocked with imported lager.*"

lagniappe (lanyap) LOUISIANA FRENCH [from American Spanish *la ñapa* the gift, from Quechua, something added] *noun* something given as a bonus or gratuity: "*The morning after the Great Panhandle Mishandle, instead of doing election postmortems, the news industry received a spectacular lagniappe: a fractious postelection campaign, made and played for TV.*" (*Time,* November 20, 2000).

lagoon (lăgoon) FRENCH [from *lagune,* itself from Italian *laguna* pit, pool, ultimately from Latin *lacus* lake] *noun* a large pool of shallow water, often alongside a much larger body of water: "*Some ghostly night when hides the moon, / I slip into the milk-warm water / And softly swim the stale lagoon*" (Robert Service, *Ballads of a Bohemian,* 1921).

laisser-faire *See* LAISSEZ-FAIRE.

laissez-aller (lesay-alay), **laisser-aller** FRENCH [allow to go] *noun* carelessness, abandon, absence of restraint.

laissez-faire (lesay-fair), **laisser-faire** FRENCH [let do, allow to act] *noun* a practice, philosophy, or doctrine allowing an individual, company, or industry to behave with complete freedom of choice and action (often referring to economic policy): "*Where your Priest has no tongue but for plate-licking: and your high Guides and Governors cannot guide; but on all hands hear it passionately proclaimed: Laissez faire; Leave us alone of your guidance, such light is darker than darkness; eat you your wages, and sleep!*" (Thomas Carlyle, *Sartor Resartus,* 1833–34). ~*adjective* of or relating to such a practice, philosophy, doctrine, or policy: "*In the 20th century, in western economies, laissez-faire policies have been largely abandoned for mixed economies*" (*Macmillan Encyclopedia*).

laissez-passer (lesay-pasay) FRENCH [let pass] *noun* (*plural* **laissez-passers**) a permit, a pass allowing an individual to go through a checkpoint: "*The Government, which is only a simple administration, has only hitherto been called upon to put in practice the old adage, Laissez faire, laissez passer, in order to favor that irresistible instinct which pushes the people of America to the west*" (William Makepeace Thackeray, *Paris Sketch Book of Mr. M. A. Titmarsh,* 1840).

lama (lahmă) TIBETAN [from *blama*] *noun* a Buddhist monk or religious teacher of Tibet or Mongolia: "*The streets of New York were crowded that year* with Hindu seers, lamas from Tibet, and all other manner of eastern sages."

lamé (lah<u>may</u>) FRENCH [laminated, from Old French *lame* gold or silver wire, ultimately from Latin *lamina* thin sheet] *noun* a type of brocaded fabric in which the yarns are interwoven with metallic thread. ~*adjective* of or relating to such fabric: *"His sister looked sensational in a gold lamé dress."*

lamentoso (lamen<u>tōsō</u>) ITALIAN [lamenting] *adverb* (in music) mournfully. ~*adjective* (in music) mournful: *"The band played a lamentoso air in response to the general mood of depression that had settled on everyone."*

lamia (<u>lay</u>meeă) LATIN [from *lamyros* gluttonous, referring to the Lamia, a devouring monster of Greek legend with a woman's body] *noun* (*plural* **lamias** or **lamiae,** <u>lay</u>miee) a female demon, a witch.

lamina (<u>lam</u>ănă) LATIN [layer] *noun* (*plural* **laminas** or **laminae,** <u>lam</u>inee, <u>lam</u>inī) a layer, a thin plate or scale: *"The pigment epithelium has traditionally been considered as a layer of the retina"* (T. L. Lentz, *Cell Fine Structure,* 1971).

landau (<u>lan</u>dow, <u>lan</u>dō) GERMAN [after Landau, Bavaria] *noun* a four-wheeled, horse-drawn carriage with removable front and rear hoods and a raised seat for the driver (as originally made in Landau, Bavaria): *"A shining landau stopped before the entrance. The*

lady rose. I took her hand, and bowed" (O. Henry, *Strictly Business,* 1910).

Landsturm (<u>lant</u>shterm) GERMAN [land storm] *noun* (*plural* **Landstürme,** <u>lant</u>shtermă) conscription in time of war; a reserve force called up at such a time (especially in German-speaking countries).

Landwehr (<u>lant</u>vair) GERMAN [land defense, militia] *noun* militia, reserve forces (especially in German-speaking countries).

langlauf (<u>lang</u>lowf) GERMAN [long run, from *lang* long and *Lauf* race] *noun* a cross-country ski race: *"The langlauf competition was hotly contested by all the Nordic teams."*

langoustine (<u>lang</u>ăsteen) FRENCH [diminutive of *langouste* lobster, itself from Old Provençal *lagosta,* ultimately from Latin *locusta* locust] *noun* a Norway lobster (especially when considered as a food item): *"Unfortunately the menu did not include the local speciality of langoustines."*

lapis lazuli (lapis <u>laz</u>(h)ălee) LATIN [from *lapis* stone and *lazulum,* from Arabic *lazward*] *noun* a semiprecious stone of a rich azure color, or the color azure itself: *"The ring comprised a small piece of lapis lazuli in a gold setting."*

lapsus (<u>lap</u>săs) LATIN [fall, slip] *noun* a lapse, an error, a slip: *"Now if the*

'court,' and 'camp,' and 'grove,' be not /
Recruited all with constant married men,
/ Who never coveted their neighbor's lot, /
I say that line's a lapsus of the pen. . ."
(Lord Byron, *Don Juan*, 1819–24).

lapsus calami (lapsăs ka̲lămī) LATIN
[slipping of the reed] *noun phrase* a
slip of the pen, a written error.

lapsus linguae (lapsăs li̲ngwee) LATIN
[slipping of the tongue] *noun phrase* a
slip of the tongue, a verbal error.

lapsus memoriae (lapsăs me̲moriee)
LATIN [slipping of the memory] *noun
phrase* a slip of the memory, a lapse
of memory.

lardon (la̲hrdăn), **lardoon** (lahdo̲on)
FRENCH [piece of fat pork, from Old
French *lard* bacon] *noun* (in French
cuisine) a strip of bacon or salt pork
that is inserted into another piece of
meat, poultry, or game to provide
extra fat and flavoring.

largesse (lahrzhes̲, lahrje̲s), **largess**
FRENCH [generosity, ultimately from
Latin *largus* liberal in giving] *noun*
generosity, liberality, or an instance of
such generosity or liberality: "*The procession was brought to a close, by some
dozen indomitable warriors of different
nations, riding two and two, and haughtily
surveying the tame population of Modena:
among whom, however, they occasionally
condescended to scatter largesse in the form
of a few handbills*" (Charles Dickens,
Pictures from Italy, 1846).

larghetto (lahrge̲tō) ITALIAN [a little
largo, somewhat slow] *adverb* (in
music) fairly slowly (to be played
slower than andante). ~*adjective* (in
music) slow. ~*noun* a passage of
music written to be played at a fairly
slow pace.

largo (la̲hrgō) ITALIAN [slow, broad,
ultimately from Latin *largus* large,
abundant] *adverb* (in music) very
slowly, with dignity. ~*adjective* (in
music) very slow, dignified. ~*noun* a
passage of music written to be played
at a very slow, dignified pace.

lariat (la̲reeăt) SPANISH [from *la reata* the
rope, ultimately from *reatar* to tie again]
noun a lasso used to catch or tether
livestock: "*The stranger looped his lariat
over the saddle and dismounted slowly.*"

larmoyant (lahrmo̲iyănt, lahrmoi-
yo̲n(g)) FRENCH [tearful, from *larmoyer*
to be tearful] *adjective* lachrymose,
tear-jerking, sentimental: "*He told her
a somewhat larmoyant tale about lost love
and then demanded supper in loud tones.*"

larva (la̲hrvă) LATIN [ghost, mask] *noun*
(*plural* **larvas** or **larvae,** la̲hvee, lahvī̲)
the immature, wingless form of
numerous insects prior to development into the adult form.

larynx (la̲rinks) GREEK [*larugx*] *noun*
(*plural* **larynxes** or **larynges,** lărin̲-
jeez) the upper part of the trachea
or windpipe in air-breathing verte-
brates that in many species contains

the vocal chords: *"The soprano was unable to appear due to an infection of the larynx."*

lasagne (lăzanyă) ITALIAN [plural of *lasagna,* probably ultimately from Latin *lasanum* chamber pot] *noun* a form of pasta shaped into thin sheets or broad strips, or a recipe incorporating such pasta layered with cheese, tomatoes, meat, and other ingredients.

lascar (laskăr) PORTUGUESE [from Hindi *lashkari* military, from *lashkar* army] *noun* an Indian sailor: *"The Lascar pretended that six years before, during a stay at Vanikoro, he had seen two Europeans that belonged to some vessels that had run aground on the reefs some years ago"* (Jules Verne, *20,000 Leagues Under the Sea,* 1870).

lasso (lasō, lăsoo) SPANISH [from *lazo,* itself from Latin *laqueus* snare] *noun* (*plural* **lassos** or **lassoes**) a leather rope with a running noose at one end used for catching livestock. ~*verb* to capture an animal using a lasso: *"They managed to lasso the last two steers and drag them back to the corral."*

latex (layteks) LATIN [fluid] *noun* (*plural* **latexes** or **latices,** laytăseez) a milky fluid obtained from various trees and plants and used in the manufacture of rubber, gutta-percha, and other products, or a form of synthetic rubber or plastic used in clothing, paint manufacture, etc.: *"All the top swimmers favor latex swimwear."*

laudator temporis acti lowdaytăr tempăris aktī) LATIN [a praiser of times past] *noun phrase* a person who praises the way things were in the past.

laureate (loreeăt) LATIN [from *laureatus* crowned with laurel, from *laurea* laurel wreath] *noun* a person who has received official honors in recognition of some achievement, usually in the academic sphere: *"Nature crowded them for him with imagery such as no Laureate could copy in the cold mosaic of language"* (Oliver Wendell Holmes, *Elsie Venner,* 1859–60). ~*adjective* of or relating to someone who has received official honors in recognition of his or her achievements.

laus Deo (lows dayō) LATIN [praise to God] *interjection* praise be to God. ~*abbreviated form* **L.D.**

lava (lahvă) ITALIAN [from Latin *labes* fall] *noun* molten rock from a volcano or from cracks in the earth's surface: *"Lava gushed from fissures in the side of the volcano."*

lavabo (lăvahbō) LATIN [I shall wash, from *lavare*] *noun* a ceremony during the Roman Catholic Mass in which celebrants ritually wash their hands after offering oblations, or the prayer spoken at this point in the Mass. May also refer more generally to any handbasin, washroom, or lavatory.

layette (layet) FRENCH [baby linen, diminutive of *laye* box, drawer, from

Middle Dutch *laege*] *noun* a complete set of clothing, bedding, and other items for newborn babies obtained in advance of the birth of a child: *"She began to assemble a layette in advance of the happy event."*

lazaretto (lazăretō) ITALIAN [from *lazareto,* derived from Nazaretto, a quarantine station by the Santa Maria di Nazaret church in Venice and from *lazaro* leper] *noun* a hospital or other institution for patients suffering from leprosy or other infectious diseases, or more generally any place of quarantine: *"Why, my dear, what would any man think of having his house turned into an hotel, habited by freaks who discharge his servants, borrow his money, and insult his neighbors? This place is shunned like a lazaretto!"* (Willa Cather, *The Troll Garden and Other Stories,* 1905).

l'chaim (lokhīm), **lechayim** HEBREW [to life] *interjection* to your health, to life (a drinking toast).

L.D. *See* LAUS DEO.

Lebensraum (laybănzrowm) GERMAN [living space] *noun* additional territory required by a nation in order to continue economic development or to defend the overall interests of the state or other community (usually referring specifically to the argument on these lines quoted by Nazi Germany as justification for territorial expansion before and during World War II).

lechayim *See* L'CHAIM.

lector (lektăr, lektor) LATIN [reader, from *legere* to read] *noun* an assistant who reads lessons during a religious service; may also refer to a reader or lecturer at a college or university: *"The lector droned on and on, his voice seeking out plaintive echoes in the far reaches of the cathedral vault."*

lederhosen (laydărhōzăn) GERMAN [from Middle High German *Leder* leather and *Hosen* trousers] *noun* leather shorts with suspenders, of a type traditionally worn in Bavaria and neighboring Alpine areas: *"The only aspect of the role he did not like was the fact that he had to wear a pair of tight-fitting German lederhosen."*

legato (ligahtō) ITALIAN [tied, bound, past participle of *legare* to bind] *adverb* (in music) smoothly. ~*adjective* (in music) smooth, connected. ~*noun* a passage of music written to be played in a smooth manner, or the practice of playing music in such a manner.

legerdemain (lejărdămain) FRENCH [from Middle French *léger de main* light of hand] *noun* sleight of hand, trickery, deception, adroitness, skill. ~*adjective* of or relating to such deception or trickery: *". . .you juggling mountebank! This is some legerdemain trick of yours to get off from the performance of your promise, as you have so often done before"* (Walter Scott, *The Antiquary,* 1816).

legionnaire (leejă<u>nair</u>), **legionaire** FRENCH [from *légionnaire,* ultimately from Latin *legionarius* legionary] *noun* a member of a legion (such as the French Foreign Legion): *"The former legionnaires meet once a year for a formal reunion dinner at which they exchange memories of past glories."* ~*noun* **Legionnaire** a member of the American Legion.

legume (<u>leg</u>yoom, <u>lig</u>yoom) FRENCH [from *légume,* ultimately from Latin *legumen* legumunious plant, pulse, itself from *legere* to gather] *noun* a vegetable or the fruit or seed of a leguminous plant used for food; can also refer to leguminous plants in general.

leitmotiv (<u>līt</u>mōteef), **leitmotif** GERMAN [leading motive, from *Leitmotiv,* from *leiten* to lead and *Motiv* motive] *noun* a basic recurring theme or image underlying a piece of music, opera, or literary work: *"The repeated use of this leitmotiv throughout the work helps to unify the whole composition."*

lento (<u>len</u>tō) ITALIAN [slow, ultimately from Latin *lentus* sluggish, slow] *adverb* (in music) slowly. ~*adjective* (in music) slow. ~*noun* a piece of music written to be played at a slow pace.

leprechaun (<u>lep</u>răkon) IRISH GAELIC [from *leipreachán* little person, itself ultimately from Old Irish *luchorpán,* from *lu* small and *chorp* body] *noun* a breed of mischievous elf or goblin in Irish folklore reputed to know the location of hidden treasure: *"The story goes that the old man offended a leprechaun and was at once carried off to a subterranean kingdom, never to return."*

lèse-majesté (layz-<u>ma</u>jăstee, lez-<u>ma</u>jăstee, leez-<u>ma</u>jăstee), **lese majesty** FRENCH [from *lese majesté,* ultimately from Latin *laesa majestas* injured majesty] *noun* (*plural* **lèse-majestés**) disrespect, insulting behavior, an affront to dignity or status (originally high treason or another serious offense committed against a sovereign or sovereign power): *"Such an act of lèse-majesté could not go unpunished."*

l'état, c'est moi (layta say <u>moi</u>) FRENCH [the state, it is I, quoting the French king Louis XIV (1638–1715)] *noun phrase* I am the state (meaning, the control of the state, company, organization rests with me); typically quoted in criticism of someone who believes he or she wields supreme power.

lettre de cachet (letră dă ka<u>shay</u>) FRENCH [letter of seal] *noun phrase* (*plural* **lettres de cachet**) a sealed letter, a letter with an official seal (often referring to one granting permission for a person to be detained without trial or sent into exile).

levee (<u>lev</u>ee) FRENCH [from *levée* act of raising, feminine past participle of *lever* to raise] *noun* an embankment or ridge raised to prevent flooding; can also refer to such an embankment built up naturally by silting: *"Water finally poured over the top of the levee and the town was rapidly inundated."*

levée en masse (levay on(g) <u>mas</u>), **levy en masse** FRENCH [rising in mass] *noun phrase* (*plural* **levées en masses** or **levies en masse**) a mass uprising (usually referring to a popular or military uprising or mobilization against an invader or other external enemy).

leviathan (lă<u>vī</u>thăn) HEBREW [*liwyathan* coiling up] *noun* a biblical sea monster and hence any large seagoing creature or anything huge or vastly complicated: *"You wonder for a long time how she goes on, for there seems to be nobody in charge of her; and when another of these dull machines comes splashing by, you feel quite indignant with it, as a sullen cumbrous, ungraceful, unshiplike leviathan: quite forgetting that the vessel you are on board of, is its very counterpart"* (Charles Dickens, *American Notes*, 1842). ~*adjective* huge, vast, massively complicated.

levy en masse *See* LEVÉE EN MASSE.

lex (leks) LATIN [law] *noun* (*plural* **leges**, <u>lee</u>jeez) law, statute.

lex aeterna (leks ay<u>ter</u>nă) LATIN [eternal law] *noun phrase* eternal law, the law of God.

lexicon (<u>lek</u>săkahn, <u>lek</u>săkăn) GREEK [from *lexikon*, neuter of *lexikos* of words] *noun* (*plural* **lexicons** or **lexica**, <u>lek</u>săkă) a dictionary or other alphabetically arranged wordbook containing the vocabulary of a language, or more generally any inventory, record, or repertoire: *"'I'll be better able to tell you when I find out what it is,' said Priscilla, casting aside a Greek lexicon and taking up Stella's letter"* (Lucy Maud Montgomery, *Anne of the Island*, 1915).

lex loci (leks <u>lō</u>see) LATIN [law of the place] *noun phrase* the law of the country where a contract is made or where some other event relevant to a legal case takes place.

lex talionis (leks tăleeōnis) LATIN [law of recompense] *noun phrase* the law of retaliation, "an eye for an eye."

liaison (<u>lee</u>ăzăn, lee<u>ay</u>zon) FRENCH [joining, linking, connection, from *lier* to bind] *noun* a close (often sexual) relationship between two individuals; more generally any cooperative interrelationship involving two or more parties: *"Their liaison lasted several years but eventually foundered over their inability to compromise."*

lib. *See* LIBRETTO.

liberté, égalité, fraternité (libairtay aygalitay fra<u>ter</u>nitay) FRENCH [liberty, equality, fraternity] *noun phrase* liberty, equality, brotherhood (an expression of the ideals of freedom originally coined as a slogan of French revolutionaries in the late 18th century):

"The young man died with the words 'liberté, égalité, fraternité' on his lips."

libido (libeedō) LATIN [desire, lust, longing, from *libere* to please] *noun* sexual desire, or the psychic drive in general: *"He complained that his libido needed a boost."*

libretto (libretō) ITALIAN [diminutive of *libro* book] *noun* (*plural* **librettos** or **libretti,** libretee) the text for an opera, musical, or other form of theatrical entertainment with music, or an actual book or booklet containing this: *"The libretto of the opera had lain forgotten on top of the wardrobe for some 50 years."* ~*abbreviated form* **lib.**

licit (lisit) LATIN [from *licitus* permitted, past participle of *licere* to be permitted] *adjective* permitted, lawful.

lido (leedō) ITALIAN [shore, beach, from Latin *litus*] *noun* a bathing beach, beach resort, or an outdoor swimming pool open to the public: *"He saw them together on the Lido and (those writing fellows are horrible) he wrote what he calls a vignette (I suppose accidentally, too) under that very title"* (Joseph Conrad, *The Arrow of Gold,* 1919).

lied (leed) GERMAN [song] *noun* (*plural* **lieder,** leedăr) an art song performed by a solo voice with piano accompaniment (as developed by Austrian and German Romantic composers of the 19th century).

lien (lēn, leeăn) FRENCH [bond, tie, fetter, ultimately from Latin *ligare* to bind] *noun* a legal charge, right, or obligation concerning property that usually comes to an end only when some debt or other duty is finally discharged: *"Mr. Casaubon was out of the question, not merely because he declined duty of this sort, but because Featherstone had an especial dislike to him as the rector of his own parish, who had a lien on the land in the shape of tithe. . ."* (George Eliot, *Middlemarch,* 1871–72).

lieu (loo) FRENCH [place, stead, ultimately from Latin *locus* place] *noun* place, stead. ~*adverb* **in lieu** instead. ~*prep.* **in lieu of** instead of, in the place of: *"The company offered replacement tickets in lieu of refunding the money she had paid."*

limbo (limbō) LATIN [ablative of *limbus* border, edge] *noun* a supernatural region between hell and heaven where unbaptized souls must spend eternity, according to Roman Catholic theology, and, by extension, any indeterminate place that lies between two more definite locations or any state of uncertainty, oblivion, or passivity: *"The family was condemned to remain in agonizing limbo until the court came to its decision."*

limousine (limăzeen, limăzeen) FRENCH [cloak, after Limousin, France] *noun* a large, luxurious car, often one in which the driver is separated from the passengers by a glass partition: *"On her 10th birthday she persuaded her parents to hire a limousine in which she could ride round town, waving to her envious friends."*

lingerie (<u>lon</u>zhăray, <u>lon</u>jăray, <u>lon</u>zhăree, <u>lon</u>jăree) FRENCH [from Middle French *linge* linen, ultimately from Latin *lineus* made of linen] *noun* underwear and nightwear for women: *"Lingerie and nightwear are now on sale on the top floor of the store."*

lingua franca (lingwă <u>fran</u>kă) ITALIAN [Frankish language] *noun phrase* (*plural* **lingua francas** or **linguae francae,** lingwee <u>fran</u>kee) a common language adopted as a means of communication among people who speak various different native languages (originally a mixture of Italian, French, Spanish, Greek, Turkish, and Arabic formerly spoken in ports around the Mediterranean): *". . .not understanding a word of German, Latin, or French, he had been obliged to have recourse to his Greek, Turkish, and the Lingua Franca, which did not procure him much in the country he was traveling through; his proposal, therefore, to me was, that I should accompany him in the quality of secretary and interpreter."* (Jean-Jacques Rousseau, *Confessions,* 1782–89).

linguine (lin<u>gwee</u>nee), **linguini** ITALIAN [plural of *linguina,* diminutive of *lingua* tongue] *noun* (in Italian cuisine) a variety of pasta shaped into narrow ribbons, or a dish of such pasta.

liqueur (li<u>kăr</u>, li<u>kyoo</u>ăr) FRENCH [from Old French *licour* liquid] *noun* a strong, sweetened alcoholic drink flavored with spices, fruit, herbs, or other substances.

literati (litără<u>rah</u>tee) ITALIAN [from Latin *literatus* literate] *plural noun* the intelligentsia, the educated class, especially people interested in literature and the arts: *"The prize committee's announcement received a cool reception among the city's literati."*

literatim (litără<u>rah</u>tim), **litteratim** LATIN [letter for letter, from *littera* letter] *adverb* letter for letter, literally: *"Now this is fine—it is rich!—and we have half a mind to punish this young scribbler for his egotism by really publishing his effusion verbatim et literatim, as he has written it"* (Edgar Allan Poe, "Ligeia," 1833). ~*adjective* letter for letter, literal.

litterae humaniores (litărī hyoomanee-<u>or</u>ayz) LATIN [more humane letters] *plural noun* the humanities.

litterateur (litără<u>ter</u>, litra<u>ter</u>), **littérateur** FRENCH [person of letters, ultimately from Latin *litterae* letters, literature] *noun* a literary person (usually referring to a professional writer of literature or literary critic): *"Among her numerous suitors was Julien Bossuet, a poor litterateur, or journalist of Paris"* (Edgar Allan Poe, "The Premature Burial," 1844).

litteratim *See* LITERATIM.

llano (l<u>ah</u>nō, <u>l</u>anō) SPANISH [plain, ultimately from Latin *planum* plain, level] *noun* an open grassy plain (often referring specifically to the grasslands of central America or SW United States).

locale (lō<u>kal</u>) FRENCH [local] *noun* a locality, a place, especially the setting or site of a story or event: *"'To Friendship, sir!' said Miss Vere; 'and why on this gloomy and sequestered spot, rather than elsewhere?' 'O, the propriety of the locale is easily vindicated,' replied her father, with a sneer'"* (Walter Scott, *The Black Dwarf,* 1816).

loc. cit. *See* IN LOCO CITATO.

loch (lokh, lok) SCOTTISH GAELIC [akin to Latin *lacus* lake] *noun* a lake or inlet of the sea largely surrounded by land (usually referring specifically to such bodies of water in Scotland): *"The road along the edge of the loch is usually busy with buses and cars carrying tourists hoping to catch a glimpse of the legendary monster."*

loco (l<u>ō</u>kō) SPANISH [crazy] *adjective* (slang) mad, crazy.

loco citato *See* IN LOCO CITATO.

locum tenens (lōkăm <u>tee</u>nenz, lōkăm <u>ten</u>enz) LATIN [holding a place] *noun phrase* (*plural* **locum tenentes,** lōkăm <u>tin</u><u>en</u>teez) a temporary substitute, a person who assumes the duties and responsibilities of another on a tem-

porary basis (usually a doctor or member of the clergy): *"A locum tenens was called in to cover for the doctor, who was recovering from his operation."* ~*abbreviated form* **locum.**

locus (l<u>ō</u>kăs) LATIN [place, locality] *noun* (*plural* **loci,** l<u>ō</u>see, l<u>ō</u>kī, l<u>ō</u>kee) a place, location, center of attention.

locus classicus (lōkăs <u>kl</u>asikăs) LATIN [classic passage, classical place] *noun phrase* (*plural* **loci classici,** lōkee <u>kl</u>asăsī, lōkee <u>kl</u>asăkī, lōkee <u>kl</u>asăkee) a classic example (often referring to a written passage considered a standard authority on or illustration of a particular subject).

locus standi (lōkăs <u>stan</u>dee) LATIN [place of standing] *noun phrase* (*plural* **loci standi,** lōkee <u>stan</u>dee) legal term for an acknowledged or recognized position or status or the right of a person to be heard by a court.

loggia (l<u>ō</u>jeeă, l<u>o</u>jă) ITALIAN [lodge] *noun* a roofed open gallery or arcade, often overlooking an open court: *"We sat chatting cheerily in the library last night, and she wouldn't let me look into the loggia, where she was making Christmas preparations"* (Mark Twain, *What is Man and Other Essays,* 1906).

logos (l<u>ō</u>gōs) GREEK [word, speech] *noun* (*plural* **logoi,** l<u>ō</u>goi) (in ancient Greek philosophy) the rational principle that governs the universe; also, in Christian theology, the Word of

God: *"There are those who have seen the rim and outer seeming of the logos there are those who have glimpsed and in enthusiasm possessed themselves of some segment and portion of the Logos. . ."* (Sinclair Lewis, *Babbitt*, 1922).

longueur (long<u>er</u>) FRENCH [length] *noun* a period of dullness or tedium, usually referring to a boring passage in a written work or musical composition: *"We had a pleasant evening, although the play had its longueurs."*

loofah (<u>loo</u>fǎ) ARABIC [from *luf*] *noun* a tropical plant of the gourd family belonging to the genus *Luffa,* or the fibrous skeleton of its fruit (traditionally used as a sponge to scrub the skin): *"He rubbed his back vigorously with a loofah and then washed off the suds with clean water."*

loquitur <u>lok</u>witǎr) LATIN [he says, from *loquor* to speak] *verb* he/she speaks. ~*abbreviated form* **loq.**

lorgnette (lorn<u>yet</u>) FRENCH [from *lorgner* to take a sidelong look at, to squint at] *noun* a pair of spectacles or opera glasses mounted on a handle: *"The old lady squinted at the child through her lorgnette and frowned."*

lotus (<u>lō</u>tǎs), **lotos** GREEK [from *lotos*] *noun* (*plural* **lotuses**) (in Greek legend) a fruit that induces a state of dreamy forgetfulness in anyone who eats it (sometimes identified as the fruit of the jujube or elm tree). Also

the name of a genus of leguminous herbs or shrubs and of various water lilies with significance in ancient Egyptian and Hindu art.

louche (loosh) FRENCH [cross-eyed, ultimately from Latin *luscus* blind in one eye] *adjective* dubious, shifty, disreputable: *"The next time she came home she was accompanied by a rather louche young man whom her parents disliked intensely."*

louver (<u>loo</u>vǎr), **louvre** FRENCH *noun* a shutter with wooden or plastic slats designed to allow the passage of air into a room but to exclude rain or sun or ensure privacy (originally a similar structure placed on the roof of medieval buildings to provide ventilation).

lucus a non lucendo (lookǎs a non look<u>en</u>dō) LATIN [a grove from its not shining] *noun phrase* an illogical or absurd derivation or piece of reasoning (in this instance based upon the coincidental similarity of the Latin words *lucus* grove and *lucere* to shine).

ludicrous (<u>loo</u>dikrǎs) LATIN [from *ludicrus* sportive, from *ludus* play, sport] *adjective* amusingly absurd, ridiculous, laughable, foolish: *"He tried to adopt a heroic pose, but only succeeded in making himself look ludicrous."*

ludo (<u>loo</u>dō) LATIN [I play] *noun* a children's board game played with dice and counters.

Luftwaffe (<u>luuft</u>vafä, <u>luuft</u>wafä) GER-MAN [air force] *noun* the German air force between the years 1935 and 1945.

luge (loozh) FRENCH [sled] *noun* a small sled or toboggan used in competitions on specially designed downhill courses, or the sport itself: *"He came off the luge at a terrifying speed on the fastest part of the run."* ~*verb* to ride on such a sled or toboggan.

lumbago (lum<u>bay</u>gō) LATIN [from *lumbus* loin] *noun* a form of muscular rheumatism affecting the lumbar region of the back.

lumpen (<u>lum</u>păn) GERMAN [from *Lumpen* rags, tatters] *adjective* of or relating to individuals who belong to a subclass of society characterized by poverty and ignorance.

lumpenproletariat (lumpănprōlă<u>tair</u>-eeăt) GERMAN [from *Lumpen* rags, tatters, and French *prolétariat* poor

working class, coined by the German political writer Karl Marx (1818–83)] *noun* the poverty-stricken, uneducated masses.

lusus naturae (loosăs <u>na</u>tyoorī, loosăs <u>na</u>tyooree) LATIN [game of nature] *noun phrase* a freak of nature, a natural curiosity. ~*abbreviated form* **lusus.**

luxe (luks) FRENCH [luxury, from Latin *luxus* luxury] *noun* elegance, luxury.

lycée (lee<u>say</u>) FRENCH [ultimately from Greek *lukeion* gymnasium] *noun* a public secondary school maintained by the government in a French-speaking country.

lyceum (<u>lī</u>see<u>ă</u>m, <u>lī</u>seeăm) GREEK [from *lukeion* gymnasium, after the Lyceum grove of Apollo Lykeios near Athens where Aristotle taught pupils] *noun* a lecture hall, or an association organizing educational talks, concerts, and other events.

_m_

M. _See_ MONSIEUR.

macabre (măkahb, măkahbră, măkah-bă) FRENCH [deathly, ghastly, from _danse macabre_ dance of death, originally _danse de Macabré_ dance of Maccabaeus] _adjective_ gruesome, ghastly, grim, unpleasant, dreadful, concerning death: _"The clouded moon cast a macabre light over the dreadful scene."_

macaroni (makărōnee), **maccaroni** ITALIAN [from _maccheroni,_ plural of _maccherone,_ ultimately from Greek _makaria_ barley food] _noun_ (_plural_ **macaronis** or **macaronies**) a variety of pasta shaped into hollow tubes, or a dish of such pasta served with cheese and other ingredients.

macédoine (masădwahn) FRENCH [Macedonian, referring to the mixed ethnic groups who lived in the empire of the Macedonian king Alexander the Great] _noun_ a mixture of chopped fruit or vegetables; by extension, any confused mixture or medley: _"The meat came with a macédoine of lightly cooked vegetables."_

machete (măshetee, măchetee) SPANISH [from _macho_ hammer] _noun_ a large, broad-bladed knife used to hack a way through undergrowth, as a weapon, and for various other purposes: _"Several of the terrorists carried lethal-looking machetes with shiny silver blades."_

machismo (măcheezmō, măkeezmō, măkismō, măchizmō) SPANISH [masculinity, from _macho_ male] _noun_ exaggerated masculinity or masculine pride, toughness.

macho (machō) SPANISH [male] _adjective_ aggressively male, ostentatiously virile, tough: _"This film will go down well with those who like their heroes macho and well-muscled."_

machtpolitik (makhtpoliteek), **Machtpolitik,** GERMAN [power politics] _noun_ power politics, the use of force to achieve political aims.

macramé (măkrahmay), **macrame** FRENCH [from Turkish _makrama_ napkin, tablecloth, towel, ultimately from Arabic _miqramah_ coverlet, bedspread] noun a variety of lace or other fabric made by knotting threads or cords in geometrical patterns. ~*adjective* of or relating to macramé fabric.

macro (mǎkrō) GREEK [from *makros* long] *adjective* large; large-scale, comprehensive (often used in combination with other words): "*Such considerations are relatively unimportant on the scale of international macroeconomics.*"

madame (mǎdǎm, mǎdam, mǎdam), **madam** FRENCH [my lady] *noun* (*plural* **madames** or **mesdames,** maydam, maydahm) a courtesy title used for a married or mature woman: "*The shop assistant bowed politely. 'Perhaps madame would care to follow me.'*" ~*abbreviated form* **Mme.**

madeleine (mǎdǎlǎn, mǎdǎlayn) FRENCH [possibly after the French pastry cook Madeleine Paumier] *noun* a small rich sponge cake flavored with lemon and baked in the shape of a shell.

mademoiselle (madmwǎzel, madǎmwǎzel, madǎmǎzel, mamzel) FRENCH [my young lady] *noun* (*plural* **mademoiselles** or **mesdemoiselles,** maydmwǎzel, maydǎmwǎzel, maydǎmǎzel) a courtesy title for a young unmarried girl or woman. ~*abbreviated form* **Mlle.**

Madonna (mǎdonǎ) ITALIAN [from Old Italian *ma donna, my lady*] *noun* the Virgin Mary, or a statue or pictorial representation of her; also used a respectful form of address for an Ital-

ian woman: "*The Madonna has been returned to the church for the first time since it disappeared during the war.*"

madrigal (mǎdrigǎl) ITALIAN [unaccompanied song, from *madrigale,* ultimately from Latin *matricalis* mother] *noun* a part-song for a small number of unaccompanied voices.

maelstrom (mayǎlstrom) DUTCH [whirling stream, from *malen* to grind, to whirl around, and *strom* stream] *noun* a powerful whirlpool, or more generally any turbulent or disruptive state of affairs: "*What passed during that night—how the boat escaped from the eddies of the maelstrom—how Ned Land, Conseil, and myself ever came out of the gulf, I cannot tell.*" (Jules Verne, *20,000 Leagues Under the Sea,* 1870).

maestoso (mīstōsō, mīstōzō) ITALIAN [majestic, from Latin *majestas* majesty] *adverb* (in music) majestically. ~*adjective* (in music) majestic, stately: "*Then Kadijah announces to the populace the Prophet's interviews with the Angel Gabriel (maestoso sostenuto in F Major)*" (Honoré de Balzac, *Gambara,* 1837).

maestro (mīstrō) ITALIAN [master, ultimately from Latin *magister* master] *noun* (*plural* **maestros** or **maestri,** mīstree) an eminent composer, orchestra conductor, teacher of music, or other distinguished figure in the arts: "*All the musicians in the orchestra have the greatest respect for their esteemed maestro.*"

maffia   *See* MAFIA.

maffioso   *See* MAFIOSO.

mafia (<u>ma</u>feeă), **maffia** ITALIAN [boldness, bragging] *noun*   a Sicilian secret society, or an equivalent criminal organization in the United States or elsewhere; may also refer to any organization or group of people suspected of using underhand or criminal tactics: *"The bosses of the company have been accused of acting like some kind of mafia outfit."*

mafioso (mafee<u>ō</u>s<u>ō</u>, mafee<u>ō</u>z<u>ō</u>), **maffioso** ITALIAN [from *mafia* boldness, bragging] *noun* (*plural* **mafiosos** or **mafiosi,** mafee<u>ō</u>see, mafee<u>ō</u>zee)   a member of the mafia: *"When he carried his violin case to work he was immediately arrested on suspicion of being a mafioso."*

magazine (<u>ma</u>găzeen, magă<u>zeen</u>) FRENCH [from *magasin,* ultimately from Arabic *makhzan* storehouse] *noun*   a warehouse or storeroom where munitions or other supplies are kept or a holder for bullets, photographic film, or other materials. Alternatively, a periodical publication or radio or television program containing miscellaneous articles and stories.

magi   *See* MAGUS.

magma (<u>mag</u>mă) GREEK [thick unguent, from *massein* to knead] *noun* (*plural* **magmas** or **magmata,** magmahtă)   molten rock beneath the crust of the earth or another planet or, more generally, any paste of solid and liquid material or sediment.

magna cum laude (magnă kăm <u>low</u>dă, magnă kăm <u>lo</u>dee) LATIN [with great praise] *adverb phrase*   with great distinction: *"Their son graduated magna cum laude."* ~*adjective phrase* with great distinction.

Magnificat (ma<u>gni</u>fikat, man<u>yi</u>fikat) LATIN [he/she magnifies, from *magnificare* to magnify] *noun*   the prayer spoken by the Virgin Mary at the Annunciation (Luke 1:46–55) and the canticle or hymn based on this, or more generally any expression of religious devotion: *"Robert of Sicily, brother of Pope Urbane / And Valmond, Emperor of Allemaine, / Apparelled in magnificent attire, / With retinue of many a knight and squire, / On St John's eve, at vespers, proudly sat / And heard the priests chant the Magnificat. . ."* (Henry W. Longfellow, "King Robert of Sicily," 1863).

magnifico (ma<u>gni</u>fik<u>ō</u>, man<u>yi</u>fik<u>ō</u>) ITALIAN [magnificent] *noun* (*plural* **magnificos** or **magnificoes**)   a distinguished or eminent person, usually one who holds high office, a grandee.

magnifique (manee<u>feek</u>) FRENCH [magnificent] *adjective*   wonderful, great: *"The chef smacked his lips with satisfaction and with a cry of 'magnifique!' grasped his assistant in his huge embrace."*

magnum (<u>mag</u>năm) LATIN [neuter of *magnus* great] *noun* a large wine bottle with a capacity of 1.5 liters (1.6 quarts): "*The winner will be presented with a magnum of champagne.*"

magnum opus (magnăm <u>ō</u>păs) LATIN [great work] *noun phrase* (*plural* **magnum opuses** or **magna opera,** magnă <u>ō</u>pără, magnă <u>ō</u>pără) a masterpiece, the greatest work of a particular artist, composer, or writer: "*His last symphony is generally considered his magnum opus.*"

magus (<u>may</u>găs) LATIN [from Greek *magos*] *noun* (*plural* **magi,** <u>may</u>jī) a member of the priesthood of ancient Medea or Persia; can also refer more generally to an astrologer, sorcerer, or wise man (usually referring to one of the three wise men, the Magi, who paid homage to the newborn Jesus): "*The practical intellects of the world did not much heed him, or carelessly reckoned him a metaphysical dreamer: but to the rising spirits of the young generation he had this dusky sublime character; and sat there as a kind of Magus, girt in mystery and enigma...*" (Thomas Carlyle, *Life of John Sterling,* 1851).

maharaja (mahă<u>rah</u>jă, mahă<u>rah</u>zhă), **maharajah** HINDI [great raja, great king] *noun* a Hindu prince with a status above that of rajah: "*The maharaja greeted the party at the entrance to his palace.*"

maharani (mahă<u>rah</u>nee), **maharanee** HINDI [from *maharajni,* great rani,

great queen] *noun* the wife of a maharaja, or a Hindu princess with a status above that of rani.

maharishi (mahă<u>ree</u>shee, mahah<u>ree</u>-shee) SANSKRIT [from *maharsi* great seer, from *mahat* great and *rsi* sage] *noun* a Hindu sage or spiritual teacher: "*Every sentence that passed from the maharishi's lips was studiously written down and eagerly communicated to his devotees.*"

mahatma (mă<u>hat</u>mă) SANSKRIT [great soul, from *mahatman* great-souled] *noun* a person who is widely revered as being wise or high-minded, also a courtesy title for such a person.

Mahdi (<u>mah</u>dee) ARABIC [from *mahdiy* he who is rightly guided, from *hada* to guide aright] *noun* a Muslim messiah or messianic leader.

mahjong (mah<u>zhon</u>(g), mah<u>jon</u>(g)), **mahjongg** CHINESE [from dialect *ma jiang* sparrows, after the sparrow design on some mahjong counters] *noun* a game of Chinese origin played by four persons with 136 or 144 rectangular tiles and dice.

maillot (<u>mī</u>ō, <u>may</u>ō) FRENCH *noun* tights worn by dancers or gymnasts; may also refer to a jersey or to a woman's one-piece bathing suit.

maiolica *See* MAJOLICA.

maison (<u>may</u>zon(g)) FRENCH [house] *noun* a house, usually referring to a fashion house or other commercial enterprise.

maison de couture (mayzon(g) dă koo<u>toor</u>) FRENCH [house of fashion] *noun phrase* a fashion house: *"The established maisons de couture have produced a bewildering variety of designs for the coming winter season."*

maisonette (mayză<u>net</u>), **maisonnette** FRENCH [from *maisonnette*, diminutive of *maison* house] *noun* a small house or self-contained apartment (usually on more than one floor): *"Such maisonettes are much sought-after by newlyweds and others working in the city."*

maître d'hôtel (maytră dō<u>tel</u>, metră dō<u>tel</u>, mayt dō<u>tel</u>, met dō<u>tel</u>), **maitre d'hôtel** FRENCH [master of hotel] *noun phrase* (plural **maîtres d'hôtel**) a headwaiter, head cook, steward, or majordomo of a hotel or restaurant: *"The maître d'hôtel showed them to a quiet table in a secluded corner of the main restaurant."* ~abbreviated form **maître d'** (maytră <u>dee</u>, metră <u>dee</u>).

majolica (mă<u>jo</u>likă), **maiolica** (mă<u>yo</u>likă, mī<u>yo</u>likă) ITALIAN [from *maiolica*, after *Maiorica* Majorca] *noun* a type of richly colored Italian earthenware pottery with a decorated tin glaze.

major (<u>ma</u>jăr) LATIN [greater, from *magnus* great, large] *noun* an adult who has reached majority, a person of full legal age. ~*adjective* greater in rank, number, size, or importance,

superior, considerable, serious: *"News of a major earthquake disaster is coming in."*

majordomo (majăr<u>dō</u>mō) SPANISH [from *mayordomo*, ultimately from Latin *major domus* chief of the house] *noun* a steward or butler, the head of the staff of a large household or the person in charge of arrangements for a particular event: *". . .Etienne saw the bailiff, the captain and lieutenant of the guard, with certain of their men-at-arms, the chaplain, the secretaries, the doctor, the majordomo, the ushers, the steward, the huntsmen, the gamekeeper, the grooms, and the valets"* (Honoré de Balzac, *Hated Son*, 1831–6).

makimono (maki<u>mō</u>nō) JAPANESE [rolled object] *noun* a horizontal Japanese scroll painting.

malade imaginaire (malahd imajă<u>nair</u>, malahd imazhă<u>nair</u>) FRENCH [imaginary invalid] *noun phrase* (plural **malades imaginaires,** malahd imajă<u>nair</u>, malahd imazhă<u>nair</u>) a hypochondriac, a person with an imaginary illness: *"Joly was the 'malade imaginaire' junior. What he had won in medicine was to be more of an invalid than a doctor"* (Victor Hugo, *Les Misérables*, 1862).

maladroit (mală<u>droit</u>) FRENCH [badly skilled, from *mal* bad and *adroit* skilled] *adjective* inept, clumsy, awkward: *"It is easy enough to spoil the lives of our neighbours without taking so much trouble: we can do it by lazy acquiescence* *and lazy omission, by trivial falsities for which we hardly know a reason, by small frauds neutralised by small extravagances, by maladroit flatteries and clumsily improvised insinuations"* (George Eliot, *The Mill on the Floss,* 1860).

mala fide (mală fidee, mală fidă) LATIN [with bad faith] *adverb phrase* with or in bad faith, fraudulently. ~*adjective phrase* deceitful, malicious, fraudulent, dishonest.

mala fides (mală fideez, mală fidayz) LATIN [bad faith] *noun phrase* bad faith, an intent to deceive, cheat, or defraud.

malaise (mălayz, malayz) FRENCH [discomfort] *noun* a sense of unease or a general feeling of ill health, lack of energy, debility, possibly marking the onset of a disease: *"To-day, in mysterious malaise, he raged or rejoiced with equal nervous swiftness, and to-day the light of spring was so winsome that he lifted his head and saw"* (Sinclair Lewis, *Babbitt,* 1922).

malapropos (mălăprăpō) FRENCH [from *mal à propos* badly to the purpose, not to the point] *adverb* inappropriately, inopportunely. ~*adjective* inappropriate, inopportune, unreasonable: *"'And I know that he was suspelled or expended, I don't remember which, but it was something bad, and Aunt Clara cried,' added Jamie all in one breath, for he possessed a fatal gift of making malapropos remarks, which caused him to*

be a terror to his family" (Louisa May Alcott, *Rose in Bloom,* 1876).

malaria (mălaireeă) ITALIAN [from *mala aria* bad air] *noun* a disease transmitted by the bite of anopheline mosquitos carrying parasitic protozons of the genus *Plasmodium* that induces periodic attacks of fever and chills.

mal de mer (mal dă mer, mal dă mair) FRENCH [malady of sea] *noun phrase* seasickness: *"She spent the entire voyage confined to her cabin by mal de mer."*

mal du pays (mal doo pay) FRENCH [sickness of the country] *noun phrase* homesickness.

mal du siècle (mal doo seeyekăl) FRENCH [dislike of the century] *noun phrase* world weariness, weariness of life, disgust with the world.

malentendu (malontondoo) FRENCH [misheard] *noun* a misunderstanding, a mistake. ~*adjective* mistaken, misapprehended.

malgré (malgray, malgray) FRENCH [despite] *preposition* despite, in spite of, notwithstanding: *"I had, as I said, left the podesta with Sheeny's portmanteau, and, unwilling to part with some of the articles it contained—some shirts, a bottle of whisky, a few cakes of Windsor soap, etc. etc.,—I had carried it thus far on my shoulders, but now was compelled to sacrifice it malgré moi"* (William M.

Thackeray, *The Adventures of Major Gahagan,* 1838).

mambo (<u>mahm</u>bō) AMERICAN SPANISH [probably from Haitian creole *mambo* to talk] *noun* a ballroom dance of Latin American origin, similar to the rumba and the cha-cha.

mamma mia (mahmă <u>mee</u>ă) ITALIAN [my mother] *interjection* my mother! (an exclamation of surprise or amazement): *"The new car drew gasps of 'mamma mia!' from several of the automotive writers attending the event."*

mammon (<u>mam</u>ăn) LATIN [from Greek *mamona,* ultimately from Aramaic *mamona* riches] *noun* material wealth or possessions, a personification of money and other riches: *"'Well, he thought that since he couldn't serve God and Mammon he'd better stick to Mammon,' said Miss Cornelia crisply"* (Lucy Maud Montgomery, *Anne's House of Dreams,* 1917).

mammoth (<u>mam</u>ăth) RUSSIAN [from *mamont* or *mamot*] *noun* an example of a genus of extinct Pleistocene elephants characterized by long curving tusks and hairy coats and, by extension, anything vast or monumental in scale or difficulty. *~adjective* vast, huge, immense, daunting: *"The engineers were faced with a mammoth task and little time to do what was necessary."*

mañana (man<u>yan</u>ă, mă<u>yah</u>nă) SPANISH [tomorrow, from *cras mañana* tomor-row early, ultimately from Latin *mane* in the morning] *noun* tomorrow, the indefinite future: *"In this country everything gets put off until 'mañana,' which could mean anything from tomorrow to some time next month or even later." ~adverb* at an unspecified time in the future.

mand *See* MANDAMUS.

mandala (<u>man</u>dălă) SANSKRIT [from *mandalam* circle] *noun* in Hindu or Buddhist religion, a circular geometrical symbol representing the universe.

mandamus (man<u>daym</u>ăs) LATIN [we command, from *mandare*] *noun* (*plural* **mandamuses**) a writ from a superior court ordering an inferior body to carry out an official act or duty: *"A mandamus was once moved for, says Doctor Burn, to compel the churchwardens and overseers to sign a certificate; but the court of King's Bench rejected the motion as a very strange attempt"* (Adam Smith, *Wealth of Nations,* 1776). *~abbreviated form* **mand.**

mandarin (<u>man</u>dărin) CHINESE [from Sanskrit *mantrin* counsellor, from *mantra* counsel] *noun* a public official, a bureaucrat (originally referring to officials of the Chinese Empire but now taken more generally to apply to senior civil servants or government officials): *"Rose said she would be kind; but had not the least idea how to entertain the queer guest, who looked as if he had* *walked out of one of the rice-paper land-scapes on the wall, and sat nodding at her so like a toy Mandarin that she could hardly keep sober"* (Louisa May Alcott, *Eight Cousins,* 1875).

mandolin (mandălin, mandălin), **mandoline** ITALIAN [from *mandolino,* diminutive of *mandola*] *noun* a musical instrument of the lute family.

manège (manezh, mănezh, manayzh), **manege** FRENCH [from Italian *maneggio* training of a horse, ultimately from Latin *manus* hand] *noun* the art of horsemanship or a place where such skills are taught; may also refer to the movements or paces of a trained horse.

manet (manet) LATIN [he/she remains] *verb* he/she remains on stage (stage direction).

manga (mangă) JAPANESE *noun* a Japanese comic book or story in cartoon strip form.

mange-tout (monzh-too, monj-too) FRENCH [eat-all] *noun* (plural **mange-touts**) a form of pea in which the peas are cooked and eaten in their pods.

mangrove (mangrōv) PORTUGUESE [from *mangue* mangrove, itself from Spanish *mangle*] *noun* a tropical maritime tree or shrub of the genus *Rhizophora* that often grows in dense masses forming mangrove swamps: *"Venomous snakes and alligators are just two of the dangers awaiting those who* are foolish enough to wander into the mangroves."

mania (mayneeă, maynyă) GREEK [madness, from *mainesthai* to be mad] *noun* a state of excitement, passion, or enthusiasm amounting to mental disorder or frenzy; may also refer to the object of such a passion or desire: *"She revealed a mania for detail, for getting the little things right."*

manifesto (manăfestō) ITALIAN [denunciation, from *manifestare* to show, to display] *noun* (plural **manifestos** or **manifestoes**) a written declaration of beliefs, intentions, or views issued by an individual, political party, or other organization: *"I wrote and published a manifesto in the Review, in which I took the very highest ground in his behalf, claiming for him not mere acquittal, but praise and honour"* (John Stuart Mill, *Autobiography,* 1873).

manna (mană) GREEK [from Aramaic *mannâ,* ultimately from Hebrew *man*] *noun* a miraculous supply of food provided by God for the Israelites during their flight from Egypt and hence any apparently miraculous and unexpected gift or supply of good things: *"To the hard-pressed industry the new government order was manna from heaven."*

mannequin (manăkin) FRENCH [figurine, from Dutch *mannekijn* little man] *noun* a dressmaker's, tailor's, or artist's dummy, or a person who models clothing.

mano a mano (mahnō a mahnō) SPAN-ISH [hand to hand] *adjective phrase, adverb phrase* hand to hand, face to face. ~*noun phrase* a confrontation.

manoir (manwah) FRENCH [manor, from *manoir* to dwell] *noun* a French manor house.

ma non troppo (mah non tropō) ITAL-IAN [but not too much] *adverb phrase* (in music) but not too much.

manqué (mon(g)kay) FRENCH [missed, past participle of *manquer* to lack, from Italian *manco* lacking, left-handed] *adjective* would-be, unfulfilled, frustrated, failed, unsuccessful: *"He denies it, but I suspect he is a novelist manqué."* ~*noun, feminine* **manquée.**

mantilla (manteeyă, mantilă) SPANISH [diminutive of *manta* cloak, ultimately from Latin *mantellum* mantle] *noun* a light scarf or shawl of a type traditionally worn by women in Spanish and Latin American countries, usually covering the head and shoulders: *"The black lace Maud has just taken off the green one will do to edge the violet, and with your nice silk mantilla you are complete, don't you see?"* (Louisa May Alcott, *An Old-Fashioned Girl,* 1870).

mantra (mantră) SANSKRIT [sacred counsel, from *manyate* to think] *noun* in Hinduism and other eastern philosophies a mystical incantation, invocation, or prayer and thus, by extension, any watchword, personal slogan, or belief: *"Caution in all things is her personal mantra."*

maquette (maket) FRENCH [from Italian *macchietta* speck, ultimately from Latin *macula* spot] *noun* a small preliminary model of a building or sculpture: *"Each architect will be required to produce a maquette of the finished building for consideration by the competition judges."*

maquillage (makeeyahzh) FRENCH [from *maquiller* to stain, from Old French *mascurer* to darken] *noun* makeup, cosmetics.

maquis (makee) FRENCH [from Italian *macchia* thicket] *noun* (*plural* **maquis,** makee, makeez) dense, scrubby undergrowth of the type commonly found around the shores of the Mediterranean and on the island of Corsica; may also refer to the Corsican guerrilla fighters who resisted German invasion from the safety of the maquis during World War II: *"Few patrols dared to venture into the maquis in pursuit of the resistance groups who used it as a base for their subversive activities."*

marathon (marăthon) GREEK [after Marathon, Greece, where the Greeks defeated the Persians in 490 B.C., the news of the victory being rushed to Athens by a long-distance runner] *noun* a long-distance race run over a course of 26 miles 385 yards (42.2 kilometers); by extension, any endurance contest or challenge that requires prolonged effort or concentration: *"The setbacks turned the project into something of a marathon for members of the research team."*

Mardi Gras (mahrdee grah) FRENCH [fat Tuesday] *noun phrase* a carnival or other festivity marking Shrove Tuesday; may also refer more generally to any carnival or fair: *"The streets were crowded with people enjoying the Mardi Gras."*

mare clausum (mahray klowzăm, mahray klorzăm) LATIN [closed sea] *noun phrase* (*plural* **maria clausa,** mahreeă klowză, mahreeă klorză) a body of water that is under the exclusive jurisdiction of one nation and barred to others: *"The Russians declared the sea a mare clausum and challenged any foreign vessels venturing into it."*

mare liberum (mahray leebărăm) LATIN [free sea] *noun phrase* (*plural* **maria libera,** mahray leebără) a body of water that is open to all nations.

margarine (marj(ă)răn, marjăreen), **margarin** FRENCH [ultimately from Greek *margaron* white of pearl] *noun* a food product derived from vegetable oils and cultured skimmed milk, often used as a butter substitute.

marginalia (mahjănayleeă) LATIN [marginal things, from *marginalis*] *plural noun* marginal notes in a text or, more generally, anything of a nonessential or peripheral nature: *"Details of variant readings of the text may be found in the marginalia."*

mariachi (mareeahchee) MEXICAN SPANISH [possibly from French *mariage* marriage] *noun* a Mexican street band or individual member of such a band, or the type of music played by such musicians: *"No wedding in this part of the world would be complete without a mariachi band."*

mariage blanc (mareeazh blon(g)) FRENCH [white marriage] *noun phrase* (*plural* **mariages blancs**) a marriage in which the partners have no sexual relationship.

mariage de convenance (mareeazh dă konvănons) FRENCH [marriage of convenience] *noun phrase* (*plural* **mariages de convenance**) a marriage of convenience, a marriage contracted for the purposes of financial gain, expediency, or reasons other than mutual affection or love: *"The merging of the two businesses was considered a mariage de convenance by shareholders in both concerns."*

mari complaisant (maree komplayzon(g)) FRENCH [complacent husband] *noun phrase* (*plural* **maris complaisants**) a husband who is aware of his wife's adultery but chooses to tolerate it.

marijuana (marăwahnă), **marihuana** MEXICAN SPANISH [from *mariguana* or *marihuana,* perhaps from the names *Maria Juana* Mary Jane] *noun* the dried leaves and flowers of the hemp or cannabis plant, which have an intoxicating effect when smoked in cigarettes or chewed.

marimba (mărimbă) BANTU [xylophone] *noun* a type of percussion instrument of southern African origin, resembling a xylophone.

marina (măreenă) ITALIAN/SPANISH [of the sea, ultimately from Latin *marinus* marine] *noun* a harbor or mooring place with facilities for yachts or pleasure boats.

marinade (marănayd) FRENCH [from *mariner* to pickle, to marinate, perhaps ultimately from Italian *marinare* to marinate] *noun* a savory sauce in which meat, fish, and other food is soaked before cooking. *~verb* to soak food in a savory sauce before cooking it; to marinate: *"Leave the meat to marinade in the sauce overnight."*

marionette (mareeănet) FRENCH [puppet, from Marion, a diminutive of Marie] *noun* a puppet operated by hand, strings, or wires: *"Computer-originated images are gradually taking the place of hand-operated marionettes in children's television and films."*

marmite (mahrmīt, mahrmeet) FRENCH [hypocritical, in allusion to the hidden contents of the lidded cooking pot, from *marmotter* to mutter and *mite* cat] *noun* an earthenware cooking pot.

marque (mahrk) FRENCH [mark, from *marquer* to mark, to brand] *noun* a brand or make of product: *"This car bears the emblem of one of the most famous marques in the automotive industry."*

mascara (măskără) SPANISH [from *maschera* mask] *noun* a cosmetic for coloring the eyelashes: *"He could tell from the state of her mascara that she had been crying again."*

massage (masahzh, masahj) FRENCH [rub down, from *masser* to massage, from Arabic *massa* to stroke] *noun* the practice of rubbing, kneading, tapping, and stroking the skin for therapeutic or pleasurable purposes. *~verb* to administer a massage or, alternatively, to flatter someone or to manipulate data or figures: *"The government has been accused of massaging the figures relating to illegal immigrants."*

masseur (maser) FRENCH [one who massages, from *masser* to massage, from Arabic *massa* to stroke] *noun* a person who gives massages. *~noun, feminine* **masseuse** (maserz) a female masseur.

massif (maseef, masif) FRENCH [from *massif* massive] *noun* a substantial mountain or group of mountains: *"Dark clouds loomed over the peaks of the massif."*

mastaba (mastăbă), **mastabah** ARABIC [from *mastabah* stone bench] *noun* an ancient Egyptian tomb rectangular in shape with sloping walls and a flat roof: *"The first archaeologist to locate the king's mastaba was a Frenchman with relatively little knowledge of ancient Egypt."*

matador (matădor) SPANISH [one who kills, from *matar* to kill, ultimately from Latin *mactator* slayer] *noun* a bullfighter who actually kills the bull in a bullfight: *"The entry of the matador is usually greeted with a roar of cheering and salutes from the crowd."*

matelot (matlō, matălō) FRENCH [ultimately from Middle Dutch *mattenoot* bedmate] *noun* a sailor: *"I had been given to understand long before that he had the rating of a second-class able seaman (matelot leger) in the fleet which sailed from Toulon for the conquest of Algeria in the year of grace 1830"* (Joseph Conrad, *Some Reminiscences*).

mater (matăr, maytă) LATIN [mother] *noun* mother.

materfamilias (maytărfămileeăs) LATIN [mistress of the house, from *mater* mother and *familia* household] *noun* a woman who is the head of a household or family. See also PATERFAMILIAS.

materia medica (matereeă medikă) LATIN [medical matter, from Greek *hule iatrike* healing material] *noun phrase* drugs, medicines, and other ingredients used as medical remedies, or the study of such substances: *"Dr. Duncan's lectures on Materia Medica at 8 o'clock on a winter's morning are some-*

thing fearful to remember" (Charles Darwin, *Autobiography*, 1887).

matériel (matееriel), **materiel** FRENCH [material] *noun* the equipment, supplies, ammunition, or other apparatus used by an army or other organization or institution: *"The wagons were loaded high with guns and other matériel for the western front."*

matinee (matănay), **matinée** FRENCH [from *matin* morning, ultimately from Latin *matin* morning, after the goddess of morning Matuta] *noun* a theatrical performance or film showing or social event that takes place in the daytime (especially an afternoon performance): *"Demand for tickets was so high that the management decided to add several extra matinees."*

matrix (maytriks) LATIN [female animal used for breeding] *noun* (*plural* **matrixes** or **matrices,** maytriseez) the womb, or any place in which something can develop and grow; can also refer in mathematics to a rectangular array of figures arranged in rows and columns: *"The little, interesting shapes had vanished from the scene; all that remained was a vast, dark matrix of sorrow and tragedy. . ."* (D. H. Lawrence, *Sons and Lovers*, 1913).

matzo (mahtsă, mahtsō), **matzah** YIDDISH [from *matse,* from Hebrew *massah* cake of unleavened bread] *noun* (*plural* **matzos,** mahtsăz, mahtsōz, or **mat-**

zoth, <u>mah</u>tsot, <u>mah</u>tsoth) unleavened bread eaten at Passover.

mausoleum (mosǎ<u>lee</u>ǎm, mozǎ<u>lee</u>ǎm) LATIN [from Greek *mausoleion,* after the 4th-century B.C. ruler Mausolus of Caria with reference to his magnificent tomb at Halicarnassus] *noun* (*plural* **mausoleums** or **mausolea,** mosǎ<u>lee</u>ǎ, mozǎ<u>lee</u>ǎ) a large tomb, usually comprising a substantial stone structure for housing the dead above ground: *"Strange goings-on have been reported in the vicinity of the family's vast old mausoleum, ranging from ghostly lights to unearthly shrieks."*

mauvais quart d'heure (movay kah <u>der</u>) FRENCH [bad quarter of an hour] *noun phrase* (*plural* **mauvais quarts d'heure**) an unpleasant or unfortunate but shortlived period of time: *"The new administration has has a rough ride lately, but senators know that every president is doomed to suffer a mauvais quart d'heure from time to time."*

maven (<u>may</u>vǎn), mavin YIDDISH [from *meyvn,* itself from Hebrew *mebhin* understanding] *noun* an expert, someone with expert knowledge, a connoisseur.

maxima cum laude (maksimǎ kǎm <u>low</u>day) LATIN [with the greatest praise] *adverb phrase* with greatest distinction (referring to awards for academic excellence). *~adjective phrase* with greatest distinction.

maximum (<u>mak</u>simǎm) LATIN [neuter of *maximus* greatest, largest] *noun* (*plural* **maximums** or **maxima,** <u>mak</u>simǎ) the greatest value, amount, or quality, or the highest point or upper limit possible. *~adjective* highest, greatest, largest: *"The bombing was intended to cause the maximum possible disruption."*

mayday (<u>may</u>day) FRENCH [from *m'aider* help me] *noun* a distress call (as used in radio messages): *"The wireless operator radioed a single mayday an hour later but failed to give details of the ship's position or condition."*

mayonnaise (<u>may</u>ǎnayz, mayǎ<u>nayz</u>) FRENCH [from *mahonnais,* after Mahon, capital of Minorca] *noun* a thick dressing made with egg yolks, vegetable oils, vinegar or lemon juice, and seasonings.

mazel tov (<u>mah</u>zǎl tof, <u>mǎ</u>zǎl tof), **mazal tov** YIDDISH [good star, from Hebrew *mazzal* star] *interjection* good luck! congratulations!

mazourka *See* MAZURKA.

mazuma (mǎ<u>zoo</u>mǎ) YIDDISH [from *mazume* cash, from *zimmen* to prepare] *noun* (slang) money, cash.

mazurka (mǎ<u>zer</u>kǎ), mazourka (mǎ<u>zoor</u>kǎ) POLISH [*mazurek,* after the Masuria region of Poland] *noun* a Polish folk dance in triple time resembling the polka, or music written in the same tempo: *"Prince Schegolskoy, a kammerjunker, had just come from Petersburg then . . . he danced the mazurka with me and wanted to make me an offer next day"* (Fyodor Dostoyevsky, *Crime and Punishment,* 1866).

mea culpa (mayă <u>kul</u>pă) LATIN [my fault, from the Christian prayer *confiteor*] *interjection* it is my fault, I am to blame: *"And now Lady Midlothian had punished it after another fashion, and Alice went out of the Countess's presence with sundry inward exclamations of 'mea culpa,' and with many unseen beatings of the breast"* (Anthony Trollope, *Can You Forgive Her?,* 1864). ~*noun phrase* an admission of personal fault or blame.

mecca (<u>me</u>kă) ARABIC [after Mecca, Saudi Arabia, referring to the city's status as a site of pilgrimage for Muslims] *noun* a focus of activity or attention: *"Memphis is a mecca for Elvis fans from around the world."*

medallion (mă<u>dal</u>yăn), **medaillon** FRENCH [from *médaillon,* itself from Italian *medaglia* medal] *noun* a large medal or a decorative panel or tablet bearing a portrait, figure in relief, or other emblem: *"The medallion fetched a record price when it was auctioned in London recently."*

media (<u>mee</u>deeă) LATIN [plural of *medium* middle, intermediate] *noun* the press or television, radio, newspapers, and magazines in general: *"The media have bombarded the president's office with demands for interviews all week."* See also MEDIUM.

medico (<u>me</u>dikō) ITALIAN/SPANISH [ultimately from Latin *medicus* physician] *noun* a physician, doctor, medical practitioner: *"With some curiosity as to what could have sent a brother medico to us at such an hour, I followed Holmes into our sanctum"* (Arthur Conan Doyle, "The Resident Patient," 1893).

mediocre (meedee<u>ō</u>kăr) FRENCH [from *médiocre,* itself from Latin *mediocris,* from *medius* middle and Old Latin *ocris* stony mountain] *adjective* of moderate or low quality, value, performance, or ability, indifferent, second-rate, unexceptional, ordinary: *"The quality of the finished product was mediocre at best."*

medium (<u>mee</u>deeăm) LATIN [neuter of *medius* middle, intermediate] *noun* (*plural* **mediums** or **media,** <u>mee</u>deeă) a middle or average condition or degree; can also refer to a substance used as a means of transmission of a force or effect, to a means of artistic expression, to a means of communication, information, or entertainment, or to anything or anyone that acts as an intermediary or agency between others. See also MEDIA.

medusa (mă<u>doo</u>să, mă<u>dy</u>oosă, mă<u>doo</u>ză, mă<u>dy</u>ooză) GREEK [after the legendary gorgon Medousa, who had snakes for hair and could turn any mortal beholder to stone] *noun* a terrifying or ugly woman: *"I thought Medusa had looked at you, and that you were turning to stone."* (Charlotte Brontë, *Jane Eyre,* 1847).

meerschaum (<u>meer</u>shăm, <u>meer</u>shom) GERMAN [from *Meer* sea and *Schaum* foam, ultimately from Persian *kef-i-darya* sea foam] *noun* a traditional German tobacco pipe with a curved stem and large bowl made from speiolite or hydrated magnesium silicate clay.

mega (<u>me</u>gă) GREEK [great, from *megas* large] *interjection* (slang) great! cool! excellent! awesome!; often combined with other words as an intensifier. ~*adjective* (slang) great, large.

megalomania (megă<u>lō</u><u>may</u>neeă, megă-<u>lō</u><u>may</u>nyă) GREEK [enthusiasm for great things] *noun* a delusive belief in one's own importance or influence in the world, or a mania for grandiose projects and effects.

megalopolis (megă<u>lop</u>ălis) GREEK [a great city] *noun* a large city or heavily populated metropolitan area.

meiosis (mī<u>ō</u>sis) GREEK [a lessening, from *meioun* to diminish, from *meion* less] *noun* (plural **meioses,** mī<u>ō</u>seez) understatement, a figure of speech in which the importance or scale of something or someone is underemphasized (the opposite of hyperbole); can also refer to a cellular process concerning the organization of chromosomes in gamete-producing cells.

melancholia (melăn<u>kō</u>leeă) GREEK [from *melankholia* melancholy, from *melas* black and *khole* bile] *noun* pathological depression, or a general melancholy, pensiveness, foreboding, depression of the spirits: *"If no one visits me soon, I shall die of melancholia."*

mélange (may<u>lonzh</u>, me<u>lahnj</u>) FRENCH [mixture, blend, from *mêler* to mix] *noun* a mixture or medley of miscellaneous items or elements.

melee (<u>me</u>lay, <u>may</u>lay), **melée, mêlée** FRENCH [conflict, struggle, from *mêler* to mix] *noun* a confused struggle or contest, a chaotic hand-to-hand fight, or more generally any confused mixture of disparate elements or state of turmoil: *"But Uncas, who had vainly sought him in the melee, bounded forward in pursuit; Hawkeye, Heyward and David still pressing on his footsteps"* (James Fenimore Cooper, *The Last of the Mohicans,* 1826).

membrum virile (membrăm vi<u>ree</u>lee) LATIN [male member] *noun phrase* the penis.

memento (mă<u>men</u>tō) LATIN [remember, imperative of *meminisse* to remember] *noun* (plural **mementos** or **mementoes**) something that serves to remind a person of something; a keepsake, a souvenir, a warning.

memento mori (mă<u>men</u>tō <u>mor</u>ee, mă<u>men</u>tō <u>mor</u>ī) LATIN [remember to die] *noun phrase* remember you must die; can also refer to something that serves to remind a person of his or her own mortality: *"He kept the bullet as a kind of memento mori, producing it at dinner parties when the hilarity of other guests began to irritate him."*

memo   *See* MEMORANDUM.

memoir (memwahr) FRENCH [from *memoire* memory, from Latin *memoria*] *noun* an autobiographical or biographical record, a memorandum, or an official note or report: *"She wrote an interesting memoir about her early life but refused to reveal any details about her first marriage."*

memorabilia (memărăbileeă, memărăbeeleeă, memrăbilyă, memărăbeelyă) LATIN [things that deserve remembrance, neuter plural of *memorabilis* memorable, from *memorare* to bring to mind] *plural noun* mementos, souvenirs, and relics that provoke memories: *"The old man's house was full of memorabilia dating back to his youth."*

memorandum (memărandăm) LATIN [to be remembered, neuter singular of *memorandus,* gerundive of *memorare* to bring to mind] *noun* (*plural* **memorandums** or **memoranda,** memărandă) a written reminder, note, record, or communication: *"The extent of the secretary of state's involvement in the affair was exposed in a memorandum to his assistant."* ~*abbreviated form* **memo** (memō).

memsahib (memsahb, memsaheeb) HINDI [from English *ma'am* and Hindi *sahib* master] *noun* a courtesy title addressed to a white European woman of high status living in India: *"Lispeth took to Christianity readily, and did not abandon it when she reached womanhood, as do some Hill girls. Her own people hated her because she had, they said, become a memsahib and washed herself daily; and the Chaplain's wife did not know what to do with her"* (Rudyard Kipling, "The Convert," 1888).

ménage (maynahzh) FRENCH [household, housekeeping, from Old French *mesnage* dwelling, ultimately from Latin *mansio* mansion] *noun* a household, a domestic establishment; can also refer to housekeeping or housework.

ménage à trois (maynahzh a twa, menahzh a twa) FRENCH [household of three] *noun phrase* a domestic arrangement in which three people live together in the same household (usually understood to imply a sexual relationship involving a husband and wife and the lover of one or both of them): *"The ménage à trois that the writer set up with his two lovers became the subject of much local gossip."*

menagerie (mănajăree, mănazhăree) FRENCH [from *ménagerie,* management of a household or farm] *noun* a collection of exotic animals or a zoo or other place where they are kept for exhibition; by extension, any collection of diverse individuals, animals, or birds: "*A substantial portion of the tycoon's fortune was devoted to maintaining his menagerie of wild animals and birds.*"

menhir (menheer) FRENCH [long stone, from Breton *men* stone and *hir* long] *noun* a prehistoric standing stone or monolith: "*The countryside in this part of France is dotted with menhirs, many of them standing in groups of two or three huge stones resting on one another.*"

meniscus (măniskăs) GREEK [*meniskos* crescent] *noun* (*plural* **meniscuses** or **menisci,** măniskee) the convex or concave upper surface of a liquid in a tube caused by surface tension; by extension any crescent or crescent-shaped body (such as a lens with crescent-shaped section).

menopause (menăpoz) FRENCH [from *ménopause* cessation of menstruation, from Greek *men* month, moon and *pausis* stopping, pause] *noun* the period in a woman's life when menstruation ceases: "*Side effects of menopause can easily be mistaken for symptoms of disease.*"

menorah (mănoră) HEBREW [candlestick] *noun* a candelabrum with seven or nine candles, as traditionally used in Jewish religious celebrations.

mensch (mensh) YIDDISH [from *mentsh* human being, from Old High German *mennisco* person] *noun* a person of integrity, rectitude, or honor.

menses (menseez) LATIN [months, plural of *mensis* month] *noun* menstruation or the menstrual flow.

mens rea (menz reeă) LATIN [guilty mind] *noun phrase* criminal intent: "*The prosecutors must establish that the defendant had the appropriate mens rea if they are to have any hope of securing a guilty verdict.*"

mens sana in corpore sano (menz sahnă in korporay sahnō) LATIN [a sound mind in a sound body, from *Satires X* by Juvenal (c. A.D. 60–117)] *noun phrase* a healthy mind in a healthy body.

mentor (mentor, mentăr) GREEK [after the legendary character Mentor, tutor to Odysseus's son Telemachus] *noun* a tutor, coach, guide, or trusted counselor or adviser: "*. . .the occurrence at the mess, petty if it were, was a welcome one to that peculiar conscience assigned to be the private mentor of Claggart*" (Herman Melville, *Billy Budd,* 1924).

menu (menyoo) FRENCH [small, detailed, ultimately from Latin *minutus* minute] *noun* a list of dishes from which a diner may choose at a restaurant or hotel; can also refer more generally to any choice of options (especially in relation to computer operations): "*There were no vegetarian items on the menu.*"

merci (mairsee) FRENCH [thank you] *interjection* thanks.

meringue (mărang) FRENCH [of unknown origin, possibly from German *Mering* cake of Mehringen] *noun* a sweet dessert topping or confection comprising egg whites and sugar that have been beaten until stiff and then baked.

mesa (maysă) SPANISH [table, from Latin *mensa* table] *noun* a steep, flat-topped, tablelike geological formation of a type commonly found in the deserts of SW United States.

mésalliance (mayzalyons, mayzălĭăns), mesalliance FRENCH [misalliance] *noun* a marriage or other match contracted between members of different social classes and thus considered unsuitable: *"To a mesalliance of that kind every globule of my ancestral blood spoke in opposition"* (Ambrose Bierce, *Can Such Things Be?* 1893).

mesdames *See* MADAME.

mesdemoiselles *See* MADEMOISELLE.

messiah (măsīă), **Messiah** GREEK [from *massias,* ultimately from Hebrew *mashiah* anointed one, from *mashah* to anoint] *noun* a savior or spiritual leader who is expected to redeem his people (often referring specifically to Jesus Christ): *"Members of the cult regarded Jones as a messiah but failed to recognize the dangers he represented."*

messieurs *See* MONSIEUR.

mestizo (mesteezō) SPANISH [mixed, ultimately from Latin *miscere* to mix] *noun* (*plural* **mestizos** or **mestizoes**) a person of mixed European and Native American ancestry. ~*noun, feminine* **mestiza** (mesteeză) a female of mixed European and Native American ancestry.

metamorphosis (metămorfōsis) GREEK [transformation, from *metamorphoun* to transform] *noun* (*plural* **metamorphoses,** metămorfōseez) a change or transformation in form, structure, appearance, shape, character, condition, or circumstance or the process by which such a change takes place (often referring specifically to biological processes): *"The commercial center of the city has undergone a complete metamorphosis in the last six months."*

metastasis (mătastăsis) GREEK [*mathistanai* to change, to remove] *noun* (*plural* **metastases,** mătastăseez) a change in position, state, or form (often referring specifically to the spread of cancer and other diseases within the body).

metathesis (metăthăsăs) GREEK [*metatithenai* to transpose] *noun* (*plural* **metatheses,** metăthăseez) a change of condition or place; may also refer to the transposition of letters, syllables, or sounds in a word or to a chemical reaction involving the interchange of atoms between two different molecules.

Methuselah (măth(y)oozălă) HEBREW [after Methuselah, the biblical patriarch and ancestor of Noah who lived in the age of 969] *noun* a very old man: *"He may get the job, although critics consider him a bit of a Methuselah."* Also, a large wine bottle with a capacity of 6 liters (6.5 quarts).

métier (metyay, meteeay), **metier** FRENCH [trade, occupation, from Latin *ministerium* work, ministry] *noun* trade, vocation, profession, forte: *"Providing helpful advice is his métier; actually doing something is generally beyond his capabilities."*

metro (metrō), **Metro** FRENCH [from *métro,* abbreviated form of *chemin de fer métropolitain* metropolitan railroad] *noun* a subway or underground railroad (sometimes referring specifically to the Paris subway system): *"Commuters were unable to get into the metro because of smoke from the fire."*

metropolis (mătropălis) GREEK [mother city, from *meter* mother and *polis* city] *noun* (*plural* **metropolises** or **metropoles,** mătropăleez) a city or large urban area, often the chief city or capital of a state, province, or country: *"But, in the first place, New York was a metropolis, and perfectly aware that in metropolises it was 'not the thing' to arrive early at the opera..."* (Edith Wharton, *The Age of Innocence,* 1920).

meum et tuum (mayăm et tooăm) LATIN [mine and yours] *noun phrase* legal term for the principle of private property.

meunière (me(r)nyer) [abbreviated form of *à la meunière* in the manner of a miller's wife] *adjective* rolled in flour and sautéed in butter (usually referring to fish recipes).

mezzanine (mezăneen, mezăneen) FRENCH [mid-story, from Italian *mezzanino,* ultimately from Latin *medianus* middle, median] *noun* an intermediate story of a building connecting two larger stories; may also refer to the lowest of the balconies in a theater: *"...water closet on mezzanine provided with opaque singlepane oblong window, tipup seat, bracket lamp, brass tierod brace, armrests, footstool and artistic oleograph on inner face of door..."* (James Joyce, *Ulysses,* 1922). ~*adjective* of or relating to such an intermediate story or balcony.

mezza voce (metsah vōchay) ITALIAN [half voice] *adverb phrase* (in music) in a moderate tone, restrained, at medium volume. ~*adjective phrase* (in music) in a moderate tone, restrained, at medium volume.

mezzo forte (metsō fortay, medsō fortee) ITALIAN [half strong] *adverb phrase* (in music) moderately loudly. ~*adjective phrase* (in music) moderately loud.

mezzo piano (metsō peeahnō, medsō peeahnō) ITALIAN [half soft] *adverb* *phrase* (in music) moderately softly. ~*adjective phrase* (in music) moderately soft.

mezzo-soprano (metsō-săp̲r̲a̲hnō) ITALIAN [middle soprano, from *mezzo* half and *soprano* soprano] *noun* (*plural* **mezzo-sopranos** or **mezzo-soprani,** metsō-săp̲r̲a̲hnee) a female singer or other woman with a voice between that of soprano and contralto. ~*adjective* of or relating to such a voice.

miasma (mīa̲z̲mă, meea̲z̲mă) GREEK [pollution, defilement, from *miainein* to pollute] *noun* (*plural* **miasmas** or **miasmata,** mīa̲z̲mătă, meea̲z̲mătă) a vaporous exhalation, emanation, influence, or atmosphere, typically noxious, polluting, or corrupting in character: *"The historic atmosphere was there, certainly; but the historic atmosphere, scientifically considered, was no better than a villainous miasma"* (Henry James, *Daisy Miller,* 1879).

micro (mīkrō) GREEK [from *mikros* small] *adjective* microscopic, very small.

mignon (meenyon) FRENCH [small and sweet] *adjective* small and delicately pretty. ~*adjective, feminine* **mignonne.**

migraine (mīgrayn) FRENCH [sick headache, from Latin *hemicrania* pain in one side of the head, from Greek *hemikrania,* from *hemi* half and *kranion* cranium] *noun* a medical condition in which sufferers are afflicted by severe, throbbing headaches and possibly nausea and vomiting: *"She decided to stay at home because she felt a migraine coming on."*

mikado (mika̲h̲dō) JAPANESE [honorable gate] *noun* an emperor of Japan: *"It is situated in the bay of Yeddo, and at but a short distance from that second capital of the Japanese Empire, and the residence of the Tycoon, the civil Emperor, before the Mikado, the spiritual Emperor, absorbed his office in his own"* (Jules Verne, *Around the World in 80 Days,* 1873).

miles gloriosus (meelayz gloreeō̲săs) LATIN [boastful soldier] *noun phrase* (*plural* **milites gloriosi,** meelătayz gloreeō̲see) a boastful soldier (formerly a stock character of stage comedy).

milieu (meely̲ă̲, mily̲o̲o) FRENCH [midst, from Old French *mi* middle and *lieu* place] *noun* (*plural* **milieus** or **milieux,** meely̲ă̲, mily̲o̲o, meely̲ă̲z, mily̲o̲oz) the background, setting, or environment for an event or development; may also refer to a particular social class or group of people sharing similar ideas and outlook: *"He felt secure within his own social milieu."*

militia (mălĭshă) LATIN [military service, the military] *noun* a body of civilians who receive military training and can be called up to assist the regular armed forces in times of emergency, the reserves, or national guard: *"The militia was called out to help ward* off the possibility of border incursions." Also refers to a self-styled paramilitary force that engages in rebel or terror activities.

mille-feuille (meel-foi) FRENCH [a thousand leaves] noun (in French cuisine) a dish comprising layers of puff pastry and filling (of jam, cream, salmon, or other ingredients).

millefleur (meelfler, meelfloor), **millefleurs** FRENCH [from *mille fleurs* a thousand flowers] noun decorated with a pattern of tiny flowers or plants (usually referring to tapestry, porcelain, or other media); may also refer to a perfume distilled from the blooms of a mixture of flowers.

millennium (măleneeăm) LATIN [a thousand years, from *mille* thousand and *annus* year] noun (plural **millenniums** or **millennia,** măleneeă) a period of 1,000 years, or the 1,000th anniversary of something: "*No one was really sure how to celebrate the start of the new millennium.*"

mimesis (mămeesăs, mīmeesăs) GREEK [imitation, from *mimeisthai* to imitate, from *mimos* mime] noun (plural **mimeses,** mămeeseez, mīmeeseez) imitation or mimicry.

minaret (mināret) TURKISH [*minare,* from Arabic *manarah* lighthouse] noun a tall tower of a mosque from the balcony of which the faithful are called to prayer in the Islamic world: "*The calls

of the muezzin from the minaret echoed round the whole quarter.*"

minestrone (minăstrōnee, minăstrōn) ITALIAN [from *minestrare* to serve, dish up, ultimately from Latin *minister* servant] noun a thick soup made with vegetables, beans, pasta, and herbs.

minimum (minimăm) LATIN [neuter of *minimus* smallest] noun (plural **minimums** or **minima,** minimă) the smallest value, amount, or quality, or the lowest point or lowest limit possible. ~adjective lowest, least, smallest: "*He failed to make the minimum weight for the heavyweight division.*"

minor (mīnăr) LATIN [smaller, younger] adjective inferior, lesser, lower in importance or position. ~noun a person below the age of legal responsibility: "*There are strict penalties for those who serve alcohol to minors.*"

minus (mīnăs) LATIN [less, neuter of *minor* smaller] preposition less, diminished by, without, deprived of, lacking: "*That is the final figure minus the cost of the refreshments.*" ~adjective negative.

minuscule (minăskyool, minăskyool) FRENCH [minute, tiny, from Latin *minusculus* rather small] adjective very small, minute, insignificant: "*He felt minuscule under the shadow of the Himalayas.*"

minutia (mănoosheeă, mīnoosheeă) LATIN [trifles, details, from *minutia* smallness] *noun* (*plural* **minutiae,** mănooshiee, mīnoosheeī) minor or trivial detail or matter.

minyan (<u>min</u>yăn) HEBREW [number, count] *noun* (*plural* **minyans** or **minyanim,** minyă<u>neem</u>) a quorum of 10 adults required for communal worship by Jewish tradition.

mir (meer) RUSSIAN [community] *noun* a peasant village commune in prerevolutionary Russia.

mirabile dictu (mărahbălee <u>dik</u>too) LATIN [wonderful in the saying] *interjection* wonderful to relate, strange to say: *"This year—mirabile dictu!—produced but one novel; and it is not impossible that the author had taken deeply into his mind, though he would not immediately act upon them, certain hints about the danger of 'overcropping,' which have been alluded to as dropping from his publishers in 1823"* (J. G. Lockhart, *The Life of Sir Walter Scott,* 1837–38).

mirage (mi<u>rahzh</u>) FRENCH [illusion, from *mirer* to look at, ultimately from Latin *mirare* to wonder at] *noun* an optical illusion often taking the appearance of a body of water in the distance and, by extension, anything illusory and unattainable: *"As usual, his hopes of wealth and a big house by the sea had turned out to be nothing more than a mirage."*

mis *See* MISERERE.

miscellanea (misă<u>lay</u>neeă, misă<u>lay</u>nyă) LATIN [mixed things, from the neuter plural of *miscellaneus,* from *miscellus* mixed] *plural noun* a miscellany of diverse objects, writings, or articles: *"The latest volume of the great man's writings include some of his last poems, among other miscellanea."*

mise-en-scène (meez-on-<u>sen</u>, meez-on-<u>sayn</u>), **mise en scène** FRENCH [putting in scene] *noun phrase* (*plural* **mise-en-scènes**) a setting or the scenery for a theatrical production or, more generally, the context or milieu for an event or occurrence: *"As a director he had definite ideas about the mise-en-scène he wanted for the production."*

miserere (miză<u>reer</u>ee, miză<u>rair</u>ee, miză<u>rer</u>ee) LATIN [have pity, from *misereri* to be merciful, from *miser* wretched] *noun* the 50 Psalm in the Vulgate, or a musical setting of it, or a cry for mercy, a general lament or complaint: *"He then, in the plainest terms, advised me to have recourse to the discipline of flagellation, every Friday, using the cat-o'-nine-tails on my bare shoulders for the length of time that it would take to repeat a Miserere"* (Wilkie Collins, *A Fair Penitent,* 1857). ~*abbreviated form* **mis.**

misericordia (măzeră<u>kor</u>deeă, măseră<u>kor</u>deeă) LATIN [pity, mercy, from *misericors* merciful] *noun* mercy, compassion: *"The women, screaming 'Misericordia!' ran right into the room, and, falling on their knees against the* walls, began to cross themselves convulsively" (Joseph Conrad, *Nostromo*, 1904).

misogyny (me<u>soj</u>ănee) GREEK [from *misein* to hate and *gyne* woman] *noun* hatred of women: *"As he grew older he grew more and more decided in his misogyny."*

missile (<u>mis</u>ăl) LATIN [from *missilis* something that can be thrown, from *mittere* to throw] *noun* a stone, artillery shell, bullet, rocket, or other object that can be thrown or projected over a considerable distance (often referring specifically to ballistic or guided missiles): *"The biggest threat to the city was perceived to come from the enemy's mobile missile launchers."*

mistral (<u>mis</u>trăl, mi<u>strahl</u>) FRENCH [master wind, from Provençal *mistral* masterful, ultimately from Latin *magistralis* of a teacher] *noun* a cold, dry, northerly wind that blows across southern France during the winter season: *"There were few tourists on the seafront now that the mistral had started to blow."*

Mlle. *See* MADEMOISELLE.

Mme. *See* MADAME.

moccasin (<u>mok</u>ăsăn) ALGONQUIAN [from *mockasin*] *noun* a soft leather shoe or boot with no heel of a type traditionally worn by Native Americans and trappers: *"The infant padded about the house in soft-soled fur-lined moccasins."*

moderato (modă<u>rah</u>tō) ITALIAN [from Latin *moderatus*] *adverb* (in music) at a moderate pace: *"'Allegro!' he called out to the postilions at every ascent. 'Moderato!' he cried as they descended"* (Alexandre Dumas, *The Count of Monte Cristo*, 1844–45). ~*adjective* (in music) moderate, at a moderate pace.

modicum (modikăm) LATIN [a moderate amount, neuter of *modicus* moderate, from *modus* mode, measure] *noun* a small or moderate portion or quantity, a limited amount: *"She hoped to emerge from the affair with at least a modicum of self-respect."*

modiste (mō<u>deest</u>) FRENCH [from *mode* mode, style] *noun* a person who makes and sells fashionable clothing, hats, and other items: *"'Ah, but you see some of these sensible inventions come from the brain of a fashionable modiste, who will make you more lovely, or what you value more—'stylish' outside and comfortable within"* (Louisa May Alcott, *Eight Cousins*, 1875).

modulus (<u>mod</u>yoolăs) LATIN [a small measure, diminutive of *modus* mode] *noun* (*plural* **moduluses** or **moduli**, <u>mod</u>yoolee) (in physics) a coefficient; (in mathematics) a number divided into another number in a congruence relation; (in architecture) a unit of length by which proportions are expressed.

modus (mōdăs) LATIN [way, method] noun (plural **modi,** mōdī) a method, way, procedure.

modus operandi (mōdăs opărandee, mōdăs opărandī) LATIN [mode of operating] noun phrase (plural **modi operandi,** mōdee opărandee, mōdee opărandī, mōdī opărandee, mōdī opărandī) a method or procedure, a way of doing things: "An example of the lawyer's modus operandi was provided by his treatment of his client."

modus vivendi (mōdăs vivendee, mōdăs vivendī) LATIN [mode of living] noun phrase (plural **modi vivendi,** mōdee vivendee, mōdee vivendī, mōdī vivendee, mōdī vivendī) a manner of living, a way of life, a practical working arrangement: "One would almost have supposed Henchard to have had policy to see that no better modus vivendi could be arrived at with Farfrae than by encouraging him to become his son-in-law" (Thomas Hardy, The Mayor of Casterbridge, 1886).

mogul (mōgăl), **moghul** PERSIAN [from mughal, from Mongolian mongyol mongol] noun an Indian Muslim of Mongolian, Turkish, or Persian descent or, more generally, a magnate or prominent personality in business or the media: "Small concerns like theirs are at the mercy of the Wall Street moguls."

mohair (mōhair) ITALIAN [from mocaiarro, from Arabic mukhayyar] noun a type of fabric or yarn made from the silky coat or fleece of the Angora goat.

~adjecitve of or relating to such fabric: "She refused to part with her old mohair coat."

moi (mwa) FRENCH [me] pronoun me, I, myself.

moire (mwahr) FRENCH [from mouaire mohair] noun a watered fabric (usually mohair or silk). ~adjective of or relating to such fabric: "We see the ladies go out shopping . . . waiting while they make the nice young clerks pull down tons and tons of silks and velvets and moire antiques and those things. . ." (Mark Twain, The Innocents Abroad, 1869).

moiré (moray, mwahray), **moire** (moray, mwahray, mwah) FRENCH [from moirer to give a watered appearance to] noun a watered fabric or a fabric or other material with a rippled or wavy texture, or appearance; can also refer to the shimmering patterns produced when geometric patterns are superimposed on each other slightly out of alignment.

mollah See MULLAH.

molto (moltō) ITALIAN [neuter of multus much] adverb (in music) very, much: "'Signor Kirkwood well,—molto bene,' said Paolo. 'Why does he keep out of sight as he does?' asked the doctor" (Oliver Wendell Holmes, Mortal Antipathy, 1885).

momentum (mōmentăm, mămentăm) LATIN [movement] noun (plural

momentums or **momenta**, mōmĕntă, mămĕntă) the impetus or force generated by a body in motion: *"The momentum of a pendulum is governed by certain fundamental laws of physics."*

mon ami (mon ămee) FRENCH [my friend] *noun phrase* (*plural* **mes amis**, mez ămee) my friend.

mon cher (mon shair) FRENCH [my dear] *noun phrase* my dear.

mondaine (mondayn) FRENCH [fashionable, worldly] *noun* a fashionable woman, a woman of the world: *"It is many weary months before the small English lady—etiquette-bound as the most world-worn mondaine—is at home in foreign 'society'"* (*Westminster Gazette*, May 28, 1902). ~*adjective* fashionable worldly.

monocoque (monăkok) FRENCH [from *mono* one and *coque* eggshell] *noun* a type of vehicle construction in which the body and chassis are one or in which the outer covering bears all the load: *"Many modern boat designers favor the inbuilt strength and simplicity of the monocoque."*

monologue (monălog), **monolog** FRENCH [speaking alone, from Greek *mono* one and *logos* speaking] *noun* a drama or part of a drama in which just one character speaks, a soliloquy: *"He delivered the monologue in a single spotlight from the edge of the stage."*

monsieur (măsyer) FRENCH [my lord, sir] *noun* (*plural* **messieurs**, mesyă) a Frenchman of high social status, or a conventional term of address for any gentleman. ~*abbreviated form* **M.**

monsignor (mănseenyor, mănseenyăr) ITALIAN [my lord, from *monsignore*, from French *monseigneur*] *noun* (*plural* **monsignors** or **monsignori**, monsaynyoree) an honorific title borne by Roman Catholic priests or prelates: *"Upon this the duke . . . communicated his designs to eight of his most trusted followers, among whom were Don Michele and the Monsignor d'Euna, who was afterwards cardinal. . ."* (Niccolò Machiavelli, *The Prince*, 1532).

monsoon (monsoon) DUTCH [from *monssoen*, from Portuguese *monção*, from Arabic *mawsim* time, season] *noun* the rainy season in tropical and subtropical climates, characterized by strong winds and heavy rainfall: *"The onset of the monsoon was signaled by towering rainclouds and a rising wind."*

mons pubis (monz pyoobăs) LATIN [pubic eminence] *noun phrase* (*plural* **montes pubis**, monteez pyoobăs) a rounded mass of fatty tissue above the pubic bones (usually referring to females).

monstre sacré (monstră sakray) FRENCH [sacred monster] *noun phrase* (*plural* **monstres sacrés**) a controversial, eccentric, or otherwise notable public figure who generally provokes strong, often antagonistic, feelings.

mons veneris (monz ven̆aris) LATIN [mountain of Venus] *noun phrase* the mons pubis in the female; can also refer to the ball of the thumb.

montage (montazh, montahj) FRENCH [assembly, putting together, from *monter* to mount] *noun* (in the arts) a collection of images gathered together in a single composition; may also refer to a series of film clips edited together in a movie or, more generally, to any heterogeneous mixture: *"Her latest work is a montage of monochrome images projected onto the wall of a cathedral."*

mont de piété (mon dă peeaytay), mont-de-piété FRENCH [mount of piety, from a mistranslation of Italian *monte di pietà* loan of pity] *noun phrase* (*plural* **monts de piété**) a pawnbroker's shop, especially a state-run organization lending money to the poor at reasonable rates of interest: *"Valuable effects were there daily sold for a twentieth part of their original cost, and the vicomtesse saw her little stores diminish daily; for the Mont de Piété was obliged to regulate its own proceedings by the received current values of the day"* (James Fenimore Cooper, *Autobiography of a Pocket-Handkerchief*, 1843).

montera (montairă), **montero** (montairō) SPANISH [hunter, from *monte* mountain] *noun* a round hat with ear flaps, as traditionally worn by hunters in Spain and elsewhere.

mon vieux (mon(g) vyă) FRENCH [my old man] *noun phrase* my old friend.

moquette (moket) FRENCH [possibly from Italian *mocaiardo* mohair] *noun* a fabric with a velvety pile used for carpets and upholstery.

morale (măral, mărahl) FRENCH [from *moral*] *noun* the emotional or mental attitude of an individual or group: *"The morale of the team dipped with the news that their captain had been injured and would be unable to play in the big game."*

moratorium (morătoreem) LATIN [thing causing delay, neuter of *moratorius* dilatory, from *morari* to delay] *noun* (*plural* **moratoriums** or **moratoria,** morătoreeă) a respite or suspension of activity or a formally authorized postponement in the fulfillment of an obligation or repayment of a debt: *"The government has placed a moratorium on further research until the possible risks involved have been evaluated."*

morceau (morsō) FRENCH [from *morsel* morsel, ultimately from Latin *mordere* to bite] *noun* (*plural* **morceaux,** morsō, morsōz) a brief literary or musical work: *"There were several side-dishes on the table, containing what appeared to be the ordinary French rabbit—a very delicious morceau, which I can* *recommend"* (Edgar Allan Poe, "The System of Dr. Tarr and Prof. Fether," 1845).

mordant (<u>mor</u>dănt) FRENCH [biting, present participle of *mordre* to bite, ultimately from Latin *mordere* to bite] *adjective* biting, caustic, cutting, incisive, acute, pungent, sarcastic: "*As a reviewer she was renowned for her mordant critiques of contemporary fashion and design."*

mores (<u>mor</u>ayz, <u>mor</u>eez) LATIN [plural of *mos* custom] *plural noun* habits, manners, morals, and attitudes (often in relation to a particular society or group): "*The mores of teenagers today are all too often the subject of concern to their elders."*

morgue (morg) FRENCH [mortuary, after the Parisian mortuary called La Morgue] *noun* a place where dead bodies are kept before burial or disposal: "*The family was shocked to hear that the old man's body had mysteriously vanished from the morgue."* By extension, any place where there is nothing going on; can also refer to a store of clippings, photographs, or other archive material in a newspaper office, film studio, etc.

morituri te salutant (mori<u>too</u>ree tay salootont), **morituri te salutamus** (mori<u>too</u>ree tay salootahmăs) LATIN [we who are about to die salute you] *interjection* the traditional salute of Roman gladiators to the Roman emperor before fighting in the arena (often quoted by people facing a daunting challenge of some kind): "*Often far away there I thought of these two, guarding the door of Darkness, knitting black wool as for a warm pall, one introducing, introducing continuously to the unknown, the other scrutinizing the cheery and foolish faces with unconcerned old eyes. Ave! Old knitter of black wool. Morituri te salutant"* (Joseph Conrad, *Heart of Darkness,* 1902).

moron (<u>mor</u>on) GREEK [neuter of *moros* foolish, stupid] *noun* a stupid, foolish, or mentally retarded person: "*Most people agree that young men who indulge in such mindless vandalism are morons and barbarians."*

mot (mō) FRENCH [word, saying] *noun* a quip or a pithy or witty saying: "*The evening produced several memorable mots, which were duly jotted down for the benefit of posterity."* See also BON MOT.

motif (mō<u>teef</u>) FRENCH [motive] *noun* a central or recurring theme in a musical composition, literary work, or speech: "*The design of the fabric was based around the central motif of a fire-breathing dragon with red and gold scales."*

mot juste (mō <u>joost</u>) FRENCH [right word] *noun phrase* (*plural* **mots justes,** mō <u>joost</u>) an appropriate choice of word or phrase: "*He paused briefly in his talk, trying to find the mot juste to express what he was attempting to explain."*

motto (mŏtō) ITALIAN [word, from Latin *muttire* to mutter] *noun* (*plural* **mottos** or **mottoes**) a word, phrase, or sentence adopted by an individual, family, or organization as a personal slogan, as reproduced on coats of arms, official seals, and so on; may also refer to any maxim adopted as a rule of conduct or guiding principle: *"He liked to tell friends that his family motto was 'far better not.'"*

motu proprio (mōtoo prōpreeō) LATIN [by one's own motion] *adverb phrase* of one's own accord, of one's own volition: *"What the Council had done was merely to assent to a definition of the dogma of the Infallibility of the Roman Pontiff which Pius IX had had issued, proprio motu, a few days before"* (Lytton Strachey, *Eminent Victorians*, 1918). ~*noun phrase* a papal edict addressed by the pope to the Roman Catholic Church or a part of it.

moue (moo) FRENCH [pout] *noun* a grimace or pout: *"She made a moue of grave disappointment."*

moussaka (moosăkah, moosakă), **mousaka** GREEK [from *mousakas*, itself from Arabic *musakka*] *noun* (in Middle Eastern cuisine) a dish of ground meat and sliced eggplant in a seasoned cheese sauce.

mousse (moos) FRENCH [froth, moss] *noun* a chilled light dessert dish made with whipped flavored milk or cream, gelatin, and egg whites.

moustache *See* MUSTACHE.

muchacho (moochahchō) SPANISH [probably from *mocho* cropped, shorn] *noun* a boy or young man (often addressed to male servants). ~*noun, feminine* **muchacha** (moochahcha) a girl, young woman, or young female servant.

muesli (myoozlee) GERMAN [diminutive of German *Mus* soft food, mush] *noun* a breakfast cereal of Swiss origin, incorporating nuts, rolled oats, and fruit.

muezzin (mooezăn, myooezăn, mwezăn) ARABIC [from *muaddin* proclaimer, from *addana* to call to prayer] *noun* a Muslim public crier who summons the faithful to prayer five times a day from the minaret of a mosque: *"There—still high elevated above the rest of the company, to whom he vivaciously cries—he seems some Turkish Muezzin calling the good people to prayers from the top of a tower"* (Herman Melville, *Moby-Dick*, 1851).

mufti (muftee) ARABIC [possibly from *mufti* interpreter of Islamic law] *noun* ordinary civilian dress (as opposed to military uniform, clerical dress, or other official garb).

mujahideen (moojahideen), **muja-hedin, mujahedeen** ARABIC [plural of *mujahid* person who wages holy war] *plural noun* guerrilla fighters dedicated to the cause of Islam.

mulatto (m(y)ălātō, m(y)ălahtō)
SPANISH [from *mulato* young mule,
from *mulo* mule] *noun* a person of
mixed black and white descent.
~*noun, feminine* **mulatta** (m(y)ălātă,
m(y)ălahtă) a female of mixed black
and white descent.

mullah (muulă), **mulla, mollah**
TURKISH [from *molla*, itself from Arabic *mawla* master, lord] *noun* a
scholar or teacher of Islamic law and
doctrine: *"He made Kim learn whole
chapters of the Koran by heart, till he
could deliver them with the very roll and
cadence of a mullah"* (Rudyard Kipling,
Kim, 1901).

multum in parvo (măltăm in pahvō)
LATIN [much in a little thing] *noun
phrase* much in little (referring to
something that is small in scale but
much bigger in significance), as in *"a
multum-in-parvo pocket-knife"* (Thomas
Hardy, *The Hand of Ethelberta,* 1876).

mumbo jumbo (mămbō jămbō)
MANDINGO [after Mumbo Jumbo, a
masked deity of the Mandingo peoples of W Africa] *noun* gibberish or
nonsensical, meaningless language or
ritual; may also refer to superstition
or witchcraft: *"Many doctors still consider alternative remedies a load of
mumbo jumbo."*

mummy (mămee) ARABIC [from
mumiyah bitumen] *noun* an
embalmed body or one that is unusu-
ally well preserved: *"They found the*

*mummy in near-perfect condition inside its
gold sarcophagus."*

muse (myooz) GREEK [from *mousa*]
noun one of the nine sister god-
desses of Greek mythology who provide inspiration in the arts and
sciences and hence any source of
inspiration: *"He complained that his
muse had deserted him and that he was
going out for a drink."*

musique concrète (myoozeek konkret)
FRENCH [concrete music] *noun phrase*
a style of modern electronic music in
which recorded natural and instrumental sounds are combined and modified to form a musical composition.

mustache (măstash, măstash), **moustache** FRENCH [from Old Italian *mustaccio,* ultimately from Greek *moustaki,*
from *mystax* upper lip, moustache]
noun hair grown by some men above
the upper lip.

mustachio (măstasheeō, măstahsheeō)
SPANISH [from *mostacho,* itself from
Italian *mustaccio*] *noun* a mustache
(usually referring to a particularly
large and luxuriant one): *"His face,
greatly sunburnt, was more than half hidden by whisker and mustachio"* (Edgar
Allan Poe, "The Murders in the Rue
Morgue," 1841).

mutatis mutandis (myootahtăs
myootandăs) LATIN [with the things
that must be changed having been
changed] *adverb phrase* with the nec-

essary changes having been made, with consideration of the respective differences: *"What is said of the army here is to be taken also to apply, mutatis mutandis, to the air force and the navy"* (S. E. Finer, *Man on Horseback,* 1962).

muzhik (moo<u>zek</u>, moo<u>zik</u>), **muzjik** RUSSIAN *noun*   a peasant in prerevolutionary Russia: *"A czarina who should see a muzhik trying on her imperial son's blue ribbon would wear no other face"* (Victor Hugo, *Les Misérables,* 1862).

myopia (mī<u>ō</u>peeǎ) GREEK [blinked sight] *noun*   nearsightedness, short-sightedness; may also refer more generally to any lack of foresight or vision.

myriad (<u>mir</u>eead) ITALIAN [from *myrioi* countless, ten thousand] *noun*   a great number   ~*adjective* innumerable, without number: *"She was faced with myriad choices."*

mysterioso (misteeri<u>ō</u>sō) ITALIAN [mysterious] *adverb* (in music)   with mystery, in a mysterious manner.

mystique (mi<u>steek</u>) FRENCH [mystic system] *noun*   an atmosphere of mystery or reverence surrounding a place, personality, object, or event: *"The mystique surrounding European royalty has remained largely intact despite recent attacks by the press."*

mythos (<u>mi</u>thos) GREEK [from *muthos* story, myth] *noun* (*plural* **mythoi,** <u>mi</u>thoi)   a myth or mythology in general; may also refer to the plot or theme of a book or play.

naan *See* NAN.

nabob (<u>nay</u>bob) PORTUGUESE [from *nababo*, ultimately from Arabic *naib* governor] *noun*   an Indian provincial governor of the Mogul Empire; by extension, any person possessing great wealth or occupying a position of importance (usually referring to someone with strong Indian connections): "...*Signor Torre del Greco, who extinguished Vesuvius by pouring into it the Bay of Naples; Spahi, the Persian ambassador; and Tul Wil Shan, the exiled nabob of Nepaul, whose saddle is the new moon*" (Ralph Waldo Emerson, "Manners," 1844).

nacelle (nă<u>sel</u>) FRENCH [small boat, ultimately from Latin *navis* ship] *noun* a streamlined bulge on an airplane wing or fuselage housing an engine or other item of machinery, or alternatively the basket or car of a balloon or airship. May also refer more generally to any similar bulge on a motor vehicle or boat.

nacho (<u>nah</u>chō, <u>nach</u>ō) SPANISH [possibly from *nacho* flat-nosed or a diminu-

tive of the name Ignacio, after the Mexican chef Ignacio Anaya] *noun*   a tortilla chip coated with melted cheese, peppers, or spices: "*Nachos are the latest trendy snack on the bar menu.*"

nad *See* NADIR.

nada (<u>nah</u>dă, <u>nad</u>ă) SPANISH [nothing, from Latin *res nata* insignificant thing] *noun*   nothing, non existence: "*The man shrugged his shoulders. 'There is no money left. Nothing. Nada. Zilch.'*"

nadir (<u>nay</u>deer, <u>nay</u>dăr) FRENCH [from Arabic *nazir* opposite] *noun*   the lowest point of something (in astronomy, the area of a sphere opposite the zenith): "*In the most illustrious lives as in the most obscure, in animals as in secretary-generals, there is a zenith and there is a nadir, a period when the fur is magnificent, the fortune dazzling*" (Honoré de Balzac, *Bureaucracy*). ~*abbreviated form* **nad.**

naïf (nī<u>eef</u>), **naif** FRENCH [inborn, natural, ultimately from Latin *nativus* native] *noun*   a naive person, an innocent. ~*adjective* naive.

naissant (na̲ysont) FRENCH [being born] *adjective* in an early stage of development, coming into being: *"This is just one of several naissant projects being considered by the company."*

naive (nı̄eev), **naïve** FRENCH [innocent, gullible, from *naif* inborn, natural, ultimately from Latin *nativus* native] *adjective* innocent, credulous, gullible, unsuspecting, unaffected, unsophisticated: *"She is more naive than she pretends."*

naïveté (nı̄eevta̲y, nı̄eeva̲ta̲y, nı̄eevtay, nı̄eeva̲tay), **naivete, naiveté** FRENCH [inborn character, from *naif* inborn, natural] *noun* a naive comment or attitude or naivety in general.

nan (nahn), **naan** HINDI [from Persian] *noun* a variety of round, flat, unleavened bread commonly eaten in the Indian subcontinent.

narcissism (na̲hr̲sisiza̲m) GREEK [after the legendary Narcissus, who fell in love with his own reflection] *noun* self-love, an obsessive admiration of or approving interest in oneself: *"After his coworkers accused him of narcissism he hardly dared even look in a mirror."*

narcosis (nahrkō̲sis) GREEK [from *narkosis* benumbing, itself from *narkoun* to make numb] *noun* (*plural* **narcoses,** nahrkō̲seez) a state of unconsciousness or stupor as induced by drugs.

natura abhorret vacuo (nachoŏră abhoret va̲kyoŏ) LATIN [nature shrinks back from something empty] *noun phrase* nature abhors a vacuum.

natura naturans (nachoŏră na̲chyooranz) LATIN [creating nature] *noun phrase* the creative power of nature: *"But taking timely warning, and leaving many things unsaid on this topic, let us not longer omit our homage to the Efficient Nature, natura naturans, the quick cause, before which all forms flee as the driven snows . . ."* (Ralph Waldo Emerson, *Essays,* 1841).

nausea (no̲zeeă, no̲seeă, no̲zhă, no̲shă) LATIN [seasickness, ultimately from Greek *nautes* sailor] *noun* a feeling that one is going to vomit; can also refer more generally to any sensation of loathing or disgust.

n.b., N.B. *See* NOTA BENE.

né *See* NÉE

nebbish (ne̲bish) YIDDISH [from *nebekh* poor, unfortunate, from Czech *nebohý*] *noun* a weak or ineffectual person. ~*adjective* weak, timid, ineffectual.

nebula (ne̲byălă) LATIN [mist, cloud] *noun* (*plural* **nebulas** or **nebulae,** ne̲byălee, ne̲byălı̄) in astronomy, a galaxy or a cloud of interstellar gas or dust; can also refer more generally to any hazy image or cloud: *"They placed the calf beside its mother again, took up* *the lantern, and went out, the light sinking down the hill till it was no more than a nebula"* (Thomas Hardy, *Far From the Madding Crowd,* 1874).

necrophilia (nekrăfileeă) GREEK [fondness for corpses] *noun* an erotic interest in sexual intercourse with dead bodies.

necropolis (nekropălis) GREEK [city of the dead] *noun (plural* **necropolises, necropoles,** nekropăleez, **necropoleis,** nekropălīz, or **necropoli,** nekropălī, nekropălee) a cemetery, especially in an ancient town or city: *"The step drew nearer, and a guardian in a braided cap walked listlessly through the room like a ghost stalking through a necropolis"* (Edith Wharton, *The Age of Innocence,* 1920).

necrosis (năkrōsis, nekrōsis) GREEK [state of death, from *nekroun* to kill] *noun (plural* **necroses,** năkrōseez, nekrōseez) the death or decay of an organ or tissue through disease or injury.

nectar (nektăr) GREEK [from *nektar,* the legendary drink of the gods in Greek and Roman mythology] *noun* a sweet or delicious liquid, often referring specifically to the sweet excretions of certain plants, as collected by bees to make honey.

née (nay), **nee** FRENCH [feminine of *né* born, past participle of *naître* to be born] *adjective* born (referring to the

maiden name of a woman before marriage). *~adjective, masculine* **né** (nay) formerly called (referring to the original name of a person, group, organization, or country).

negligee (neglăzhay, neglăzhay), **negligé** FRENCH [from *négligé,* past participle of *négliger* to neglect] *noun* a light dressing gown for women, usually made of sheer material; can also refer more generally to casual or informal attire: *"She gave her mother a hideous pink negligee for her birthday."*

nem. con. *See* NEMINE CONTRADICENTE.

nemesis (nemăsis) GREEK [retribution, after Nemesis, the Greek goddess of divine retribution] *noun (plural* **nemeses,** nemăseez) an act of retribution or punishment, or the agent of this: *"But, clearly, the old order was already in part reversed. The Nemesis of the delicate ones was creeping on apace"* (H. G. Wells, *The Time Machine,* 1895).

nemine contradicente (neminay kontrădikentay) LATIN [no one contradicting] *adverb phrase* unanimously, with no one dissenting. *~abbreviated form* **nem. con.**: *The resolution was passed nem con.*

neon (neeon) GREEK [neuter of *neos* new] *noun* an inert gaseous element used in electric lighting, the lights themselves, or the lighting thus produced. *~adjective* of or relating to such lighting or to colors reminiscent of vibrant neon lighting: *"All the operating rooms now have neon lighting."*

ne plus ultra (nay plăs <u>ă</u>ltră, nee plăs <u>ă</u>ltră) LATIN [no more beyond] *noun phrase* (*plural* **ne plus ultras**) the acme, apex, or highest point; the ultimate achievement or example of something: *"A little south of east was Palos, where Columbus weighed anchor, and farther yet the pillars which Hercules set up; concerning which when we inquired at the top of our voices what was written on them,——for we had the morning sun in our faces, and could not see distinctly,——the inhabitants shouted Ne plus ultra (no more beyond). . ."* (Henry David Thoreau, *Cape Cod,* 1865).

n'est-ce pas? (nes <u>pa</u>) FRENCH [is it not?] *interrogative* is that not so?

Nestor (<u>nes</u>tă, <u>nes</u>tor), **nestor** GREEK [after Nestor, an aged king of Pylos in Greek legend respected for his advice to the Greeks at Troy] *noun* a wise old man or a person who has the status of a leading figure or patriarch in a particular field.

net (net) FRENCH [neat, clean, clear] *adjective* free from all charges or deductions. *~noun* a clear amount, profit, weight, or price. *~verb* to yield or receive as profit: *"He hopes to net in excess of a million before the end of the year."*

netsuke (<u>net</u>skee, net<u>soo</u>kee) JAPANESE *noun* (*plural* **netsuke** or **netsukes**)

an intricately carved toggle of ivory, wood, etc., originally suspended by a cord from the sash of the traditional Japanese kimono.

neurosis (noo<u>rō</u>sis, nyoo<u>rō</u>sis) GREEK [*neuron* nerve] *noun* (*plural* **neuroses,** noo<u>rō</u>seez, nyoo<u>rō</u>seez) a mild mental or emotional disturbance affecting the personality or, more generally, any state of anxiety or obsession: *"His neurosis got worse and worse through the winter."*

neuter (<u>noo</u>tăr, <u>nyoo</u>tăr) LATIN [neither] *adjective* neither male or female; neutral or impartial. *~noun* something that is neither male or female; or someone or something that is neutral, imperfectly developed, or castrated. *~verb* to castrate, to spay or otherwise to deprive someone or something of power or potency.

nevus (<u>nee</u>văs) LATIN [birthmark] *noun* (*plural* **nevi,** <u>nee</u>vī) a birthmark, mole, or other blemish on the skin.

nexus (<u>nek</u>săs) LATIN [binding, linking, from *nectere* to bind] *noun* (*plural* **nexus** or **nexuses,** <u>nek</u>săsăz) a connection, a link; a cluster or connected series; may also refer to the center or focus of something: *". . .how a book,* Le Control Social, *had the effect of making Frenchmen begin to drown one another cannot be understood without an explanation of the causal nexus of this new force with the event"* (Leo Tolstoy, *War and Peace,* 1863–69).

niche (nich) FRENCH [recess, retreat, from *nicher* to nest, ultimately from Latin *nidus* nest] *noun* a recess, alcove, or cranny; a place or position in which a person or thing is snugly or comfortably lodged, a position of advantage in a marketplace etc., a place of safety or retreat: *"The partnership has occupied a prominent niche in the market for several months now."* ~*verb* to place in a niche.

nickel (nĭkăl), **nickle** SWISS GERMAN [probably from German *Kupfernickel* copper demon, from *Kupfer* copper and *Nickel* goblin] *noun* a hard silver-white metal commonly used in alloys and as a catalyst. ~*verb* to coat or cover with nickel.

nihil ad rem (nīhil ad rem, nihil ad rem) LATIN [nothing to the matter] *adjective phrase* irrelevant, beside the point.

nihil obstat (nīhil obstat, nihil obstat) LATIN [nothing hinders] *adjective phrase* (in the Roman Catholic Church) approval from an official censor indicating that a book is free of doctrinal or moral error and, more generally, any statement of official approval.

nil (nil) LATIN [from *nihil* nothing] *noun* nothing, zero.

nil desperandum (nil despărandăm) LATIN [nothing to be despaired, quoting the *Odes* of Horace (65–8 B.C.)] *interjection* do not despair, never despair.

nimbus (nimbăs) LATIN [cloud, rainstorm] *noun* (*plural* **nimbuses** or **nimbi,** nimbee) a cumulus raincloud or more generally any cloud, vapor, atmosphere, or halo: *"In about a minute and a half I was fringed out with an electrical nimbus that flamed around for miles and miles and lit up all space like broad day"* (Mark Twain, *Captain Stormfield,* 1909).

ninja (ninjă) JAPANESE [preserving person, from *nin* preserve, endure and *ja* person] *noun* (*plural* **ninja** or **ninjas**) a fighter trained in Japanese martial art (originally a class of mercenaries trained as assassins and saboteurs in 14th-century Japan).

nirvana (nervahnă, nărvahnă) SANSKRIT [a blowing out, extinguishing] *noun* a state of bliss or of spiritual enlightenment (inspired by the liberation of the soul achieved after death according to Buddhist philosophy): *"That shop is nirvana for those in search of high fashion at bargain prices."*

nisei (neesay, neesay) JAPANESE [second generation] *noun* (*plural* **nisei** or **niseis**) a child of Japanese immigrants to the United States (usually referring to one who has been born and educated in the U.S.).

nisi (nīsī) LATIN [unless] *adjective* not final (a legal term indicating that a court order or decree, etc. will take effect at a stipulated time, all other conditions having been fulfilled or no challenges to it having been received): *"'Well; and what is it about?' he said after kissing her. 'That the decree nisi in the case of Phillotson versus Phillotson and Fawley, pronounced six months ago, has just been made absolute'"* (Thomas Hardy, *Jude the Obscure*, 1895).

No (nō), **Noh** JAPANESE [ability, talent] *noun* a stylized form of classical Japanese drama incorporating masked characters, dance, and song.

noblesse (nōbles) FRENCH [nobility, ultimately from Latin *nobilis* well-known, highborn] *noun* nobility of rank or birth, the aristocracy (especially with reference to the nobility of France).

noblesse oblige (nōbles ōbleezh) FRENCH [nobility obligates] *noun phrase* the belief that nobility of rank or birth brings with it obligations to maintain high standards of personal morality and honor: *"It is your name, and you cannot be rid of it. It is yours of right, as my name has been mine of right; and not to assert it, not to live up to it, not to be proud of it, would argue incredible baseness. Noblesse oblige"* (Anthony Trollope, *Lady Anna*, 1873–4).

nocturne (noktern) FRENCH [nocturnal, from Latin *nocturnus*] *noun* a work of art depicting evening or night, or (in music) a composition for the piano that is pensive or dreamlike in character: *"Play me something. Play me a nocturne, Dorian, and, as you play, tell*

me, in a low voice, how you have kept your youth" (Oscar Wilde, *The Picture of Dorian Gray*, 1891).

Noel (nōel), **Noël** FRENCH [from *noël* Christmas, carol, ultimately from Latin *natalis* birthday] Christmas, or a Christmas carol.

Noh *See* NO.

noir (nwahr) FRENCH [black] *adjective* black (often with reference to black humor).

noisette (nwazet, nwăzet) FRENCH [diminutive of *nois* choice cut of meat, ultimately from *noix* nut] *noun* a small cut of lean meat.

nol. con. *See* NOLO CONTENDERE.

nolens volens (nōlenz vōlenz) LATIN [unwilling willing] *adverb phrase* whether willing or not, willy-nilly.

noli me tangere (nōlee mee tanjăree) LATIN [do not touch me] *noun phrase* (*plural* **noli me tangeres**) a warning against touching or interfering with something or someone; may also refer to an object or person that should not be touched or alternatively to a pictorial representation of Jesus Christ appearing to Mary Magdalene after the resurrection.

nolle prosequi (nolee prosekwee) LATIN [to be unwilling to pursue] *noun phrase* a legal term indicating that no further action is to be taken in regard to a particular case or suit. ~*abbreviated form* **nolle pros.** *or* **nol. pros.**

nolo contendere (nōlō kontĕndăree) LATIN [I do not wish to contend] *noun phrase* (*plural* **nolo contenderes**) a legal term indicating that a defendant in a case has decided neither to admit nor to deny the charges. ~*abbreviated form* **nol. con.**

nol. pros. *See* NOLLE PROSEQUI.

nom de guerre (nom dă gair) FRENCH [war name] *noun phrase* (*plural* **noms de guerre**) a pseudonym or assumed name under which a person takes part in some enterprise: *"How odd and unfair it is: wicked impostors go around lecturing under my nom de guerre and nobody suspects them; but when an honest man attempts an imposture, he is exposed at once"* (Mark Twain, *Life on the Mississippi,* 1883).

nom de plume (nom dă ploom) FRENCH [pen name] *noun phrase* (*plural* **noms de plume**) a pseudonym or assumed name under which a person publishes a piece of writing: *"She decided to release her second novel under a nom de plume."*

nom de théâtre (nom dă tayahtră) FRENCH [theatrical name] *noun phrase* (*plural* **noms de théâtre**) a pseudonym or stage name under which a person performs in the theater.

nomen (nōmen) LATIN [name] *noun* (*plural* **nomina,** nŏmină) name (usually referring to a person's surname).

nomen dubium (nōmen doobeeăm) LATIN [doubtful name] *noun phrase* (*plural* **nomina dubia,** nŏmină doobeeă) in taxonomy, a doubtful or uncertain identification of a specimen, recognizing the possibility that the identification may be incorrect.

nomen nudum (nōmen noodăm, nōmen nyoodăm) LATIN [naked name] *noun phrase* (*plural* **nomina nuda,** nŏmină noodă) in taxonomy, a proposed name for a group of species details of which have yet to be officially published.

nonchalance (nonshalons, nonshalons) FRENCH [carelessness, heedlessness, from *nonchaloir* to disregard] *noun* unconcern, indifference, coolness: *"The family greeted the news with nonchalance."*

nonchalant (nonshalon(g), nonshalon(g)) FRENCH [careless, heedless, from *nonchaloir* to disregard] *adjective* unconcerned, indifferent, cool, casual, unexcited: *"His nonchalant manner infuriated her."*

non compos mentis (non kompăs mentis) LATIN [not having mastery of one's mind] *adjective phrase* not of sound mind, not in one's right mind, mentally disturbed: *"Several of the younger partners began to speculate that the old* man was non compos mentis." ~ abbreviated form **non compos.**

nondescript (nondăskript) LATIN [from non not and descriptus described] adjective without distinguishing features, dull, drab: "They agreed that the office should be decorated throughout in fairly nondescript colors."

non licet (non liset) LATIN [it is not lawful] adjective phrase not permitted, unlawful.

nonpareil (nonpărel) FRENCH [not alike] noun someone or something that is considered unique or without equal. ~ adjective of or relating to someone or something without equal, unique, unrivaled: "'Then she is as honest and genuine as she looks,' rejoined my guardian, 'and it is impossible to say more for her.' 'She's Colour-Sergeant of the Non-pareil battalion,' said Mr. Bagnet. . .'" (Charles Dickens, Bleak House, 1852–53).

non placet (non playset, nōn playset) LATIN [it does not please] noun phrase a negative vote against a proposal, an expression of dissent.

nonplus (nonplăs) LATIN [from non plus not more] verb to perplex, baffle, puzzle, put at a loss: ". . .Rose was one of the children who observe and meditate much, and now and then nonplus their friends by a wise or curious remark" (Louisa May Alcott, Eight Cousins, 1875).

non sequitur (non sekwiter, non sek-witoor) LATIN [it does not follow] noun phrase (plural **non sequiturs**) a statement or conclusion that does not follow logically on from what preceded it: "The professor is well known for his non sequiturs and illogicalities." ~ abbreviated form **non seq.**

non troppo (non tropō) ITALIAN [not too much] adverb phrase (in music) not too much, without excess. ~ adjective phrase (in music) not too much.

noodle (noodăl) GERMAN [from Nudel] noun a variety of pasta shaped into long ribbons or strings.

nosh (nosh) YIDDISH [from naschn, from Middle High German naschen to nibble] noun (informal) a snack or light meal, or food in general; may also refer to a restaurant or snack bar. ~ verb (informal) to eat a snack or light meal.

nostalgia (nostaljă, năstaljă, năstahljă) GREEK [homesickness, from nostos return home and algeo to be in pain] noun sentimental yearning for times past, real or imagined: "Nostalgia is a pastime best enjoyed by the very old."

nostrum (nostrăm) LATIN [from noster our] noun (plural **nostrums**) a patent medicine of a secret or dubious character and hence any unproven remedy, panacea, or pet scheme: ". . .and now all the inheritance is to pass away, merely because one good worthy gentleman would not be contented to enjoy his horses, his hounds, and his bottle of claret, like thirty or forty predecessors, but must . . . try every new nostrum that has been tabled by the quackish improvers of the time" (J. G. Lockhart, *Life of Sir Walter Scott,* 1837–38).

nota bene (nōtă benee, nōtă beenee) LATIN [mark well] *verb phrase* note well, observe particulary. ~*abbreviated forms* **n.b., N.B.**

notabilia (nōtăbileeă) LATIN [things worthy of note, plural of *notabilis* notable] *plural noun* notable items, things worthy of notice: *"This website specializes in theatrical notabilia."*

nougat (noogăt) FRENCH [from Old Provençal *nogat,* ultimately from Latin *nux* nut] *noun* a variety of confection in which pieces of nut or fruit are embedded in sugar paste.

nous (noos) GREEK [mind, intellect] *noun* mind, reason, intelligence, common sense: *"She does not have sufficient nous to solve the problem for herself."*

nouveau (noovō, noovō) FRENCH [from Middle French *novel* new] *adjective* new, recently arrived or acquired, fresh, up to date.

nouveau riche (noovō reesh) FRENCH [new rich] *noun phrase (plural* **nouveaux riches,** noovō reesh) a rich person whose wealth has been relatively recently acquired; a parvenu, an

upstart: *"The nouveaux riches have few real friends, and their greatest enemies are others among their number."* ~*adjective phrase* of or relating to the newly rich.

nouveau roman (noovō rōmon(g)) FRENCH [new novel] *noun phrase (plural* **nouveaux romans**) a novel written in a postmodern prose style that rejects formalities of plot and characterization.

nouvelle (noovel) FRENCH [new] *noun* a short novel, a novella.

nouvelle cuisine (noovel kwizeen) FRENCH [new cooking] *noun phrase* a style of cookery that emphasizes the use of light, healthy sauces, fresh ingredients, and attractive presentation of food: *"Lavishly finished photographs of nouvelle cuisine dishes are an essential ingredient of most bestselling magazines."*

nouvelle vague (noovel vahg) FRENCH [new wave] *noun phrase (plural* **nouvelles vagues**) a cinematic style originating in France in the late 1950s and characterized by the use of innovative camera work and relatively unknown actors; since revived periodically in describing various new trends and movements in the arts.

nova (nōvă) LATIN [feminine of *novus* new] *noun (plural* **novas** or **novae,** nōvee, nōvī) astronomical term for a star that suddenly increases massively in brightness and then fades gradually to its original dim state: "*Astronomers have identified three new novas as a result of their latest search in deep space.*"

novella (nōvelă, năvelă) ITALIAN [feminine of *novello* new] *noun* (*plural* **novellas** or **novelle,** nōvelee) a short novel: "*His novellas were generally better received than his longer works.*"

nuance (nooons, nyooons) FRENCH [shade, hue, from *nuer* to make shades of color, ultimately from Latin *nubes* cloud] *noun* a subtle quality or variation, a nicety: "*They preserve a social tradition of which I should be sorry to lose the least perfume. Of course I don't expect you, just at first, to feel the difference, to see the nuance*" (Edith Wharton, *The Reef,* 1912).

nubile (noobīl, nyoobīl) FRENCH [from Latin *nubilis* marriageable, itself from *nubere* to marry] *adjective* (of a woman) marriageable, sexually attractive: "*He was one of those comedians who always seemed to be surrounded by nubile young hopefuls.*"

nucleus (nookleeăs, nyookleeăs) LATIN [kernel, nut] *noun* (*plural* **nucleuses** or **nuclei,** (nookleeī) a central point around which everything else gathers or revolves; can also refer more specifically to the kernel of a cell or to the core of an atom.

nuit blanche (nwee blonzh) FRENCH [white night] *noun phrase* (*plural* **nuits blanches**) a sleepless night: "*The weeks passed half-real, not much pain, not much of anything, perhaps a little relief, mostly a nuit blanche. Paul went restless from place to place*" (D. H. Lawrence, *Sons and Lovers,* 1913).

nulli secundus (nălee sekundăs) LATIN [second to none] *adjective phrase* the first-class, of the first rank.

numero uno (noomărō oonō, nyoomărō oonō) ITALIAN [number one] *noun phrase* number one; the best, most important, or prominent person or thing: "*Her grandfather likes to think he is still numero uno in the organization.*"

nunc dimittis (nungk dămitis) LATIN [now lettest thou depart, from the opening words of the Song of Simeon in Luke 2:29–32] *noun phrase* a canticle or prayer said at evensong and compline, or music written to accompany this; may also refer generally to any dismissal or permission to depart.

nunchaku (nănchăkoo, nănchahkoo) JAPANESE [from Okinawa dialect] *noun* in Japanese martial art, a type of weapon comprising two sticks connected by a short strap or chain.

nuncio (nănseeō, nuunseeō) ITALIAN [from *nunzio,* ultimately from Latin *nuntius* messenger] *noun* a papal legate who represents the papacy in a foreign country or who undertakes special missions on behalf of the Pope: "*I arranged with the Nuncio . . .*

that we should receive written information of Romayne's state of health, and on that understanding we returned to England" (Wilkie Collins, *The Black Robe,* 1881).

nymphomania (nimfămayneeă, nimfă-maynyă) GREEK [madness of the bride, from *numph* bride and *mania* madness] *noun* excessive sexual desire in the female.

O

O.A.M.D.G.   *See* OMNIA AD MAJOREM DEI GLORIAM.

ob.   *See* OBIIT.

obbligato (oblăgahtō), **obligato** ITALIAN [obligatory, past participle of *obbligare* to oblige] *adjective* (in music) obligatory, indispensable, not to be omitted. ~*noun* (*plural* **obbligatos** or **obbligati**, oblăgahtee)   a passage of music written to accompany a solo or the main melody. ~*abbreviated form* **obb.**

obi (ōbee) JAPANESE [belt] *noun*   a sash worn round the waist as part of traditional Japanese dress: *"Carpenters had torn out the partition between front parlor and back parlor, thrown it into a long room on which she lavished yellow and deep blue; a Japanese obi with an intricacy of gold thread on stiff ultramarine tissue, which she hung as a panel against the maize wall. . ."* (Sinclair Lewis, *Main Street,* 1922).

obiit (ōbeeit), **obit** LATIN [he/she/it died] *noun*   (in epitaphs) died. ~*abbreviated form* **ob.**

obiit sine prole (ōbeeit sinay prōlay), **obit sine prole** LATIN [he/she/it died without offspring] *noun phrase*   (in genealogy) died without offspring. ~*abbreviated form* **o.b.s.p., o.s.p.**

obit   *See* OBIIT.

obiter (ōbită) LATIN [meanwhile, incidentally] *adverb*   in passing, by the way. ~*adjective* incidental.

obiter dictum (ōbităr diktăm) LATIN [something said by the way] *noun phrase* (*plural* **obita dicta,** ōbită diktă)   an incidental remark, observation, or opinion: *"The judge made his opinion clear in an obiter dictum, but this cannot be considered a precedent for future cases."*

obit sine prole   *See* OBIIT SINE PROLE.

objet d'art (obzhay dar) FRENCH [art object] *noun phrase* (*plural* **objets d'art**)   a work of art, an object of artistic value, a curio: *"The store window was full of trinkets and objets d'art."*

object trouvé (obzhay troovay) FRENCH [found object] *noun phrase* (*plural*

objets trouvé) a natural object, usually found by chance, that is considered to have artistic or aesthetic value in itself.

obligato *See* OBBLIGATO.

obscurum per obscurius (obskyoorăm per ob<u>skyoor</u>iăs) LATIN [the obscure by the still more obscure] *noun phrase* (in logic) an explanation of the obscure that is even more obscure than what it attempts to explain.

o.b.s.p. *See* OBIIT SINE PROLE.

ocarina (okă<u>reen</u>ă) ITALIAN [from *oca* goose (referring to its gooselike shape)] *noun* a crude musical wind instrument comprising an oval body with several fingerholes and a mouthpiece: *"The child picked up the ocarina and produced three ethereal, piping notes."*

odalisque (<u>o</u>dălisk) TURKISH [*odalik* chambermaid, from *oda* chamber] *noun* a female slave or concubine in a harem; may also refer more generally to any sexually attractive female: *"He beheld about her shoulders the amber tresses of the 'Odalisque bathing'; she had the long waist of the medieval chatelaines; she resembled, too, the 'Pale Woman of Barcelona'; but above all she was the Angel!"* (Gustave Flaubert, *Madame Bovary,* 1857).

odeon (<u>o</u>deeăn), **odeum** GREEK [from *oideion* place for song] *noun* (*plural* **odeons** or **odea,** <u>o</u>deeă) a theater, concert hall, or cinema.

odium (<u>o</u>deeăm) LATIN [hatred, from *odisse* to hate] *noun* opprobrium, infamy, disrepute, unpopularity, hatred, detestation; may also refer to the state of being hated or disliked or to an object inspiring such feelings: *"It took many years for the party to shake off the odium of corruption following accusations of electoral fraud."*

odyssey (<u>o</u>dăsee) GREEK [after Homer's epic poem the *Odyssey,* describing the voyages of Odysseus] *noun* an epic or lengthy voyage or period of wandering (actual or spiritual): *"She had not realized that research into her family history would take her on such a remarkable odyssey through her country's history."*

Oedipus complex (<u>e</u>dăpăs kompleks, <u>ee</u>dăpăs kompleks) GREEK [after the legendary Oedipus, the prince of Thebes, unknowingly killed his father and married his mother] *noun phrase* (in psychology) a personality disorder in which the subject becomes obsessively jealous or hostile toward the parent of the same sex or feels sexual desire for the other parent.

oeil-de-boeuf (er dă <u>băf</u>) FRENCH [ox's eye] *noun phrase* (*plural* **oeils-de-boeuf**) a small, round window or alternatively a small antechamber in a palace.

oesophagus *See* ESOPHAGUS.

oestrus *See* ESTRUS.

oeuvre (<u>er</u>vră) FRENCH [work, product] *noun*   a literary or artistic work, or a large body of work (usually referring to the life work of an artist, composer, or writer): *"The first symphony is still considered the maestro's most significant oeuvre."*

ogre (<u>ō</u>găr) FRENCH [giant who feeds on human flesh, probably after Orcus, a god of the underworld in classical mythology] *noun*   a hideous monster or cannibalistic giant; by extension, any person or object that inspires dread, terror, or loathing: *"Youngsters today shrug off tales of terrifying witches and flesh-eating ogres that would have had children in a former era shivering with dread."*

olé (ō<u>lay</u>) SPANISH [hurray] *interjection* bravo! (shout of approval at some feat or accomplishment, traditionally shouted as a salute by crowds at bullfights).

olim (<u>ō</u>lim) LATIN [formerly] *adverb* formerly, at one time, in times past.

olla podrida (olă po<u>dree</u>dă) SPANISH [rotten pot] *noun phrase* (*plural* **ollas podridas**)   (in Spanish and Latin American cuisine) a richly seasoned meat and vegetable stew containing a wide variety of ingredients; may also refer more generally to any miscellany or medley of incongruous objects.

oloroso (olă<u>rō</u>sō) SPANISH [fragrant] *noun*   a full-bodied medium-sweet Spanish sherry.

olympiad (ă<u>lim</u>peead) GREEK [after Olympia, Greece, where the Olympic Games were held in ancient times] *noun*   the celebration of the Olympic Games, held every four years; it referred originally to the four-year intervals between the games: *"The last olympiad proved a financial and public relations triumph and set a new standard for future organizers."*

Olympian (ă<u>lim</u>peeăn) GREEK [after Olympia, Greece, where the Olympic Games were held in ancient times] *adjective*   of or relating to the Olympic Games or to Olympus, the home of the gods in classical mythology; may also refer more generally to anyone whose imposing character or remarkable achievements suggest godlike status: *"The blacksmith drew himself up to his full height and glared with Olympian fury at his tormentors."*

om (ōm) SANSKRIT [from the syllables *a, u, m,* representing the three main Hindu deities] *interjection*   mantra intoned by Hindus and Tibetan Buddhists during meditative contemplation of ultimate reality.

ombudsman (<u>om</u>buudzmăn) SWEDISH [from *ombud* representative] *noun* (*plural* **ombudsmen**)   a government official or other authority who investigates complaints against other public officials and bodies: *"It has just been announced that the affair is to be investigated by the ombudsman."*

O.M.D.G. *See* OMNIA AD MAJOREM DEI GLORIAM.

omega (ō<u>may</u>gă, ō<u>meg</u>ă, ō<u>mee</u>gă) GREEK [from *ō mega* large o] *noun* the last letter of the Greek alphabet, used to indicate the end or the last of a series.

omelette (<u>om</u>lăt, <u>om</u>ălăt), **omelet** FRENCH [from Middle French *alumelle* knife blade, ultimately from Latin *lamina* thin plate] *noun* a dish made with eggs beaten and fried, often with vegetables, cheese, or other ingredients: *"Supper comprised nothing more than an omelette and a slice of bread."*

omertà (ōmer<u>tah</u>) ITALIAN [dialect variant of *umiltà* humility] *noun* the code of silence observed by members of the mafia and other similar criminal organizations.

om mani padme hum (ōm mănee pădmay <u>hoom</u>) SANSKRIT [oh goddess Manipadma] *interjection* mantra intoned by Tibetan Buddhists as a prayer or aid during meditation.

omnia ad Majorem Dei Gloriam (omneeă ad mīyorăm dayee <u>glo</u>reeăm) LATIN [all to the greater glory of God] *noun phrase* everything to the greater glory of God (the motto of the order of St. Francis). ~*abbreviated forms* **O.A.M.D.G., O.M.D.G.**

omnia vincit amor *See* AMOR VINCIT OMNIA.

omnibus (<u>om</u>nibăs) LATIN [for all, dative plural of *omnis* all] *noun* a book or television or radio program in which several stories or episodes are brought together: *"Some new stories will appear in an omnibus of the great man's writings to be published next month."* ~*adjective* of or relating to a publication or program containing several items.

on dit (on(g) <u>dee</u>), **on-dit** FRENCH [one says, it is said] *noun phrase* (*plural* **on dits**) a piece of gossip, a rumor.

onomatopoeia (onămătă<u>pee</u>ă) GREEK [from *onomatopoiia* making of a word] *noun* the formation of a word through imitation of the sound associated with the subject in question. The sound of the word suggests its meaning: *"The words 'buzz,' 'hiss,' and 'cuckoo' are examples of onomatopoeia."*

onus (<u>ō</u>năs) LATIN [burden, load] *noun* (*plural* **onuses,** <u>ō</u>năsiz) a burden, duty, obligation, or blame; the burden of proof: *"Now that the allegations have been made public, the onus is on the government to prove it acted correctly."*

op. *See* OPERA; OPUS.

op. cit. *See* OPERE CITATO.

opera (<u>op</u>ără) ITALIAN [work] *noun* a form of musical drama consisting of recitatives, arias, and choruses with full orchestral accompaniment, or an example of this; may also refer to a theater or other organization presenting such performances: *"For many people, a night at the opera is an experience only to be enjoyed if someone else is paying."* ~abbreviated form **op.**

opéra bouffe (opără <u>boof</u>) FRENCH [from Italian *opera buffa* comic opera] *noun phrase* a genre of satirical comic opera.

opera buffa (opără <u>boo</u>fã) ITALIAN [comic opera] *noun phrase* a genre of farcical comic opera of a type popular in Italy in the 18th century.

opéra comique (opără ko<u>meek</u>) FRENCH [comic opera] *noun phrase* a form of opera in which musical passages are interspersed with spoken dialogue.

opera seria (opără <u>ser</u>eeă) ITALIAN [serious opera] *noun phrase* (*plural* **operas seria** or **operie serie**) a form of opera dealing with heroic or mythological characters or incidents.

opere citato (opăray si<u>tah</u>tō) LATIN [in the work cited] *adverb phrase* (in bibliographical references) in the work previously cited. ~*abbreviated form* **op. cit.**

operetta (opă<u>ret</u>ă) ITALIAN [diminutive of *opera* work] *noun* a genre of romantic comic opera; a short light opera: *"The two men each wrote several operettas with other partners before starting on their celebrated collaboration."*

opprobrium (op<u>rō</u>breeăm) LATIN [disgrace, infamy, from *opprobare* to reproach] *noun* (*plural* **opprobriums** or **opprobria**) contempt, distaste, reproach, or something giving rise to disgrace or shame: *"Bartle spoke these last words in a rasping tone of reproach, and looked at Vixen, who poked down her head and turned up her eyes towards him with a keen sense of opprobrium. . ."* (George Eliot, *Adam Bede,* 1859).

optimum (<u>op</u>tămăm) LATIN [best] *adjective* greatest, best, most favorable: *"Everything has been carefully planned to ensure the optimum chance of the safe return of the shuttle to earth."* ~*noun* the greatest amount or degree possible.

opus (<u>ō</u>păs) LATIN [work, deed] *noun* (*plural* **opuses,** <u>ō</u>păsiz, or **opera,** opără) an artistic work (especially in reference to a musical composition): *"No one expected the composer's next opus to take the form of a comic opera."* ~*abbreviated forms* **op., Op.**

opus Dei (ōpăs <u>day</u>ee) LATIN [work of God] *noun phrase* God's work (usually referring specifically to the obligation of the human race to pay worship to God); also the name of a Roman Catholic organization founded in Spain in 1928.

orangery (<u>or</u>ănjree, <u>or</u>injree), **orangerie** FRENCH [from *oranger* orange tree] *noun* a greenhouse, conservatory, or other structure suitable for the cultivation of orange trees: *". . .the servant . . . led him by way of the orangery to my uncle's private apartments"* (Joseph Conrad, *Some Reminiscences*).

oratorio (orătoreeō) ITALIAN [after the Oratory of St. Philip Neri in Rome, from Latin *oratorium* oratory] *noun* a variety of musical composition featuring full choir and orchestra, usually based on a religious or biblical story and staged without costumers or scenery: *"The choir performs an oratorio in the local church at Christmas every year."*

ordre du jour (ordră doo zhoor) FRENCH [order of the day] *noun phrase* an agenda for a meeting or day's proceedings.

oregano (ărĕgănō, orăgahnō) SPANISH [wild marjoram] *noun* a perennial mint (*Origanum vulgare*) used as seasoning or in the form of an aromatic oil; can also refer to plants of the genera *Lippia* and *Coleus*.

origami (orăgahmee) JAPANESE [paper folding, from *ori* fold and *kami* paper] *noun* the Japanese art of folding paper into the shape of birds or animals: *"The art of origami is taught to children throughout Japan starting at primary school age."*

osso bucco (osō bookō) ITALIAN [pierced bone] *noun phrase* (in Italian cuisine) a dish comprising a shin of veal with marrowbone cooked in wine.

o.s.p. *See* OBIIT SINE PROLE.

ostinato (ostănahtō) ITALIAN [obstinate, from Latin *obstinatus*] *noun* (*plural* **ostinatos** or **ostinati**, ostănahtee) (in music) a melodic passage that is repeated throughout a musical composition. ~*adjective* repeated over and over again, recurring.

Ostpolitik (ostpolitik) GERMAN [east policy] *noun* politics dealing with the countries of eastern Europe, formerly under Soviet domination.

o tempora! o mores! (ō tempără ō morayz) LATIN [o the times! o the manners!, quoting the *Catilinam* of Cicero (106–43 B.C.)] *interjection* oh what times! what manners! (usually lamenting the standards of the contemporary world).

ottava (otahvă) ITALIAN [octave] *adverb* (in music) an octave higher or lower than written. ~*adjective* (in music) an octave higher or lower than written.

ottava rima (otahvă reemă) ITALIAN [octave rhyme] *noun phrase* (*plural* **ottava rimas,** otahvă reemăz) (in heroic poetry) a stanza of eight-, 10-, or 11-syllable lines in which the first six lines rhyme alternately and the last two form a rhyming couplet: *"Wherefore, as a memorial of them, I bought there several Legends of Female Saints and Martyrs, and of other Ladies quite the reverse, and held up as warnings; all of which are* *written in ottava rima, and sold for three halfpence apiece"* (Thomas Carlyle, *Life of John Sterling,* 1851).

ottocento (otōchentō) ITALIAN [eight hundred] *noun* the 19th century in Italy, with particular reference to Italian culture of that period.

ottoman (otămăn) FRENCH [probably from Italian *ottomano,* itself after Osman, I founder of the Ottoman Empire] *noun* an upholstered seat, couch, or sofa, usually lacking a back; may also refer to an upholstered footstool or to a variety of corded silk or rayon fabric: *"Take the armchair, Miss Cuthbert. Anne, you sit here on the ottoman and don't wiggle"* (Lucy Maud Montgomery, *Anne of Green Gables,* 1908).

oubliette (oobleeet) FRENCH [from *oublier* to forget] *noun* a small dungeon with a trapdoor opening, in which prisoners may be confined and forgotten: *"The royal prisoner was threatened with incarceration in the castle oubliette if he refused to sign the charter."*

outrance (ootrahns) FRENCH [excess, from *outrer* to pass beyond] *noun* the last extremity, the utmost: *"The battle will be a l'outrance, sith the said offence was of a deadly sort, admitting of no composition"* (Mark Twain, *A Connecticut Yankee in King Arthur's Court,* 1889).

outré (ootray) FRENCH [exaggerated, past participle of *outrer* to carry to excess] *adjective* bizarre, unconventional, eccentric: *"The more outré and grotesque an incident is the more carefully it deserves to be examined, and the very point which appears to complicate a case is, when duly considered and scientifically handled, the one which is most likely to elucidate it"* (Arthur Conan Doyle, *The Hound of the Baskervilles,* 1902).

ouzo (oozō) GREEK *noun* an aniseed-flavored Greek liqueur.

ovum (ōvăm) LATIN [egg] *noun* (*plural* **ova,** ōvă) the female reproductive egg, cell, or gamete.

oxymoron (okseemorăn) GREEK [neuter of *oxymoros* pointedly foolish] *noun* (*plural* **oxymorons** or **oxymora,** okseemoră) a saying, expression, or word in which apparently contradictory elements or ideas are combined: *"The phrase 'a loving enemy' was just one of several oxymorons that peppered his speech."*

oyez (ōyes, ōyez, oiyay, ōyay), **oyes** FRENCH [hear ye, imperative plural of *oïr,* from Latin *audire* to hear] *interjection* hear this! (as uttered by town criers, court officers, etc.).

oy vay (oi vay) YIDDISH *interjection* ejaculation expressing surprise, despair, or delight.

p. *See* PIANO.

p.a. *See* PAR AVION; PER ANNUM.

P.A. *See* PAR AVION.

pace (pay̱see, paẖchay, paẖkay) LATIN [with peace, ablative of *pax* peace] *preposition* with all due respect to, with due deference to.

pacha *See* PASHA.

pachuco (pǎcho̱oko̱) SPANISH [flashily dressed] *noun* a Mexican American youth with a taste for fashionable clothing (usually referring to members of Mexican American gangs); can also refer to the slang argot used by such gangs.

pachyderm (pa̱kiderm) GREEK [*pachydermos* thick-skinned] *noun* an elephant, rhinoceros, hippopotamus, pig, or other example of thick-skinned nonruminant hoofed mammals.

pacifico (pǎsi̱fiko̱) SPANISH [peaceful] *noun* a person of peaceful character or intentions, a pacifist: *"Journalists*

detected a waning in the influence of the pacificos in the senate."*

paddy (pa̱dee) MALAY [from padi] *noun* rice, or a piece of wetland in which rice is grown.

padre (paẖdray, paẖdree) SPANISH/ ITALIAN/PORTUGUESE [from Latin *pater* father] *noun* a priest; often referring to a chaplain in the armed forces: *"The padre was summoned to give the dying man the last rites."*

padrone (pǎdro̱nee) ITALIAN [protector, owner, from Latin *patronus* patron] *noun* (*plural* **padrones,** pǎdro̱neez, or **padroni,** pǎdro̱nee) a master, boss, employer, or patron; may also refer to an Italian hotel proprietor or innkeeper: *"But this: that I, a confidential man and a Corsican, should have to ask your pardon for bringing on board your vessel, of which I was Padrone, a Cervoni, who has betrayed you—a traitor!—that is too much"* (Joseph Conrad, *The Mirror of the Sea,* 1906).

paean (pee̱ăn) GREEK [hymn of thanksgiving addressed to Apollo, from

Paian, the Greek name for Apollo] *noun* a tribute or expression of praise, triumph, or thanksgiving: *"This quickly took us out of range of Red-Eye, and the last we saw of him was far out on a point of land, where he was jumping up and down and chanting a paean of victory"* (Jack London, *Before Adam*, 1906).

paedophilia *See* PEDOPHILIA.

paella (pay<u>e</u>lă, payay(l)ă) SPANISH [pot, pan, ultimately from Latin *patella* small pan] *noun* (in Spanish cuisine) a dish of rice, meat, seafood, and vegetables flavored with saffron.

pagoda (pă<u>gō</u>dă) PORTUGUESE [temple, probably ultimately from Persian *butkada* idol temple] *noun* a Buddhist or Hindu temple or sacred building, usually taking the form of a tower with several stories and upcurving roofs; can also refer to any other tower of a similar design.

pajamas (pă<u>jah</u>măz, pa<u>ja</u>măz), **pyjamas** HINDI [from Persian *pa* leg and *jama* garments] *plural noun* a two-piece garment designed to be worn in bed; may also refer to a similar lightweight garment worn as casual wear. ~*abbreviated form* **p.j.'s.**

paladin (pă<u>lă</u>din) FRENCH [from Italian *paladino* courtier, from Latin *palatinus* officer of the palace] *noun* a heroic champion or knight errant: *"Stories are still told of the great deeds performed by the paladins of Charlemagne's court."*

palais de danse (palay dă <u>dons</u>) FRENCH [palace] *noun phrase* dance palace, public ballroom. ~*abbreviated form* **palais.**

palazzo (pă<u>lats</u>ō) ITALIAN [from Latin *palatium* palace] *noun* (*plural* **palazzos** or **palazzi,** pă<u>lats</u>ee) a palace, mansion, or other large house in Italy, or in the Italian style: *"But, without this occupation, the life of Vronsky and of Anna, who wondered at his loss of interest in it, struck them as intolerably tedious in an Italian town; the palazzo suddenly seemed so obtrusively old and dirty. . ."* (Leo Tolstoy, *Anna Karenina*, 1874–76).

palette (pă<u>lă</u>t) FRENCH [diminutive of *pale* spade] *noun* a wooden or plastic tray on which artists mix paints; and, by extension, any range of colors, elements, or effects: *"As a film director he had learned to master the use of a wide-ranging palette of emotional effects."*

palisade (pă<u>lă</u>sayd) FRENCH [from *palissade,* from Latin *palus* stake] *noun* a pointed stake or row of pointed stakes used as a defensive barrier: *"The river slid along noiselessly as a shade, the swelling reeds and sedge forming a flexible palisade upon its moist brink"* (Thomas Hardy, *Far From the Madding Crowd*, 1874).

palladium (pă<u>lay</u>deeăm) GREEK [*palladion* statue of Pallas Athena] *noun* (*plural* **palladiums** or **palladia,** pă<u>lay</u>deeă) a statue of Pallas Athena that was venerated in classical times as the guardian of Troy; since applied to anything considered a safeguard or protection.

palomino (palămeenō) SPANISH [from Latin *palumbinus* like a dove] *noun* a horse with a tan-colored coat and white mane and tail, or a light tan color.

pampas (pampăs) SPANISH [from Quecha *pampa* plain] *plural noun* a grassy plain, a prairie (usually referring specifically to the extensive grasslands of South America): *"There are few cowboys working in the traditional way on the pampas of South America today."* May also refer to a yellow-green color.

panacea (panăseeă) GREEK [*panakeia* cure-all, from *panakes* all-healing] *noun* a remedy for all ills, a universal remedy, a cure-all: *"Her faith in her solution as a panacea for the world's ills was touching but shortlived."*

panache (pănash) FRENCH [from Italian *pennachio* plume, tuft, ultimately from Latin *pinnaculum* small wing] *noun* a small tuft of feathers on a hat or helmet and, by extension, flamboyance, style, verve, or confidence: *"They made their entrance with a certain panache, swords jangling and capes flapping in the breeze."*

panatela (panătelă), **panatella, panetela** SPANISH [a long thin biscuit, ultimately from Latin *panis* bread] *noun* a long, slender variety of cigar.

pancetta (panchetă) ITALIAN [diminutive of *pancia* belly, paunch] *noun* (in Italian cuisine) a variety of unsmoked bacon.

pandemic (pandemik) GREEK [*pandemos* of all the people] *noun* a widespread outbreak, as of disease or panic: *"Fears were raised that the cases already reported would inevitably multiply and develop into a pandemic."* ~*adjective* widespread, worldwide, universal.

pandemonium (pandămōneeăm) GREEK [evil spirit] *noun* hell, the infernal regions; may also refer more generally to any state of uproar, disorder, or tumult.

pandit *See* PUNDIT.

Pandora's box (pandorăz boks) GREEK [after the legendary box of Pandora from which were released all the evils of the world] *noun phrase* a source of unforeseen troubles: *"She little realized what a Pandora's box she had opened when she brought up the subject of his first wife."*

panegyric (panăjīrik) GREEK [*paneyrikos* of or for a festival assembly] *noun* a eulogy, a hymn of praise: *"Such men . . . who take all their kindness as a matter of course, and not as a subject for panegyric"* (George Eliot, *Adam Bede,* 1859).

panem et circeneses (panăm et serkenzeez, panăm et kerkenzayz) LATIN [bread and circuses] *noun phrase* bread and circuses, symbolizing food and entertainment (the provision of which has cynically been thought to be sufficient to keep the common populace under control since classical times).

panetela   *See* PANATELA.

panic (<u>pa</u>nik) GREEK [from *panique,* itself from Greek *panikos* of Pan] *noun* a state of frenzy, uncontrollable fear, or terrified confusion (originally ascribed in classical times to the influence of the god Pan). ~*verb* to throw into such a state of frenzy, fear, or confusion.

panorama (pană<u>ra</u>mă, pană<u>rah</u>mă) GREEK [from *pan* all and *horama* sight] *noun* a wide-ranging, comprehensive, or all-round view, a cyclorama; may also refer to a continually changing scene: *"The vantage point offered a stunning panorama, with an unbroken view to the horizon in all directions."*

pantheon (<u>pan</u>theeăn) GREEK [after the Pantheon temple in Rome, from the Greek *pantheion* temple of all gods, from *pan* and *theos* god] *noun* a temple dedicated to all the gods or otherwise honoring the dead; may also refer to the most celebrated persons connected with a particular profession, art, trade, or sport: *"His name joins that of other greats in the pantheon of baseball."*

panzer (<u>pan</u>zăr, <u>pant</u>săr) GERMAN [tank, armor, coat of mail, from Old French *panche* belly] *noun* a tank (usually referring to the tanks of the German army in World War II): *"The German panzers rolled across the border at dawn and met little resistance."* ~*adjective* of or relating to a panzer tank or panzer tank force.

papabile (papa<u>bee</u>lee, papa<u>bi</u>li) ITALIAN [likely to be pope] *adjective* of or relating to someone who is considered a likely candidate for pope. ~*noun* (*plural* **papabili,** papa<u>bee</u>lee) a likely candidate for pope.

paparazzo (papă<u>rat</u>sō) ITALIAN [after a fictional photographer called Paparazzo in the film *La Dolce Vita* (1960) by Federico Fellini (1920–93)] *noun* (*plural* **paparazzi,** papă<u>rat</u>see) an independent or freelance press photographer who specializes in photographing the rich and famous, regardless of their consent: *"The princess was hounded by paparazzi all her life."*

papier-mâché (payper mă<u>shay</u>, papyay ma<u>shay</u>) FRENCH [chewed paper] *noun* a mixture of pulped paper and glue or flour used as a modeling material. ~*adjective* of or relating to such material; can also refer more generally to anything artificial, fake, or unreal.

papillote (papee<u>yōt</u>, papee<u>lōt</u>) FRENCH [from *papillon* butterfly] *noun* a greased paper wrapper in which meat or other food is cooked: *"The fish was cooked en papillote."* ~*adjective* of or relating to such a wrapper.

papoose (pa<u>poos</u>) NARRAGANSETT [from *papoòs*] *noun*   a young child or baby (originally one of Native American parentage).

paprika (pă<u>pree</u>kă) HUNGARIAN [from Serbo-Croat *papar* ground pepper] *noun*   a condiment made from the ground dried pods of cultivated sweet peppers. ~*adjective* of or relating to a dish flavored with paprika.

papyrus (pă<u>pī</u>răs) GREEK [*papuros* paper reed] *noun* (*plural* **papyruses** or **papyri**, pă<u>pī</u>ree)   a variety of sedge (*Cyperus papyrus*) grown in the Nile Valley and, by extension, a form of paper made from such grasses or anything written on scrolls made of this material. ~*adjective* of or relating to such grasses or paper made from them: *"Instead of speech with a Pythia or a Sibyl, they will sell you a plain papyrus leaf, hardly dry from the stalk, and bid you dip it in the water of a certain fountain, when it will show you a verse in which you may hear of your future"* (Lew Wallace, *Ben Hur*, 1880).

par (pahr) LATIN [one that is equal, a match] *noun*   equality, a common level, an average norm, or an accepted standard (specifically a golf term, and used more generally by extension): *"His game was below par last season."*

par.   *See* PARENTHESIS.

paralysis (pă<u>ra</u>lăsis) GREEK [wrong loosening, from *paralyeing* to loosen, to disable] *noun* (*plural* **paralyses**, pă<u>ra</u>lăseez)   a loss of the ability to feel or move; by extension, any powerlessness or inability or failure to act.

paranoia (pară<u>noi</u>ă) GREEK [madness, derangement, from *paranous* demented] *noun*   a mental disorder characterized by delusions of grandeur or of persecution or involving obsessive distrust of others.

paraphernalia (parăfă<u>nay</u>lyă) GREEK [*parapherna* bride's property beside the dowry] *plural noun*   an individual's personal belongings or, more generally, any miscellaneous collection of accessories, effects, equipment, or furnishings: *"The lorry was loaded with all the paraphernalia necessary for an Arctic expedition."*

parasol (<u>par</u>ăsol) FRENCH [from Italian *parasole,* from *parare* to shield and *sole* sun] *noun*   a light, portable sunshade resembling an umbrella: *"Each of the ladies carried a parasol to shield their delicate skin from the blazing sun."*

paratha (pă<u>rah</u>tă) HINDI *noun* (in Indian cuisine)   a flat cake of unleavened bread.

par avion (pahr <u>a</u>veeăn) FRENCH [by airplane] *adverb phrase*   by air (relating to letters and other items to be sent by airmail). ~*abbreviated from* **P.A., p.a.**

par éminence (pahr emă<u>nons</u>) FRENCH [by eminence] *adverb phrase*   preeminently.

parenthesis (pă<u>ren</u>thăsis) GREEK [act of inserting, from *parentithenai* to insert] *noun* (*plural* **parentheses,** pă<u>ren</u>thăseez) a digression or explanatory word or phrase inserted into a text to provide additional information: *"'Not much, I fear,' returned my mother. 'Not so much as I could wish. But Mr. Copperfield was teaching me —' ('Much he knew about it himself!') said Miss Betsey in a parenthesis"* (Charles Dickens, *David Copperfield,* 1849–50). ~*abbreviated form* **par.**

par excellence (pahr eksă<u>lons</u>) FRENCH [by excellence] *adjective phrase* the best of its kind, preeminent: *"He is a great guy, and a raconteur par excellence."* ~*adverb pharase* particularly, above all others.

par exemple (pahr e<u>gsom</u>pă̆l) FRENCH [for example] *adverb phrase* for example, for instance. ~*abbreviated form* **p.e., p. ex.**

parfait (pahr<u>fay</u>) FRENCH [perfect] *noun* a frozen flavored custard made with whipped cream and syrup, or a dessert comprising layers of ice cream, fruit, syrup, and whipped cream and usually served in a tall glass.

pariah (pă<u>rī</u>ă) TAMIL [from *paraiyan* hereditary drummer] *noun* a member of a low caste in India; by extension, any social outcast: *"After the scandal he became a pariah, barred from all the houses in fashionable Boston."*

pari passu (paree <u>pa</u>soo, <u>pa</u>ree pasoo) LATIN [with equal step] *adverb phrase* at an equal rate of progress, equally, on an equal footing, side by side, without bias: *"The proceeds of the deal will be distributed pari passu between the relatives."*

parka (<u>pah</u>kă) ALEUT [skin jacket, from northern Russian dialect] *noun* a hooded weatherproof jacket (as originally worn by Eskimos).

parole (pă<u>rōl</u>) FRENCH [word, promise, ultimately from Latin *parabola* speech, parable] *noun* the release of a convicted prisoner on condition of good behavior: *"When he had communicated this bright idea, which had its origin in the perusal by the village cronies of a newspaper, containing, among other matters, an account of how some officer pending the sentence of some court-martial had been enlarged on parole, Mr. Willet drew back from his guest's ear..."* (Charles Dickens, *Barnaby Rudge,* 1841). Can also refer to a password or watchword known only to sentries or guards. ~*verb* to release a prisoner on parole.

parquet (<u>pahr</u>kay, pahr<u>kay</u>) FRENCH [small enclosure, from *parc* park] *noun* a type of flooring consisting of inlaid wood blocks; can also refer to the ground floor in a theater or to the area immediately in front of the stage. ~*verb* to lay a floor of wooden blocks.

parterre (pahr<u>tair</u>) FRENCH [from *par terre* on the ground] *noun* a formal ornamental garden or a level area on which a house of village is built; can also refer to the ground floor of a theater: *"The charms of a parterre are daily be-rhymed in verse, and vaunted in prose, but the beauties of a vegetable garden seldom meet with the admiration they might claim"* (Susan Fenimore Cooper, *Elinor Wyllys*, 1846).

parthenogenesis (pahrthănōjenăsis) GREEK [*parthenos* virgin and Latin *genesis genesis*] *noun* reproduction in which the egg develops without being fertilized (common among certain classes of plants and invertebrates).

partim (pahrtim) LATIN [in part] *adverb* in part.

parti pris (pahrtee pree) FRENCH [side taken] *noun phrase (plural* **partis pris**) prejudice, bias, partiality, a preconceived opinion. ~*adjective phrase* prejudiced, biased, partial.

partita (pahrteetă) ITALIAN [divided into parts, from *partire* to divide] *noun (plural* **partitas** or **partite**, pahrteetay) (in music) an instrumental suite comprising variations written for a solo player or chamber ensemble.

parvenu (pahrvănoo, pahrvănyoo) FRENCH [one who has arrived, past participle of *parvenir* to arrive] *noun* a person who has only recently acquired wealth, status, or power; an upstart, one of the nouveaux riches. ~*noun, feminine* **parvenue** a female

parvenu. ~*adjective* of or relating to such an upstart: *"Only old Catherine Mingott, with her absence of moral prejudices and almost parvenu indifference to the subtler distinctions, might have bridged the abyss. . ."* (Edith Wharton, *The Age of Innocence*, 1920).

pas (pa) FRENCH [pace, step, from Latin *passus* step] *noun* right of precedence, the right to go first; can also refer to a step in classical dance.

pas de chat (pa dă sha) FRENCH [step of cat] *noun phrase* a catlike forward-springing leap in classical ballet: *"The dancer executed a perfect pas de chat and struck a pose of cheerful defiance at the front of the stage."*

pas de deux (pa dă dă, pa dă doo) FRENCH [step of two] *noun phrase* a duet for two dancers; may also refer to a relationship or activity in which two people or things participate: *"The lovers were engaged in a kind of pas de deux, oblivious of everyone around them."*

pas devant (pa dăvon(g)) FRENCH [not in front of] *adverb phrase* not in front of the children (or others present), not appropriate in present company.

pasha (pahshă, pashă, păshah), **pacha** TURKISH [from *pasa,* ultimately from Persian *padshah* king, lord] *noun* a person of consequence or high office in northern Africa or Turkey: *"And Lansing and Strefford were left to watch the departure of the happy Pasha ensconced* *between attentive beauties"* (Edith Wharton, *Glimpses of the Moon*, 1922).

paso doble (pasō dōblay) SPANISH [double step] *noun phrase* (*plural* **paso dobles**) a brisk ballroom dance based on Latin American rhythms, or the music accompanying this.

pasquinade (paskwănayd) FRENCH [from Italian *pasquinato,* after Pasquino, the name of a statue in Rome where lampoons were posted] *noun* a satire or lampoon, usually anonymous.

pass. *See* PASSIM.

passé (pasay) FRENCH [past, past participle of *passer* to pass] *adjective* outmoded, outdated, behind the times, antiquated, past one's prime: *"The philosophy of the interwar generation was dismissed as passé by the enfants terribles that emerged after the liberation."*

passe-partout (paspertoo, paspahrtoo), **passepartout** FRENCH [pass everywhere] *noun* a master key or pass that allows the holder to cross borders at will; can also refer to a frame or border in which a picture may be displayed.

pas seul (pa se(r)l, pa săl) FRENCH [solo step] *noun phrase* (*plural* **pas seuls**) a dance or sequence of steps for a solo performer.

passim (pasim, pasăm) LATIN [scattered, from *passus,* past participle of *pandere* to spread] *adverb* mentioned here and there, mentioned in various places (in bibliographical notes). ~*abbreviated form* **pass.**

pasta (pahstă) ITALIAN [ultimately from Greek *paste*] *noun* (in Italian cuisine) a form of processed wheat flour and egg dough made in a range of shapes and used in a wide variety of dishes; may also refer to any dish in which pasta is a main ingredient: *"Pasta figures prominently among the favorite dishes of today's children."*

pastiche (pasteesh) FRENCH [from Italian *pasticcio* pasty] *noun* a composite work of art incorporating selections from other works, or a work of art created in imitation of the style of another artist, author, or composer.

pastille (pastăl, pastil) FRENCH [from Latin *pastillus* small loaf] *noun* a flavored or medicated lozenge or candy: *". . .its rooms and passages steamed with hospital smells, the drug and the pastille striving vainly to overcome the effluvia of mortality"* (Charlotte Brontë, *Jane Eyre,* 1847).

pastis (pastees) FRENCH [jumble] *noun* a French liqueur flavored with aniseed.

pastorale (pastărahl, pastăral) ITALIAN [shepherdlike, from *pastore* shepherd] *noun* (*plural* **pastorales** or **pastorali,** pastărahlee) an opera or other instrumental or vocal composition on a rural theme.

pastrami (păstrahmee) YIDDISH [from Romanian *pastrama* pressed and cured meat, possibly of Turkish origin] *noun* a highly seasoned shoulder cut of smoked beef.

pâté (patay), **pate** FRENCH [paste] *noun* a rich spread made with chopped or seasoned meat, liver, or fish.

pâté de foie gras (patay dă fwah gra) FRENCH [pâté of fat liver] *noun phrase* (*plural* **pâtés de foie gras**) a rich pâté made with fatted goose liver.

patella (pătelă) LATIN [diminutive of *patina* shallow dish] *noun* (*plural* **patellas** or **patellae**, pătelee, pătelī) a kneecap; can also refer in botany, zoology, etc. to any panlike or cuplike shape: *"The x-ray clearly showed a fracture of the patella."*

pater (patăr) LATIN [father] *noun* father; may also be used as an abbreviated form of paternoster.

paterfamilias (patărfămileeăs, pahtărfămileeăs, paytărfămileeăs) LATIN [from *pater* father and *familias* household] *noun* (*plural* **patresfamilias,** patreezfămileeăs, pahtreezfămileeăs, paytreezfămileeăs) the father of a family, the head of a household.

paternoster (pahtărnostăr, patărnostăr) LATIN [from *pater noster* our father, from the opening words of the Lord's Prayer] *noun* the Lord's Prayer, or music written to accompany it; can

also refer to any form of words recited as a prayer or charm.

pathétique (patheteek) FRENCH [moving] *adjective* (in music) moving, with feeling.

pathos (paythos, paythōs, pathōs) GREEK [feeling, emotion, suffering, from *pathein* to experience, to suffer] *noun* a feeling or expression of sympathy or pity, or something that evokes pity, compassion, or tenderness: *"The pathos of the plight of the refugees was inescapable and overwhelming."*

patina (păteenă, pătănă) ITALIAN [shallow dish] *noun* a green film that appears naturally on copper or bronze with time through oxidation and hence any surface shine or gloss that an object acquires with age or exposure to acids: *"He glanced once at his favorite tree, elm twigs against the gold patina of sky, and fumbled for sleep as for a drug"* (Sinclair Lewis, *Babbitt*, 1922).

patio (pateeō) SPANISH [outdoor space] *noun* a courtyard, terrace, or other area adjoining a house that is suitable for various outdoor activities, such as eating meals or relaxing in the sun: *"She was waiting for her husband on the patio, a cocktail in each hand."*

patisserie (pătisăree) FRENCH [from *pâtisserie* pastry, bakery, from *pasticier* to make pastry, ultimately from Latin *pasta* paste] *noun* a pastry or a bakery where French pastries are made or sold: *"A good patisserie is an essential feature of the typical French townscape."*

patois (<u>pat</u>wah) FRENCH [rough speech, possibly from Old French *patoier* to handle roughly] *noun* (*plural* **patois,** <u>pat</u>wahz) a nonstandard dialect, the language of a particular social group or trade, jargon.

patron (<u>pay</u>trăn) FRENCH [from Latin *patronus* defender] *noun* a person who acts as guardian, supporter, or protector of a cause, artist, social event, or institution; can also refer to a customer or client of a particular establishment or institution or to the proprietor of a restaurant or inn: *"The theater has many wealthy and influential patrons and can rely upon their support if the show is slow to take off."*

pavane (pă<u>van</u>), **pavan** FRENCH [from Italian dialect *panano* of Padua] *noun* a formal, stately court dance of the 16th century, or music written to accompany this.

pax (paks, pahks) LATIN [peace, harmony] *noun* peace, especially peace in international relations; may also refer to the kiss of peace during the Mass.

pax Romana (paks rō<u>mah</u>nă, pahks rō<u>mah</u>nă) LATIN [Roman peace] *noun phrase* the period of peace and prosperity that existed under the rule of ancient Rome; may also refer generally to ancient Roman culture and civilization.

pax vobiscum (paks vō<u>bis</u>kăm, pahks vō<u>bis</u>kăm) LATIN [peace with you] *interjection* peace be with you: *"As he opened the door, the Milesian features of Father McShane presented themselves, and from their center proceeded the clerical benediction in Irish-sounding Latin, Pax vobiscum!"* (Oliver Wendell Holmes, *Elsie Venner,* 1859–60).

paysan (pay<u>zan</u>) FRENCH [country] *noun* a peasant or a person from the country (usually in a French-speaking country). ~*adjective* peasant style: *"This paysan style of cookery has become very popular among chefs in recent years."*

p.c. *See* PERCENT.

p.d. *See* PER DIEM.

p.e. *See* PAR EXEMPLE.

peccadillo (pekă<u>dil</u>ō) SPANISH [little sin, diminutive of *pecado* sin] *noun* (*plural* **peccadillos** or **peccadilloes**) a minor vice, a trifling offense or petty fault: *"The papers are always full of revelations about the peccadillos of public figures."*

peccavi (pe<u>kah</u>vee) LATIN [I have sinned] *interjection* an acknowledgment of sin or error: *"'O, I say, Maggie,' said Tom at last, lifting up the stand, 'we must keep quiet here, you know. If we break anything, Mrs. Stelling'll make us cry peccavi'"* (George Eliot, *The Mill on the Floss,* 1860). ~*noun* an admission or confession of sin or error.

pedophilia (peedăfileeă) GREEK [*pai* child and *philia* loving] *noun* perverse sexual desire for children: *"The old man disappeared from the area after he was accused of pedophilia."*

peignoir (paynwahr, penwahr) FRENCH [garment worn while combing the hair, from *peigner* to comb] *noun* a woman's loose dressing gown, bathrobe, or negligee.

peloton (pelăton) FRENCH [from Latin *pila* ball] *noun* the main pack or field of riders in a bicycle race.

penchant (penchănt) FRENCH [present participle of *pencher* to incline, ultimately from Latin *pendere* to weigh] *noun* a strong inclination or taste, a liking or leaning for something: *"They were going from end to end of the country in all manner of useful missionary capacities; their penchant for wandering, and their experience in it, made them altogether the most effective spreaders of civilization we had"* (Mark Twain, *A Connecticut Yankee in King Arthur's Court*, 1889).

pendulum (pendyoolăm, penjoolăm) LATIN [hanging thing, from *pendulus* hanging, swinging] *noun* (*plural* **pendulums** or **pendula**, pendyoolă, penjoolă) a weight suspended in such a way that it can swing freely from side to side under the force of gravity (as employed in clocks); can also refer more generally to anything that oscillates between opposites: *"Public opinion is the pendulum by which political success is measured in a modern democracy."*

penetralia (penătrayleeă) LATIN [innermost things, neuter plural of *penetralis* inner] *noun* the innermost or most private, hidden parts or recesses of someone or something: *"'Yea,' was the concise reply of the Cameronian leader, in a voice which seemed to issue from the very penetralia of his person"* (Walter Scott, *Waverley*, 1814).

penne (penay) ITALIAN [plural of *penna* pen, quill] *noun* a variety of pasta shaped into diagonally cut cylinders, or a dish incorporating such pasta.

pensée (ponsay) FRENCH [thought] *noun* a thought, idea.

pension (penshăn) FRENCH [ultimately from Latin *pendere* to pay] *noun* a boardinghouse or small hotel offering accommodation at a fixed rate (in France or various other European countries): *"She sought seclusion from the public gaze in a shabby pension in unfashionable central France."*

pentathlon (pentathlăn, pentathlahn) GREEK [five contests, from *penta* five and *athlon* contest] *noun* an athletic event in which contests compete in five different disciplines (cross-country, running, fencing, shooting, horseback riding, and swimming).

per (per) LATIN [through, by] *preposition* through, by means of, for each, during, according to, as instructed: *"Please carry out the tasks per the directions on the sheet provided."*

per annum (per anăm) LATIN [through the year] *adverb phrase* annually, yearly, every year, for each year, by the year: *"The enterprise brings in over two million dollars per annum."* *~abbreviated forms* **p.a., per an.**

per ardua ad astra (per ahrdyooă ad astră) LATIN [through difficulties to the stars] *noun phrase* through difficulties to the stars (the motto of Britain's Royal Air Force). See also AD ASTRA PER ARDUA.

per capita (per kapită) LATIN [by heads] *adverb phrase* for each person, by each person, equally among individuals. *~adjective phrase* for each person, by each person: *"The jury is considering paying a per capita sum to all those who are represented in the lawsuit."*

percent (persent), **per cent** LATIN [from *per centum* by hundred] *adjective phrase* in the hundred, for or in every hundred. *~abbreviated form* **p.c.**

per contra (per kontră) LATIN [by the opposite side (of the ledger)] *adverb phrase* on the contrary, by way of contrast, on the other hand. *~abbreviated form* **per con.**

per diem (per deeăm, per dīăm) LATIN [by the day] *adverb phrase* daily, each day, by the day, day by day: *"And having*

finished burnishing his arms, he sate down patiently to compute how much half a dollar per diem would amount to at the end of a six months' campaign. . ." (Walter Scott, *A Legend of Montrose,* 1819). *~noun phrase* (*plural* **per diems**) a daily payment, fee, or allowance. *~abbreviated form* **p.d.**

perdu (perdoo, perdyoo), **perdue** FRENCH [lost, past participle of *perdre* to lose] *noun* out of sight, concealed, hidden, undiscovered, unnoticed, secluded.

père (pair) FRENCH [father] *adjective* father, senior, older.

perestroika (perăstroikă) RUSSIAN [restructuring, reconstruction] *noun* the economic and bureaucratic reform program that was introduced in the Soviet Union in the 1980s; may also refer to any economic or political reorganization: *"A policy of cultural perestroika is needed to revitalize the arts in modern eastern Europe."*

pergola (pergălă) ITALIAN [from Latin *pergula* projecting roof, from *pergere* to come forward] *noun* a trellis, arbor, or other similar structure: *"They found the old man sitting in a rocking chair in the pergola, a gun resting on his lap."*

peripeteia (perăpăteeă, perăpătīă), **peripetia** GREEK [falling around, from *peripiptein* to fall around, to change suddenly] *noun* an abrupt reversal of circumstances or change of fortune.

periphrasis (părifrăsăs) GREEK [*periphrazein* to declare] *noun* (*plural* **periphrases,** părifrăseez) circumlocution, a roundabout means of expression.

per mensem (per mensăm) LATIN [by the month] *adverb phrase* monthly, each month, by the month, every month.

perpetuum mobile (perpetyooăm mōbili, perpetyooăm mōbilay) LATIN [perpetually moving thing] *noun phrase* perpetual motion or a machine that runs by perpetual motion.

per pro *See* PER PROCURATIONEM.

per procurationem (per prokyoorateeōnăm) LATIN [by agency] *adverb phrase* by proxy, on the authority of a deputy or agent. ~*abbreviated forms* **per pro, p.p.** Strictly speaking when used in a letter the abbreviation *p.p.* should precede the name of the person signing the letter. "In modern usage the abbreviation is frequently interpreted as 'for and on behalf of' and placed before the name of the person on whose behalf the letter is signed. This 'incorrect' sequence is so well-established that the correct usage could lead to misunderstanding" (*Bloomsbury GoodWord Guide,* edited by Martin H. Manser).

per se (per say, per see) LATIN [by itself] *adverb phrase* in or by itself or themselves, intrinsically, as such:

"*Should computer hacking per se be outlawed as a crime?*"

persiflage (persiflahzh) FRENCH [from *persifler* to banter, from *per* through and *siffler* to whistle] *noun* lighthearted, frivolous conversation; banter, teasing.

persona (persōnă) LATIN [actor's mask, character in a play] *noun* (*plural* **personas** or **personae,** persōnee, persōnī) an individual's character or personality; a public or private guise or role: "*The great actor's last appearance was in the persona of a mouse in an eminently forgettable Broadway comedy.*"

persona grata (persōnă grahtă, persōnă grată) LATIN [an acceptable person] *noun phrase* (*plural* **persona grata** or **personae gratae,** persōnee grahtee) an individual who is considered personally acceptable or admissible (usually relating to the status of individuals in diplomatic relations).

persona non grata (persōnă non grahtă, persōnă non grată) LATIN [an unacceptable person] *noun phrase* (*plural* **persona non grata** or **personae non gratae,** persōnee non grahtee) an individual who is considered personally unacceptable or inadmissible (often relating to the status of individuals in diplomatic relations): "*The authorities decreed that the journalist was now persona non grata, and he made preparations to leave the country.*"

personnel (persănel) FRENCH [staff, from Latin *personalis* personal] *plural noun* the employees or staff of an organization or company: *"The personnel of the organization will have to be reduced by half if these financial targets are to be met."*

per stirpes (per sterpeez) LATIN [by descendants, from *per* through and *stirps* family, descendants] *adverb phrase* by stocks or branches (legal term referring to the assignment of equal shares among the inheritors of an estate).

pesto (pestō) ITALIAN [pounded, from *pestare* to pound] *noun* (in Italian cuisine) a sauce made with fresh crushed basil, garlic, pine nuts, grated cheese, and olive oil.

pétillant (petiyon(g)) FRENCH [sparkling, lively] *adjective* slightly sparkling (of wine).

petit bourgeois (pătee borzhwah) FRENCH [little citizen] *noun phrase* (*plural* **petits bourgeois**) a member of the petite bourgeoisie (the lower middle class). ~*noun phrase, feminine* **petite bourgeoise** (păteet borzhwahz) a female member of the petite bourgeoisie. ~*adjective phrase* of or relating to the petite bourgeoisie, conventional.

petite (păteet) FRENCH [little, feminine of *petit*] *adjective* trim, slight, small (usually referring to a woman's figure): *"She was an attractive girl with blonde hair and a petite figure."*

petite bourgeoisie (păteet borzhwahzee) FRENCH [little bourgeoisie] *noun phrase* the lower middle class, characterized by limited, conventional opinions and attitudes: *"The country's leaders were terrified of offending the petite bourgeoisie, and decided not to act."*

petit four (petee for, pătee for) FRENCH [small oven] *noun phrase* (*plural* **petit fours** or **petits fours**) a small cake or biscuit (often served with coffee at the end of a meal).

petit mal (pătee mal) FRENCH [little sickness] *noun phrase* epilepsy in its milder form: *"The emperor's advisers were worried that one day their leader would display the symptoms of petit mal in public."* See also GRAND MAL.

petit pain (pătee pan(g)) FRENCH [little bread] *noun phrase* (*plural* **petits pains**) a small bread roll.

petit point (pătee pwan(g)) FRENCH [small point] *noun phrase* a tent stitch or a piece of embroidery made with such small stitches.

petits pois (pătee pwah) FRENCH [small peas] *plural noun* small young green peas.

p. ex. *See* PAR EXEMPLE.

phaeton (fayătăn) GREEK [after Phaëthon, the son of the sun god Helios in Greek legend, his name from *phaethon* shining] *noun* a light four-wheeled horse-drawn open carriage; subsequently applied to touring cars: *"Yonder, where that phaeton with the well-clipped pair of grays has stopped—standing at their heads now—is a Yorkshire groom. . ."* (Charles Dickens, *American Notes,* 1842).

phalanx (fāylanks, falanks) GREEK [battle line] *noun* (*plural* **phalanxes** or **phalanges,** faylanjeez, falanjeez) a formation of troops in close array; by extension, any closely massed body of people, animals, or things: *"The protesters were faced with a phalanx of police officers backed by a rank of armored vehicles."*

phallus (falăs) GREEK [*phallos* penis, symbol of the penis] *noun* (*plural* **phalluses** or **phalli,** falī, falee) the penis, or a representation or symbol of the penis.

pharmacopoeia (farmăkăpeeă), **pharmacopeia** GREEK [*pharmakopoiia* preparation of drugs] *noun* a book describing drugs and their preparation, or a stock of such drugs.

phenomenon (fănomănăn) GREEK [*phainesthai* to appear] *noun* (*plural* **phenomenons** or **phenomena,** fănomănă) an observable happening, event, or fact, especially one that is considered out of the ordinary: *"The new book gives fresh scientific explanations of natural phenomena."* Can also refer to individuals who have distinguished themselves through their talent or intelligence.

phobia (fōbeeă) GREEK [*phobos* fear] *noun* an exaggerated or irrational fear or dislike of someone or something: *"Her anxiety about calories amounts almost to a phobia toward food of all kinds."*

phoenix (feeniks) GREEK [from *phoinix*] *noun* (*plural* **phoenixes**) in classical mythology, a bird that every 500 years burns itself to ashes in a fire in order to rise reborn from the flames; can refer more generally to anyone or anything that rises anew after some setback or disaster: *"The city has risen like a phoenix from the ashes of the old town."*

phylum (fīlăm) GREEK [*phylon* tribe, race] *noun* (*plural* **phylums** or **phyla,** fīlă) a primary division of the animal or plant kingdoms; also applicable in classifying languages: *"Prof. Huxley . . . says that he considers the phylum or lines of descent of the Vertebrata to be admirably discussed by Haeckel, although he differs on some points"* (Charles Darwin, *The Descent of Man,* 1871).

physique (făzeek) FRENCH [physical, bodily, ultimately from Latin *physicus* of nature] *noun* the physical structure and characteristics of an individual: *"The ladies present admired the strongman's magnificent physique."*

pi (pī) GREEK [from *pei,* an abbreviation of *periphereia* periphery] *noun* the 16th letter of the Greek alphabet; also the name for the mathematical number expressing the ratio of the circumference of a circle to its diameter and of a symbol representing this.

pianissimo (peeănisămō) ITALIAN [very softly] *adverb* (in music)   to be played or sung very softly. *~adjective* (in music) very soft. *~noun* (*plural* **pianissimos** or **pianissimi**, peeănisămee) (in music) a very soft passage. *~abbreviated form* **pp**.

piano (peeanō, peeahnō) ITALIAN [soft, ultimately from Latin *planus* smooth] *adverb* (in music)   to be played or sung softly. *~adjective* (in music) soft *~abbreviated form* **p**. *~noun* a keyboard instrument (a pianoforte) capable of being played either softly or loudly, the metal strings within the body being sounded by hammers operated when the keys are depressed and the volume being controlled by the pressure on the keys and through the use of foot pedals.

piazza (peeatză) ITALIAN [broad street] *noun* (*plural* **piazzas** or **piazze**, peeatzee)   a large open square in the middle of a town or city (usually referring to Italian towns); may also refer more widely to any roofed gallery or arcade: *"The piazza was suddenly full of dancing, singing people."*

picaresque (pikăresk, peekăresk) FRENCH [from Spanish *picaresco*] *adjective*   of or relating to a rogue or rascal; may also refer to a type of novel written in a wandering, illogical style:

"His square face was confident, his foxy mustache was picaresque" (Sinclair Lewis, *Main Street,* 1920).

picnic (piknik) FRENCH [from *pique-nique,* of unknown origin] *noun*   an excursion during the course of which those present eat a meal they have brought with them in the open air. *~verb* to take part in such an open-air meal.

picot (peekō) FRENCH [small point, from *piquer* to prick] *noun*   a small loop of ribbon or lace forming part of an ornamental edging to a fabric.

pièce de résistance (pies dă rezistons, pies dă rayzistons) FRENCH [piece of resistance] *noun phrase* (*plural* **pièces de résistance**)   the chief attraction, the main event or most important item (often referring to the principal dish of a meal): *"The dessert turned out to be the chef's pièce de résistance."*

pièce d'occasion (pies dokayzhăn) FRENCH [a piece of occasion] *noun phrase* (*plural* **pièces d'occasion**)   a literary or musical work created for a particular occasion.

pièce noire (pies nwahr) FRENCH [black piece] *noun phrase* (*plural* **pièces noires**)   a play or film with a gloomy, pessimistic, or tragic tone.

pièce rose (pies rōz) FRENCH [rosy piece] *noun phrase* (*plural* **pièces roses**) a play, film, or other artistic work with an entertaining, optimistic tone.

pied-à-terre (peeayd ă <u>tair</u>) FRENCH [foot to ground] *noun phrase* (*plural* **pieds-à-terre**) a temporary lodging or occasional residence; a home base: "*They live in the countryside but have a pied-à-terre in London.*"

pierrot (pee<u>ă</u>rō), **Pierrot** FRENCH [diminutive of *Pierre* Peter] *noun* a white-faced clown of traditional French pantomime, typically dressed in a loose-fitting all-white costume: "*She decided to buy a small pierrot doll to take home as a souvenir.*"

pietà (peeay<u>tah</u>), **Pietà** ITALIAN [pity, from Latin *pietas* piety] *noun* an artistic representation of the Virgin Mary grieving over the crucified Christ.

pilaf (pi<u>laf</u>, <u>pee</u>laf), **pilaff, pilau** (pi<u>low</u>, <u>pee</u>low), **pilaw** (pilaw, <u>pee</u>law) TURKISH [from Persian *pilav* boiled rice and meat] *noun* (in Middle Eastern and Indian cuisine) a dish of seasoned rice and meat, fish, and vegetables.

piña colada (peenyă kă<u>lah</u>dă), **pina colada** (peenă kă<u>lah</u>dă) SPANISH [strained pineapple] *noun phrase* an alcoholic drink made with rum, pineapple juice, and cream of coconut.

pince-nez (pans <u>nay</u>) FRENCH [from *pincer* to pinch and *nez* nose] *noun* spectacles that are clipped to the nose by a spring: "*His aunt, as aunts are all too apt to do, stared at him witheringly over her pince-nez.*"

pinetum (pī<u>nee</u>tăm) LATIN [pine grove, from *pinus* pine] *noun* (*plural* **pineta,** pī<u>nee</u>tă) a plantation of pine trees or other coniferous trees: "*The pinetum includes many rare species.*"

pinto (pintō) SPANISH [spotted, painted] *noun* (*plural* **pintos** or **pintoes**) a horse or pony having a coat with white patches. ~*adjective* pied, mottled, skewbald.

pinxit (pink̲sit) LATIN [he/she painted] *noun* he/she painted it (referring to the artist of a painting). ~*abbreviated form* **pinx., pnxt.**

pipette (pi<u>pet</u>), **pipet** FRENCH [diminutive of *pipe* pipe, cask] *noun* a tube into which a small quantity of liquid or gas can be withdrawn and retained for measuring, as widely used in scientific laboratories: "*The professor drew some of the liquid up into a pipette and scrutinized the contents quizzically.*"

piquant (<u>pee</u>kon(g)) FRENCH [stinging, stimulating, present participle of *piquer* to prick, to sting] *adjective* spicy, tasty, appetizing, tart, bitter, pungent; may also refer to a character who is deemed witty or provocative: "*The meat was served in a wonderful piquant sauce.*"

pique (peek) FRENCH [from *piquer* to prick] *noun* resentment, wounded vanity, annoyance: *"She flounced out of the room in a fit of pique."* ~*verb* to irritate, provoke, offend, annoy, vex.

pirouette (pirooet) FRENCH [whirl, possibly from *pivot* pivot and *girouette* weathervane] *noun* a rapid full turn of the body (as in ballet). ~*verb* to spin the body in such a manner: *"And gayest of all was Mrs. Darling, who would pirouette so wildly that all you could see of her was the kiss, and then if you had dashed at her you might have got it"* (J. M. Barrie, *Peter Pan,* 1904).

pis aller (peez alay), **pis-aller** FRENCH [to go worst] *noun phrase* (*plural* **pis allers,** peez alay, peez alayz) an expedient, a last resort.

pissoir (piswahr) FRENCH [from *pisser* to urinate] *noun* a public urinal (especially one in a French-speaking country).

piste (peest) FRENCH [track, from *pistare* to trample down, to pound] *noun* a downhill ski run: *"The avalanche threatened to engulf several skiers on the piste."*

pita (peetă), **pitta** GREEK [bread, cake] *noun* (in Mediterranean and Arab cuisine) a flat oval-shaped unleavened bread often eaten stuffed with meat or vegetables.

piton (peeton(g)) FRENCH [eye-bolt] *noun* a metal spike or peg used in mountaineering to secure ropes to a rock or ice surface.

più (pyoo, peeoo) ITALIAN [plus] *adverb* (in music) more.

pizza (peetză) ITALIAN [possibly from Old High German *bizan* to bite] *noun* (in Italian cuisine) a flat dough base topped with cheese, tomato, meat, vegetables, or other ingredients and baked.

pizzeria (peetsăreeă) ITALIAN [from *pizza*] *noun* a restaurant or other establishment where pizzas are made or served: *"The pizzeria has become a popular meeting place for students."*

pizzicato (pitsikahtō) ITALIAN [plucking, past participle of *pizzicare* to pluck] *noun* (*plural* **pizzicatos** or **pizzicati,** pitsikahtee) a piece of music plucked rather than played with a bow. ~*adverb* (in music) plucked. ~*adjective* (in music) plucked.

p.j.'s *See* PAJAMAS.

placebo (plăseebō) LATIN [I shall please] *noun* (*plural* **placebos** or **placeboes**) a medication or other treatment that soothes a patient psychologically without having any real effect on any actual physical complaint; can also refer more generally to anything that soothes or placates: *"This announcement by the president is nothing more than a placebo designed to calm worried supporters."*

placet (pla̱yset, pla̱ket) LATIN [it pleases] *noun* an expression or vote of approval or assent.

plaque (plak) FRENCH [metal sheet, from *plaquier* to plate, from Middle Dutch *placke* piece] *noun* a flat plate or tablet of metal, porcelain, wood, or other material: *"The president unveiled a plaque in memory of the soldiers who died in the war."* Can also refer to an ornamental brooch, ornament, or badge.

plat du jour (pla dă zhoor) FRENCH [plate of the day] *noun phrase* (*plural* **plats du jour**) a dish that is identified as the dish of the day in a restaurant.

plateau (pla̱tō, pla̱tō) FRENCH [platter, from *plat* flat, ultimately from Greek *platus* broad, flat] *noun* (*plural* **plateaus** or **plateaux**, pla̱tōz, pla̱tōz) a level area of elevated tableland; can also refer to any period, condition, or level of stability: *"She felt she had reached a plateau in her life and could not see any way forward."*

platonic (plă̱tonik, playto̱nik) GREEK [from *platonikos*, after the Greek philosopher Plato (c. 427–c. 347 B.C.)] *adjective* of or relating to the philosophy of Plato; more generally, of or relating to love that is free from physical desire: *"The evidence suggests that their relationship remained purely platonic."*

platoon (plă̱toon) FRENCH [from *peloton* little ball] *noun* a military unit comprising two or more squads; can also refer more generally to any group of people working or acting together: *"A platoon of soldiers was sent into the wood to flush out any remaining survivors."*

plaudit (plo̱dit) LATIN [from *plaudere* to applaud] *noun* a round of applause or expression of approval: *"The cast graciously acknowledged the plaudits of the spectators before leaving the stage."*

plaza (pla̱ză, plahză) SPANISH [from Latin *platea* broad street] *noun* a public square or other open area in a town or city; can also refer to a shopping center.

plebs (plebs) LATIN [common people] *plural noun* the common people, the populace, the ordinary citizens. ~*adjective* **plebeian** of or relating to the common people.

plectrum (plektrăm) GREEK [*plektron*, from *plessein* to strike] *noun* (*plural* **plectrums** or **plectra**, plektră) a pick used for playing a guitar or other string instrument.

pleno jure (pleenō jooăree) LATIN [with full right] *adverb phrase* with complete authority.

plenum (plenăm, pleenăm) LATIN [neuter of *plenus* full] *noun* (*plural* **plenums** or **plena**, plenă, pleenă) a full meeting of a legislative body or other association or group; can also refer to the full membership of an organization: *"The matter will be discussed at the next full plenum of the executive committee."*

plethora (pl̲ethără) GREEK [*plethore* fullness, from *plethein* to be full] *noun* a state of superfluity, overabundance, profusion, glut, or excess.

plié (pleea̲y) FRENCH [past participle of *plier* to bend] *noun* a ballet pose in which the dancer adopts a stance with knees bent, back straight, and feet out-turned.

plus (plus) LATIN [more] *preposition* with the addition of: *"That is the basic figure, so plus taxes the total comes to $10,000."* ~*adjective* of a quantity more than zero. ~*noun* something additional.

plus ça change (ploo sa sh̲anzh) FRENCH [abbreviation of *plus ça change, plus c'est la même chose* the more things change the more they are the same thing, originally coined by the French journalist Alphonse Karr (1808–90)] *noun phrase* the more things change, the more they remain the same.

p.m. *See* POST MERIDIEM; POST-MORTEM.

pnxt. *See* PINXIT.

poco (p̄ōkō, pokō) ITALIAN [little, from Latin *paucus* few] *adverb* (in music) somewhat, to a slight degree.

poco a poco (p̄ōkō a p̲ōkō, pokō a pokō) ITALIAN [little by little] *adverb phrase* (in music) gradually, little by little.

podium (p̄ōdeeăm) LATIN [balcony, height] *noun* (*plural* **podiums** or **podia,** p̄ōdeeă) a dais, lectern, or raised platform for the use of a public speaker or orchestra conductor (originally a raised area in amphitheaters of the classical world): *"Several shots were fired at the podium before the security men managed to disarm the intruder."*

pogrom (p̄ōgrăm, p̄ōgra̲hm) RUSSIAN [devastation] *noun* a systematic massacre or program of persecution directed against a civilian population (usually referring to massacres of Jewish people): *"Millions died in the pogroms organized by Stalin's underlings."*

point d'appui (pwan(g) dap̲wee) FRENCH [point of support] *noun phrase* (*plural* **points d'appui**) base, foundation, prop; may also refer to a fulcrum or strategic point.

pointe (pwan(g)t) FRENCH [from *pointe du pied* tiptoe] *noun* (in ballet) a pose in which the dancer balances on tiptoe (*on* or *en pointe*).

pointillism (pwa̲nteelisăm, poi̲n-tălisăm), **pointillisme** FRENCH [from *pointiller* to stipple] *noun* an impressionistic artistic technique in which color is applied in small strokes or dots.

polder (po̲ldăr) DUTCH [from Middle Dutch *polre*] *noun*   an area of low-lying land that has been reclaimed from the sea, a lake, or other body of water (usually applying to certain areas of the Netherlands): *"Changes in the climate threaten to return the polders of the Low Countries to the sea."*

polenta (pōle̲ntă, păle̲ntă) ITALIAN [pearl barley] *noun*   (in Italian cuisine) a paste, dough, or porridge made from cornmeal (originally pearl barley or barley meal).

politburo (po̲litbyoorō), **politbureau** RUSSIAN [from *polibyuro,* from *politicheskoe byuro* political bureau] *noun*   the executive committee of a Communist party; by extension, any group in control of an organization or state.

politesse (polite̲s) FRENCH [cleanness, ultimately from Italian *pulire* to polish, to clean] *noun*   formal politeness, decorousness, good manners.

politico (păli̲tikō) ITALIAN/SPANISH [from Latin *politicus* political] *noun* (*plural* **politicos** or **politicoes**)   a politician or political activist: *"The union has been infiltrated by politicos belonging to extremist parties of the left."*

polka (po̲lkă) CZECH [either from *Polka* Polish woman, feminine of *Polak* Pole, or from *pulka* half-step] *noun*   a lively ballroom dance ultimately of Bohemian origin, or music written to accompany this: *"She would have been more so if she had*

seen her reprehensible brother-in-law dancing a triumphal polka down the hall with Rose in honor of having silenced the enemy's battery for once" (Louisa May Alcott, *Eight Cousins,* 1875).

polonaise (polăna̲yz) FRENCH [feminine of *polonais* Polish] *noun*   a formal processional dance of Polish origin, or music written to accompany this.

poltergeist (po̲ltărgīst) GERMAN [noisy ghost, from *poltern* to knock, to disturb, and *geist* spirit] *noun*   a variety of ghost that communicates its presence through rappings and the moving of furniture and other objects rather than through actual manifestation: *"The family complained that the poltergeist was keeping them awake at night, and they insisted on being moved to a new house."*

pompon (po̲mpon) FRENCH [from *pompe* tuft of ribbons] *noun*   an ornamental ball of wool, ribbons, or silk worn as a decoration for clothing or hats.

poncho (po̲nchō) SPANISH [from Araucanian *pontho*] *noun*   a blanket-like or waterproof cloak with a hole that can be slipped over the head: *"When the sky clouded over, the hiker was glad he had packed his poncho."*

pons asinorum (ponz asino̲răm) LATIN [bridge of asses, referring to a geometry proposition put forward by the Greek mathematician Euclid (fl. 300

307

B.C.)] *noun phrase* a stumbling block or a test of ability of understanding.

poodle (<u>poo</u>dăl) GERMAN [from *Pudel,* abbreviation of *Pudelhund,* from *pudeln* to splash and *hund* dog] *noun* one of a breed of dogs with characteristically thick curly coats, sometimes elaborately trimmed.

poppadam (<u>pop</u>ădăm), **popadam, poppadam, poppadum** TAMIL [from *pappatam,* possibly from *paruppa atam* lentil cake] *noun* a circular wafer of crispy spiced dough eaten with curry or other Indian food.

poppycock (<u>pop</u>eekok) DUTCH [from dialect *pappekak* soft dung] *noun* nonsense, rubbish: *"The major insisted that he had never heard such poppycock in all his life."*

por favor (por fa<u>vor</u>) SPANISH [for a favor] *adverb phrase* please, if you please.

port de bras (por dă <u>bra</u>) FRENCH [carriage of the arm] *noun phrase (plural* **ports de bras)** technique relating to movement of the arms in ballet.

portfolio (port<u>fo</u>leeō) ITALIAN [from *portafoglio,* from *portare* to carry and *foglio* sheet, leaf] *noun* a set of documents, drawings, or photographs, or a case in which these are carried: *"The art student carried his work home from school in a portfolio under his arm."* Can also apply to the collective responsibilities of functions of a government official or other figure of authority or to the various securities held by an investor in the stock market.

portico (<u>por</u>tikō) ITALIAN [from Latin *porticus* porch, from *porta* gate] *noun (plural* **porticos** or **porticoes)** a colonnade, covered walkway, or a covered entrance to a building: *"It stood at one end of the main street, its classic portico and small-paned windows looking down a flagged path between Norway spruces to the slim white steeple of the Congregational church"* (Edith Wharton, *Ethan Frome,* 1911).

portiere (port<u>yer</u>, <u>por</u>teeă) FRENCH [from *portière]* *noun* a curtain hanging across a doorway as a screen or to keep out drafts.

portmanteau (port<u>man</u>tō) FRENCH [from *portemanteau,* from *porter* to carry and *manteau* mantle, cloak] *noun (plural* **portmanteaus** or **port-manteaux,** port<u>man</u>tō, port<u>man</u>tōz) a large suitcase or bag: *"As he reached the foot of the slope, an elderly horseman, with his portmanteau strapped behind him, stopped his horse when Adam had passed him, and turned round to have another long look at the stalwart workman in paper cap, leather breeches, and dark-blue worsted stockings"* (George Eliot, *Adam Bede,* 1859). ~*adjective* of or relating to a term created by combining two other words: *"'Smog' is a portmanteau word, formed from 'smoke' and 'fog.'"*

posada (păsahdă SPANISH [from *posar* to lodge] *noun* an inn or hotel in a Spanish-speaking country.

poseur (pōzer) FRENCH [poser, from *poser* to pose] *noun* a person who makes out to be something other than he or she really is; an affected person, a fraud, a snob, a show-off: *"Even his best friends admit that he has always been a bit of a poseur."* ~*noun, feminine* **poseuse** (pōzerz) a female poseur.

posse (posee) LATIN [to have power, from *posse comitatus* power of the country] *noun* a group of people recruited to assist a sheriff in times of emergency, usually to pursue criminals; may refer more generally to any band of people working together in pursuit of a common interest: *"There was no shortage of volunteers to join the posse to hunt down the infamous gunfighter."*

post bellum (pōst belăm), **postbellum** LATIN [after the war] *adjective phrase* of or relating to the period immediately following a war.

post coitum (pōst koităm, pōst kōităm) LATIN [after intercourse] *adjective phrase* following sexual intercourse. ~*adverb phrase* following sexual intercourse.

post factum (pōst faktăm) LATIN [after the fact] *adverb phrase* retrospective, after the event.

post hoc (pōst hok) LATIN [after this] *adverb phrase* henceforth, after this.

~*adjective phrase* consequent, after the fact.

posthumous (poschămăs, postyămăs, postyoomăs), **posthumus** LATIN [from *postumus* late-born, last] *adjective* after the death of the person concerned: *"Both officers received posthumous medals for their courage in rescuing wounded men under fire."*

post meridiem (pōst mărideeăm) LATIN [after noon] *adjective phrase* after the hour of noon, in the afternoon or evening, between midday and midnight. ~*abbreviated form* **p.m., P.M.**

postmortem (pōst mortăm) LATIN [after death] *noun* an autopsy; may also refer more generally to any analysis of an event after it has ended: *"An official postmortem failed to reveal the cause of the accident."* ~*adjective phrase* after the death of the person concerned, after the event. ~*adverb phrase* **post mortem** after death. ~*abbreviated form* **p.m.**

post partum (pōst pahrtăm), **postpartum**, **postpartum** LATIN [after birth] *adjective phrase* following childbirth, relating to the period after birth.

postscriptum (pōstskriptăm) LATIN [written after, from *postscribere* to write after] *noun* (*plural* **postscripta**, pōstskriptă) a postscript, a note added at the end of a letter, article, or other work: *"I offered him the report on the 'Suppression of Savage Customs,' with* the postscriptum torn off." (Joseph Conrad, *Heart of Darkness*, 1902). ~*abbreviated form* **PS.**

potage (po<u>tahzh</u>) FRENCH [what is put in a pot, from *pot* pot] *noun* a thick soup: "'*Will you take some potage, Miss ah—Miss Blunt?' said Mr. Crawley. 'Capital Scotch broth, my dear,' said Sir Pitt, 'though they call it by a French name'*" (William Makepeace Thackeray, *Vanity Fair*, 1847–48).

pot-au-feu (pot ō <u>fă</u>) FRENCH [pot on the fire] *noun (plural* **pot-au-feux**) (in French cuisine) a dish of boiled meat and vegetables.

pot pourri (pō pă<u>ree</u>, pō pă<u>ree</u>), **pot-pourri** FRENCH [rotten pot] *noun* a mixture of dried flower heads and petals, herbs, and spices that are placed in a room in order to fill it with scent; can also refer more generally to any medley or miscellaneous collection: "*The book is a pot pourri of recollections and memories of a bygone age.*"

pouf (poof), **pouffe** FRENCH [from *pouf* something inflated] *noun* an ottoman, a footstool, a large firm cushion.

poulet (poo<u>lay</u>) FRENCH [chicken] *noun* a chicken (especially in reference to a chicken-based dish).

pour encourager les autres (por onkoorahzhay layz <u>o</u>tră) FRENCH [to encourage the others, quoting the French writer Voltaire (1694–1778)] *adverb phrase* as an example to others (usually referring to the punishment or humiliation of an individual as a lesson to others to do better): "*The general feeling was that the captain had been sacrificed pour encourager les autres.*"

pourparler (porpahr<u>lay</u>) FRENCH [to discuss] *noun* a preliminary discussion (especially with regard to international diplomacy).

pousse-café (poos ka<u>fay</u>) FRENCH [push coffee, coffee chaser] *noun* an after-dinner drink in which several differently colored liqueurs are poured into a glass so as to form separate layers.

powwow (<u>pow</u>wow) NARRAGANSETT [from *powwaw* shaman] *noun* a Native American medicine man or shaman; can also refer to a traditional Native American ceremony or social gathering and, by extension, to any social get-together or discussion meeting. ~*verb* to hold a social gathering or discuss something: "*Tom Sawyer called the hogs 'ingots,' and he called the turnips and stuff 'julery,' and we would go to the cave and powwow over what we had done, and how many people we had killed and marked*" (Mark Twain, *The Adventures of Huckleberry Finn*, 1884).

pp. *See* PIANISSIMO.

p.p. *See* PER PROCURATIONEM.

praecognitum (preekog<u>nee</u>tăm) LATIN [something learned beforehand, from *praecognoscere* to know beforehand] *noun* (*plural* **praecognita,** preeko<u>gnee</u>tă) something that must be known before something else can be understood.

praenomen (pree<u>nō</u>măn) LATIN [pre-name] *noun* (*plural* **praenomens** or **praenomina,** pree<u>nom</u>ănă) a first name, a forename, a personal name (originally the first of the three names borne by males in ancient Rome).

praesidium   *See* PRESIDIUM.

praetorium (pree<u>tor</u>eeăm) LATIN [from *praetorius* belonging to a praetor] *noun* (*plural* **praetoria,** pree<u>tor</u>eeă) the quarters of the praetorian guard in Rome; by extension, the court or palace of any ruler in classical times or the tent of a Roman general in a military camp.

praline (<u>prah</u>leen, <u>pray</u>leen) FRENCH [after the French soldier Marshal de Plessis-Praslin (1598–1675), whose cook created the first praline mixtures] *noun* a confection made from chopped nuts and caramelized sugar, or a chocolate filled with such a mixture.

praxis (<u>prak</u>săs) GREEK [action, doing, from *prassein* to do, to practice] *noun* (*plural* **praxes,** <u>prak</u>seez) action, practice, customary way of doing things; may also refer to the exercise of a particular art, science, or skill.

précis (pray<u>see</u>, <u>pray</u>see) FRENCH [pre-cise] *noun* (*plural* **précis,** <u>pray</u>seez) a concise summary of the main points of an argument or theory: *"Students were asked to prepare a précis of the inaugural speech."* ~*verb* to summarize something.

premier (pră<u>meer</u>, pră<u>mee</u>ăr, pree<u>mee</u>ăr, <u>pre</u>meeăr) FRENCH [first, chief, leading] *adjective* the first in importance, rank, or quality; the earliest. ~*noun* a prime minister, a chief minister, head of state: *"Plans are being made for a summit conference between the president and the premiers of several European countries."*

premier cru (pră<u>mee</u>ă <u>kroo</u>, prămyă <u>kroo</u>) FRENCH [first growth] *noun phrase* (*plural* **premiers crus**) a top-quality wine.

premier danseur (pră<u>mee</u>ă don<u>ser</u>, prămyă don<u>ser</u>) FRENCH [first dancer] *noun phrase* (*plural* **premiers danseurs**) the principal male dancer in a ballet company. ~*noun phrase, feminine* **première danseuse** (pră<u>mee</u>ă don<u>serz</u>, prămyă don<u>serz</u>) the principal ballerina in a ballet company.

premiere (<u>prem</u>eeair), **première** FRENCH [feminine of *premier* first] *noun* a first performance or exhibition of something: *"Many of Hollywood's finest turned out for the premiere of the film."* ~*adjective* principal, first, chief, leading. ~*verb* to present a first performance or exhibition of something.

presidium (pre<u>sid</u>eeăm, pre<u>zid</u>eeăm), **praesidium** RUSSIAN [from *prezidium,* ultimately from Latin *praesidium* garrison] *noun* (*plural* **presidiums** or **presidia,** pre*si*deeă, pre*zi*deeă) the executive committee of an organization or state (especially, formerly, a communist state): *"The matter will be brought before the presidium next week."*

prestissimo (pre*tis*ămō) ITALIAN [from *presto* quick] *adverb* (in music) faster than presto. ~*adjective* very fast.

presto (*pres*tō) ITALIAN [fast, soon, ultimately from Latin *praesto* at hand] *interjection* there! voila! see!: *"There was not one thing to remind us that we were in Russia. We walked for some little distance, reveling in this home vision, and then we came upon a church and a hackdriver, and presto! the illusion vanished!"* (Mark Twain, *Innocents Abroad,* 1869). ~*adverb* (in music) quickly, fast; immediately, suddenly. ~*adjective* (in music) fast, rapid; immediate, sudden. ~*noun* a piece of music written to be played at a rapid pace.

prêt-à-porter (pret a por*tay*) FRENCH [ready to wear] *noun* ready-to-wear clothing, off-the-rack clothes, ready-made. ~*adjective* of or relating to ready-to-wear clothing.

pretzel (*pret*ză l) GERMAN [from *Brezel,* ultimately from Latin *bracellus* bracelet] *noun* a German variety of hard, glazed, salted bread traditionally baked in loose knots and other shapes.

preux chevalier (pră shă*vale*eă) FRENCH [valiant knight] *noun phrase* a chivalrous knight, a gallant knight.

prie-dieu (pree-*dyă*) FRENCH [pray God] *noun* (*plural* **prie-dieux**) a prayer stool with a raised shelf at which the faithful kneel to pray in church; can also refer to a type of low armless upholstered chair with a low seat and a high straight back.

prima ballerina (preemă bală*reen*ă) ITALIAN [leading ballerina] *noun phrase* the principal ballerina in a ballet company; a ballerina of the first rank: *"As a girl she had dreamed of the moment when she would advance into the spotlight in the pink tutu of a prima ballerina."*

prima donna (preemă *don*ă) ITALIAN [first lady] *noun phrase* a principal female singer in an opera company or concert group; can also refer to any person who is known for being self-important, vain, over-sensitive, petulant, or temperamental: *"Because of the financial pressures, few directors have much patience with prima donnas in the modren theater."*

prima facie (prīmă *fay*shee, preemă *fay*shă, prīmă *fay*see, preemă *fay*seeă) LATIN [at first sight] *adverb phrase* at first view, on the face of it, on the surface. ~*adjective phrase* valid, true, self-evident, apparent, legally satisfactory: *"To many people, the suspect's attempts to flee the scene were prima facie evidence of his guilt."*

primogenitor (prīmōjĕnătă) LATIN [from *primus* first and *genitor* begetter] *noun* ancestor, forefather.

primum mobile (prīmăm mōbălee, preemăm mōbălee) LATIN [first moving thing] *noun phrase* (*plural* **primum mobiles**) a prime mover, a main fount of activity, energy, or motion.

primus inter pares (prīmăs intă pahreez, preemăs intă pahreez) LATIN [first among equals] *noun phrase* first among equals.

prix fixe (pree feeks, pree fiks) FRENCH [fixed price] *noun phrase* an entire meal that is charged at a fixed price, a fixed-price menu: "*The restaurant has two menus, one à la carte and the other operating on a prix fixe basis.*"

pro (prō) LATIN [for, in favor of] *noun* an argument or evidence in favor of a proposition or theory: "*We could spend all evening debating the pros and cons of the situation.*" ~*preposition* for, in support of, in favor of. ~*adjective* supporting, favoring. ~*adverb* in favor, favoring, in affirmation.

pro bono publico (prō bōnō publikō) LATIN [for the public good] *adjective phrase* for the good of society, in the interests of everyone (often referring to legal work done for no fee). ~*abbreviated form* **pro bono.**

procès-verbal (prōsay verbahl) FRENCH [proceedings, verbal trial] *noun* (*plural*

procès-verbaux, prōsay verbō) an official written record of legal or other proceedings.

proconsul (prōkonsăl) LATIN [from *pro consule* for the consul] *noun* a governor or military commander of a province of ancient Rome; may also refer to an administrator of a colony, dependency, or occupied territory: "*Do you know, I always, from the very beginning, regretted that it wasn't your sister's fate to be born in the second or third century A.D., as the daughter of a reigning prince or some governor or proconsul in Asia Minor*" (Fyodor Dostoyevsky, *Crime and Punishment,* 1866).

profiterole (prăfitărōl) FRENCH [diminutive of *profit* profit] *noun* a small puff pastry with a cream or other filling, often covered in chocolate sauce.

pro forma (prō formă) LATIN [for form, in accordance with form] *adjective phrase* for the sake of form, as a matter of form, as a formality ~*noun* an invoice sent in advance of goods supplied: "*Full details of the shipment are given on a pro forma sent separately by post.*"

progenitor (prōjenătăr, prăjenătăr) LATIN [from *progignere* to beget] *noun* a direct ancestor or forefather; may refer more generally to any originator, predecessor, or precursor: "*This other-self of mine is an ancestor, a progen-*

itor of my progenitors in the early line of my race, himself the progeny of a line that long before his time developed fingers and toes and climbed up into the trees" (Jack London, *Before Adam,* 1906). ~*noun, feminine* **progenitrix** (prōjĕnătriks, prăjĕnătriks) a female ancestor or forebear.

prognosis (prognōsis) GREEK [foreknowledge, from *progignoskein* to know before] *noun (plural* **prognoses,** prognōseez) a forecast, prediction, or prognostication (often referring to the predicted course of a disease): *"The doctor was kind, but his prognosis was not good."*

proletariat (prōlătaireeat) FRENCH [from *prolétariat,* ultimately from Latin *proles* progeny] *noun* the laboring class or, more generally, the lower social classes in society: *"But as a member of a revolutionary proletariat—which he undoubtedly was—he nourished a rather inimical sentiment against social distinction"* (Joseph Conrad, *The Secret Agent,* 1907).

promenade (promănayd, promănahd) FRENCH [a walk, form *promener* to take for a walk] *noun* a place to walk or ride; may also refer to a formal ball or to a procession of guests at such a ball. ~*verb* to walk about in public, or as if in public view.

pronto (prontō) SPANISH [from Latin *promptus* prompt] *adverb* promptly, immediately, quickly, without delay.

propaganda (propăgandă) ITALIAN [that which must be spread, after the *congregatio de propaganda fide* organization of the Roman Catholic Church, which works to propagate Catholic faith] *noun* information, rumor, ideas, or doctrines that are deliberately promoted in order to further or to undermine a particular cause, person, or organization. Can also refer to the process of spreading such information.

prophylactic (profălaktik) GREEK [from *prophylaktikos,* from *prophylassein* to be on guard] *noun* something that wards off disease or prevents pregnancy (often referring to specifically to a condom). ~*adjective* of or relating to the prevention of disease or pregnancy.

pro rata (prō rahtă) LATIN [according to the rate, from *pro rate parte* in accordance with the calculated part] *adverb phrase* proportionately, in proportion: *"Any profits arising from the investment will be distributed pro rata."* ~*adjective phrase* proportional, shared proportionally. ~*abbreviated form* **p.r.**

proscenium (prăseeneem, prōseeneem) GREEK [*proskenion* in front of the scene] *noun (plural* **prosceniums** or **proscenia,** prăseeneeă, prōseeneeă) the stage in ancient Greek and Roman theaters; in the modern theater it can refer either to the front part of the stage in front of the curtains or, more often, to the arch that frames the stage itself, dividing the playing area from the forestage and the auditorium: *"The role of the conventional proscenium has changed out of all recognition in modern theater, with numerous performances taking place in the round and even in the midst of audiences."*

prosciutto (prōshootō) ITALIAN [from *presciutto* ham, from *prae* pre and *asciutto* dried out] *noun* (*plural* **prosciuttos** or **prosciutti,** prōshootee) a variety of dry-cured spiced Italian ham.

prosit (prōzăt, prōsăt), **prost** (prōst) GERMAN [from Latin *prosit* may it be beneficial] *interjection* good health, cheers (a German drinking toast).

prospectus (prăspektăs, prōspektăs) LATIN [prospect, outlook, from *prospicere* to look forward] *noun* (*plural* **prospectuses,** prăspektăsăz, prōspektăsăz) a brochure, pamphlet, or preliminary document containing a forecast and other details about a future project, enterprise, or literary work or describing a stock offering or a mutual fund: *"The company's prospectus was impressive, but the investors still had their doubts."*

prosthesis (prostheesis, prosthăsăs) GREEK [*prostithenai* to add to] *noun* (*plural* **prostheses,** prostheeseez) an artifical limb or other artificial replacement for a body part.

protean (prōteeăn, prōteeăn) GREEK [after the classical Greek sea god Pro-

teus, who could change his shape at will] *adjective* versatile, variable: *"Donald appeared not to see her at all, and answered her wise little remarkes with curtly indifferent monosyllables, his looks and faculties hanging on the woman who could boast of a more Protean variety in her phase, moods, opinions, and also principles, than could Elizabeth"* (Thomas Hardy, *The Mayor of Casterbridge,* 1886).

protégé (prōtezhay, prōtăzhay) FRENCH [protected person, past participle of *protéger* to protect] *noun* a pupil, an individual who enjoys the protection, patronage, sponsorship, or guidance of another more experienced or influential person: *"He spent years as the CEO's protégé, patiently awaiting the day when he would step into the limelight himself."* ~*noun, feminine* **protégée.**

pro tempore (prō tempăree) LATIN [for a time] *adverb phrase* for the time being. ~*abbreviated form* **pro tem.**

proviso (prăvīzō) LATIN [provided, past participle of *providere* to provide] *noun* (*plural* **provisos** or **provisoes** a clause or article detailing a condition, qualification, stipulation, limitation, or exception in an agreement or legal document: *"To this Lady Tringle added her proviso, that she should have the choice"* (Anthony Trollope, *Ayala's Angel,* 1881).

proximo (proksămō) LATIN [from *proximo mense* in the next month] *adjective* of or relating to the next month. ~*abbreviated form* **prox.**

PS *See* POSTSCRIPTUM.

pseudo (<u>soo</u>dō) GREEK [false] *adjective* false, fake, counterfeit, spurious; can also refer to a person who is affected or pretentious. ~*noun* a person who pretends to be more than he or she is (especially intellectually). Often combined, as a prefix, with other words, e.g., *pseudo intellectual, pseudoscience.*

psyche (<u>sī</u>kee) GREEK [from *psukhe* soul, spirit, ghost, breath] *noun* the mind, the soul, the self, the ego, the personality.

pucka *See* PUKKA.

pudendum (pyoo<u>den</u>dăm) LATIN [from *pudendus* something shameful, gerundive of *pudere* to be ashamed] *noun* (*plural* **pudenda,** pyoo<u>den</u>dă) the external genitalia (usually referring to females).

pueblo (<u>pweb</u>lō, poo<u>eb</u>lō) SPANISH [village, ultimately from Latin *populus* people] *noun* a Native American communal dwelling typical of those found in certain parts of the SW United States; also, a Native American village in the same region.

puisne (<u>pyoo</u>onee) FRENCH [born afterward, younger] *adjective* subordinate, inferior, junior, associate, later.

puissance (<u>pwee</u>sons, <u>pyoo</u>ăsons) FRENCH [power, from *puissant* power-

ful] *noun* power, authority, influence, sway: *"And after these King Arthur for a space / And through the puissance of his Table Round, / Drew all their petty princedoms under him"* (Alfred, Lord Tennyson, *Idylls of the King,* 1859).

pukka (<u>pă</u>kă), **pucka** HINDI [from *pakka* cooked, ripe, mature] *adjective* genuine, authentic, real, reliable, first-class: *"Honest, sir, this is a pukka antique Queen Anne bedstead."*

puma (<u>p(y)oo</u>mă) SPANISH [from Quechua] *noun* a cougar, a mountain lion.

pumpernickel (<u>păm</u>părnikăl) GERMAN [from *pumpern* to break wind and *Nickel* goblin] *noun* a variety of dark, heavy German bread made from wholemeal rye flour.

pundit (<u>păn</u>dit), **pandit** HINDI [from *pandita* learned] *noun* a teacher or learned person; by extension, a critic or other informed observer or expert: *"Political pundits are predicting an overwhelming victory for the president."*

purdah (<u>per</u>dă) URDU [from *parda* screen, veil] *noun* the seclusion of women from the public gaze in orthodox Muslim and Hindu society (in private quarters or with faces hidden by veils in public) and hence any state of seclusion or enforced isolation: *"The released hostages are being kept in purdah until they have been fully debriefed."*

puree (pyoo<u>ray</u>, pyoo<u>ree</u>), **purée** FRENCH [from *purée,* itself from *purer* to purify, to strain] *noun* a thick paste made from pulped vegetables, fruit, or other ingredients. ~*verb* to prepare such a paste.

putsch (puch) SWISS GERMAN [insurrection] *noun* a secretly plotted and usually unexpected and possibly violent attempt to overthrow a government or eliminate political opponents: *"Most of the political opposition was eliminated in a putsch later that spring."*

putto (<u>puu</u>tō) ITALIAN [boy, probably ultimately from Latin *putus* boy] *noun* (*plural* **putti,** <u>puu</u>tee) a representation of a naked or seminaked boy, angel, or cherub (a standard character of Renaissance art).

putz (puutz, puts) GERMAN [decoration, from Yiddish] *noun* (slang) a fool or an unpleasant person (originally slang for a penis).

pyjamas *See* PAJAMAS.

pylon (<u>pī</u>lon) GREEK [gateway, from *pyle* gate] *noun* a steel tower or mast, or any towerlike structure; may also refer to the massive gateways found at many ancient Egyptian sites: *"Through a dromos of sphinxes and couchant double-winged lions she was borne, and set down before Oraetes sitting on a throne specially erected at the sculptured pylon of the palace"* (Lew Wallace, *Ben Hur,* 1880).

pyromania (pīrō<u>may</u>neeă, pīrō<u>may</u>nă) GREEK [madness for fire] *noun* an obsessive urge to start fires.

pyrrhic (<u>pi</u>rik) LATIN [after Pyrrhus, a king of Epirus whose army suffered heavy casualties against the Romans at Apulum in 279 B.C.] *adjective* at too great a cost (usually referring to victories gained only with heavy losses to the winning side): *"The press hailed the success of the negotiations, but everyone knew it was a pyrrhic victory."*

Q.E.D. *See* QUOD ERAT DEMONSTRAN-
DUM.

Q.E.F. *See* QUOD ERAT FACIENDUM.

q.s. *See* QUANTUM SUFFICIT.

quadrille (kwo<u>dril</u>, kwă<u>dril</u>) FRENCH
[small square, from Spanish *cuadrilla*
square block, from *cuadro* square] *noun*
a riding display or alternatively a
square dance for four couples (or
music written to accompany such a
dance): *"'. . .you can have no idea what a
delightful thing a Lobster Quadrille is!'
'No, indeed,' said Alice. 'What sort of a
dances is it?'"* (Lewis Carroll, *Alice's
Adventures in Wonderland,* 1865).

quaere (<u>kwir</u>ee) LATIN [to ask, imperative of *quaerere* to question, to inquire]
noun a query, a question.

quant. suff. *See* QUANTUM SUFFICIT.

quantum (<u>kwon</u>tăm) LATIN [neuter of
quantus how much, how great] *noun*
(*plural* **quanta,** <u>kwon</u>tă) an amount,
quantity, portion, share, part. ~*adjective* large, significant, abrupt: *"Recent*

*advances in electronics represent a quan-
tum leap in technology."*

quantum meruit (kwontăm <u>mer</u>ooit)
LATIN [so much as he/she has
deserved] *noun phrase* as much as he
or she is entitled to (usually relating to
sums of money due for services rendered or work done).

quantum sufficit (kwontăm <u>să</u>fisit)
LATIN [as much as suffices] *noun phrase*
as much as is needed, to a sufficient
extent. ~*abbreviated forms* **q.s., quant.
suff.**

quarantine (<u>kwor</u>ănteen) FRENCH
[from *quarantaine,* from *quarante* forty]
noun a period of isolation (originally
lasting 40 days) that may be imposed
on any person, animal, or ship to prevent the spread of disease or pests:
*"The dog was kept in quarantine until it
was clear that it was not infected."* ~*verb* to
place a person, animal, or ship in isolation to prevent the spread of disease
or pests.

quark (kwahrk) GERMAN [curd] *noun* a
low-fat curd cheese of German origin.

319

quartier (kahrtya͟y) FRENCH [from Latin *quartus* fourth] *noun*   a quarter, district, area (usually of a city): *"My father gave me a profuse allowance, and I might have lived (had I chosen) in the Quartier de l'Etoile and driven to my studies daily"* (Robert Louis Stevenson, *The Wrecker*, 1892).

quarto (kwort͞o) ITALIAN [from *quartus* fourth] *noun*   a size of paper measuring 9½ by 12 inches (241 by 305 mm), or a book printed on pages of this size: *"The maps were printed on quarto pages and had lost little of their original color."*

quasi (kwa͟yz͞ī, kwa͟ys͞ī, kwa͟hzee, kwa͟hsee) LATIN [as it were, just as if] *adjective*   resembling, virtual (often used in combination with other words): *"It was clear to him that the police suspected him of running a quasi-casino in his restaurant."* ~*adverb* seemingly, in some sense.

quattrocento (kwotr͞o chent͞o), **quatrocento** ITALIAN [four hundred] *noun* the 15th century (usually relating to Italian history or the arts). ~*adjective* of or relating to the 15th century. See also CINQUECENTO.

quel (kel), **quelle** FRENCH [what] *adjective* what: *"Quelle horreur!"*

quelque chose (kelka͟ sh͞oz) FRENCH [some thing] *noun phrase* something, something extra, the necessary extra thing: *"I think the whole outfit still lacks quelque chose, but I can't quite put my finger on it."*

quenelle (ka͟nel) FRENCH [from German *Knödel* dumpling] *noun* a poached dumpling of ground meat or fish served in a cream sauce.

que sera, sera   *See* CHE SARÀ, SARÀ.

questionnaire (kwescha͟nair, kwestya͟nair) FRENCH [list of questions, from *questionner* to question] *noun*   a document comprising a series of questions, a survey based on such a series of questions: *"She was accosted in the street by an overbearing woman carrying a questionnaire about her shopping habits."*

queue (kyoo) FRENCH [tail, from Latin *cauda*] *noun*   chiefly British, a waiting line of people, vehicles, messages, or tasks; may also refer to a braid of hair worn at the back of the head. ~*verb* to wait in line or to organize people or things into a line, to be dealt with in order: *"The old woman refused to queue for a ticket, complaining that she had paid in advance specifically in order not to be kept waiting in line."*

quiche (keesh) FRENCH [from Alsatian dialect *Küchen* cake] *noun* a savory pie made with milk, eggs, cheese, and other ingredients.

quidnunc (kwidnănk) LATIN [from *quid nunc?* what now?] *noun*   a busybody, a gossip.

quid pro quo (kwid prō <u>kwō</u>) LATIN [what for what] *noun phrase* (*plural* **quid pro quos, quids pro quos,** or **quids pro quo**) something for something, one thing in return for another, a deal by which something is given or received in exchange for something else: *"Most companies will inevitably expect something in return for relaxing the rules on lunch breaks—some kind of quid pro quo."*

quién sabe (kyen <u>sah</u>bā) SPANISH [who knows?] *interjection* who knows?

quieta non movere (kweeaytă nōn mō<u>vai</u>ree) LATIN [not to disturb calm things] *noun phrase* let a sleeping dog lie, leave well enough alone.

quietus (kwī<u>ee</u>tăs, kwī<u>ay</u>tăs) LATIN [from *quietus est* he is quit] *noun* death or a cessation of activity; may also refer to the final settlement of a debt or obligation: *"The guns fell silent, and for several hours the whole front line was in the grip of an uneasy quietus."*

quis custodiet ipsos custodes? (kwis kăs<u>tō</u>diet ipsos kăs<u>tō</u>deez) LATIN [who will guard the guards?, quoted from the *Satires* of Juvenal (c. 60–117 A.D.)] *interjection* who will guard the guards themselves? (or, who will check that the guards themselves observe the law?).

quisling (<u>kwis</u>ling) NORWEGIAN [after Vidkun Quisling (1887–1945), the Norwegian prime minister who was executed for collaborating with the Nazis during World War II] *noun* a collaborator with the enemy, a traitor: *"Accused by his workmates of being a coward and a quisling, the youth ran from the building and hid in the parking lot."*

qui vive (kee <u>veev</u>) FRENCH [long live who? (used as a challenge by French sentries)] *noun phrase* a state of alertness, awareness, or watchfulness.

quoad (<u>kwō</u>ad) LATIN [as far as, as much as] *preposition* in regard to, with respect to.

quod erat demonstrandum (kwod erat demon<u>stran</u>dăm) LATIN [which was to be proven] *noun phrase* what had to be demonstrated, which was to be proved. *~abbreviated form* **Q.E.D.**

quod erat faciendum (kwod erat fashee<u>en</u>dăm, kwod erat fakee<u>en</u>dăm) LATIN [which was to be done] *noun phrase* what had to be done, which was to be done. *~abbreviated form* **Q.E.F.**

quodlibet (<u>kwod</u>lăbet) LATIN [what pleases, from *quod* what and *libet* it pleases] *noun* a point or thesis advanced for discussion; may also refer in music to any lighthearted, humorous composition or medley.

quod vide (kwod <u>vee</u>day) LATIN [to see] *verb phrase* (*plural* **quae vide,** kwī <u>vee</u>day) see this, which see (used in bibliographical references). *~abbreviated form* **q.v.**

quo jure (kwō yooray, kwō jooray) LATIN [with what right?] *adverb phrase* by what right?, by what authority?

quondam (kwondăm, kwondam) LATIN [at one time, formerly] *adjective* former, sometime: *"The animal itself was as peaceful and well-behaved as that father of all picture-wolves, Red Riding Hood's quondam friend, whilst moving her confidence in masquerade"* (Bram Stoker, *Dracula*, 1897).

quorum (kworăm) LATIN [of which] *noun* a group of people (usually referring to the minimum number of individuals required to attend a meeting of an organization in order to satisfy requirements of legal competence): *"The number of members at the meeting was three people below the quorum, so it had to be abandoned."*

quota (kwōtă) LATIN [what part in number, from *quota pars* how great a part] *noun* a proportional part or share; may also refer to a maximum number, amount, or quantity allowed: *"The government announced measures to make sure that the quota of immigrants allowed into the country was not exceeded."*

quo vadis (kwō vahdis) LATIN [to what place are you going? (recalling the words spoken by Christ to Peter when the latter tried to leave Rome to escape execution] *verb phrase* where are you going?

q.v. *See* QUOD VIDE.

r. See RECTO.

rabbi (<u>ra</u>bī) HEBREW [my master] *noun* the leader of a Jewish congregation; may also refer to a master or teacher, specifically a scholar who expounds upon Jewish law: *"The rabbi was waiting for them at the synagogue."*

raconteur (rakon<u>ter</u>, rakon<u>toor</u>) FRENCH [from *raconter* to tell] *noun* a teller of anecdotes and stories: *"In manner, something of the grand seigneur still clung to him, so that he even ripped you up with an air, and I have been told that he was a raconteur of repute"* (J. M. Barrie, *Peter Pan,* 1904). ~*noun, feminine* **raconteuse** (rakon<u>terz</u>) a female teller of anecdotes and stories.

radius (<u>ra</u>ydeeăs) LATIN [ray] *noun* (*plural* **radiuses** or **radii,** <u>ra</u>ydeeī) a straight line running from the center of a circle or sphere to the circumference or surface; can also refer figuratively to any bounded or circumscribed area: *"A simple calculation produced both the radius and the circumference of the circle."*

raffia (<u>ra</u>feeă) MALAGASY [after a palm of the genus *Raphia*] *noun* the soft fiber of palm leaves that is commonly used in basketwork and other crafts.

raga (<u>rah</u>gă) SANSKRIT [color, tone] *noun* a melodic pattern or mode in traditional Indian music, or an improvisation based upon a traditional raga: *"Like many Western musicians of his generation, he became interested in learning the techniques of the Indian raga, even traveling to India itself to hear such music played in its original context."*

ragout (ra<u>goo</u>) FRENCH [from *ragoûter* to revive the taste] *noun* (in French cuisine) a rich, highly seasoned stew of meat and vegetables; may also refer more generally to any mixture of miscellaneous items: *"Here are also some dolphins' livers, which you take to be ragout of pork"* (Jules Verne, *20,000 Leagues Under the Sea,* 1870).

raison d'état (rezon(g) day<u>ta</u>) FRENCH [reason of state] *noun phrase* (*plural* **raisons d'etat**) a reason connected with the interests of the state or national security.

raison d'être (rezon(g) detră) FRENCH [reason to be] *noun phrase* (*plural* **raisons d'être**) a reason, motivation, or justification for the existence of a thing: *"She was more than just a lover to him, she was his raison d'être."*

raisonné (rayzonay) FRENCH [past participle of *raisonner* to reason] *adjective* reasoned out: *"It has given us a catalogue raisonné of the substances found upon our planet, and shown how everything living and dead is put together from them"* (Oliver Wendell Holmes, *Medical Essays,* 1883).

raita (rīeetă) HINDI [from *rayta*] *noun* (in Indian cuisine) a dish of chopped vegetables in yogurt or curd.

raj (rahj) HINDI [from Sanskrit *rajya*] *noun* rule, sovereignty (usually referring specifically to British rule in India in the 19th century—the Raj): *"Memories of the Raj are still strong in aristocratic Indian society."*

raja (rahjă, rahjah, rahzhă, rahzhah), **rajah** HINDI [from Sanskrit *rajan* king, probably ultimately from Latin *rex* king] *noun* an Indian prince or king; also applied to rulers and other persons of authority in Malaysian and Javanese society: *"The raja arrived with all the panoply appropriate to his status."*

raku (rahkoo) JAPANESE [ease, enjoyment] *noun* a variety of Japanese pottery with a lead glaze.

rallentando (ralăntandō) ITALIAN [slowing down, from *rallentare* to slow down again, to abate] *adverb* gradually decreasing in speed. ~*adjective* slowing down.

Ramadan (ramădahn) ARABIC [month of dryness] *noun* the sacred ninth month of the Muslim year, during which the faithful fast and observe other restrictions between the hours of sunrise and sunset.

ramekin (ramkin, ramăkin), **ramequin** FRENCH [from Low German *ram* cream] *noun* an individual portion of cheese or some other appetizing food prepared in a small dish, and thus also the dish itself: *"The chef expertly poured the prepared mixture into exquisite china ramequins from which the guests ate using delicate silver spoons."*

rampant (rampănt) FRENCH [present participle of *ramper* to climb] *adjective* widespread or otherwise unchecked, wild, extravagant, unrestrained. May also refer in heraldry to the pose of a lion, bear, or other creature depicted standing on its left hind leg with forelegs raised and head in profile: *"The family shield features a black lion rampant against a white background."*

ranchero (ranchairō) SPANISH [rancher, from *rancho* small ranch] *noun* a rancher or ranch hand (usually working on a ranch in Mexico): *"The saloon was packed with cowboys and rancheros,* *their clothes and hair the color of the dust in which they had ridden all day."*

rani (<u>rah</u>nee), **ranee** HINDI [queen, from Sanskrit *rajni,* feminine of *rajan* king] *noun* an Indian queen, or the wife (or widow) of a rajah.

rapido (<u>ra</u>pidō, ra<u>pee</u>dō) ITALIAN [rapidly] *adverb* (in music) rapidly. ~*adjective* (in music) rapid.

rappel (ră<u>pel</u>, ra<u>pel</u>) FRENCH [recall, from *rapeler* to recall] *verb* (in mountaineering) to execute a controlled descent by sliding down a rope, to abseil. ~*noun* a descent down a rope, an abseil.

rapport (ra<u>por</u>, ră<u>por</u>) FRENCH [from *rapporter* to bring back] *noun* a relationship, typically one in which those concerned are in harmony or agreement or otherwise share the same outlook or feelings: *"The two strangers quickly fell into conversation and soon established an easy rapport."*

rapporteur (rapor<u>ter</u>) FRENCH [reporter, from *rapporter* to bring back] *noun* a person who communicates reports of a meeting or other proceedings. ~*noun, feminine* **rapporteuse** (rapor<u>terz</u>).

rapprochement (ra<u>proshmon</u>(g)) FRENCH [from *rapprocher* to bring together] *noun* the establishment, or reestablishment, of harmonious relations between two parties: *"Reports*

from the negotiations in Washington suggest that the two sides may finally have reached a rapprochement."

rara avis (rairă <u>ay</u>văs, rahră <u>ay</u>văs) LATIN [rare bird] *noun phrase* (*plural* **rara avises** or **rarae aves,** rahrī <u>ah</u>vayz) a rarity, a remarkable person or thing.

ratatouille (rata<u>too</u>ee, rata<u>twee</u>) FRENCH [from *ratouiller* to disturb and *tatouiller* to stir] *noun* (in Provençal cuisine) a stew made from tomatoes, eggplant, onions, green peppers, herbs, and (sometimes) meat.

rathskeller (<u>rats</u>kelăr) GERMAN [from *Ratskellar* city-hall basement restaurant] *noun* a bar or restaurant housed in a cellar or basement.

ratio (<u>ray</u>shō, <u>ray</u>sheeō) LATIN [reckoning, reason] *noun* the quotient of two numbers or other mathematical expressions, or, more generally, the proportional relation between two or more things: *"The ratio of money invested to profit made has changed for the better in recent months."*

ratio decidendi (raysho desi<u>den</u>dee) LATIN [reason of deciding] *noun phrase* (in law) the reason or grounds for a decision.

rationale (rashă<u>nal</u>) LATIN [neuter of *rationalis,* from *ratio* reason] *noun* a reasoned statement of principles, or the basis or underlying reason for something: *"There seemed to be no way to understand the rationale behind such actions."*

ravioli (raveeōlee) ITALIAN [plural of *raviolo* little turnip] *noun* (in Italian cuisine) a dish of pasta squares stuffed with meat or cheese or other filling, usually served in sauce.

ravissant (ravison(g)) FRENCH [from *ravir* to seize, to enchant] *adjective* ravishing, delightful, enchanting.

re (ree, ray) LATIN [ablative of *res* thing] *preposition* with regard to, regarding, concerning, in the case of. See also IN RE.

realpolitik (rayalpoliteek), **Realpolitik** GERMAN [from *real* real and *Politik* politics] *noun* practical politics, political realism (as opposed to theoretical or ideological politics): "*Such humanistic considerations have little impact in the world of modern realpolitik.*"

rebus (reebăs) LATIN [by things] *noun* (*plural* **rebuses**) a representation of a word, syllable, or phrase by pictures or other symbols.

réchauffé (rayshōfay) FRENCH [warmed-over, reheated] *noun* a rehash, or a dish of reheated food. ~*adjective* rehashed, reheated.

recherché (răshairshay, răshairshay) FRENCH [select, past participle of *rechercher* to seek out] *adjective* choice, rare, exotic, or, more negatively, obscure, affected, pretentious: "*'Twixt the original and Oriental decorations, the strange and delicious food, and the personal-*ities both of the distinguished guests, the charming hostess and the noted host, never has Zenith seen a more recherché affair than the Ceylon dinner-dance given last evening by Mr. and Mrs. Charles McKelvey to Sir Gerald Doak*" (Sinclair Lewis, *Babbitt*, 1922).

recipe (resăpee) LATIN [take, from *recipere* to take, to receive] *noun* a prescription or formula; often referring to a set of instructions and ingredients for making something (commonly relating to cookery): "*No one seemed to realize that what she was suggesting was a recipe for disaster.*"

recitativo (resătateevō) ITALIAN [from *recitare* to recite] *noun* (*plural* **recitativos** or **recitativi**, resătateevee) (in music) recitative.

réclame (rayklahm) FRENCH [advertising, from *réclamer* to appeal, to ask for] *noun* showmanship, publicity, or public acclaim.

reconnaissance (rekonăsons) FRENCH [recognition] *noun* a preliminary scouting or examination of a position, area, or situation for military or other purposes: "*Two aircraft were dispatched to carry out a reconnaissance of the front line.*"

recto (rektō) LATIN [ablative of *rectus* right] *noun* a right-hand page in a book or other document. ~*abbreviated form* **r.** See also VERSO.

rector (rektăr) LATIN [leader, director, from *regere* to direct] *noun* a Protestant clergyman or a Roman Catholic priest in charge of a church or congregation; can also refer to the head of certain educational establishments: *"The rector of the university dismissed the allegations in a statement released to the press later that day."*

reculer pour mieux sauter (răkyoolay por meeă sortay) FRENCH [to draw back in order to leap better] *noun phrase* a tactical withdrawal made in order to launch a new assault on something, a setback that can be turned to one's own advantage.

redingote (redingōt) FRENCH [from English *riding coat*] *noun* originally, a long double-breasted overcoat for men; now applied to long coats for women (usually with a cutaway front or a front panel in a contrasting color): *". . .about two o'clock we behold him, 'in walnut-coloured great-coat, redingote noisette,' descending through the Place Vendome. . ."* (Thomas Carlyle, *History of the French Revolution,* 1837).

redivivus (redăīvăs, redăveevăs) LATIN [reused, renewed] *adjective* reborn, brought back to life, resurrected.

reductio ad absurdum (ridăkteeō ad abserdăm, ridăksheeō ad abserdăm) LATIN [reduction to the absurd] *noun phrase* reduction to the point of absurdity; in logic, the refutation of a proposition by following it through to ridiculous extremes.

reductio ad impossible (ridăkteeō ad imposibeelay) LATIN [reduction to the impossible] *noun phrase* reduction to the point of impossibility; in logic, the refutation of an argument by taking it to its impossible conclusion.

referendum (refărendăm) LATIN [something to be referred, from *referre* to refer] *noun* (*plural* **referendums** or **referenda,** refărendă) a plebiscite or popular vote, often seeking approval of a measure already passed or proposed by a government or other legislative body: *"Any changes to the constitution would have to be approved by referendum."*

regalia (răgaylyă) LATIN [kingly thing, neuter plural of *regalis* regal] *noun* the emblems or symbols of royalty; may also refer to any insignia or accouterments associated with authority or indicative of elevated status, or to any costume worn on a special occasion: *"They loved to travel to London to see the state occasions with officials dressed in regalia."*

regatta (răgată) ITALIAN [from *regata* contest, struggle] *noun* a boat race, or series of races: *"The king was a regular participant in yachting regattas off the Isle of Wight."*

regime (rayzheem, rejeem), **régime** FRENCH [system, ultimately from Latin *regimen*] *noun* a method of government, or a particular government in power; may also refer more generally to any system or pattern of action: *"The new regime has yet to win international recognition."*

regimen (rejămăn, rezhămăn) LATIN [rule, from *regere* to rule] *noun*　a systematic plan or regulated mode of life or course of action, such as a diet or course of exercise; may also refer generally to any regime or government: *'He attacked his noble guest without scruple on the severity of his regimen"* (Walter Scott, *The Antiquary,* 1816).

regina (rejīnă) LATIN [queen] *noun* queen, a reigning female monarch.

regisseur (rayzhiser), **régisseur** FRENCH [from *régir* to direct, ultimately from Latin *regere* to rule] *noun* a person who presents a work of theater or ballet; an artistic director.

regius (reejăs) LATIN [royal, from *rex* king] *adjective*　royal (indicating that a university professorship was bestowed originally by royalty or by virtue of royal patronage): *"He was appointed Regius Professor of Philosophy at the relatively young age of 33."*

regnum (regnăm) LATIN [from *regnare* to reign] *noun* (*plural* **regna,** regnă) kingdom.

Reich (rīk, rīsh) GERMAN [kingdom, state] *noun* (*plural* **Reiche,** rīkă)　a state or empire, usually referring specifically to the Holy Roman Empire (the First Reich, ended 1806), the National German Empire (the Second Reich, 1871–1919), or the Third Reich in Nazi Germany (1933–45).

rel.　*See* RELIQUIAE.

relais (rălay) FRENCH *noun* (in France) a café or restaurant, sometimes also offering accommodation.

relievo (rileevō) ITALIAN [from *rilevare* to raise] *noun*　relief, a style of molding or carving in which figures are sculpted on a flat background.

religieuse (rălijeeerz, rălizheeerz) FRENCH [from *religieux* religious] *noun* a nun or other woman belonging to a religious order: *"Here Reposes in God, Caroline de Clery, a Religieuse of St. Denis aged 83 years—and blind"* (Mark Twain, *A Tramp Abroad,* 1880).

religieux (rălijeeă, rălizheeă) FRENCH [religious] *noun*　a monk or other man belonging to a religious order.

religioso (relijeeōzō) ITALIAN [religious] *adverb* (in music)　with religious feeling. ~*adjective* devotional, religious.

reliquiae (relikweeī, relikwiee) LATIN [from *relinquere* to leave behind] *noun* relics, remains of the dead: *"It was left to the lawyers to sort out the reliquiae of the estate."* ~*abbreviated form* **rel.**

remanet (remănet) LATIN [it remains] *noun*　(in law) a case that remains to be heard.

renaissance (<u>ren</u>ăsons, ră<u>nay</u>sons) FRENCH [rebirth] *noun*   the revival of the arts and culture that took place in Europe in the postmedieval period, and hence any revival or rebirth: *"Interest in early chamber music has undergone something of a renaissance in the last decade."*

rencontre (ron(g)<u>kon</u>tră) FRENCH [encounter, fight] *noun*   a clash, combat, or other hostile meeting between opposed parties.

rendezvous (<u>ron</u>divoo, <u>ron</u>dayvoo) FRENCH [meeting place, from *rendez-vous* present yourselves] *noun* (*plural* **rendezvous,** <u>ron</u>divooz, <u>ron</u>dayvooz) a prearranged meeting, or the place where such a meeting is to take place. ~*verb* to meet at a prearranged place and time: *"The raiding party was supposed to rendezvous with the Resistance at midnight, but no one turned up."*

rentier (<u>ron</u>tyay) FRENCH [from *rente,* ultimately from Latin *rendita* paid] *noun*   a person whose income comes from property or investments.

repartee (reper<u>tee</u>, repahr<u>tee</u>, repahr<u>tay</u>) FRENCH [from *repartir* to retort] *noun*   a witty, clever reply, or light, witty conversation: *"She quickly tired of his empty-headed repartee and sought more rewarding company."*

repechage (repă<u>shahzh</u>, repă<u>shahzh</u>) FRENCH [from *rêpechage* second chance, reexamination, from *rêpecher* to fish

out, to rescue] *noun* (in sport) a trial heat in which losers in an early round have another chance to qualify for the later stages of a competition. ~*adjective* of or relating to such a heat.

repertoire (<u>rep</u>ătwah) FRENCH [from *répertoire* repertory] *noun*   a selection of rehearsed performances, skills, methods, or fields of knowledge from which a performer or theatrical company and so forth may choose: *"A slight smile passed over Polly's face as she returned her thanks for the new pupil, for she remembered a time when Mrs. Shaw considered her 'sweet songs' quite unfit for a fashionable young lady's repertoire"* (Louisa May Alcott, *An Old-Fashioned Girl,* 1870).

répétiteur (repeti<u>ter</u>, repeti<u>toor</u>) FRENCH [tutor, coach] *noun*   a music coach, or a person who conducts ballet or opera rehearsals.

replica (<u>rep</u>likă) ITALIAN [repetition, from *replicare* to repeat] *noun*   an accurate reproduction or copy of something: *"The revolver was only a cheap replica, but at a distance it looked just like the real thing."*

répondez s'il vous plaît (rayponday seel voo play) FRENCH [reply, if you please] *verb phrase*   please reply. ~*abbreviated form* **R.S.V.P.**

reportage (repăr<u>tahzh</u>, report<u>ahzh</u>, ri<u>por</u>tăj) FRENCH [from *reporter* to report] *noun*   reporting of the news, or the style or manner in which the news is reported: *"Standards of reportage vary from paper to paper and all too often tend to reflect the journalistic and abilities and style of the editor."*

repoussé (răpoo<u>say</u>, ră<u>poo</u>say) FRENCH [pushed back] *noun* a form of decorative metalwork, in which patterns are raised in relief by hammering or pressing on the reverse side. ~*adjective* of or relating to such metalwork.

reprise (ră<u>preez</u>) FRENCH [renewal, repeat, from *reprendre* to take back] *noun* a repetition, recapitulation, renewal, or resumption of an action, performance, or theme: *"A lack of time saved them from a reprise of the whole performance."*

requiem (<u>rek</u>weeăm, <u>rayk</u>weeăm) LATIN [from *requies* quiet, rest, the first word of the introit of the Latin mass for the dead] *noun* a mass for the dead, or a solemn chant or dirge in honor of the dead (or a musical setting of this): *"The composer's requiem ranks among the greatest works of the century."*

requiescat (rekwee<u>es</u>kat, raykwee<u>es</u>kat) LATIN [may he (or she) rest] *interjection* rest (a prayer for the repose of the dead).

requiescat in pace (rekwee<u>es</u>kat in pahchay, raykwee<u>es</u>kat in pahchay) LATIN [may he (or she) rest in peace] *interjection* rest in peace (a prayer for the repose of the dead): *"God help him,*

over whose dead soul in his living body must be uttered the sad supplication, Requiescat in pace!" (Oliver Wendell Holmes, *Elsie Venner,* 1859–60). ~*abbreviated form* **R.I.P.**

res cogitans (rayz <u>kog</u>itanz, rayz <u>koj</u>itanz) LATIN [thinking thing] *noun phrase* the mind, the soul, something that thinks.

reservoir (<u>re</u>zervwahr) FRENCH [tank, holder, from *reserver* to reserve] *noun* a supply, reserve or store of something (often referring specifically to an artificial lake where water is stored for the public supply): *"The commission has a reservoir of funds for such projects."*

res gestae (rayz <u>ges</u>tī, reez <u>jes</u>tee) LATIN [things done] *noun phrase* (in law) the facts of a case; can also refer more generally to events in the past, things done, achievements.

residuum (ră<u>zid</u>jăwăm) LATIN [the remainder, from *residuus* remaining] *noun* (*plural* **residuums** or **residua**, ră<u>zid</u>jăwă) residue or remainder, something left over: *"An unexplained residuum of change must be left to the assumed uniform action of those unknown agencies, which occasionally induce strongly marked and abrupt deviations of structure in our domestic productions"* (Charles Darwin, *The Descent of Man,* 1871).

res ipsa loquitur (rayz ipsă <u>lok</u>witer) LATIN [the matter itself speaks] *noun* *phrase* (in law) the facts speak for themselves.

res judicata (rayz joodi<u>kaht</u>ă) LATIN [judged matter] *noun phrase* (in law) a case that has been decided by a court and cannot be reopened.

res non verba (rayz non <u>ver</u>bă) LATIN [things not words] *noun phrase* deeds not words, action not talk.

res publica (rayz <u>puub</u>likă) LATIN [public affair] *noun phrase* a commonwealth, a republic, the state.

restaurant (<u>rest</u>ărănt, <u>rest</u>ront) FRENCH [present participle of *restaurer* to restore] *noun* a place where meals and other refreshments can be bought and eaten: *"A new Italian restaurant has opened opposite the railroad station."*

restaurateur (restără<u>ter</u>), **restauranteur** (restăron<u>ter</u>) FRENCH [ultimately from Latin *restaurator* restorer] *noun* the owner or manager of a restaurant: *"By day he was Quigg, the restaurateur. By night he was the Margrave—the Caliph—the Prince of Bohemia. . ."* (O. Henry, *Strictly Business*, 1910).

restitutio in integram (resti<u>choo</u>tiō in intăgram) LATIN [restoration to the uninjured state] *noun phrase* (in law) the restoration of an injured party or parties to their former condition.

résumé (<u>rez</u>ămay, reză<u>may</u>, <u>ray</u>zămay, rayză<u>may</u>) FRENCH [resumed, past participle of *résumer* to resume] *noun* a summary or abstract (often referring specifically to a person's curriculum vitae): *"She gave him a quick résumé of the plot so far and sat back to watch his reaction."*

resurgam (re<u>zer</u>gam) LATIN [I shall rise again] *interjection* (among Christians) I shall rise again (signifying belief in resurrection of the faithful after death): *"Her grave is in Brocklebridge churchyard: for fifteen years after her death it was only covered by a grassy mound; but now a grey marble tablet marks the spot, inscribed with her name, and the word 'Resurgam'"* (Charlotte Brontë, *Jane Eyre*, 1847).

reticule (<u>ret</u>ikyool) FRENCH [ultimately from Latin *reticulum* network] *noun* a woman's purse or small net bag closed by a drawstring; can also refer in optics to a grid of fine lines arranged in the eyepiece of sights or other optical instruments.

retina (<u>ret</u>ănă, <u>ret</u>nă) LATIN [probably ultimately from *rete* net] *noun* (*plural* **retinas** or **retinae,** <u>ret</u>ănee, <u>ret</u>ănī) the sensory membrane lining the eye that receives images formed by the lens and communicates them to the brain: *"Such injuries to the retina usually heal themselves within a few weeks."*

retroussé (ră<u>troo</u>say, ră<u>troo</u>say) FRENCH [turned-up, past participle of *retrousser* to turn up] *adjective* turned-up (usually referring to the shape of a person's nose).

retsina (ret<u>see</u>nă) GREEK [from *retine* pine resin] *noun* a resin-flavored Greek white wine.

revanche (ră<u>vonsh</u>) FRENCH [from Middle French *revenche* revenge] *noun* revenge, retaliation (usually relating to policies concerning the reclamation of lost territory).

reveille (re<u>vă</u>lee) FRENCH [from *réveillez*, imperative of *réveiller* to awaken] *noun* a bugle call, drum roll, or other signal marking the time to get up, as in military camps: *"The two soldiers were ordered to report to the commander at reveille the following morning."*

revenant (<u>re</u>vănănt, <u>re</u>vănon(g)) FRENCH [one returning, present participle of *revenir* to return] *noun* a person or spirit who returns after death or after a long absence, a ghost; may also refer to a person whose character or behaviour recalls a past age: *"For granting even that Religion were dead . . . or that it now walked as goblin revenant with Bishop Talleyrand of Autun; yet does not the Shadow of Religion, the Cant of Religion, still linger?"* (Thomas Carlyle, *History of the French Revolution,* 1837).

reverie (<u>re</u>văree, <u>rev</u>ree) FRENCH [from *rêverie* daydream, from *rêver* to dream] *noun* a daydream, an idle fancy or an abstract, dreamy, meditative state of mind: *"She went into a reverie, trying to imagine herself on a beach with the sound of the waves in her ears."*

revue (ră<u>vyoo</u>) FRENCH [review, survey] *noun* a variety of theatrical entertainment comprising songs, sketches, and dancing: *"Toward the end of her career she became a star of cabaret and revue."*

rex (reks) LATIN [king] *noun* king, a reigning male monarch.

rhadamanthine (radă<u>manth</u>īn) GREEK [after Rhadamanthus, the son of Zeus and Europa in Greek mythology, who became a judge in the underworld] *adjective* inflexibly severe or strict: *"As a judge he dispensed justice with rhadamanthine rigor, becoming notorious for the length of sentences he imposed."*

rhombus (<u>rom</u>băs) GREEK [*rhombos* lozenge] *noun* (*plural* **rhombuses** or **rhombi,** <u>rom</u>bī, <u>rom</u>bee) a parallelogram with four equal sides and two acute and two obtuse angles: *". . .in this artiste's hands meat assumed the flavor of fish, fish of mushrooms, macaroni of gunpowder; to make up for this, not a single carrot went into the soup without taking the shape of a rhombus or a trapezium"* (Ivan Turgenev, *A Hunter's Notes,* 1847–51).

ricksha (<u>rik</u>shah), **rickshaw** JAPANESE [from *jinrikisha* person-power vehicle] *noun* a traditional Japanese hooded two-wheeled vehicle drawn by one or two people: *"A ricksha conveyed the ambassador to the residency."*

ricochet (<u>ri</u>kăshay) FRENCH [to rebound] *noun* a rebound. *~verb* to rebound, glance off, bounce back: *"The bullet ricocheted off the oil barrel and hit the light, throwing the whole room into complete darkness."*

ricotta (ri<u>ko</u>tă) ITALIAN [recooked, from *ricuocere* to cook again] *noun* a variety of Italian soft, white, unripened, unsalted whey cheese; may also apply to a type of cheese made from whole or skimmed milk.

rictus (<u>rik</u>tăs) LATIN [open mouth, from *ringi* to open the mouth] *noun* the mouth orifice; a gaping grin or grimace: *"A rictus of cruel malignity lit up greyly their old bony faces"* (James Joyce, *A Portrait of the Artist as a Young Man,* 1914–15).

rien ne va plus (reean(g) nă va <u>ploo</u>) FRENCH [no more goes] *interjection* no more bets (announcement made by the croupier in roulette when the wheel starts to spin).

rigatoni (rigă<u>to</u>nee) ITALIAN [from *rigato* furrowed] *noun* (in Italian cuisine) a type of pasta shaped into hollow fluted tubes.

rigor mortis (rigăr <u>mor</u>tis) LATIN [stiffness of death] *noun phrase* the stiffening of the body that takes place after death: *"Rigor mortis had set in, and it was with difficulty that the corpse was wrestled into a body bag."*

rijsttafel (<u>ri</u>stahfăl) DUTCH [from *rijst* rice and *tafel* table] *noun* (in Indone-sian cuisine) a meal comprising various meat, vegetable, and seafood dishes accompanied by rice.

rinforzando (rinfort<u>sand</u>ō) ITALIAN [present participle of *rinforzare* to strengthen] *adverb* (in music) a sudden crescendo. ~*adjective* with a sudden crescendo.

rio (<u>ree</u>ō) SPANISH [river] *noun* river.

R.I.P. *See* REQUIESCAT IN PACE.

riposte (rip<u>ost</u>) FRENCH [counterthrust, from Italian *riposta* answer] *noun* a swift or clever retaliatory remark, retort, or action: *"'Pace gives life,' was the riposte"* (Oscar Wilde, *The Picture of Dorian Gray,* 1890). ~*verb* to make such a retort or retaliatory response.

risorgimento (reezorji<u>ment</u>ō) ITALIAN [rising again, from *risorgere* to rise again] *noun* (*plural* **risorgimentos** or **risorgimenti**, reezorji<u>men</u>tee) a revival or renaissance (often referring specifically to the Risorgimento movement that resulted in the unification of Italy in the 19th century).

risotto (ri<u>zot</u>ō) ITALIAN [from *riso* rice] *noun* (in Italian cuisine) a seasoned dish of rice cooked in meat stock.

risqué (ri<u>skay</u>) FRENCH [risky, past participle of *risquer* to risk] *adjective* daring, indelicate, improper, indecent: *"The old man made a few risqué remarks* *about the waitress but otherwise behaved himself reasonably well."*

rissole (ri̱sōl) FRENCH [from Old French *ruissole,* ultimately from Latin *russus* red] *noun*   a variety of meatball coated in breadcrumbs and fried.

ritardando (ritahrda̱ndō) ITALIAN [present participle of *ritardare* to slow down, ultimately from Latin *retardare* to retard] *adverb*   (in music) slowing in tempo. ~*adjective* becoming slower.

rite de passage (reet dǎ pa̱sahzh) FRENCH [rite of passage] *noun phrase* (*plural* **rites de passage**)   a landmark in life marking the transition from one state of being to another, or a ceremony or ritual celebrating this: *"Getting one's first car is one of those rites de passage that seems commonplace enough to the person concerned, but it is much more significant to the parents."*

ritornello (ritorne̱lō) ITALIAN [from *ritorno* return] *noun* (*plural* **ritornellos** or **ritornelli**, ritorne̱lee)   a short instrumental refrain or interlude in a musical composition.

riviera (riveeai̱rǎ, rivya̱irǎ)) ITALIAN [coast, after the Riviera coast of SE France] *noun*   a coastal resort area: *"In the perpetual purposeless rush of their days, the feverish making of winter plans, hurrying off to the Riviera or St. Moritz, Egypt or New York, there was no time to hunt up the vanished or to wait for the laggard"* (Edith Wharton, *Glimpses of the Moon,* 1922).

rivière (riveeai̱r, rivya̱ir) FRENCH [river] *noun*   a necklace of diamonds or other precious stones.

robe de chambre (rōb dǎ sho̱mbrǎ) FRENCH [bedroom robe] *noun phrase*   a dressing gown or negligée: *"Undressing is a woe; our robe de chambre / May sit like that of Nessus, and recall / Thoughts quite as yellow, but less clear than amber"* (Lord Byron, *Don Juan,* 1819–24).

robot (rō̱bot, rō̱bǎt) CZECH [*robota,* forced labor; the word was originally used as part of the title of a play, *R.U.R.* (Rossum's Universal Robots), written in 1920 by the Czech playwright Karel Čapek] *noun*   a machine that can do mechanical routine work; a person who behaves in a mechanical manner; automaton.

roche moutonnée (rosh mootǎna̱y) FRENCH [fleecy rock, from *roche* rock and *mouton* sheep] *noun phrase* (*plural* **roches moutonnées**)   a rocky outcrop that has been rounded and smoothed by glacial erosion.

rococo (roko̱kō, rōkǎ̱kō) FRENCH [from *rocaille* pebblework] *noun*   an artistic or musical style featuring fanciful curved forms and elaborate decoration. ~*adjective* of or relating to such an artistic or musical style; ornate, elaborate, extravagant, florid: *"The picture frame was an extraordinary rococo affair in dark mahogany, complete with trailing vines and fruit."*

rodeo (rōdeeō, rădayō) SPANISH [corral, from *rodear* to surround, ultimately from Latin *rotare* to rotate] *noun* a roundup of livestock, or a public demonstration or competition in which riders display their skills at roping cattle or breaking horses: *"He narrowly escaped serious injury at his first rodeo when he was tossed straight over the rails by a bucking stallion."*

rogan josh (rōgăn josh) URDU [from *rogan jos* or *raugan-jos* stewed in ghee] *noun phrase* (in Indian cuisine) a dish of curried meat cooked in a spicy sauce.

roi fainéant (rwa fayneeon(g)) FRENCH [do-nothing king] *noun phrase* (*plural* **rois fainéants**) a person who exercises power in name only, or who is too lazy to exercise any power he or she actually has.

roi soleil (rwa solay) FRENCH [sun king] *noun phrase* (*plural* **rois soleils**) an eminent person (often referring specifically to Louis XIV of France, who adopted the Sun as an emblem).

role (rōl), **rôle** FRENCH [roll] *noun* the part or character played by an actor in a theatrical production, or any assigned function or part in a process or organization: *"The butler was destined to play an important role in the scenes that were to follow."*

roman à clef (rōmon(g) a klay) FRENCH [novel with a key] *noun phrase* (*plural* **romans à clef**) a novel in which real events or people are thinly disguised as fiction.

roman à thèse (rōmon(g) a tayz) FRENCH [novel with a thesis] *noun phrase* (*plural* **romans à thèse**) a novel that presents or argues a particular thesis, a novel with a strong didactic intent.

roman de geste (rōmon(g) dă zhest) FRENCH [romance of heroic deeds] *noun phrase* (*plural* **romans de geste**) an epic poem on chivalric or heroic themes, chanson de geste: *"The adventures of Charlemagne and his paladins became the subject of many a roman de geste and are still told today."*

roman-fleuve (rōmon(g) fle(r)v) FRENCH [river novel] *noun* (*plural* **romans-fleuves**) a novel based on a leisurely exploration of family life (or of some other close-knit community).

roman policier (rōmon(g) poleeseeay) FRENCH [police novel] *noun phrase* (*plural* **romans policiers**) a detective story, particularly one by a French author.

rondeau (rondō, rondō) FRENCH [from *rond* round] *noun* (*plural* **rondeaux,** rondō, rondōz) a verse form usually comprising 10 or 13 lines, in three stanzas, with the the first line used as a repeated refrain; may also refer to a type of popular song of medieval French origin: *"At that moment Lloyd Mallam, the poet, owner of the Hafiz Book*

Shop, was finishing a rondeau to show how diverting was life amid the feuds of medieval Florence, but how dull it was in so obvious a place as Zenith" (Sinclair Lewis, *Babbitt*, 1922).

rondo (rondō) ITALIAN [from French *rond* round] *noun* a piece of instrumental music with a repeating refrain or theme, often comprising the last movement of a concerto or sonata.

rosé (rōzay) FRENCH [pink] *noun* a pale red-colored table wine made from red grapes from which the skins have been removed during fermentation. ~*adjective* pinkish or pale red in color: *"The sky had turned a delicate rosé color and the mountains had taken on a distinct purple hue."*

Rosh Hashanah (rōsh hăshahnă, rosh hăshahnă) HEBREW [head of the year] *noun* the Jewish New Year.

roster (rostă) DUTCH [from *rooster* grid iron] *noun* an itemized list or register of personnel, duties to be performed, or events to take place: *"The Regiment would sooner be struck off the roster than forego their distinction"* (Rudyard Kipling, "The Rout of the White Hussars," 1888).

rostrum (rostrăm) LATIN [beak, from *rodere* to gnaw, also applied to the prow of a ship and hence to a platform in the Forum of ancient Rome decorated with the prows of defeated enemy ships and used by public orators] *noun*

(*plural* **rostrums** or **rostra,** rostră) a platform or piece of staging from which a person may deliver a speech or performance (often referring specifically to the stand from which a conductor directs an orchestra): *"As the speaker mounted the rostrum a large over-ripe tomato exploded with satisfying gusto against the microphone stand."*

rota (rōtă) LATIN [wheel] *noun* a list or roster of persons, or a tally of tasks or duties in a fixed order of rotation: *"He checked the rota pinned to the noticeboard and saw that he was already late to help with the evening meal."*

rôti (rotee) FRENCH [roast] *noun* (in French cuisine) a dish of roasted meat. ~*adjective* roasted.

rotisserie (rōtisăree, rōtisree) FRENCH [from *rôtir* to roast] *noun* a type of oven in which food may be rotated on a spit while being roasted; may also refer to a restaurant or shop serving barbecued or roast meats.

rotunda (rōtăndă) LATIN [feminine of *rotundus* round, circular] *noun* a circular building, typically topped by a dome; may also refer to a large circular hall or other area in a hotel or other public building: *"The corridor opened out on the central rotunda of the library, where the main reading room was situated."*

roué (rooay) FRENCH [broken on the wheel (referring to the punishment thought by some to be suitable for pleasure-seeking profligates)] *noun* a rake, a debauchee, a man with a reputation for dissolute living: *"Her father had for years cultivated the air of an old roué, though in reality he was usually in bed by ten o'clock with a good book and a cup of cocoa."*

rouge (roozh) FRENCH [red] *noun* a reddish cosmetic powder or cream used to color the cheeks or lips: *"The little girl watched intently as her mother dabbed a little rouge on her cheeks."* ~*verb* to color the cheeks or lips with rouge.

rouge-et-noir (roozh ay nwahr) FRENCH [red and black] *noun phrase* a card game in which bets are placed on a table marked with two red and two black diamond spots.

roulade (roolahd) FRENCH [act of rolling, from *rouler* to roll] *noun* (in French cuisine) a cooking technique in which food is prepared in the form of a roll and served sliced: *"The meal was finished with generous slices of ice cream roulade."*

rouleau (roolō) FRENCH [from *rôle* roll (referring originally to the roll of paper from which actors formerly learned their parts)] *noun* (*plural* **rouleaus** or **rouleaux,** roolō, roolōz) a small roll or cylinder of coins or other objects: *"Early in the morning, the rouleau of gold was left at my door in a little box, with my name on the outside"* (Charles Dickens, *A Tale of Two Cities,* 1859).

roulette (roolet) FRENCH [small wheel, from *rouelle* wheel] *noun* a gambling game played with a revolving wheel divided into numbered compartments, participants betting on the number where a spinning ball will finally come to rest; may also refer to the revolving wheel itself.

routier (rooteeay) FRENCH [ultimately from Latin *rumpere* to break] *noun* a long-distance truck driver in a French-speaking country.

routine (rooteen) FRENCH [habit, from *route* traveled way] *noun* a habitual, customary, or regular method of doing things: *"The athlete disliked any interruption to her time-honored training routine."* ~*adjective* habitual, commonplace, ordinary.

roux (roo) FRENCH [browned, from *beurre roux* brown butter] *noun* a mixture of flour and butter used to thicken soups and sauces.

R.S.V.P. *See* RÉPONDEZ S'IL VOUS PLAÎT.

rubella (roobelă) LATIN [feminine of *rubellus* reddish] *noun* German measles.

Rubicon (roobikăn) LATIN [after the Rubicon river in northern Italy, which Julius Caesar crossed with his troops in 49 B.C., thus declaring his challenge against the Senate] *noun* a decisive, irrevocable step; can also refer to any boundary or limitation: *"With this deci-*

sion the president effectively crossed the Rubicon: if he failed to win the day there would be no going back."

rubric (<u>roo</u>brik) LATIN [from *rubrica* red earth] *noun*   the title, heading, instructions, or similar material at the beginning of a text (formerly often printed in red); may also refer to any gloss or other explanatory material in a text: *"'We Confess a Mistake' was the rubric above the leader, and she uttered a cry of triumph, for she thought the mistake was what she had just been reading, and that the editorial would apologize for the incomprehensible journalistic error upon the first page"* (Booth Tarkington, *The Conquest of Canaan,* 1905).

ruche (roosh) FRENCH [beehive, ultimately from Latin *rusca* tree bark] *noun* a frill, pleat, or gathered strip of fabric suitable for use as trimming for a dress or curtains: *"A cluster of tea-rose buds at the bosom and a ruche reconciled Meg to the display of her pretty, white shoulders, and a pair of high-heeled silk boots satisfied the last wish of her heart"* (Louisa May Alcott, *Little Women,* 1868).

rucksack (<u>ruk</u>sak, <u>rook</u>sak) GERMAN [from *Rucken* back and *Sack* sack] *noun* a knapsack: *"The rucksacks were piled up in the corner and all the members of the party sat down to eat."*

rumba (<u>răm</u>bă) SPANISH [probably of African origin] *noun* a Cuban-style ballroom dance, or music written to accompany it.

ruse de guerre (rooz dă <u>gair</u>) FRENCH [ruse of war] *noun phrase* a trick to deceive an enemy in time of war; by extension, any justifiable ruse or trick: *"Her lover forgave himself for his low deception on the grounds that it was a simple ruse de guerre."*

rus in urbe (rus in <u>er</u>bay) LATIN [the country in the city] *noun phrase* an impression of the countryside transported into an urban area (such as through the planting of trees): *"The painting of an idyllic landscape on the side wall of a decrepit tenement constituted a feeble attempt to create the impression of rus in urbe."*

S. *See* SENOR; SIGNOR; SIGNORA.

S.A., s.a. *See* SINE ANNO.

Sabbath (sabăth) HEBREW [from *shab-bath* rest] *noun* the seventh day of the week, traditionally a time of rest and worship (Sunday among Christians, Saturday among Jews): *"There was much resistance to opening stores on the Sabbath."*

sabot (sabō, sabō) FRENCH [from Old French *çabot,* ultimately from Arabic *sabbat* sandal] *noun* a traditional wooden shoe or type of sandal with a wooden sole and sides.

sabotage (sabătahzh, sabătahj) FRENCH [from *saboter* to make a noise with sabots, to destroy with sabots (wooden shoes)] *noun* a deliberate act of destruction of property, typically as part of a campaign to hinder an enemy; may also refer more generally to any subversive or destructive act. ~*verb* to commit an act of sabotage: *"The men decided to sabotage the management's attempts to regain control of negotiations."*

saboteur (sabăter) FRENCH [from *saboter* to make a noise with sabots, to destroy with sabots (wooden shoes)] *noun* a person who commits acts of sabotage.

sabra (sahbră) HEBREW [from *sabbar* prickly pear] *noun* a native born Israeli.

sachet (sashay) FRENCH [diminutive of *sac* bag, ultimately from Latin *saccus*] *noun* a small bag or packet: *"There was a plentiful supply of sachets of soap and shampoo in the washroom."*

sadhu (sahdoo), **saddhu** SANSKRIT [good man] *noun* a Hindu holy man or sage.

saeva indignatio (sīvă indignahteeō) LATIN [fierce indignation] *noun phrase* strong indignation (usually in response to human folly).

safari (săfahree) KISWAHILI [from Arabic *safar* journey] *noun* a journey, tour, or expedition; a hunting trip in pursuit of wild animals. ~*adjective* sand-colored, beige (the color of traditional safari clothes): *"In the end he chose a broad-brimmed hat and a safari-colored jacket for the trip."*

saga (sahgă) OLD NORSE [tale, saw] *noun* a prose narrative recounting heroic events and figures of Icelandic and Norwegian legend; by extension, any lengthy tale of epic character: *"It took some time but eventually they prevailed upon their hostess to share with them the epic saga of her early love life."*

sahib (saheeb, sahib, saheeb) HINDI [from Arabic *sahib* master, friend] *noun* sir, master (term of respect for Europeans used in colonial India).

sake (sakee, sahkee), **saké** JAPANESE *noun* a Japanese alcoholic drink made from fermented rice.

salaam (sălahm) ARABIC [peace] *noun* a salutation or ceremonial greeting used in the East (often in the form of a low bow, with the right hand placed on the forehead): *"Abdulla understood the meaning of that silence, and rose to take leave with a grave salaam"* (Joseph Conrad, *Almayer's Folly,* 1894). *~verb* to make such a greeting.

salami (sălahmee) ITALIAN [plural of *salame,* from *salare* to salt] *noun* a type of highly seasoned pork and beef sausage.

salle (sal) FRENCH [room] *noun* a hall or other large room.

salon (salon(g)) FRENCH [from Italian *salone,* itself from *sala* hall] *noun* a drawing room, living room, or reception room; may also refer to a fashionable social gathering or exhibition of artistic works held in such surroundings and, by extension, to any fashionable business establishment or shop: *"I want to come back to London. I want to have a charming house here. I want to have a salon"* (Oscar Wilde, *An Ideal Husband,* 1895).

salsa (salsă) SPANISH [sauce, ultimately from Latin *salsus* salted] *noun* a spicy sauce made from tomatoes, onions, and hot peppers; may also refer to a modern variety of Caribbean dance music and dance style associated with such music: *"The sounds of salsa music and laughter drifted out of the harbor-front bars."*

salut (saloo) FRENCH [salute, ultimately from Latin *salutare* to greet] *interjection* a greeting, salutation, or toast.

salute (săloot, salootay) ITALIAN [salute, ultimately from Latin *salutare* to greet] *noun* a greeting, salutation, or toast.

sal volatile (sal volatilee) LATIN [swift salt] *noun phrase* smelling salts (ammonium carbonate).

samba (sambă, sahmbă) PORTUGUESE *noun* a Brazilian dance of African origin or a Latin American ballroom dance based on it; may also refer to music written to accompany it: *"They danced the samba until the sun rose over the distant mountains."*

samizdat (s<u>am</u>izdat) RUSSIAN [abbreviated from of *samizdatel'stvo,* from *sam* self and *izdatel'stvo* publishing house] *noun*　an underground press or a clandestine system of publishing and distributing literature that has been officially suppressed (originally referring to such activity in the former Soviet Union).

samosa (s<u>ă</u>m<u>ō</u>s<u>ă</u>) PERSIAN/URDU *noun* (in Indian cuisine)　an appetizing triangular pastry filled with meat or vegetables.

samovar (s<u>am</u>ăvahr) RUSSIAN [self-boiler, from *samo* self and *varit'* to boil] *noun*　a traditional Russian tea urn, commonly made of copper: *". . .the drawing room, a large room with dark walls, downy rugs and a brightly lighted table, gleaming with the light of candles, the whiteness of napery, the silver of the samovar and the tea service of transparent porcelain"* (Leo Tolstoy, *Anna Karenina,* 1874–76).

sampan (s<u>am</u>pan) CHINESE [three boards, from *saam* three and *baan* board, plank] *noun*　a flat-bottomed Chinese boat steered by a stern oar or oars: *"A large sampan floated majestically out of the harbor on the evening breeze."*

samurai (s<u>a</u>măr<u>ī</u>, s<u>a</u>myăr<u>ī</u>) JAPANESE [warrior] *noun*　a member of the tra-

ditional Japanese military caste or feudal nobility. *~adjective* of or relating to the samurai class of warriors: *"The old man took down the samurai sword that hung over the fireplace and held it out to his visitor for inspection."*

san (san) JAPANESE [diminutive of *sama* honorable] *noun*　a courtesy title affixed to a person's name or other titles.

sanatorium (sănăt<u>o</u>reeăm) LATIN [healing place, neuter of *sanatorius* curative] *noun* (*plural* **sanatoriums** or **sanatoria,** sănăt<u>o</u>reeă)　an institution where the sick may receive therapy or medical treatment; may also refer to a health resort or to a medical center within a school or other establishment: *"The school sanatorium was crowded with victims of the virus." ~abbreviated form* **san.**

sanctum (s<u>ank</u>tăm) LATIN [neuter of *sanctus* sacred, holy] *noun* (*plural* **sanctums** or **sancta,** s<u>ank</u>tă)　a sacred place, a private study or retreat from the world: *"'I beg your pardon, Mr. Traddles . . . I was not aware that there was any individual, alien to this tenement, in your sanctum'"* (Charles Dickens, *David Copperfield,* 1849–50).

sanctum sanctorum (s<u>ank</u>tăm sankt<u>or</u>ăm) LATIN [translation of Hebrew *qodes haqqodasim* holy of holies] *noun phrase* (*plural* **sancta sanctorum,** sanktă sankt<u>or</u>ăm)　the holy of holies (the most holy place) in the Jewish

341

Temple in ancient Jerusalem, or a sacred shrine in any church or temple; may also apply to any sanctum or private retreat.

sangfroid (son(g)fwah), **sang-froid** FRENCH [cold blood] *noun* composure, coolheadedness, impertubability, equanimity, self-possession (especially under pressure): *"His lack of reaction to her anger was typical of his British 'stiff upper lip' and old-fashioned sangfroid."*

sangria (sangreeă) SPANISH [bleeding] *noun* a Spanish drink made with sweet red wine, fruit, spices, and soda water.

sans (sonz, sanz) FRENCH [without, ultimately from Latin *sine* without, influenced by *absentia* absence] *preposition* without, devoid of.

sansculotte (sanzkoolot, sanzkyoolot), **sans-culotte** FRENCH [from *sans-culotte* without knee-breeches, referring to members of the lower classes in late-18th-century France] *noun* a radical political extremist, revolutionary, or anarchist (referring originally to republican radicals at the time of the French Revolution); may also refer more generally to any member of the lowest ranks of society.

sans-gêne (son(g) zhen) FRENCH [without embarrassment] *noun phrase* lack of self-restraint, disregard of polite conventions.

sans pareil (son(g) paray) FRENCH [without equal] *adjective phrase* without equal, unequaled: *"He built a reputation as a linguistic authority sans pareil."*

sans peur (son(g) per) FRENCH [without fear] *adjective phrase* without fear, fearless.

sans souci (son(g) soosee) FRENCH [without worry] *adjective phrase* carefree.

saraband (sarăband), **sarabande** FRENCH [from Spanish *zarabanda* (ultimately of oriental origin)] *noun* a stately Spanish court dance in triple time, or music written to accompany it.

sarape *See* SERAPE.

sarcoma (sahrkōmă) GREEK [*sarkoma* fleshy growth, from *sarkoun* to grow flesh] *noun* (*plural* **sarcomas** or **sarcomata,** sahkōmătă) a malignant growth or tumor: *"The doctors examined the sarcoma and decided to operate without delay."*

sarcophagus (sahkofăgăs) GREEK [*sarkophagos* flesh-eating stone (referring to the belief that dead flesh could be consumed by limestone)] *noun* (*plural* **sarcophaguses** or **sarcophagi,** sahkofăgī) a stone coffin or, more generally, a coffin of any kind: *"The sarcophagus of the pharoah was removed, along with other grave goods, later that day."*

sari (sahree), **saree** HINDI [from Sanskrit *sati* strip of cloth] *noun* a traditional Indian dress for women comprising a long piece of cotton, silk or other lightweight cloth wrapped over the shoulder and around the waist: *"The bride wore a richly decorated gold sari, her hair covered by a bright red silk shawl."*

sarong (sărong) MALAY [sheath, quiver] *noun* a skirt or dress comprising a long strip of cloth wrapped around the body (traditionally worn by both men and women of the Malay Archipelago and parts of the Pacific but now more widely worn as beachwear for women).

sarsaparilla (saspărilă, sasăpărilă) SPANISH [from *zarzaparrilla,* from *zarza* bush, bramble and *parilla,* diminutive of *parra* vine] *noun* a soft drink flavored with an extract from the dried roots of a tropical plant of the genus *Smilax.*

sartor resartus (sahrtor resahrtăs) LATIN [the tailor retailored, from the title of the work by Thomas Carlyle (1795–1881) first published in 1833–34] *noun phrase* a person when considered as being molded by the society in which he or she lives.

sashay See CHASSÉ.

Satan (saytăn) HEBREW [adversary] *noun* the Devil, the chief evil spirit in Judaic and Christian religions.

satay (satay) MALAY [from *satai* or *sate*] *noun* (in Indonesian and Malaysian cuisine) a dish comprising pieces of meat grilled on a skewer served with spicy peanut sauce.

satsuma (satsoomă, satsămă) JAPANESE [after the former Japanese province of Satsuma] *noun* a variety of seedless, thin-skinned tangerine, and the tree from which it comes.

saturnalia (satănayleeă, saternaylyă) LATIN [neuter plural of *saturnalis* of Saturn] *noun* the festival of Saturn in ancient Rome and thus, by extension, an unrestrained celebration or orgy: *"They had been so for generations, and it was only gradually that the Cambridge Saturnalia were replaced by the decencies and solemnities of the present sober anniversary"* (Oliver Wendell Holmes, *Over the Teacups,* 1891).

satyagraha (sătyahgrăhă, sătyăgrăhă) SANSKRIT [from *satya* truth and *agraha* persistence] *noun* a policy of passive resistance (often specifically referring to the nonviolent political campaigns of Mahatma Gandhi against British rule in India): *"The policy of satyagraha won the mahatma many reluctant admirers in the West."*

satyr (saytăr) GREEK [from *satyros*] *noun* a race of woodland deities of Greek mythology described as half human and half goat or half horse and as having lascivious natures; may also refer more generally to any lecherous or lascivious male: *"In his private life the great man showed all the gross tastes of a Grecian satyr."*

sauerkraut (<u>sow</u>ărkrowt) GERMAN [from *sauer* sour and *Kraut* greens] *noun* a traditional German dish of finely chopped pickled salted cabbage.

sauna (<u>so</u>nă, <u>sō</u>nă,) FINNISH *noun* a hot steam bath in which steam is produced by pouring water on hot stones: *"By mid-afternoon the heat of the sun had turned the engine shed into a sauna."*

sauté (so<u>tay</u>, sō<u>tay</u>) FRENCH [past participle of *sauter* to jump] *noun* a dish that has been fried quickly in hot fat. ~*adjective* of or relating to food prepared in such a way. ~*verb* to fry food quickly in hot fat.

sauve qui peut (sōv kee pă) FRENCH [save himself whoever can] *noun* a general panic, headlong flight, a disordered stampede, a case of everyone for themselves: *"'Sauve qui peut, is my motto,' continued Mr. Stryker. 'I shall take care of myself; though I have no objection that the rest of the world should profit by my excellent example; they may improve on my model, if they please'"* (Susan Fenimore Cooper, *Elinor Wyllys,* 1846).

savanna (să<u>va</u>nă), **savannah** SPANISH [from *zavana,* from Taino *zabana*] *noun* an extensive treeless plain; may also refer to a tropical or subtropical grassland with scattered trees: *"Purple*

rainclouds piled up toward the west, their shadows spreading across the savanna."

savant (sa<u>von(g</u>), să<u>vant</u>, sa<u>vănt</u>) FRENCH [knowing, present participle of *savoir* to know] *noun* a learned person, a sage, a scholar: *"This thought comes to me as, sitting on a bench near the band-stand, I see an old savant who talks to all the children"* (Robert Service, *Ballads of a Bohemian,* 1920).

savoir faire (savwah <u>fair</u>), **savoir-faire** FRENCH [to know how to do] *noun phrase* assured confidence in social situations, the ability to know how to behave, tact: *"It would be doing injustice to Miss Wardour's savoir faire, to suppose she was not aware that such a question would lead to an answer of no limited length"* (Walter Scott, *The Antiquary,* 1816).

savoir vivre (savwahr <u>veev</u>ră), **savoir-vivre** FRENCH [to know how to live] *noun phrase* knowledge of the ways of the world, sophistication, etiquette.

sayonara (sī<u>yă</u><u>nah</u>ră) JAPANESE [if it be so] *interjection* good-bye, farewell. ~*noun* a good-bye, a farewell.

sc. *See* SCULPSIT.

scagliola (skal<u>yō</u>lă, skal<u>yo</u>lă) ITALIAN [little chip, diminutive of *scaglia* chip of marble] *noun* a variety of imitation marble used for flooring, columns, and other items: *"For the morning sun fell aslant on the great glass globe with gold fish in it, which stood on a scagliola pillar in* front of the ready-spread bachelor breakfast-table, and by the side of this breakfast-table was a group which would have made any room enticing" (George Eliot, Adam Bede, 1859).

scampi (<u>skam</u>pee) ITALIAN [plural of scampo lobster] noun   a large shrimp or number of shrimp (often referring to a dish of shrimp served in a garlic sauce or breadcrumbs).

scenario (să<u>nah</u>reeō) ITALIAN [from Latin scaenarium place for erecting stages, itself from scena stage] noun the plot or synopsis of a play, film, opera, or novel, or more generally any planned or possible sequence of future events: "This latest turn of events suggested a whole new scenario."

schadenfreude (<u>shah</u>dănfroydă), **Schadenfreude** GERMAN [from Schaden damage, harm and Freude joy] noun pleasure derived from the difficulties of others.

schema (skeemă) GREEK [from skhema shape, form] noun (plural **schemas** or **schemata,** skee<u>mă</u>tă, skee<u>mah</u>tă)   an outline, synopsis, plan, diagram, model, or framework of something.

schemozzle   See SHEMOZZLE.

scherzando (skert<u>sand</u>ō) ITALIAN [joking, from scherzare to joke] adverb   (in music) playfully, in a joking manner. ~adjective   playful, sportive. ~noun (plural **scherzandos** or **scherzandi,** skert<u>san</u>dee) a playful piece of music.

scherzo (skertsō) ITALIAN [joke] noun (plural **scherzos** or **scherzi,** <u>skert</u>see)   a lively passage of instrumental music written in a humorous, playful style: "For my misty meditation, at the second changin-station, Suffered sudden dislocation, fled before the tuneless jar Of a Wagner obbligato, scherzo, doublehand staccato" (Rudyard Kipling, "As the Bell Clinks," 1886).

schizophrenia (skitsă<u>free</u>neeă) GREEK [divided mind, from schizein to split and phren mind] noun   a psychotic disorder in which the subject exhibits signs of a split personality.

schlemiel (shlă<u>meel</u>), **shlemiel** YIDDISH [from shlemil, ultimately from the Hebrew name Shelumiel God is my welfare] noun   a fool, a clumsy or unlucky dolt.

schlepp (shlep), **schlep, shlep** YIDDISH [probably from German schleppen to drag] verb   to toil along, to drag, haul, or carry: "The youth shrugged his shoulders and schlepped down the street, scraping up dust with his boots."

schlock (shlok), **shlock** YIDDISH [probably from shlak apoplectic stroke, itself from shlogn to strike] noun   goods or other material of inferior quality. ~adjective poor, trashy, inferior.

schloss (shlos), **Schloss** GERMAN [castle] noun   a castle (usually referring to one in a German-speaking country): "They walked about the streets and the wooded hills, they drove in cabs, they boated on the river, they sipped beer and coffee, afternoons, in the Schloss gardens" (Mark Twain, A Tramp Abroad, 1880).

schmaltz (shmolts), **schmalz, shmaltz** GERMAN [from *Schmalz* rendered fat, lard] *noun* sentimentality (usually referring to excessive sentiment in writing or music): *"The schmaltz that permeated popular music in the immediate postwar period came to an abrupt end with the advent of rock 'n' roll."*

schmatte *See* SHMATTE.

schmooze (shmooz), **shmooze** YIDDISH [from *shmues* chat, itself from Hebrew *shemuoth* news, rumor] *verb* to gossip or chat informally. ~*noun* informal chat or gossip.

schmuck (shmuk), **shmuck** YIDDISH [from *shmok* penis] *noun* a fool, a jerk, a simpleton: *"After this last outburst, all present agreed that the stranger was some schmuck from out of town and that it would be best just to ignore him."*

schnapps (shnaps), **schnaps** GERMAN [from *Schnaps* dram of liquor] *noun* strong Holland gin, or a spirit resembling it.

schnell (shnel) GERMAN [fast, quick] *interjection* quickly! *adverb* fast, quickly.

schnitzel (shnitzăl) GERMAN [shaving, chip, slice] *noun* (in German cuisine)

a seasoned veal cutlet fried in breadcrumbs.

schnorrer (shnorăr) YIDDISH [from German, *Schmurrer* beggar] *noun* a beggar, a scrounger, a parasite.

schnozzle (shnozăl), **shnozzle** YIDDISH [from *shnoits* snout] *noun* a nose. ~*abbreviated form* **schnozz**.

schola cantorum (skōlă kantorăm) LATIN [school of singers] *noun phrase* (*plural* **scholae cantorum**, skōlee kantorăm, skōlay kantorăm,) a singing school, a choir school, or a group of singers; can also refer to the area in which the choir sits in early church buildings.

schtick *See* SHTICK.

schuss (shoos) GERMAN [shot] *noun* (in skiing) a straight downhill run at top speed. ~*verb* to ski down a slope at top speed.

schwarmerei (shvermărī), **schwärmerei** GERMAN [from *schwärmen* to swarm] *noun* excessive sentiment or enthusiasm (often referring to youthful infatuation with someone or something).

Schweinhund (shvīnhănt, shwīnhănt), **schweinhund** GERMAN [pigdog] *noun* swine, pig, bastard (as a term of abuse).

scilicet (skeeliket, sīlăset, silăset) LATIN [surely, from *scire* to know and *licet* it is permitted] *adverb* to wit, namely, that is to say. *~noun* a specifying clause in a document or agreement.

scintilla (sin<u>ti</u>lă) LATIN [spark] *noun* a spark, a trace, a minute particle, a tiny amount: *"Not a scintilla of these was lost on Porthos; and at every one he uttered an exclamation which betrayed to his friend that he had not lost sight of the idea which possessed his brain"* (Alexandre Dumas, *Twenty Years After*, 1845).

scire facias (sīree <u>fay</u>sheeăs) LATIN [you should cause to know] *noun phrase* a judicial writ requiring a party to show why a judgment or other decision should not be enforced against them.

scirocco *See* SIROCCO.

scriptorium (skrip<u>tor</u>eeăm) LATIN [from *scribere* to write] *noun* (*plural* **scriptoriums** or **scriptoria,** skrip<u>tor</u>eeă) a room in a medieval monastery where manuscripts were copied out by scribes, hence any writing room: *"The young scholar was taken to the scriptorium, where he might see the older monks at work on sacred texts."*

sculpsit (<u>skul</u>psit) LATIN [he/she carved it] *verb* he or she carved or engraved it (used to identify the sculptor responsible for a particular work). *~abbreviated form* **sc., sculp., sculps.**

S.D., s.d. *See* SINE DIE.

séance (<u>say</u>ons, say<u>ons</u>) FRENCH [sitting, from *seoir* to sit] *noun* a spiritualist meeting during which sitters attempt to communicate with the spirit world: *"The four of them agreed to hold a séance to attempt to contact the ghost of the notorious pirate."*

sec (sek) FRENCH [dry, ultimately from Latin *siccus* dry] *adjective* (of champagne) moderately dry. *~noun* a moderately dry champagne: *"The butler returned from the cellar with a bottle of sec."*

secretaire (sekră<u>tair</u>) FRENCH [from *sécretaire*, ultimately from Latin *secretum* secret] *noun* a writing desk or bureau with a range of drawers, pigeonholes, and (sometimes) secret compartments in which letters and other documents are kept: *"But his confidential friend and attendant, Monsieur Fiche, proved that the ring had been presented to the said Madame de Belladonna two days before the Marquis's death, as were the bank-notes, jewels, Neapolitan and French bonds, &c., found in his lordship's secretaire and claimed by his heirs from that injured woman"* (William Makepeace Thackeray, *Vanity Fair*, 1847).

secretariat (sekră<u>tair</u>eeat) FRENCH [from *sécretariat* office of secretary, ultimately from Latin *secretarius* confidential officer] *noun* the office of secretary, or the clerical or administrative staff of a large organization (often referring to a government department): *"Orders for the immediate* *evacuation of the village were issued by the secretariat."*

segno (<u>say</u>nyo) ITALIAN [sign] *noun* (*plural* **segnos** or **segni,** <u>say</u>nyee) (in music) a sign indicating the position from which a passage of music is to be repeated.

segue (<u>seg</u>way, <u>say</u>gway) ITALIAN [there follows, from *seguire* to follow] *verb* to proceed from one piece of music to another without a pause: *"The best radio disc jockeys can segue from one record to another with such skill that it is impossible to tell where one song ends and another begins."* ~*noun* an unbroken transition from one piece of music, subject, activity, level, or condition to another.

seicento (say<u>chen</u>to) ITALIAN [six hundred] *noun* the 17th century (usually in relation to Italian arts and culture).

seigneur (sayn<u>yer</u>, sen<u>yer</u>) FRENCH [senior, elder] *noun* a man of rank or authority, a gentleman, an aristocrat (originally referring specifically to the lord of a feudal manor): *"'Will your cousin come south this year, to that beautiful villa of his at Cannes?' . . . 'A grand seigneur combined with a great connoisseur,' opined the other heavily"* (Joseph Conrad, *The Arrow of Gold,* 1919).

semiosis (simee<u>o</u>săs, semee<u>o</u>săs, semī<u>o</u>săs) GREEK [observation of signs, from *semeioun* to observe signs] *noun* the process of signification (variously

applied in language, linguistics, or biology).

semper fidelis (sempăr fi<u>day</u>lis) LATIN [ever faithful] *adjective phrase* always dependable, always trustworthy (motto of the United States Marine Corps). ~*abbreviated form* **semper fi.**

semplice (<u>sem</u>plichay, <u>sem</u>plichee) ITALIAN [from Latin *simplex* simple] *adjective* (in music) simple, plain. ~*adverb* (in music) simply, plainly.

sempre (<u>sem</u>pray) ITALIAN [from Latin *semper* always] *adverb* (in music) always, throughout.

senatus populusque Romanus (senahtăs popyooluskway ro<u>mah</u>năs) LATIN [the senate and Roman people] *noun phrase* the senate and the Roman people (as quoted in official decrees). ~*abbreviated form* **S.P.Q.R.**

senhor (sin<u>yor</u>) PORTUGUESE [superior, lord, from Latin *senex* old] *noun* (*plural* **senhors** or **senhores,** sin<u>yor</u>eezh, sin<u>yor</u>eez) respectful form of address for a man (especially one in a Portuguese-speaking country). ~*abbreviated form* **Snr.**

senhora (sin<u>yor</u>ă) PORTUGUESE [mistress, feminine of *senhor* superior, lord, from Latin *senex* old] *noun* respectful form of address for a married woman (especially one in a Portuguese-speaking country). ~*abbreviated form* **Snra.**

senhorita (seenyăreetă) PORTUGUESE [young lady, diminutive of *senhora* mistress] *noun* respectful form of address for an unmarried woman (especially one in a Portuguese-speaking country). ~*abbreviated form* **Snrta.**

senior (seenyăr) LATIN [older, from *senex* old] *noun* a person of superior rank or standing; may also refer to a senior citizen. Also, term designating a man whose son's name is identical to his. ~*abbreviated form* **Sr.**

senor (saynyor), **señor** SPANISH [lord, master] *noun* (*plural* **senors** or **señores,** saynyorayz) respectful form of address for a man (especially one in a Spanish-speaking country). ~*abbreviated forms* **S., Sñr., Sr.**

senora (saynyor), **señora** SPANISH [lady, feminine of *señor* lord, master] *noun* (*plural* **senoras** or **señoras,** saynyoraz) respectful form of address for a married woman (especially one in a Spanish-speaking country). ~*abbreviated forms* **Sñra., Sra.**

senorita (saynyăreetă), **señorita** SPANISH [young lady, diminutive of *señora* lady] *noun* (*plural* **senoritas** or **señoritas,** saynyăreetăz) respectful form of address for an unmarried woman (especially one in a Spanish-speaking country): "*The senoritas gathered in a tight knot as the guitars struck up for the first dance.*" ~*abbreviated forms* **Sñrta., Srita., SRTA, Srta.**

sensu stricto (sensoo striktō), **stricto sensu** LATIN [in the strict sense] *adverb phrase* strictly, strictly speaking. ~*adjective phrase* in a strict sense.

sententia (sentenshă) LATIN [feeling, opinion, from *sentire* to feel] *noun* (*plural* **sententiae,** sentenshiee) an aphorism, maxim, or saying.

senza (senză) ITALIAN [probably from Latin *absentia* absence] *noun* (in music) without.

sepia (seepeeă) GREEK [cuttlefish, ink] *noun* a faded brown color (reminiscent of the brown color of the ink released by cuttlefish). ~*adjective* of or relating to such a color (often referring to sepia-tinted photographs, drawings etc): "*It reminded me of a sepia painting I had once seen done from the ink of a fossil Belemnite that must have perished and become fossilized millions of years ago*" (H. G. Wells, *The Time Machine,* 1895).

seppuku (sepookoo, sepăkoo) JAPANESE [abdomen-cutting, from *setsu* to cut and *fuku* abdomen] *noun* hara-kiri.

sepsis (sepsis) GREEK [decay, from *sepein* to putrefy] *noun* (*plural* **sepses,** sepseez) blood poisoning, a toxic condition caused by bacterial infection (often referring specifically to setpicemia): "*The surgeon did what little he could, but sepsis had set in and the task appeared hopeless.*"

seq. *See* SEQUITUR.

sequestrator (se̱kwăstraytăr) LATIN [one who receives as a third party, a trustee] *noun* (in law) a person who takes legal possession of another's property and holds it temporarily until a debt is paid or other claims have been met.

sequin (se̱ekwin) FRENCH [from Italian *zecchino*, ultimately from Arabic *sikkah* die, coin] *noun* a small shiny metal or plastic disc used as a decoration for clothing and accessories: *"She came down to dinner in a green dress covered in sequins."*

sequitur (se̱kwiter) LATIN [it follows] *noun* a consequence or logical conclusion. *~abbreviated form* **seq.**

seraglio (săra̱lyō, săra̱hlyō) ITALIAN [from *serraglio* enclosure, ultimately from Turkish *saray* palace, mansion] *noun* a harem, or the palace of a sultan; may also refer to the women of a harem: *"But if not, I will first strangle you—I learned the art from a Polonian heyduck, who had been a slave in the Ottoman seraglio—and then seek out a mode of retreat"* (Walter Scott, *A Legend of Montrose*, 1819).

serape (săra̱hpee, săra̱pee), **sarape** SPANISH [from Mexican Spanish *sarape*] *noun* a brightly colored woolen shawl draped around the shoulders (as worn by men in Central American countries).

seraph (se̱răf) HEBREW [back formation of *seraphim* order of angels] *noun* (*plural* **seraphim,** se̱răfim, se̱răfeem, **seraphs**) a member of the highest order of angels in celestial hierarchies.

serenade (seră̱nayd) FRENCH [from *sérénade* song in the open air, itself from Italian *serenata,* from *sereno* clear, calm] *noun* a song or instrumental composition addressed to a lover or other individual; can also refer to a musical composition written for a small instrumental group. *~verb* to address such a composition to a lover or other individual: *"Each evening the lovers were serenaded by a nightingale singing in the bushes below their balcony."*

seriatim (sireea̱ytăm) LATIN [in a series, from *series* chain, from *serere* to join] *adverb* in a series, serially, in succession, one by one: *"I take two volumes (and no man could do it in less) to examine the theories of all the philosophers in the world, ancient and modern, on the Vital Principle. I take two more (and little enough) to scatter every one of the theories, seriatim, to the winds"* (Wilkie Collins, *After Dark,* 1856). *~adjective* following in a series.

serum (se̱erăm) LATIN [whey] *noun* (*plural* **serums** or **sera,** se̱eră) a watery fluid, such as whey, blood serum, or plant juices: *"Fresh supplies of blood serum were rushed to the hospital when the scale of the emergency became evident."*

serviette (serveȩt) FRENCH [a towel, from *servir* to serve] *noun* a table napkin: *"The table was laid with fine china and crisp white serviettes in silver rings."*

sesquipedalia (seskwăpădaylyă) LATIN [from *sesquipedalis* a foot and a half] *plural noun* long, multisyllabic words.

settecento (seteechentō) ITALIAN [seven hundred] *noun* the 18th century (usually with reference to Italian art and culture of the period).

sforzando (sfortsahndō, sfortsandō) ITALIAN [from *sforzare* to force] *adjective* (in music) forceful, with emphasis. ~*adverb* to be played with special emphasis, forcefully. ~*noun* (*plural* **sforzandos** or **sforzandi,** sfortsahndee, sfortsandee) a note, or sequence of notes intended to be played in such a manner.

sfumato (sfoomahtō) ITALIAN [past participle of *sfumare* to evaporate] *noun* (in painting) a hazy or blurred outline, a gradual shift in tone or color. ~*adjective* painted in a hazy, soft, indistinct manner.

sgraffito (skrafeetō, zgrafeetō) ITALIAN [past participle of *sgraffire* to scratch away] *noun* (*plural* **sgraffiti,** zgrafeetee, skrafeetee) an artistic technique in which an image is created by scratching away a top layer of clay or plaster to expose a different color beneath (usually relating to pottery); may also refer to a piece of pottery decorated in such a manner.

shah (shah) PERSIAN [king] *noun* title formerly borne by the ruler of Iran (originally Persia).

shaikh *See* SHEIKH.

shako (shakō, shaykō) HUNGARIAN [*csákó* peaked, ultimately from German *Zacken* peak, point] *noun* (*plural* **shakos** or **shakoes**) a style of peaked military hat with a high crown plume: *"The captain removed his plumed shako and bowed low to the ladies as they advanced into the room."*

shalom (shahlom, shălom) HEBREW [peace] *interjection* peace (used as a greeting or farewell).

shaman (shahmăn, shaymăn) RUSSIAN [from Tungusian *saman*] *noun* a priest, medicine man, or healer who professes to have communication with the spirit world and to be able to use magic to cure illnesses or foretell the future: *"The old woman rejected the advice of the doctors and instead called in the local shaman."*

shammy *See* CHAMOIS.

shampoo (shampoo) HINDI [from *capo,* imperative of *capna* to press] *noun* a soapy preparation with which the hair (or carpets or other fabrics) can be washed. ~*verb* to wash the hair (or carpets or other fabrics) with soap: *"She says she will stay in tonight and shampoo her hair."*

sharia (sha<u>ree</u>ă), **shari'a, shariat, sheria, sheriat** ARABIC [from *shar'iah* lawfulness] *noun* the body of Islamic law derived from the Koran: *"The new government insisted upon strict observance of the sharia throughout the country."*

sharif (shă<u>reef</u>), **shareef, shereef, sherif** ARABIC [from *sarif* illustrious, noble] *noun* a person who claims descent from Muhammad through his daughter Fatima—thus, by extension, any ruler or other figure of authority in an Arabic country. ~*noun, feminine* **sharifa** (shă<u>reef</u>ă) the wife of a sharif.

shashlik (shahsh<u>lik</u>, shahsh<u>lik</u>), **shashlick, shaslik** RUSSIAN [from *shashlyk,* probably ultimately from Crimean Tatar *šiš* skewer] *noun* (in eastern European and Asian cuisine) a kebab of seasoned mutton.

shebeen (shă<u>been</u>) IRISH [from *síbín* illicit whiskey] *noun* an unlicensed drinking den or other establishment where alcohol is sold illegally: *"Rumor had it that the men met together each night at an illegal shebeen, but the police never found out where it took place."*

sheesh kebab *See* SHISH KEBAB.

shegetz (<u>shā</u>gits) YIDDISH [*sheygets* non-Jewish boy, from Hebrew *sheques* blemish, abomination] *noun* (*plural* **shkotsim,** <u>shkort</u>sim) insulting term for a non-Jewish man or boy, or for a Jewish man or boy who is judged to have lapsed in his religious obligations.

sheikh (sheek, shayk), **sheik, sheykh, shaikh** ARABIC [from *shaykh* old man, chief, ultimately from *šāka* to grow old] *noun* an Arab chief or other figure of authority, such as the head of a family or community.

shekel (<u>shek</u>ăl) HEBREW [from *sheqel,* itself from *saqal* to weigh] *noun* in historical and modern Israel, a coin equivalent to a certain weight of gold or silver, and thus money or riches in general: *"You are a Jew, and of the line of David. It is not possible you can find pleasure in the payment of any tax except the shekel given by ancient custom to Jehovah"* (Lew Wallace, *Ben Hur,* 1880).

shemozzle (shă<u>moz</u>ăl), **schemozzle** YIDDISH [from Hebrew *shellomazzal* bad luck] *noun* a confused muddle or altercation, uproar. ~*verb* to make a hasty retreat, to escape.

sherbet (<u>sher</u>băt), **sherbert** (<u>sher</u>bărt) TURKISH [from Persian *sharbat,* from Arabic *sharbah* drink] *noun* a cold drink made with sweetened fruit juice or effervescent sherbet powder; alternatively, a fruit-flavored ice made with milk, egg white, or gelatin. *See also* SORBET.

sheria, sheriat *See* SHARIA.

sherpa (<u>sher</u>pă) TIBETAN [from *sharpa* inhabitant of an eastern country] *noun* a member of a Nepalese people inhabiting the southern Tibetan Himalayas, long known for their skill as mountain climbers and guides: *"The sherpas get little recognition for risking their lives accompanying international expeditions up Himalayan peaks."*

sherry (<u>sh</u>eree) SPANISH [from *sherris,* itself named after Xeres (now Jerez) in southern Spain] *noun* a fortified blended wine grown in southern Spain.

sheykh *See* SHEIKH.

shiatsu (shee<u>at</u>soo), **shiatzu** JAPANESE [finger pressure, abbreviated form of *shiatsuryoho,* from *shi* finger, *atsu* pressure and *ryoho* treatment] *noun* a type of massage in which specific areas of the body are kneaded with the fingers and palms.

shibboleth (<u>sh</u>ibălăth, <u>sh</u>ibăleth) HEBREW [from *shibbolet* stream, flood] *noun* a catchword or slogan that is associated with a particular group, sect, or class but is generally derided by others as being devoid of meaning, a truism or platitude; can also refer to a custom or usage that is peculiar to a particular group, class, or nationality: *"It was as if she had just awakened to the assurance she was beloved. That was the shibboleth—the cry by which she sounded the closed depths of her love and called to the stricken life of a woman's insatiate vanity"* (Zane Grey, *Call of the Canyon,* 1924).

shiksa (<u>shik</u>să), **shikse** YIDDISH [feminine of *sheygets* non-Jewish boy, from Hebrew *sheqes* blemish, abomination] *noun* insulting term for a non-Jew-

ish woman or girl, or for a Jewish woman or girl who is judged to have lapsed in her religious obligations.

shillelagh (shă<u>lay</u>lee), **shillalah** IRISH [after Shillelagh, Ireland] *noun* a cudgel: *"The constable laid out the last of the troublemakers with a hefty blow of his shillelagh."*

shish kebab (<u>shish</u> kăbahb), **sheesh kebab** TURKISH [from *şişkebabi,* from *şiş* spit and *kebab* roast meat] *noun phrase* (in Turkish cuisine) a dish comprising pieces of marinated meat and vegetables cooked on a skewer.

shivaree *See* CHARIVARI.

shlemiel *See* SCHLEMIEL.

shlep *See* SCHLEPP.

shlock *See* SCHLOCK.

shmaltz *See* SCHMALTZ.

shmatte (<u>shma</u>tă), **schmatte** YIDDISH [from *schmatte,* itself from Polish *szmata* rag] *noun* rag (usually referring to ragged clothing).

shmooze *See* SCHMOOZE.

shmuck *See* SCHMUCK.

shnozzle *See* SCHNOZZLE.

shogun (<u>sho</u>găn) JAPANESE [from *shōgun* general, from Chinese *jiang jun* general] *noun* an hereditary military ruler or warlord in Japan prior to the mid-19th century: *"The shoguns wielded supreme power among their followers but dissipated much of their energy in petty squabbles with their rivals."*

shtick (shtik), **shtik, schtick** YIDDISH [from *shtik* pranks, piece] *noun* a stage routine, gimmick, or gag; can also refer to a person's individual interest or activity.

shtoom (shtăm) YIDDISH [from German *stumm* silent] *adjective* silent, dumb, mute: *"The gang members agreed to keep shtoom if they were questioned by the police."*

shufti (shooftee, shăftee), **shufty** ARABIC [from *sufti* have you seen?, from *safa* to see] *noun* a look, a glance, a peep: *"They decided to have a quick shufti round the building to see if anyone was left inside."*

sibyl (sibăl) GREEK [from *sibulla* prophetess] *noun* a female seer or prophetess of ancient Greece or Rome; subsequently applied more generally to any female fortuneteller, sorceress, or wise person: *"The emperor consulted a sibyl to find out what the future might have in store for him."*

sic (sik) LATIN [so, thus] *adverb* thus, so written, as follows (usually indicating that something unlikely, questionable, or misspelled has been copied exactly from the original).

sic passim (sik pasim) LATIN [thus, so throughout] *adverb phrase* so throughout, the same wherever found (referring to a recurring word or idea in a particular text or other work).

sic semper tyrannis (sik sempăr tīranis) LATIN [thus always to tyrants] *interjection* this is how tyrants end (as quoted by John Wilkes Booth as he assassinated Abraham Lincoln in 1865, and since adopted as the motto of the state of Virginia).

sic transit gloria mundi (sik tranzit gloreeă măndee) LATIN [thus passes away the glory of the world, as quoted by the German religious writer Thomas à Kempis (1380–1471)] *interjection* see how worldly glory and success does not last.

siddha (sidhă) SANSKRIT *noun* (in the Jain religion) a person who has attained a high level of spiritual perfection.

siècle (seeekăl) FRENCH [century, ultimately from Latin *saeculum* generation] *noun* a century, or more generally an age or era: *"With the coronation of the new king began a siècle d'or in French history."*

sieg heil (zeek hīl) **Sieg heil** GERMAN [hail victory] *interjection* hail victory (shout of acclamation adopted by the German Nazi party in the 1930s). ~*noun* such a shout of acclamation: *"The protestors laid siege to the governor's* office, daubing slogans on the walls and soluting him mockingly with sieg heils."

sierra (si<u>e</u>ră, seea<u>ir</u>ă) SPANISH [saw, ultimately from Latin *serra* saw] *noun* a range of mountains, especially one with a jagged, sawlike outline: "*She colored invisibly, with a warmth against which the breeze from the sierra seemed to have lost its cooling power in the sudden melting of the snows*" (Joseph Conrad, *Nostromo,* 1904).

siesta (see<u>e</u>stă) SPANISH [from Latin *sexta hora* sixth hour, noon] *noun* a midday or afternoon nap or short rest, particularly one taken in a hot country: "*He always took a siesta after lunch in the bars of Barcelena.*"

siffleur (si<u>f</u>lăr) FRENCH [whistler, from *siffler* to whistle] *noun* a person who whistles (especially one who entertains publicly by whistling). ~*noun, feminine* **siffleuse** (si<u>f</u>lerz).

signor (seen<u>yor</u>, <u>seen</u>yor) ITALIAN [from *signore,* ultimately from Latin *senior* superior, lord] *noun* (*plural* **signors** or **signori,** seen<u>yor</u>ee) title of respect addressed to a man of superior social standing. ~*abbreviated forms* **S., Sig.**

signora (seen<u>yor</u>ă) ITALIAN [feminine of *signore,* ultimately from Latin *senior* superior, lord] *noun* (*plural* **signoras** or **signore,** seen<u>yor</u>ay) title of respect addressed to a married woman of superior social standing. ~*abbreviated forms* **S., Sig.**

signorina (seenyo<u>reen</u>ă) ITALIAN [young lady, diminutive of *signora,* ultimately from Latin *senior* superior, lord] *noun* (*plural* **signorinas** or **signorine,** seenyo<u>reen</u>ee) title of respect addressed to an unmarried woman of superior social standing.

silhouette (silă<u>wet</u>) FRENCH [after the French controller of finances and author Étienne de Silhouette (1709–67), possibly in reference to the shortlived tenure of his office] *noun* a dark image seen against a lighter background, or the outline of a person or object. ~*verb* to depict someone or something in outline: "*The castle loomed over them, silhouetted against the setting sun.*"

silo (<u>sī</u>lō) SPANISH [from Latin *sirus,* ultimately from Greek *siros* pit] *noun* a cylindrical bin, pit or tower used to store silage, crops, or other material; can also refer to an underground storage silo for guided missiles: "*At noon they drove into her first farmyard, a private village, a white house with no porches save a low and quite dirty stoop at the back, a crimson barn with white trimmings, a glazed brick silo, an ex-carriage-shed, now the garage of a Ford, an unpainted cow-stable . . .*" (Sinclair Lewis, *Main Street,* 1920).

s'il vous plaît (seel voo <u>play</u>) FRENCH [if it pleases you] *adverb phrase* please, if you please. ~*abbreviated form* **S.V.P.**

simile (<u>sim</u>ălee) LATIN [something similar, from the neuter of *similis* like, similar] *noun* a figure of speech in which two otherwise dissimilar things are compared (usually introduced by "as" or "like"): "'As sharp as mustard' and 'as quiet as a mouse' are similes."

simpatico (simpatikō) ITALIAN / SPANISH [sympathetic, ultimately from Latin *sympathia* sympathy, itself from Greek *sumpathes* having a fellow-feeling] *adjective* sympathetic, congenial, agreeable, likable: "*Ray Kennedy used to know about all their little doings, but since his death there was no one whom the Mexicans considered simpatico*" (Willa Cather, *The Song of the Lark*, 1915).

sine (sīn) LATIN [from *sinus* curve] *noun* a trigonometric function equal to the ratio between the length of the side opposite an acute angle in a right-angled triangle and the length of the hypotenuse.

sine anno (sīnay anō) LATIN [without a year] *adverb phrase* undated. ~*abbreviated forms* **S.A., s.a.**

sine causa (sīnay kozǎ, sīnay kowzǎ) LATIN [without cause] *adverb phrase* for no reason.

sine die (sīnay deeay) LATIN [without day] *adverb phrase* indefinitely, without a date being fixed for a future meeting or action: "*The court adjourned sine die.*" ~*adjective* indefinite. ~*abbreviated forms* **S.D., s.d.**

sine prole (sīnay prōlay) LATIN [without offspring] *adverb phrase* without issue, without children: "*He died sine prole.*" ~*abbreviated form* **S.P., s.p.**

sine qua non (sīnay kwah nōn) LATIN [without which not] *noun phrase* something essential, something indispensable: "*Humility is the sine qua non of their religion.*" ~*adjective phrase* essential, indispensable.

sinfonia (sinfōneeǎ, sinfǎneeǎ) ITALIAN [from Latin *symphonia* symphony, instrumental harmony, ultimately from Greek *sumphonos* harmonious] *noun* an overture to a larger musical composition; may also refer to a small-scale symphony or to a small orchestra.

sinfonia concertante (sinfǎneeǎ konsertantay) ITALIAN [symphony in concerto style] *noun phrase* a concerto written for more than one solo instrument.

sinfonietta (sinfǎnyetǎ, sinfōnyetǎ) ITALIAN [diminutive of *sinfonia*, from Latin *symphonia* symphony, instrumental harmony, ultimately from Greek *sumphonos* harmonious] *noun* a relatively small-scale symphony; may also refer to a small symphony orchestra.

singspiel (singspeel, zingshpeel) GERMAN [from *singen* to sing and *Spiel* play] *noun* (*plural* **singspiels** or **singspiele**, singspeelǎ, zingshpeelǎ) a genre of musical entertainment combining songs and comic dialogue that became popular in Germany in the late 18th century.

siren (sīrăn) GREEK [sea nymph, after the Sirein of Greek mythology] *noun* a half female and half bird sea creature traditionally believed to lure sailors to their death by drowning through their beautiful singing and, by extension, any dangerously beautiful or seductive woman; may also refer to any mechanical or electronic device that emits a loud wailing sound as a warning of danger. ~*adjective* enticing, alluring, seductive: *"To many people's surprise the new leader appeared immune to the siren charms of ultimate power."*

sirocco (sărokō), **scirocco** (shărokō) ITALIAN [from Arabic *sharq* east] *noun* a hot dry wind that blows from North Africa into the northern Mediterranean region at certain times of year; may also be used to refer to similar oppressive hot winds in other parts of the world: *"The sirocco came early that year, driving tourists out of the coastal resorts."*

sitzkrieg (sitskreeg), **Sitzkrieg** GERMAN [seat war, sitting war, from *sitzen* to sit and *krieg* war, imitating *blitzkrieg* lightning war] *noun* a war or other confrontational situation in which no actual hostilities are taking place or in which a major conflict is avoided.

si vis pacem, para bellum (see vis pahchem pară belăm) LATIN [if you want peace, prepare for war] *verb*

phrase if you wish for peace, get ready for war.

ski (skee) NORWEGIAN [from Old Norwegian *skith* stick of wood] *noun* one of a pair of narrow strips of wood, metal, or plastic material fastened to the shoes and used to glide over snow or water; may also refer to runners attached to vehicles for similar purposes. ~*verb* to glide over snow or water while wearing skis.

skoal (skōl) DANISH [from *skaal* cup, bowl] *interjection* a drinking toast—health!

slainte (slahntshă) GAELIC [from *slàinte mhór* good health] *interjection* a drinking toast—health!

slalom (slahlăm) NORWEGIAN [from *slalåm* sloping track] *noun* (in skiing) a zigzag downhill course in which competitors must steer through flags or other markers: *"She fell in the downhill event, but took second place in the slalom."* ~*verb* to ski downhill on a zigzag course delineated by flags or other markers.

smorgasbord (smorgăsbord) SWEDISH [from *smörgås* sandwich and *bord* table] *noun* a buffet including a wide variety of hot and cold dishes, such as meat and fish dishes, pickles, cheeses, and salads; by extension, any mixture of diverse elements: *"The committee came up with a compromise, a smorgasbord of initiatives and resolutions."*

smorzando (smort<u>san</u>dō) ITALIAN [present participle of *smorzare* to extinguish] *adverb* (in music) dying away. ~*noun* (*plural* **smorzandos** or **smorzandi,** smort<u>san</u>dee) a passage of music in which the sound dies away.

Snr. *See* SENHOR.

Sñr. *See* SENOR.

Snra. *See* SENHORA.

Sñra. *See* SENORA.

Snrta. *See* SENHORITA.

Sñrta. *See* SENORITA.

sobriquet (<u>sō</u>brikay, <u>sō</u>briket, sōbri<u>kay</u>, sōbri<u>ket</u>), **soubriquet** FRENCH [nickname] *noun* a nickname or epithet: *". . . as he had a rather flighty and dissolute mode of conversing, and furthermore avowed that among his intimate friends he was better known by the sobriquet of 'The Artful Dodger,' Oliver concluded that, being of a dissipated and careless turn, the moral precepts of his benefactor had hitherto been thrown away upon him"* (Charles Dickens, *Oliver Twist*, 1837).

sofa (<u>sō</u>fǎ) ARABIC [from *suffah* long bench] *noun* a long upholstered seat or couch with a back and two arms: *"The dog curled up on the sofa and regarded them both with a baleful eye."*

soi-disant (swah-dee<u>zon(g)</u>) FRENCH [saying oneself] *adjective* so-called, self-styled, supposed, would-be: *"He was too little of an aristocrat to join the club of Royal True Blues, and too little of a democrat to fraternise with an affiliated society of the soi-disant Friends of the People, which the borough had also the happiness of possessing"* (Walter Scott, *The Antiquary*, 1816).

soigné (swahn<u>yay</u>), **soignée** FRENCH [past participle of *soigner* to take care of] *noun* well-groomed, sleek, elegant: *"She was accompanied by a young man in a bottle-green velvet suit, well-spoken and soigné in appearance."*

soiree (swah<u>ray</u>), **soirée** FRENCH [evening period, ultimately from Latin *serus* late] *noun* a party or other social gathering held in the evening: *"My aunt is holding a little soiree on Thursday evening and I promised I would go."*

solarium (sō<u>la</u>reeǎm, sǎ<u>lai</u>reeǎm) LATIN [sun porch] *noun* (*plural* **solariums** or **solaria,** sō<u>la</u>reeǎ, sǎ<u>lai</u>reeǎ) a glass-enclosed porch or other room; may also refer to a room where guests or patients may be exposed to real or artificial sunlight.

solitaire (<u>so</u>litair, soli<u>tair</u>) FRENCH [from Latin *solitarius* solitary, alone] *noun* a card or board game played by a single player; may also refer to a ring or other piece of jewelry set with a single diamond, or to a person who lives a solitary life: *"He selected a magnificent solitaire for his wife and a gold watch for his daughter."*

solo (sōlō) ITALIAN [alone, from Latin *solus*] *noun* a musical composition for a lone voice or instrument or any other kind of performance presented by a single performer. *~adverb* alone: *"He was scheduled to fly solo for the first time the following afternoon." ~adjective* singlehanded, sole, unaccompanied. *~verb* to perform alone.

sombrero (sombrairō) SPANISH [from *sombra* shade] *noun* a wide-brimmed hat traditionally worn in Mexico and other parts of Central America: *"The field workers all wore huge straw sombreros to protect them from the blazing heat."*

sommelier (sămelyay) FRENCH [pack animal driver, ultimately from Latin *sagma* packsaddle] *noun* a wine waiter.

sonata (sănahtă) ITALIAN [that which is sounded, from *sonare* to sound] *noun* an instrumental musical composition for one or two instruments, usually comprising three or four contrasting movements; a musical form that comprises the statement, development, and recapitulation of two or more themes.

sonatina (sonăteenă) ITALIAN [diminutive of *sonata* that which is sounded, from *sonare* to sound] *noun* (*plural* **sonatinas** or **sonatine,** sonăteenee) a small-scale or simplified sonata.

son et lumière (son ay loomyair) FRENCH [sound and light] *noun* an open-air theatrical entertainment comprising a recorded narration with accompanying light and sound effects, usually presented in a historical building or site: *"The history of the town was told in a spectacular son et lumière staged below the castle walls."*

sophomore (sofămor, sofmor) GREEK [possibly from *sophos* wise and *moros* foolish] *noun* a second-year student at a university, college, or secondary school: *"I feel as if I didn't belong anywhere yet. I put in my Freshman and Sophomore years at Redmond two years ago"* (Lucy Maud Montgomery, *Anne of the Island,* 1915).

soprano (săpranō, săprahnō) ITALIAN [from *sopra* above] *noun* (*plural* **sopranos** or **soprani,** săpranee, săprahnee) the highest singing voice in a choir, belonging to boys, women, and castratos; may also refer to a musical instrument with a high range. *~adjective* of or relating to a soprano or a soprano part: *"Despite his unpromising appearance the boy was revealed to have a superb soprano voice."*

sorbet (sorbay, sorbit) FRENCH [ultimately from Turkish *serbet* sherbet] *noun* a fruit-flavored ice (variously served as a dessert or between courses to clear the palate): *"The children finished the meal with lemon sorbets and another round of milkshakes."* See also SHERBET.

sordino (sordeenō) ITALIAN [from *sordo* silent, ultimately from Latin *surdus* deaf, mute] *noun* (*plural* **sordini,** sordeenee) a mute used to change the sound of a musical instrument.

sortie (sortee, sortee) FRENCH [going out, from *sortir* to escape] *noun* a small-scale raid, sally, or foray launched against an enemy (especially one mounted from a defensive position); may also refer more generally to any outing or exploratory trip: "*However, on his second sortie, on the 27th of November, Gideon Spilett, who had ventured a quarter of a mile into the woods, toward the south of the mountain, remarked that Top scented something*" (Jules Verne, *The Mysterious Island,* 1874). ~*verb* to launch an attack upon an enemy.

sostenuto (sostănootō) ITALIAN [past participle of *sostenere* to sustain] *adverb* (in music) sustained, prolonged. ~*adjective* sustained, prolonged. ~*noun* (*plural* **sostenutos** or **sostenuti,** sostănootee) a passage of music in which the notes are sustained or prolonged.

sotto voce (sotō vōchee) ITALIAN [from *sottovoce* under voice] *adverb phrase* under the breath, in an undertone, very softly. ~*adjective phrase* under the breath, in a low voice, silent: "*The attorney made one or two sotto voce observations to his assistant and then stood to address the court.*"

sou (soo) FRENCH [ultimately from Latin *solidus* solid] *noun* a five-centime piece, or more figuratively a tiny

sum of money: "*I wouldn't give you a sou for that old car of yours.*"

soubrette (soobret) FRENCH [from Provençal *soubreto* conceited, from *soubret* coy] *noun* a coquettish young woman or lady's maid (usually referring to such a character in a stage comedy or comic opera): "*Susan appeared after breakfast in the study, her head bound with a kerchief of bright pattern . . . so that she suggested something between a gypsy, a jaunty soubrette, and the fille du regiment*" (Oliver Wendell Holmes, *The Guardian Angel,* 1867).

soubriquet *See* SOBRIQUET.

soufflé (sooflay, sooflay) FRENCH [past participle of *souffler* to blow, to puff up] *noun* (in French cuisine) a sweet or savory dish including egg yolks and beaten egg whites among the ingredients that is baked until it puffs up. ~*adjective* of or relating to such a dish.

soupçon (soopson(g), soopson(g)) FRENCH [suspicion] *noun* a trace, a bit, a tiny amount: "*He accepted her version of events, but later admitted to harboring a soupçon of doubt.*"

sous (soo) FRENCH [under, from Latin *subtus* below, under] *adjective* assistant, subordinate, deputy: "*Preparation of the meal became the responsibility of the sous-chef.*"

souvenir (soovăneeăr, soovăneeăr) FRENCH [to remember, ultimately from Latin *subvenire* to come to mind] *noun* a memento, reminder, keepsake: *"The box was stuffed with postcards, photographs, letters, and various souvenirs of childhood holidays."*

soviet (sōviet, soviet) RUSSIAN [from *sovet* council] *noun* an elected legislative council in a communist country (usually referring to the former Soviet Union); also used more generally to refer to the government and people of the former Soviet Union. ~*adjective* of or relating to a soviet system, or to the Soviet Union itself.

sovkhoz (sovkoz, sovkos), **sovkhos** RUSSIAN [from *sovetskoe khozyaistvo* soviet farm] *noun* (*plural* **sovkhozes** or **sovkhozy,** sovkozee, sovkosee) a state-owned farm in the former Soviet Union (specifically one in which the workers were paid wages).

S.P., s.p. *See* SINE PROLE.

spaghetti (spăgetee) ITALIAN [plural of *spaghetto,* itself from *spago* cord, string, ultimately from Latin *spacus*] *noun* a variety of pasta made in long slender strings and thus, by extension, a dish of such pasta (variously cooked with meats, sauces, and other ingredients).

spécialité de la maison (spesyalitay dă la mayzon(g)), **specialité de la maison** FRENCH [specialty of the house] *noun phrase* the house specialty, a dish presented as the best that a particular restaurant has to offer; may also refer

more generally to any unusual or distinctive thing, quality, or skill: *"Highly illustrated wildlife books are the spécialité de la maison."* ~*abbreviated form* **spécialité.**

specie (speeshee, speesee) LATIN [from *in specie* in kind] *noun* cash, money in the form of coin: *"She was glad to own the bracelet, and enchanted with the effect it produced on her slim wrist; yet, even while admiring it, and rejoicing that it was hers, she had already transmuted it into specie, and reckoned just how far it would go toward the paying of domestic necessities"* (Edith Wharton, *Glimpses of the Moon,* 1922).

specter (spektăr) FRENCH [ghost, from *spectrum* appearance] *noun* a ghost, an apparition; may also refer to anything of an illusory or imaginary nature.

spectrum (spektrăm) LATIN [appearance] *noun* (*plural* **spectrums** or **spectra,** spektră) the band of colors into which light splits when passed through a prism; may also refer to any range or sequence of things, ideas, or interests.

speculum (spekyălăm) LATIN [mirror, from *specere* to look at] *noun* (*plural* **speculums** or **specula,** spekyălă) a mirror, reflector, or other medical instrument used to inspect bodily orifices or canals.

sphinx (sfinks) GREEK [after the Sphinx winged monster of Greek mythology, probably from *sphiggein* to draw tight] noun (*plural* **sphinxes** or **sphinges,** s<u>fin</u>jeez) a winged female monster with a woman's head and a lion's body that was reputed to kill anyone who could not answer the riddle it posed; by extension, may also refer to any puzzling or enigmatic object or person: *"Misery and death, this was certain; beyond that we knew not, and I confess I was very much afraid. But as I realized then, it is useless to question that eternal Sphinx, the future"* (H. Rider Haggard, *Allan Quatermain,* 1887).

spiel (speel, shpeel) GERMAN [from *spielen* to play] *noun* chatter, talk (especially the patter or glib persuasiveness of a salesperson, fraudster, or con artist): *"The old man sighed deeply and abruptly told the salesman to cut the spiel and tell him the price."* ~*verb* to talk persuasively, to deceive through glib talk.

spiritoso (spir<u>ă</u>t<u>ō</u>s<u>ō</u>) ITALIAN [spirited] *noun* (in music) animated, lively.

spirituel (spirich<u>ă</u>w<u>el</u>, spiree<u>twel</u>), **spirituelle** FRENCH [spiritual] *adjective* refined, witty, sprightly, ethereal.

sportif (s<u>por</u>tif) FRENCH [sporting] *adjective* sporty, sports-loving, designed for or suitable for sports or casual wear.

S.P.Q.R. *See* SENATUS POPULUSQUE ROMANUS.

Sprechgesang (<u>shprek</u>gezan(g)) GERMAN [speech song] *noun* (in music) a

style of vocal delivery halfway between speech and song.

spritzer (s<u>pritz</u>ăr) GERMAN [from *spritzen* to splash] *noun* an alcoholic drink comprising white wine and soda water.

spritzig (s<u>pritz</u>ig) GERMAN [from *spritzen* to splash] *adjective* sparkling (referring to wine).

spumante (spoo<u>man</u>tee) ITALIAN [sparkling, abbreviated from *Asti spumante*] *noun* a sparkling white wine made in the Italian province of Asti.

sputnik (s<u>puut</u>nik, s<u>put</u>nik) RUSSIAN [traveling companion] *noun* an artificial satellite (as applied to early Soviet spacecraft): *"With the launch of the first sputniks, the space race was on."*

sputum (s<u>pyoo</u>tăm, s<u>poo</u>tăm) LATIN [neuter past participle of *spuere* to spit] *noun* (*plural* **sputa,** s<u>pyoo</u>tă, s<u>poo</u>tă) spittle, saliva, mucus, and other excretions from the respiratory passages.

Sr. *See* SENOR.

Sra. *See* SENORA.

Srita., SRTA, Srta. *See* SENORITA.

Stabat Mater Dolorosa (stahbat mahtăr dolăr<u>ō</u>să) LATIN [the grieving mother was standing] *noun phrase* the opening words of a hymn on the subject of the Virgin Mary at Christ's cross; may also refer to a musical setting of this hymn. ~*abbreviated form* **Stabat Mater.**

staccato (stăkahtō) ITALIAN [detached, past participle of *staccare* to detach] *adjective* disconnected, disjointed, abrupt, jerky: "*A series of staccato taps on the west window brought Anne flying in from the yard, eyes shining, cheeks faintly flushed with pink, unbraided hair streaming behind her in a torrent of brightness*" (Lucy Maud Montgomery, *Anne of Green Gables,* 1908). ~*adverb* in a disconnected, disjointed manner. ~*noun* a passage of music written to be played in a disconnected, disjointed manner. ~*abbreviated forms* **stac., stacc.**

stadium (staydeeăm) LATIN [from Greek *stadion*] *noun* (*plural* **stadiums** or **stadia,** staydeeă) a large sports arena with tiered seating for spectators: "*The stadium was packed for the big championship game between the two local teams.*"

stalag (stalag) GERMAN [abbreviated from *Stammlager* base camp] *noun* a prison camp (usually referring to such a camp for captured enemy soldiers in Nazi Germany).

stanza (stanză) ITALIAN [abode, room] *noun* a verse of other group of lines from within a longer poem: "*All but the first few opening stanzas of this epic work were lost in a fire a century later.*"

stasis (staysăs, stasăs) GREEK [*histasthai* to stand] *noun* (*plural* **stases,** stayseez, staseez) a static state, a condition of equilibrium or stagnation: "*Events may soon hand young George a victory that eluded old George. But other, more profound things have altered. First, the belief in a new world order that saw an international coalition of forces voyage to the Gulf and a United Nations freed from cold war stasis, sanction action*" (*Guardian,* February 20, 2001).

status (staytăs, statăs) LATIN [standing, rank, from *stare* to stand] *noun* a state or condition of someone or something; can also refer to the standing or rank of a person within a community or before the law, or more generally to a state of affairs: "*The lieutenant delivered his status report as soon as he reached the base.*"

status quo (staytăs kwō, statăs kwō) LATIN [state in which] *noun phrase* an existing state of affairs: "*These events, though alarming, are not expected to alter the status quo.*"

stein (stīn) GERMAN [from *Steingut* stoneware] *noun* a large beer mug (typically one made from earthenware); can also refer to the amount of beer held by such a mug.

stela (steelă), **stele** (steelee) GREEK [*stele* standing stone] *noun* (*plural* **steles** or **stelae,** steelee) a carved or inscribed stone pillar or slab recording the deeds of monarchs or other information about the ancient world (sometimes also serving as a gravestone).

steppe (step) RUSSIAN [from *step*] *noun* an extensive treeless plain (often referring to the grasslands of southeastern Europe and central Asia): "*Snowstorms swept the steppe for days at a time, making travel impossible.*"

stet (stet) LATIN [let it stand, from *stare* to stand] *verb* leave unchanged, do not delete (used as an instruction on corrected manuscripts or other text).

stigma (stigmă) GREEK [*stizein* to tattoo, to prick] *noun* (*plural* **stigmas** or **stigmata,** stigmahtă, stigmătă) a brand, stain, or mark of shame or disgrace; may also refer specifically to the wounds sustained by Christ on the cross: "*They hint that all whales always smell bad. Now how did this odious stigma originate?*" (Herman Melville, *Moby-Dick,* 1851).

stiletto (stăletō) ITALIAN [diminutive of *stylo* stylus, dagger] *noun* (*plural* **stilettos** or **stilettoes** a dagger with a long, slender blade; may also refer to a pointed instrument used to pierce holes in fabric, or to the high, tapering heel of some women's shoes.

stimulus (stimyălăs) LATIN [spur, incentive] *noun* (*plural* **stimuluses** or **stimuli,** stimyălī, stimyălee) a stimulant, an incentive, something that incites, provokes, or arouses: "*It is hoped that*

this investment will prove a stimulus to growth throughout the industry."

stipendium (stīpendeeăm) LATIN [stipend, wages] *noun* (*plural* **stipendiums** or **stipendia,** stīpendeeă) salary, pay: "*The old man is paid a small stipendium to look after the family graves.*"

stirps (sterps) LATIN [stem, stock, lineage] *noun* (*plural* **stirpes,** sterpayz, sterpeez) a branch of a family of plants, animals, or people, or an individual from whom others are descended.

stoic (stōik) GREEK [from *stoikos* of the portico, referring to the Painted Portico at Athens where Zeno taught his pupils] *noun* a person who subscribes to the philosophical view that the individual should be free of all passion and guided by natural law (after the teaching of the Greek philosopher Zeno); may refer more generally to any person who seems unmoved by pain or pleasure. ~*adjective* of or relating to stoic principles: "*The child received the news with stoic indifference.*"

stoop (stoop) DUTCH [from *stoep* step] *noun* a small porch, platform, or veranda at the top of some steps in front of the entrance to a house, townhouse, or apartment building: "*Her parents were waiting for her on the stoop.*"

strabismus (străbizmăs) GREEK [*strabismos* squinting condition, from *strabos* squint-eyed] *noun*   an eye condition in which binocular vision is impaired.

stratum (<u>stray</u>tăm, <u>strat</u>ăm) LATIN [spread, bed, from *sternare* to spread out] *noun* (*plural* **stratums** or **strata,** <u>strah</u>tă, <u>strat</u>ă) a layer or bed of rock, earths, or tissue; also used more generally to refer to any of a series of layers, levels, stages, or gradations.

stretto (<u>stret</u>ō), **stretta** (<u>stret</u>ă) ITALIAN [narrow, close] *noun* (*plural* **strettos** or **stretti,** <u>stret</u>tee)   (in music) a part of a fugue in which voices or subjects overlap; may also refer to the final section of a piece of music, typically played at an increasingly fast pace.

stricto sensu   *See* SENSU STRICTO.

strudel (<u>strood</u>ăl, <u>shtrood</u>ăl) GERMAN [whirlpool] *noun*   a type of pastry comprising thin layers of flaky pastry rolled and baked, with a fruit or cheese filling.

stucco (<u>stă</u>kō) ITALIAN [from Old High German *stukki* crust] *noun* (*plural* **stuccos** or **stuccoes**)   a fine plaster used for decorative architectural moldings, or the moldings themselves; can also refer to a coarse plaster or cement used to coat exterior walls.

stupa (<u>stoo</u>pă) SANSKRIT [from *stūpa*] *noun*   a dome-shaped Buddhist shrine.

stupor (<u>stoo</u>pă, <u>styoo</u>pă) LATIN [stupidity, astonishment, from *stupere*] *noun* a state of dullness, apathy, lethargy, stupefaction, or inability to think: *"Most of the passengers slumped in their seats with expressions of stupor."*

Sturm und Drang (shterm uunt <u>dran(g)</u>) GERMAN [storm and stress, after the title of a play by German playwright Friedrich von Klinger (1752–1831)] *noun phrase*   an 18th-century movement in German literature characterized by strong emotions and the conflict between the individual and society; may also refer more generally to any state of turmoil or emotional turbulence.

stygian (<u>stij</u>ăn) GREEK [from *stygios,* after the River Styx, which was believed to flow through the underworld of Greek mythology] *adjective* of or relating to the River Styx, or, more generally, dark, gloomy, forbidding, hellish: *"In the meanwhile all the shore rang with the trump of bullfrogs, the sturdy spirits of ancient wine-bibbers and wassailers, still unrepentant, trying to sing a catch in their Stygian lake—if the Walden nymphs will pardon the comparison ..."* (Henry David Thoreau, *Walden; or, Life in the Woods,* 1854).

stylus (<u>stī</u>lăs) LATIN [from *stilus* spike, pen] *noun* (*plural* **styluses** or **styli,** <u>stī</u>lī)   an instrument used for writing, marking, or incising; may also refer to the needle used to play vinyl records or to various needle-like cutting implements.

suave (swahv) FRENCH [pleasant, sweet, from Latin *suavis* gentle] *adjective* sophisticated, urbane, gracious, smooth: *"The popular image of the secret agent is a suave young man in sunglasses and a finely tailored suit, but the reality is different."*

subito (s<u>oo</u>bitō) ITALIAN [suddenly, from *subitus* sudden] *adverb* (in music) suddenly, abruptly, quickly.

sub judice (săb y<u>oo</u>dikay, săb j<u>oo</u>dăsee) LATIN [under a judge] *adverb phrase* before the court, currently under consideration by the court (and therefore not to be discussed elsewhere): *"He declined to comment further as the matter was still sub judice."*

subpoena (săbp<u>ee</u>nă) LATIN [from *sub poena* under penalty] *noun* a legal writ requiring a person to appear before a court. ~*verb* to serve a writ on someone requiring them to attend a court.

sub rosa (săb r<u>ō</u>ză) LATIN [under the rose, a reference to the rose as a symbol of the Egyptian god Horus, representing secrecy] *adverb phrase* secretly, in confidence: *"The deliberations of the committee were highly sensitive, and it was understood by all present that their discussions were strictly sub rosa."* ~*adjective* secret, confidential.

sub specie aeternitatis (săb spekee ayternă<u>tah</u>tis) LATIN [under the aspect of eternity] *adverb phrase* in its essential form or nature; viewed in a universal perspective.

substratum (sub<u>stray</u>tăm, sub<u>strat</u>ăm) LATIN [spread underneath, neuter of *substratus*, from *substernere* to spread under] *noun* (*plural* **substratums** or **substrata,** sub<u>stray</u>tă, sub<u>strat</u>ă) an underlying layer or level, a foundation or basis: *"The evening sun seemed to shine more yellowly there than anywhere else this autumn—stretching its rays, as the hours grew later, under the lowest sycamore boughs, and steeping the ground-floor of the dwelling, with its green shutters, in a substratum of radiance which the foliage screened from the upper parts"* (Thomas Hardy, *The Mayor of Casterbridge,* 1886).

sub voce (săb v<u>ō</u>chay) LATIN [under the word] *adverb phrase* under the given word or heading (as used in text references). ~*abbreviated form* **s.v.**

succès de scandale (săksay dă skan<u>dal</u>) FRENCH [success of scandal] *noun phrase* something that becomes a popular success through the notoriety it attracts: *"The writers enjoyed a succès de scandale with their next show, which featured full frontal nudity."*

succès d'estime (săksay de<u>steem</u>) FRENCH [success of esteem] *noun phrase* something that attracts critical praise but fails to win popular favor.

succès fou (săksay <u>foo</u>) FRENCH [mad success] *noun phrase* a huge success.

succubus (săkyăbăs), **succuba** LATIN [from *succubare* to lie under] *noun* (*plural* **succubuses** or **succubi,** săkyăbī, săkyăbee) a demon, particularly one supposed to assume female form in order to seduce men while they sleep: *"The poet went mad in his old age, refusing to sleep for fear that he would be preyed upon by a succubus."*

suede (swayd), **suède** FRENCH [from *gants de Suède* Swedish gloves] *noun* leather with a soft napped surface. ~*adjective* made of suede.

sui generis (sooī jenăris, sooee jenăris) LATIN [of its own kind] *adjective phrase* unique, peculiar, in a class by itself: *". . . as for the Lords o' Session . . . I would have ye ken, for your ain regulation, that to raise scandal anent them, whilk is termed to murmur again them, is a crime sui generis,—sui generis, Mr. Deans—ken ye what that amounts to?"* (Walter Scott, *The Heart of Midlothian*, 1818).

sui juris (sooī jooris, sooee yooris) LATIN [of one's own right] *adjective phrase* of full legal age and capacity, legally responsible for one's own affairs.

suite (sweet) FRENCH [retinue, ultimately from Latin *sequere* to follow] *noun* retinue, the personal staff of a monarch or other dignitary; may also refer to a set or series of rooms, matching furniture, musical compositions, or other things considered as constituting a single unit: *"There were just enough people left in the long suite of rooms to make their progress conspicuous . . ."* (Edith Wharton, *The House of Mirth,* 1905).

sukiyaki (skeeyahkee, sookeeyahkee) JAPANESE [from *suki* slice and *yaki* broil] *noun* (in Japanese cuisine) a dish of fried beef and vegetables cooked in soy sauce and sugar.

sultan (săltan) ARABIC [ruler, power] *noun* title borne by the monarch of a Muslim country. ~*noun, feminine* **sultana** (săltahnă) the wife or other close female relative of a sultan.

summa cum laude (sămă kăm lowdă, sămă kăm lowdee, sămă kuum lordă) LATIN [with highest praise] *adverb phrase* with highest distinction (usually referring to a degree, diploma, or other academic qualification): *"She graduated summa cum laude but had great difficulty finding a job in which she could apply her knowledge."* ~*adjective phrase* with highest distinction.

summum bonum (sămăm bōnăm) LATIN [highest good, as defined by the Roman orator Cicero (106–43 B.C.)] *noun phrase* (*plural* **summa bona,** sămă bōnă) (in philosophy) the supreme good.

sumo (soomō) JAPANESE [from *sumō*] *noun* a Japanese style of wrestling in which two opponents attempt to force each other out of the ring or to the ground.

suppressio veri (săpresheeō <u>vair</u>ī) LATIN [suppression of what is true] *noun phrase (plural* **suppressiones veri,** săpresheeōneez <u>vair</u>ī) (in law) a misrepresentation of the truth, suppression of true facts.

supra (<u>soo</u>pră) LATIN [above, beyond, before] *adverb* above, earlier in the text (used in written documents); can also mean besides or in addition to. ~*adjective* additional, extra.

suprême (soo<u>prem</u>) FRENCH [supreme, ultimately from Latin *superus* upper] *noun* (in French cuisine) a rich cream sauce in which chicken and other meats may be prepared.

supremo (să<u>preem</u>ō, soo<u>preem</u>ō) SPANISH [from *generalissimo supremo* supreme general, from Latin *supremus* uppermost] *noun* a supreme leader or commander in chief, a person who occupies a position of ultimate rank or authority: *"The only person who can make such a decision is the supremo himself."*

sursum corda (sersăm <u>kord</u>ă) LATIN [up hearts, from the opening words of the Eucharistic prayer or a corresponding versicle] *noun phrase* lift up your hearts; also applied more generally to any cry of exhortation or to anything inspiriting.

sushi (<u>soo</u>she) JAPANESE *noun* (in Japanese cuisine) a dish of cold rice and vinegar shaped or rolled into small pieces mixed or topped with raw fish or shellfish, and sometimes wrapped in seaweed.

susurrus (să<u>să</u>răs) LATIN [hum, whisper] *noun* a low murmur, rustling, or whispering (often suggestive of malicious rumors or an undercurrent of discontent): *"This was their rural chapel. Aloft, through the intricate arches / Of its aerial roof, arose the chant of their vespers, / Mingling its notes with the soft susurrus and sighs of the branches"* (Henry W. Longfellow, *Evangeline,* 1847).

suttee (su<u>tee</u>, <u>su</u>tee) SANSKRIT [from *sati* faithful wife, from *sat* good] *noun* the Hindu tradition that a man's wife should willingly throw herself onto the funeral pyre of her husband when he is cremated; may also refer to a woman who immolates herself in this way: *"The family expected that his widow would commit suttee in the time-honored manner, but when the fire was lit she was nowhere to be found."*

suum cuique (sooăm <u>kwee</u>kway) LATIN [to each one's own] *noun phrase* to each his due, to each his own.

s.v. *See* SUB VOCE.

svelte (svelt) ITALIAN [*svelto* plucked, past participle of *svellere* to pluck out] *adjective* slender, lithe, sleek; may also refer to a person who is noted for his or her urbanity or suavity.

S.V.P. *See* S'IL VOUS PLAÎT.

swami (<u>swah</u>mee) HINDI [from Sanskrit *svamin* master, lord] *noun* a Hindu mystic or religious teacher.

swastika (<u>swos</u>tikă) SANSKRIT [from *svasti* well-being] *noun* a form of a cross of ancient origin with all four arms extended at right angles in a clockwise direction (originally a symbol of good luck but now reviled as a symbol of Nazi Germany in the 1930s and 1940s).

symbiosis (simbee<u>ō</u>săs, simb<u>ī</u><u>ō</u>săs) GREEK [*symbioun* to live together] *noun* (*plural* **symbioses,** simbee<u>ō</u>seez, simb<u>ī</u><u>ō</u>seez) a cooperative relationship between two dissimilar organisms (or persons, communities, or organizations) from which both parties gain some advantage: *"The two species benefit from the symbiosis that exist between them—one getting food and the other, protection."*

sympathique (simpa<u>teek</u>) FRENCH [sympathetique] *adjective* agreeable, likeable, suitable (of a person, place, or situation): *"The old lady found her*

nephew very sympathique and promised herself she would leave him some money in her will."

symposium (simp<u>ō</u>zeeăm) GREEK [*symposion,* from *sympinein* to drink together] *noun* (*plural* **symposiums** or **symposia,** simp<u>ō</u>zeeă) a formal meeting or conference during which speeches are made and ideas exchanged on a particular subject or group of subjects; may also refer to a publication comprising a collection of essays or papers on a particular subject.

synopsis (să<u>nop</u>sis) GREEK [comprehensive view, from *synopsesthai* to be going to see together] *noun* (*plural* **synopses,** să<u>nop</u>seez) an abstract, outline, or condensed summary of a narrative, treatise, or plot: *"She sent the publisher a synopsis of her new novel but did not get an immediate reply."*

synthesis (<u>sin</u>thăsis) GREEK [*sytithenai* to put together] *noun* (<u>sin</u>thăseez) the combination or joining together of separate parts or elements into a coherent whole.

t. *See* TEMPORE.

tableau (tablō, tablō) FRENCH [picture] *noun* (*plural* **tableaus** or **tableaux**) a picture or a striking grouping of figures in a picture, on the stage, or elsewhere: *"One of her hands was stretched towards him involuntarily, and it was in that attitude that he long remembered her . . . one hand out-stretched like that of a figure in a tableau. . ."* (Booth Tarkington, *Conquest of Canaan*, 1905).

tableau vivant (tablō veevon(g)) FRENCH [living picture] *noun phrase* (*plural* **tableaux vivants**) a grouping of one or more motionless, posed, silent figures upon a stage (often depicting some scene from literature or legend): *"Young men flocked to see the scandalous tableaux vivants staged there, ogling at nude models arranged in classical scenes."*

table d'hôte (tahbăl dōt) FRENCH [host's table] *noun phrase* (*plural* **tables d'hôte**) a meal of several courses served to guests at a hotel or other eating place at a fixed price (and sometimes also at a fixed time).

taboo (tăboo), **tabu** TONGAN [from *tabu*] *noun* a social convention or other prohibition against saying or doing something (originally because of fear of punishment by the supernatural): *"That evening she decided to break the family taboo against speaking one's mind."* ~*adjective* of or relating to something that is considered forbidden, banned, or socially improper.

tabula rasa (tabyălă rahză, tabyălă rahsă) LATIN [scraped tablet] *noun phrase* (*plural* **tabulae rasae,** tabyălī rahzī, tabyălī rahsī) a tablet from which written symbols have been scraped away and thus, by extension, a blank mind or anything in a pristine state: *"If one once allows the possibility of making all the past a tabula rasa—no property, no family—then labor would organize itself. But you have nothing. . ."* (Leo Tolstoy, *Anna Karenina*, 1874–76).

tacet (tahket, tayset, taset) LATIN [is silent, from *tacere* to be silent] *adverb* (in music) be silent (instruction to a player to remain silent during a particular passage). ~*noun* silence, pause.

tacit (<u>ta</u>sit) LATIN [from *tacitus* silent] *adjective* silent, expressed without words or speech, implied, inferred, understood: *"She seemed to shrink from the tacit condemnation of Rosamond's opinion which such a confidence on her part would have implied."* (Wilkie Collins, "After Dark," 1856).

taco (<u>tah</u>kō) SPANISH *noun* (in Mexican cuisine) a fried tortilla rolled and filled with seasoned meat, cheese, beans, and other ingredients.

taedium vitae (teedeeăm <u>vī</u>tee, tīdeeăm <u>wee</u>tī) LATIN [weariness of life] *noun phrase* weariness of life, loathing of life, suicidal boredom: *"...as Domitian, had wandered through a corridor lined with marble mirrors, looking round with haggard eyes for the reflection of the dagger that was to end his days, and sick with that ennui, that terrible taedium vitae, that comes on those to whom life denies nothing . . ."* (Oscar Wilde, *The Picture of Dorian Gray*, 1890).

tae kwon do (tī <u>kwon</u> dō, tī kwon <u>dō</u>) KOREAN [art of hand and foot fighting, from *t'ae* to trample, *kwon* fist, and *to* way] *noun phrase* a martial art similar to karate (of Korean origin).

tagliatelle (talyă<u>te</u>lay) ITALIAN [from *tagliare* to cut] *noun* fettucine, a variety of pasta shaped into narrow strips.

tai chi (tī <u>chee</u>), **t'ai chi** CHINESE [abbreviated from *tai chi chuan* extreme limit boxing] *noun phrase* ancient Chinese system of meditative exercise.

taiga (<u>tī</u>gă) RUSSIAN [from Mongolian *taiga*] *noun* an area of swampy coniferous forest (usually referring to the area between the steppes and tundra of Siberia): *"The wildlife of the taiga has only recently attracted the attention of documentary filmmakers."*

tallith (<u>tah</u>lăs, <u>ta</u>lăt, <u>ta</u>lăth), **tallis** HEBREW [cover, cloak] *noun* (*plural* **talliths** or **tallithim**) a shawl with fringed corners worn over the shoulders by Jewish men during morning prayers.

Talmud (<u>tah</u>lmăd, <u>ta</u>lmăd) HEBREW [from *talmudh* instruction] *noun* the central texts of Jewish tradition, comprising the Mishnah and the Gemara: *"'But it was written—in the Talmud—that you should involve yourself in the inscrutable and gloomy Fate which it is my mission to accomplish, and which wreathes itself—e'en now—about in temples"* (Charles Dickens, *Martin Chuzzlewit*, 1843).

Tamagotchi (tamă<u>go</u>chee) JAPANESE [lovable egg] *noun* trade name for a type of electronic toy programmed to imitate the demands and behavior of a pet animal.

tamale (tă<u>mah</u>lee) SPANISH [from Mexican Spanish *tamal,* from Nahuatl *tamalli* steamed cornmeal dough] *noun* (in Mexican cuisine) a dish of seasoned ground meat rolled and steamed in cornmeal dough and corn husks.

tandoori (tan<u>door</u>ee) HINDI [from *tandur* tandoor oven] *adjective* (in Indian cuisine) of or relating to a dish cooked over charcoal in a tandoor (a cylindrical clay oven): *"We ate some delicious chicken tandoori, followed by ice cream and coffee."* ~*noun* a dish cooked over charcoal in a tandoor (a cylindrical clay oven).

tango (tan<u>gō</u>) SPANISH [possibly of African origin] *noun* a syncopated Latin American ballroom dance, or music written to accompany it: *"His attempts to dance the tango provoked laughter at the tables."* ~*verb* to perform such a dance.

tant mieux (ton(g) <u>myǎ</u>) FRENCH [so much better] *interjection* so much the better: *"I have bundled together this manuscript, and have added to it a few more verses, written in hospitals. Let it represent me. If I can find a publisher for it, tant mieux. If not, I will print it at my own cost. . ."* (Robert Service, *Ballads of a Bohemian*, 1920).

tanto (tan<u>tō</u>) ITALIAN [so much, from Latin *tantum* so much] *adverb* (in music) so, so much.

tant pis (ton(g) <u>pee</u>) FRENCH [so much worse] interjection so much the worse: *"'Tant pis!' said her Ladyship, 'I hope it may do her good!' Then, in a lower tone, but still loud enough for me to hear, 'I*

noticed her; I am a judge of physiognomy, and in hers I see all the faults of her class'" (Charlotte Brontë, *Jane Eyre*, 1847).

tantra (tan<u>trǎ</u>) SANSKRIT [wrap] *noun* an example of Buddhist or Hindu religious writing (typically on the subjects of mysticism, mediation, or sexual practices).

tao (dow, tow) CHINESE [way, path] *noun* (in Taoist philosophy) the guiding principle of all reality, as evidenced by the processes of nature, and the path of virtuous conduct an individual should follow in order to achieve harmony with the universe.

tapas (<u>ta</u>pas) SPANISH [plural of *tapa* cover] *plural noun* hors d'oeuvres, appetizing snacks (as served with drinks in Spanish bars).

taramasalata (tarǎmasǎ<u>lah</u>tǎ) GREEK [from *taramas* preserved roe and *salata* salad] *noun* (in Greek cuisine) a dish of pink-colored creamy paste made from the smoked roe of gray mullet or cod combined with olive oil, lemon juice, and garlic.

tarantella (tarǎn<u>telǎ</u>), **tarantelle** ITALIAN [after Taranto, Italy] *noun* a lively Italian folk dance traditionally believed to be effective as a cure for the bite of a tarantula spider, or music written to accompany it.

tarboosh (tah<u>boosh</u>), **tarbush**, **tarbouche** ARABIC [from Turkish *tarbus*, itself from Persian *sarpus,* from *sar* head and *pus* cover] *noun* a tasselled red felt hat resembling a fez widely worn by Muslim men (sometimes as part of a turban): *"Then he pushed his way in among the crowd, a veritable beauty of a man in the finest apparel, wearing tarboosh and turban and a long-sleeved robe purfled with gold"* (Richard Burton, *Arabian Nights,* 1885–88).

tarot (tarō) FRENCH [from Italian *tarocchi,* itself of unknown origin] *noun* a set of 78 playing cards used for fortunetelling purposes. ~*adjective* of or relating to tarot cards.

tartine (tahrteen) FRENCH [from *tarte* tart] *noun* a slice of toast served spread with butter or jam.

tastevin (tastăvon(g)) FRENCH [from *tâtevin* wine-taster] *noun* a shallow cup (often silver) used for tasting wines.

tatami (tatahmee) JAPANESE *noun* (*plural* **tatami** or **tatamis**) a straw mat used as a floor covering in Japanese homes.

taverna (tavernă) GREEK [from Latin *taberna* tavern] *noun* a café or bar (especially one in Greece): *"The tavernas were full of drunken soccer fans roaring their club anthems into the night."*

Te Deum (tay dayăm, tee deeăm) LATIN [from *te deum laudamus* thee, God, we praise] *noun phrase* (*plural* **Te Deums**) we praise you God, the opening words of a liturgical hymn of praise to God, and thus the hymn itself or any celebration of thanksgiving.

teepee *See* TEPEE.

telamon (telămăn) GREEK [*telamones,* after the mythological hero Telamon] *noun* (*plural* **telamones,** telămōneez) a male statue used as a supporting column in classical architecture.

telekinesis (telikăneesis, telikīneesis) GREEK [movement at a distance] *noun* the production of motion in objects by spiritual or supernatural rather than physical means: *"Telekinesis seemed to be the only explanation left for the movement of the chair across the room."*

telos (telos, teelos) GREEK [end, probably from *tellein* to accomplish] *noun* (*plural* **teloi**) an ultimate end, aim, or purpose.

temp. *See* TEMPO; TEMPORE.

tempera (tempără) ITALIAN [temper, from *temperare* to temper] *noun* a process of painting using pigment mixed with egg yolk or other mediums rather than oil; may also refer to the pigment itself: *"He bought a fine Renaissance portrait of an Italian matron in tempera."*

tempo (tempō) ITALIAN [time, from Latin *tempus* time] *noun* (*plural* **tempos** or **tempi,** tempee) the pace at which a piece of music is played, or more generally the speed at which anything is done: *"Maggie could look at Stephen . . . and he could even ask her to play his accompaniment for him, since Lucy's fingers were so busy with that bazaar-work; and lecture her on hurrying the tempo, which was certainly Maggie's weak point"* (George Eliot, *The Mill on the Floss*, 1860). ~*abbreviated form* **temp.**

tempore (<u>tem</u>poray) LATIN [in the time of] *preposition* in the time of (referring in chronologies to the reigns of particular monarchs when the exact dates are obscure). ~*abbreviated forms* **t., temp.**

tempus fugit (tempăs <u>fyoo</u>jit, tempăs <u>fyoo</u>zhit) LATIN [time flees] *interjection* time flies, time passes quickly: *"The author of the famous saying Tempus fugit (you understand Latin, of course) was, I take leave to think, an idle man"* (Wilkie Collins, "The Legacy of Cain," 1889).

tenet (<u>ten</u>ăt, <u>teen</u>ăt) LATIN [he holds, from *tenere* to hold] *noun* a belief, opinion, or principle generally accepted as true (usually referring to ideas common to the members of a particular organization or profession): *"Lord Fawn, at Fawn Court, could not do wrong. That was a tenet by which she was obliged to hold fast"* (Anthony Trollope, *The Eustace Diamonds*, 1873).

tenor (<u>ten</u>ăr) LATIN [uninterrupted course, from *tenere* to hold] *noun* the general course, drift, or character of

something; can also refer to a male with the highest natural adult singing voice or to a musical instrument with a range below that of alto: *"The tenor of the conversation changed after the chasm between their philosophical outlooks became apparent."* ~*adjective* of or relating to a tenor voice.

tepee (<u>tee</u>pee), **teepee, tipi** DAKOTA SIOUX [from *ti* to dwell and *pi* used for] *noun* a conical tent of cloth or hides stretched over a frame of poles, a wigwam (as used by American Plains Indians): *"The chief received his guests in his tepee, surrounded by his most trusted advisers."*

tequila (tăk<u>ee</u>lă) SPANISH [after Tequila, Mexico] *noun* an Mexican liquor distilled from the fermented mash of agave.

terminus (<u>ter</u>mină̆s) LATIN [boundary, end] *noun* (*plural* **terminuses** or **termini,** term<u>in</u>ī, term<u>in</u>ee) an ultimate goal or destination (often a station or other finishing point of a travel route); may also refer to the tip or extremity of something: *"This was the terminus of the 'Cape Cod Railroad,' though it is but the beginning of the Cape"* (Henry David Thoreau, *Cape Cod*, 1865).

terminus ad quem (termină̆s ad <u>kwem</u>) LATIN [end to which] *noun phrase* a destination, purpose, or goal; may also refer to a deadline or other finishing point.

terminus ante quem (terminăs antee kwem) LATIN [end before which] *noun phrase* the finishing point of a period, the latest possible date that something could have happened.

terminus a quo (terminăs ah kwō) LATIN [end from which] *noun phrase* a point of origin, a starting point.

terminus post quem (terminăs pōst kwem) LATIN [end after which] *noun phrase* the earliest possible date that something could have happened, the earliest possible start of a period.

terpsichorean (terpsikăreeăn, terpsikoreeăn) GREEK [after Terpsichore, the Greek muse of dancing and choral song] *adjective* of or related to dancing: "*Young children spent many hours being trained in music and the terpsichorean arts.*"

terra alba (teră albă) LATIN [white earth] *noun phrase* white pulverized gypsum (as used in various manufacturing processes); may also refer to pipeclay, kaolin, magnesia, and other substances.

terracotta (terăkotă) ITALIAN [from *terra cotta* baked earth] *noun* a fired reddish glazed or unglazed clay used for earthenware, or an item of pottery or decorative ware made from such material. ~*adjective* of or relating to terracotta material, or reddish-brown in color: "*The tree grew in a vast terracotta pot decorated with classical figures.*"

terra firma (teră fermă) LATIN [solid land] *noun phrase* dry land, firm ground: "*The sailors were glad to reach terra firma at last.*"

terra incognita (teră inkogneetă, teră inkognătă) LATIN [unknown land] *noun phrase* (*plural* **terrae incognitae,** terī inkogneetī) unknown territory, an unexplored field of study or knowledge: "*From this point on the researchers were in terra incognita.*"

terra nova (teră nōvă) LATIN [new land] *noun phrase* new land, newly reclaimed land.

terrazzo (tăratzō, tăratsō) ITALIAN [terrace, balcony] *noun* (*plural* **terrazzi,** tăratzee, tăratsee) a polished mosaic floor made with chips of marble or granite set in mortar.

terrine (tăreen, tereen) FRENCH [earthenware pot, from Old French *terrin* earthen, from Latin *terra* earth] *noun* a tureen or earthenware dish in which food is prepared; can also refer to a mixture of meat, fish, or vegetables cooked or served in a terrine: "*They were served a cold salmon terrine for their first course.*"

tertium quid (tersheeăm kwid, terteeăm kwid) LATIN [a third something, from Greek *triton ti* some third thing] *noun phrase* a middle course between two choices, something intermediate between two things, a third party: "*For these reasons, and for* *others which need not appear, I decline to state positively whether there was anything irretrievably wrong in the relations between the Man's Wife and the Tertium Quid"* (Rudyard Kipling, "At the Pit's Mouth," 1888).

terza rima (tertsă <u>ree</u>mă) ITALIAN [third rhyme] *noun phrase* a verse form comprising rhyming triplets of iambic pentameters (the middle line of each triplet rhyming with the first and third lines of the following triplet): *"As a poet he was unsurpassed as a master of epic verse, most of which was composed in terza rima."*

tessera (<u>te</u>sără) LATIN [probably from Greek *tessares* four (a reference to the four corners of tablets or tiles)] *noun* (*plural* **tesserae,** <u>te</u>săree, <u>te</u>sărī) a small tablet, tile, or block (as used in mosaic work or, in ancient Rome, for tickets and tallies): *"After arranging the watches, he ordered the tessera to be given to the rest of the troops; when the bugle sounded for the second watch they were to muster round him in silence"* (Livy, *History of Rome,* first century B.C.).

testimonium (testă<u>mō</u>neeăm) LATIN [evidence, testimony] *noun* (*plural* **testimoniums** or **testimonia,** testă<u>mō</u>neeă) (in law) a concluding clause of a document detailing the manner of its execution; may also refer more generally to any official certificate or to a letter supporting the suitability of an individual for holy orders.

tête-à-tête (tayt ă <u>tayt</u>, tet ă <u>tet</u>) FRENCH [head to head] *noun* a private conversation between two parties: *"As the girl's father, he felt it was time he had a tête-à-tête with his daughter's close friend."* ~*adjective* face-to-face. ~*adverb* privately, face-to-face.

tetragrammaton (tetră<u>gra</u>mătăn) GREEK [four letters, neuter of *tetragrammatos* having four letters] *noun* the four Hebrew letters (YHWH or JHVH) used to represent the name of God.

T.G.V. *See* TRAIN À GRANDE VITESSE.

theatrum mundi (theeatrăm <u>măn</u>dee) LATIN [theater of the world] *noun phrase* the representation of life as a theatrical entertainment, the theater as a mirror of the world.

thé dansant (tay don<u>son</u>(g)) FRENCH [dancing tea] *noun phrase* (*plural* **thés dansants**) a tea dance.

thesaurus (thă<u>so</u>răs) LATIN [treasury, store, collection, from Greek *thesauros*] *noun* (*plural* **thesauruses** or **thesauri,** thă<u>so</u>rī, thă<u>so</u>ree) a type of dictionary that lists words and their synonyms (and, sometimes, antonyms); may also refer to a classified list of terms or keywords relating to a particular subject: *"Each student will be expected to buy a good dictionary and a thesaurus."*

thesis (<u>thee</u>săs) GREEK [act of laying down] *noun* (*plural* **theses,** <u>thee</u>seez) a position or proposition advanced for discussion and proof (often in the form of a dissertation or essay based on research by the author): *"Those who heard him read his Thesis at the Medical Commencement will not soon forget the impression made by his fine personal appearance and manners, nor the universal interest excited in the audience..."* (Oliver Wendell Holmes, *Elsie Venner*, 1859–60).

thespian (<u>thes</u>peeăn) GREEK [after Thespis, the earliest recognized actor in Greek classical theater] *noun* an actor: *"Vergil Gunch thundered, 'When we manage to grab this celebrated Thespian off his lovely aggregation of beautiful actresses—and I got to admit I butted right into his dressing-room and told him how the Boosters appreciated the high-class artistic performance he's giving us. . .'* (Sinclair Lewis, *Babbitt*, 1922). ~*adjective* of or relating to the theater.

threnos (<u>three</u>nos) GREEK [funeral lament] *noun* (*plural* **threnoi,** <u>three</u>noi) a song of lamentation, an elegy, or threnody.

thug (thug) HINDI [from *thag* thief] *noun* a gangster, a hoodlum, a ruffian: *"The bar owner worried that he would be visited by thugs if he did not pay the protection money demanded."*

tiara (tee<u>ah</u>ră) GREEK [crown] *noun* a decorative (often expensively bejewelled) headband worn by women: *"She lifted her hand to the tiara of bright jewels radiant on her head, and, plucking it off with a force that dragged and strained her rich black hair with heedless cruelty, and brought it tumbling wildly on her shoulders, cast the gems upon the ground"* (Charles Dickens, *Dombey and Son*, 1846–48).

tic (tik) FRENCH [from Italian *ticchio*] *noun* an involuntary facial twitch or mannerism; may also be used more generally of any unconscious quirk of language or behavior: *"The suspect was described as tall and thin, with a shock of red hair and a pronounced tic."*

tic douloureux (tik doolă<u>roo</u>, tik doolă<u>ră</u>) FRENCH [painful tic] *noun phrase* a painful spasm (especially of the facial muscles), trigeminal neuralgia: *"Mr. Weller communicated this secret with great glee, and winked so indefatigably after doing so, that Sam began to think he must have got the tic douloureux in his right eyelid"* (Charles Dickens, *Pickwick Papers*, 1836).

tika (<u>tee</u>kă, <u>ti</u>kă) HINDI [from Hindi *tika* or Panjabi *tikka*] *noun* a mark on the forehead (especially of a woman) identifying a Hindu's caste or social status.

tikka (<u>ti</u>kă, <u>tee</u>kă) PANJABI *noun* (in Indian cuisine) a dish of spiced meat or vegetables cooked on a skewer.

tilak (<u>tee</u>lăk) SANSKRIT [from *tilaka*] *noun* a mark on the forehead identifying a Hindu's caste or social status.

tilde (<u>til</u>dă) SPANISH [from Latin *titulus* title] *noun* the diacritical mark (as on ñ) used in certain languages such as Spanish and Portuguese to indicate a palatal nasal sound or nasalization.

timbre (<u>tam</u>băr, <u>tam</u>bră), **timber** FRENCH [bell struck by a hammer, from Greek *tymbanon* kettledrum] *noun* the resonance, tone, or other qualities or characteristics of a particular sound, voice, or instrument: *"There was an interval of a second or two between each word, and a sort of 'ring, ring, ring,' in the note of the voice, like the timbre of a bell"* (Rudyard Kipling, "In the House of Suddhoo," 1888).

timpani (<u>tim</u>pănee) ITALIAN [plural of *timpano* kettledrum] *plural noun* a set of kettledrums.

tinnitus (<u>tin</u>ităs) LATIN [ringing, from *tinnire* to ring] *noun* a medical condition resulting in a continuous ringing in the ears.

tipi *See* TEPEE.

tirade (<u>ti</u>rayd, ti<u>rayd</u>) FRENCH [shot, from Italian *tirare* to draw, to shoot] *noun* a prolonged outburst of denunciation (usually referring to haranguing, vehement speech, typically one full of insults and invective): *"I stared at her. How provoking she was! So I went on to finish my tirade"* (Joseph Conrad, *Chance*, 1914).

tirailleur (tir<u>i</u><u>yer</u>) FRENCH [from *tirailler* to fire in skirmishing order] *noun* a sharpshooter or skirmisher (usually referring to such troops in the French army during the Napoleonic Wars): *"A line of French tirailleurs approached the British positions from the south but were easily beaten off."*

tiramisu (tiră<u>meesoo</u>, tirămi<u>zoo</u>) ITALIAN [from *tira mi su* pull me up] *noun* (in Italian cuisine) a dessert dish made with ladyfingers, mascarpone cheese, powdered chocolate, and espresso.

tiro *See* TYRO.

tisane (ti<u>zan</u>) FRENCH [ultimately from Greek *ptisane* crushed barley] *noun* an infusion of dried herbs or other ingredients used to make herbal teas or other drinks (often consumed for their supposed medicinal qualities).

toccata (tă<u>kah</u>tă) ITALIAN [touched, from *toccare* to touch] *noun* a virtuoso musical composition for organ and harpsichord (or other keyboard instruments): *"On the balcony, late in the evening, while the others were listening indoors to the low modulations of a young composer who had embroidered his fancies on Browning's 'Toccata,' Susy found her chance"* (Edith Wharton, *Glimpses of the Moon*, 1922).

tofu (<u>to</u>foo) JAPANESE [from Chinese *doufu,* from *dou* beans and *fu* rot, turn sour] *noun* bean curd.

toga (<u>to</u>gă) LATIN [gown, garment] *noun* a loose wrap or gown (of a type worn originally by citizens in ancient Rome): *"They unearthed the statue of a Roman patrician, complete with flowing toga."*

toilette (twah<u>let</u>) FRENCH [diminutive of *toile* cloth] *noun* the process of dressing and grooming; may also refer to a particular costume or style of dress: *"The old lady insisted upon finishing her toilette before going downstairs to be interviewed by the detectives."*

tokamak (tō<u>kă</u>mak), **tokomak** RUSSIAN [from *toroidal'naya kamera s aksial'nym magnitnym polem* toroidal chamber with an axial magnetic field] *noun* a toroidal device for producing controlled nuclear fusion.

tombola (tom<u>bō</u>lă) ITALIAN [*tombolare* to tumble, to turn a somersault] *noun* a lottery drum from which winning tickets are drawn.

ton *See* HAUT TON.

tonneau (ton<u>ō</u>, tun<u>ō</u>) FRENCH [barrel, cask] *noun* (*plural* **tonneaus** or **tonneaux**) the seating compartment of an automobile (or the rear area of such a compartment); may also refer to the removable hood of a convertible automobile: *"Her eyes, shining under a white veil, met his for just the instant before she was quite by, and when the machine had passed a little handkerchief waved for a moment from the side of the tonneau where she sat"* (Booth Tarkington, *His Own People,* 1907).

tontine (<u>ton</u>teen) FRENCH [after Italian banker Lorenzo Tonti (1635–95)] *noun* a financial arrangement in which investors contribute equally to a common fund to be inherited by the sole survivor of the group.

topee (tō<u>pee</u>, <u>tō</u>pee), **topi** HINDI [hat] *noun* a pith helmet: *"Several men wore sunhats or topees to protect themselves from the glare."*

toque (tōk) FRENCH [soft hat, from Spanish *toca* headdress or Portuguese *tocca* cap] *noun* a style of soft, brimless hat for women: *"The pale blue haze of an autumn day crept between the tree-trunks of the Park and made a background for the gray dress, the black velvet toque above the black hair, and the resolute profile"* (Rudyard Kipling, *The Light That Failed,* 1890). May also refer to the tall, brimless hats traditionally worn by chefs.

Torah (<u>tor</u>ă) HEBREW [instruction, teaching] *noun* the five books of the Pentateuch; the sacred texts and rabbinical interpretation of Jewish religious law and wisdom.

torchère (tor<u>shair</u>) FRENCH [from *torche* torch] *noun* a tall ornamental stand for a candlestick.

toreador (<u>to</u>reeădor) SPANISH [from *torear* to fight bulls, from *toro* bull] *noun* a bullfighter: *"Her new lover arrived at the party in the dress of a Spanish toreador."*

torque (tork) FRENCH [from Latin *torquere* to twist] *noun* a twisting or turning force: *"This machine measures the amount of torque put on an aircraft's wing."* ~*verb* to twist or cause to twist.

torso (<u>tor</u>sō) ITALIAN [stock, stalk, from Latin *thyrsus* stalk] *noun* (*plural* **torsos** or **torsi,** <u>tor</u>see) the trunk of the human body (excluding the head and limbs); may also refer to anything incomplete or mutilated: *"The police announced the discovery of a human torso in the river and requested information from possible witnesses."*

torte (<u>tor</u>tă, tort) GERMAN [tart, pastry, probably from Italian *torta* cake] *noun* (*plural* **tortes** or **torten,** <u>tor</u>tăn) a frosted cake or tart made with eggs, nuts, or dry breadcrumbs.

tortellini (tortă<u>lee</u>nee) ITALIAN [plural of *tortellino* small cake, from *torta* cake] *plural noun* a variety of pasta shaped into small squares, rolled into rings, and filled with meat or cheese.

tortilla (tor<u>tee</u>yă) SPANISH [diminutive of *torta* cake] *noun* (in Mexican cookery) a round, thin cake made with unleavened cornmeal or wheat flour bread, usually filled with meat, cheese, or beans.

totem (<u>tō</u>tăm) ALGONQUIAN [from *ototeman* his totem] *noun* an object venerated as the emblem of a family, clan, or tribe (or a carved or painted depiction of such an object): *"Kim, with slightly raised head, was still staring at his totem on the table, when the chaplain stepped on his right shoulder-blade"* (Rudyard Kipling, *Kim,* 1901).

toties quoties (tōteeayz <u>kwō</u>teeayz) LATIN [so often as often] *adverb phrase* as often as, repeatedly, as occasion demands.

toto caelo (tōtō <u>sī</u>lō) LATIN [by the whole heaven] *adverb phrase* in an entirely different fashion, utterly.

touché (too<u>shay</u>) FRENCH [touched, past participle of *toucher* to touch] *interjection* good thrust! (acknowledgment of a hit in fencing and, by extension, of any success, accusation, witticism, or rejoinder).

toupee (too<u>pay</u>) FRENCH [from *toupet* forelock] *noun* a wig or other hairpiece worn to conceal a bald patch: *"The wind dislodged the old man's toupee, giving him a comic air."*

tour de force (toor dă <u>fors</u>) FRENCH [feat of strength] *noun phrase* (*plural* **tours de force**) a remarkable performance or feat of skill, ingenuity, or strength: *"The following year he delivered a tour de force in the role of Hamlet."*

tournedos (ternă<u>dō</u>) FRENCH [from *tourner* to turn and *dos* back] *noun* a small fillet of beef cut from the tenderloin.

tourniquet (ternăket) FRENCH [turnstile, from *tourner* to turn] *noun* a bandage or other device applied to a limb to check blood flow: *"The nurse tied a tourniquet around the girl's arm to stop the bleeding."*

tout de suite (toot <u>sweet</u>) FRENCH [all in succession, immediately] *adverb phrase* immediately, at once, now, right away: *"'I want someone over here tout de suite,' he roared, before slamming the phone down."*

tout ensemble (toot on(g)<u>som</u>blă) FRENCH [everything together] *noun phrase* the overall effect, the whole thing (referring to a work of art, for example).

tout le monde (too lă <u>mond</u>) FRENCH [all the world] *noun phrase* all the world, everybody.

tragedienne (trăjeedee<u>en</u>) FRENCH [from *tragédienne* actress in tragedy] *noun* an actress who plays roles in tragic drama: *"As a tragedienne she has few equals on the modern stage."*

trahison des clercs (trayzon(g) day <u>clairk</u>) FRENCH [treachery of the clerks, from the book *La Trahison des Clercs* (1927) by Julien Benda] *noun phrase* the treason of intellectuals (through the betrayal or compromise of academic standards, for political or other motives).

train à grande vitesse (tran(g) a grond vee<u>tes</u>) FRENCH [high speed train] *noun phrase* a high speed train in France. ~*abbreviated from* **T.G.V.**

trait (trayt) FRENCH [act of drawing] *noun* a distinguishing quality, mannerism, peculiarity: *"His jealousy of his wife is not his most endearing trait."*

tranche (tronch) FRENCH [slice, from *trancher* to cut] *noun* a portion or installment of something (usually relating to finance); can also refer to a block of shares or bonds: *"The payment will be made in three tranches."*

tranche de vie (tronch dă <u>vee</u>) FRENCH [slice of life] *noun phrase* a representation of real life (usually relating to literature or art).

trattoria (trată<u>ree</u>ă) ITALIAN [from *trattore* restaurateur, from *traiter* to treat] *noun* (*plural* **trattorias** or **trattorie,** trată<u>ree</u>ay) a restaurant (especially an Italian-style restaurant): *"They spent each evening of their vacation at the local trattoria."*

trauma (<u>trow</u>mă, tromă) GREEK [wound] *noun* (*plural* **traumas** or **traumata,** <u>trow</u>mătă) a physical wound or injury; may also refer to a state of mental disorder resulting from emotional or physical stress: *"This childhood trauma continued to haunt her in adult life."*

trecento (tray<u>chen</u>tō) ITALIAN [three hundred] *noun* the 14th century (especially in relation to Italian culture of the period).

trek (trek) AFRIKAANS [from Dutch *trekken* to pull, to haul] *noun* a journey, trip, or migration (originally a journey undertaken by ox wagon). ~*verb* to undertake an arduous journey (originally by ox wagon), to migrate: *"They trekked for miles through the jungle before they found the crash site."*

tremolo (tremălō) ITALIAN [tremulous, from Latin *tremere* to tremble] *noun* (in music) vibrato, a tremulous or vibrating effect produced by a musical instrument or voice.

très (tray) FRENCH [very] *adverb* too much, very. ~*adjective* very: *"Her outfit was judged très chic by those who ought to know."*

triage (treeahzh, treeahzh) FRENCH [sorting, sifting, from *trier* to sort out] *noun* the sorting of patients into three categories on arrival at a hospital or emergency aid station according to the nature and severity of their injury or illness; may also be applied to the sorting and prioritization of projects, commodities, and so on.

tricorne (trīkorn), **tricorn** FRENCH [three-cornered] *noun* a three-cornered hat, a cocked hat. ~*adjective* of or relating to such a hat.

tricot (treekō, trīkăt) FRENCH [from *tricoter* to knit] *noun* a fine warp-knitted fabric used in clothing, or a form of twilled cloth made from wool or wool and cotton.

trio (treeō) ITALIAN [from *tre* three] *noun* a set of three objects or people; may also refer to a musical composition written for three voices or instruments: *"The three men decided to form a trio, playing jazz in clubs all along the west coast."*

triptych (triptik), **triptyque** GREEK [from *triptychos* having three folds] *noun* a picture painted on three folding panels and, by extension, anything comprising three parts: *"The painting comprises a triptych, painted on three huge wooden panels."*

triskaidekaphobia (triskădekăfōbeeă) GREEK [*treiskaideka* thirteen and *phobos* fear] *noun* fear of the number thirteen.

triste (treest) FRENCH [sad, from Latin *tristis* sad] *adjective* sad, melancholy, mournful, miserable, wistful, dull.

tristesse (treestes) FRENCH [sadness, sorrow] *noun* sadness, sorrow, melancholy, unhappiness.

triumvir (trīămver) LATIN [from *trium virum* of three men] *noun* (*plural* **triumvirs** or **triumviri,** trīămverī, trīămveree) a member of a commission or ruling body of three (i.e., a triumvirate).

trivia (triveeă) LATIN [plural of *trivium* place where three roads meet, influenced by *trivialis* trivial, commonplace, vulgar] *plural noun* unimportant details or facts, trifles: *"The book unearthed a lot of trivia about the great man's private life but little about his real character."*

troika (troikă) RUSSIAN [group of three, from *troe* three] *noun* a Russian carriage or vehicle drawn by three horses abreast; by extension, any group of three people or things (especially a ruling body comprising three people): *"The prime minister, the defense minister, and the war minister formed a troika, effectively running the country without reference to others."*

trompe l'oeil (tromp loi, tromp loiee) FRENCH [deceive the eye] *noun phrase* a technique in visual art by means of which a viewer is tricked into thinking what is painted is real; an optical illusion: *"The staircase had been decorated with a trompe l'oeil view designed to deceive a visitor into thinking he was entering a vast temple."* ~*adjective* of or relating to such an effect.

troppo (tropō) ITALIAN [too much] *adverb* (in music) too much.

trottoir (trotwah) FRENCH [from *trotter* to trot] *noun* a sidewalk, a pavement.

troubador (troobădor) FRENCH [composer, from *trobar* to compose] *noun* an itinerant poet or musician of a class who wandered parts of France and northern Italy in the medieval period, celebrating chivalry and courtly love, and, by extension, any poet or musician.

troupe (troop) FRENCH [company, herd, band] *noun* a company, group, troop (of performers): *"She joined a troupe of traveling actors and, despite her young age, was allowed the occasional solo spot."* ~*verb* to gather or travel in a group.

trousseau (troosō, troosō) FRENCH [outfit, diminutive of *trousse* bundle] *noun* (*plural* **trousseaus** or **trousseaux**) the clothes, linen, household goods, and other possessions of a bride at the time she gets married: *"Her trousseau included a lot of kitchenware and other practical items."*

tsar *See* CZAR.

tsunami (soonahmee) JAPANESE [harbor wave, from *tsu* harbor and *nami* wave] *noun* (*plural* **tsunami** or **tsunamis**) a tidal wave (the result of an earthquake of volcanic eruption): *"People living along the coast had little chance to escape the terrifying tsunami that surged in from the ocean."*

tumulus (toomyălăs, tyoomyălăs) LATIN [from *tumere* to swell] *noun* (*plural* **tumuli,** toomyălī, toomyălee, tyoomyălī, tyoomyălee) an artificial hillock or mound (often marking the site of an ancient grave or barrow):

"*Archaeologists opened the tumulus but found little evidence of anything pre-Roman.*"

tundra (tă̱ndră) RUSSIAN [marshy plain] *noun*   a cold, treeless plain with a marshy surface over permafrost, typical of arctic and subarctic regions or to mountain areas above the treeline: "*Special skills are needed to survive in the tundra for more than a few days.*"

tu quoque (too kwōkee, tyoo kwōkee) LATIN [you too] *noun phrase* (*plural* **tu quoques**)   you too (a retort redirecting a charge or criticism at the person who made it).

tutor (tootăr, tyootăr) LATIN [protector] *noun*   a person who acts as instructor, guide, or teacher to another. ~*verb* to instruct, guide, or teach another: "*He was a great performer and had been tutored by the best in the business.*"

tutti (tootee) ITALIAN [all] *adverb*   (in music) all together. ~*adjective* all together.

tutu (tootoo) FRENCH [from *cucu* backside, diminutive of *cul* buttocks] *noun*   a short skirt with stiffened frills of a type worn by ballet dancers.

tycoon (tīkoon) JAPANESE [from *taikun* great lord, prince, from Chinese *da* great and *jun* prince] *noun*   a wealthy businessman or magnate (originally a shogun of imperial Japan): "*We were told that her uncle is a tycoon somewhere out east.*"

typhoon (tīfoon) PORTUGUESE [from *tufão,* possibly from Greek *tuphon* violent storm, influenced by Chinese *tai fung* big wind] *noun*   a tropical cyclone or whirlwind: "*Three ships were lost in a typhoon that struck the islands three days later.*"

tyro (tīrō), **tiro** LATIN [from *tiro* young soldier] *noun*   a novice, a beginner.

tzigane (seegahn) HUNGARIAN [*czigány*] *noun*   a Hungarian Gypsy, a Romany. ~*adjective* of or relating to Hungarian Gypsies or Gypsy culture (especially Gypsy music).

u

über alles (oobăr <u>a</u>lez) GERMAN [above all] *adverb phrase* over everything else, above all else (usually associated with the former German national anthem, first verse: *"Deutschland über alles"*).

Übermensch (<u>oo</u>bărmensh) GERMAN [over person, from the title of a philosophical treatise by Friedrich Nietzsche (1844–1900)] *noun* (*plural* **Übermenschen,** <u>oo</u>bărmenshăn) superman (representing a supreme form of human being): *"The notion of a kind of aryan super human, or Übermensch, was taken up with enthusiasm by the Nazi leadership."*

uberrima fides (yooberimă <u>fi</u>deez) LATIN [of the fullest faith] *noun phrase* the utmost good faith, complete honesty (used chiefly as a legal term).

ubi sunt (oobee <u>soont</u>) LATIN [where are they] *noun phrase* (*plural* **ubi sunts**) nostalgia for the past, for vanished times, people, or places.

ubi supra (oobee <u>soo</u>pră) LATIN [where above] *adverb phrase* where mentioned above, in the page or passage previously referred to (used in bibliographical references). ~*abbreviated form* **u.s.**

u.d. *See* UT DICTUM.

uitlander (<u>oo</u>tlandăr, <u>oo</u>tlahndăr) AFRIKAANS [from Middle Dutch *utelander* outlander, foreigner] *noun* a foreigner (formerly referring specifically to a person of British origin living in the Transvaal or Orange Free State): *"The Boers resented the presence of so many uitlanders, chiefly Britons, in their villages and violence was inevitable."*

ukelele *See* UKULELE.

ukiyo-e (ookeeōy<u>ay</u>) JAPANESE [fleeting world, from *ukiyo* fleeting and *yo* world] *noun* a movement in Japanese art of the 17th, 18th, and 19th centuries, typically depicting domestic and everyday scenes.

ukulele (yookăl<u>ay</u>lee), **ukelele** HAWAIIAN [jumping flea, from *uku* flea and *lele* jumping] *noun* a small four-stringed guitar originally of Portuguese origin but usually associated with Hawaii, where such instruments became very popular: *"The girl's grandfather had enjoyed a career as a singer in revue, often accompanying himself on a battered old ukulele."*

ult. *See* ULTIMO.

ulterior (ul<u>tee</u>reeăr) LATIN [father, beyond] *adjective* further, future, remoter, thither; may also refer to something that goes beyond what is openly said or otherwise revealed: *"Several observers suspected that the president had an ulterior motive."*

ultima ratio (ultimă <u>rah</u>teeō, ultimă <u>ray</u>sheeō) LATIN [the last plan] *noun phrase* the last resort, the final argument, the final sanction.

ultima Thule (ultimă <u>thyoo</u>lee) LATIN [farthest Thule] *noun phrase* the most remote part or limit of the discoverable world, formerly identified as Ireland, Norway, or Iceland but originally a reference to the northernmost region of ancient Greece; may also refer generally to any remote objective or point.

ultimatum (ultă<u>may</u>tăm) LATIN [neuter of *ultimatus* final] *noun* (*plural* **ultimatums** or **ultimata,** ultă<u>may</u>tă) a final demand or proposition, the refusal of which will result in the end of negotiations or other immediate action: *"The invaders delivered an ultimatum, demanding the surrender of all surviving forces before midnight."*

ultimo (ul<u>tă</u>mō) LATIN [in the last, from *ultimo mense* in the last month] *adjective* of or relating to the preceding month: *"'We will then,' continued my father, 'resume the subject of mine of the 1st ultimo, to which you sent me an answer which was unadvised and unsatisfactory'"* (Walter Scott, *Rob Roy,* 1817). ~*abbreviated form* **ult., ulto.**

ultra (<u>ul</u>tră) LATIN [beyond, above, exceeding] *adjective* extreme, radical, excessive. ~*noun* an extremist, a radical (usually with reference to politics): *"The new policy failed to attract the support of ultras within the party."*

ultra vires (ultră <u>vi</u>reez) LATIN [beyond power] *adverb phrase* beyond the power or scope of a particular legislative authority or other legal body or official: *"The government's decision was declared ultra vires by the courts."*

umbilicus (um<u>bi</u>likăs, umbă<u>li</u>kăs) LATIN [navel] *noun* (*plural* **umbilicuses** or **umbilici,** ăm<u>bi</u>likee, ămbă<u>li</u>see) navel, bellybutton; may refer more generally to the core or center of something.

umbra (<u>um</u>bră) LATIN [shade, shadow] *noun* (*plural* **umbras** or **umbrae,** <u>um</u>bree, <u>um</u>brī) a shaded area (often referring specifically to the shadow cast by a celestial body); sometimes also used to refer to an inseparable companion or other person who persistently shadows someone else: *"Radio communication with the* *spacecraft was temporarily lost as it passed through the moon's umbra."*

umlaut (<u>uum</u>lowt) GERMAN [from *um* around and *Laut* sound] *noun* a vowel change in which the sound is influenced through assimilation with the following syllable, or the diacritical mark, (as on *ä*) representing such a change.

Umwelt (<u>um</u>velt) GERMAN [environment] *noun* the environment, the surrounding world, milieu.

Untermensch (<u>uu</u>ntărmensh) GERMAN [under person] *noun* (*plural* **Untermenschen,** <u>uu</u>ntămenshăn) a racially inferior person (usually associated with the racial policies of Nazi Germany).

uomo universale (wōmō yooniver-s<u>ah</u>lee) ITALIAN [universal man] *noun phrase* (*plural* **uomini universali,** wōmini yooniver<u>sah</u>lee) a person with knowledge of or expertise in a wide range of fields, a Renaissance man: *"The count liked to think of himself as a uomo universale, although his critics considered him a pompous dilettante."*

urbi et orbi (erbee et <u>or</u>bee) LATIN [for the city and the world] *adverb phrase* (relating to proclamations issued by

the Roman Catholic Church) to be observed by Roman Catholics around the world.

urbs (erbz) LATIN [city] *noun* the city, modern urban society: *"Trends in modern rock are dominated by the urbs."*

u.s. *See* UBI SUPRA; UT SUPRA.

ut dictum (oot <u>dik</u>tăm) LATIN [as said] *adverb phrase* as directed. ~*abbreviated forms* **u.d., ut dict.**

ut infra (oot <u>in</u>fră) LATIN [as below] *adverb phrase* see below (used in bibliographical references). ~*abbreviated form* **ut inf.**

utopia (yoot<u>ō</u>peeă) GREEK [after Utopia, the idealized island society envisaged by Sir Thomas More (1478–1535) in his treatise *Utopia* (1516), from Greek *ou* no and *topos* place] *noun* an imaginary place or situation in which ideal conditions prevail: *"The new regime represented a kind of utopia for scientists eager to pursue research without official interference."*

ut supra (oot <u>soo</u>pră) LATIN [as above] *adverb phrase* see above, as previously (used in bibliographical references). ~*abbreviated forms* **u.s., ut sup.**

V

v. *See* VERSO; VERSUS; VIDE.

vacuum (<u>va</u>kyoom, <u>va</u>kyooăm) LATIN [vacant, neuter of *vacuus* empty] *noun* (*plural* **vacuums** or **vacua,** <u>va</u>kyooă) an empty space, a void or state of isolation; also used as an abbreviation of vacuum cleaner: *"His resignation left a vacuum in the party leadership."* ~*adjective* of or relating to a vacuum. ~*verb* to use a vacuum cleaner or some other device capable of creating a vacuum.

vade in pace (vaydee in <u>pah</u>chay) LATIN [go in peace] *verb phrase* go in the peace of God.

vade mecum (vaydee <u>mee</u>kăm, vahdee <u>may</u>kăm) LATIN [go with me] *noun* (*plural* **vade mecums**) a manual or other small reference book; may also refer to anything useful habitually carried about the person: *"Over the course of their holiday the wine guide became their vade mecum."*

vae victis (vī <u>vik</u>tis) LATIN [woe to the conquered, quoting the Roman historian Livy (59 B.C.–A.D. 17)] *interjection* woe to the vanquished (a demand for an enemy to be humiliated after defeat).

vale (<u>vah</u>lay) LATIN [from *valere* to be well] *interjection* farewell, good-bye. ~*noun* a greeting or farewell.

valet (va<u>lay</u>, <u>va</u>lay, <u>va</u>lăt) FRENCH [young nobleman, page, ultimately from Latin *vassallus* manservant] *noun* a man's personal servant, or a person employed by a hotel or other institution to perform various domestic services on behalf of customers: *"But I quitted France five years ago, and, wishing to taste the sweets of domestic life, took service as a valet here in England"* (Jules Verne, *Around the World in 80 Days*, 1873). ~*verb* to act as a valet to someone, or to clean something for a customer (typically clothes or the customer's car).

valet de chambre (valay dă <u>shom</u>bră) FRENCH [chamber valet] *noun phrase* (*plural* **valets de chambre**) a man's personal servant, whose duties typically include care of clothes and other domestic chores: *"The duke sent a message via his valet de chambre."*

391

valet de place (valay dă plas) FRENCH [manservant of place] *noun phrase* a courier, a person who acts as a guide for tourists.

Valhalla (valhală) OLD NORSE [*Valholl* hall of the slain, from *valr* battle-slain warriors and *holl* hall] *noun* (in Norse mythology) the great hall of Odin in which dead heroes feast with the gods and recount their adventures; may also refer more generally to heaven or the afterlife: *"The Vikings showed no fear, dying in the full expectation of dining with the gods in Valhalla."*

valise (vălees) FRENCH [from Italian *valigia*, itself from Latin *valesia*] *noun* a suitcase or portmanteau: *"That evening Miss Barry gave Diana a silver bangle bracelet and told the senior members of the household that she had unpacked her valise"* (Lucy Maud Montgomery, *Anne of Green Gables*, 1908).

vamoose (vămoos) SPANISH [from *vamos* let us go] *verb* to leave quickly, to make a rapid exit: *"The kids vamoosed as soon as they saw the owners returning."*

Vanitas (vanitas) LATIN [vanity] *noun* (in 17th-century Dutch art) a still life featuring various emblems of mortality and the transience of life.

vanitas vanitatum (vanitas vanitahtăm) LATIN [vanity of vanities, as quoted in Ecclesiastes] *interjection* vanity of vanities (quoted as a caution against human pride and reminding

the ambitious of the futility of existence): *"Ah! Vanitas Vanitatum! which of us is happy in this world? Which of us has his desire? or, having it, is satisfied?"* (William Makepeace Thackeray, *Vanity Fair*, 1847–48).

vaporetto (vapăretō) ITALIAN [diminutive of *vapore* steamboat] *noun* (*plural* **vaporettos** or **vaporetti**, vapăretee) in Venice a motorboat used as a form of public transport on a canal (usually for short journeys): *"The party opted to take the vaporetto to the square of St. Mark's."*

vaquero (vakairō) SPANISH [from *vaca* cow] *noun* a cowboy or cattle driver in Spanish-speaking Central or South America: *"In this gorgeous uniform, with his bull neck, his hooked nose flattened on the tip upon a blue-black, dyed moustache, he looked like a disguised and sinister vaquero"* (Joseph Conrad, *Nostromo*, 1904).

varia lectio (vaireeă lekteeō) LATIN [different reading] *noun phrase* (*plural* **variae lectiones**, vaireeī lekteeōneez) a variant reading (of a text).

variorum (vaireeōrăm, vahreeōrăm) LATIN [of various persons, abbreviated from *editio cum notis variorum* edition with notes of various persons] *noun* an edition of a text (often the complete works of an author) published together with notes or variant readings. ~*adjective* of or relating to such an edition: *"During the whole bygone* *week he had been resolving to set this after-noon apart for a special purpose,—the re-reading of his Greek Testament—his new one, with better type than his old copy, fol-lowing Griesbach's text as amended by numerous correctors, and with variorum readings in the margin"* (Thomas Hardy, *Jude the Obscure,* 1895).

vaudeville (v̲o̲rdvil, v̲ō̲dvil, v̲o̲rdăvil, v̲ō̲dăvil) FRENCH [light comedy song, ultimately from *vau-de-Vire* valley of Vire (an area in NW France formerly well known for such music)] *noun* a theatrical entertainment comprising a series of varied musical, comedy, and other acts: *"Many stars of vaudeville suc-cessfully made the transition to film com-edy."* ~*adjective* of or relating to such an entertainment.

vaya con Dios (v̄ı̄ya kon d̲ee̲os) SPANISH [go with God] *interjection* God go with you.

vedette (ved̲et̲) FRENCH [from Italian *vedetta,* itself from *vedere* to see and probably ultimately from Spanish *velar* to keep watch] *noun* a mounted sen-tinel posted in front of a military posi-tion, a scout; may also refer to a light patrol boat or launch.

veld (velt, felt), **veldt** AFRIKAANS [from Dutch *veld* field] *noun* open grass-land (usually referring to the grassy plains of South Africa): *"To the left stretched a vast expanse of rich, undulating veld or grass land, whereon we could just make out countless herds of game or cattle,*

at that distance we could not tell which" (H. Rider Haggard, *King Solomon's Mines,* 1885).

veleta (văl̲ee̲tă), **valeta** SPANISH [weathervane] *noun* a fast-paced tra-ditional Spanish round dance in which couples dance alongside one another.

veloce (vayl̲ō̲chay) ITALIAN [from Latin *velox* quick] *adverb* (in music) quickly, rapidly. ~*adjective* quick, rapid.

velour (văl̲oo̲r), **velours** FRENCH [vel-vet, ultimately from Latin *villus* hair] *noun* a variety of heavy fabric resem-bling velvet.

vendetta (vend̲et̲ă) ITALIAN [revenge, from Latin *vindicta* vengeance] *noun* a blood feud, a prolonged campaign of vengeance waged by one family, orga-nization, or individual against another: *"I had some talk with him about the war times; but presently the discourse fell upon 'feuds,' for in no part of the South has the vendetta flourished more briskly, or held out longer between warring families, than in this particular region"* (Mark Twain, *Life on the Mississippi,* 1883).

venez-ici (vănayz-ee s̲ee̲) FRENCH [come here] *adjective* seductive, alluring, tempting.

veni, vidi, vici (waynee weedee w̲ee̲kee, vaynee veedee v̲ee̲chee) LATIN [I came, I saw, I conquered, as quoted by Julius Caesar (100–44 B.C.) on his victory over Pharnaces, king of Pontus, at

Zela in 47 B.C.] *interjection*   I came, I saw, I conquered.

venire facias (vănīree f<u>ay</u>sheeăs) LATIN [to cause to come] *noun phrase* a judicial writ ordering a sheriff to assemble a body of suitable people from which a jury may be chosen.

ventre à terre (vontră a <u>tair</u>) FRENCH [belly to the ground] *adverb phrase* prone, flat on the ground; may also refer to depictions of animals in flight, with their legs horizontal to the ground.

venue (<u>ven</u>yoo) FRENCH [coming, from *venir* to come] *noun*   a location where an entertainment or other event takes place: *"The stadium was confirmed as the venue for the big match of the season after the program of refurbishment was completed early."*

Venus (<u>vee</u>năs) LATIN [after Venus, the Roman goddess of love] *noun*   the goddess of love; may also be used to refer to any women who is admired for her beauty or charm.

vera causa (veeră <u>kow</u>ză) LATIN [true cause] *noun phrase* (*plural* **verae causae,** veerī <u>kow</u>zī) (in philosophy)   the real cause of something happening.

veranda (vă<u>ran</u>dă), **verandah** HINDI [from Portuguese *varanda* railing, balustrade, ultimately from Latin *vara* rod] *noun*   an open-sided gallery or portico attached to the outside of a

building: *"Her grandparents were waiting in the shade of the veranda."*

verbatim (ver<u>bay</u>tăm) LATIN [word for word, from *verbum* word] *adverb* word for word, in the exact words, precisely: *"At the heart of the bill, introduced on December 2 last year, is the new definition [of terrorism] copied verbatim from the FBI"* (*Guardian,* May 10, 2000).

verbatim et literatim (verbaytăm et litără<u>rah</u>tăm) LATIN [word for word and letter for letter] *adverb*   exactly as written. ~*adjective* exactly as written. ~*abbreviated form* **verb. et. lit.**

verboten (ver<u>bō</u>tăn) GERMAN [forbidden] *adjective*   forbidden, prohibited, not allowed.

verbum sapienti (verbăm sapee<u>en</u>tee) LATIN [abbreviated from *verbum sapienti sat est* a word to the wise is sufficient] *interjection*   enough said, a wise person does not need to be told everything in order to understand. ~*abbreviated form* **verbum sap., verb. sap.**

Verfremdungseffekt (ver<u>frem</u>dăngse-fekt) GERMAN [alienation effect, coined by German playwright Bertold Brecht (1898–1956)] *noun*   alienation effect, distancing effect (a theatrical theory that argues that an audience should not be allowed to become emotionally involved in what they are shown, so that they may absorb any polemic message more clearly).

verismo (vay<u>reez</u>mō) ITALIAN [verism] *noun* realism (usually relating to realism or naturalism in the arts, particularly in Italian opera of the late 19th/early 20th centuries.

vérité (verătay) FRENCH [truth, abbreviated from *cinema vérité*] noun filmmaking in which the highest standards of realism are aimed for.

verkrampte (ver<u>kramp</u>tă), **verkramp** AFRIKAANS [cramped, narrow] *adjective* politically or socially conservative, reactionary (usually relating to South African politics). ~*noun* a reactionary, a political conservative.

vermicelli (vermă<u>che</u>lee, vermă<u>se</u>lee) ITALIAN [plural of *vermicello*, diminutive of *verme* worm] *noun* (in Italian cuisine) a variety of pasta shaped into long fine strings: "*Katusha and Mary Pavlovna, both wearing top-boots and with shawls tied round their heads . . . vied with one another, offering their goods, hot meat pie, fish, vermicelli, buckwheat porridge, liver, beef, eggs, milk*" (Leo Tolstoy, *Resurrection*, 1899).

Véronique (verăneek), **Veronique** FRENCH [after the personal name *Véronique* Veronica] *noun* any dish prepared with white seedless grapes.

vers de société (vair dă sōseeătay) FRENCH [society verse] *noun phrase* a

type of ironic light verse usually dealing with fashionable, topical issues.

vers d'occasion (vair do<u>kay</u>zhon(g)) FRENCH [verse of occasion] *noun phrase* occasional verse, light verse written to celebrate a particular event.

vers libre (vair <u>lee</u>bră) FRENCH [free verse] *noun phrase* (*plural* **vers libres**, vair <u>lee</u>brăz) free verse, poetry that rejects the usual conventions of rhyme, meter, and so on: "*Many poets of the older generation deplored the explosion in vers libre that took place after the war.*"

verso (<u>ver</u>sō) LATIN [abbreviated from *verso folio* the page being turned, from *vertere* to turn] *noun* a left-hand page in a book (or the reverse side of a coin). ~*abbreviated form* **v.** See also RECTO.

versus (<u>ver</u>săs, <u>ver</u>săz) LATIN [against, towards] *preposition* against, in contrast to: "*This last conflict was in essence a final confrontation based on the old world versus the new.*" ~*abbreviated form* **v.**, **vs.**

vertex (<u>ver</u>teks) LATIN [whirl, crown, summit, from *vertere* to turn] *noun* (*plural* **vertexes** or **vertices**, <u>ver</u>tăseez) the point of a figure opposite the base; the highest point or summit of something: "*Our courses were converging like the sides of an angle, the vertex of which was at the edge of the fog-bank*" (Jack London, *The Sea-Wolf*, 1904).

vertigo (<u>ver</u>tigō) LATIN [from *vertere* to turn] *noun* a sensation of giddiness or confusion (as induced by fear of heights): *"The effort was too great; he began to sway from side to side, as from vertigo, and before I could spring from my chair to support him his knees gave way and he pitched awkwardly forward and fell upon his face"* (Ambrose Bierce, *Can Such Things Be?* 1893).

verve (verv) FRENCH [fancy, animation] *noun* spirit, enthusiasm, vivacity, vitality, energy: *"The band played with verve as the evening came to a close."*

vestigium (vestijeeăm) LATIN [footprint, track] *noun* (*plural* **vestigia,** vestijeeă) a vestige, a trace (often referring to a vestigial structure in anatomy).

veto (veetō) LATIN [I forbid] *noun* (*plural* **vetoes**) an official prohibition, an interdiction, a final decision that nullifies an earlier one (often relating to a blockage placed upon a governmental or legislative vote or act): *"That I have some claim to the exercise of a veto here, would not, I believe, be denied by any reasonable person cognizant of the relations between us. . ."* (George Eliot, *Middlemarch,* 1871–72). ~*verb* to impose such a prohibition or interdiction.

vexata quaestio (veksahtă kwīsteeō, veksaytă kwīsteeō) LATIN [vexed question] *noun phrase* (*plural* **vexatae quaestiones,** veksahtee kwīsteeōneez) a vexed question, something under debate: *"These queries, I confess,*

are not easily answered: at all events, a satisfactory reply to them might cost more trouble than would, if properly considered, the whole vexata quaestio to which they have reference" (Edgar Allan Poe, "The Rationale of Verse," 1843).

v.i. See VIDE INFRA.

via (vīă, veeă) LATIN [way] *preposition* by way of, by means of, through the medium of: *"She traveled to Australia via Singapore."*

Via Dolorosa (vīă dolărōză) ITALIAN [sorrowing way] *noun phrase* the route through Jerusalem taken by Christ as he carried his cross to the crucifixion and thus, by extension, any prolonged or arduous trial or ordeal.

via media (vīă meedeeă, veeă maydeeă) LATIN [middle way] *noun phrase* a middle way, a compromise.

vibrato (vibrahtō, vībrahtō) ITALIAN [past participle of *vibrare* to vibrate] *noun* (in music) a tremulous effect produced by rapid variation in pitch. ~*adverb* tremulously.

viceroy (vīsroi) FRENCH [from *vice-roi* in place of the king] *noun* a governor or other ruler of a country, colony, or province who acts as representative of an absent monarch: *"And so unmeasureable is the ambition of princes, that he seemed to think of nothing less than reducing the whole empire of Blefuscu into a province, and governing it, by a viceroy ..."*

(Jonathan Swift, *Gulliver's Travels,* 1726).

vice versa (vīsee ver̲s̲ă, vīs ver̲s̲ă) LATIN [the position being reversed] *adverb phrase* conversely, with the order reversed: *"This sauce goes well with fish, and vice versa."* ~*abbreviated form* **v.v.**

vichyssoise (vishee̲s̲w̲a̲h̲z̲, veeshee-s̲w̲a̲h̲z̲) FRENCH [from *vichyssois* of Vichy, abbreviated from *crème vichyssoise glacée iced* cream soup of Vichy] *noun* (in French cuisine) a cold soup made with leeks or onions, potatoes, cream, and chicken stock.

victor ludorum (viktă loo̲d̲o̲r̲ăm) LATIN [victor of the games] *noun phrase* the overall winner of a competition (usually relating to sports): *"After this last victory he was crowned victor ludorum."*

vide (vī̲d̲ee, vee̲d̲ay) LATIN [imperative singular of *videre* to see] *verb* see, refer to (a direction to a reader to consult a particular passage or text). ~*abbreviated forms* **v., vid.**

vide ante (vīdee a̲n̲tee, veeday a̲n̲tay) LATIN [see before] *verb phrase* see above, see previous (a direction to a reader to consult an earlier passage in a text).

vide infra (vīdee i̲n̲fră, veeday i̲n̲fră) LATIN [see below] *verb phrase* see below (a direction to a reader to consult an subsequent passage in a text). ~*abbreviated form* **v.i.**

videlicet (videl̲ăset, vīdel̲ăset, viday-liket) LATIN [it is permitted to see, from *videre* to see and *licet* it is permitted] *adverb* that is to say, namely, to wit: *"One of the Macphersons, named Alexander, one of Rob's original profession, videlicet, a drover, but a man of great strength and spirit. . ."* (Walter Scott, *Rob Roy,* 1817). ~*noun* an explanatory note (usually referring to a note in a legal document). ~*abbreviated form* **viz.**

video (vi̲d̲eeō) LATIN [I see, from *videre* to see] *adjective* of or relating to the electronic transmission or reception of visual images. ~*noun* abbreviation for video recorder, videocamera, or videotape: *"The whole incident was caught on video."*

vide supra (vīdee s̲o̲o̲pră, veeday s̲o̲o̲pră) LATIN [see above] *verb phrase* see above (a direction to a reader to consult a previous passage in a text). ~*abbreviated form* **v.s.**

vie en rose (vee on(g) r̲ō̲z̲) FRENCH [life in rose, often associated with the song "La vie en rose" sung by French singer Edith Piaf (1915–63)] *noun phrase* life as seen through rose-tinted spectacles, a naive view of the world.

vi et armis (vee et a̲h̲r̲mees) LATIN [by force and arms] *adverb phrase* violently, by force of arms.

vigilante (vijă̲l̲a̲n̲tee) SPANISH [watchman, guard, from Latin *vigilans,* from *vigilare* to keep watch] *noun* a member of a volunteer committee of ordinary citizens assembled to suppress crime and punish lawbreakers in a particular locality (usually when the authorities are perceived to have failed to do so): *"The police warned that they would not tolerate the presence of vigilantes in the area."* ~*adjective* of or relating to such vigilante groups or actions.

vigneron veenyăr̄ōn(g̣)) FRENCH [from *vigne* vine, vineyard] *noun* a winegrower, a person who grows grapevines.

vignette (vinyet, veenyet) FRENCH [small vine, diminutive of *vigne* vine] *noun* a scene, anecdote, sketch, or episode (as in a film or story); may also refer to an ornamental design on the title or chapter pages of a book, to an architectural decoration comprising intertwined leaves or branches, or to a portrait photograph or other picture in which the central image fades at the edges into the background: *"After calling at one or two flat places, with low dams stretching out into the lake, whereon were stumpy lighthouses, like windmills without sails, the whole looking like a Dutch vignette, we came at midnight to Cleveland, where we lay all night, and until nine o'clock next morning"* (Charles Dickens, *American Notes*, 1842).

villa (vĭlă) LATIN [country house] *noun* a large country house or estate (often referring to the houses of wealthy citizens of ancient Rome); may also refer to a vacation home or to relatively modest rural or suburban detached or semidetached residences (usually with their own yard or garden space): *"They used the money to buy a substantial villa on the French Riviera."*

ville (vil) FRENCH [town] *noun* a town or village.

vim (vim) LATIN [accusative of *vis* strength] *noun* enthusiasm, energy, spirit: *"'I wouldn't give a dog I liked to that Blewett woman,' said Matthew with unusual vim"* (Lucy Maud Montgomery, *Anne of Green Gables,* 1908).

vin (van(g)) FRENCH [wine] *noun* wine (especially French wine).

vinaigrette (vinăgret) FRENCH [from *vinaigre* vinegar] *noun* a dressing for meats, fish, or salad made with oil and vinegar, onions, parsley, and herbs; may also refer to a small ornamental box used to store smelling salts or other aromatic preparations: *"'But this treating servants as if they were exotic flowers, or china vases, is really ridiculous,' said Marie, as she plunged languidly into the depths of a voluminous and pillowy lounge, and drew toward her an elegant cut-glass vinaigrette"* (Harriet Beecher Stowe, *Uncle Tom's Cabin,* 1852). ~*adjective* of or relating to a dish served with such a dressing or sauce.

vin blanc (van(g) blon(g)) FRENCH [white wine] *noun phrase* white wine (especially white wine of French origin): *"Then when he had drunk up the bottle of petit vin blanc, she gave him her hand, and took him up to the drawing-room. . ."* (William Makepeace Thackeray, *Vanity Fair,* 1847–48).

vindaloo (vindăloo) PORTUGUESE [probably from Indo-Portuguese *vinh d'alho* wine of garlic] *noun* a highly spiced curried dish of Indian origin made with meat or fish and incorporating garlic and vinegar among other ingredients: *"The restaurant is particularly famous for its fiery vindaloos, which only the bravest diners can look in the eye."* ~*adjective* of or relating to such a curry.

vin de table (van(g) dă tahblă) FRENCH [table wine] *noun phrase* wine suitable for drinking with a meal: *"She ordered some cheap vin de table, considering this homecoming hardly worthy of better fare."*

vin du pays (van(g) dă pay) FRENCH [wine of the country] *noun phrase* a wine of local origin.

vingt-et-un (vantayăn(g)) FRENCH [twenty-one] *noun* the card game blackjack (or pontoon).

vinho verde (veenō verdee) PORTUGUESE [green wine] *noun phrase* a Portuguese wine with a greenish color (indicating that it has been bottled early in the maturing process).

vino (veennō) ITALIAN/SPANISH [wine, from Latin *vinum* vine] *noun* wine.

vin ordinaire (van(g) ordănair) FRENCH [ordinary wine] *noun phrase* cheap, ordinary table wine suitable for everyday consumption (rather than more expensive classic vintages): *"They dined off bread and cheese washed down with a very acceptable if modest vin ordinaire."*

vin rouge (van(g) roozh) FRENCH [red wine] *noun phrase* red wine (especially red wine of French origin).

virago (vărahgō) LATIN [manlike woman, from *vir* man] *noun* (*plural* **viragos** or **viragoes**) a fierce or brash, overbearing woman; a woman of great strength, courage, or indomitability: *"All he discovered was a strange, fat woman, a sort of virago, who had, apparently, been put in as a caretaker by the man of affairs"* (Joseph Conrad, *The Arrow of Gold,* 1919).

virgo intacta (vergō intaktă) LATIN [untouched virgin] *noun phrase* a virgin, a female who has never had sexual intercourse: *"The police doctor declared the girl was still virgo intacta, and the charge of rape was dropped."*

virtu (vertoo) ITALIAN [from *virtù* virtue] *noun* a love of or enthusiasm for curios or works or art; may also refer to curios or objets d'art themselves: *"With the cessation of the call, the gallery was cleared of the soldiery; many of whom, as they dared not appear in the ranks with visible plunder in their hands, flung what they had upon the floor, until* *it was strewn with articles of richest virtu"* (Lew Wallace, *Ben Hur,* 1880).

virtuoso (vertyoo͞osō, vertyoo͞ozō) ITALIAN [virtuous, skilled] *noun* (*plural* **virtuosos** or **virtuosi,** vertyoo͞osee, vertyoo͞oee) a person with interest or expertise in a particular field, especially the fine arts; a connoisseur. *~adjective* expert, skilled: *"Her dreams of fame as a virtuoso violinist were dashed by the injuries she received in the accident."*

virus (vīrəs) LATIN [venom] *noun* an infective microorganism or complex molecule that reproduces in living cells, especially one that causes disease in humans, animals, or plants; may also refer to a disease caused by such microorganisms or more generally to anything that tends to corrupt or poison: *"The panic spread like a virus through the population."*

vis (vis) LATIN [strength] *noun* (*plural* **vires,** vīreez) force, power, energy.

visa (veeză, veesă) LATIN [*videre* to see] *noun* an official endorsement on a passport permitting the holder passage: *"They had to queue for hours to get the necessary visas to enter the country."*

vis-à-vis (veez-a-vee, vees-a-vee) FRENCH [face-to-face] *preposition* face-to-face with, in relation to, as compared with, regarding. *~noun* a counterpart or opposite number; may also refer to a date, partner, or escort or to a private conversation between two partners. *~adverb* opposite, face to face.

viscera (visără) LATIN [from *viscus* organ] *plural noun* the internal organs of the body; may also refer more generally to the interior or inner contents of something: *"He meant to be a unit who would make a certain amount of difference toward that spreading change which would one day tell appreciably upon the averages, and in the mean time have the pleasure of making an advantageous difference to the viscera of his own patients"* (George Eliot, *Middlemarch,* 1871–72).

vista (vistă) ITALIAN [sight, from *visto,* past participle of *vedere* to see] *noun* a prospect or extensive view of something (real or imaginary): *"This discovery opened up new vistas for research scientists around the globe."*

vis viva (vis vīvă) LATIN [living force] *noun phrase* the principal in mechanics that the power of an object equals its weight or mass multiplied by the square of its velocity.

viva (veevă) ITALIAN/SPANISH [long live, ultimately from Latin *vivere* to live] *interjection* hurrah! long live! (an expression of acclamation or approval, often followed by the name of the person or ideal being landed).

vivace (veevahchay, veevahchee) ITAL- IAN [vivacious] *adverb* (in music)

brisk, spirited, vivacious. *~adjective*
brisk, spirited, vivacious.

vivarium (vīv<u>ah</u>reeăm) LATIN [park,
preserve, warren, from *vivus* alive]
noun (*plural* **vivariums** or **vivaria,**
vīv<u>ah</u>reeă) a terrarium for small animals or fish.

vivat (<u>vī</u>vat, <u>vee</u>vat) LATIN [may he or
she live, from *vivere* to live] *interjection*
hurrah! long live! (an expression of
acclamation or approval): *"And as soon
as they had got out, in their soaked and
streaming clothes, they shouted 'Vivat!' and
looked ecstatically at the spot where
Napoleon had been but where he no longer
was and at that moment considered themselves happy"* (Leo Tolstoy, *War and
Peace,* 1863–69).

viva voce (vīvă <u>vō</u>see, veevă <u>vō</u>chay)
LATIN [with the living voice] *adverb
phrase* by word of mouth, orally.
~adjective phrase oral: *"The old crude
viva voce system of Henchard, in which
everything depended upon his memory, and
bargains were made by the tongue alone,
was swept away"* (Thomas Hardy, *The
Mayor of Casterbridge,* 1886). *~noun
phrase* an oral examination. *~abbreviated form* **viva** (vīvă), **v.v.**

vive (veev) FRENCH [may he, she, or it
live, from *vivre* to live] *interjection* hurrah! long live! (an expression of acclamation or approval): *"There were four
French delegates in a brake and one, a plump
smiling young man, held, wedged on a stick,
a card on which were printed the words: Vive*

l'Irlande!" (James Joyce, *A Portrait of the
Artist as a Young Man,* 1914–15).

vive la différence (veev la dif<u>ă</u>rons)
FRENCH [long live the difference] *interjection* long live the difference (usually celebrating the differences
between the two sexes).

vixit (<u>vik</u>sit) LATIN [he/she lived] *verb*
he/she lived (inscribed on tombstones before the deceased person's
dates).

viz. See VIDELICET.

vodka (<u>vod</u>kă) RUSSIAN [from *voda*
water] *noun* a strong, colorless
liquor made from a mash of rye,
wheat, other cereals, or potatoes.

vogue (vōg) FRENCH [style, fashion,
ultimately from *voguer* to row (originally a reference to rowing styles)]
noun popularity, fashion, style, or
something that is recognized as being
currently popular or in fashion: *"Mr.
Trabb then bent over number four, and in a
sort of deferential confidence recommended
it to me as a light article for summer wear,
an article much in vogue among the nobility and gentry. . ."* (Charles Dickens,
Great Expectations, 1860–61).

voilà (vwal<u>ah</u>), **voila** FRENCH [see there,
there it is] *interjection* there! (expression drawing attention to something
just completed or revealed): *"'Voila!' she
exclaimed as she whipped the cloth off the
finished cake."*

voir dire (vwar <u>deer</u>) FRENCH [to speak the truth] *noun phrase*   (in law) a preliminary examination of a witness or juror to establish their competency to take part in a case; may also refer to an oath taken by a witness or juror that they will speak the truth.

vol-au-vent   (vol-ō-<u>von(g</u>),   <u>vol</u>-ă-von(g)) FRENCH [flight in the wind] *noun*   a small round pastry shell filled with meat, fish, or seafood in sauce (served hot or cold): *"The guests will be offered champagne cocktails and vol-au-vents on the terrace."*

volens (<u>vō</u>lenz) LATIN [willing] *adjective* (in law) consenting (usually to the risk of injury).

volente Deo (volentee <u>day</u>ō) LATIN [God willing] *adverb phrase*   God willing.

volk (folk), **Volk** AFRIKAANS [from Dutch *volk* people, race] *noun*   the people (often referring specifically to the Afrikaner population of South Africa or to the German nation during the Nazi period).

volte-face (volt <u>fas</u>) FRENCH [from Italian *voltafaccia* about-face, from *voltare* to turn] *noun*   an about-face, a reversal in policy, opinion, or attitude: *"The press attacked this apparent volte-face in government policy."*

vomitorium (vomi<u>tor</u>eeăm)   LATIN [neuter of *vomitorius* vomitory (referring to the disgorging of spectators)] *noun* (*plural* **vomitoria**, vomi<u>tor</u>eeă) a passage or other entrance leading to or from the seats in an amphitheater, stadium, or theater.

voodoo (<u>voo</u>doo), **Vodun** LOUISIANA CREOLE [from *voodou,* itself probably from Ewe *vodu* demon, guardian spirit] *noun*   a folk religion of Haiti derived ultimately from African polytheism and ancestor worship; may also refer to a spell, charm, or hex, or to black magic practices in general. ~*adjective* of or relating to such worship or rituals, or to black magic in general: *"The voodoo cult continues to flourish despite the condemnation of local churches."*

Voortrekker (<u>vor</u>trekăr) AFRIKAANS [from *voor* before and *trekken* to trek] *noun*   a Boer pioneer, especially one of the South African settlers of Dutch descent who joined the Great Trek of 1838.

vorlage (<u>for</u>lahgă) GERMAN [forward position] *noun* (*plural* **vorlages** or **vorlagen,** <u>for</u>lahgăn)   the position assumed by a skier, with the body leaning forward but with the heels still resting on the skis.

vortex (<u>vor</u>teks) LATIN [whirlpool] *noun* (*plural* **vortexes,** <u>vor</u>teksez, or **vortices,** <u>vor</u>tăseez)   a mass of particles, fluid, or vapor revolving about an axis; may also refer to any scene of frenetic activity or to anything else resembling a whirlpool or eddy: *"Now his imagination spun about the hand as* about the edge of a vortex; but still he made no effort to draw nearer" (Edith Wharton, *The Age of Innocence,* 1920).

vox populi (voks pop̲yooli̅, voks pop̲-yoolee, voks pop̲ălee) LATIN [voice of the people] *noun phrase* popular sentiment, general opinion.

voyeur (voi̲er) FRENCH [one who sees, from *voir* to see] *noun* a person who obtains sexual gratification from clan-destine observation of sexual activity; may also refer to any person who probes into the private affairs of others: *"The accusation that the professor was a secret voyeur caused considerable unrest among parents of students at the college."*

vs. *See* VERSUS.

v.s. *See* VIDE SUPRA.

v.v. *See* VICE VERSA; VIVA VOCE.

wadi (<u>wo</u>dee) ARABIC [from *wadiy* river bed, valley] *noun* a shallow depression in a desert region, or the bed or a stream or river that is dry at certain times of year: *"The rain filled the wadi and within minutes the landscape was transformed."*

wagon-lit (vagon(g)-<u>lee</u>) FRENCH [from *wagon* railroad car and *lit* bed] *noun* (*plural* **wagon-lits** or **wagons-lits,** vagon(g)-<u>lee</u>, vagon(g)-<u>leez</u>) a railroad sleeping car (usually referring to the rail systems of France or other continental European countries).

wallah (<u>wo</u>lă), **walla** HINDI [one in charge, from Sanskrit *pala* protector] *noun* a person who is associated with a particular job or other activity (typically a relatively low-ranking servant).

Walpurgisnacht (val<u>per</u>găsnakt) GERMAN [Walpurgis Night, named after the English St. Walburga (died 779)] *noun* (in German-speaking countries) the eve of May Day, when witches are reputed to assemble for a secret Sabbath each year; occasionally also used to refer to any nightmarish or orgiastic situation.

wampum (<u>wom</u>păm) ALGONQUIAN [abbreviated form of *wampumpeag,* from *wampan* white and *api* string] *noun* strings of beads and polished shells as formerly used as money by native Americans and hence, by extension, money in general: *"Had she never worn that painted robe before? Was it the first time that these strings of wampum had ever rattled upon her neck and arms?"* (Oliver Wendell Holmes, *The Guardian Angel,* 1867).

wanderjahr (<u>von</u>dăyahr), **Wanderjahr** GERMAN [wander year, from *wander* wander and *Jahr* year] *noun* (*plural* **wanderjahrs** or **wanderjahre,** <u>von</u>dăyahră) a year of wandering or travel (usually referring to one undertaken by a young person or apprentice).

wanderlust (<u>won</u>dărlăst) GERMAN [desire for wandering, from *wandern* to wander and *Lust* desire] *noun* an enthusiasm for wandering or travel: *"Her father was periodically seized with a* wanderlust that took the family around the world."

wazir (wăzeeăr) ARABIC [helper] *noun* a vizier, a high-ranking state official of the Ottoman Empire.

Wehrmacht (vairmakt) GERMAN [defense force] *noun* the German armed forces (specifically relating to the German army in the years 1935–45).

weltanschauung (veltanshowăn(g)), **Weltanschauung** GERMAN [world view, from *Welt* world and *Anschauung* view] *noun* (*plural* **weltanschauungs** or **weltanschauungen,** veltanshowănăn) a comprehensive view of the world, a philosophical viewpoint that encompasses the whole of world history or civilization: *"These ideas were slowly transformed over the years into a weltanschauung that became the old man's gospel and creed."*

weltpolitik (veltpolitik), **Weltpolitik** GERMAN [world politics] *noun* international politics or policy: *"The journal was full of opinions about the lastest developments in weltpolitik."*

weltschmerz (veltshmerts), **Weltschemrz** GERMAN [world pain] *noun* apathy or mental distress at the state of the world; also used more generally to refer to any mood of sentimental yearning or sadness: *"'I wonder —' Carol was plunged back into last night's Weltschmerz. 'I wonder if these farmers*

aren't bigger than we are?'" (Sinclair Lewis, *Main Street*, 1920).

westpolitik (vestpolitik), **Westpolitik** GERMAN [west policy] *noun* the policy of former communist eastern European countries toward increased political and trading links with Western nations: *"The progress of westpolitik was slow at first but gathered pace as individual governments began to realize the opportunities for economic advancement."*

wickiup (wikeeăp), **wickyup** ALGONQUIAN [from *wikiyapi* lodge, dwelling] *noun* a form of temporary wigwam-like hut or shelter made of brushwood (as used originally by nomadic Native Americans of the West and Southwest United States): *"Ten steps away was a little wickiup, a dim and formless shelter of rags and old horse-blankets, a dull light showing through its chinks"* (Mark Twain, "Double-Barreled Detective Story," 1902).

wiener schnitzel (veenăr shnitzăl, weenăr snitzăl) GERMAN [Viennese cutlet] *noun phrase* (in German cuisine) a breaded veal cutlet or escalope.

wigwam (wigwam) ALGONQUIAN [dwelling] *noun* a rough hut consisting of hides, mats, rush, or bark laid over an arched framework of poles (as used as temporary housing by native Americans of the Great Lakes region): *"You can trim up to any extent, and be as free and easy as squaws in a wigwam, for* *this corner is set apart for you ladies and we never cross the line uncle is drawing until we ask leave"* (Louisa May Alcott, *Eight Cousins,* 1875).

wissenschaft (<u>vi</u>senshaft), **Wissenschaft** GERMAN [knowledge, scholarship] *noun* the pursuit of knowledge or learning.

wok (wok) CHINESE [from *wohk*] *noun* (in oriental cuisine) a deep bowl-shaped frying pan.

wonton (<u>won</u>ton) CANTONESE [from *wahn-tan*] *noun* (in Chinese cuisine) a small pocket of dough with an appetizing filling (usually served in soup).

wunderbar (<u>vă</u>ndăbahr) GERMAN [wonderful] *interjection* wonderful! excellent! great! ~*adjective* wonderful, excellent, great.

wunderkind (<u>vă</u>ndărkint, <u>wă</u>ndărkint), **Wunderkind** GERMAN [wonder child] *noun* (*plural* **wunderkinds** or **wunderkinder,** <u>vă</u>ndărkindă, <u>wă</u>ndărkinda) a child prodigy, a person who excels at something while still relatively young: *"The young painter quickly won recognition as a wunderkind of the New York art scene."*

wurst (werst, wersht), **Wurst** GERMAN [mixture] *noun* (in German cuisine) German or Austrian sausage.

x, y

xenophobia (zenăf̲ō̲beeă, zeenăf̲ō̲beeă) GREEK [fear of foreign things, from *xénos* stranger and *phobos* fear] *noun* fear or hatred of foreigners: *"These writings illustrate how patriotism can be transformed into xenophobia."*

yakuza (yăkoōză) JAPANESE [gangster, from *ya* eight, *ku* nine and *za* three (the lowest possible hand in a Japanese gambling game)] *noun* a member of a Japanese crime organization, a gangster involved in organized crime in Japan: *"Frustrated by his work as a lawyer's clerk, he dreamed of becoming a yakuza."*

yang (yang) CHINESE [sun, masculinity] *noun* (in Chinese philosophy) the masculine principle in nature, associated with heat, dryness, or light.

yantra (y̲antră) SANSKRIT [supporter, fastener, from *yam* to hold, to support] *noun* a geometric design used as an aid in meditation.

yarmulke (y̲ahmăkă), **yarmelke** YIDDISH [from Polish *jarmulka* and Ukrainian *yarmulka* skullcap, probably from Turkish *yağmurluk* rainwear] *noun* a prayer cap of the type traditionally worn by male Orthodox Jews.

yashmak (y̲ashmak), **yasmak**, **yashmac** ARABIC [from Turkish *yaşmak* to hide oneself] *noun* a veil of the type worn by Muslim women in public to conceal all of the face except the eyes: *"Why do they hide their ears with seaweed hair? And Turks their mouth, why? Her eyes over the sheet, a yashmak"* (James Joyce, *Ulysses,* 1922).

yenta (y̲entă), **yente** YIDDISH [after the personal name Yente] *noun* a gossip, a busybody, a person who meddles in the affairs of others.

yeshiva (y̲asheevă), **yeshivah** HEBREW [from *y̅ā̲sh̅ā̲b* to sit] *noun* (*plural* **yeshivas** or **yeshivot,** y̲asheevot) a Jewish college or seminary where students are offered instruction, especially in sacred texts.

yeti (y̲etee) TIBETAN [from *yeh-teh* little manlike creature] *noun* abominable snowman (a legendary apelike creature supposed to live in remote parts of the Himalayas): *"Numerous magazines* *published the photographs, which purported to show the footprints of a yeti."*

yin (yin) CHINESE [moon, femininity] *noun* (in Chinese philosophy) the feminine principle in nature, associated with cold, dampness, or dark.

ylang-ylang (eelan(g)-eelan(g)) TAGALOG [from *ilang-ilang*] *noun* a tree of tropical Asia, *Cananga odorata,* prized for a perfume obtainable from its greenish-yellow leaves.

yoga (yōgă) SANSKRIT [from *yogah* union, yoking, from *yunakti* he yokes] *noun* a Hindu philosophy, the aim of which is the attainment of peace and understanding through suppression of physical and mental activity; can also refer to a system of exercises designed to increase physical self-control and spiritual well-being: *"Classes in yoga are available at several local venues."*

yoghurt *See* YOGURT.

yogi (yōgee) SANSKRIT [from *yogah* union, yoking] *noun* a person who practices yoga; also used to refer more generally to any person noted for his or her wise, mystical, or contemplative character: *"'Beggars a plenty*

have I met, and holy men to boot, but never such a yogi nor such a disciple,' said the woman" (Rudyard Kipling, *Kim,* 1901).

yogurt (yōgărt), **yoghurt** TURKISH [from *yoğurt]* *noun* a semisolid food made from fermented whole or skimmed cow's milk and milk solids, often mixed with fruit or flavorings: *"The company is working on a new line of lowfat yogurts."*

Yom Kippur (yōm kipoor, yom kipoor, yom kipăr) HEBREW [day of atonement] *noun* the holiest Jewish holiday marked by fasting and prayer: *"Business was suspended for the feast of Yom Kippur."*

yoni (yōnee) SANSKRIT [vulva] *noun* Hindu symbol based on a stylized representation of the female genitalia and used to identify the female principle in nature.

yurt (yert), **yourt** RUSSIAN [from *yurta,* itself from Turkic *jurt]* *noun* a type of circular tent made from skins or felt stretched over a lattice framework (as used by nomads in central Asia); sometimes also applied to a hut partly sunk into the surrounding earth and covered with soil and turf.

zabaglione (zahbălyōnee) ITALIAN [possibly ultimately from Latin *sabaia* an Illyrian drink] *noun* (in Italian cuisine) a whipped dessert made with egg yolks, sugar, and Marsala wine.

zaftig (zaftig, zoftig), **zoftig** YIDDISH [from *zaftik* juicy, succulent, itself from German *saftig* juicy] *adjective* plump, well-rounded (usually referring to a woman's figure).

zeitgeist (zītgīst), **Zeitgeist** GERMAN [time spirit, from *Zeit* time and *Geist* spirit] *noun* the prevailing spirit of the time (variously taking in the morals, culture, and intellectual fashions of a particular era): *"Often have I fancied how, in thy hard life-battle, thou wert shot at, and slung at, wounded, hand-fettered, hamstrung, browbeaten and bedevilled by the Time-Spirit (Zeitgeist) in thyself and others. . ."* (Thomas Carlyle, *Sartor Resartus,* 1833–34).

Zen (zen) JAPANESE [religious meditation, from Chinese *chan* meditation] *noun* a form of Buddhism in which devotees aspire toward enlightenment through meditation and self-contemplation: *"She took up Zen during her 50s and still enjoys meditation, even though she has long since lost interest in Eastern mysticism."*

zenana (zănahnă) HINDI [ultimately from Persian *zan* woman] *noun* in India and neighboring countries, the part of a house where women live in seclusion; a harem.

zephyr (zefăr) GREEK [after Zephyrus, god of the west wind in Greek mythology] *noun* a light breeze (especially one blowing from the west): *"He felt a zephyr curling about his cheek, and turned. It was Bathsheba's breath—she had followed him, and was looking into the same chink"* (Thomas Hardy, *Far from the Madding Crowd,* 1874).

zeugma (zoogmă) GREEK [yoking] a figure of speech in which a word modifies or governs two or more words when it applies to only one of them or is appropriate to each one but in a different way: *"Charles Dickens's sentence 'Mr. Pickwick took his hat and his leave' is an example of zeugma."*

zither (<u>zi</u>thăr), **zithern** GREEK [from Greek *kithara* stringed musical instrument] *noun*   a string instrument with a flat body and 30 to 40 strings: *"The plangent strumming of a zither filled the evening quiet."*

zoftig   *See* ZAFTIG.

zollverein (<u>zol</u>vărīn), **Zollverein** GERMAN [customs union, from *Zoll* toll and *Verein* union] *noun*   a tariff union, a trading arrangement under which participating states abandon customs duties between themselves, while maintaining them with regard to states outside the union (referring originally to the tariff union that was set up between German states in the 19th century).

zombie (<u>zom</u>bee) BANTU [ghost] *noun* one of the undead (a person raised from the dead by voodoo or other supernatural power and obliged to wander the earth as a menacing automaton); may also refer more generally to any person who seems to have lost all self-will or otherwise acts in an apathetic, unresponsive manner: *"The news of his mother's death seemed to have reduced him to little more than a zombie."*

Index

ersatz
feldsher
fest
Festschrift
flak
flügelhorn
foehn
Fraktur
frankfurter
Frau
fräulein
führer
Gastarbeiter
Gasthaus
gegenschein
gemutlich
geopolitik
gesellschaft
gestalt
gestapo
gesundheit
glockenspiel
Götterdämmerung
Graf
hände hoch
hausfrau
Heimweh
Herr
Herrenvolk
hinterland
ich dien
jäger
jawohl
Jugendstil
Junker
kaffeeklatsch
kaiser
kamerad
kapellmeister
kaput
katzenjammer
kinder, kirche, küche
kindergarten
kirsch
kitsch
knackwurst
knapsack
kobold

kohlrabi
kriegspiel
kultur
Kulturkampf
Kulturkreis
kümmel
kursaal
lager
landau
Landsturm
Landwehr
langlauf
Lebensraum
lederhosen
leitmotiv
lied
Luftwaffe
lumpen
lumpenproletariat
machtpolitik
meerschaum
muesli
nickel
noodle
Ostpolitik
panzer
poltergeist
poodle
pretzel
prosit
pumpernickel
putsch
putz
quark
rathskeller
realpolitik
Reich
rucksack
sauerkraut
schadenfreude
schloss
schmaltz
schnapps
schnell
schnitzel
schuss
schwarmerei
Schweinhund

sieg heil
singspiel
sitzkrieg
spiel
Sprechgesang
spritzer
spritzig
stalag
stein
strudel
Sturm und Drang
torte
über alles
Übermensch
umlaut
Umwelt
Untermensch
verboten
Verfremdungseffekt
vorlage
Walpurgisnacht
wanderjahr
wanderlust
Wehrmacht
weltanschauung
weltpolitik
weltschmerz
westpolitik
wiener schnitzel
wissenschaft
wunderbar
wunderkind
wurst
zeitgeist
zollverein

GREEK
acme
acropolis
Adonis
aegis
aeolian
aeon
agape
agnostic
agora
agoraphobia
alpha

amazon
amnesia
anabasis
analgesia
analysis
anaphrodisiac
anathema
androgynous
android
anti
antipodes
antithesis
aphasia
aphrodisiac
apocrypha
apologia
apotheosis
arcadia
Argus
Armageddon
asphyxia
aura
automaton
bathos
beta
bibliomania
bouzouki
bulimia
calliope
carcinoma
Cassandra
catachresis
catalysis
catastrophe
catechesis
catharsis
catheter
chaos
charisma
chiasmus
chimera
Chi-Rho
coma
cosmos
criterion
delphic
delta
diaeresis

INDEX

sui juris
summa cum laude
summum bonum
suppressio veri
supra
sursum corda
susurrus
suum cuique
tabula rasa
tacet
tacit
taedium vitae
Te Deum
tempore
tempus fugit
tenet
tenor
terminus
terminus ad quem
terminus ante quem
terminus a quo
terminus post quem
terra alba
terra firma
terra incognita
terra nova
tertium quid
tessera
testimonium
theatrum mundi
thesaurus
tinnitus
toga
toties quoties
toto caelo
triumvir
trivia
tumulus
tu quoque
tutor
tyro
uberrima fides
ubi sunt
ubi supra
ulterior
ultima ratio
ultima Thule
ultimatum

ultimo
ultra
ultra vires
umbilicus
umbra
urbi et orbi
urbs
ut dictum
ut infra
ut supra
vacuum
vade in pace
vade mecum
vae victis
vale
Vanitas
vanitas vanitatum
varia lectio
variorum
veni, vidi, vici
venire facias
Venus
vera causa
verbatim
verbatim et litteratim
verbum sapienti
verso
versus
vertex
vertigo
vestigium
veto
vexata quaestio
via
Via Dolorosa
via media
vice versa
victor ludorum
vide
vide ante
vide infra
videlicet
video
vide supra
vi et armis
villa
vim
virago

virgo intacta
virus
vis
visa
viscera
vis viva
vivarium
vivat
viva voce
vixit
volens
volente Deo
vomitorium
vortex
vox populi

**LOUISIANA
CREOLE**
voodoo

MALAGASY
raffia

MALAY
amok
caddy
gong
gutta-percha
ketchup
kris
paddy
sarong
satay

MALDIVIAN
atoll

MANDINGO
mumbo jumbo

MAORI
haka
kai
kia-ora
kiwi

MONGOLIAN
Dalai Lama

NARRAGANSETT
papoose
powwow

NEPALESE
Gurkha
kukri

NORWEGIAN
fjord
kraken
krill
quisling
ski
slalom

OLD NORSE
berserk
saga
Valhalla

PANJABI
bhangra
tikka

PERSIAN
ayatollah
baksheesh
bazaar
caravanserai
hafiz
houri
mogul
samosa
shah

POLISH
mazurka

PORTUGUESE
albino
auto-da-fé
bossa nova
favela
infanta
infante
junta
lascar